Best Wishes
"Pepper" Jane Davis
Catcher 1944/53
#7 — HOF 11/5/88

"DIRT IN THE SKIRT"

BY LAVONE PEPPER PAIRE DAVIS

Started 1940 – Finished 2000?

Well, would you believe 2004 –

Or – maybe more?

Maybe 2005 or 6 or even 7?

Unless, of course, I've gone to heaven!

Well, I guess the date is 2008?

Never fear, cause I'm still here,

Everything is fine! It's definitely 2009!

Peoria Red Wings VS Racine Bells 1946
Pepper Paire bat in hand and Sophie Kurys hitting the
"Dirt In The Skirt"

AuthorHouse™
1663 Liberty Drive
Bloomington, IN 47403
www.authorhouse.com
Phone: 1-800-839-8640

© 2009 Pepper Paire Davis. All rights reserved.

No part of this book may be reproduced, stored in a retrieval system, or transmitted by any means without the written permission of the author.

First published by AuthorHouse 11/10/09

ISBN: 978-1-4490-4379-7 (sc)
ISBN: 978-1-4490-4378-0 (dj)

Library of Congress Control Number: 2009911405

Printed in the United States of America
Bloomington, Indiana

This book is printed on acid-free paper.

DEDICATION

This book is dedicated to my mom, Tessie. Mom was competitive. She was a rebel. She believed that if you tried hard enough, if you never gave up, anything was possible. And you never, ever had to be ashamed of trying. Her competitiveness and desire to win was born in me. Mom gave up her day in the sun so I could have my night with the stars! She was my best friend, my biggest supporter and always my greatest fan. If there was a Hall of Fame for moms, "Mom" would be there.

Hortense Theresa La Page
Born 1908 - Died 1959 - Christmas Day

LETTER OF APPRECIATION

There are so many people that helped me make this book a reality that I can not do justice to all of them! You know who you are and if I haven't thanked you in words, I thank you all from the bottom of my heart.

Thanks to my husband Bob who gave me my son, William, who has always been the light of my life. And to Phyllis, his wife, who turned that light on. And to my grandson, Riley, who shines so brightly in it!

To Robbie, who explained to me the mystery of my life when she told me I was a "Procrastinator Perfectionist!"

To my bro Joe and his gal Sal and their kids – they are my rocks. He always knows everything I don't and maybe more! Thank you, Jeannine – I wouldn't have made the deadline without you. Thanks to all of my family and to my little bro Russ and his wife Jo Ann.

To my daughter Susan and her husband Ralph. To my mountain kids from their Valley Grandma! To my #1 grandson, "Scoot," who shared his life with me and his gal Jil.

To Ricker Dicker Do and Paula Walla Poo -- the book would not have happened without you! To ESPN Sue and her Choir Boy – my Sacramento family.

To James and his sweet family – thanks so much for sharing your wonderful talent and precious time with me! To Marge and Kammie who were there for me when I needed them. And the beat goes on and on!

Thanks to Loozie Woozie from Pepper Wepper! And thanks to all of my teammates -- those upstairs and the few left downstairs. Hey gals, we did it! I'm still all for one and one for all – and a very proud All American! Thank you Georgie Girl and my pal Joie.

Of course, I can't forget the "Big Umpire in the Sky," who calls all the plays! Thank you, Lord!

Last, but not least, thanks for all of my fans out there! Baseball wouldn't be any fun without you!

-- Lavone Pepper Paire Davis
P.S. Don't forget to buy the book! Ha!

QUOTE FROM PENNY MARSHALL:

"The rare courage and style displayed by the young ladies of the 'All American Girls Professional Baseball League' was truly remarkable. They dealt with double standards, personal tragedies and the specter of an ugly war looming over them; all the while they were completing a rough, physical schedule and playing through painful injuries that would keep some of their male counterparts of today moaning on the bench.

"I felt it was important to make 'A League Of Their Own' to tell you about this unique part of women's sports history that had been swept under the rug for 50 years. We only had time for the tip of the iceberg. Pepper's documented pictures and memories will give you the whole ball game. She'll take you back with her for a peek into yesterday and show you the warm, wonderful, innocent world we have lost. Thanks to Pepper, the truth came through in the movie, as it does in the book. It will inspire you to laugh with her, love with her, cry with her and play baseball with her. You might not want to hit the 'Dirt In The Skirt,' but you will enjoy reading about it. The unusual story will slide off the pages of this book and into your heart!"

QUOTE FROM TOM HANKS:

"Pepper knows baseball! She also loves baseball! What makes her so special and unique though, is that she played baseball! Professional, heat throwing, swing for the fences drag bunt, double steal, line drive to the left field baseball! The kind of baseball that separates those that 'do' from those that only 'talk.' For this reason, Pepper Davis and all the players of the 'All American Girls Professional Baseball League' have stories as rich as any in the game. And Pepper knows how to tell them."

DIRT IN THE SKIRT
Table of Contents

Chapter 1   My Field of Dreams – On my way to Cooperstown Hall of Fame Museum! Flashbacks of my life and my Mom.

Chapter 2   The Glass House – Buster and Busted – The Great Depression including Mom's marriage.

Chapter 3   Up a Tree With Hoover's Chickens – Poultry Politics – Pop enters.

Chapter 4   All the Way With the WPA – FDR and nickels to clink together.

Chapter 5   Hard Times and Softball – "Take my Brother!" – Baseball and softball teams.

Chapter 6   From Hot Dogs to Hot Tamales – Conflict at school and beginning of road trips.

Chapter 7   The Dynamic Duo – Faye and me –adventures and misadventures.

Chapter 8   Nightmare Alley – The crash and the hand of G-d.

Chapter 9   The Big Event – Joe joins up – P-38s – Howard Hughes and the Ambulance Corp.

Chapter 10   A War and a League Are Born – Out of gas in Brentwood – purple pants and red hair.

Chapter 11   Cal-Can-Do! – 1944 spring training –AAGPBL – Minneapolis Millerettes.

Chapter 12   Buzz Me Mr. Blue – Baseball games – broken bones and back home with the "Hell Diver."

Chapter 13   There's No Place Like Home (If It's Your House) – Mom and the house – Joe and Bob and B-24s – "Into the wild blue yonder."

Chapter 14   Where You Going, Easter? Spring Training 1945, Chicago, Illinois, Wrigley – The rookie from Rainbow Creek.

Chapter 15   The Great One – Max Carey and curve balls – I live up to my name.

Chapter 16   A Charming Experience – Ups and downs of spring training – chaperones and charm school – publicity – a song is born.

Chapter 17 The Bubble-Gum Pink Daisies – Uniforms – Ft. Wayne, Indiana – war games -- Percy Jones General Hospital – the mayor and the "Cacapot."

Chapter 18 He Was Definitely a Foul Ball! -- Romantic games and baseball games – the War – the cemetery and the Caca House.

Chapter 19 Fear Strikes Out, and Love Does, Too! – Joe's B-24 bomber is down – FDR is too! V.J. Day, August 15, 1945, and Harry S. Truman.

Chapter 20 Jim Thorpe's Thunderbirds! Winter '45 – The great Olympic champ – disastrous Pascagoula spring training 1946.

Chapter 21 No Buttons No Bows – Just Bugs and Bats and Belles (The Joint Was Jumping)– Spring training and a surprise – Pascagoula, Mississippi 1946.

Chapter 22 It Just Keeps Getting Better – Marnie – Murphy – Jimmy and fishing and winning.

Chapter 23 For Whom the Belles Toiled – Behind the dish again -- Murphy and Willie – winning baseball – the surprise visitor!

Chapter 24 The Catcher Who Didn't Drop the Ball – The Peaches and the Belles duke it out for the championship – Trouble in paradise – Playing hurt.

Chapter 25 Stormin' Norman – Mom and Norman – Howard Hughes and the "Spruce Goose" – Havana, Cuba, 1946.

Chapter 26 The Crash and I Don't Mean Wall Street – Betrayed again -- Grand Rapids and a wounded Chick – my Grand Rapids buddies.

Chapter 27 Jaws (A Whale of a Fish Tale) – Dorth from the North and go fish – Ziggy and John and Tex and a rough year with the Grand Rapids Chicks.

Chapter 28 Latin Knights and All American Women – South America Tour 1948 – Submarine maneuvers – John's doghouse – wine capers.

Chapter 29 Reconditioned Chick – Joe's St. Louie Woman – Russell feels the draft – Mom's visit.

Chapter 30 Big Daddy Wore Cement Scuffies (Sopranos Relatives) – Faye, Tex and me and the "Mafia" – she flipped her biscuit – St. Louis and Tea Kettle Beer.

Chapter 31 The End of the Caca Era – Chick adventures – Grand Rapids gunslingers – "holy suffering – jumped up".

Chapter 32 Bear Hunting With a Stick – California, here we come!

Chapter 33 One More Time -- My little Rambler – Betrayed again – Home to heal again.

Chapter 34 Let the Good Times Roll – From Jimmie Foxx to the Silver Fox – A Chick becomes a Daisy – I spoke with spooks!

Chapter 35 On the Rocks With the Silver Fox – Foul play – apartments and parties – Home and Hughes Aircraft – Bowling and Bob!

Chapter 36 There is Life After Baseball – and Death! Baseball ends – A man becomes "the love of my life" – Dad and Mary and Marlin Manor – "Black Christmas."

Chapter 37 A Whole New Game – Dad and Mary – Willie is born – Bobby and Suzy and G-d and the grunion.

Chapter 38 Hair Today – Gone Tomorrow – Hairy or harried??? Times raising teenagers – wife and mother and cooking – Pepper Paire disappears – enter Mrs. Lavone Davis.

Chapter 39 Shake and Bake -- Bob blamed me – And the freight train crashed – The ghosts take over.

Chapter 40 Single With Shingles – A new breakdown and low point in my life.

Chapter 41 On a Roll – Downhill (Who Purloined the Feline?) – Patches – Scoot and Suzy – Betty and John.

Chapter 42 Happy Days Are Here Again – Chicago reunion 1982 – David Hartman – the All Americans are back!

Chapter 43 You Win One, You Lose One – A Penny for your thoughts – The big C – Hall of Fame dream reborn – Willie and Phyllis tie the knot.

Chapter 44 The Tooth, the Whole Tooth, Nothin' But the Tooth! – Cooperstown and Penny – Clarky Barky – the curtain falls.

Chapter 45 Showtime -- Party time – Chicago tryouts – slip and slide and glow and glide – Geena Davis.

Chapter 46 To the Set, By the Jet – Food and fun – movie comes to life – real reels.

Chapter 47 Truth or Dare – Foul or Fair – Technical advisor, for real, finally – Riley.

Chapter 48 Something Old is Something New – Penny's house – TV calls – "sneak premiere" – "Chitty Chitty Bang Bang."

Chapter 49 It Ain't Over 'Til It's Over -- The premiere and the press round table and me – the MVP!

Chapter 50 I Sang! It's Over! Isn't It? – Fan Fest and San Diego All Star Game in 1992 – Hall of Fame signers – It's all right for girls to play baseball!

The End – believe it or not! (for now)

Chapter 1
My Field of Dreams

"Journey's End! Cooperstown"
11/5/88

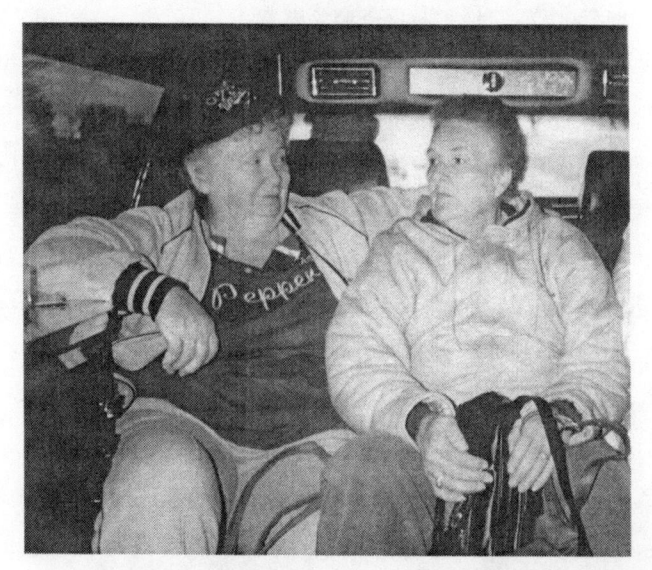

"Pepper Paire Davis"   `All the way Mae'
"The Catcher"   "Faye Dancer"

Baseball Hall of Fame Cooperstown, NY

It was a slinky, big black limousine -- the kind that movie stars and Arab sheiks ride around in; big enough for eight average-sized people, but our six bulky bodies pretty well filled the luxurious interior. Now, that's a six-pack for you! As the limo sped on toward mid-New York state, I looked at the faces around me and thought, "Boy, do they look old!" How we had changed in the last 45 years. I had to look hard into their eyes to fully recognize them. I stared at Tiby, thinking how different she looked. Her long, pale blond hair was now short and gray. It was cut in a cereal bowl style with bangs hanging down to her water blue eyes. Her eyes hadn't changed much, except these days they squinted over Ben Franklin glasses. "Don't touch that button!" she ordered Faye, shaking a finger at her! "You might eject us!" Faye responded with a cherubic smile, ignoring Tiby (and that hadn't changed either). Faye pushed the button and WHAM!, out came a fully-stocked bar. "Aha!" she crowed. "Champagne ma' dears?" she offered in the polished voice of a country lady. Forty-five years hadn't stolen the twinkle from her eyes nor her soul. We all gave our enthusiastic approval! After all, this was a special occasion. So, Faye began to pour for us "but none for herself." She had given up drinking years before.

    I turned to look out the window and watched the upstate New York countryside slide by. I was greeted by a breathtaking view of rolling green hills topped here and there with white patches of snow. Giant trees wearing their glorious fall dresses of red, gold and purple were reaching for the sky like colorful exclamation points. What I'd heard was true! This part of New York was truly beautiful this time of year! It was November 3, 1988.

    Staring out the window, I caught a glimpse of a road sign. My heart stopped! "Cooperstown – 60 miles" -- a simple sign and such a short distance. But, I'd been on the journey how long? And dreaming of being there for a lifetime. Was it really true? Was I finally getting there after all these years? Studying my reflection in the window, much as I had studied my companions earlier, I realized I hadn't really seen myself for as long as I hadn't seen them. The reflection that stared back at me had close-cropped white, but still curly hair, faded blue eyes and the same round face. Well, actually it was much more rounded now. With a start, I realized if my hair was long and black, I'd look just like my Mom! Her image, and fragments of stories I had heard, and memories of my own, invaded the window reflection. I closed my eyes and my mind drifted back.

Ride Tessie Ride!

A slender girl came riding up astride a sleek, white Indian pony. Her fancy ruffled dress and petticoat were hiked up showing her tanned shapely legs and shoeless bare feet gripping the pony's naked white belly. The crowd gasped! Shocking! No young lady rode a horse like that! The starter had the gun poised above his head. He stared at her, mouth agape. Finally, he mumbled uncertainly, "I don't know about this ... young lady?" She glared at him, her dark brown eyes flashing fire! Breathing deeply and tying the strings of her new pink bonnet firmly under her chin, she pointed to the sign nailed to a nearby post. It read: "Three-mile race – open to anyone with guts enough to ride." Defiantly, she said: "Well, Mister? I'm anyone! And I've got guts enough to ride!" Taken by her desire, the crowd allayed its initial shock and roared their approval. "Let her ride! Let her ride!" came the cries from the people that milled around the dusty road. Seizing the moment, the girl screamed, "SHOOT!," her 15-year-old shrill voice cracking. Without thinking, the starter fired and they were off! The girl led from the start, her black hair spilling out from under her pink bonnet. Her body molded to the speeding horse. Over the rocks they flew, never stumbling -- and outdistancing her nearest competitor, a "cowboy" on a "big black" with each stride. The pony splashed through a stream without slowing. Then he zigzagged through the trees with the girl ducking under the low-hanging branches. They rounded the bend and raced over the dusty road, flying down the homestretch! They were one, the pony and the girl. The hooves of the little pony didn't seem to even touch the ground as they sped to their common goal – the finish line!

The pink bonnet was now flying straight back surrounded by a flowing mass of black hair. The strings clung tenuously to the girl's thin neck by a single knot. Then, not a quarter of a mile from the finish line, it happened! The knot holding the strings gave way and the bonnet flew off, tumbling back down the dusty road. The girl gave one quick glance over her shoulder. The "big black" was a hundred yards behind. Jerking back hard on the reins, she pulled her pony to a sliding stop! She literally yanked him up off the ground and turned him around in a swirling cloud of dust! They made the 180-degree turn and streaked back down the road making a wide circle to the hat. Without slowing him, the girl slid down the side of the pony, clinging to him with a one-handed grip on his mane and a bare heel over his back. As the pony swooped by her bonnet, she grabbed it, and in an amazing display of balance and strength, pulled her body back up onto the pony. As they completed the circle, the cowboy on the "big black" had drawn even with them. They were both racing at full speed toward the approaching finishing line! The girl and her pony molded into one flying blur as they laid flat out down the stretch, matching the "big black," stride for stride! With only 10 yards to go, they were neck and neck! Communicating to the pony by the sheer will of her body, the girl begged him for one last torturous effort. The gallant little pony responded with a final lunge! They won – by a nose! As they triumphantly crossed the finish line, the crowd went wild!

  The little girl anxiously waited for the people to quiet down so that the judges could present her with the prize. When the noise finally subsided, one of the judges asked her, "What are you going to do with all that money, little girl?" Fifty dollars was a large sum of money for a young girl in those days. The little girl drew herself proudly up, took a deep breath, and the words came pouring out loud and clear: "I'm gonna buy a bathing suit! And, and then I'm goin' to California!" She raised a grimy little fist triumphantly in the air and continued: "Then I'm gonna train by swimming in the ocean!" She looked around at the people, her fist still clutching the now dirty, crumpled-up pink bonnet. Waving the bonnet, she finished defiantly, "And then, I'm going to win the diving and swimming medals in the Olympic games!" The year was 1918. The high-spirited, beautiful young girl was Tessie LaPage, from Hot Springs, South Dakota. She was my Mom!

  Tessie kept her word about coming to California. The dark-eyed, dark-haired young beauty from South Dakota trekked the then- monumental journey to the City of the Angels, but this time she rode the "Iron Horse" instead of her pony! Hard as it was to do so, she had to leave her beloved pony in South Dakota. She was following her dream, by coming to this land by the sea, to train for the 1924 Olympic tryouts.

Tessie was accompanied by, guided by, and completely dominated by, Emma LaPage, my Grandma. "Ma," as she was called, was a full-figured, upright woman of 57 years. She'd had my mom "Tessie" at the mature age of 42. She ruled the 15 year old with an iron hand. I think one of the reasons they came to California was because Ma wanted to get away from Grandpa Louie LaPage. I never did know the real story there. But Ma used the reason that she had to bring old family friend, "Waddy Hoover," out to California to be admitted to the "Old Soldiers Home"; that's what the Veterans Administration was called in those days. This move would also give young, spirited Tessie a chance at her Olympic dream.

Ma must have had a hidden bankroll because young Tessie's 50 bucks alone couldn't have done it. So, they made the move to 1535 Pontius Ave., Sawtelle, California, now known as sophisticated West Los Angeles. Pontius Avenue was located right at the foot of the Veterans Home and was destined to be a two-grandma street. Because, unbeknownst to Ma and Tessie, down at the other end of the block, on the other side of the street, resided the "Paire" family from Melrose, Montana. The Paire family had taken up residence on Pontius Avenue to be company to (my grandpa to be) Joe Paire who was also admitted to the "Old Soldiers Home." There was only a handful of National Veterans homes in the United States at that time. The year was approximately 1921. The Old Soldiers Home in California was fairly new and relatively uncrowded in comparison to the other regional homes around the country.

The Paire family consisted of two brothers and their mother. Charles E. Paire, my Dad-to-be, who was a smooth talkin', silver-tongued ladies man. His tall, lanky brother, Uncle Jim, who was shy and reserved, and their little, round Danish-speaking mother, Christina Bodina Paire. Rumor had it that my Grandpa Paire had rescued Grandma Paire from the back of a Mormon bishop's wagon in Utah. As the story goes …

The Mormons were known on occasion to swoop down on the towns and snatch up the women right off the streets. In a cloud of dust and thundering horse hooves, they would carry the women off -- never to be seen, nor heard from again. Quite a story! I know, but Dad had a million of 'em. Some were true and some were a product of his creative imagination. I think I inherited some of that imagination.

Across the street from the Paire house was the pumping plant that supplied the area with water. Charles E. Paire maintained and serviced the plant. Ahh, yes! Paire, the plumber. You do not pronounce the "e" in Paire. Charles was quite a catch for some lucky young lady! It didn't take him long to notice shy, soft-spoken Tessie LaPage. She had big brown eyes, a fully rounded figure and pale white skin; her long black satin hair curled gently to her waist. She could have easily posed for a Mona Lisa portrait. With the innocence of youth shining out of her eyes, she turned many a young man's head. No wonder my Dad used to strut by, a block out of his way, to go home. And no wonder my Grandma used to watch him – Charles, the eligible bachelor who was fully employed and drove a Duesenberg. He always wore his hat pushed back from his face with a lock of curly brown hair conveniently out of place, giving him a charming boyish look that belied his age. His piercing blue eyes and his glib silver tongue often had a hypnotic effect on women. "Ma" was no exception. She fell under his spell. It didn't matter that he was 32 years old and my mom, Tessie, was only 15. Charles was a mature kind of a catch every mother wanted for her daughter in those days.

Tessie didn't pay too much attention to him at first. She was too busy with her swimming and diving training for the Olympic games. Tessie and Ma rode the streetcar daily to Santa Monica Beach. Once there, Tessie would swim the three miles out to the breakwater and back. Next, they would walk two miles to Venice where Mom would practice her diving at the indoor Venice Plunge for two to three hours; then the return trip home. Dad got to timin' things. He would meet them at Santa Monica Boulevard and walk the three blocks home with them. Ma was more and more impressed and flattered by the attention of this dandy.

Indeed, Charles cut quite a figure! He was small in stature, about 5'8", but well-built and always, when not working, immaculately attired. He loved to dress in white -- from his snap-brim Panama hat to his shiny patent-leather shoes. Sometimes a silver-handled cane dangled eloquently from his crooked arm – for looks only. I think one of the reasons he took such pleasure in being well-dressed was because he was a plumber. The nature of his job was such that he wanted to distance himself from it when not working. If you looked deeply into those piercing eyes you could see a mischievous twinkle lurking there. He had a rebel streak in him, which was evident by the sign on the back of his Model-T work truck. It read: *"Paire the Plumber – Your crap is my Bread and Butter"* -- quite a bold statement for the 1920s! Charles was worldly and woman-wise. He also had the brains to court Ma in order to win the heart of young Tessie. All Tessie heard from her mother was that Charles was so very handsome, how refined he was, and he had a job, and a car, and a house. Ma sang his praises morning, noon and night and it finally took effect!

The young impressionable teenager never had a chance! Suddenly, she found herself married to a man more than twice her age, one she hardly knew. It was destined for disaster from the beginning! Meantime, Ma had met slow talkin', pipe smokin' straight-back Ottis Rhea from Missouri. Grandpa Louie became history, and Ottis Rhea and Ma got married. They became Ma and Ote Rhea forever, it seemed.

Mom moved across the street to live with the Paires. It was the beginning of a nightmare for her! She still went to the beach every day. But now she usually walked the three miles because Dad didn't approve of her riding on the streetcar alone. He would refuse to give her streetcar money and accused her of being a brash woman. Ma Rhea wouldn't interfere. Soon came the discovery that Charles was quite a drinker, a fact he had kept hidden before the marriage. Also, Uncle Jim was a full-blown alcoholic, but at least he was nice and quiet about it. Dad wasn't, and sometimes he would get verbally abusive. Mom wanted to go back home. But Ma, who also took a little nip now and then, was still on Charles' side. So, Mom kept trying to make it work, and of course, the inevitable happened.

Mom got pregnant and my beloved brother came into the world. Mom was just 16 and she had a little baby boy to look after and care for. He was christened "Joseph Louis Paire" after his Granddad but Mom called him "Jody." She would pack-up baby Jody and take him to the beach with her, still trying to hang onto her Olympic dream. She had become friends with many of the people who lived in the area and while Mom continued her training, her friends watched baby Jody.

More than once, Tessie begged Ma to let her come back home because life with Charles Paire was getting worse. He would come home in the middle of the night smelling of booze and cheap perfume. He'd wake her up and try to make love to her. If she refused, he would drag her out of bed to argue about it. Grandma Christina Bodina was well into her 80s and no help to young Tessie. She didn't speak English and only understood a few words. She would just shake her head, hold her hands out helplessly and continue doing a little cookin' and cleanin'. She spent the rest of her time sitting in her rocker, dreaming of the past, I guess? Maybe she wished she'd gone with the Mormon bishop? So, poor little Mom struggled on. She'd gotten herself a part-time cooking job at the beach, still trying to keep her dream alive.

But, alas, it was not meant to be. Although she had fought hard against it, she found herself pregnant, this time with me. With that came the harsh realization that her Olympic dream had ended. At the tender age of 17, she would now have two small children to raise with virtually no help from anyone. She was never bitter. She took it like the champion she always was; put her hopes and dreams away and poured her heart into being the most wonderful mother in the world. She still went to the beach and swam when she could get away. But now it was because she loved it so much – I guess that's what kept her going!

On May 29, 1924, 18 months after Joe's arrival, I was born in the big brass bed at Ma and Ote's house, the same 1535 Pontius Ave. that is now a Pacific Bell parking lot. That reference as a birthplace gets quite a few looks! My Dad told it like: my Mom pulled out some of his curly brown locks by the roots when I was being born. My Mom told it like: the doctor just made it in time. And Dad didn't show up at all until it was over, and he was less than sober when he got there. My Grandma Rhea told it like: she was Florence Nightingale and the doctor

8

wasn't much help. And me, what can I tell you? I was only just being born. But I'll bet ya I was looking around for first base!

My Mom was reading a French novel when I was born, so I became Lavone Agnes (the middle name is after an aunt) Paire. Despite the French in me, "Lavone" was a name that never did fit me. When I was little, I guess I kinda looked like an angel. I had a kewpie doll face, my hair was in tight Shirley Temple ringlets – only it was platinum blond. I had big blue eyes with long silky eyelashes that annoyed me when I blinked. Yeah, I've seen the pictures. But boy, I know I wasn't any angel! Things were pretty much a blur in those days. But, I can remember sitting on the curb at the age of about two and seeing my Dad come running down the street. He was hollering. And he was mad! It scared me. He shouted at me: "Where is your brother, Jody?" and, "When I find him – I'm gonna kill 'im!" I looked up with that scared little angel face and said, "Don't 'killie' me, Daddy!" That made Dad laugh and got Jody off the hook for not running Dad's errand. I was to hear that story many times down through the years. By now, Mom had really had it with Dad! Even Ma had begun to realize it was a bad deal. Ma still had a soft spot for Charlie, but she knew now that he was neither a good father, nor a good husband.

The end came one night when Dad came home in the wee hours. Drunk again, he climbed into bed with Mom who was fast asleep. He'd brought a drunken buddy home with him and he crawled in alongside of Dad and the two men passed out. Mom was sleeping away and didn't know what was going on. Dad woke up first, looked around and shoved the guy out of bed. He started screaming at Mom, accusing her of infidelity! That did it! Mom hit him with an iron skillet, grabbed us kids and headed across the street to Ma and Ote's house. Dad got a two-inch scar out of it. He told everyone he got it in World War I, fighting in the trenches of France. Mom said he never left the States. At any rate, Mom didn't let him talk his way out of that one. That was the end of their May-December marriage.

We weren't destined to last too long at Ma and Ote's house either, because Ma was more dominating than ever. Ottis Rhea, her hubby, would be the first to tell you that. Grandpa Ote looked like Abraham Lincoln, but Ma never did free him! He just couldn't keep up with her.

Maybe that's why he acted so grumpy at times; actually he was a pretty nice old guy. Somehow, the two households remained friendly, at least on the surface.

Dad soon picked himself up another wife – a Mexican gal named Margaret Tapia. She was "Maggie" to us and she was good to us! In the meantime, Mom had met self-proclaimed "Bohunk," Jesse Blazek, at the Saturday night dances with Ma and Ote. "Bohunk" was a nickname for Bohemian; and "Pop," as he later became known to us, was very proud of his old world heritage. Actually, "Bohunk" was more of a slang putdown than a nickname. Some people today might not realize there was plenty of racial prejudice around those days, also. The blacks didn't invent it. The Irish were dubbed "Micks"; the Chinese were referred to as "Chinks"; the Mexicans had "Spicks" hung on them; the Jewish people got the delightful tag of "Sheenies" or "Kikes"; the Italians were "Wops"; and the Indians were still called "Savages." But it was dealt with differently -- at least by Pop anyway. He didn't shoot off his mouth or react with violence. He dealt with it by proving with his actions that he was as good or better than any man. He was fiercely proud of being an American.

My brother Jody and I were now old enough to remember what was going on. We loved living at Ma and Ote's house. We were fascinated by Grandma Rhea's bright, auburn-colored hair. She wore it immaculately knotted in the back. She wore it like a queen wears a crown. It was always such a mystery to us how it stayed so eternally neat and so eternally red -- until the wig came off years later, revealing the gray underneath! There were many more mysteries at Ma and Ote's for us.

There was the big round crock that was stored under the sink. A cheese cloth covered the contents, which was an ever-present batch of home brew that had little cubes of white fluffy yeast floating on top. Sometimes Pop and Ote couldn't wait for it to get ripe so they would slip a dipper into it and start sampling. After bawling them out properly for jumpin' the gun, Ma and Mom would usually join the samplin' and they'd all wind up as sick and green as the beer. Grandma Rhea would make root beer for us kids, too. We would get to help put the brass caps on the dark brown bottles. We'd be samplin' too! It didn't matter that it was warm. It just tasted wonderful. We'd get to help put the caps on the beer bottles too, if it lasted long enough to bottle.

I remember the backyard as huge with lots of trees in it. There were trees of all kinds -- a peach tree, a fig tree, an apricot tree, a walnut tree, a loquat tree and a Satsuma plum tree. We loved to help pick the fruit, and we would usually wind up eating ourselves sick. There were also boysenberry and blackberry bushes; concord grapevines and a white lattice arbor that had tiny, little, beautiful red and yellow primroses climbing all around it. There were many other flowers scattered throughout the yard, like the multicolored dahlias and the pink and white carnations, and the red, red geraniums, just to name a few. It was like a make-believe fairyland to us. But, the biggest and most fascinating thing of all was this giant, scary, mystery tree. It had big, shiny, green leaves and bore huge green eggs that would turn black. Then the black eggs would soften and drop, covering the ground with a giant, black, velvety blanket. Everybody said they were poison. So every year, Grandpa Rhea had to hire a man with a truck to haul 'em off. Jody and I used to speculate at what kind of monster might hatch out of those eggs? Imagine that! Boy, would I love to have that giant avocado tree in my backyard now!

Well, like I say, everything was going along smoothly until one Saturday night. Ma and Ote, Mom and Pop, my Dad "Charlie" and his new wife, Maggie, all went to the dance together. Somehow, Pop and Dad got into a fight. Of course it involved booze as this was the time of prohibition. Everyone was choosing sides and arguing. Grandpa Ote, who was slightly inebriated, took a break from the arguing and went into the alley to relieve his kidneys. Someone called the police. Grandpa Ote got caught taking his leak and wound up in jail. Pop got the blame for the call. Actually, I think Dad did it to get even. Anyway, Mom stood up for Pop and Ma stood up for Charles. They argued bitterly and we wound up moving out in a huff. And that's when we went to live in, what I remember as, the glass house.

Christina Bodina
"Grandma Paire"

Cousin Geneva, Grandma Rhea, Charles Paire (Dad) with his Dusenberg

Dad & Grandma Rhea in front of my birthplace 1535 Pontius Ave. Sawtelle, CA

Aunt Mayme
Before she found religion

Aunt Mayme &
Mom, Age 3

Chapter 2
"The Glass House"

The "Glass House" in Sawtelle on Cotner Avenue was only a couple of miles from Ma and Ote's house, but we weren't going to see them for a while because things had to cool down. I remember it as the glass house because it had lots of doors and windows and everything seemed to be made of glass. Pop wanted to move in with us, but he wasn't ready to commit. Seems like he had to deal with giving up women for a woman and going from "caddy" to "Daddy" and "cab driver" to "breadwinner" and "family man." That was a big jump! Since Mom wouldn't go for it without the ring and the vows, Pop did a disappearing act.

So, little brown-eyed, Mona Lisa Mom was left to go it alone. Forgetting her Olympic dream, she faced being a bus-ridin', hashslingin' waitress with two little babies to support and care for. Quite a task for the young, inexperienced teenager! It was 1927 and I was only three at the time. It wasn't until many years later that I realized what Mom went through. She had a quiet, inner faith that, I guess, gave her the courage to deal with all the tough, outer things. Of course, I don't remember too much about those days. Things were pretty hazy. But certain memories seem to stand out clearly. One thing I remember was that Mom was still going to the beach to swim in the ocean, only now she took us with her. She would put us on her back and we would each grab a shoulder and she would swim out a mile and a half to the breakwater and back. All we had to do was kick our feet. She was still a very powerful swimmer.

I remember across the street from our house there were these huge, empty fields filled with tall, wild grass. It towered over the heads of Jody and me. We used to crawl around in it, flatten out the grass and make rooms and paths to play in. It was there I remember having our first dog. He was a beautiful German shepherd and his name was "Buster." Mom would look out the windows and although she couldn't see us in the tall grass, she always knew where we were because she could see Buster's tail just waggin' away. What a smart, wonderful dog our Buster was. He did all the routine tricks with ease: rolling over, playing dead, shaking hands and speaking. He could walk on his hind legs, count for you and we even taught him to climb a ladder. It was the era of famous movie dogs. There was Rex, the wonder dog -- he was sort of a mutt as I remember. Rin Tin Tin was another one. He was also a German shepherd. But Buster was much prettier and much smarter. Buster would have made Lassie look like Dumbo. It took us a while to teach him to climb a ladder, but, man, he got it down pat! We would find out much later how important the ladder climbing trick was for my bro and me.

Buster was my first love. He was the reason that in all the following years growing up always included a dog in our family. He used to sleep with his head on the pillow between Jody and me. Buster was always such a comfort to Mom. She had to work long and hard hours and she could count on him to take care of us. She knew he would never let anything hurt us. My aunt would come over and watch us while Mom was at work. We were allowed to play in our yard and across the street in the grass. Like all kids, we occasionally broke the rules and went out of bounds. Most of the time we got away with it without harm. But one time we didn't!

There was this irrigation ditch way down at the end of the block. Of course, we were supposed to stay away from it. But, against Jody's objections, I had to go investigate on my tricycle. My bro and Buster followed me. When we got there, I saw a plank across the ditch. Well, to little Miss Daredevil "Poulet" (French for "little chicken," as my Dad called me) that was a red flag! I had to ride my trike across the plank! The back wheels barely made it and halfway across the inevitable happened. Kerplunk! Off I went into the ditch with a lot of screamin' and splashin'. It was about five feet deep and over my head. Stunned by the 10-foot fall, I lay silent with my face straight down in water. My bro Jody slid down the sandy side and waded in after me. He grabbed me by my arms and pulled my face out of the water. Then he started sinking down into the soft, sandy bottom. He was trying to hold both of our heads out of the water and holler for help at the same time. But no one was around. The world was so different then. It seemed so much smaller and much less crowded. It was like we were in a vacuum. I could hear Jody's voice sounding like it was echoing down a long, dark tunnel. Soon, poor, little Jody was losing his fight. His little chin was slipping under the muddy water, his little legs were frantically scratching and scrambling. But that was only digging him in deeper and deeper into the muddy bottom. Yet, he still wouldn't let go of me! And he never would have! I was hanging in his arms like a limp dishrag. We would have gone to a watery, muddy grave together.

Then a sharp sound penetrated the darkness of my mind. It was Buster's familiar barking, echoing down that long, dark tunnel. Jody heard it too. "Come on, Sissy! Open your eyes, Sissy! Help me! Buster is here! He'll save us!" I struggled with all my might and I got my eyes open. "Come on, Sissy! Kick your feet, Sissy," he pleaded. Well, I started kicking and we got our heads back up out of the water. But, by now Jody was just too tired and we weren't gonna make it. We weren't goin' anywhere except maybe down the drain. I started to black out again, but was startled out of it by a huge splash. The next thing you know, we were moving toward the bank. Buster had slid down the side, jumped into the water and grabbed Jody by the back of his suspenders. He was towing us! We were both kicking again and we made it to the side of the bank. The three of us lay there exhausted. Buster was in the middle and we were wrapped all around him! We were just one, big knot of slimy mud and water and there was a lot of kissin' and huggin' and tail waggin' going on. I don't know how long we laid there just catching our breath, but suddenly, in a startling moment, things became very clear in my mind and I realized something terrible was happening. There was a soft rustling sound and the water was creeping up on us. I didn't know what was happening, but Jody knew. They were filling the ditch with water. I can still see Jody's face 'til this day. The snot was running out his nose and the tears were streaking down his muddy cheeks. I remember watching him as he took a slippery, little Napoleon stance and pointed his stubby finger at Buster commanding fiercely, "Go, Buster! Go!" I said, "Go get Mom!" Buster struggled up, tail between legs, and looked at me pleading for an excuse to come back. And I did as I often did, I imitated my big bro. I pointed my finger at him and I screamed in my little four-year-old falsetto voice, "Buster, go! Buster, go get Mommy!" He had a Herculean task ahead of him because he couldn't hold his footing in the soft, sandy mud. He'd struggled up three or four excruciating feet and find himself buried up to his shoulders then he'd slip back down. Over and over he tried. It was getting darker now. We were starting to lose our footing. As the water rose, we'd float out with the current and pull ourselves back by Buster's tail. But Buster's strength was going. His efforts were getting weaker. Jody was silent again. I knew he was praying. His face was turned up and he was staring at the sky. I was too far gone to cry. It was hard just to breathe in the wet, shivering darkness. Buster finally gave up and lay down, whimpering softly. We both looked at my brother's face for help, as I have done all my life. His faith has always seen me through! He patted my head with a muddy, little fist, looking down with that loving smile and he stared up again searching for an answer.

As the last of the sun flashed across the sky and lit the other side of the ditch, the golden rays reflected in a strange, reverent way on Jody's face. It was as if a light went on. His eyes popped wide open! His little face screwed up into a ball and he started screaming and pointing across the ditch. "Buster! Buster! Climb the ladder! Climb the ladder, Buster!" We were on the soft side of the ditch! The other side was a pile of rocks. Jagged edges were sticking out like a stairway, leading up like a ladder. Jody again pointed and screamed, "Buster! Buster! Go! Go! Go climb the ladder!" He shoved a whimpering Buster into the water urging Buster, "Climb the ladder! Climb the ladder! Go get Mom!" He was alternately pleading and screaming commands.

Buster paddled across the current, dragged himself out of the water and lay shivering for a moment. Then he jumped up and made his way up the rocks with leaps and bounds. When he got to the top, he shook himself mightily and, looking down at us, he gave a loud scolding series of barks, telling us to hang on. He flipped his muddy tail, spun around and took off. In the meantime, Jody had found a tough, scraggily, little muddy root that refused to die. He managed to hold us to the shore by clinging to the root with one hand and tightly wrapping his arm around me. But the water was rising rapidly and the current was getting stronger. We knew it wouldn't take long and it would be over our heads even if we could hang on!

We found out afterward that when Buster got back to the house, the front door was closed. He ran to the kitchen back door and started jumping up against the screen barking frantically. No one paid any attention to him. My aunt, who was a little afraid of him anyway, was fixing dinner.

First she tried to shush him. Then she tried to close the door on his frantic barking. They say he jumped through the screen! Growling and snarling, he grabbed my aunt's apron and tried to drag her to the door. God only knows what might have happened if Mom hadn't walked in the front door. She ran to the kitchen screaming at Buster, "What are you doing, Buster? What are you doing?" She grabbed him and pulled him off my frightened aunt. Then, with horror, she realized he was wet and covered with mud! "My God, Buster! What happened? Where are the kids?" Buster turned around and took off yelping and leaping and looking back pleading with his eyes for Mom to follow him. And they came!

Mom slid down the bank and took us in her arms and held us close, soothing us softly as only she could do. There was a lot of noise and excitement going on as the neighbors came running to help. But we didn't care, we were in the magic circle of Mom's arms. All was right with the world again! I guess I drifted off in an exhausted sleep. Mom said I mumbled something about "Breakwater, Mommy! Breakwater, Mommy! Swim, Mommy, swim!"

I guess you could call it a happy ending, except it didn't end there. My beloved bro Jody became very ill after our excursion in the ditch. He'd had pneumonia as a baby and again at the age of three. The cold, wet struggle we'd had in the ditch did his lungs in again. He came down with lobar pneumonia for the third time. In those days, that was it, "Strike three," so they said. A little five-year-old boy wasn't supposed to survive pneumonia for the third time! Indeed, there came a time when Jody's weary, little body was wracked with fever and chills alternately. That's when the doctor said he could do no more. He told us it was in God's hands and he didn't expect Jody to make it through the night. The fever would reach a peak and it would kill him if we couldn't break the congestion in his lungs.

Well, I know it was in God's hands, but it was my Mom who put those hands to work. She put hot towels on his chest and then cold towels. She boiled the water on the stove in a washtub. In between times, she made poultices. She called them "mustard plasters" and she covered his chest with them when he was shivering and shaking. We wrapped blankets and our bodies around him, holding him to keep him warm and willing him to keep breathing. I put cold rags on his head while Mom held him. She lifted him in and out of the bathtub countless times, alternately cooling and warming him that way. Her faith and her strength were unbelievable!

For three days and three nights, he was not supposed to see the light of the dawn. But the morning after the third night his fever finally broke. His body cooled and he opened his soft, brown eyes and smiled at us. Then he started coughing up the green poison that was killing him. It wasn't over, but it was beat! It took a while, but he finally got well. Once again, we crawled the tall grass in the fields and made our playhouses, we rode our trikes, played with

Buster and, of course, played baseball. We were always together. God gave me such a great gift when he made my brother. I couldn't, and still can't, imagine life without him.

For a while we pretty much just cleaned out the peanut butter and jelly jars, licked the cake and frosting bowl clean and went about our way, just growing up. Life was good again, but it didn't stay that way. It seemed that something was always popping up to upset the apple-cart. Like the time I crawled over a hunk of glass. I cut my knee to the bone, but I made it through it. Then there was the time I got home early from school and got the front door key from my aunt. I was going to surprise Mom by doing the dishes, but I broke the door key off in the door. I thought it was an unforgiveable crime and the end of the world! Mom just laughed and hugged me, telling me she loved me more than that old key. She was so warm and wonderful. To this day I can feel her love! Anyway, time passed and then the big baddy happened.

Our beloved Buster disappeared! We combed the neighborhood day and night calling his name, but we never found him. Pop had come back into our lives again and he drove us miles and miles in his taxicab looking for Buster. We knew it had to be foul play because Buster would never have left us on his own. Different people had tried to buy him at times, especially one particular guy who worked for the studios. That man disappeared at the same time as Buster. Buster's loss broke all our hearts. He was a part of us and life was lonely and scary without him. The nights were cold and long and scary without him. We missed his warm body that had always been in the middle of the bed with us. We missed him playing ball with us. He was always the designated "chaser" when the ball got by us. Of course, we always had a tussle getting the ball back. Our Buster was the first of a long, long line of doggies that came into our lives bringing us so much loyalty and such love and joy. Then eventually we all suffered such heartbreak when we lost them. But they always left us beautiful memories to cherish!

I don't know whether it was because of the loss of Buster or whether Pop just missed us so much, but anyway, he gave in. He brought the ring and he said the words and we were a family – one that was to last through thick and thin! So, now we needed a bigger house! Anyway, there were too many things around there that reminded us of our beloved Buster. It was time to move and move we did, into a cute, little white house on Corinth Avenue. We were still in Sawtelle, but closer to Santa Monica Boulevard so Mom could take the streetcar for transportation. Pop had to use his car day and night to earn a living. He drove a cab all night and caddied or worked pick-up jobs all day. Things were getting worse in our world again. Financially, Pop was struggling around the clock just to come home with a nickel or a dime, a quarter at the most. The writing was on the wall. Mom had to go to work again. Pop didn't want her to, but sooner or later he had to face the reality. He was killing himself and we still weren't making it. Life was tough!

Aunt Amanda & Uncle Bonner's
Bus

Hortense Theresa LaPage
Age 16

Buster

Bro Joe & Me (5&4) After falling in Ditch
"Sawtelle"

Chapter 3
Up a Tree with Hoover's Chickens

In the big outside world changes were taking place. We were in the '30s and the United States was trying to poke its head out of the Depression and Herbert Hoover was in the White House promising a chicken in every pot. Mom was a Democrat and she didn't like Hoover and his Republican troops. She thought they had an oil well and we got the shaft. They got the white meat and we got the feathers. She really got aggravated about that chicken thing! To make matters worse, one time when she was driving along behind a guy with a "Chicken in a pot" bumper sticker, he cut her off and she had to swerve to miss him. She ran the car right into a little tree. The tree bent over and the car was suspended up there in the air stuck on the tree! Mom was leaning out the window shaking her fist and screaming, "I'll give you a chicken in every pot! And you know which end of it!" It was a funny sight, and it happened right down at the end of our block, so we got to see it!

Politics used to be great fun between Republicans and Democrats. It was just old-fashioned, downright bad mouthin'. But it was based on truth and it was always face to face and with an explanation of what was done right and what was done wrong! When it was over, everybody pulled hard for the winner. Believe it or not. I think politicians were almost honest in those days. Ya, and you know what? Being a lawyer was considered a respectable job and an honorable profession. In today's world, some members of the legal profession are seen in a different light. But despite Hoover and the Republicans' scheme of "the rich get richer" so they can give the "poor" cheap jobs, things were improving slightly. Of course, they couldn't have gotten much worse, or we couldn't have survived. Funny thing about a depression, when you're really poor you kinda don't notice it, because you don't have anything to lose. I think I just figured out that poor people are happier than rich people.

I remember when Jody and I used to go with Mom and Pop down to the lima bean fields. In those days Sawtelle pretty much ended at Pico Boulevard, south of that was farmland. After the harvest we would sift through the hulls and find the discarded beans. Then Mom would put together the best bowl of beans that you ever dipped a lip on! All she had to do was touch it and it became the best food in the world. When we were living really high on the hog (that meant we had an extra 25 cents to spare) we would drive over to Culver City to Helms Bakery and get a 50-pound flour sack full of day-old goodies. Breads and cookies and cakes! Oh boy! What pure heaven. After we ate all the stuff, Mom would make us clothes out of the flour sacks.

Life just seemed so clean and simple those days. We didn't know how tough it was because we weren't used to anything else. But, you know what? We always had love and laughter and no fear. No matter how bad it got, we knew Mom and Pop would find a way. I know now how hard it must have been for them. They must have laid awake nights trying to figure out a way for us to survive. But when the dawn broke, Pop was out looking for a way to make a quarter or 50 cents, and Mom would greet us with a smile and a hug, and there would be something good on the table to eat. She surely must be in a very special place in heaven waiting for us and finding a way to make it good for everybody. Pop is up there too. Mom probably sneaked him in the back door and he's looking around trying to pick up an extra quarter. You know what? I think Dad is there, too, because he probably smooth talked St. Peter into letting him in.

Meanwhile, Jody and I were managing to do some growing up while we were working our way through school. The first school I can remember was Sawtelle Boulevard Grade School. It was in an area where a lot of Mexican families were living. Unfortunately for us, there was a language barrier and a total lack of communication. That coupled with their jealousy and resentment led to bad feelings. We didn't know why they didn't like us, then. Now I know. It was because we were white, and even though we had very little, it was still more than they had! So we were constantly in the minority and consistently having to defend ourselves. I was pretty feisty, but my bro Jody was kind-hearted, patient and peaceful. He never wanted to hurt anyone. He wouldn't even step on a bug. He would pick it up and put it in a safe place. Later on in high school he became President of the World Friendship Club. Then when war came he got his ulcers worrying about the innocent people he had to drop his B-24 bombs on. But, anyway, back to grade school. The Mexican kids would pick on him like crazy because he didn't want to fight. This went on for a while. Then one day a gang of them somehow got Jody cornered in an alley and were all ready to beat up on him. But you know what? Little sister caught up with them! And together, back to back, we fought them. Seems like there were thousands, but actually, I guess there were only five or six. We sent them out of that alley on the run with bloody noses, bruises and crying. When you face bullies and back them down, sometimes they turn and run. Fortunately for us, in those days most kids didn't have knives, guns or clubs. You just fought with fists. Your bare hands. It wasn't even kosher to kick somebody! We probably would not have survived if it had happened today. Of course, we had bloody noses and cuts and black eyes too. But as we swaggered home arm and arm, we didn't feel the pain. Jody's shirt was ripped and bloody, my coveralls were torn, muddy and bloody, but we had smiles on our faces as bright as the sunshine. When Mom ran to meet us, tears were running down her face, "What happened? What happened?" We proudly announced, "We won, Mom! We won!" Like I say, it was a different world. They didn't come back and shoot us or rape me or bomb our house. They weren't really bad kids. After that, they respected us. We even got to be friends, eventually, after we learned to speak a little Spanish. However, later when we moved to Armacost Avenue in West Los Angeles and went to school there, we had to go through it all over again with a different gang!

Well, the ugly specter of the Depression was still looming over us and times were going from bad to worse again. So Mom had to go to work. She found a job at a quaint little restaurant in Santa Monica. It was right on the beach, on Pacific Coast Highway. It was called "The Lighthouse." It wasn't actually operational, just built to look like a lighthouse. Mom worked in the front at the open-air counter as the fry-cook. It was cold, wet and hard work, but she was glad to get a job. She didn't make much salary and had to depend on the tips for her income. Pop had the same kind of thing going with his caddying and cab driving. As the money got tighter, the tips got smaller. Pop didn't really want Mom to work, but they had no choice. One good thing in those days was you could depend on your neighbors to help you out by watching your kids when they got home from school. I guess there are some of those kinds of neighbors left today. But not very many of them live around me! So I don't know about trusting them with your kids.

Mom liked working there because after a while she started getting good tips. The reason was across the street from The Lighthouse was a fancy bar and restaurant. It was owned by Thelma Todd. Ms. Todd was a glamorous movie star of the 1920s and '30s. At that time many movie stars lived in huge estate homes on the beach. Sometimes they'd go slummin' and stop in and get burgers from Mom and they tipped big! There was a lot of talk about Thelma Todd being secretly tied to the mafia. It was rumored that one of her boyfriends was a big mafia boss. There might have been some truth to it because one night in 1935 Thelma was found dead in her car in an abandoned spot on the Coast Highway! She was supposed to have committed suicide by leaving her car running and dying from carbon monoxide. Her friends and relatives all swore she loved life too much to do that! They said she would never have killed herself. The rumors persisted. There was talk that she was murdered because she was trying to get away from the mob scene. There was a big stink over the whole thing. Unfortunately, it resulted in Thelma's restaurant being closed down and the area soon became a tainted place. People stopped coming around so Mom's restaurant had to close down. What a change from today. With a reputation like that, all the scandal sheets would have headlined it and made a big deal out of it and Thelma's place probably would have become a big success. The people probably would have flocked there out of curiosity alone! As I said, it was a different world then. So through no fault of her own, Mom was out of a job. Once again, we were in financial trouble.

So it became time to move again because we couldn't afford to pay the rent on our house. Actually, we couldn't afford to pay rent, period! This time we wound up on Armacost Avenue, still in Sawtelle (West L.A.) between Wilshire and Santa Monica Boulevard. We were only six blocks from Santa Monica City limits. Mom and Pop were desperate and so our third grandma came into the picture! She was Pop's Mom and her name was Stella Blazek (pronounced Blah-zeck!). She owned the house we moved into on Armacost Avenue. This street was destined to be our home for the next 25 years. We were gonna be up and down it like a yo-yo. The first of five houses that we lived in on that street was 1451 Armacost Avenue.

Grandma Blazek let us move in because she knew Mom and Pop were having a tough time making it. We were supposed to come up with $25 a month rent -- not an easy thing to do in those days! But sometimes Grandma B. would let them slide. After getting to know Grandma B. and her family, we finally found out why Pop had stalled on the marriage. They were strict Catholics. They did not approve of a divorced woman with two kids as Pop's wife. She and her husband, Grandpa Frank Blazek, were from a part of Europe's old country originally called Bohemia. It was one of the countries that Hitler put out of business. The Blazeks were pretty old-fashioned in their ways. They had two sons: Pop and his younger brother, Uncle Steve. Uncle Steve lived at home with Grandma and Grandpa B. Grandma B. raised Pop and Uncle Steve the old country way. They both were altar boys and ruled by Grandma B.'s strict Catholic hand. She thought that by cab driving and caddying golf Pop was going down the wrong street. She also thought that Mom was the shady lady that had steered him down that street. So, she kind of ignored us for a while. Grandma B. and Grandpa B. had plenty of money. They owned several houses in Sawtelle (West L.A.). They could have made it a lot easier for us than they did. Later on in life Grandma B. kind of mellowed out. I even got to know and love her. But she and Mom never did see eye to eye. Eventually, though, they were able to gain respect for one another.

We only lived down the alley from Grandma B. and Grandpa B. They lived on Westgate Avenue, one block north of Santa Monica Boulevard. Up the street from their house was University High School. University was to be our alma mater high school. One block south from us was Brockton Avenue Grammar School. So, it indeed ended up an ideal place for us to grow up.

By now "Hoover's chickens had flown the coop" and the "Big Depression" was still in full swing. Pop lost his taxi job because nobody had the money to take a cab. He was reduced to being a caddy only and that just didn't cut it. Things were bad all over and there were more hard times ahead. I remember that sometimes Pop would dig ditches from dawn to dusk and come home maybe with just a quarter. He'd be dragging his hind end because he was so tired. He would be covered with mud and his hands would be raw and sore. Mom would cry and hug him and tell him how proud she was of him while she gently bathed and cared for his blistered hands. We would hug his legs and say "horsey-horsey, Daddy, let's play horsey." And you know what? As tired as he was, he would grab us up, plant us on his shoulders and go galloping around whistling and snorting while we laughed ourselves silly. He had a way of whistling that sounded just like a horse. It was like two or three sounds put together. It was really unique. His pain and suffering would just seem to melt away and love filled the air. When we went to bed at night we didn't know where the next meal would come from, but we always knew it would come! Joe and I never worried because we didn't ever go hungry. We knew that Mom and Pop would always take care of us! All the necessary things like clothing and shoes were a problem, but we found ways to get by. You always bought shoes way too big and they used to last in those days. When the soles wore out on you, there was always plenty of cardboard around to stick in the holes and it didn't show. You just kept the tops shined and they looked fine! Mom made pajamas and shirts of those flour sacks. They were pretty colorful, but we were used to them. It didn't matter that the clothes were worn, as long as they were clean. No matter what the food was, whatever they scraped up, Mom would make it taste good. She was the greatest cook there ever was or ever will be. Not fancy unless she wanted to be, but she could get fancy if she had to. It just seemed like all Mom had to do was touch it and it would become tasty!

We got a few things from welfare that year. It was one of the few times we ever did. Right around Christmas time we got a food box. It had some candy, some cheese and crackers and some canned stuff in it. Spam was the only meat included. Spam wasn't thought too much of in those days. Now it's kind of expensive and considered a delicacy. A lot of people like it. Back then, we looked on it as a poor imitation of meat. But Mom made it taste like the most delicious ham you ever laid a lip on. Her homemade biscuits and bread were so good that it didn't matter that it was white, uncolored margarine on them. Her stew and chili (without much meat in it, if any) would melt in your mouth. Oh, and her meatloaf, that was to die for! She even made special things for little miss picky me who wouldn't eat things like onions. Imagine that! I didn't like onions! Now I load them up into everything when I cook. But I still don't like raw onions. Boy, I bet my Mom is flipping in her grave at that one!

She would make things special for me without onions. So, what do you do with meatloaf without onions? Well, Mom knew what to do. She made a Hawaiian meatloaf out of pineapple and carrots just for me. I tried to make it. I can't get it to come out right. I can't remember how to make that one. I was too little, I guess. She constantly invented new dishes. She made all kinds of great dishes out of whatever she'd have to cook with. She could make something out of nothing, which was the one thing that was plentiful. I specifically remember one Christmas when Pop came home with a wild goose. He said he had accidentally run over it with his car. Man, he must have had to chase it for miles. That bird was so tough, you could have patched the tires with it. That dinner was one of Mom's few failures, but her wonderful dressing and her lip-smacking gravy made up for it. Later, she ground up the goose and made delicious pot pies covered with her world-class gravy. I remember she used to make cold cucumber soup. "Consumé," I guess they call it now? Well, that was unheard of in those days. "Cold consumé" was not supposed to be invented until years later. She also made a beer and cheese-whip dip. That too wasn't supposed to be invented until years later. They say that necessity is the mother of invention. Well, that mother's name was "Tessie." Speaking of inventions, that's how we got most of our toys. We invented them. If we had old skates, we made scooters out of them. All you needed was an apple box and a 2-by-4 piece of lumber about 2 to 3 feet long. You could always find an apple box behind a grocery store and pick up a piece of wood off a scrap pile where somebody was building something. Nothing was ever thrown away. We even straightened out nails and reused them. You took the skates apart then fastened the front skate wheels to the front of the 2-by-4 and the back wheels to the back. That way you could steer from the front. Then you nailed the apple box on the 2-by-4 and put handles on the top of the apple box. If you didn't put the apple box on it, it was kind of an early version of a skateboard. But with an apple box on it and handlebars, you had a coaster. Of course, you fancied them up by painting and nailing bottle caps on them. You put inside shelves in there also. Pretty cool, eh? We built some great "Soapbox Derby" cars too. Of course we built those with Pop's help. We were always going to enter "The Derby," but somehow we never did get it done. Probably because we didn't think we would win and we probably didn't have the entering fees either. We made bows and arrows out of tree limbs and string; rubber guns out of wood. We would cut out a handle and nail it to a long, narrow piece of wood. That would be the barrel of the gun. Next, we would put a clothespin on the back of the handle. Then we would cut up an old tire tube into round strips, tie knots in those round strips and stretch them out over that long barrel. Then we would fasten the rubber strips to the clothespin at the other end. Boy, if you put two knots in them, they really could smart!

      We actually didn't miss not having fancy, store-bought toys. So if we would get one for Christmas or something, it was like icing on the cake. We learned to make airplanes out of balsa wood and kites out of sticks and newspaper. We took pride in building them. We had contests to see who could build the best ones in the neighborhood. Seems to me it taught us a lot and it was fun! We didn't miss the luxurious life, because you can't miss what you never had! But you can want things and you can dream about getting them!

Grandma Rhea and Mom 1920s
Venice Beach, CA.

The Angel "Me"
5 or 6 years old
Sawtelle
1929

Venice Beach 1920s
Mom & Grandma

Theresa La Page
"Mom"

Chapter 4
All the Way With the WPA

We were holding our own until the time when there was some kind of disagreement between Mom and Pop and Grandma B. They were all involved. I don't remember what happened. All I can remember is that Pop was gone, and we were alone again. So Mom had to go back to work. Grandma Rhea and Grandpa Ote took up the slack. They didn't have a lot but they watched us kids and came up with a few dollars when they could spare it, and that made things a little easier. Mom was working at a restaurant again. She was breaking her back and making very little money. But, thank goodness, the separation didn't last very long and Pop came back home.

Times were still financially bad! It seemed like it was going to stay that way forever! But then came Franklin Delano Roosevelt (FDR), who started the WPA. God bless him! "FDR and the WPA and then everything was A'OK." WPA stood for Works Progress Administration. The New Deal era was in full swing. That was our salvation. We were finally going to have some financial stability in our lives. Pop landed a government job as a landscape engineer. He kidded about being a glorified gardener, but he was really very proud of his job. His first project was building the Arroyo Seco Freeway. It is now called the Pasadena Freeway. It went all the way from West L.A. to Pasadena and Azusa, probably about a whopping 50 miles, and we thought it was wonderful!

They used to make a big joke about the men leaning on their shovels all day long in the WPA, but I'll tell you what, that was a myth. Most of those guys were so glad to get those jobs that they worked long and hard. They built many wonderful freeways and highways. At that time, California had the best roads and freeways in the country -- better than most of the other states. Before the freeways, we had roads called speedways. These were long stretches of roads in the city where you didn't have any stop signs or signals or cross streets. You could just shoot along them without stopping. That's probably where the "freeway" idea came from.

Our family was actually starting to get a few nickels to clink together. So Pop decided to help Joe get a brand-new Schwinn bike. It was a streamlined, sparkling, shiny, silver thing of beauty. Of course, I got the old beat-up one. But that was OK, I was tickled to get it, and happy for my bro. He needed the new bike for his two paper routes. Pop made the down payment, about 10 bucks as I remember, and Joe made the monthly payments of about $2. In those days it seems like payments went on forever, and there was no interest, or extra charges added on. His paper routes made him from $10 to $15 a month -- if the people paid him, that is. Out of that he gave Mom $5 a month. Doesn't sound like much, does it? But boy, oh boy, I'll tell you what, you could buy a heck of a lot for that money.

Well, once again a Mexican gang struck. They wanted Joe's new bike. They chased him every opportunity they got when nobody was around to help. He was constantly on the run. This one time he came flying home on the bike with them behind him and misjudged a turn into a stone driveway. Whammo, he crashed into a cement wall at full speed. Fortunately, he was OK, but the bike wasn't. It wrecked the front wheel and the fork, and bent the heck out of it. Pop helped him fix it, but it was never the same after that. It kind of looked like a crab, sort of going straight ahead sideways. The only blessing was the gang finally gave up and left him alone. I guess maybe they were sorry for what they did. They weren't really bad guys, just different.

Then once again, the monkey wrench. Unexpectedly, Mom became pregnant with baby Russell. While we were all happy about a new baby, it meant that Mom had to quit working. That would make things a little tight again, moneywise. But Pop was promoted to foreman, and it did seem as if the country was starting to prosper. Things were beginning to get slightly better again. Mom and Pop and Grandma B were all getting along together, finally, so we settled in and we got comfortable.

By now we had a little Boston bull terrier and we named him "Boy." We also had a little female puppy from one of his litters and we called her "Baby." They were beautiful little guys and we cuddled up to them at night. It was a special feeling to hug their warm bodies and feel their love. It makes you feel safe and secure and teaches you to love unconditionally. I think you miss a lot by not knowing and growing up with a special pet that you love. There might be a theory out there that animals don't have souls or memories or brains, but there's no way that's true. They become a part of your heart and a part of your family. My life has been so enriched by them. As I look back all these years later, the memories are still warm and full of enjoyment and love.

We moved into a new house again, this time down the street a little and on the other side of the street, but still staying on "Armacost Alley." We now had a great big backyard with lots of trees. The lot was about 75 feet wide and 150 feet deep. Those days you got land with your home. Now you just get a two-story house on a little slab of cement with a postage stamp backyard and front yard. We even had a garage off the alley with a loft in it, which made a great clubhouse. There was a big walnut tree, among others, that was perfect for a treehouse so, of course, we built one. It had a trap door with a hanging rope ladder. It was our private hideaway place. Later on we were to have some great adventures in our treehouse.

Money was still nonexistent, but we always managed to have some fun and something to eat. One of the main reasons for eating at this time was "Mr. Jonna" and his grocery store. It was located down at the end of our street on the corner of Armacost Avenue and Santa Monica Boulevard. When we moved to 1451 Armacost Ave., Mr. Jonna and his family were our next-door neighbors. We were to be friends and neighbors for many years. Now that I look back on it, they were an unusual sort of family, to say the least.

Well, what am I saying? I guess we were an unusual family too. There was Mr. Jonna, a portly looking, little round man in his late 40s or early 50s. He had a little round face that was pinched by little round "Ben Franklin" glasses. His gray hair was immaculately trimmed in a round, cereal-bowl style. I guess it was fair to say, he was a well-rounded man! He was very soft spoken and mild mannered. He always wore a long-sleeved button-down sweater, slate blue or gray. It usually matched his hair. His pants always matched, too. They were kind of like mailman uniform pants, sort of a slate gray blue. I think Mr. Jonna might have been part saint. He led a very lonely life. I also think that he might have been a little sweet on Mom. He carried us through that big Depression.

We ran a bill for years and years at the grocery store. My Mom tried to buy only the necessities, but when she got home she always found something extra thrown in with no charge, like a piece of steak or maybe some ice cream, something Mr. Jonna knew we could not afford. Of course, we paid a few pennies on the bill now and then, but it wasn't much and it wasn't often. He carried many other families through the bad times, too. Unfortunately, when the good times came, many of them did not pay him back. We did though! That was the first thing I did when I got my first job. I paid off our bill with the Jonnas, then I paid room and board money to the folks. Mrs. Jonna was the neighborhood mystery. You never got a good look at her. We only got brief glimpses of her sneaking in and out of the shadows or peeking out from behind the curtains and drapes. She was as skinny and narrow as Mr. Jonna was round. She had long, dark scraggly hair and large, black frightened eyes that stared at you out of a ghostly white face. She always wore some sort of a flowing dress or gown and rarely did you ever hear her speak. She just sort of floated in and out of the shadows. Sometimes you could hear faint, eerie laughter. Looking back now, the poor lady must have had some unknown problems -- shades of "Jane Eyre." Then there were the kids. Katherine was the oldest. She was somewhere in her late 20s. She was a beautiful, brown-eyed gal with a friendly smile and a great infectious laugh. Yet there was always something sad about her. Perhaps her mom had something to do with that. Katherine was the one who took care of the family. There didn't seem to be any personal life for her. I used to watch for the times when Katherine would be working at the store, because she used to give me more for my money. They had this candy game called "Lucky-Bites." They were little chocolate-covered pieces, sort of like mints, only they had vanilla, chocolate or strawberry cream centers. You won prizes if you got the colored ones. Katherine used to give me tips on where the "Lucky-Bites" were. That was a fun game and they just cost 1 cent a bite and they tasted great. Well, next in line in the Jonna family was Bill Jonna. He was about Joe's age, maybe a little older, and he was a spoiled, nasty brat. He had blond hair and blue eyes. I swear he could have been Hitler's right-hand man. He was very handsome but he usually had a sullen or arrogant look on his face. He always seemed to be mad about something, particularly if he didn't get his way. He and I clashed a great deal. I wonder why? Then came Barbara -- my pal and Joe's dream girl. She was a golden-haired blond with starry blue eyes and cute little dimples. She had Shirley Temple's curls and a Shirley Temple smile. She could even tap dance like Shirley. She took lessons and then passed them on to me. I did OK, but I was much better at turning double plays than I was at the "buck and wing." We were great pals, Barb and I, even though we were such opposites. We did a lot of things together, but she was Joe's age and went to a private school, so that limited our time together. Barb was also very girly and I was a tomboy, but I tried and she tried. We played football and baseball. Barb would play, but she wasn't the greatest at it. She definitely caught and threw like a girl. She was kind of awkward at it and she wore a dress over jeans! We thought that was kind of funny, but I guess my "buck and wing" was kind of funny, too! We liked each other and for a while we were close friends. We went on diets together; we drank liquid Jell-O and black coffee. That's how I got introduced to black coffee and I still drink it that way. But not the Jell-O, yuk!

We had a clubhouse down the street behind the grocery store. It was a garage and it was filled with groceries and empty boxes. We built our office out of cardboard boxes. That's where we wrote the neighborhood newspaper. We called it "The Daily Scoop"! Now, that was a disaster because we published some things people did not want known. Soon we were out of business and we were lucky that our folks weren't sued.

After that closed down, we had meetings in our treehouse. What are secret treehouses for? Secret things, right? So, one day we were in our treehouse doing our secret thing -- which, at the time, was a biggie! Some time earlier we had made corncob pipes out of the real thing with bamboo stems and we pretended like we were smoking! Well, at the time we made them, Mom thought that was pretty cute. So now we decided to try the real thing. Either Bill or Barbara had swiped some "Twenty Grand" cigarettes and we crammed them into the green corncob pipes and lit them. We were just puffing away, coughing, gagging and laughing, but still puffing away like big people, when wham! All of a sudden, up through that trap door on the floor popped Grandma Rhea's regal head. Wow! Talk about a shock! On my meter it ranks right up there on the Richter scale with King Kong's big hand reaching in that skyscraper window and grabbing Faye Wray. We never dreamed that Ma could or would climb up that tree. She had made one of those drop-in visits and she caught us red-handed. She gave us that "Ah ha! I got you" look and now we were really going to get it. Then she spoke to us in a steely tone. "This must never happen again," and her head disappeared. We sat petrified thinking, "Oh, boy, we're really going to pay for this one." But, you know what? She didn't squeal on us. At the time, we couldn't figure that one out. Later on I realized that seeing those green corncob pipes, she knew we were going to pay one way or another. And we did! We were so sick! We threw-up for days. Mom thought we had some kind of terrible disease. Well, you know what? Neither Joe nor I ever took up smoking. Barbara didn't either. That cured us. Only Bill did, but then he would just out of meanness. I think growing up was a lot more fun in those years than it seems to be now. We played games all the time. Some of them we just made up. We played "kick the can" and "hide and seek." Like I said, we made our own toys. Also, we filled up bottle caps with mud and shot them like marbles. Of course, baseball was always around. Once in a while we got store-bought toys for Christmas. Sometimes I even got a doll, but I really didn't like playing with dolls. But you know what? My brother Joe liked them, but that was OK because later on he liked the real ones better.

    It just seemed like there was nothing you couldn't do if you tried. Everything was a challenge and it was so much fun to accept the challenge and beat it. We learned a lot. As I said, there was always a baseball game going on somewhere and wherever that game was, we always managed to find it or it would find us. We just seemed to be very busy playing hard all the time and baseball was always our first and our last choice.

    Our times with the Jonna family and my friendship with Barbara wasn't destined to last long. There were too many differences in our ages and in our lifestyles. They had private schools, music and dance lessons. Joe and I were the poor neighbors. Barbara and Katherine never treated us that way, but we felt it. And Bill, well, he let us know every chance he had that we were inferior. But that was fortunate for me because when we went through the dangerous age of being curious about sex, Bill was the one who came up with the dirty books and wanted to try things out. My dislike for him kept me out of trouble; that and my brother's watchful eye. Joe always kept a close eye on me, his beloved little sis. He always had the biggest crush on Barbara and while she was very fond of him, she told him that he was too much like a brother to be her boyfriend. Besides, we both told him at the time that he kissed oceans. Joe just "kissed oceans." In other words, he was kind of a sloppy kisser. Sally, my sister-in-law, tells me that he got over that. She surely ought to know, they just celebrated their 61st wedding anniversary. So I know he's pretty good at kissing now!

Time passed and while we remained next door to the Jonnas, we slowly grew apart. Our friendship just kind of faded away into the background. I will always remember Barbara and I know Joe will too. I will especially remember those warm, summer nights when we played games in the streets and stayed out in our front yards until 10 p.m. at night. Games like touch football, kick the can, hide and seek, and stink base. Remember "ollie ollie oxen free?" Well, the spelling might not be right and I don't know what the heck it means, but that's how it sounded. You know, when you couldn't find somebody and then you finally gave up looking for them?

We had our quiet moments, too. Sometimes when we were tired of games, Barbara and I used to lie out on their thick, manicured front lawn and make pictures in the sky out of the beautiful, snowy white clouds. I wonder if she remembers that? I wonder if she is still alive? Oh my, those were the days.

Once again it seemed like the country was working its way out of the Depression and that the happy "good time sun" was going to shine!

Dad's job was going good. He was bringing in the bucks. We got to go to a picture show (as we called it) once in a while and we were able to make fudge -- and have all the ingredients to put in it. But as usual, just when things got going good, something always hit the wringer. Disaster struck again. Pop got caught in a landslide on his freeway job and his left foot and leg got crushed. He had to have a deep hip cast put on. In those days there was no unemployment insurance protection; if Pop couldn't drive to work he simply would have lost his job. Somehow, someone had to drive him to work, wait for him and drive him back home.

Joe had two paper routes so he couldn't give those up -- we needed the money. Mom had little baby bro Russell to take care of, so she couldn't do it. So I was elected. I already knew how to drive because Joe had taught me. So I drove Pop to and from work all summer in that little, four on the floor, green Ford pickup. Can you imagine a little 11-year-old girl out there on the 405 or 101 freeways today? Joe had known how to drive from the age of eight. Dad (Charlie Paire) had taught him. That way Joe could drive when Dad was too drunk.

Through the years Dad would show up sober every now and then when Pop wasn't around. Mom would let Joe and I spend a little time with him, even though he wasn't paying alimony. She would let Joe go with him for a day sometimes, but, because of his drinking, she didn't trust him with me. She was right, too, because Joe had some harrowing times with him. You could get away with letting kids drive then, because there weren't that many cars on the roads. There also weren't nutty drivers from all over the world like there are now. Road rage was unheard of -- sort of like science fiction. It was even legal for a kid to drive when you were 15, if you had an adult relative in the car with you.

I remember Jody telling me the stories of his driving experiences with Dad. It's funny now, but it wasn't at the time. This one time, Dad picked him up in the morning and they drove around town for a while visiting Dad's old cronies. He loved showing off his son. He would polish off a couple drinks and then hit the road again. Dad also had a bottle of Muscatel wine in the car, and he was sipping on that in between stops. By mid afternoon he was pretty well smashed. They wound up in downtown Beverly Hills, stuck at a stop signal. Dad was too drunk to get the car in gear. So he finally just got out, staggered around the car and pushed "Little Jody" into the driver's seat and passed out, leaving this 8-year-old kid trying to drive a stick shift. Well, "Little Jody" did the "buck and wing" for a little while. Then he finally got the car in gear, and rock and rolled out of there. He learned to drive the hard way, cold turkey! He told me about another time, when he was only 4 years old. He and Dad were going over old "Sepulveda Pass" (there was no 405 Freeway at that time -- there was just a narrow winding road!) and Dad was barreling around a big curve. I guess he looked over just in time and saw "Little Jody" sliding out the car door. He grabbed him by his belt, just in time to save him! Seems Dad hadn't made sure that the door was closed properly. Jody never told Mom about those narrow escapes, because we loved our Dad, even though we knew he was such a stinker at times. He tried time after time to quit drinking, but he could never stick to it! He was a "Jekyll and Hyde." Great guy when he was sober and most of the time, even when he was drinking. But then once in a while he would go over the top and become a devil. I would live to regret that, years later. Anyway, by me driving Pop to work with his broken ankle, we got through the summer and Pop was able to hang on to his job. Thus, we continued to prosper, at least for the time being.

Pop Gma B, Uncle Steve
& Baby Russ

Pop, Baby Russ
& W.P.A. Gang

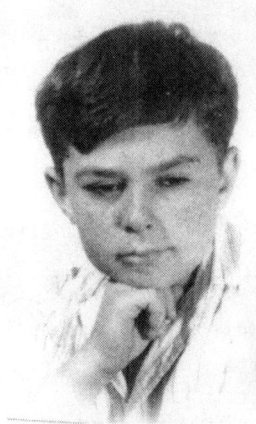

"The Thinker"   Double Trouble   "The Stinker"
                 "The Terrible Eights"

Chapter 5
Hard Times & Softball

Jody has now become Joe and I've become Sis instead of Sissy. Even though Joe was 18 months older than me, he was the kind of brother who didn't mind his little sister tagging along. In fact, he usually came and got me if I wasn't already there. We were constant companions; we laughed together, cried together and fought together. We were in constant competition in all the sports -- and I beat him a lot of the time. This shows you what a good brother he was because he still loved me.

University High School was just a block from the house and it had tennis courts. We had some old, used tennis rackets and we played tennis every day after school. We kept score and I can remember it getting up to like 214 to 215 sets. Mom always knew who won before we told her, because it was always the one leading the parade home. We played football in the streets, of course. The neighborhood gang would get together and choose up teams. This was a constant because you could play football even after it was dark. With the streetlights, you could see that big oblong football. But baseball was still our favorite game.

When we would choose up teams, Joe would tell the guys, "If you want me on the team you have to take my sister, too." I liked to kid him and say, "A year later, in order to get me they had to take you." My feet were firmly planted on the path that would take me down the road to Cooperstown. With the rough and tough sandlot experience my natural talent blossomed and I was playing aggressive softball in an industrial league at the age of 10. By the time I was 12, I had little time for anything else but school and baseball. I was playing on three different softball teams, in three different leagues, and all the teams had sponsors.

The first team I played for was sponsored by a little grocery store on Santa Monica Boulevard in Sawtelle. It was called Satinger's Grocery Store. If we won our game, we got to go over to the store and they gave us a big brown paper bag and we could fill it with anything we wanted. So I learned early that if I wanted to bring home the bacon I better win. In the other two leagues I got what was called gas money. It ranged from 75 cents to $1.50, and sometimes hamburgers and hot dogs were included. It sure didn't amount to much by today's standards, but in those days, 75 cents could buy a lot of stuff. A stamp only cost 2 cents, a paper maybe a nickel, a dozen eggs 25 cents, a loaf of bread maybe 6 cents. Milk cost maybe 6 cents a gallon and steak maybe a big 20 cents. By the time you throw in a veggie and dessert that was about 75 cents worth of stuff.

We were still pretty entrenched in the Depression so the money was a godsend. I was so proud that I was finally big enough to help the family out -- because first, last, and always, we were a family. We had been raised to share! This is one of the most valuable lessons in life that you can learn. Remember, what goes around comes around. In the Bible they say it differently; they say, "Do unto others." About this time, we gals around the country were starting to step it up and do some role modeling. Amelia Earhart was flying around the world. Shirley Temple was singing, "On the Good Ship Lollipop." Eleanor Roosevelt was starting to be heard from, and, yeah, I felt right in the swing of things!

Our grocery-store team played our home games at the old soldiers' home, technically know as The Veteran Administration Ballpark in Sawtelle. It is now known as the Jackie Robinson Stadium, West L.A. The games were free. We played for the entertainment of the old vets, our families and anybody else who wanted to drop in and watch a ballgame. I have a certificate of merit from the first chief administrator for playing there. Our girls' softball games were played at night under about one candlepower light. A steel helmet certainly would have been helpful in the outfield.

I used to have a little superstition, a little ritual I went through, to make the old boys laugh. There was a fire extinguisher hanging on the wire fence by the dugouts. When I would go past it on my way to the on-deck circle, I would stick the nose part of the hose into the fence. Then I would turn around and swing my two bats to warm up. I would pretend not to notice that one of the old geezers would sneak up and push the hose out, so it would hang down again. Then, when I would turn around and see it, I would give a puzzled look and push it in again. Well, this would go on as long as I was in the on-deck circle. If I was there long enough, at one point I would pretend frustration, and eventually anger. The old guys would bust a gut laughing.

When I think about it, I always did like to make people laugh. I guess that's something I got from my Mom. I still enjoy doing it! As I said before, there weren't too many spectators in the stands at these games. But one thing you could always be sure of was that my Mom and my family would be there. My Mom was always my most loyal and consistent rooter. Sometimes, she got excited and got into some pretty heated arguments in the grandstand -- especially if they criticized her little girl. But she was always a lady with class. I'm like Mom in a lot of ways, but I'm not too sure about the lady or that class part. I know that I got her sense of humor and that's for sure.

I was just reading an old letter I got from her in 1945 when I was back playing ball. She wrote, "You better get that charley horse out of your arm and write me or I'm going to make sure that you get one where you sit down." Through everything I did, my Mom was always on the sidelines rooting for me and my team all the way. I know that has a lot to do with how I turned out -- well, at least the good part. Pop helped in every way he could, too. He hauled our team around in that little green pickup all those nights and to all those games. Sometimes there would be four of us gals in the front seat and about five or six more in the bed of the truck! That little old baby just kept on going. I think it was about a 1923 or 1924 Chevy. They made cars and trucks in those days that just kept on going and going, like the bunny!

We sure had a lot of fun and a ton of good times at that old ballpark. It was there, I guess, where I first realized how much I loved baseball. I knew I always wanted to be a part of it, and I wasn't the only one who felt that way. Many of my teammates loved baseball just like I did. One of my teams at the "Old Soldiers Home" Ballpark was called the "Ocean Park Reds" -- we had these fire-engine red, satin uniforms. Well, our pitcher Jenny and our coach Bruno fell in love and decided to get married. We had the ceremony right there at the Old Soldiers Home Ballpark, right **at home plate!** Jenny was attractive. She was a sexy-looking gal with long blond hair. There she stood in her red satin shorts and shirt, with a white bridal veil trailing behind her long shapely legs. What a picture! Now that's real baseball love for you.

I can't remember if Bruno was a good coach or not, but I can remember he was Italian, tall, dark and handsome. He had a cute little mustache and, as so often is the case with Italians, he could sing. He reminded me of an Italian version of the old-time movie star John Boles. (If any of you out there go back as far as me in the movies you might remember him!) I even remember the song Bruno sang to Jenny at the wedding. It was called "If I Had My Way" --

and Bruno obviously had his way! It went something like this, "If I had my way, dear, forever there'd be a garden of roses for you and for me." The last line, "You'd reign all alone, like a queen on a throne. If I had my way." I guess at that time I was going through my romantic stage of growing up.

By 1936 I was in the sixth grade at Brockton Avenue grammar school. Joe had already graduated and was now going to University High. "Uni High" went from the sixth grade to the 12th. I was missing my big bro and just counting the time until I could graduate and move over to high school with him. I was pretty bored at school because I had to play all the sports with the girls only and most of them weren't very good. So I didn't hang around much after school to play kickball or baseball or whatever was going on. But there was one time I had stayed to help a teacher, and when I was walking out across the playground I heard a commotion behind me. Then I heard this loud voice bellow out! "Get out of the way or I'll knock your head off!"

I turned around and saw this lanky, wild-haired, wild-eyed, blond girl standing there, getting ready to kick the ball. I just looked at her, turned my head and kept on walking. Next thing I knew the ball went whistling by my ear, and, wham, into one of the girls on the playground. She started holding her stomach and crying! This lean, scraggly haired, blond girl goes running over and says, "Oh you big crybaby, can't you take it?"

Up comes a teacher and grabs her by the ear and says, "Faye Dancer, I told you not to kick it so hard!" The teacher dragged her away, scolding her every step of the way. "Now you've done it. I'm not warning you again. Now you can only play with the boys." This blond girl unleashed a series of swear words that we never used in school! The last I saw of her, the teacher was foaming at the mouth and dragging her into the principal's office. I thought, *Who was that*? Little did I know that Faye Dancer would someday become my very best friend down through the years.

Like I said, school was a bit of a drag. I was too smart, I guess, because I didn't want to study. So I would just get C's and B's without studying. If I was in danger of flunking anything, I would write the teacher a poem. It always worked. I would wind up with a decent grade. I was just biding time waiting to get over to University High with my bro. But, wouldn't ya know, the year I graduated they decided to make Uni High a senior high only -- grades nine through 12. So I had to detour and take the bus to Emerson Jr. High School, which was located in Westwood. Boy, I hated taking that bus trip up and back every day. In fact, I hated that school, and for no really good reason, I guess. It was just that Uni High was right next door with my bro just a block away! But I had to ride a bus three miles to Westwood Village every day, just to go to school.

Besides, there weren't my kind of people in Westwood. It had been a private school before they made them take the kids from public schools. The majority of the students ahead of me came from rich families and they were snooty and "hoity toity." I didn't mingle with them. Actually, a couple of them tried to be friends with me. I think Helen Darling and Faith De Muire (and they were just as beautiful as their names sounded) really wanted to be my friends. Later on, I read that Faith became a protégé of Howard Hughes and starred in a couple of "B" movies.

I got brave one year and wrote and acted out a little skit for one of our school plays. We had this recreation area called "The Bowl." It was just a big round area with a grandstand all around it. I put on my red satin shorts and did a musical version of "Little Red Riding Hood." About all I can remember about it is that I sang "When The Deep Purple Falls." I modified the words to fit. I remember the last line was "When the deep purple falls over sleepy garden walls, Wolfy, come back to me." Well, it caused quite a commotion and the teachers thought it was too risqué. But the kids loved it. That's when Helen and Faith tried to include me in their little clique. I wasn't comfortable with it, nor did I have the clothes to wear in their circle. I wasn't comfortable in heavy makeup like they wore, either, and I wasn't ready for the boys yet. To this day, I don't know whether they really wanted to include me in their glamorous clique or whether they were just making fun of me. I had gained a little bit of popularity and my little red riding hood thing made me a little bit of a celebrity. Maybe that attracted them for a short time. At any rate, it didn't work out.

I stayed pretty much a loner my first two years at Emerson. It wasn't until the last year that I finally met up with a friend. I used to have to wait on the corner of Armacost Avenue and Santa Monica Boulevard for the bus. One morning, I was standing there waiting for a bus and lo and behold, there stood the lanky, wild-haired, wild-eyed blond thing that I had had the brief encounter with at Brockton Avenue School. We didn't talk much at first. I really didn't want to get acquainted with her from what I remembered, and neither did she with me. But one day we had to sit together on the bus so we started talking. We agreed that Emerson was a dumb school, and we both wanted to go to University High. I discovered she could be quiet and reserved when she wanted to be. She just liked to shock people, for whatever reason -- it amused her, I guess.

We got around to talking about baseball and I found out she played softball at the Vets home also. Well, that definitely made us friends. I was a year older and in the ninth grade and she was in the eighth grade, so we only saw each other on the buses coming and going. Eventually, through fate I guess, we both wound up on my softball team at the Old Soldiers Home. Then we became real friends. We were both pretty good ball players -- two little daredevils! That combination always proved for exciting times. We really could have gotten into a lot more trouble than we did! We were either very lucky, or maybe the Lord knew that we really weren't bad and just watched over us.

There was one episode that could have really been disastrous. We found ourselves "up the creek without a paddle." That was what I call the "Los Angeles River" episode and our "point of no return adventure." Rome Carluche was the coach on another softball team. He knew that Faye and I were good ball players and he wanted us on his team. He invited us out to his little ranch in the Monterey Park area. It was out East L.A. way. He had several horses and he let Faye and me ride some of the young ones that needed breaking in and exercising. He was making points with us and getting his horses exercised at the same time. Smart guy. Anyway, Faye turned out to be a natural on a horse and I guess I inherited my ability from my Mom and her Indian pony stories, because we both could ride well.

We rode bareback and barefoot with only a rope halter. We got pretty good at it, so we got bold and this one day we rode down to the banks of the L.A. river, which was quite a ways from the ranch. We didn't think it was dangerous because everybody in California knows there's never any water in the L.A. river! So here we are, riding along the bank of the river, on this gravel path that was about 4 feet wide. It had some thick trees and brush and then a cement wall going straight up on our right side. On our left side was this steep drop down to the river.

The bank just went straight down all the way to the riverbed, which was probably a good 100 feet down, maybe even a little more.

Faye and I were talking about how we needed to start teaching our horses to go down the sides of hills, especially the one I was riding. He would always shy away from going up or down a hill. Up ahead of us we saw a big man coming toward us. He had on raggedy jeans and a raggedy shirt. He looked dirty and unshaven. We pulled our horses to a stop but he kept coming at us. He started to talk to us, "Hey, girlies, how sweet you look." His voice was syrupy and he had a strange look in his eyes. I said, "Oh, oh, Faye, let's get out of here." We both just barely had enough room to swing our horses around and when we did, there, coming out of the bushes behind us, were two dirtier, nasty-looking men.

We looked at each other and knew we were in trouble. Then we looked down that steep bank and made an unspoken choice. "You go first," I yelled. "Kick him, Faye, and pray that Smokey follows." Faye gave her horse a "Yee haw!" and a quick jerk and kicked him hard. He reared up and then plunged down the side of the bank. I kicked my horse and screamed, "Yea, Smokey! Go Smokey!" after a heart-stopping moment, he reared up, kicked back and then, thank God, he plunged down the side of that bank after Faye and her horse. What a wild, sliding, thrilling ride that was. Somehow we made it to the bottom of the river in one piece, and still on the horses! When we calmed the horses down and looked up we saw there were now about six guys standing up there. They were swearing at us and making obscene gestures. We kicked our horses again and high-tailed it out of there.

What we escaped could easily have been rape or murder or both! God was good to us! I've never forgotten that episode, and Faye hasn't either. That was the end of our riding in isolated areas. Actually, that really ended our riding careers. We made the mistake of telling our folks what happened and they wouldn't let us go anymore. Wonder why not?

Girls', Men's Nines Battle for Crowns
Twelve Games Carded

By Allen Dale

[Newspaper article text]

Pepper, Age 14

Faye and Pepper
entertaining the troops

Early Softball Buddies
"Me, Snookie, Tiby and Faye on Donkey" Not sure who's the "Jackass" here ! Tiajuana Fun
1945

Dr. Pepper Softball Team
Pepper, bottom row second from the right with
Burgess Meredith, Buddy Ebsen & Robert Preston

Ocean Park Reds - Pepper, age 14

Youngs Market Championship Team
Pepper, age 15

"Explaining The Game !"
Pepper, age 14

Chapter 6
From Hot Dogs -- to Hot Tamales

By 1940 I finally made it out of snooty Westwood and back to Sawtelle and good old University High School, and Joe and I were united again. I felt whole again! I left Faye behind me for the time being because she still had another year to finish at Emerson Jr. High. We still played on the same softball team, but we didn't see as much of one another as we had when we were going to school together. Uni High was a melting pot of all races that was so typical in most California high schools. It had a unique and beautiful campus. It was built on top of a hill that originally was part of an Indian reservation. The campus was terraced off into three different levels.

The top level was office buildings and classrooms. More classrooms were located on the middle level and it was called the grove because it had walnut trees and majestic, tall oak trees scattered throughout it. It also had a beautiful, sparkling natural stream running through it. At the far end there was a little snack bar that sold popcorn, drinks, candy and stuff like that. On that level there were also little, individual bungalow classrooms. They were used when there was an overload of students. They were fun to have, but, boy, they could really be uncomfortable at times when the weather didn't cooperate -- so it was hot in the summer and cold in the winter. They had no heating systems and the windows were the only air conditioning. But we really didn't do a lot of complaining because that was normal for the time.

The bottom level held our auditorium and our sports center. That's where the tennis courts, the gym and the football field were located. The track surrounded the football field. It was really quite a nice campus for those days. I guess that was one of the reasons why a lot of famous movie stars picked Uni High as their alma mater. Their attendance was pretty much mythical. They attended only major functions for technical requirements and publicity reasons. I'm speaking of yesterday's stars, of course. People like Mickey Rooney, Judy Garland, Linda Darnell, Ann Baxter, Jane Brian, Marshal Thompson, just to name a few. Oh, yeah, and another one you might remember as Norma Jean Baker before she became Marilyn. I know there have been many schools mentioned that she attended, but I can show you my yearbook with her

47

picture in it. I still get calls from people wanting to buy it because of that. So I know she attended Uni!

Well, now it was time for me to have another name change. I had gone from Sissy to Sis and from Peewee to Little Stuff in softball because I was usually the littlest or the youngest person on the team. Now I became Pepper. This was mainly because my curly, platinum blond hair had gone golden and now was developing a red tint to it. It was still just as curly as ever and that's a blessing that has remained with me all my life. I have always been grateful for that -- especially after I joined the All Americans as a catcher and needed about three showers a day. But, at that time, it was kind of a stigma to be a redhead. They were called hot stuff and that was definitely not desirable! The boys would tease me and call me "Red Pepper, Red Pepper." I would protest and say, "My hair is not red, it is blonde. I'm a strawberry blonde."

They would say, "Oh, no! Oh, no, it's red. You're red pepper. You're red pepper!" Eventually, the red got dropped, but the Pepper stuck. Since my personality was always much more of a pepper than my given name of Lavone, I became "Pepper Paire," a name that has always fit me much better than any of the others. The media and the fans loved it during my baseball days. Although I was dubbed other names at different times, I was destined to remain Pepper. First I became Auntie Pepper, then I became Mom Pepper and then I became Grandma Pepper. And I would dearly love to live long enough to become Great Grandma Pepper.

By the time I was 16, I was playing on three different softball teams in three different leagues. I was making seven to eight bucks a week and helping the family pay bills. It was hard juggling my schoolwork with baseball games and staying out late for those doubleheaders, traveling all over, getting home late and getting to bed late. But when I got behind in my studies, I had my built-in solution. I would do the old "write the teacher a poem" bit and wind up with a good grade. It always worked.

It was about this point that my travels began. It was the summer of 1940! I was picked for an all-star softball team to go to Mexico -- Guadalajara and Mexico City. We also played a couple of exhibition football games while we were down there -- talk about ahead of my time! That, my friends, is when I started writing this book. My original title was "From Hot

Dogs To Hot Tamales." Mom let me go on that trip, but she worried about it until I got back home safely. The trip was promoted by one of our softball coaches. He was also a promoter, but he didn't have a good track record for making money. He was toying with the idea of starting a women's football league. As you can imagine, it was considered an outrageous idea and probably more of a publicity stunt than anything else.

We had previously played a couple of football games at the Los Angeles Coliseum. There were maybe 3,000 or 4,000 people there and you could hardly see or hear them. At that time I was about 4 feet 8 inches tall and weighed maybe 100 pounds soaking wet. I was the center on offense and a linebacker on defense. The gal I was supposed to stop was Jan Woods. She was 6 feet tall and weighed 180 and was a javelin thrower in the Olympic Games. I always ended up at the bottom of the pile with my nose in the dirt.

That's when I picked up the nickname "Peewee" for a while. The announcer would say, "Well, folks, Peewee Paire is at the bottom of the pile again." My poor Mom would be sweating it out, waiting for me to get up and she'd be saying, "Oh, no, my poor little girl, she's getting flattened." Miraculously, I never really got hurt bad. Most of the time I nailed that big Amazon. I didn't wind up flat either! I'm more the Dolly Parton type.

The whole football scheme never went anywhere. Meanwhile, I was still doing all my softball things at the same time. After the end of the 1941 softball season, I went on another tour. I was really starting to get the travel bug. We toured the Midwest and played an occasional exhibition football game, but it was mainly an all-star softball tour. We called ourselves the "Hollywood All Stars." One place I especially remember is Kirkfield, Missouri. I still have newspaper clippings and a scorecard from Kirkfield in my scrapbook. Another town we played in was Tulsa, Oklahoma. That stands out as a giant memory!

When we got there, the local newspaper headlines read, "Hollywood Girls Play Tulsa Midgets Champs." We thought, "Hey, that's great! This ought to be easy. We're just playing a bunch of midgets!" Well, we found out differently. The Tulsa Midgets were the Girls World Amateur Softball Champions and they all stood more than 6 feet tall —— a little play on words there. They were dressed in men's uniforms, but they wore rubber spikes. We came out in our little red satin shorts and shirts and our metal spikes and beat the tar out of those gals. Actually, we were just a little pick-up team. Many of us were just young kids, but I can't remember losing too many of those games. We were supposed to split the gate profits and I can remember seeing some pretty big crowds. But if the tour made money, it never got as far as Mom and me. We got home with less money than we left with and counted ourselves lucky to get home. We found out from that trip just how popular softball was getting all over the USA and Mexico, too.

We breathed a big sigh of relief when we got back to good old California. As I write now and think back at all the chances I took, I wonder if I would have the courage to do it all over again. It just seemed like the natural thing to do at the time. If there was a ballgame to be played, I wanted to be there no matter where it was. If there was a challenge thrown down, I picked it up undaunted. My Mom and Pop trusted me and gave me the freedom to be there and the courage to do it. As I think about it all these years later, I realize how lucky I was.

With softball growing in popularity, our California teams became the center of attraction. We had a big league operation going on here. We had paid admission, paid umpires, great crowds, big-name sponsors like 7UP, Dr Pepper, Young's Market, Goodrich Silvertown Tires, Signal Oil and many more. Our sponsors realized the value of such cheap advertising and bought us great-looking uniforms. We were all class in our colorful satin shorts and blouses. We also had brilliant-colored matching ski pants and jackets. We didn't wear hats and we had to furnish our own spikes and gloves. We had some very talented ballplayers and some extremely good teams and leagues.

One very good reason for our success was our weather. It gave us the jump on everything. We played round the clock, year in and year out. I can remember going to the beach on Christmas and practicing sliding in the sand. This all may sound like bragging, but, as they say, "The proof is in the pudding" and the pudding was the All American Girls Baseball League. Every Californian, or every "prune picker from the land of fruits and nuts" (as we were dubbed by the other ballplayers) made it into the league with flying colors. We were so successful in California that we had three paid admission ballparks in the Hollywood area alone. Fiedler Field number one was on Third Street and Fairfax Boulevard; Beverly Stadium was on Beverly Boulevard and Second Street; and Fiedler Field number two was right on Sunset Boulevard on the strip in Hollywood. It was next to the Grauman's Chinese Theater.

In one of the leagues I played for the Melrose Grotto Restaurant. It was located in Hollywood on Melrose Boulevard right across the street from R.K.O. Studios. Sometimes we would get a free dinner there after we played our game. We were eating there this one time when Lucille Ball and Desi Arnaz came in. It was before they were married and Lucy was a glamorous showgirl. Desi was just a young, handsome bandleader from Cuba. He made some overtures to us. He wanted to play "bissball" with us. No wonder Lucy had trouble with him down through the years.

In those early softball years there were also very good men's teams that shared the billing with us. They had some great stars including baseball's Lou Novikoff. He was known as the "Mad Russian." He's in the Softball Hall of Fame and was a fine pitcher. After he switched to baseball, he became an outfielder and won five minor league batting titles. Then he wound up a great career by playing in the majors for the Chicago Cubs. Lou used to come to our games because his little sister, Mary Novikoff, pitched in our league. She was a fine pitcher and a star like her brother.

Believe it or not, we girls were the fans' favorites and we outdrew the guys all the time. The main reason for that was because we played so well — but maybe, just maybe, the fact that we looked cute in those satin shorts helped. You know what I think the real reason was? I think it was because we tried so hard, giving 110 percent all the time. I think that showed. Since we played in the heart of downtown Hollywood, we became the favorites of many movie stars. Many big stars attended our games. Mom really gave me the business one night telling me that there was a very famous movie star watching and that I was his favorite ballplayer. So, I'm guessing Clark Gable, Tyrone Power, Robert Taylor. She's laughing like crazy and saying, "No, no, guess again." Turned out to be Jimmy Durante. Well, as a teenager, I was a little crushed by that because I looked upon him as a comedian. I was looking for romance. But, hey, Jimmy, if you're up there looking down now, I thank you so much for appreciating me.

Some of the stars I remember coming out to the games were Victor Killian, Robert Preston, Burgess Meredith, Buddy Ebsen, Robert Taylor and Tyrone Power. I remember Carol Lombard was there with Clark Gable, George Raft and Brian Donlevy and really too many more to mention. They loved betting on our games. They would bet on the next pitch, whether it would be a strike or a ball. Every year we used to have a "leading men versus comedians" softball game for charity. We would play a regular game before or after. We also played donkey baseball against them. What a riot! You had to hit the ball, jump on a donkey, ride him to first base, get off the donkey, ride the donkey to the ball, get off him again, throw the ball, get back on the donkey and try to catch it. What a crazy game!

Being younger than my teammates at that time, my Hollywood nickname became "little stuff." But nothing really stuck until later on. Also, being younger, I usually wound up being the crowd favorite — add to that some ability and I guess my personality helped, too. Sometimes the stars would slip me an extra five bucks if they won money on me. My Hollywood teams were Dr Pepper and Young's Market. We were the class of the league along with Goodrich Silvertown Tires. We were always duking it out for first place with them. We were strong down the middle and we had a good catcher. We had Snookie Harrell at short and me at second. Our centerfielder was Faye Dancer -- or you might call her "All The Way Mae," as in the movie "A League of Their Own." Most of our players became stars in the All American League later on.

We had a very good pitching staff, which included Betty Luna who later played for the South Bend Blue Sox and the Rockford Peaches. Betty was a very good pitcher. She pitched a couple of no-hitters. We also had our blond bombshell, Teddy Minor. Teddy was a tall, well-built, slender, sexy-looking blonde. They were our aces. Then we had the coach's wife, Mabel. She was a heck of a good pitcher also, and we had a major smart manager, Freddy Pahler. Put that all together and we were tough to beat.

Our rivals, Goodrich Silvertown, also had future All-American greats on their team, like Dottie Wiltse Collins. She was a premier softball pitcher. They were also strong down the middle with Alma Ziegler (my buddy Ziggy) as their second baseman and a great pitcher in the All American. She was the franchise player for the Grand Rapid Chicks. They had Charlene "Shorty" Pryor, a fleet-footed centerfielder who could run the bases and slide well! They also had a good catcher and their manager was Bill Allington. Bill later managed in the All American for championship teams like the Rockford Peaches and the Fort Wayne Daisies. Bill was to become the most successful manager in the All American and was dubbed the "Silver Fox" because of his baseball brains and his silver, prematurely gray hair.

Freddy, our softball manager, would undoubtedly have been a successful manager in the All American had he chosen to go that way. But, he didn't. He and Bill disliked each other intensely so our teams naturally became great rivals. It was like the Giants and the Dodgers, always fighting it out to see who was going to win. Bill and Freddy managed in totally different ways. They were both extremely knowledgeable, but Freddy believed in teaching you by motivating you, caring for you and allowing you a certain amount of leeway. With Bill, it was his way or the highway. He could make you or break you, depending on whether or not you could take it. We had some epic battles between our two teams. We were always battling each other for the championship.

There was one Sunday night game I especially remember. We were playing each other in the championship finals and it was a tight, 0-0 contest. The house was packed and Dottie Wiltse was pitching against us. She and Teddy Minor, our blond bombshell, were duking it out. Bill Allington was pulling out all his tricks. Every time the umpire would put in a nice, new, white ball, it would soon disappear. The next thing you knew, there would be a dark-looking, well-worn ball out there by the time our team was up to bat. Well, this kept happening. Freddy would call time out and ask the umpire to throw in a new ball. At night, under softball lights, it was hard to see a ball when it got really dirty. With the speed of the pitchers out there, it was also dangerous. It was a routine thing to throw out a used one and throw in a nice, new, white one. But the new balls seemed to stay in there only as long as they came up to bat. Mysteriously, the dirty ones would reappear when Collins was on the mound and we were up to bat.

Freddy was getting madder and madder by the moment. After this went on for about two or three innings, Freddy called time, walked out and asked the umpire to look at the used ball. Freddy looked at it, carefully inspected it and then promptly threw it over the backstop and into the parking lot. Then he smugly walked back to our dugout. The umpire threw out a nice, new, white ball. Collins rubbed it up and threw one pitch, as required, and then out came Bill. He called time and asked for the ball. He looked at it, carefully inspected it and then promptly threw it over the backstop and into the parking lot. Then he handed Dottie a used one and smugly walked back to his dugout.

Well, you can guess what happened next. It went on and on, Bill throwing out the new ones and Freddy throwing out the old ones. The umpires were allowing it to happen because these were two great coaches and two prominent guys in our league. But, they finally had to stop the game because we ran out of balls. At that point the chief umpire took charge. He sent out for more balls and the game continued. As I remember, it went into extra innings and we finally won, 2-1. I think it was probably the longest game in our history. It took about four and a half hours to play. What a long night that was!

As I said before, I was playing in three different leagues. In my other leagues, the ballparks were usually free admission, except for the Fiedler Field ballparks. The other ballparks were not in the downtown Hollywood or L.A. area. The Ocean Park Reds played at the Soldiers Home ballpark, so we were the home team there. I remember one ballpark was out in East L.A., out around Slauson Avenue and Pico Boulevard. There was another park on Centinela in Inglewood. That was a cute, little wooded park area that sat down in a little dale with a lot of grass, flowers and trees. It was a really nice, well-kept diamond. It was fun to go there on a Saturday or Sunday with the whole family. Mom would take along a picnic lunch and then we'd play the game that night. The field lights were not so great. They usually consisted of a telephone pole with about a four-candle power light bulb on it. You might have three of them down each line and maybe two of them in the outfield.

Another park I played in was the Twelfth Street Park in Santa Monica. It was a multi-complex field run by the city for track and field meets and they had baseball there also. There was also midget car racing there at night. You could smell the fumes from miles away because those midget cars burned Castor oil in them. You could also hear them roaring from miles away. They were fun to watch. We usually played a late game after the races were over. The lights there were pretty good, but with all the abuse it took, the ball field was terrible. I wonder how much cancer we picked up from those fumes? Everyone had fun, of course, because we didn't have to pay to watch the races. That was yet another plus that baseball brought into my life.

"The Silver Fox" - Bill Allington
1945

Mexico City At 15
Pepper Top Most Left

Hollywood "All Stars" Softball in
summer Football in the fall

Pepper and team
mates in Mexico

55

Chapter 7
The Dynamic Duo

As my softball career progressed, I got more and more into it and played on more and more teams. Faye Dancer was destined to come back into my life. In 1941 I managed to get her on my elite Beverly Stadium team in Hollywood, so we started hanging out together again. The team we played for was sponsored by Dr Pepper -- appropriate, eh? Freddy Pfahler was still our manager. Mom and Pop and Faye's mom and pop became friends and the two families had a lot of fun together at the softball games. They would sit together and root for us. Our rooting section consisted of my Mom, Faye's mom, Olive, and Annabelle "Lefty" Lee's mom, Hazel. Lefty was a pitcher on our team and also the starting first baseman.

The moms would all root like crazy for us. The dads would just sort of hang around and jaw together. High up behind our moms sat Dottie Wiltse and "Snookie" Harrell's moms. Snookie was our shortstop and a great ballplayer, but her mom always sat with our archenemy, "Curveball" Wiltse's mom. It was a good spot for them to sit because that way their noses could stay up in the air. They would look down disapprovingly at our families rooting and hollering for us!

Sometimes, when we played the second game of a doubleheader, Faye and I would just sort of wander around and get lost. Our folks didn't know it, but while they watched the game, Faye would swipe her dad's car keys. Then we would go out to the parking lot and I would drive their brand-new 1940 two-door green Ford around. Sometimes we would race our pitcher Teddy (the blond bombshell). She had a souped-up 1936 Ford coupe. I usually won. Faye didn't drive until years later when I taught her, but she was always after me to drive. Once again, God was good to us because we never got caught, we never got a ticket and we never had an accident.

Faye and I didn't realize that we were different from Snookie and a lot of our other Californians, but we were. We were daredevils! We were great ballplayers and we loved playing the game (pardon my ego), but we loved to have a lot of fun, too. I don't think we were conceited about our skills, but we weren't backward about them either. As I read my own words, I can see how we were raised, compared with how their parents raised them, and that's part of what made us different!

We used to walk or ride our bikes to my Uncle Bonner and Aunt Amanda's house, who lived close to us. She was the same Aunt Amanda who took care of Joe and me when we were little. Uncle Bonner was my Mom's older brother. They never had any children so they would welcome our visits. They had this neat little house on a lot that was about 50 feet wide and probably 200 feet deep. The lot went all the way back from the front of their street to the railroad tracks that bordered Sepulveda Boulevard in Sawtelle. They had fruit trees, grapevines and lots of beautiful flowers. They also had chickens, ducks and rabbits, so it was a real interesting place for city kids to visit.

Uncle Bonner and Aunt Amanda made lots of clever wood craft type things, like weather vanes, trellises, cute little bird houses, garden seats, etc. Traffic was pretty heavy on Sepulveda Boulevard and there was room for cars to pull up and park all along the railroad tracks, so they had a good thing going. They did a good business. It was sort of like a fairyland to us. I learned a valuable lesson there. There was a little bird in a peach tree and he was just chirping away. Uncle Bonner had a BB gun to scare off the crows and to keep the cats and dogs from chasing the chickens and ducks. Well, I shot that BB gun at the little bird and darn if I didn't hit it. I had shot it from the back porch window. The little bird keeled over and fell out of the tree into the grass. I felt terrible. I rushed out to see if maybe it would miraculously be OK and I couldn't find it. I prayed for weeks that it would be OK and I never shot anything else while I was growing up. That's kind of the old cliché; don't shoot at anything unless you really _want_ to hit it.

Uncle Bonner had an old Model T car (about a 1918 or 1919) and he made a flat bed truck out of it! Boy, did I have fun driving that! It had two gears, one to drive forward, one to drive backwards and the brake pedal. I tell you what, you had to stand up to turn that sucker around a corner! It didn't have any top on it at all so you were pretty much exposed to the elements.

Aunt Amanda was a very good cook! She made this special concord grape pie for me. I've never heard of it before or after, but it was my favorite and it was delicious. She also made blackberry and blueberry dumplings and rhubarb pie. Boy, you just don't see those kinds of things on the menu anymore. We really had some fun times and some good eating when we were with them. We'd help them with the chores and play in the yard all day. Then we'd have a great fried chicken dinner, gravy, mashed potatoes, fresh veggies and homemade biscuits. And then those delicious desserts. We would listen to the radio, "Amos and Andy" and all those old radio programs, and eat popcorn. If it got too late and if it wasn't a school night, we would spend the night. They were modestly fixed, but to us they were rich. But I <u>did</u> have some <u>rich</u> relatives. They would be Aunt Holly and Aunt Hortense. They lived in a big stone mansion down in L.A. off Wilshire Boulevard in the high-rent district. Joe and I visited them a few times, but they would always be running in and out while we were there. So, this one time while they were gone we decided to make fudge. They sort of allowed us the run of the house. They were rich and had all the ingredients. We didn't have to leave anything out. Mom had taught us how to make fudge all kinds of ways with or without all the goodies. Well, it turned out great. It had the right look, the right smell and the right texture. It was perfect! Until we tasted it. It turns out we mistook the salt for the sugar. WOW! What a taste that was! But you know what? We ate it anyway. We always had a good time down there. But it just wasn't comfortable and we were always glad to get back home.

Our other rich relatives were Mom's sister, Aunt Sadie, and her husband, Uncle Dave. They lived in Idaho and owned cabins in Sun Valley and furniture stores in Jerome and Twin Falls. But I think they made most of their money on a string of mortuaries (we called them funeral parlors) that they owned. Mom and Joe visited them a couple of times and Joe went up there and worked for Uncle Dave one summer, but I never visited them. I guess I kind of resented the fact that they had so much and we had so little. They could have made Mom's life a lot easier. Their kids always thought that they were a lot better than us and they showed it. Well, they weren't really any better than us. Maybe they had more money, but they weren't any better. I often wonder now when I look back, if they saw my movie "A League of Their Own" and realized it was me when they read the end credits. We lost contact with them a long time ago.

Uncle Dave drove a fancy new Chrysler. When they would visit, he would pay me a dollar to wash it. Then they would go off sightseeing with Mom and Grandma Rhea and Grandpa Ote. They would go to Knotts Berry Farm, Ocean Park Pier or the beach. Uncle Dave would leave me the keys. Big mistake! Faye and I would wash and shine that sucker up and then race it up and down Wilshire Boulevard. I remember one time I went around a curve a little bit too fast and almost turned it over. I wonder if Uncle Dave ever realized why he always had to get gas every time he left our house? Once again, God was good to me!

It seems like cars could have been my downfall! I never realized how important they were in my life! The first car that Joe got to drive besides Dad's was our Grandma and Grandpa Rhea's. They had an old 1927 four-door black and purple Dodge (four on the floor). It had purple and black leather upholstery. When they got a new Dodge (it must have been about a 1936 or 1938 gold-colored coupe), they gave the old sedan to Mom. Joe got to drive it to deliver his papers. When he'd get sick with a cold or something, Mom would drive and I would hang on the running board and throw the papers while Joe directed us. What fun that was for me! That old Dodge is what Joe taught me to drive in when I was 10 or 11. Joe and I cut our teeth on California freeways. We never feared them, and because of that, we both were good drivers! Mom was a good driver, also, so I guess we came by it naturally.

While Joe was going to high school, he bought a 1932 Model A convertible with his pal, Bob Hook. They were paying for it by delivering papers on their paper routes. Bob was cute and a nice guy, but it seemed that Bob's father was involved in paying for the car and it got too complicated. Anyway, that partnership soon dissolved. I had a crush on Bob and that didn't work out either! We were pretty much in the high school scene now. Joe was in stage plays and on the football team. He was not really big enough for football. He only got in the games at the end. We called him "two-minute Joe." My bro Joe was actually a good all-around athlete, but not great. He always gave 100 percent in everything he did! I can remember that I used to wish I could be on his team so I could help him win, like when we were little! To this day my bro says, "If I had your arm, Sis, I'd be in the majors."

High school just kind of flew by with all the ballgames and all the school activities. To me school was sort of a minor thing in the background as my softball became more and more important. But I do remember this one time that Joe was in this stage play at school. It was "The HMS Pinafore," a musical production. The whole family went to the play. There was this scene where Joe was in a rowboat with some guys and they were all supposed to be rowing away. There was a painted canvas on the floor and that was supposed to be the ocean. They had kids crawling under it to make the waves. Well, one of the kids' heads popped up through the canvas ocean. There was a moment of dead silence and then Joe hollered, "Man overboard!" They pulled the kid into the boat. That bit brought the house down and became the hit line in the show.

But Joe didn't go on with drama. He was too modest and lacked self-confidence. When I look back now at the high school pictures, he was really very, very handsome. He had curly black hair, a white toothy smile with a dimple on one side and big soft brown eyes like Mom's. He was well built, too. He was not tall, but not too short either. He just didn't know how handsome he was. He didn't believe Mom and me when we would tell him. He'd have all these crushes, but he would never tell the girls. He was always very shy around girls, until he got in the service. Then he got over that. I guess a lot of guys got over that in the service.

As for me, I was still in my brother's shadow and too much into baseball to care about guys yet. Although I had some secret crushes, too, I never let the guys know either. Mostly I hung out with my baseball friends. At school my best friend was Betty Ticen. We had something in common. Her mom worked for Hollywood actress Jean Harlow. She was her social secretary. Our Mom worked for actress Louise Rainer, a two-time Academy Award winner. She won an Academy Award for "The Good Earth" and "The Great Ziegfield," back to back, I believe. I have personalized autographed pictures from both Jean Harlow and Louise Rainer. That strange business of famous people as a constant in my life was always there.

By now, I had decided to be a journalist. I was majoring in English and worked on both the school paper and the annual. My teacher was Mrs. Forrest. She told me that I had a great deal of talent and life in my writing, but she hated my undisciplined style, my careless punctuation and spelling, etc. At that time there was only one way to write -- her way was the right way! Times have changed and the right way now is not necessarily the strictly correct way; if it works, you can get away with it! I really liked my classes, but she made it so hard on me that it caused me to start disliking writing. I had always been so much better than anyone around me that I felt special, but she criticized me so much, I felt like I wasn't good anymore.

      I turned more and more to my baseball and the adventures it brought me. I became good friends with one of my teammates, Peggy Barns, on the Ocean Park Reds. Peggy was going with this cute, young guy called "Frenchy." I think Frenchy was Filipino and just didn't want to admit it. Those were different times when sometimes people were ashamed of their heritage. Frenchy had this fire-engine red Lincoln Continental Zephyr convertible. Wow! Did I feel like I was styling in that thing -- white leather upholstery, "Continental Kit" on the back and silver twin exhaust pipes that purred and rumbled. It had lots of extras and chrome all over the place. Wow! Here I go again with the cars. He had this fabulous horn. That horn played a tune, DA DA DA DA DA DA DA (to "Mary Had a Little Lamb"). Was that ever cool! In today's world I think I could have been a race car driver. Imagine "Pepper Paire's Porsche." Anyways, back to the plot. I felt sorry for Frenchy because he was such a sweet guy. Peggy was a sexy-looking redhead with a body to match and she had plenty of guys running after her. It was rumored that she cheated on Frenchy. They were supposed to be married, but I don't think they really were. Since I was "their best friend," I got caught in the middle. Like so many best friends do, I secretly developed a crush on Frenchy. Their romance only lasted a year, married or whatever, and they split up for good. Then Frenchy and I dated for a while. I thought I got what I wanted, but it wasn't the same. I was over him and he wasn't over Peggy. You have to be careful what you wish for, because so many times when you get it, you find out you don't really want it. I guess you could call Frenchy my first legitimate boyfriend. I wasn't that much into boyfriends. Baseball was my real love.

      Things started to go wrong as far as school was concerned and then it really became a drag. At this time they had this outfit called the "Girls Athletic Association" (GAA). All the best athletes were invited to join. Well, that old green-eyed devil called jealousy came into the picture and somehow word got around that I played pro softball. That was not really true; all I got for playing was a little gas money. All amateur athletes had sponsors and got gas money. I was entitled to that. But they said because there was paid admission to the games, that made me a pro and I couldn't belong to the GAA. Nor could I take part in the sports activities at school. I had to go to folk-dancing classes or play with the less talented second-string girls. Well, you can imagine how that made me feel, being far better than all of them and being left out of everything.

That system was very unfair and I think it still remains in effect today. It's somewhat like the Olympic Games and how unfairly they were run all those years. Funny thing, though -- when we would play other schools, somehow they would always manage to have an excuse to get me on the team and in the lineup. What this did was isolate me even more from my school mates. I remained pretty much a loner.

Betty Ticen

Louise Rainier

Jean Harlow

Aunt Amanda & Uncle Bonner's Trellis

Uncle Bonner and Aunt Amanda and their Model T in the 20s

Chapter 8
Nightmare Alley

About this time, Faye finally arrived at Uni High. The time was right, and Faye and I soon became best friends. She ran into all the same problems I was facing, so that made our bond closer. We were just a couple of crazy kids, and when we got together things always seemed to get exciting. When I think back now at some of the adventures we had, I marvel that we lived through it all!

One of the things we liked to do was to take the bus to the beach and go to the Santa Monica and the Ocean Park piers. Well, what amusement park pier doesn't fascinate kids? But Faye and I went a little overboard on that. We got to be friends with the man who ran the merry-go-round on the Santa Monica Pier; he would let us pay one admission and ride over and over again. Somehow, that brass ring would always come up when Faye and I were going by it. If one didn't grab it the other one did. Then we got a free ride. That merry-go-round is still down there. They have restored that old pier and the Hippodrome. What memories that holds for me.

We got to be friends with all the guys that ran the concessions. Our favorite game was knocking down these metal milk bottles with baseballs. You got three chances and if you knocked them down, you got this cute little cupie doll! We got a lot of dolls! The guy let us play for nothing because we drew a lot of people to the table, just to watch us throw the ball. Sometimes we had a little money to pay, but most of the time the guys would just let us go on the rides for free! It was a good thing that those were innocent times because we could have gotten into a lot more trouble than we did. I can still hear that old merry-go-round organ playing its heart out!

Due to the fact that we were hanging out more and more with older gals, Faye and I finally got into the dating scene. Servicemen were always available, and that's where Faye met her Johnny. He was a corporal in the Army. She stayed pretty true to him all the time he was overseas. Unfortunately, he was killed in Europe on Invasion Day! She would never be the one to admit it, but I really think he was the one guy Faye really loved and would have married.

I turned more and more away from school because it just wasn't a pleasant experience. I made sure I got passing grades and then did my other things. Those unhappy school memories still remain with me. I hear people talking about wanting to go to all these great high-school reunions! But I really lived in another world and I never had any desire to attend one. I think I mentioned I had a Catholic background but I wasn't a good one. Most of the time I missed mass for baseball games, but I wasn't a bad person and I think God knew that because he sure helped me out of a lot of tight spots. I sometimes attended mass at this little church around the corner from us called St. Sebastian's. It was all white with a little white picket fence around it and a cobblestone walk led to the wooden stairs. There were lots of archways and trellises and they were covered with little white and yellow primroses. Red and white carnations bordered everything and perfumed the air. It had huge old-fashioned swing-out windows covered with cobwebbed trails of honeysuckles. The windows allowed us to hear the happy sounds of the birds and smell the air that was so perfumed by Mother Nature. At the same time they filtered the warm rays of the California golden sun.

It felt more like you were in the Garden of Eden than a church. The pastor fit that image. He gave very simple down-to-earth sermons that made sense and didn't condemn you to damnation forever if you did something just a little bit wrong. It was a wonderful place to enjoy your relationship with God. On top of that, it was an ideal church for movie stars to attend because it was such a little hideaway church. If you looked around a pew or two you might just spot a famous movie star. It was the favorite church of many of them because of its inconspicuous, low profile.

I remember one Sunday, I just glanced up and saw a tall, well-built man in a dress Marine uniform coming down the aisle. He had this slender, fashionably dressed, black-veiled woman on his arm. They sat down in the pew in front of me. I couldn't see their faces, but when he turned his head to put his hat on the seat I almost swallowed my gum (which I shouldn't have been chewing anyway). It was Tyrone Power, the world's handsomest man. I was to figure out later that the veiled beauty on his arm was "Annabelle," the renowned French actress whom he later married. I'm afraid at that particular time my thoughts were a lot less than holy. It was a fringe benefit from God.

Speaking of God's fringe benefits, more and more, I realize, I sure got my share. I remember this one weekend when my Dr Pepper softball team was driving down to Phoenix to play the Championship Phoenix Queens. There were two carloads of us. Our manager, Freddy, and his wife, and some ballplayers were leading the way in his classy Ford convertible. Wade Weaver was our assistant coach and he was driving the second car. It was a four-door, four on the floor, 1935 Ford. Wade was also our pitcher Teddy's boyfriend. There were three in the front seat and Lil, Faye and I in the back seat. It was 5 a.m. and we'd been driving all night. We wore our uniforms -- satin shorts and blouses. We were ready to play the game.

    The desert night was cold and I had to put on my heavy suede uniform jacket. I had shifted my position from the seat to the floor and gone to sleep. Curled up, with my head and arms on the seat, I felt a big bump and it woke me and I saw that it was starting to get light. I was cramped and kept telling myself, *Wake up! Get up and sit on the seat.* But it was as if something was holding my head down and telling me, *Wait! Wait! Don't get up yet!* I don't know if any of you have ever felt the hand of God, but that's what I believe I was feeling, only I didn't know it at the time. I was actually getting mad at myself for not getting up, when it happened!

    I was trying to force my head up from whatever was holding me down, when Teddy screamed. There were screeching brakes, and the sound of Wade cursing, "My God, get over, you bastard!" The sound of smashing metal and broken glass all melted into one giant roar. The car shuddered violently and the world turned upside down. The car went rolling over and over and over. It threw me from the floor to the ceiling and back again. With my belly hitting the seat, I was unaware of any of the other bodies around me, just me. Crash, bam, hitting the floor and the seat as the car rolled over again and again. Finally, it flipped one more time and then stopped right-side up, shuddering again violently. There was complete silence for a moment. I pulled myself up from the seat and looked around. The doors had flown open on the passenger side when the car stopped. My head was still spinning. It was like my senses were returning to me, one at a time. I saw Faye and Lil tumble out on the ground and then crawl up the bank. I could see that we were in a gully of some sort and I turned to look at the front seat. Then Teddy screamed again and I saw Teddy and Holly go tearing up the side of the bank. Then I heard Wade, "Oh my God, my arm! Oh my God, my arm!" Slowly I turned my head around and I saw something that I never want to see again.

Wade was trying to open his door with his left arm. The trouble was, he didn't have one. His forearm and hand from elbow down were gone. He just had a bone sticking out and it looked blue. It was sticking out from his shoulder and the muscle and the skin was ripped to shreds and flying loose! Blood was spewing around in all directions. He just kept repeating, "Oh my God, my arm! Oh my God, my arm!" He kept trying to open the door with a hand and an arm that weren't there. Later he told us that he could have sworn that his hand was on the handle of the door and it wouldn't open. Everyone but me had gone scrambling and screaming up the hill and I wanted to scream and run up that hill right after them. I don't honestly know what kept me there, but I knew I couldn't leave him alone.

I started talking to him because he was starting to get hysterical. He was slashing at the door with his other arm and kicking at it with his feet. The blood was flying and my first-aid knowledge kicked in. My God, he was going to bleed to death! "Wade! Wade!" I screamed over his noise. "Calm down! Calm down!" Hearing me, he turned his head and became aware that I was still there. I'll never forget the look on his face — horror and fear and disbelief all mixed into one. "Calm down. Calm down, please," I pleaded, sliding over the seat and out the door. He screamed, "Don't leave me!" I said, "No. No. Wait. I won't leave you. I'm coming. We can't get our doors open. Come over to this side."

I reached in the door and grabbed his hand and pulled him gently urging. "Come on. Come on. We will lie down on the bank. I'll stop the bleeding." With me pleading, he shifted over and out on the ground and lay back with this stunned look on his face. He was very, very white and I was afraid he was going to go into shock. I started talking to him again. Taking his face in my hands, I pleaded, "Wade, help me. Look at me. Stay awake." Then I pulled my satin belt off my shorts telling him, "Now I'm going to put a tourniquet on your arm. This won't hurt."

I took my belt and wrapped it up under his arm and over the shoulder and cinched it down. It stopped the bleeding almost immediately. I was saying, "Thank you, God. Thank you, God," when I heard voices and Freddy came sliding down the bank. Seeing me covered with blood, he hollered, "My God, Pepper, are you all right?"

I said, "I'm okay. I'm okay, Freddy, but we've got to get Wade to the hospital." Leaving the rest unspoken, I looked into his eyes and he knew what I meant. Faye and Lil had come back down and they helped Freddy carry Wade up the bank and to the car. I just lay there for a moment looking at our car. It was so smashed up. It was round and miraculously sitting upright on the brake drums. The wheels were gone and the passenger doors on the right side had flown wide open. If they had opened while we were rolling over, none of us would be here to tell the story. Fortunately they didn't pop open until the car stopped. When I looked at the window that I was going to raise up and open, there was a bloody imprint of Wade's hand and arm etched in the shattered glass.

I became aware of some ugly feelings under my back and raising up, I took my heavy jacket off and turned it around. It was full of shattered sticks and pieces of bloody glass. That would have all been in my face had I been able to get up and sit down. It was God's hand that held me down.

It turned out that we were 90 miles from the nearest hospital in Wickenburg, Arizona. What a harrowing ride that was in Freddy's car. We were going 80 miles an hour or better most of the way. After an accident like that you can imagine what that did to our nerves. But it was a race to save Wade's life. He never lost consciousness. He just kept whispering, "Oh my God, my arm! Oh my God, my arm!" with tears dripping down his face. It took three days in the hospital before we knew if he was going to make it. They said the belt saved his life. We were all stiff and sore but okay, or so we thought. We played the ballgame, but I wound up in the hospital that night with stomach cramps that were diagnosed as menstruation problems. Eight years later I came up with a "bleeding chocolate tumor." They removed it, but the doctor told me it was caused by bouncing on that seat!

The accident happened because a guy in a Lincoln Zephyr coming the other way was drunk! He was swerving all over the road. He barely missed Freddy in the car ahead of us and caused Freddy to swerve off the road. But, when he got to us, we were crossing a two-lane bridge over a gully and Wade had nowhere to go. So his car sideswiped us and ripped everything off the left side of our car, including Wade's arm. Then the Zephyr flipped and went rolling down that road. We flipped sideways, went off the bridge and rolling down the gully. Wade's arm was back in the middle of the road, with his ring and watch still on it. One of our gals in Freddy's car walked back and picked it up, wrapped it up and brought it to the hospital. Unfortunately, they couldn't reattach it because it had been detached too long and there was not enough flesh left on his upper arm. They just didn't have the technology at that time to do it. The gal that picked it up later on became a nun. I think that experience influenced her.

It was so tragic for us -- we were so young. That wreck was to live with me as a nightmare for many years. Wade had been driving with his arm out the window holding the top of the car. I never drive that way, and I never let anyone else drive that way if I'm in the car with them. If I pass someone driving that way I shudder. It brings it all back! In my nightmare I'd be driving along in a car and God would say: "Pepper, if you want Wade to have his arm back, you must drive this car at 50 miles an hour (which was a great speed at that time) into a brick wall. I can't tell you if you will live or not but Wade will get his arm back." Well, I'd be revving the engine up and ready to slam into the wall at full speed and then I'd wake up shaking and wondering.

The guy in the other car was killed and he was rich, so Wade got a ton of money. But that didn't get his arm back. They had to take it off clean at the shoulder so he couldn't even have a false one. Wade was never the same after that. He became a lonely, brooding person and never talked to anyone. Finally, he just disappeared. We heard he went back to Texas to live with his folks. It took about five years for that nightmare to fade away. It left a scar on my heart and, at times like this, when I'm reflecting on the memory, it comes back. Tragic things often leave scars, but life goes on, if you're lucky -- and I was lucky -- that time!

**CHAPTER 9
THE BIG EVENT**

It was 1941 and the Depression was now definitely over, but something far worse was about to raise its ugly head. The dark specter of World War II was on its way. I'll say we didn't know it -- and we didn't -- but we were aware of some things that were going on. President Roosevelt was talking with Japan about their aggressiveness and their unhappiness; fact is, their ambassadors were in Washington having "peace talks." We knew something could possibly happen, but this was America, right? No one would dare challenge us, right? Especially not those polite, little Japanese people. So, if and when there was a war, it would be on our terms, right? We would be the ones who would decide when and where to drop the bombs! So there really wasn't anything to worry about, right?

The military, however, was beefing up the aircraft factories. They were going full-blast and that accounted for the economy swinging around and kicking the Depression clear out of sight. Everybody was having a great time, especially "Pepper and her gal friends." There were servicemen all over the place and, since I was always very patriotic, I didn't play favorites. I dated the Marines; I dated the Army; I dated the Navy; I dated the Air Corps -- all divisions. After all, it was only fair. I didn't want to cheat anybody! However, my baseball still always came first.

I tried and excelled at many sports -- including golf, tennis and bowling. But there was little opportunity for women to actively participate in any of these sports and no opportunity at all to earn any money from them. The equipment was expensive and unless you were rich, or you had a sponsor, or you were somebody's protégé, it was too expensive to play the game. It was almost impossible for a woman to pursue a career in sports -- one you could really earn a living at.

So softball remained the sport that paid for me. I was still playing in three leagues a week. By now, basically, baseball had just become a way of life for me. It remained my only outlet for my exceptional athletic ability and my competitive spirit. It was something that I just had to do, like breathing. So I made the most of it. I played half-a-dozen games a week and hung on to my dream of going to Cooperstown, even though I knew that was impossible. The guys, who I was always better than, still took a great deal of delight in telling me, "Hey, girls can't be in the Hall of Fame." Now where have I heard that before?

I was now in the 12th grade and a senior at last. I couldn't wait to get graduation over with and get on with my real life. School was so boring. Most of my older baseball friends were already out in the world and I couldn't wait to join them. There were just three of us still in school -- Faye, Mary Brown, who played on the Ocean Park Reds team, and me. We palled around together and often double and triple dated, safety in numbers, you know. Those dates, of course, came on weekends and took place before and after our beloved ballgames. Sometimes we would go to the USO and sometimes we would visit our favorite little cocktail lounges; the Starlight Room in the Biltmore Hotel, Downtown L.A., was one of our favorites.

We didn't hang out in cheap bars, only classy places that were really respectable and we were always with a date. No pick-ups. The place we really loved the best was the Casino Ballroom down at the Ocean Park Pier. It was a big palace-like ballroom with crystal chandeliers and marble columns all over the place. It was a gorgeous place and the best part was that the great swing bands played around the clock on weekends. They played for the servicemen and for the war factory workers who were on the swing shift and the graveyard shift. There was always something going on.

Admission was free for the servicemen and a whopping dollar for everyone else. If you were a good-looking gal and available and friendly, you didn't have to pay that dollar, either. The big bands would take turns playing -- Tommy and Jimmy Dorsey, Glenn Miller, Benny Goodman, Artie Shaw, Count Basie, Kaye Kaiser, Louie Armstrong, Cab Calloway. You name it, they were there. I don't think those great bands received proper credit for what they did, at least not as much as they should have! Their music was a great morale booster for everyone, especially the lonely service guys, far from home waiting to be shipped out to "God knows where," not knowing whether they would ever get back home. We went there to entertain them and to dance with them.

We went in groups for safety sake. It wasn't the big, bad, sadistic world then that it is now. The worst you could expect was that a guy might try to get fresh! You could just tell him off and dump him. But you know what? They were mostly sweet, honorable guys who treated you with respect and just wanted someone to talk to, to dance with and to hold hands with. After maybe the third date, you let him kiss you goodnight. They treated us like they hoped their sisters (whom they loved) would be treated. Of course, if we would meet someone we really connected with, we arranged to meet him again at the dance. If that went well, we might ask him to dinner at our house to meet the folks. That way it became respectable for you to date him. If he agreed, then you figured he probably didn't have any ulterior motives.

    I met Tony Ornada that way. He was a Marine sergeant stationed at El Toro Marine Base. Technically, I guess it's in Orange County, but it's down San Diego way for me. Tony was Italian, and he looked it! He had big, soft brown eyes and curly brown hair and his skin was just dark enough to give him a movie-star look. He was so handsome in his dress blues that he turned heads. I fell for Tony and he fell for me and he became my steady. His buddy, George, also connected with Mary Brown, so we became a foursome. We wound up many nights dancing the hours away until we had to drive them back to base to beat the clock.

    What a wonderful time that was. My first real love. Wow! I won't deny that we may have steamed up a few car windows. Mary and George did, too. But I can honestly tell you that a relationship was different than it is now. You saved the best for your husband -- and I did. Anyway, Mary and I were so hung up on these two guys that we decided to join the Marine Corps. We couldn't join until we were 20, though, so instead we signed up for the Women's Ambulance Corps. We drilled two nights a week, practicing drill routines and learning first aid. I became a corporal and they made Mary top sergeant. I learned then that life could be unfair. The captain told me that I was smarter and better at everything, but that Mary had a big voice and better posture. Well, she didn't have better posture, she just had smaller boobs than I did. She could square her shoulders and throw out her chest. If I did that I could have put somebody's eyes out. It wasn't Mary's fault. She felt bad about it and thought that it should have been me. I used to have to tell her what to do all the time. We practiced our drills at her house. This one time her folks were out of town and we came back to her house from our dates. We'd had a couple of drinks and we were really feeling our oats. So we decided to check out her Dad's liquor cabinet. We found this big bottle of gin! It was already open, so he won't miss a little slug or two we figured. We had been drinking "Tom Collins" before, so this fit right in. We were in the safety of Mary's house, so what's the harm? Well, one more led to two, to three, and after that, who counts? We had a great time that night ... I think? All I remember was a lot of giggling, then going to bed at about 3 a.m. We slept until about 9 a.m. Then the disaster hit. We both got so sick, throwing up, crushing headaches, more throwing up, belly aches, more throwing up. At least I made it to the bathroom. Mary didn't. I swear, when she threw up, it went about 30 feet across the room. <u>And</u> she visited all the rooms messing all of them up! Honest to God, she looked like a lizard shooting his tongue out across the room. Well, when things finally calmed down, we slept all day. Then we went about cleaning things up. That was an all-night, ugly, stinky job. Gin has a perfumed taste and smell. I could never stand it again. If I get a whiff of it, it brings it all back and up, if I'm not careful.

      For a while there, Mary and I were great friends. We liked a lot of the same things: baseball, of course; the Ambulance Corps; and especially dating guys. As far as Mary was concerned, dating guys was the highlight! As far as I was concerned, baseball was still my main love! Things were fine when we were going with Tony and George and double dating with them. But as time passed, Tony and George passed, too. When they shipped out, at first they wrote frantically and we wrote back frantically. Eventually, it got back to us that they had girls back home waiting for them. So, while we still did our patriotic duty once in a while, that information cooled things down and took the glamour away for us. Eventually, we moved on and so did they, I guess.

      After that, Mary and I started dating again and we met these two Army guys at the Ocean Park Casino and Ballroom. Eventually, we started dating them. Mary's date was an Army lieutenant and mine was a cute little blonde corporal named Johnny (Army also!). This one time we went on a picnic out in the country -- somewhere in the trees. I forget where the heck we went. The lieutenant had just one thing on his mind and Mary wasn't buying it. My little Johnny was just holding my hand and looking at me longingly with those big, blue, innocent eyes. At least, so I thought. He was certainly making my heart beat faster. The next thing you know, Mary grabs my Johnny and plants a long, open-mouthed kiss on him. We used to secretly call it "French kissing." When Johnny came up for air, he says to me with this big grin, "Gee! I wish you kissed like that." Then Mary went running off with him following her, leaving me with

"Lieutenant Octopus." Well, I put him in his place quick and easy and had him laughing when I did it, but my feelings were really hurt. When Mary and Johnny came back, they tried to make up with me, but I wasn't having any of it.

After I tamed the lieutenant down, he even wanted to date me and promised me that he would be good, but he wasn't my type. I've already told you my policy on that. I guess I didn't trust Mary either after that episode and we gradually grew apart.

Faye and I became closer friends than ever. Of course, double dating with Faye was a real adventure. You never knew what she was going to do. It could be great embarrassment or it could be great fun, depending on the mood she was in. But there was always one thing you could count on, it would never be dull. I remember this one time Faye called me about midnight and said: "Get over here, Pepper. John Agar is serenading me on my door step and he's got a cute friend with him." I said, "Yeah, yeah, yeah, and Clark Gable is over here with me." Faye said: "No really, really, Pepper. He's drunk as a skunk, and they've got a beautiful, red Cadillac convertible! They want to drive us around and they'll let me drive, too!" Well, I knew I couldn't let that happen, so I went over to check on things. Sure enough, it was true. There he was, big as life and twice as cute. The other guy wasn't bad looking either. He was also an actor, but not famous like John. John Agar was a leading man, movie star and very handsome. He was one of Shirley Temple's leading men after she "grew up"! After he got out of the Army, he starred with her in "*Fort Apache*" and they fell in love! It started out like a fairy-tale romance. Later on, they wound up getting married (but it didn't end well). At first, I was a little worried about what the guys wanted from us, but they just wanted somebody to play games with. They already had beautiful women that would sleep with them anytime they wanted. John wasn't married to Shirley Temple at the time. We weren't really surprised when their marriage broke up later. We knew John really had a drinking problem. He was very handsome and talented! He was also a very nice guy, but his habit hurt his career. He could have been a huge star! Later on, he became clean and sober and went on to have a distinguished career, but he was past his prime and did a lot of sci-fi. John was a gentleman!

By now, Faye and I were looking pretty good! Faye's hair was a pale blonde color and it was long and silky and flew in the breeze. She had big ocean blue eyes with a peaches and cream complexion. She was built well with a slender figure and beautiful legs. Of course, I used to kid her about her "fried eggs" and "my grapefruits." We were tan and fit and the epitome of the outdoor American natural beauty that was so popular then. Yes, it was actually popular to look healthy! I had filled out in all the right places and my hair was now a beautiful strawberry blonde. That's what they called hair that was gold with some red in it. I had green eyes that sometimes changed to blue and a pretty good smile. So the point being, it was OK to look healthy then. You didn't have to look pale and sick to be glamorous. The guys didn't mind being seen with us, so we had fun with the Hollywood scene for a little while. I was beginning to feel like Ginger Rogers. Everyone told me that I looked like her and I could sing and dance a little. Faye kind of resembled a healthy "Madeleine Carroll." But the "glitter" scene wasn't for us. The Hollywood drinking and sex scene wasn't for us either. It wasn't long before John and his buddy fell by the wayside, in more ways than one.

    He wasn't the only movie star I dated. There were others that I could have dated and didn't for good reasons; especially one very famous one, but I found out that he was married and lying about it so I turned him down! I was Victor Killian's favorite baseball player. He was known as the flasher on "Mary Hartman, Mary Hartman." Victor was a very distinguished character actor with a long record of good movies. "The Wake of the Red Witch," was one.

    Then there was this one time when I was driving along in my car down Victory Boulevard in Van Nuys, when this big, handsome man on this motorcycle rides up alongside of me at a stop sign. He wore a beautiful Army Air Force Captain's uniform. I was staring at him when he turned and gave me this great big cutesy smile! I said, "Hiya, Clark." And he said, "Hiya, sweetheart." Yep, Clark Gable smiled at me. I'll never forget that one!

    Our country was really gearing up for war by now! Hitler and Mussolini were raising hell in Europe and it looked like the bad guys were all teaming up. Actually, all the signs were there, but no one really wanted to believe it. We really were just playing at going to war. It couldn't really happen to us. Oh, well, we'll be "Scarlett O'Hara" and think about it tomorrow. Joe was talking about joining the Air Force Reserves and that scared the life out of me. So, oh well, I'll be "Scarlett O'Hara" again and worry about that tomorrow. That tomorrow was getting closer and closer; much closer than we realized. Of course, the California economy was now zooming!

War products were all over the place. We were building everything from military supplies and aircraft, to ships, to bombs, to guns. My baseball heroes were joining up; Joe DiMaggio, Ted Williams and Bob Feller. Of course, a few deadbeats were flying off to Canada trying to avoid the coming draft. I was still plugging along playing all the ball I could and plowing through Highschool just waiting for that final bell to ring. Joe was out of school and I needed out! It was December 1941, and my graduation was coming up pretty soon and that would provide the way out!

While that December started out like any other month, it wasn't to end that way. It would prove to be a tragic time for America and a dark chapter in our history. It would be filled with fear for the future of democracy and it would be the end of World Peace. We were still blissfully unaware of the danger and our life was going on as usual. Bro Joe was working downtown for Bank of America in a job that he really didn't like. The big event was going to be "my graduation." But a much bigger event got here first -- the unbelievable, vicious, back-stabbing attack on Pearl Harbor. It was December 7, 1941. All of our lives were about to change drastically. World War II was launched by the Japanese Navy with their cowardly, sneaky, inhuman attack on Pearl Harbor, Hawaii. Now, if that offends anyone, I'm sorry, but it's the truth. We camped by our radios at all times grieving, but not believing. Then, after hearing it again and again, we feared for our loved ones.

The war that was never to happen again was here. We were being threatened with invasion. FDR strengthened us. He promised us revenge, victory and salvation. He gave up his own life in keeping that promise. My bro, Joe, immediately joined the Air Force Reserves like so many of our brave, young men did. It didn't take long for them to call him. Nothing seemed important now but the war. Graduation came and went and the big deal was no big deal. I didn't even go to my own prom. Even after my Mom had bought this beautiful dress for me. However, I did manage to talk my date into coming to the ballgame because, you see, we had a doubleheader that night! So, he came to the ballgame and then we went dancing afterwards. It just didn't seem right to have a big celebration with so many brave Americans dead and dying!

There was the threat of being bombed at any moment. The world had become small and filled with fear. California was considered a prime target after Pearl Harbor. They were on their way to us! The Ambulance Corps stepped up its training and enlisted more recruits. My Pop became an air-raid warden and there were air-raid shelters all over the place.

Testing the air-raid sirens became mandatory and it was so scary when they blasted off. Everybody was relieved when it was all over! Except, one night, the test didn't end. We only lived three miles from Douglas Aircraft, a big defense plant. Douglas was located right next to the Santa Monica Airport. Everything was totally camouflaged like all the other airports and defense plants. There were netted pockets of anti-aircraft guns surrounding the whole area. That night, those guns started firing! The flak was falling on the roof of our house! It sounded like hail! Then, all the power went off and everything became very black. It was about 2 a.m. as I remember it! Well, we all, of course, did what we were not supposed to do. We hastily grabbed up our sweaters and coats in the dark and ran outside to stare up at the sky. No, it was definitely not hail! Our neighbors were all out on their porches or in their front yards, too. Everyone was excitedly speculating about what was happening. Mom and Pop were standing on the front porch and we heard Mom saying "Oh, my, Daddy!" That was so frightening. I was so scared. Then we hear Pop's loud voice, "Well, you're just a scaredy cat." He blustered on, "I wasn't scared. I knew everything was alright." About that time the porch light came back on. Mom starts howling with laughter, "Oh, no, you weren't scared. Oh, no, you're not a scaredy cat."

Joe and I were out in the front yard and Mom is laughing so hard we turn around to see what was so funny at a time like this. We see Pop. He had grabbed this fuzzy thing he thought was his sweater in the dark and threw it on -- only it wasn't his sweater. It was his long john red flannel underwear. He had it on upside down and backwards and he was peeking out the slit in the back. He had his arms in the legs and the arms and shoulders were dangling down, fortunately to his knees, because Pop slept in the nude. It was the funniest sight I've ever seen in my life. He looked like a one-eyed, four-legged lobster. Mom was practically rolling on the floor with laughter, "Oh, no, you weren't scared!" Pop whirls around, red arms and legs flying, and beats a hasty retreat into the house, taking all our pictures on the way in. He got out of sight before any of the neighbors saw him, but Mom never let him forget that one. "Oh, no, you weren't scared. Oh no, you're not a scaredy cat." Well, that took all our fears away. We all laughed until we cried -- even Pop. It turned a frightening experience into a priceless memory.

The next day they told us that some camouflaged weather balloons had broken loose and that's what they were shooting at. But a Marine pilot told me what really happened! He said that a flight of Japanese reconnaissance planes had flown up by way of Mexico. Had they been bombers, we were dead ducks. If the Japanese had decided to push forward at that point of the war, I think history has documented that they possibly could have gone all the way. We could be speaking Japanese in California right now. But, fortunately for us, they didn't have the confidence and they changed their game plan. Boy! Am I glad of that!

So now I was finally free. School was behind me! I was eager to get on with my <u>real</u> life in the <u>real</u> world. But my goals were totally different now. Things had changed drastically. Instead of going to UCLA and starting my career as a writer and working part time to support that, I was now committed to helping the war effort. Everything was geared to us gals taking over at home so our boys could go fight. So, "Pioneer Pepper," (though I didn't know it at the time) started looking for a difficult job. Being a hot-rodder, race car expert, why not Standard Oil? Why not a gas station? They advertised that they needed women to help the war effort! So I applied for the job. They sent me to school to learn to "check the hood," meaning check the water, the oil and the battery and kick the tires, etc. But the most important thing they wanted me to do was to smile pretty at the guys while pumping their gas and cleaning their windows. Women just didn't work in gas stations in those days! So this was quite a unique job. They furnished us with purple overalls. They clashed with my red hair, but it was effective when I smiled pretty at the men. Of course, I already knew how to do all the car things, so for a while I had a ball at my gas station job!

Me

Me & Tony
Mary & George

Tony - Russ - George

Navy

All dressed up for
the graduation party
I didn't go to

The ambulance corp "1942"
2nd Row down from top 3rd girl in

Chapter 10
A War and a League Are Born

It turned out that my first job was not only special, but it came with a special gas station, too. It was located in Brentwood, well-known as the home of the "elite of the elite." Brentwood had it all over Beverly Hills in "Old World" class. Most of the homes had been owned by the same prestigious families for generations. Many movie stars frequented my station daily. My association with famous people was to continue. You need to go back to the '40s to check out all of these names. One I remember was Brian Donlevy. I also remember John Payne as a customer! They both starred in westerns. John Payne was in a lot of other films, too, including musicals! Brian Donlevy was strictly a cowboy star at that time in his career, but later on he did other things.

Donlevy would come rolling in driving a bright, canary yellow Cadillac convertible. It had steer horns on the hood and one of those musical horns (like Frenchy's). It played "Merrily We Roll Along," while I was servicing his car. He always gave me a big smile! He wore a great big, white Stetson cowboy hat. When I was done and he was ready to "merrily roll along" he would say, "Thanks, Honey," and flip me a brand new silver dollar! That was a lot of money in those days. So, I smiled pretty in those purple overalls.

Then one day in came Tony De Marco of the Tony and Sally De Marco dancing team. They were second in popularity to Fred Astaire and Ginger Rogers. They made musicals and, while they weren't huge stars, they were well-known. Tony De Marco took one look at me in my purple overalls with my long, wavy, red hair and asked me for a date. He was small in stature and a slender man, Italian, dark and really handsome. He said he was divorced and he and Sally were just dance partners. I agreed to go out with him and gave him my number, but when I got back home and told my Mom, she told me that it wouldn't be right to go out with him! He had given me his card, so I chickened out and had Mom call him and tell him I was sick. Well, guess what? He sent me two dozen beautiful, giant, white roses and a lovely note. It said he had to go out of town for filming, but that he would be back and that he would call me.

I felt guilty for a while. I kept ducking around the corner when I thought he was coming into the station. Eventually, I just got tired of worrying about meeting up with him. It was one of the reasons I quit my job. The other reason was that the station paid minimum wages and I needed to make more money.

At this time softball had become more prominent than ever. It had become part of the war effort. All the big defense plants had teams and we played for the entertainment of the workers and the servicemen. It had become a symbol of corporate pride and excellence to have a champion softball team. One of the executives that owned some of the softball fields we played on got me a job at Lockheed Aircraft. They paid me a lot more money. If I can remember correctly, it was a mere 75 cents an hour -- and that was "some kind of pumpkins!" I went to work in the blueprint engineering department and was helping to build P-38s. I was on my way to becoming an electronic technician or maybe just "Rosie the Riveter" doing my patriotic bit and loving it.

Lockheed Aircraft was located in Burbank, which is a part of the San Fernando Valley. (I still live in the Valley, but I'm in Van Nuys now. I call it "shake and bake" country for obvious reasons.) Getting there wasn't a problem because I had transportation. My bro Joe had bought a 1939 Chevy Coupe before he went into the service. Naturally, he couldn't take it with him, so I took over the payments and we co-owned it. That little maroon beauty could really get up and go. Being the "Barney Oldfield" racecar driver, I knew how to drive it. That little car was to play a big part in our family life a little bit later on.

At this point, a lot of new people were coming into my life. It was about 15 miles to work, which was quite a distance then. It's not comparable to 15 miles on the freeways now. We had to go over the Sepulveda Pass. Actually, when I think about it, it was probably more like 20 miles. Gas rationing was in effect because of the war. So I made a few phone calls, checked it out, and we formed a car pool. There were four of us in the carpool: Eleanor Dixon, myself and two other gals. So, enter the Dixons into my life. Eleanor and I were to become very good friends and, of course, we would wind up double dating. Faye hadn't graduated yet, so we were kind of separated for a little while, but we stayed good baseball buddies and saw each other two or three times a week that way.

It just so happened that the Dixon family lived right in that very elite Brentwood section where my gas station was. The Dixons' house was an old-fashioned, cozy, country-style cottage surrounded by lots of roses and exotic plants. There were little winding streets all around the house. Right behind Eleanor's house was this sprawling ranch-style home with stables and a swimming pool. It was owned by the before-mentioned John Payne. At that time, he was married to actress Gloria De Haven. John was a big, handsome man, a movie star macho type. He made a lot of famous movies with famous actresses like Alice Faye and Sonja Henie. He and his wife dropped in for visits at Eleanor's house. That was another notch on my famous movie star belt.

The Dixon family was unique and had their own claim to fame. Mrs. Dixon was a quiet, classy lady with beautiful olive skin, dark brown hair and flashing black eyes. Eleanor was a well-stacked beauty with a demure, sweet smile, but stand back! You didn't cross her. She'd let you know if you did. Unfortunately, Eleanor had asthma from early on and was a little fragile. She had to worry about catching cold or being in a draft. Her mom worried about that, too! I think that might have accounted for Eleanor's temperamental flashes. Still, we became very good friends. We both possessed a good sense of humor. I allowed for her shortcomings and she allowed for mine.

Next on the family list came the two handsome brothers -- Billy Dixon, the younger brother, and Tommy Dixon, the older one. Billy and I didn't meet for a while because he was overseas in the Army, but I saw photos. He had that wholesome, All–American boy look -- big, brown eyes with careless locks of brown hair just kind of flying around. If you looked really close into those big, brown eyes you could see a little bit of devil lurking in there. Billy had great dimples when he smiled and muscles in all the right places. While I didn't meet Billy until later, I did get to meet his big bro, Tommy.

Tommy Dixon was probably the handsomest man I ever dated. He had the same smooth, olive skin and beautiful, soft, brown eyes. He wasn't tall, but he was tall enough, with big, wide shoulders. He was beautifully built. He had perfectly sculptured jet black hair and a flashy white smile. Tommy had tried to join up, but they wouldn't take him because he had a lung problem. Also, he was studying to be an actor and going to acting school with the still unknown Alan Ladd at the time. He had a job as a radio announcer with KHJ for a classical music program. Can you believe I think I heard Tommy's voice not too long ago on that same radio station? Tommy was not only very handsome, but he was so charming -- I believe it's called "sex appeal." Whatever you call it, Tommy had it! Along with a velvet-smooth, deep voice that could talk you into anything. He almost talked me into "something" one night, but, fortunately for me, he was a gentleman and didn't persist. Oh, my! Check out the pictures. (I don't know what happened to Pop Dixon. He was a well-kept secret and was long gone before I entered the scene.)

We had some great times, Eleanor and I, working together and double dating. The fog used to be terrible on our early morning drive to Lockheed. I was driving down Magnolia Boulevard one morning. It was only a narrow, two-lane street then and I was leading the parade because if you found a car in front of you, everybody would just get up close to the bumper and follow it. There were six to eight cars following me when I got to a narrow road and turned left. It looked like the road that turned into the plant, but the road got narrower and narrower and pretty soon I started seeing what looked like big, tall weeds! I thought, "Uh oh! These weeds didn't grow overnight." The weeds got thicker and thicker and taller and taller and I came to the realization that it was corn, not weeds! I had turned into a cornfield and, eventually, of course, it dead-ended. It squeezed us to a stop! All of those cars behind me had to back out about three miles. Boy! Did I endure some bad-mouthing and cursing and horn-honking. I stopped leading the parade after that and looked for someone to follow. At that time, the valley was crisscrossed by little, lonely roads with a lot of cornfields, walnut groves, orange groves and grapefruit groves. There was not the massive city growth there is now.

My stay at Lockheed only lasted a year. In 1944, I went to work at Western Pipe and Steel Shipyards. Pop was working there and he knew the recreation director who just happened to be baseball's very great Pepper Martin. Pepper is in the Hall of Fame and played third base for the Chicago Cubs, but he lived in California at the time. The shipyards had hired him because of the publicity angle and they wanted to have a good ball team. My Pop told him about us and how good we were. So Faye came back into my life with a bang! She and I and Betty Luna got jobs at the shipyards.

Betty was a good friend of mine and a pitcher on one of my teams. They hired us as welders' assistants. Now we didn't know the first thing about welders or their equipment or anything and we weren't supposed to. Our job was to put their softball team on the map! Our equipment consisted of Louisville Sluggers. When we got to work, we would punch in and then find some place to hide. We were just there to play baseball. For that we got 90 cents an hour. That was <u>really</u> big bucks! Of course, I have to admit that it was boring and eight hours can be a long time when you're conveniently trying to avoid somebody. The union rules were being broken because we were supposed to go to school and be certified to be a welder's assistant. But it was a common happening in those days. All the defense plants did it!

My ballplaying skills already had gotten me many things in my life and this was just another fringe benefit. So, like I said, the days were long and boring. One thing I forgot to mention is that when you changed a war job of any kind you had to get an availability certificate from your current employer. You weren't allowed to take a job from another company without it! But as long as you went from one defense job to another, there was never a problem. You just had to stay on the job for at least three months. That way, the work force stayed steady and got the job done.

One day, we had reported to work and were hiding out when Betty and I noticed that Faye was gone. She was nowhere to be seen. That could spell trouble! We started sneaking around trying to find her. We came upon this big wooden structure where they were building a ship. There was a big crowd on the ground around it and about a hundred feet up in the air we saw another crowd! They were way up on this high deck that looked like a crow's nest. They were all laughing and hollering! The people down on the ground were also pointing up and laughing. When we got a little closer and looked up -- there was Faye.

She was up there on top of that pelican's roost in her shorts and a T-shirt -- no mask, no safety equipment, no nothing else. She had bare arms and legs hanging out and she was just welding away. Sparks were flying and she was just laughing and putting on a show! Well, we tried to get her down from there. We were waving and hollering at her, but she just ignored us! Pretty soon, along came the union officials! Oh, boy! That was a tough scrape to get out of. They got her down from there and we all got hauled into headquarters. Of course, Pepper Martin came in and rescued us, but it wasn't easy! We weren't very popular at that particular moment. Somehow he got us out of the mess and we were once again in hiding.

This went on for a while but we were getting pretty tired of playing hide and seek. I was still playing in all my other leagues and dating and getting home late at night. Then I had to rise early to make that drive down to San Pedro to the shipyards. It was getting to be quite a drag for all of us. The industrial leagues were not as much fun as our commercial league, even though we did have Western Pipe and Steel in first place. The caliber of play wasn't as good and we would have many, many high scoring games. Any good ballplayer will tell you that sloppy baseball is no fun! So we were looking for a way out when fate stepped in and provided it.

The war was still escalating. Russell was acting older all the time. Pop was working hard and drinking hard, but Mom had backed off. She vowed not to take a drink until my bro Joe came back home safely. He was in training in Texas at the time. He had originally started out to be a pilot, but they had too many pilots, so now he was training to be a navigator! Then they were talking like they had too many navigators, so we didn't know where he was going to end up. But that didn't matter; all we wanted was for him to come home safely.

Unfortunately, we now had some obnoxious neighbors living next door to us who caused us a lot of problems. The owners couldn't get them out because they were on welfare with a minimum income. There were some laws which stated that you couldn't move people out unless they had a place to go. There are times when it seems like property owners don't have equal rights. They were a pain in the neck to my Mom because they were always borrowing and never returning! But Mom believed in "live and let live," so she put up with it.

I was still playing for my manager Freddy Pahler on the Dr Pepper Ball Club, and we were still playing against the Silver Fox, Bill Allington! One night after the game, Bill asked me if he could come to my house and bring some of his team and have a meeting with my folks. He said he wanted to talk to all of us about playing professional baseball. Mom thought he was nuts, but told him, "OK, come ahead." That was the beginning of it all. I was going to be re-routed on my road to Cooperstown. Bill met with me and my folks and some other ballplayers and their parents at our house. He explained that he was a scout for Philip K. Wrigley of

Wrigley's Gum. Mr. Gum was going to start a women's professional baseball league in case the major league season folded because of the war. We would be paid to do what we would rather do than eat! Imagine that!

We really didn't believe it. It was too much like a dream. But it wasn't a dream. Many things had led to this. Major league baseball was really hurting. The players were all joining up. Those who didn't were being drafted. It all took its toll. The talent was growing thin in the majors. The minor leagues were all but wiped out in the small towns. If you could throw a baseball, you were in the majors. Bill Veek, general manager and owner of the St. Louis Browns baseball team, had a midget on his team. He also had a one-armed centerfielder in his lineup. The centerfielder's name was Pete Gray. He was a good ballplayer, too. As for the midget, I don't know what kind of player he was, but he certainly must have been hard to pitch to.

We were in danger of losing our great national pastime. Fearing what that loss might do to the morale of the American people, Franklin Delano Roosevelt asked Philip K. Wrigley and Branch Rickey for help. FDR was afraid the 1943 and 1944 major league seasons might have to be canceled because of the lack of manpower. Branch Rickey and P.K. Wrigley recognized the popularity of women's softball all over the country so they thought, "Hey! We'll start a women's league! We'll teach the girls to play baseball and if the major leagues fold, they can step right into the big ballparks." So, it followed that in 1943 Mr. P.K. Wrigley, joined by his distinguished associates Ken Sells and Branch Rickey, formed the first and only women's professional baseball league.

History was in the making. The All American Girls Professional Baseball League was born. The original four teams were centered around the Great Lakes. They consisted of the Rockford Peaches from Illinois; the South Bend Blue Sox from South Bend, Indiana; the Racine Belles, from Racine, Wisconsin; and the Kenosha Comets from Wisconsin. They scouted only the Midwest that first year, but by the winter of 1943, the league was off the ground and doing well. They knew it was going to be successful, so they decided to expand the league to six teams in 1944. That's when California came on the scene. They sent scouts all over the United States and Bill Allington was the California scout. He wound up picking only seven out of 10 of us gals who were at that meeting, and much to my surprise, I was one of them. So, this wasn't a dream, it was really going to happen.

Even though I had many things going on in April 1944, without any hesitation, I stepped out of my defense job at the shipyards and into the pages of history. At 18 years old, I was now going to be an "All American Girl." A whole new era was beginning. I would have to prove myself, but my Cooperstown dream was reborn. Wow! What great adventures were ahead of me!

Besides me, Bill picked Thelma "Tiby" Eisen, Faye Dancer, Alma Zeigler, Annabelle Lee, Dorothy "Snookie" Harrell and Dottie Wiltse. Though we played on different teams in California, we were all acquainted and actually good friends off the ballfield. Now we had a common bond. We thought we had died and gone to heaven. While it was wonderful, it was pretty scary, too. We were all young. Eighteen was a lot younger and more innocent than it is today. I had always lived at home with my folks and so had the other girls. Now we were going to leave the nest, leave town and go out and do something no woman had ever done before.

I realize now that it took a lot of courage. We could not have done it without the love and support of our families. My number one fan, my Mom, told me that she knew that I could do it and that she wanted me to do it for her! She had given up her Olympic dream for Joe and me, but I knew just how much she would miss me and how much she would miss seeing me play. She was so very proud of me and so was Pop. He would miss me, too. My little brother, Russell, was already missing his big bro Joe a lot; now he was going to lose his sis. These things were all to change Russell and make him grow older much ahead of his time. My Mom missed Joe and worried a great deal about him. Now she would have to worry about me, too.

It was hard, but I packed my bags and I swallowed the lump in my heart and headed for the train station. I had no idea that the journey I was embarking on was going to last 10 years and then continue on 40 years later at a big reunion in Chicago! Then, another six years after that it would lead to Cooperstown and extend to a movie that was going to make us world famous. We were going to be in a "League of Our Own." Of course, we didn't know it then. It's funny how often people who are making history do not realize it until after they become history. That is what happened to many of our fine ladies, my baseball friends. Many did not live to see us go to Cooperstown and they did not live to see this very wonderful movie become an immensely popular classic! I guess I shouldn't say they didn't see it, because I'm sure they are up on cloud nine looking down and enjoying it with us.

      We didn't know what was ahead of us on that historic day in April 1944. We didn't know if we would make it and we definitely didn't know we'd be making history. What we did know was that we were doing something very important for the war effort and that we were ready. So when we headed for the train station that morning we didn't know just how hard it was going to be. I remember thinking on my way to the train depot: "Well, we've got two weeks to make it and surely I can make it. And if I don't make it, my way is paid home and I've got nothing to lose!" But deep down inside of me I knew I did have a lot to lose. I wanted my Mom to be proud of me! I wanted my family to be proud of me! Most of all, I wanted to do my best for the war. I vowed to work just as hard as I could and I prayed I could make it!

BEVERLY STADIUM
(Formerly Fiedler Field)
The HOME of GIRLS SOFTBALL
Beverly & La Cienega   Tel. BR. 2-3251
(Toll Free)

SCHEDULE
Double Header Every Evening
FIRST GAME 7:45 P.M.

1939

"Tommy Dixon"
Handsomest guy
I ever dated
1943

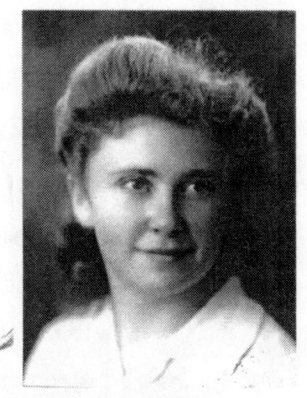

Me - 1942
Graduate

P-38 LIGHTNING

Winter 1944 We left the tree up
until July

1942

L. A. SOFTBALL PARK
Slauson near Western
L. A. SOFTBALL PARK GIRL PLAYERS
— BENEFIT —
Field Events — Double Header
SELECT MISS SOFTBALL OF 1940
ADMISSION 20c   1 P.M., Oct. 13, 1940

N° 483

1940

Mom & Joe 1944   Joe 1942

BENEFIT GAME   N° 1316
BEVERLY STADIUM
BEVERLY AT LA CIENEGA...PHONE BRADSHAW 2-3251
WEDNESDAY, SEPT. 3, 1941
AMERICAN LEAGUE DOUBLE - HEADER
General Admission 20c

Winter 1944

Chapter 11
Cal-Can-Do!

It wound up being quite an eerie ride to the station that morning. Faye and her folks were following us in their little green Ford. Pop kept checking on them in the mirror. My Mom was quiet, trying to keep from crying. Little bro Russell was quiet, and I know he was thinking how he was going to miss me and my spoiling him. Even my Pop was quiet. I'm sure he was thinking about the many ballgames he drove us all to. You already know what was in my heart! When we got there, in Downtown L.A., we drove right up to the front steps of Union Station -- you could do that in those days. I started looking around for the other gals. We were all to meet at the steps and wait for Bill Allington. The Silver Fox was bringing us our tickets! Faye and I hopped out first and were unloading luggage when we heard Ziggy's familiar whistle. Looking around, we spotted the other gals behind a huge pile of luggage. We dragged our suitcases over and added them to the pile. There was a lot of laughing and jabbering going on! The dads all went to park the cars! While there were only seven of us, we had 40 suitcases!

Our moms were all standing together over at one side looking like they were attending a funeral. Pretty soon, Bill Allington showed up and spotted us and our luggage. He gave a little whistle and sarcastically observed, "That's an awful lot of luggage for two weeks." That's not all the good news he had. He then proceeded to tell us he was going to be there when we got there and that he had been picked to manage one of the teams and was flying to Chicago that same day. Well, we all gulped a little and I hoped silently that I did not get on his team. Then we got a porter to help with the luggage and headed for the train! We were going on the Silver Streak Streamliner and we were all pretty excited about that!

All too soon, it was time to go. We were giving our moms last-minute instructions and they in turn were giving us last-minute warnings and orders and rules: "Don't talk to strange men; drink plenty of milk; get plenty of rest. Write! Write! Write!" etc. The dads were kind of quiet, just standing around, making swinging motions and small talk. "Hit that apple. Make us proud," etc. Everybody had tears in their eyes and in their voices. At the last minute everyone broke down and there was a lot of hugging and kissing and crying!

The porters were urging us to get on the train, so we finally climbed aboard the streamliner and it started slowly moving out. We leaned out the windows and doors, waving and throwing kisses as long as we could. I can still see my Mom's smiling face, with the tears streaming down it. What courage it took for her to let me go. I could hear Pop's horsy whistle, even above all the train noise, and I could read my poor little brother Russell's eyes -- he had such a lost look. I knew what he was thinking. His big bro Joe was gone and now me! He was starting to retreat into his own little fantasy world. I don't know how my Mom kept smiling that day through her tears, because I knew what was in her heart. Her little boy Joe was grown up and overseas fighting. She had the fear of losing him to deal with. Now her baby girl was leaving her and, even though she wanted me to go, I knew she was agonizing! You know what? I was agonizing in my heart, too, thinking of the pain that I was causing her. After we got over our crying, we all just sat very quietly for a while, thinking our own thoughts. All of us were wondering what was ahead. All of us were scared half to death.

Pretty soon, however, curiosity got the best of us. We started investigating and, of course, we found a club car! We also found that it was loaded with servicemen, and good-looking servicemen of all varieties: sailors, Marines, soldiers, etc. Every one of them was leaving home, too, and they were just as scared and lonesome as we were. They were anxious just to talk to somebody, to laugh and to smile a little. So, hey! We perked up! Things didn't really seem so tragic. The trip no longer seemed lonesome for the servicemen or for us!

Eighteen was the legal drinking age and Cuba Libras (a la the Andrew Sisters' Rum and Coca-Cola) tasted very good, so we started having fun! That first night we all indulged a little and drowned our sorrows. It was a three-day train trip to Chicago at that time and we were nervously looking forward to our arrival. With the help of the servicemen, we weathered the trip pretty well -- dancing a little bit at night in the club car, playing cards during the day, eating in the diner. It was all new to us, and it was quite an adventure. So we kept pretty busy and we were all pretty pooped out by the time we got to Chicago. Forgive me but, speaking of "pooped out," the trains at that time were equipped with bathrooms that had "potties" that just opened up and dumped the contents on the tracks. When the train was in the station, they would lock the bathroom doors and ask you not to use them unless it was an emergency. So we learned a new song -- don't know where it came from, but the main verse went like this:

> We encourage constipation
> While the train is in the station,
> Harvest moon is shining,
> I love you!

(A little 1940s sense of humor there! I think the melody was part of a classic called "Syncopation.")

When we finally arrived in Chicago we had to grab all the luggage, fight our way through the station and find our bus! We were going to the twin cities of Peru and LaSalle, Illinois. It was a couple of hours' ride outside of Chicago and that's where spring training was being held. It seemed an eternity, but the bus finally pulled up to this quaint, little hotel in Peru. When we checked in at the desk, they gave us this big package with all our instructions in it! There were a lot of little booklets telling us what was going on. It had meal tickets in it and all kinds of schedules and rules. The hotel was an old, two-story building with stairs only -- kind of like your bed and breakfast hotels today, but without any luxuries.

I was assigned a room with Faye and Ziggy. There were three cots in the room and a bathroom down the hall. There were stairs and more stairs all over the place. We found out a little bit later that there was another more modern hotel for the vets at a nearby location. At first, we got pretty upset about that, but then we were just rookies so we figured we had to pay our dues! It was all kind of like a dream. Memories of that first year do not stand out as vividly in my mind as memories of some of the other years. I guess part of the reason for that is because I'd like to forget some of the things that happened.

My thoughts wandered all over the place. Everything kind of boiled down to getting up at dawn -- or so it seemed -- using our breakfast coupons, and then going out to the ballpark. When you got there, there were a lot of guys running around in flannel baseball uniforms. They all had big clipboards and were making notes, which we would have killed to see. We also saw chaperones standing around in their little Marine-like uniforms; we wondered how that was going to be? The managers, who were all ex-big leaguers, were picking ballplayers and lining up teams. We did a lot of throwing and catching the ball and then tried out for different positions.

The diamond facilities were not the greatest, but they were passable. There were no fences, so you had to run down a lot of baseballs in the cow pastures. We didn't play too many real games. It was mostly just hard work and a lot of practice sessions. Our hotel was old and not what we expected. Outside of Faye's escapades, things were pretty quiet! Nothing much memorable happened to me. I was still trying to be good and worried a lot about making the team. But Faye kept things lively for everybody by staying out late and climbing up coal bins to get in the windows to keep from getting caught by the chaperone.

One thing was very clear: We California gals had a jump on everybody because we were already in good playing shape. That set the stage for the everlasting feud between the conservative, snobby, Midwestern vets and the cocky California rookies. Our California leagues went year-round because of our great weather. Because of that we had some mighty fine teams with some very talented ballplayers. We could go to the beach even in the winter and practice running and sliding in the sand. We played beach volleyball until we dropped. This kept our muscles hard and our legs strong and, of course, we sported some great tans. The Midwesterners hated us for that -- the loud mouths and cockiness didn't help, either!

Baseball skills were not the only requirement. Wrigley didn't want the image of women imitating men, so femininity was stressed at all times. There was even a charm-school session that had to be cut short because of the scheduled exhibition games. We weren't too happy when we found out that we had strict dress-code requirements: No slacks, no shorts and no jeans in public at any time. No smoking or drinking in public, except for two beers after the ballgame with your meal and that had to be in a very discreet place approved by the chaperone or by the managers. Our hair had to be shoulder length or longer and groomed neatly at all times. If your hair was up in pin curls or anything like that, your head had to be covered with a babushka -- that means "scarf" in Polish, I think.

We had to walk, talk and act like a lady at all times. There were even some ridiculous suggestions for the ballgames, like putting soap under your fingernails to keep them from getting dirty. Well, the managers dumped that one in a hurry. They didn't want bubbles coming up when you got hot and sweaty and maybe you would throw a bubble to first base instead of the ball. But the biggest shocker of all times was our uniform! It was the early 1940s and Mr. Wrigley knew that if he put a woman in a man's uniform, playing a man's game, no one would pay to come through those gates to watch. So they gave us a dress-like uniform in pastel colors and we had cutesy little team names hung on us like Blue Sox, Comets, Belles, Peaches and Chicks. Of course, they didn't mind that our bare legs showed in those short, ballerina, tunic-like uniforms. We discovered that we had to be this cute little baby doll, but go out there and play baseball with the skills of a guy. Quite a double standard, wouldn't you say?

I didn't know it at the time, but for the next 10 years of my life the name of the game was to be "All American Baseball." I was to learn that to be an "All American Girl" meant that you were totally dedicated to your teammates, to the fans and to the games! We were committed to doing our best at all times! We really believed that "All American" meant American, not like a super sports star, but American like the flag -- red, white and blue, and stars and stripes forever. "The Chevy at the levee," "Mom's apple pie" and "home cooking." Because of the war, we felt that it was our job to get out there and entertain the people and help keep our country's morale high. Our loved ones were overseas fighting and some of them were dying in this "bloody, stabbed-in-the-back" war.

We played when we were sick and we played when we were hurt. We didn't have any room to sit out a game. We only had 16 ballplayers and that included our pitching staff -- 16 that is, if everybody was healthy. Most of the time we had somebody injured. Major league ball clubs carry 15 pitchers alone in spring training and 12 most of the year. We played whatever position we were asked to play. We had a four-month season and we played between 120 and 130 ballgames during a season and traveled at the same time. If the team needed a first baseman, you played first base. If they needed a shortstop, you played shortstop. If they needed a catcher, you got behind the plate, and so on. If, by chance, the bus broke down, you pushed it. That happened more than once. If we had a day off -- and that was rare -- you could bet your bottom dollar we would be playing an afternoon or an evening exhibition game at a military base for the guys. If we weren't doing that, we were making up rain-outs. Can you imagine the overpaid, underplayed, millionaire wimps of today doing that? Of course, I don't mean wonderful ballplayers like Tony Gwynn, Cal Ripkin Jr., Nolan Ryan, Duke Snider, Joe Di Maggio, Harmon Killebrew, Ted Williams and Hank Aaron, to name a few.

When I signed my contract, I found out that my starting salary was going to be $75 a week. I was thrilled! That was a great deal of money in the 1940s. Remember, 65 or 75 cents an hour was considered prime wage. Of course, we only made that money for a four-month season. So that kept us from getting rich. But then I found out that we also got a whopping $2.25 a day meal money when we were on the road. You could actually eat on that. You could get breakfast for a quarter, lunch for the same and a decent dinner for 75 cents. So there was money left over.

Some of the gals lived on their meal money and sent their paychecks home. We all sent money home to help out. All our traveling expenses, hotels, and so on, were paid! We traveled mostly by charter buses and there were some harrowing tales to tell because they were old buses and I mean old buses -- 1930 vintage or earlier. The league cities were picked so you could reach them on an overnight bus trip. Sometimes it took 10 to 12 hours to get to the next town. Because of the war and gas rationing, the buses had speed governors on them so they could only go 50 miles an hour, tops! The armed forces took up all the public transportation facilities, so that was the only way we could go.

The league was expanding this year from four to six teams. The teams from the prior year were the Kenosha (Wisconsin) Comets and Racine (Wisconsin) Belles, the South Bend (Indiana) Blue Sox and the Rockford (Illinois) Peaches. This year they were adding the Milwaukee Chicks from Wisconsin and the Minneapolis Millerettes from Minnesota to the league. When spring training broke up, we found out that Faye, Dottie Wiltse, Annabelle Lee and I were assigned to the Minneapolis Millerettes. Ziggy and Tiby were assigned to the Milwaukee Chicks. Well, the names weren't so bad -- our name, anyway, the Minneapolis Millerettes. We were named after their minor league ball club, the Millers. But our uniforms were killers! They were bubble-gum pink. Our manager turned out to be Bubber Jonnard. He was an ex-pitcher for the New York Giants. He also had a twin brother who caught for them. Bubber was a good guy, but he liked to drink. He was great with the pitchers and catchers, but he lacked a little in overall general knowledge of baseball.

We found ourselves headed up north to Minneapolis to the "Land of a Thousand Lakes." Looking back now, the fact that Minneapolis was so far off the beaten path made traveling difficult and expensive. It was an overnight train trip to the other ballparks that would eventually prove to take too much of everything -- too much time, too much trouble and too much money. That was going to be our undoing. Since we were an expansion team, we weren't supposed to be very good that year.

We did have an interesting combination of ballplayers! Like I said, we only had 16 ballplayers on our roster. We had (maybe) two good starting pitchers, sometimes three. The rest of the staff was made up of infielders and outfielders with good arms. One of them would come in on the mound when we needed somebody else to throw and the pitcher would go play their position. If they were knocked out, they would just go back to their regular position and somebody else would give it a try. We just moved around the field like checkers. Eventually, the real pitcher might even get to sit down!

Anyone with a good arm had a shot at pitching. Better still, if they couldn't do anything else, hey! Make a pitcher out of them! Every pitcher was a starting pitcher and they were called pitchers, period! They started usually every second or third night. It took a lot to get knocked out of the game, so there were some pretty high scoring games because of that. Boy! How about all the fancy titles they have for pitchers today! Starter, mid-reliever, short reliever, long reliever, closer, stopper, etc. What a difference. I'm really surprised that they don't have someone to ride the bus for them! They could call them butt relievers!

When we arrived in Minneapolis we found that it was a beautiful city with lots of lakes (as advertised!). We also found out that there were lots of nice people there. The players stayed with prominent families in their team's town. There were always a lot of people on a waiting list to have an All American stay with them. It was sort of like being adopted. Faye and I got very lucky and stayed at the home of this Swedish family named Thornston. They had a big, rambling, three-story house right on the lake. They had a big, 18-foot Chris Craft, some little outboard fishing boats and their own private dock and pier. They were great fans and the whole family came to every ballgame. And they let us use their boats and their cars! They threw barbecues for us and even had Hawaiian luaus for us. They were really great people. They treated us like family.

It wasn't because of the fans that we eventually didn't make it in Minneapolis. We had a pretty good, all-around team. Our catcher was a good receiver, but coming in from softball, her arm wasn't the greatest and she had a hard time throwing to second base. But then, most of the catchers did until they managed to build up their arm strength! (If they ever did.) Like I told you, our pitchers really earned their money. Dottie Wiltse was our ace. She won 20 games that first year. Once she pitched both games of a doubleheader and won them both. That happened more than once in our league by other pitchers. Annabelle Lee, another one of our California products, was a knuckleballer, and she threw a bunch of dipsy-doodle stuff. She pitched a perfect game in 1944. Her nephew, Bill Lee, was called "Spaceman Lee." He pitched in the major league and won a lot of games for the Montreal Expos in 1950.

We also had a wonderful outfield. They could cover a lot of ground. Our leftfielder was Helen Callaghan from Vancouver, Canada. We called her "Cally." I would guess her height at maybe 4 feet 6 inches. Her hair alone was 4 feet tall! Cally probably weighed about 102 pounds. She was a feisty little gal, a little banty rooster, but, boy, could she swing that pine! She used a mighty big bat. It was 36-inch, 36-ounce Ted Williams, Louisville Slugger. Now that is a big bat even for today's big-money swingers. Most of your major leaguer players today use a 33- or 34-inch bat. Cally had great wrist action. She was petite, but powerful with a big swooping swing.

Her son, Casey Candale, played in the majors. Cally taught him to play. His swing and his batting stance are just like his mom's.

Cally could really pick them up and lay them down. She stole a lot of bases -- more than 100 that year. But she wouldn't slide. She would go into the base standing straight up and come to a hard abrupt stop. You would want to hide your eyes, hoping her knees and ankles would hold up. If Cally would have learned to slide, no one could have thrown her out. She also had a strong arm and got a good jump on the ball in the outfield. She was a fine outfielder and a good hitter and won a couple of batting titles.

Faye Dancer was our centerfielder and a super outfielder. You already know all about her and how good she was. After being trained by those baseball coaches, she picked up some of the fine points that she might have missed along the way. Then she became arguably, what could have been and should have been called the best ballplayer in the league. But some people would dispute that because of her antics and her personal habits. Faye and I were destined to become partners in crime in the "All American." We were going to get away with a lot of mischief because we didn't do anything really bad and we were pretty darn good ballplayers. You never knew what Faye was going to do and you still don't. She was dubbed "All the Way Faye" in the All American -- partially because of that, but mainly because she would go all the way as a ballplayer, crash into a wall or whatever it took to win a ballgame. That's when we started calling ourselves "caca faces" -- actually, we still do. I won't explain that here, but I think you can guess!

I know I've talked about her ability before, but it's worth repeating! Faye was as explosive as Jose Canseco at the plate and the same type of hitter. Strike out or homerun. She could also dump a bunt down and beat it out. She stole a lot of bases and she could slide with the best of them. Her weakness at the plate was that she was strictly a fastball, bad ball hitter. Just throw her a curve or a change-up or a strike down the middle and you got her out. She probably had more pure, natural talent than any other player in our league and she ran like a gazelle. Sometimes when a ball is hit, boom! You know that there's no doubt about it; it's going over the outfielder's head. Well, I have never seen anybody take one look and turn their back on the ball the way Faye did; then grab that ball out of the sky while running full speed, taking it over either shoulder; then leap up, spin around and come down and throw a strike to home plate. She had a bullet arm.

Sometimes, she'd be right up against the centerfield fence and instead of relaying the ball, she would throw it 300 feet in the air to the catcher, making an outfielder out of the catcher. The catcher had to catch the ball and tag the runner at the same time. Now that wasn't such a great thing to do and Faye knew better. She just did it to excite the crowd and the throw was usually perfect. She was a great crowd pleaser. Faye was <u>very</u> superstitious — as were a lot of us! Superstitions were definitely a part of our game! Maybe it was part belief and part fantasy, but that way we could use them as crutches. It was a way to get your mind off the bad things.

Later on, I'll write in more detail about the superstitions because we had some funny ones. One of Faye's was collecting glass eyes, whether they would be human, horses, teddy bears, or whatever! She would run around the grandstands convincing people to rub her glass eye so she could get a base hit. She was actually benched at one time for being "overly superstitious."

Faye's mode of dress was all her own. She used to wear her hat with the brim turned up. Her socks were turned down very low, about 4 inches above her shoes. They almost looked like anklets! Her uniform skirt somehow wound up being very short and pinned close to her thighs. Her belt buckle turned to the back. Sometimes she'd come running in from the outfield and call "time" right in the middle of a pitch and give the ump a big smile and say, "Hi." She'd then take a drink of water and wave to the fans and go running back out to her position. If time was called to pull the pitcher and another one was coming in, or if there was any other kind of delay, you could see Faye doing cartwheels in the outfield. (Shades of Ozzie Smith.)

As I said, we were going to be in hot water a lot! The funny thing was they thought I was the instigator, because Faye always looked so innocent. "Who me?" Even though we were an expansion team and not expected to go anywhere, we had other ideas. We were a strong team because we were made up mainly of Canadians and Californians. We had mainly

Canadians and Californians in our starting lineup. The Canadians were Helen Callahan and her sister, Margie, who played third base, and two Canadian pitchers, Audrey Haynes and Dodie Barr. Then there was Penny O'Brien, who played the outfield, and another utility player, Yolande Teillet, who caught and played the outfield. The California contingent consisted of Faye and me, Annabelle Lee and Dottie Wiltse.

We had Vivian Kellogg from Michigan at first base and "Bird Dog" Jackson was our right fielder. We had two local gals from Minneapolis: Lorraine Borg, catcher and Peggy Torreson, third base. Audrey Kissel was our little, black-haired, pig-tailed, dark-eyed second baseman. Audrey was from the Midwest. Some of the other teams laughed at us and dubbed us "Cal Cans," but the laughter stopped after the season got going. Our expansion team of misfits added a third dimension to that name; we became "Cal Can Do," and we did! Despite having to stand up on those all-night train trips, we did a lot of winning and we were constantly planting our feet into first place. In the first half we were definitely a team to be reckoned with.

I told you about our manager, Bubber Jonnard, but I didn't tell you about our chaperone. We called her "Ida Red" -- it was similar sounding to her real name, which will remain a secret. There was a cowboy song that was very popular that year. It went something like, "Ida Red, Ida Red, I'm plumb fool about Ida Red." Well, Faye and I got the whole team singing it! The problem was, Ida really didn't belong in baseball. She belonged somewhere else serving tea. She was a petite little gal and a little long in the tooth. She tried very hard, but she wasn't cut out for the job. For one thing, she was too easy to fool! Also, she was really "man conscious." To be frank, she did some really dumb things.

We weren't destined to last long in Minneapolis because the odds were stacked against us. The other owners didn't like that expensive, overnight train trip, and the media didn't help us out in any way. We only had a little band of 500 to 800 loyal fans that even knew about us! Most of the sportswriters would either make fun of us or not write about us at all. You might say that while the writing was not in the papers, it was on the wall!

Faye Dancer

Faye & I

Lefty - Me - Ziggy

Annie Meyers 15 yrs old w/her father

L-R Dottie-Me Ziggy-Faye and Tiby

Chappy, Me, Dottie, Tex

Spring Training Hotel

Whitey-Faye-Carolyn Morris

Bubber Jonnard & Max Carey

Cal-Can-Do-L-R-Frnt row
Me - Bubber - Chappy - Audrey K

Chapter 12
Buzz Me -- Mr. Blue

Baseball was and still is a macho sport. Nobody connected with the major leagues wanted to admit that girls could play baseball, except Wrigley, and we were just a wartime commodity to him. Unfortunately, most of the media agreed with the general consensus! That was the main reason we didn't make it in the big cities. But in the smaller towns, in the Midwest, we ruled! The fans loved us, and we loved them! We were first in their hearts, and they demanded that we be first on their sports pages!

For the short time we were in Minneapolis, we liked it a lot! We played our games at the Nicolet Avenue ballpark. It was the home of the minor league ball team we were named after. I'm told that it's not there anymore!

Across the street from the ballpark was a great restaurant called the President's Café. After the game, we could go there and have a nice dinner! They had a backroom where we could hide and relax with a couple of beers! We even had transportation around town. The Minneapolis fans gave me a little red 1922 Model T truck. They had "Pepper Paire" painted in white on the doors on each side and "water bucket" painted on the back. I knew how to drive it because it was like my Uncle Bonner's. We had one heck of a good time riding around in that little jalopy in our hometown. It hardly used any gas at all. It had those old-fashioned pedals for reverse and forward. It also had the spark and choke on the wheel! I still had to stand up to turn the corner, but what fun we had with that old Model T. Boy, do I wish I had it now. It would probably be worth $100,000, or more. Maybe like a million! (See the pictures.)

So, we were having fun and winning some ballgames until that fatal road trip came along. We had planted our feet in first place and we might have kept them there, because we were determined to win! Who knows what might have happened if lady luck had not dealt us a bad hand. The first thing that went wrong was that Peggy and Lorraine, the local Minneapolis gals, quit. Peggy was going to be cut from the team and Lorraine was her buddy, so she quit with her in protest. That was strike one! We didn't have another catcher at the time, but we had a rookie who could play a decent shortstop. So, stupid me, I volunteered to go behind the dish and try catching.

Catching was always a big problem in our league because pitchers had to learn how to hold runners on, and it was a long way down to second base (much longer than in softball). I had a strong arm and I could make the throw, so I went behind the plate for the team's sake. Since I was an infielder, I caught with my infielder's glove. I paid the price for that. I have fingers that point in all directions at the same time. I was leading the league in fielding percentage as a shortstop and I was also leading in doubles and high in RBIs when I went behind the plate. Faye was leading the league in stolen bases and home runs, and playing a great centerfield. We were a big part of the season the team was doing so well.

Then the powers that be decided that the Minneapolis Millerettes were expendable. The rest of the league voted to drop the Minneapolis franchise because it was too far off the beaten path. This made it too costly for the rest of the teams to travel to. That was strike two! So, for the second half of the 1944 season, we became a traveling team and called ourselves the "Minneapolis Orphans." I wrote a poem about that. From then on, we would be living on chartered buses and in old hotels. Boy, what great fun that was going to be! We were orphans and that meant our entire life was on that bus and in those hotels, and on the ballfield! One day after another! There was no time for rest and relaxation. It was a constant rat race with no one rooting for us. We were together 24 hours a day, with little or no privacy. It's a wonder we didn't kill each other!

No matter who we were playing or where we were going, we were the visiting team. We had a bus trip to get there and we landed in a hostile environment. If we played Saturday night in Rockford, after the game we'd travel all night long to Grand Rapids, and maybe get there by 10 a.m. Sunday morning. Then, if we had time, we would go to the hotel and drop off the luggage. If not, we would get in uniform on the bus, go directly to the ballpark and play a Sunday afternoon doubleheader. If we did get in early in the morning, our hotel rooms wouldn't be ready and we'd have to sleep in the lobby until they were.

There were no new vehicles made in 1944 because of the war. As far as we knew, there simply weren't any new buses, period! Most likely we got one that was made in the early 1930s or before. You could bet that it was pretty rickety. If it broke down, we pushed it. If we were too far out in the boonies, we spent many nights lying on the side of the road waiting for a tow truck. It happened a lot. Of course, there was no such thing as a potty on the bus. So, if we got stuck out in the wilderness, well, hopefully there was a tall grassy hill nearby, or a cornfield, or something of that nature. You had to be very careful and watch out for poison oak and for varmints (big or little)! You had to love baseball to go through what we did. Baseball was like a religion to me then and it still is. But, some of the players today are doing things that are starting to make me a nonbeliever. For most of us, the game came first. In my opinion, that is what's wrong with all organized sports today. Some players put themselves first. They're millionaires, and they're not dry behind the ears yet. But, they don't want anybody telling them what to do. I personally don't think that works. My kids were brought up to learn values and respect. Maybe it's easier to have values and respect when you're poor as opposed to being rich. They've got guys today in the major leagues that need at least one day off a week. They're already tired when the season starts. You read about them getting their second wind. Well, where the hell did their first wind go? When I read about some complaints and know the salaries they make, I really have to wonder how long baseball will survive.

Life had definitely gotten a lot tougher for us. Strike two had arrived with a vengeance! They didn't even let us go back for our belongings. We didn't have time because we were playing baseball every single day and night. Eventually, all our stuff was shipped to us, but it never caught up with us. It just followed us around from hotel to hotel. We wound up having to buy a lot of extra clothes. I gave my little red Model T (though it broke my heart) to our batboy in Minneapolis, and he was thrilled to death to get it. He was a senior in high school and didn't have a car!

Perhaps I should explain our league a little here. The first year they called it "All American Softball." Then it went to baseball -- "All American Girls Baseball League" in the second year.

We were playing a game that was a cross between baseball and softball. The pitching was still underhanded and the mound was 40 feet from home plate. Max Carey said, "You could add 50 to 75 points to our batting average in comparison with the major leaguers." That was because, just when we were getting to know the game, it would change again. It seemed like the pitcher was right on top of you, right down our throat, when she threw. We were still pitching underhanded, as in softball, but we had to hold runners on as in baseball.

The field dimensions and the ball were different from baseball. In the beginning, we used an 11¾-inch ball, much like a softball. But it was as hard as a baseball. For that matter, ask anyone who plays softball if the ball is soft. They'll tell you it's not! Our ball was made deliberately not to carry in the air. It had a hard plastic center, but it was string wound down to the core. That made it smart when it hit you. The outfielders could play in because it didn't carry in the air. You lost a lot of hits that way. The field dimensions favored the pitchers. You could get thrown out at first base on a line drive to right field. That was routine. I've even seen fast runners get thrown out at first base on a line drive to centerfield, if the outfielder knew her hitter and would take a chance and play short.

The base paths were longer than softball and the first baseman and the third baseman could play deep. They could knock the ball down and still throw you out. Ninety percent of us could bunt the ball well and hit the dirt when needed despite those skirts. We were taught to get the jump on the ball by reading the pitcher and her moves to first base. We were taught the art of base stealing. We could have given a lot of today's major leaguers lessons. Anyway, back to Minneapolis ...

When the Minneapolis Millerettes became that road team, all of the fun seemed to go out of the game. We were still trying, but everything and everybody was against us! Even the umpires! Seemed like they were all named "Homer"!

I was doing OK but I was never more than a mid-speed runner before I was a catcher and catching was slowing me down more. But I could still get that extra base when we needed it because I played heads-up baseball most of the time. Except for one night in Racine, and it cost me. Strike three was coming up for me, Faye and the Orphans! We were playing the Racine

Belles and the first night there, our substitute shortstop and Faye collided in the outfield going for a little pop fly. Faye went down with a back injury. They put her in an ambulance and took her to the Kenosha Hospital. Kenosha was only a few miles from Racine, so I went to see her that night after the ballgame. I told her, "Move over lazy bones, you look too comfortable." Bad judgment on my part. I even told her, "I bet the food was good." That was another mistake.

Well, the next night, our pitchers were getting tattooed all over the place. The Racine Belles were whopping us 17-0. The Racine coach was a famous ex-hockey player by the name of Johnny Gottselig. He played for the Chicago Blackhawks at one time, and he managed like a hockey player. Racine had a runner on third base and a ground ball was hit back to our third baseman, Margie Callahan. Being that many runs ahead of us, the coach should not have sent the runner home. Ordinarily, she would have been out by about 30 feet. But Margie threw the ball halfway to China, down the first base line. I stepped up and out of the runner's way and was watching the ball. The base runner, who was an overzealous, under-brain-powered gal, thought I was going for the ball when I stepped toward first base. She jumped straight into me. I was looking down the first base line trying to see where the ball had gone, and not watching when she planted a knee on both sides of my neck. My collarbone snapped like a wishbone and I went down with a terrible pain in my left shoulder. They helped me up and I walked off the field trying to keep from groaning and passing out. I had this horrible burning feeling in my left shoulder, and the rest of me didn't feel too good, either.

Our chaperone, who again shall remain nameless, (I know she's not going to like this) didn't want to wreck the uniform. I told you about these uniforms. They were not made for playing baseball. They had a tight tunic top with a small zipper on the side. The tunic unbuttoned but you still couldn't get out of it without unzipping the side. Then, since it was fitted, you had to pull the thing up over your head to get it off. Now, our penny-wise and pound-foolish chaperone, instead of cutting the uniform off me, insisted that I raise my arms up over my head. Then she pulled that uniform off me! I could feel my collarbone breaking more. Again, you could hear it pop! And the pain almost knocked me out. That turned it into a really bad break.

That was it! I was through for the day and, as it turned out, for the rest of the year. So, that night I made the trip to Kenosha to the hospital! I found out that it wasn't so dang comfortable and that the food stunk! There I was, lying flat on my back in the emergency room, and I heard this commotion outside the door. In comes Cacapot Faye, free-wheeling it in a wheelchair, laughing and pointing a finger at me. "Hey, I knew you couldn't stay away," she hollered. She was only there for a minute, but she was firing questions, "How the hell are you? What are you doing here?"

Well, "Big Mama," the head nurse, showed up yelling, "Hey, you! What are you doing here? Back to bed with you. You know you don't belong here!" Big Mama looked like she was about 10 feet tall and she was built like Shaquille O'Neal. She grabbed Faye's wheelchair and jerked her out of there, I can still see her now. Faye's mouth flew open and her feet flew up in the air, along with her nightgown, and she was gone. It was the only time I ever saw anyone get the best of Faye. I had to laugh in spite of the pain. We didn't know it at that time, but we were both going to be out for the rest of the year. And as we went, so went the team. We were a great part of the offense and the defense. Without us, they soon dropped out of contention and fell to last place. Strike three! You're out! That's where everybody had expected us to be anyway.

What a disappointment that was! It was a nightmare for both of us. It was like being in a strange world, in limbo. We couldn't play and we didn't know when we would get to play again. They had a horse doctor in charge of the ballplayers (that's what I called him). He was probably in his 80s and had an attitude about women. They just shouldn't exist (that was his attitude), especially as ballplayers. He was an old baseball man and women ballplayers were completely beyond his comprehension. He didn't X-ray my shoulder, he didn't tape my shoulder or put a cast on it. He just looked at it, poked at it and moved my arm around (just to hear me scream, I think). Then he put what he called an "iron cross" on my back. It was a harness-like thing, a sort of padded metal cross. I'll tell you, "cross" was a good name for it because I suffered like I was nailed to it! It simply didn't hold anything in place. There was constant movement and pain in my shoulder. I felt like something was sticking in me all the time. I had to sleep in my chair sitting up. There was too much pain to lie down and rise up again.

The doctor shall remain nameless, but we called him Dr. Stone Fingers. When I complained about the pain, he did nothing. His attitude was that I was just a little girl who couldn't take pain and there was nothing really the matter with me. At the end of three weeks, when I was supposed to be almost healed, he finally took some X-rays. Then he found out that the bone had slipped and was jabbing me all the time! It was hemorrhaging and everything had to be reset. That put me out for the rest of the year. Treated properly, I would have been out for just four to five weeks. But, there was so much damage done internally, that my collarbone had barely started to knit! The same thing happened with Faye. He didn't X-ray her, either. His attitude was, "You should be playing now!" She was to suffer the rest of her life with back problems that probably could have been avoided. We couldn't play and didn't know when we could play. If we went home, we wouldn't be paid. There was no health insurance to protect us. We had to be available for play, or we couldn't collect our salary. We were kind of in limbo. We were hurt, lonely and feeling left out. When our team came to town to play games, we found out who our real friends were, and they weren't the ones we thought, either. A couple of them still owe me money. They borrowed money from me while they dated and yet they didn't have the time for a "crippy" who had a thing on her back that made her look funny. That iron cross thing belonged in a torture chamber of the medieval days.

There was one consolation, at least. A lot of good-looking men lived in the Kenosha area. So, with the help of our Kenosha buddies, we managed to do a little bit of partying and cause some trouble. We were really too severely injured to enjoy much of anything, but another good thing came out of it, too. That's when I wrote "The All American Girls Professional Baseball Song." I wrote the words down and I was working on the music in my head, like I always did. I didn't get it finished, but I had it pretty well worked out in my head. We stayed at the home of Jack Rice, one of our umpires. He and his wife lived in Kenosha! Since he was on the road a lot and took his wife with him, they let us stay there. As a catcher that was a hard pill to swallow (stay at an umpire's house?) Ugh!

Jack was a pretty good guy and maybe one of the better umpires in the league, and that helped. It was good for them. They had us at their house to watch it. It was good for us because it was a lot better than those funky old hotels. So, it worked out OK for everybody. It really turned out to be a tough, long year for both Faye and me. By now, we were pretty bored and pretty homesick. The only thing that kept me going was my Mom. She wrote me faithfully two to three times a week and didn't gripe too much when she would only get short answers back. I had an excuse, right? The broken collarbone!

I still have some of Mom's letters. I was just reading one the other day in which she sent me all her love and then told me that they were going to move. The house that we had rented all those years was going to be sold. The folks had tried to find another place on Armacost Alley, but nothing was available. I knew Mom was unhappy with that because we had lived on that street a long time. That's where our memories were. I remember I vowed I would try to help her do something about that!

One good thing about the move was that they found a house on Wellesley Avenue, only three or four streets over from Faye's house. Faye lived on a little street called Walnut Lane, just around the corner. We were at the end of a cul-de-sac. There was a big vacant field and then there was California's first drive-in theater on the corner of Olympic Boulevard and Bundy Avenue. The Dancer house was actually a part of Harold Lloyd's movie set at one time, and it was moved there after they were through with it.

That long, dragged-out miserable season finally came to an end, and we booked passage on the streamliner home, along with all the rest of the Californians. I'll tell you, we were all pretty happy to be heading home. I got rid of the albatross cross from my back, but I was still weak and mending and Faye still had to wear her back brace. Though her back appeared to be getting well, hers was a more serious injury. We were a happy group as we headed back home. California natives are never really happy anywhere else.

That club car was still hooked onto that train and it was still full of servicemen! So, it was a fun trip home. I met a very handsome Marine pilot. His name was a little funky, George Jerko. I was having a little problem thinking about if I married him how "Pepper Jerko" would sound. Maybe, like something to eat? But, I decided I could live with it and set my sights on him. He was about 6 feet tall, well-built and extremely handsome. Actually, he looked kind of like a golden-skinned young Dana Andrews. He had brown, wavy hair and blue, blue eyes. Really looked kind of like a Greek god, and maybe that was because he was Greek.

It turned out that he flew a Helldiver on a Navy carrier and was going to be stationed at that familiar El Toro Marine Base just down the road from us. What a wonderful small world it was. He seemed to like me a lot, although I had a little competition with Annabelle Lee, but I thought I won that battle. When I look at those old pictures, I can see that Annabelle and I resembled each other a lot. We both had long, curly red hair, green eyes and a round smiling face. But she was shorter than I was, more petite. I was more the healthy, All-American beauty type that was so popular in those days. At least I've been told that.

The train wound its way through those majestic mountains and passed through the purple desert into all those beautiful orange groves, and finally found its way into L.A. and Union Station. I kissed George goodbye, after making sure he knew my phone number by heart, and jumped off that train and into my Mom's and Pop's arms. It sure felt good to have my Mom baby me with her tender, loving care. Soon my shoulder healed completely, and it didn't figure to bother me in the future, as far as baseball was concerned. Even though the bone had slipped and left a big lump there. Fortunately, it wasn't my throwing arm.

I resumed my home-style of living by getting a job in a defense plant and becoming "Rosie the Riveter" again, dating new guys, and, of course, getting fat on my Mom's cooking. I also worked some of it off playing all my winter softball leagues. I was keeping in shape for the All-American Girls Professional Baseball League spring training.

I had given up on hearing from my Greek God George, when after about a month, he finally remembered my phone number and called. He had been on maneuvers, he said, training to go overseas and wasn't allowed to call anyone (so he said). We made a date and he came down that weekend. He got along great with my folks, and I was thinking something might come of this. We went dancing and we were "Fred and Ginger" together. We even liked the same drink, rum and Coca-Cola (a la the club car). He stayed that weekend at my house, and slept on the couch. In those days they always did that. Then I drove him downtown to the bus station. As we waved goodbye, he flashed that white, white smile and hollered, "I'll buzz you."

I thought he meant he would call me. Well, I soon found out differently. A few days later, Mom and I were in the kitchen doing the dishes one morning and we heard this plane flying overhead. I commented on how it must have been going to land somewhere because it was so low. That plane was flying so low that it made the house vibrate. The next thing you know it was back again, sounding even closer. I said, "Mom, I bet he's in trouble." We ran out the front door and stood by the palm tree and shaded our eyes as we looked up. Sure enough, here comes this plane again, circling us. When it came by again I swear it was so low you could see the white of the pilot's teeth as he smiled. I know he was less than a hundred feet off the ground. My Mom panicked and said, "He's going to crash! He's going to crash!"

Then it dawned on me that it was George in his Helldiver and he was buzzing me! I put my arms around my Mom and, laughing like crazy, explained. She still was ready to start digging her way to China when he finally waved and took off. Boy, he broke a million rules on that one! But what fun that was for me. He told me later he was able to find us because of the drive-in theater and the palm tree in our front yard. But the really funny part came later. Faye called me the next day and she told me her dad was really mad because some idiot in an airplane circled the neighborhood. The plane threw oil all over his backyard. Well, I told Faye who it was and we got a great laugh out of the whole thing. I never did admit it to her dad.

George made for an interesting winter. We heated up the car windows in that little Chevy at times. He came over about every other weekend saying he had duty when he couldn't make it. But he didn't show up for our date this one weekend. He called me later and I found out that he had crashed in his Helldiver when a tire blew on a landing. He was able to crawl away from the plane before it exploded into flames. He had a few burns and a broken arm. He was a very lucky man. Then he came over and stayed for a week at my house before he headed home to Philadelphia to his folks. He was talking about me meeting his folks and making with the marriage talk. But, I still didn't give it up. Even though I was infatuated with him, everything seemed just too perfect. Something wasn't right.

It was a good thing I had that feeling because after he got home, I never heard from him again. It upset me, but I soon got over it because so much was going on in my life. We didn't compare notes until years later. But I found out that every other weekend he was dating Annabelle Lee and giving her the same line. What a hoot! And they say girls are fickle. So, George "Jerko" lived up to his name!

One reason I forgot about "El Jerko" was because we got some great, great news. My bro, Joe, was coming home to California. He was going to be stationed at March Field in Riverside. Joe was now a radio gunner on a B-24 Bomber. That's what they needed most so that's what they made him. Your way is never right. The Army's way is always right! Joe didn't care. He just wanted to do his job and get home again. Mom and Pop and little Russell and I were doing cartwheels. Even our little Boston bull Jerry was happy about the whole thing. We didn't want to think about that final stop at March Field. That was going to complete his training and we knew what that meant! We just became Scarlett O'Hara again and decided not to worry about that until tomorrow.

Mom & Me
getting buzzed!

1944 Pepper,
Broken Collarbone

1944 Minneapolis Millerettes

Faye looking
innocent!

Tex & Me

Umpire
Jack Rice

All-American Girls Professional
Baseball League 1943-1954
1944 Millerettes

Nicolette Field

Bathing Beauties
Helen C, Audrey,
Faye, Me and Dottie

"Dolly Pepper Parton
of the league"

"My Red Wagon"

The Silver Fox
and his Peaches

The Minneapollis Orphans

Stylin
L-R--Audrey K- Dottie - Faye - Me-

113

Chapter 13
There's No Place Like Home! (If It's Your House)

It was just a couple of days before Thanksgiving and we waited by the telephone, hoping that Joe would be home by turkey day and that we would have a real Thanksgiving. The Army never told you anything that you wanted to know until after you didn't need to know it which was then too late. (Wow, that one sounded like a "Yogi Berraism.") Finally, the phone rang and I heard my Mom's cry of joy. "Joe! Joe! It's him. Oh, thank God, it's my boy. He's home." My bro Joe was at the downtown Los Angeles Greyhound Bus Depot and we were in that car and on our way before the phone hit the receiver. I'm not even sure if Mom hung it up.

That trip to the bus depot was something else. That was the only time I ever heard Mom say, "Daddy, can't you go faster? Hurry up! Hurry up!" Usually it was, "Daddy, don't go so fast! You're going to get us a ticket." It took about an hour to get there, but we finally made it. I cannot describe to you the overwhelming joy in my heart when I saw my bro standing there on the steps, waiting for us. He looked so handsome in his Army Air Force uniform. He had his ever-loving duffle bag over his shoulder and the widest smile in the whole world on his face.

Mom was out of the car before it stopped, tears streaming down her face, running to meet him. He grabbed a hold of that duffle bag and ran to meet her. Pop, Russ and I got out and just stood there watching Mom and Joe hugging. We were all crying and no one was talking, at least for the moment. Joe buried his head on Mom's shoulder to hide his tears. But the silence didn't last long. Then we all charged him. Somehow it seemed like we all fit into Mom's arms again. Joe and my eyes met and we were little kids again and safe in that warm circle of Mom's loving arms. What a wonderful feeling that was. (Writing this has brought it all back to me and I have to stop for a while because the tears are running down my face.)

The trip back home went a lot faster. Everybody was talking at the same time. Little bro Russell was beaming and blabbering and I was laughing and blabbering. Joe was trying to answer all our questions at once. Mom was back to normal, with her backseat driving.

"Daddy, you're going too fast again. Watch out! See that truck?" Once in a while, Pop would answer back a few unprintable words and tell her to pipe down and let him drive. But he was smiling all the time.

That was a wonderful winter. Everything cooperated, even the weather. We had such great times, and such wonderful holidays. You learn the true meaning of the holidays when something like that happens. I had temporarily taken a job at the W.P. Fuller paint store in Santa Monica as a sales lady, just as a break from electronics. The money wasn't as good but it was close to home. The hours were better and I had more free time to spend with my family. I was classed as a sales lady, but basically my job turned out to be decorating the store windows. I liked that a lot. It allowed me to express my artistic nature. I made most of the props myself and I saved them a lot of money. I did some little cutesy holiday things, like Santa Claus sliding into home plate and being tagged out. With some cutesy little paint sayings like, "There won't be any runs with Fuller Paint!" (Something like, that.)

I might have had a future in that if I had stuck to it. But baseball would have interrupted that career like it did all the others for that 10-year period. For the time being, the job fit me perfectly. When Joe was home, he could drop me off and do his running around in our car and then come back and get me. Or, I would ride home with a friend by the name of Billie Naglehoff. She was a cute little blond gal. We got along great and often double dated. I introduced her to my bro Joe and they hit it off immediately. Joe liked her a lot. The feeling was mutual, so they started dating. That worked out great because Joe was bringing home different guys from March Field, where he was stationed. He'd bring a different guy from his B-24 Bomber crew every weekend. I dated them and if there was more than one, I got them dates with Faye, or Eleanor, or Dottie, or somebody.

We were all having a great time, dancing, bowling and going to the movies. Sometimes we would hang around the house with the folks and have a barbecue in the backyard. We'd play lawn darts, listen to music or play cards. We liked listening to radio programs. I don't know why, but it seemed like there were a lot of things to do in those days that were fun and didn't cost any money. Of course, everyone enjoyed Mom's cooking. There was always some fantastic food to look forward to, whether it was her killer devil's food cake, or her wonderful meatloaf, or maybe her wonderful pot roast and gravy, or the barbecued steaks. It didn't matter, it was all wonderful.

The crew from Joe's bomber squadron was all from different states. It helped to fill the void and it kept them from feeling so lonely, to come to our home and be a part of our family. I wasn't seriously dating anyone. I remember Dan Topping. He was the special gunnery sergeant on the crew. He was a very handsome little guy. I had fun with him. Then one time, my bro brought Bob Snyder home. Bob was the nose gunner on the B-24. It was a dangerous job and he made sure he told me about it. Bob was from New York and he was a typical New Yorker. I was from California and I was a typical Californian. I personally think that New Yorkers and Californians are just natural opposites. They don't mix ... sort of like oil and water.

We engaged in verbal battle from the very beginning. Both Californians and New Yorkers think that they're lucky and that their state is the greatest state there is. We fought over everything. We fought over whose pizza was better. We fought over whose weather was better. We jitterbugged beautifully together, but he called it the New Yorker, and I called it the California Shuffle. It just went on and on. There wasn't anything we didn't argue about. Well, we spent so much dang time arguing, the next thing you know, we had fallen in love. We no longer switched around our weekends with our dating. Joe and Billie had become an item, and there was only Bob for me with his big, brown, cocker spaniel eyes and his wonderful, full white smile. He looked so handsome in his uniform. We became secretly engaged and I promised to wait for him.

Meanwhile, I think Joe and Billie might have had a future, too. I know she had fallen hard for Joe. But my bro had met a gal in St. Louis while he was in training there. He was still thinking of her and he was too honorable to take advantage of Billie. So, that romance really wasn't going anywhere. I think Billie had great hopes that it would. We really had some good times that spring. We did all the normal things that everybody did in those days. We went to the beach together. The boys came along when I went down to work out in the sand to get my legs ready for spring training. We went to ballgames, of course, as well as free concerts in the park. As I said before, there seemed to be an awful lot of things to do then, that didn't cost any money.

They still had the great bands down there on the Ocean Park Pier, performing at the Casino Ballroom. That was always a thrill. Dancing was such a big part of my life then. I loved it and I was good at it. I think if I had not been so crazy about baseball and if it hadn't been for the All American league, I might have gone for some kind of future in show business. But, I couldn't give up my baseball. I loved it too much!

Time was moving along and we just sort of toughed it out during the weekends. Even though she wasn't showing it, or wasn't talking about it, I knew Mom was thinking, "How much longer do we have?" We knew sooner or later that Joe and Bob would be making that trip up to San Francisco and they would be flying out. But, like I say, we just kept on being Scarlett O'Hara and we didn't talk about that. We knew that it was going to happen but we refused to admit it. Except at night, when the lights were out and we were lying there and not able to sleep. I would wind up saying my prayers over and over. I know that's when Mom was thinking about it too. Joe and I loved our little 1939 Chevy. We tooled all around town in it. It was only a coupe but it had a little jump seat in the back.

It was just perfect for Joe and me and Bob and Billie. But, much as we loved it, we got to talking about it and we decided it was expendable. We knew we could get a good buck for it because used cars were at a premium. The manufacturers were making tanks, trucks, guns and all kinds of vehicles for the war. They were not making any new cars. Our car was expendable because I couldn't take it back east with me, at least not yet (because I wasn't a star). Joe would be leaving and he certainly couldn't take it with him, so he had no need for it. The folks had an old car, but it ran well, so they didn't need it.

We knew that Mom had always wanted a home to call her own (she had never owned one). She had this house spotted, right next to where we had lived all those years. She knew that it would be up for sale soon because she knew the history. That's where our obnoxious neighbors lived. They were still on welfare. Not because they needed it, but just because they didn't want to work. They didn't take care of anything. The house and the yard were a mess. They were always behind in their rent. The guy that owned it was tired of trying to collect. When we lived next door, he would come knocking at our house, looking for them. Because of the welfare laws, the only way to get them out was to sell. Mom was watching that house with an eagle eye.

Underneath all that mess she knew there was a great house. It was on a big lot, about 75 x 150 feet, and had a big grassy front yard. There was a big cement front porch with lots of stone pillars to sit on. Later on, Pop glassed that in for another bedroom. There were fruit and walnut trees in the backyard and everything was fenced in. It had a big double garage with a back alley entrance and it even had a greenhouse. It was perfect for the folks. Three bedrooms with beautiful hardwood oak floors and, best of all, the house was at the perfect location. It was one block south of Wilshire Boulevard on Armacost Avenue, the street of Mom's dreams.

So Joe and I decided to sell our car so they could have the down payment on the house. Mom was in seventh heaven! They could have never raised enough money any other way. Pop was still working at the shipyards. But, it took all their money to meet expenses and pay rent. Rent was very high then, because of the war. There were no instant loans or credit cards or any of that kind of stuff. Banks required collateral and if you didn't have a home, you didn't have that. You had to pay a third down on all big purchases like a home or a car.

So, while Mom was in heaven in one way, in another way she wasn't. We never talked about Joe's leaving. We all knew it was coming soon, but we didn't know how soon. While it was wonderful thinking about selling the car and buying the house, it was not wonderful to think about why we were doing it. We were all living on borrowed time. We got through February and into March, and then it happened. The news none of us wanted to hear came. Bob and Joe came home that weekend and by the look on their faces, we knew. They were under secret orders and couldn't really tell us anything, just that they were going to join the war effort and that soon they would be flying out.

It was a sober and quiet ride back to the bus station that weekend. I couldn't bear to look at Joe's back as they walked away from us. We stayed and watched them board the March Field Air Force bus, and we watched until the bus was out of sight. We had all tried frantically to have a good time and act like nothing was wrong that weekend. There had been a lot of brave faces and a lot of silent tears. Then, it was an even quieter ride back home. I rode back with an arm around my Mom, knowing that when Bob and Joe flew out over the Pacific, they would be taking both our hearts with them. But, God was kind to us and he provided us with a diversion, something else to think about.

That very next week, Mom found out that the house had been put up for sale. They were asking $5,000 -- that is not a misprint! And it was well worth it. But due to the tenants insulting everybody and the lousy condition of the house, nobody was bidding on it. Mom was waiting with bated breath for the right opportunity. Time after time, it didn't sell. She finally called them and put in an offer of $3,000. They came back with $4,000! Mom said $3,300, and they said, sold!

That meant that we now had to sell the car, but we had a little time while it went through escrow. This was fortunate because the car got stolen and was found stripped down near Long Beach. But, we had good insurance and they had to completely restore it. So, it turned out to be a break because the car was now like new and worth more money. We needed top dollar and we got it -- $1,100 on the button. That was lots of money in those days. There was the one-third down payment and the payments were only $25 a month. That was a lot less than their rent had been. So, we were finally able to pay Mom and Pop back for all the wonderful things they did for us. After Mom's death in 1959, Pop sold the house for $25,000. Real estate in California was always like gold, and it still is. Only it just takes a lot more gold to buy it now!

Well, now my time was getting short, and we weren't talking about that either, but Mom knew I had to be leaving, too. So, I quit my job and spent my time helping Mom clean up the mess. That place really needed a lot of work before they could move in. We were going up there every day, working on the house, fixing and cleaning, and shoveling out the debris. Russ would come up with us and work outside, digging weeds and cleaning up the yard. Mom and I got everything ready to paint. We scraped, cleaned and sanded. Then Pop would do the painting when he got home from the shipyards.

Pop was a painter in his spare time and he was pretty good at it. The only thing about his painting was if he was using red paint and any was left over, everything would be painted red! If he was using blue paint and any was left over, everything would be blue. He and Mom used to go around and around about that one. Anyway, Pop worked the graveyard shift because he made extra money. So, he would help us until about three or four in the afternoon, then he had to eat and get some sleep. But first, we'd always sit out in the backyard and admire everything. We'd have a couple of beers together, then Pop would eat his dinner and go to sleep until it was time to get up and drive to work. It took a huge effort to get that place livable, but it was worth it. Little bro Russell was as happy as a clam. The street he grew up on was ours again. He was going to have his own little room. He was roaming the neighborhood looking for old friends and making new ones. At that time, he was about 10, going on 50. His wardrobe was something else. He wore old-fashioned vests with suit coats and jeans. A watch and chain would be hanging out of the vest pocket. He always wore a hat and carried a cane. He had all kinds of hats: straw hats, top hats, Derbies, etc. He was retreating again from his childhood, knowing that Joe was gone and that I would soon be leaving. That was his way of dealing with losing us. There were furniture stores and antique stores and all kinds of cute little art stores up and down Wilshire Boulevard. Russ made friends with one of the owners of an antique store, Andrew Ottostead. Andrew was about 50, so he and Russ got along great. When we would go up to the house to work, Russ would help for a while, under protest, then he would disappear. But we always knew where to find him. He would be at Andrew's. He worked for Andrew sometimes. He got mostly merchandise for his pay instead of money. He did get a little money sometimes, but mostly he would get his hats, canes, watches, etc.

Well, the time came and I had to go. I can still see my Mom on her hands and knees, scrubbing those hardwood floors, with steel wool to get the grime off, and looking up at me with tears in her eyes. But she was smiling and trying to make it easy on me, like she always did. I'd been helping her scrub, so I knew it was a tough, back-breaking job and hard on the knees. I also knew that the brunt of the whole work would now fall on Mom. But, at least she finally had her house, and that was making her happy! Maybe working that hard kept her from thinking too much. Maybe it kept her heart from hurting too much. I needed to report to spring training on time to get my two-week salary. So, I had to go. The last-minute instructions came, "Now you write, you hear?"

"Yes Mom, I will." I hugged her hard and ran out of the house, so we both wouldn't break down. Russ had disappeared, as usual. Pop had to go off to work and I felt terrible leaving Mom so lonely and so vulnerable. But, I had to go. Baseball was calling me, and I could never resist that call. This time we were flying and Faye's folks were driving us to the airport. My mind was a jumble because so much had happened. But on the way there, I began to get that old feeling again. I had been temporarily distracted from my baseball by Joe and Bob, and Mom and the house. But now I started to get excited again. Baseball was calling me, and I never could resist that siren. For 10 years, I simply could not resist that call!

Mom"Tess" & Jerry

Me and my smilen Bob

Me, Joe and Boots under protest

Pepper practicing her swing

Mom & Mickey

Little Russell

The Car that bought the house

Mickey

Boots

Mom's Dream House

Chapter 14
Where You Going, Easter?
(1945 Spring Training in Chicago!)

"Where you going, Easter?" That's baseball talk for, "What team are you gonna be with?" Meaning, are you gonna be traded? Where you gonna be on Easter, in April? That was one of the things that was going through my mind on that long hard drive through traffic to the Los Angeles Airport. I knew 1945 was going to be a special year. That 1944 winter was the first of many time periods marking what I was to discover could be such an eternity. When a season ended and I would return to California, even though I worked and dated and bowled and got fat on Mom's cooking, subconsciously I was in limbo. I was always just waiting for the baseball season to begin again, waiting for that siren to call me. It was like I had two lives, one on the road and one at home.

Later on, after I was an established star, there would be pre-season and post-season tours to cut into that limbo time. In 1945, however, I was anxious and nervous because I still had to prove myself. The 1944 season had barely begun when that collision at home plate broke my collarbone and abruptly ended it for me. Everything now seemed like a fantasy in my mind. I couldn't believe that I'd be playing baseball every day and/or night, just like the big leaguers. And getting paid good money for doing something that I would rather do than eat anyway. Getting my picture taken, signing autographs, seeing write-ups and pictures in the daily papers. Staying in big, fancy hotels and being pointed out as a celebrity. Not to mention all the cute guys hanging around, wanting to meet us and take us out to dinner after the games.

Everything was so much fun! But, the best part of all was the hard-fought, competitive baseball. Beating my buddies was compulsive for the total commitment on the field and the bragging rights off the field. What a life! That's why I was chomping at the bit. I was more than ready to show the world, Pepper had come to play! My broken collarbone had healed and besides, it was my left shoulder. Being a right-hander, I didn't figure to have any throwing problems. I'd put plenty of work in at the beach with the rest of the California gals, getting that big jumpstart on the rest of the league. The sunny weather allowed us to be at the beach all winter and the running and sliding playing volleyball in the sand kept our legs in shape. It was going to be great fun to report to spring training and show off my beautiful tan to my white-skinned teammates.

I was jolted out of my thoughts by a huge airplane flying over and screaming at us. We were almost at LAX. Mr. Dancer negotiated the traffic and dropped us off at the terminal. Tiby and Ziggy were already there, waiting for us. Faye said her goodbyes, hugged and kissed her folks, and then we went down the ramp and climbed into a big DC-4. It seemed like Chicago was a long way off in those days. I swear, it's moved closer today. After all the usual annoying delays, off we went into the wild blue yonder. But, the blue didn't last long. It turned to black as we landed in Dallas, just ahead of a tornado.

We were temporarily grounded, so we watched the storm from the airport windows. Lightning flashed everywhere and the thunder was deafening. As we watched, a little Piper Cub tried to come in for an emergency landing. We could see the lightning bolts silhouetting it. The plane struggled mightily and the storm was bucking the little plane all around the sky. The battle only lasted about 10 minutes and the little plane finally lost, crashing at the outskirts of the airport. We never knew the outcome. All the power went out and everything went pitch black.

That was an auspicious start for our journey, one that would have made a seasoned flyer nervous, and we were far from seasoned, pickled maybe, but not seasoned (a little joke there). The storm finally passed over the area and we took off again (after everyone hastily took out flight insurance). This time we made it all the way to Chicago. As soon as we picked up our luggage at O'Hare, we grabbed a cab and headed for the Allerton Hotel. It was located right on Lake Michigan. That's where we would be staying for the 1945 spring training. The baseball fields were right across the street from the hotel. (Incidentally, the hotel is still there but the fields are not.)

When we got to the hotel, we unloaded our bags and sat around the lobby waiting for our room assignments. Posters and pictures hung from the walls and easels all over the lobby advertising the "All American Girls Professional Baseball League." Just like that, I was beginning to feel like a celebrity again. Faye began to read the advertisements aloud to us, and when Faye read aloud, it was pretty loud. "Hey," she bellowed, "There's going to be six teams again this year. Wow! What a ball we'll have."

Tiby, who was off to one side studying a poster, looked disapprovingly at Faye. She shushed her and then called to Zig and me. "Come here," she ordered. When we came over she pointed, "Look, there's Max Carey." We did a double take and Ziggy said, "Hey, there's the great man, coach of the 1944 champion Milwaukee Chicks!" She patted Tiby on the back and said, "I sure hope he's our manager this year, too!" They had won the league championship in 1944 with Max as their coach, but we had heard rumors that things were going to change this year.

Despite winning the championship, Milwaukee wasn't bringing the team back. Like Minneapolis, it was too far off the beaten path. They also had no media support and didn't draw well. I muttered reverently, "Max is a cinch to be in the Hall of Fame! You guys were so lucky to play for him." Max had practically rewritten baseball's record books. He was the stolen base leader, he had the most hits in a single ballgame, the most runs scored, on base the most times in a game, and so on.

Faye had joined us by now and she said, "Boy, I hope I get on his team." I gave her a look and said laughingly, "Hey, you steal enough bases now without really learning how." She was staring over my shoulder and didn't respond. Her blue eyes widened and her mouth dropped open. "Wow, would you look at that?" she bellowed, and began to laugh. I turned around just in time to see the revolving doors spin out this gal who looked like she came right out of the "Grapes of Wrath." She strolled in with a barefooted nonchalance. Her shoes hung over her shoulder by the strings. She had on faded blue overalls with one strap hanging loose, the pant legs were rolled up unevenly and underneath the overalls she wore a weather-beaten, long sleeved plaid shirt with the cuffs turned up. Her blond straw hair was tied in a ponytail with a string and she had a battered baseball cap pulled down over her eyes. "Grapes of Wrath" or not, everything looked scrubbed clean.

Reaching the center of the lobby, she dropped her beat-up carpetbag and stared in wonderment, as if she had stumbled into the Taj Mahal. Ziggy gave one of her patented low whistles. The gal heard it, spotted our smiling faces, and barefooted it over to us. She pushed her hat back as she reached me and drawled, "Howdy, y'all." She shifted her weight a little, smiled a lopsided smile and stuck out a well-worn work hand to shake. She went on, "I'm Trudy Hatcher from Rainbow Creek, Tennessee. Who be you? Be you ballplayer or movie star?"

The twinkle in her bright blue eyes told me that she knew a lot more than she let on. Never being one to pass on the opportunity for a little fun, I fired back, "Hey, I'm both. Ginger Rogers at your service. But call me Pepper Paire for short, as in the best shortstop in the U.S. of A., and I'm from sunny California." Taking her hand, I continued, "Ballplayers sign up over here." I led her over to the line at the reception desk, ignoring the sly looks and giggles we got on the way. I knew what they were thinking. This year there was going to be a great emphasis on femininity. Everything we read and heard pointed to that. Even if she could hit like Babe Ruth, this gal didn't have a chance.

My thoughts were interrupted by a couple of brass-buttoned bellboys who came up with our keys and gathered up our luggage. They called to us, "Walk this way, ladies." I waved to Trudy whose nonchalance now had flown the coop. She looked scared and lonely standing in that line. I thought about how I would feel if I were all alone. So, I yelled at her, "See you later, Trudy. I'll give you a call." Her face brightened and she waved back enthusiastically. We followed the bellboys, Indian-trail style, with Faye mimicking their "Walk this way, ladies" a la the Marx Brothers. We climbed into the elevator and learned we were on the 17th floor. "Woo-wee," Faye exclaimed. "I'm glad we're not walking."

"Yeah," I agreed, a little nervously. Seventeen floors was real high up for California gals. At that time, earthquake-prone California tended to keep their buildings short. I believe they were limited to seven stories. We wound up with adjoining rooms. Faye and Tiby were in one and Ziggy and I were in the other. Annabelle and Dottie were together on another floor. We thought that was neat because we could open up the doors and run back and forth.
Ah, what to do? Four fun-loving, young gals far from home in a big, classy hotel? Well, of course, call room service! We ordered hamburgers and fries, and since the legal drinking age was 18, we had a beer apiece.

The cost of $5 plus a 25-cent tip almost choked us. That was spending money for a week. We decided to let Wrigley foot the bill after that. We did have to admit it was classy. Little round silver plates, with little round silver lids and little round hamburger patties, with little round buns. They were served on one of those fancy rolling carts by a couple more of those guys with their fancy brass-buttoned hotel uniforms. The lids came in handy later when we played "McNamara's Band" with them.

With all the gabbing and unpacking, and calling home to let everybody know we made it okay, we didn't hit the sack until after midnight. By then I was so excited I couldn't sleep. I turned my light back on and sat up to check out the package I'd been given at the desk. It was a big plastic bag with all kinds of papers and booklets in it, including a meal book with breakfast and dinner coupons. Wow! I exclaimed, "Zig, are you awake? We've got to be dressed and down in the hotel dining room at 7 a.m. for breakfast and then out at the ball field by 8 a.m."

Zig looked at me from the other bed. "I know," she answered with a groan. "That's why I'm trying to get some sleep." She pulled the sheet over her head. I tried again. "Did you see the schedule? It's really rough." This time Zig rolled over, turned her back on me and snapped a trio of orders. "Shut up, turn off the light and go to sleep."

"OK, OK," I grumbled. I switched off the light and put my head down on the pillow. "But I know I can't go to sleep," I muttered. The next thing I knew, the alarm was ringing. Somehow because of the time change, we screwed up setting our clocks. We were going to be late. Hustling our showers, we dressed and rushed down to the dining room, spikes and all, to cash in our breakfast coupons. By then it was 7:45 a.m. and everybody had eaten and gone. They made us take off our spikes and gave us some quick toast, orange juice and milk. Then they shoved us out the door pointing to the park across the street.

It was damp and misty and we could barely see a group of people huddled together under the trees. No one had told us that April mornings around Lake Michigan could be so cold and wet. Putting our spikes back on, we clanked across the street to join the group under the trees. When we got there, we discovered that all the Midwesterners were warmly dressed in jeans and sweatshirts. They looked perfectly smug and comfortable. Up we come, this group of Californians in our skimpy little T-shirts and shorts, and with our little blue legs hanging out. So much for showing off our tans! Some of the veterans were laughing at us. But we didn't let them laugh long.

The laughter stopped when they saw us play ball. In fact, that first day pretty much set the tone again and renewed the long-lasting feud between us "cocky, loud-mouth" Californians and the "redneck, snobby" Midwesterners. Looking around, I could see that this was really a big professional recreational complex. I could make out what looked like four diamonds through the mist, one in each corner of the complex. The mist was lifting a little now and the sun was trying to poke its head through. Everything looked so green and smelled so clean. I could see small white butterflies fluttering around the outfield. It was hard to believe. Was I dreaming?

About that time, a harsh shrill whistle blew and jarred me out of my reverent state. A loud voice boomed out, "OK gals, let's move." Orders called for everyone to take two complete laps around the half-mile track before and after practice. This was the start. I judged there to be about 300 gals all together and we began moving off in little groups. It didn't help our popularity any to have Faye beat everybody badly on the first trip around. We were all cheering for her and my gopher-toothed friend Zig was whistling her on with encouragement. So, as an encore, she did the second lap backwards and still beat everybody.

After running, we were divided into four groups; about 75 gals and five to six coaches per group. The coaches were walking around the diamond with clipboards filled with rosters and rules. And let us not forget the chaperones. They were present, too, about six of them. We knew by now that, though they came in different sizes and they may not be designated as such, a thorn by any other name, was still a chaperone. Some would be bad, some would be great, but all had to be endured. They were a necessary part of the game plan.

After finishing our running, we all huddled in a shivering group around the mound wondering what came next. My thoughts were flying all over the place and I wondered if everybody else was as nervous as me. I took a look around, checking out the various get-ups. Some of the gals had on shorts and halters and some wore jeans. I even saw a sun suit or two. Boy, what a conglomeration, I thought! There were skinny little girls and some big, raw-boned, tough-looking gals. There were some frail-looking, white-meat Canadians with their pale faces bundled up and some smug-looking, pale-faced Midwesterners. Then, of course, we tan-skinned Californians with our well-rounded, brown legs.

The hairdos were something else, too. Some of the gals had their hair in curlers. Some wore bandanas on their heads, or "babushkas," as they were called. Some wore baseball caps or sun visors. Faye's long, blond, shoulder-length hair was limp with dew. Tiby's blond hair also hung straight and limp. Even Ziggy's brown perm was drooping. I thanked the Lord again for my curls. I had my strawberry-blond hair braided, Daisy Mae style, and tied with white gauze bows. In the middle of my hairdo evaluation, a man's voice rang out with authority from behind me. "Listen up, girls." It startled me enough to the point I jumped up and whirled around, and there stood the "Great One."

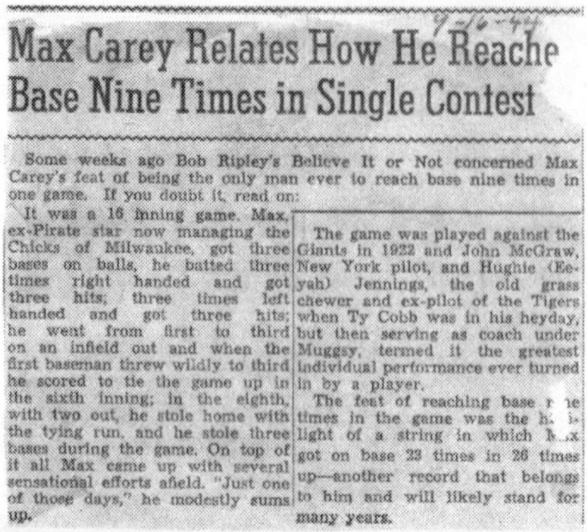

Max Carey Relates How He Reached Base Nine Times in Single Contest

Some weeks ago Bob Ripley's Believe It or Not concerned Max Carey's feat of being the only man ever to reach base nine times in one game. If you doubt it, read on:

It was a 16 inning game. Max, ex-Pirate star now managing the Chicks of Milwaukee, got three bases on balls, he batted three times right handed and got three hits; three times left handed and got three hits; he went from first to third on an infield out and when the first baseman threw wildly to third he scored to tie the game up in the sixth inning; in the eighth, with two out, he stole home with the tying run, and he stole three bases during the game. On top of it all Max came up with several sensational efforts afield. "Just one of those days," he modestly sums up.

The game was played against the Giants in 1922 and John McGraw, New York pilot, and Hughie (Eeyah) Jennings, the old grass chewer and ex-pilot of the Tigers when Ty Cobb was in his heyday, but then serving as coach under Muggsy, termed it the greatest individual performance ever turned in by a player.

The feat of reaching base nine times in the game was the highlight of a string in which Max got on base 23 times in 26 times up—another record that belongs to him and will likely stand for many years.

Lefty Lee

Dottie Wiltse

Dottie Collins (Wiltse), Tex Lessing, Bird Dog Jackson, Viv Kellogg

Fort Wayne Ball Club

Max, Pepper, Lefty, Marnie, Zig & Snookie Front

Max Carey Getting last laugh

Getting in shape Santa Monica, CA winter 45

All of us Prune Pickers made it 1945

130

Chapter 15
The Great One

There in the center of the diamond was the legendary Max Carey, standing tall and foreboding. He wore a faded Pittsburgh Pirates uniform and was holding the biggest clipboard in organized baseball under his arm. I would have loved to get a look at those notes. Max started reading off names in alphabetical order. Everybody answered "Here," as they had in school days. When he got to my name, he asked, "Who is Pepper Paire?"

I blushed and held up a finger, answering with a soft, "Here." Max peered at me over horn-rimmed glasses and said, "Come up here."

I stepped out from the group and walked up to him. He stood more than 6 feet tall and had no trouble looking down at my 5-foot-5-inch frame. "Well, well," he said. He paused as he pushed his hat back, and then he continued, "All the way from L.A., huh? Tell me, just what kind of fruit is a Pepper Paire anyway?"

That really brought the laughter from the ranks. I was used to being kidded about my name, but Max was pushing it. Before I had time to think, I snapped back at him, pointing to the ball in his pocket, "Just hand me that apple," I said emphatically, "and I'll show you."

Max grabbed my wrist, turned my hand over and broke out laughing. "Hey, you couldn't throw a ball with those short stubby fingers. You must have to shot put it."

That did it! My arm was a thing of pride to me. I felt I could throw better than most women, and most men, for that matter. The "fighting Irish" in me came out, leaving the "loving French" behind. I didn't care where I was or who was there or what the situation was. It didn't help that everybody else was laughing at me, even my friends. They all thought that everything was pretty funny. "OK, OK," I snarled at him. "Just give me the ball, Buddy, if you really want to know!" I was so mad I was sputtering.

"Well, well, simmer down," he said, a smile still hovering around the corners of his mouth. He handed me the ball, pulled his glove out from his back pocket and walked about 10 feet back, chuckling all the way. "Think you can make it this far?"

Well, I knew I was in the soup by now, but I wasn't about to back down. When in doubt, charge! So, I popped off, "Hey, a big leaguer like you shouldn't need a glove for a shot put."

The smile disappeared from Max's face. He nodded, "You're right." He dropped the glove and held out his hand. "Well, Pepper," he said through a smirk, "Let me have it."

I could just visualize the ball hitting him right smack in the middle of that smirk. So, I hauled back and fired the ball as hard as I could, right at his chops. Well, Max made no effort to catch it. He just stepped aside and watched it zip by. It went smoking down the line about a hundred feet, skidded, bounced a couple of times and rolled, and rolled, and rolled. Max watched it in dead silence until it came to a stop. Then he turned to me, shook his head and said, "Well, not bad, Pepper! Not bad at all." Then he added, "For a rookie, and a girl at that. Now, let's see if you can run that far? Go get it," he commanded. He hesitated and then he repeated, "Go get it, Cannon!"

I took off on a dead run, grinning at him as I passed him. I knew that I was OK. I had a bond with him. From that day on, Max always kidded with me. I took it because I found out that Max never kidded anyone he didn't like or didn't think would make it. Reaching the ball, I picked it up and started trotting back.

On the way back, I witnessed a very strange sight. Out in centerfield, Faye, Ziggy and Tiby were running around wildly, leaping and jumping awkwardly in the air, stabbing at the sky with their gloves. They were making some really strange moves, none that I'd ever seen in baseball before. When I got back to Max, I asked him, "Do you want me to go out there and do whatever it is they are doing?" Curiosity got the better of me and I asked, "Well, what the heck are they doing?"

Max gave me an innocent look and said, "Well now, Pepper, your buddies thought you were having such a good time, I sent them out there to catch those little white butterflies and have some fun of their own." He winked at me, threw an arm over my shoulder and said, "Let's go see if your bat's as good as your arm." "Or your mouth," he added. He led me over to the batting cage and aimed me at the bat rack and said, "Pick your poison." Then he headed out to the mound. He started throwing to warm up his arm.

I was nervous and dry mouthed. Checking out the bats, I was pleasantly surprised to find they were Louisville Sluggers and not softball bats! Gleefully, I picked a 33-ounce bat with a slim handle. Hardball bats were much easier to hit with for me. I grabbed a couple more bats and stood in the on-deck circle, swinging all three. That way, when I stopped and dropped two, it would make my bat seem light and pick up my bat speed.

Looking around, I saw that the coaches had infielders lined up three to four deep, hitting ground balls to them. They were all taking turns. I looked for Californians. They weren't hard to find, being the noisiest ones out there, chattering encouragement to each other. Ziggy and Snookie were at short. Tiby and Faye were in centerfield and Annabelle Lee (how's that name for a southpaw pitcher?) was over on the sidelines throwing with other pitchers. I was saying silent prayers for everyone when I noticed Trudy in line for her turn at first base. She flashed her lopsided smile and hollered, "Hi ya, movie star."

Max looked over at her, and I could see the disapproval on his face. She still had on her "Grapes of Wrath" outfit, with no shoes. I could see she didn't have a glove, and it was her turn next. Max was still warming up so, I quickly grabbed my mitt, ran behind the cage and yelled, "Trudy." I waved the glove at her and she trotted toward me and I tossed it to her saying, "Hey, this glove never misses." She caught it deftly with one hand, nodded her thanks and went back to first base.

Seeing that Max was ready to throw, I stepped into the batter's box. He said, "How about it, Pepper? Do you want me to take it easy on ya?"

"Well, heck no, Mr. Carey," I answered. "I'm ready when you are. Just watch yourself, and give me your best shot." He looked at me and then tossed a big fat one right in my favorite spot, knee high on the inside corner. I nailed it on the button, lining it down the third base line. I hadn't learned to keep my mouth shut yet, so I popped off, "Hey, that's at least a triple."

Max didn't respond, not in words anyway. He called for another ball and began rubbing it up. This time he took a wind-up. "Oh! Oh," I thought, and sure enough, he turned loose a fastball express right at my head. I hit the dirt fast! I could see him laughing in his glove as I got up and dusted myself off. I just smiled at him, choked up on my bat a little bit, gave a little tap on home plate and waited. The next pitch was right down the middle with plenty of smoke on it, but I was ready. I lined it right back through the box. Max swiped for it as he ducked. But he only succeeded in knocking his cap off, as the ball whistled by his ear. He turned his back to me and watched the ball streak out to centerfield. I think his face was about two shades whiter, although he was acting very nonchalant.

He threw me about 10 more pitches, some inside, some outside, and I showed him I could hit the ball where it was pitched. I took the outside pitches to right field and I pulled the inside pitches down the third base line. "Well, that's OK," Max yelled. "As a matter of fact, that was pretty good! Let's see what you can do with this one."

By this time, I was getting pretty cocky. The coaches had all stopped hitting balls and were watching me. The gals, too. All eyes were on me hitting pitches from Max Carey. I figured Max was going to throw me another "fastball express" or some "chin music," as we called it. So, I dug in and I vowed to myself, I'm really going to step into this thing and belt it! Here comes the ball, looks big and fat and right in my favorite spot, right at my knees in the center of the plate. I took a mighty swing, visions of a gigantic home run flashed through my mind.

Suddenly, the ball was gone! It curved sharply and dropped in the dirt. I missed it so badly that I lost my balance and fell flat on my rump. From that lonely position, I could see Max laughing at me, as was everyone else. I got up with a sheepish grin, brushing myself off and muttering, "OK, OK, you got the last laugh, Max." I was to learn that he always did. But silently, I vowed to myself that I would learn to hit that curve ball.

Putting my bat back in the rack, I looked around for Trudy. She was just getting her turn at first base. So, I walked over to watch and wait for my glove. Well, I swear, no matter how they tried (and they did try), they couldn't throw one by her. She dug it out of the dirt, came off the bag for a tag when the throw was down the line and stretched out like a ballet dancer on a clothesline. Moving about gracefully and naturally, flipping the ball over her shoulder to the coach without even looking. The only way they could get the ball by her was to throw it so high it landed in the stands.

Moving off first base to make way for the next gal, she tossed me my glove, winked and said, "Thanks, Pepper! That mitt of yours is a dandy."

I thought, "Wow! What could she do with a first baseman's mitt?" I caught my glove with a smile and ran out to do my thing. I found myself alternating with my pal Ziggy at shortstop. We both did pretty well fielding ground balls cleanly and making good throws, even handling the half-hops pretty well. That went on for a while and we were getting pretty tired. Thankfully, somebody finally blew a whistle and called "Lunch."

Walking off the field behind Zig, I noticed that she was limping. By now the sun was out in full force and we were sweating up a storm. "Zig," I called out and pointed to a shady tree. She headed for the tree and I went over to the dugout to get the lunches. They were all neatly stacked in boxes. So, I grabbed a couple and joined Zig under the tree. She had her shoe off and her sock had a hole in the heel revealing a big blister. "Wow! That's a whopper!" I said. "Ziggy, you'd better stay off that foot."

"But I haven't made it yet," she worried. I understood her concern but I knew that she couldn't play much longer with that blister. But, first things first. We inspected our boxed lunches: two sandwiches, a piece of fruit, juice and milk. "What? No dessert?" I complained as I was stuffing a ham sandwich in my mouth. Missing breakfast had taken its toll.

We were busy munching our lunch and didn't see or hear Max Carey come up behind us until he spoke. "Well, how are the two California hot shots?"

Without being prompted he saw Ziggy's foot. "Oh, oh," he exclaimed. "Look at the bubble. No more for you today, young lady. Go back to the hotel and take care of that foot." Zig objected but finally gave in. As she limped dejectedly across the park toward the hotel in her stocking feet, I couldn't help but feel sorry for her. Before the day was over my sympathy turned to envy. The rest of that day was a killer. We fielded ground balls endlessly. We tried out for different positions and somehow squeezed in more batting practice. We practiced bunting and running them out. We even sandwiched in a five-inning ball game. It seemed that 5 o'clock would never come. But mercifully it finally did. Then we still had to complete those two final laps around the track! Faye beat everybody again, and then it was finally over.

Three hundred hind ends were dragging when we plunked back across the street that night. We had much less energy than when we hotfooted it over in the morning. Taking off our spikes, we headed into the hotel. It was all I could do to shove that revolving door around. Tiby and Faye were behind me and they got a free ride. Something looked funny inside but I was too tired to dwell on it, so I just staggered over to the elevators and stood leaning on the button. I felt a hand on my shoulder, Faye said, "Forget it, Pepper, the power's out. The elevators are down."

"Oh no!" I moaned, with more emotion than I figured I had left in me. "Not 17 flights of stairs."

Faye nodded her sweat-streaked face. I nodded my equally grimy face back in disbelief. She stuck out an arm and said, "Come on, Cacaface." We linked elbows and looked for the door marked "stairs." Max Carey's back was just disappearing through it when we spotted it. So, we staggered over to the door and stumbled through it. Our shoes and our gloves were hanging over our shoulders, Trudy style, by the shoestrings. Max was ahead of us as we started up the stairs. At the second floor he turned and said cheerfully, "Well, I'm getting off here, girls. What floor are you on?"

With looks that could kill, we groaned in unison, "17th!"

He repeated, "17th floor?" and then added lightly, "Oh well, girls, it's good for your legs." Then he disappeared through the second-floor door. It took us half an hour to make it up those 17 flights. We would struggle up a couple, then sit down and rest. After sitting a minute or two, we would look at each other and say, "It's good for your legs!" and up we would go. We finally got to our rooms and collapsed. Tiby and Ziggy were already sprawled out across their beds. Zig's foot was propped up on a pillow with a slipper on it. What a lovely way to finish the day (or so we thought)! But our ordeal wasn't over.

The phone soon rang and one of the chaperones called to remind us that we had charm school at 7 p.m. Naturally, formal dress was required. Then we found out that charm school was back down on the seventh floor. That just happened to be where the Midwesterners were staying. We got pretty well stressed out about that and our first case of chaperone hatred set in. It was 6 o'clock, so if we wanted to eat, we had to shower, dress and hustle down 17 flights of stairs to the dining room, eat and then climb seven flights back up to charm school. Well, Zig and I passed on the food. We let Faye and Tiby get ready first. Then we got ready.

Now, we're not talking about skirts, blouses and bobby socks here. We're talking cocktail dresses or suits, nylons, even girdles, and 3-inch heels. The whole works.

For me, it meant putting my hair in an upsweep, a fake flower behind my ear, earrings and, of course, add the makeup to that. Well, after a lot of groaning and complaining and helping each other with zippers and makeup, Zig and I finally made it out the door. Then we had to walk down the 10 flights of stairs. As we went down those stairs, we sure as heck didn't wear our heels. We carried our shoes. Zig had a shoe and a slipper on.

When we got to the charm-school room, we stopped, put our shoes on, and edged in. We found seats in back of the class. They were passing out little booklets titled, "How a Girl Professional Ballplayer Becomes a Star." It was complete with illustrations. It had a bunch of cutesy little tips on how to catch a man. Plus, it had room for note taking. We all thumbed through it and laughed. On the first page it said, "Ladies learn to giggle politely." It also said, "Ladies don't perspire, they glow" and "Ladies don't walk, they glide." I busted out with "Oh, great! All day long we swing, sweat and slide, and all night they want us to giggle, glow and glide!"

Well, that got a big laugh from everyone except Ms. Uptight, our teacher. Her name was really Miss Updyke. We, of course, had rechristened her. She glared at me and started passing out more material. We calmed down and the teacher started her first lesson. It was on diction and, of course, gliding and glowing and giggling. Oh boy! This was going to be something else!

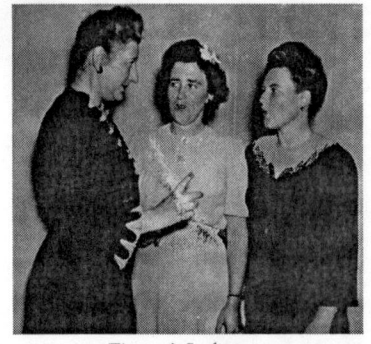

Ziggy & Lefty
"R-ooling The Ball"

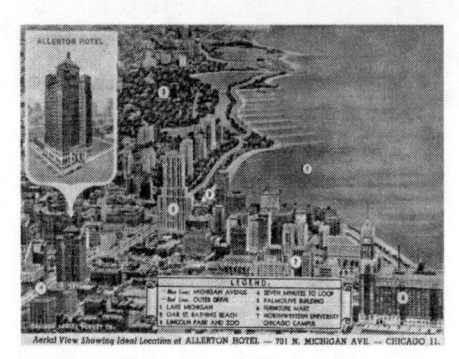

Allerton Hotel-Chicago, Ill

How a *Ball Player* becomes a ★STAR★

All American Charm School

Getting in shape at the beach
Me-Lefty-Snookie

Dottie-Betty-Snookie-Lefty
Faye & Datewiler
Prune Pickers that made it

Chapter 16
A Charming Experience

"Miss Uptight" was in the middle of explaining glowing and gliding, and so on, when the door slammed open and there stood Trudy. A stunned silence fell over the room. Faye leaned over and loudly whispered, "I guess that's her good outfit?" Trudy had on a skirt that resembled a used gunnysack. It was clean, but still a used gunnysack. Her blouse was crumpled and sleeveless. It would have buttoned up all the way except some of the buttons were missing. So, it flapped open at the top. Her ponytail was now tied with a big, red, faded bow that looked like it came out of a funeral parlor, or a Jim Beam Whiskey bottle. Completing the outfit, she wore white bobby socks that slouched sloppily because the elastic was shot. So, they hung down over her worn out "Minnie Mouse" shoes. A fashion plate she was not.

Trudy spotted me, nodded with a grin and repeated her lobby greeting, saying to the room, "Howdy y'all. I'm Trudy Hatcher from Rainbow Creek, Tennessee." Then, directing her question to Ms. Uptight, she added, "Be you the teacher?"

Well, poor Ms. Uptight was gasping for breath. Trudy turned back to the class and with a laugh said, "My, oh my, don't y'all look purdy? Be you ballplayers or be you movie stars?"

Holding up our charm-school booklets, we answered in a chorus, "We be movie stars!"

When she got her composure back, Ms. Uptight seated Trudy next to me and went on with the show. Actually, it turned out to be more of a three-ring circus than a show. We were supposed to roll our R's with round sounds as in "RRRrroll the ball. BBBbbounce the ball. Well, teach got Ziggy out there with a book on top of her head to glide. Now, there was Ziggy walking on one high heel and one slipper at a lopsided gate with a book placed defiantly on her head. "RRRrroll the ball, bbbbbounce the ball," she said, and then the inevitable happened -- Zig dropped the proverbial ball, although in this case, of course, it was a book. We all roared with laughter.

Next, it was my turn. I was all set to show them how it was done, being the sophisticated Californian that I was. But, I found out that it wasn't too easy to balance a book on top of an upsweep hairdo and a fake flower. I finally got it up there and took my first step, only to discover that stairs and the grueling workout had taken its toll, in the form of a charley horse. I made a grab for my leg as the cramp hit me and I started hopping around yelling, "Ouch, ouch, ouch!"

Well, the book, the hair and the fake flower all came tumbling down just like Humpty Dumpty. That brought the house down again. Ms. Uptight, who was not having an easy time controlling the class, excused me from my exercise and I limped back to my seat. They have very fancy names for what we called charley horses in those days, like strained hamstrings, ruptured ligaments, abdominal strains and so on. Yeah, and they've got fancy salaries to go with them.

Next came Trudy's turn. The book kept falling off and her conversation went something like this, "Y'all roll that there ball, y'all bounce that there ball." The laughter in the room was increasing with each verse. "Shucks, teacher," Trudy went on, "my head's not flat like the book. It's kind of round, you know?" She popped the book back on her head and solved the problem of keeping it there by holding it with one hand. She thrust the other hand out to keep her balance. So, she was walking around like a tightrope walker, to the delight of the appreciative audience. As she walked, she drawled, "Heck, that book won't bounce or roll any dang way. Why don't y'all read the dang thing to us any who?"

Well, that did it for her, although the class would have liked to keep her up there all night. But, Ms. Uptight, who was quickly living up to the name we had given her, angrily grabbed the book and pointed Trudy to a chair. By now, you would have thought that Ms. Uptight would have given up. But, she hadn't. She looked at her list and she said, "Well now, I will pick a pretty name. Now, let's see, here's one ... Faye Katherine Dancer. What a lovely name." She glanced around trying to locate the young lady with the lovely name.

Faye made a motion to indicate that it was her.

"What a lovely name," she cooed again. She asked, "Do you prefer to be called Faye or Katherine, my dear?"

Faye stood up and bellowed out with what was a natural voice for her, "Actually, I prefer Cacaface, my dear!" Of course, we all got pretty silly about that. Faye grabbed the book and planted it on her head. Her ankles were turning out with the high heels. They were not part of her normal mode of dress. Needless to say, she was not as graceful as Ms. Uptight had hoped she would be. She went about bellowing. "Roll the damn ball. Bounce the damn ball." Well, the next thing you know, the book fell to the floor and Faye followed it with, "Oh sh-t, I dropped the damn thing." (I hope this doesn't offend anybody, but that's really what our "All The Way Faye" said.)

That did it. We all erupted into howling laughter again. The teacher's face turned into a brilliant shade of red. Shaking her finger at Faye, she said, "Young lady, we do not use profanity."

Faye shook her finger right back and innocently said, "Well, I don't either, I use Taboo — perfume, that is!"

Ms. Uptight, now completely representative of her new name, exploded, "Out, out, out, all of you, you, you ... " She was fumbling for the right words.

Trudy hollered, "Oh, oh, Teach, no cuss words!" Ms. Uptight was pretty much beyond words anyway. But, she managed to point to the door and hissed, "Ballplayers, ballplayers, class dismissed!"

Those words were music to our ears. We were out the door in nothing flat. Zig and I somehow managed to gimp back up the 10 flights of stairs. Actually, it kind of helped to work out the knot in my leg. Besides, we were laughing so hard that it didn't seem so bad.

As soon as we got back to the room, I hit the tub to soak my leg. Zig joined me in the bathroom, sitting on the john with her heel propped up, soaking it in the wash basin. We were making fun of each other when the phone rang. Tiby picked it up and we heard, "Yes, Ms. Doodle, yes, Ms. Doodle, no, Ms. Doodle." Zig's and my eyes met and we groaned, now what?

Tiby said, "Yes, Ms. Doodle" several more times and then hung up. We were expecting the worst when Tiby appeared at the door, "Hey crips," she said. "We get a break tomorrow. We don't eat breakfast until 8 a.m. and there's no practice in the morning. We go to the hotel recreation room at nine for uniform assignments and publicity pictures." Ignoring our cheers she went on, "Oh yeah, I forgot to tell you, the elevators are working now, you could have ridden back up here." Well, I threw my soap at her and Ziggy kicked water at her from the wash basin before she could escape out of the room. But boy, we were happy about that.

The next morning, you can bet, Ziggy and I were early for breakfast. We were starved and we consumed a ballplayer's breakfast about the size of home plate. Then we went over to take the elevator down to the basement where the recreation room was located. When the elevator doors opened, out came Trudy. She had her overalls on and her carpetbag in her hand. Seeing the look on her face I knew she had been cut. She set her bag down and stuck out a scrubbed clean hand and said, "Well, Ginger, see you in the movies." Taking her hand, I started to tell her how sorry I was. But, I could see the tears starting to form in her eyes, so I just squeezed her hand hard and said, "I'll leave a pass at the door for the best ballplayer in town."

"Thanks friend," she murmured softly and she picked up her bag and headed toward the door. Watching that straight back move away, I couldn't help but think they had made a mistake there. There was a real classy lady inside that body. I berated myself. I should have called her. I looked at Zig and Faye looked at me. We were all thinking the same thing. Zig said, "Can't we do something, gals?"

I said, "Well, I guess we could try."

Faye bellowed out, "Hey, Trudy!"

Trudy turned around and I flipped her our key. "Catch it!" I hollered.

She instinctively grabbed it, looking at me wondering. I continued, "Meet you later in our room. The game's not over yet."

Hope filled her face as the elevator doors snapped closed. We all vowed to take charm school a little more seriously.

Life, Liberty and the Pursuit of Look!

When we got down to the recreation room, the place was jumping. Some of the gals came up to us babbling excitedly, "Hey, girls, Life magazine is here." The area was crawling with reporters and photographers. Life, Liberty and Look magazines were all represented and sports writers were scribbling notes all over the place. We knew we had new uniforms this year and we had been dreading this. We had tried to forget about the uniforms until now. Last year was bad enough but we heard they were going to be worse this year.

We weren't really ready to experience them but, ready or not, they handed them out to us. They were satin shorts and lightweight, long-sleeved jerseys to wear under the uniform. The uniform itself was a big one-piece, tunic-like dress, with a flap that buttoned across the chest. It was tight around the waist but the skirts were flared and had little short zippers on the side. They were hard to get in and out of. We still had to take them off over our head. They made us look like a cross between ballerinas and ice skaters. All that was bad enough, but the colors made it even worse: bright yellow, lime green, peach, baby blue and worst of all, that old bubble-gum pink!

And the hats, well, they resembled something like half of an Easter basket. They were nothing like a real baseball hat. They had to be pinned on and they still flopped in the breeze. Faye held up her uniform howling in disbelief, "Look at these! How can we play ball in this?"

I gave her a look, tapped her on the chest and warned, "Remember Trudy?"

She shut up in a hurry. We all went into the dressing room to put on our uniforms. After a whole lot of griping, teasing and admiring ourselves in the mirrors, we came out self-consciously holding our skirts down. Wearing shorts was something we were used to, but, we had to get used to this tiny skirt over them, again. Somehow it made it seem indecent to bend over (and drafty, too). We checked out the Midwestern vets and they all seemed right at home in the uniforms. So, we relaxed a little bit figuring we'd get used to them again. We had last year, sort of, anyway.

The rookies were all huddled together in one corner and told to wait. One-year players were still considered rookies so that meant us, too. In the meantime, the vets gave us smug looks, as they were being interviewed and photographed. I whispered to Tiby, "So much for us getting into Life or Look."

"You never know," she snapped back at me. "Just shut up and wait."

I was getting bored, so I started looking around and I spotted a piano in the corner. I sneaked over to it, sat down on the bench and plunked a key, looking around to see if anybody heard or cared. There was such bedlam with all the chattering and cameras flashing that no one was paying any attention to me. So, I began fooling around. I don't play the piano but I do write songs. First, I get an idea. Then I work on it in my head and then I write the words down on paper. Next, I sing little melodies in my head until things seem to fit together just right. Then, I pick out the notes on the piano.

I remembered the song I had written in Kenosha last year for the league, when I was out with my broken collarbone. I started to hum the melody and then I sang a line I remembered, "We're all for one, we're one for all, we're All Americans." One finger was plunking it out as I went. Then I was joined by another voice. A little gal with long brown hair and brown eyes was standing beside me. "I like that," she said. "My name is Robin. Want me to help you? I play the piano." She finished with a smile.

I found a pencil and paper and wrote the words down for her. Then I would sing what I wanted and Robin would pick out the notes on the piano. This went on for a little while. Time was no problem since the press were ignoring the rookies anyway. Finally, I got it like I wanted it. I grabbed a bat and made like it was a guitar. We were ready to perform when the Cacapot came walking up. "Hey, what's happening?" she wanted to know.

"Remember that song I wrote when we were hurt in Kenosha?" I asked.

She nodded, "Oh yeah, the League song, right?"

I laughed, "Yeah, that's right. You want to hear it?"

"Wait, wait," she said. She turned around and yelled out in loud, raucous tones, "Hey! Everybody! Pepper wrote us a song. Hey! Everybody! Over here!" She continued the barrage until we had a group of 25 or 30 gals around us. I was in my element, on the stage strumming on my Louisville Slugger guitar and wearing a big grin. I was ready to perform. Singing my song for the first time, I asked, "Ready Robin?"

She repeated, "Ready!" and enthusiastically played a little fanfare. Then I sang out:

Batter up, hear that call.

The time has come for one and all

To play ball.

We're the members of the All American League.

We come from cities near and far.

We've got Canadians, Irishmen and Swedes.

We're all for one, we're one for all.

We're All Americans.

Each girl stands, her head so proudly high.

Her motto do or die.

She's not the one to use or need an alibi.

Our chaperones are not too soft, they're not too tough.

Our managers are on the ball.

We've got a President who really knows his stuff.

We're all for one, we're one for all.

We're All Americans.

When I finished, there was nothing but dead silence. Oh, Lord, I thought I had bombed. But when I looked around, the faces of the girls told me something else. They looked stunned and happy and proud, all at once. Some even had tears in their eyes. One began to clap, then another and another, and soon they were all cheering and applauding. At that moment we were, "One for all and all for one, and All Americans." In the middle of the applause,

145

I heard a voice say, "Hold it." I looked up and the flash of a camera blinded me. It was the photographer from Life magazine.

"Wow!" he said. "That was great." He shot a couple more pictures of Robin and me, and then Max called for Faye, Dottie, Ziggy, Tiby and Annabelle Lee to join us. Reporters interviewed us and more photographers shot pictures. Tiby gave me an "I told you so" look and the other gals all stared enviously at us. Life magazine was a real big deal. We couldn't wait to tell our folks. There was a great write-up about the league in the June 1945 issue of Life, complete with photos. My songwriting picture almost made the cover. But Bill, the cute photographer, got it in too late and missed the deadline. At least that's what he told me over a cup of coffee. He wanted me to go out with him, but we weren't allowed to go out at that time. Cute as he was, I was afraid to break the rules.

When we got back to the room, there was Trudy waiting for us. Flushed with success and giddiness, we made a phone call to Max. We pleaded a lot, begged a lot and threatened a little, and finally we got Trudy a little extra time. We promised Max we would take her shopping to change her image. Basically, Max was a good guy. Besides, he knew Trudy could play. So, he gave us a week to make a lady out of her. We had our hands full with baseball all day and charm school and photos all night, but we knew we could do it. When we got to bed each night, we were really bushed.

Gals were being cut every day, but by now we knew all the Californians were going to make it, and we knew that Trudy was going to make it, too. Because, now she dressed like us, with tweed skirts, Ship and Shore blouses or sweaters, saddle shoes and, of course, those ever-loving bobby socks. She was still a little bit awkward walking around in her new shoes, and her English wasn't teatime talk yet, but she pretty much kept quiet in public. Besides, she turned into a graceful swan on the baseball field and all the coaches wanted her on their team.

Everything was a learning process during those first two weeks and there sure was an awful lot to learn. The game rules and dimensions were very different from softball. We still had the big ball, but unofficially pitching was sidearm, as well as underhand. So, we were introduced to drops, and back door curves, sinkers and screwballs. Major leaguers will tell you that these are the hardest pitches to hit. Some of them still can't hit them. Leading off the bases was new to us. In softball it wasn't allowed. Softball games were seven innings and we played nine. That was a long time, especially when you played a doubleheader.

The first game was always seven innings, but the second was nine. It used to be that way in the majors, too. When you add in some extra-inning games, it really made for a long day or a long night. Finally, the big day arrived. "Allocation Day" they called it. We called it "Judgment Day." We found out that the team lists were posted in the recreation room. We all raced down there frantically searching for our names. Faye Dancer found our names first. She was laughing when she came to me, "Cacapot, we're Fort Wayne Daisies."

"Oh no!" I moaned. "Not the bubble-gum pink uniforms!" Sure enough, Faye, Annabelle Lee, Dottie and I were all on the Fort Wayne list. But not my buddy Ziggy. I was looking for my pal's name when she came running up. "Hey, Pepper," she cried enthusiastically, "I'm a Grand Rapids Chick." Tiby was right behind her shouting, "Me, too!"

"Well, I'm a Daisy!" I said, dejectedly rolling my eyes. But we all hugged and cried. We figured at least we made it. Trudy made it, too. We helped her find her name. She was a Racine Belle. So, everybody was happy. Later on, that same day, I found out that our coach was a famous ex-big leaguer also. His name was Bill Wambsganns, or "Wamby" as he called himself. He shortened his name, because the newspapers never spelled it right. Bill was the only ballplayer to make an unassisted, triple play in a World Series. He still is, I think. "Oh great," I thought. "He will probably be a lot like Max Carey!" Boy! Was I wrong! I found out that same day that "Wamby" was a Presbyterian minister in his spare time! And a serious one, too! With that news, I looked over at Faye and wondered how strong a constitution Coach Wamby had? And if my friend would drive that poor preacher to drink before the season was over!

CHARM SCHOOL and training camp is run for All-Americans at Peru, Ind. The girls are taught how to make the most of their looks as well as play ball. Above, Carolyn Morris models for Tyyne De Luoma.

QUEENS OF SWAT

"PEPPER" FRONT ROW - MIDDLE - WEARING Saddle SHOES"

Look Magazine
1945

Chapter 17
The Bubble-Gum Pink Daisies

Allocation Day was the end of spring training and the next day we said our tearful goodbye's to our new friends and to our old friends on other teams. We climbed on those ever-loving buses, two teams to each bus. We were to do a short little exhibition tour on the way to our new towns. After all, it was four days until the season opener, so God forbid we should have a day off! That would be a waste of time, right? They got their money's worth out of us!

We found out that we lucked out! Our traveling companions were the ex-Milwaukee Chicks, now the Grand Rapids Chicks. So, we would be traveling with my buddy Ziggy and also Tiby. This year they were being coached by Benny Meyers. Max Carey, "The Great One", was now president of the league. Benny Meyers was also an ex-major league player and a great guy. Their chaperone was a Canadian ex-player by the name of Dottie Hunter. Dottie was tough and we were to find that out the hard way, but she was fair, and a great gal! Then, of course, we had our manager, part-time preacher, Bill Wamby, and a gal from Indiana named Ellen Townsen, who was our chaperone. She was an unknown element to us and it's too bad it didn't stay that way.

Off we went, our first stop being Percy Jones General Hospital in Battle Creek, Michigan. They put us in one of the many Army barracks on the base. It was a two-story wooden frame building with lots of rooms down the hallways. It was filled with Army cots and big bathrooms and showers at the end of each hallway. After we got unpacked, they took some of us on a tour of the hospital. I volunteered to go. I knew that it was going to be tough and hard to take, because I knew we were going to see many injured boys. Some didn't even know who they were. They were in a coma. Some were so badly injured you wanted to cry. But, you had to smile and try to cheer them up with sweet talk, and pat their hands and kid with them. Some of them didn't have hands to pat. We were told the hospital specialized in brain surgery and operations to correct mental problems. You couldn't help but think of your loved ones and hope and pray that they wouldn't end up this way.

After that we went out and played our exhibition ballgame. A lot of the guys walked us back to the barracks after the ballgame, laughing, talking and admiring our uniforms (of course) with all that bare leg showing. Ruth "Tex" Lessing made a date with one of the guys to meet him later that night at the dance they were having for us. He was a cute young blond guy with a short buzz. We called it a crew cut. He was wide-eyed and innocent looking. You could see a big red scar on his head, under the hair that was trying to grow back in. I don't believe he was even shaving yet because he still had golden fuzz on his pale face. He didn't look like he was 18, but he had to be. Well, Tex was tired that night and she asked me to tell the kid she was sick and couldn't go. She told me, "Now, you take care of my sweet young thing."

I laughed and said OK. When we got to the dance, there he was, waiting for her. I told him she couldn't make it, and he got a funny look on his face and said angrily, "People shouldn't make promises and not keep their word." But then he seemed to get over it. We had a good time just dancing and talking and laughing. We had a 12 o'clock curfew, so when we left the dance, he asked if he could walk me back and I said sure. There was a group of soldiers that wanted to escort us back, and we knew there was safety in numbers.

We had to walk down the middle of this long line of barracks. I was just jabbering away, talking about my bro and California and so on, when I noticed that he was kind of lagging back a little. I turned to him and started to say let's catch up when he grabbed me and pulled me in between two barracks. We were out of sight of the gang ahead of us. He was holding me with one hand and arm, and a leg with some kind of karate hold. I was not a weakling, but I couldn't move, and he still had a free hand. He put his fingers around my neck with his hand and I could feel him squeezing my throat. I thought, oh, oh, I'm in trouble!

He was saying, "That blond girl, Tex, she shouldn't have lied to me," and he started gritting his teeth. I tried not to panic, and tried to change the subject by asking him about his mom and family. He smiled with kind of a faraway look in his eyes and started telling me what a great time he used to have, picking off little puppies and little kittens with his 22-caliber rifle — picking them off from his porch. Then I <u>knew</u> I was in trouble. I don't know what might have happened from there if Faye hadn't missed me and turned around. She started yelling, "Pepper, where are you?" He relaxed his hold for a minute and I twisted away from him and ran out to the group. You bet I didn't lag behind after that. He followed me with a mad look on his face.

When we got back to the barracks, it was a warm evening and Tex and a couple of the other gals were out on the balcony. They were waving at us and laughing at us. This young kid turned red in the face and started shaking his fist at her and screaming at her, "You lied to me! You lied to me!" He was practically foaming at the mouth and was trying to climb up the side of the building, trying to get at her. The other guys grabbed him and hustled him off. We all high-tailed it into our barracks, locking the doors behind us. The chaperone wanted to know what was going on, so I told her, and I showed her! I still had his fingerprints on my throat.

We always had midnight curfews, but during exhibition games there wasn't always a bed check. This time the chappy decided she'd better check this night. Sure enough, one of our gals wasn't in yet! It was getting late and we all stayed up, just milling around and getting real worried. One o'clock came, almost 2 o'clock and then here she comes, sneaking in. The lights went on, the chaperone grabs her and starts shaking her, "Where have you been?" We were all leaning over the balcony hollering, "Where you been?"

She was a Canadian with a fiery temper and she got real angry and exploded, "What the bloody hell's the matter? You'd think I killed somebody." Well, I won't use any names because the gal has denied that it ever happened ... but it did. She was fine. She just had a great time on her date. But it scared the heck out of the rest of us. Come to think about it, that wasn't the only time that Tex got me in trouble with a date. That little rascal!

I guess I'd better describe our team a little bit. We still had our basic gang of "Cal Cans" that we had the year before. Maybe there were a few subtracted and a few added. We had Vivian Kellogg from Brooklyn, Michigan. She was our hard-hitting first baseman, a fine ballplayer and a good hitter. She was tall, with blond hair and a little shy smile. Actually, at first, "Kelly" was quite a shy person, but we took care of that later on.

Then we had Irene Runky, who immediately became "Runky Dunk." She was a smiling, black-haired, black-eyed Pollock from Chicago. "Runky Dunk" had a habit of making basket catches (that means catching the ball down low and short, going with it and sinking to your knees). She also had a habit now and then of juggling the ball maybe two or three times, but she always managed to catch it before it hit the ground. She would come running in, and we would all be saying, "Runky Dunk, you scared the life out of us. Cut that out?" She'd flash that big wide smile and say in Chicago-ese, "Hey, just wanted to 'give da crowd a trill!'"

Then, of course, my friend Ruth "Tex" Lessing was our catcher. She was born in San Antonio in 1925 and was one year younger than me. Tex had joined the "League" in 1944 and had taken over when I was injured -– with Tex behind the plate I knew I could relax and go back to shortstop. Tex was beautiful inside and outside. She was also a very talented catcher, probably the last position you would expect her to play. She looked more like a model than a catcher, but she couldn't be bothered with that nonsense. She immediately established herself as a hard-nosed catcher who could hit when it counted and get the job done. She had platinum-blond hair, shoulder length, with just the right amount of waves, and it curled up so cute on the bottom. She had brilliant blue eyes that stood out against her movie-star complexion and natural eyebrows (no need for makeup). Tex had a dazzling smile that turned the world around, with just a hint of a dimple. Her voice was low and sexy, but slow, with a prominent Texas drawl. With her, it was perfect! She was slender and built well, but her walk was improved by charm school. She had that long-legged Texas stride. She also had a sense of humor that wouldn't quit and a "Texas talent" for telling long tales. She, Faye and I were instant soulmates. The season of the "Cacapot Era" and the Cacapot connection was born (actually "Caca" was a Texas expression). "Caca everything!"

We were all pretty excited and just waiting to check out our new town, but we had one more military stop to make and we were all pretty nervous about it. We were scheduled to play an exhibition game at Fort Sheridan, which was in the Chicago area. In the end, we had no problem there. We didn't need to worry. The guys were great and appreciative and gentlemen. As a matter of fact, out of all those years and all those exhibition games, the Percy Jones General Hospital incident was the only trouble we ever had, and then it wasn't that bad. The poor guy just needed help. So, we really didn't have anything to complain about.

At long last, we were finally on our way to our next home. Fort Wayne, Indiana, and to our ... ugh, ugh, ugh ...bubble-gum pink uniforms. We all wanted to check out our new town and get going with our baseball, but first we had to find places to stay. The first night we stayed at the Van Orman Hotel. Harold Van Orman was president of our Fort Wayne ball club. He put us up and bought us dinner that first night, at which time he provided a list of people who wanted to have an "All American Girl" stay in their home.

We had one day to get settled in and the season would open. Of course, coach Bill had us scheduled for a heavy practice session that one day, 10 a.m. to 3 p.m., with no lunch break! That's one thing we found out about Coach Wamby. His answer to everything was practice. He never got tired of hitting balls at us. He hit them until we dropped. Never mind that we had to find a place to live or get unpacked. Opening Day was Sunday and so we had to report to the ballpark at 9:30 a.m. because it was a 2 o'clock Sunday afternoon doubleheader. Ah, what a guy!

The fact that there was very little time worked in our favor though, because there was a house listed with an upstairs flat for rent: three bedrooms, a kitchen and bathroom. I don't think that they would have let a bunch of us stay together, if we didn't have the time element. But we talked them into letting Tex, Faye and me stay together. Then we recruited Kelly from Michigan and our other Californians, Annabelle Lee and Dottie Wiltse, and we got the flat. Our landlady was a sweet old widowed gal. Her name was Mrs. Rollins and she needed the money. That was only $5 a week, apiece. But six times five was 30, so that meant $120 a month. In those days that was big bucks! So it was a good deal for <u>all</u> of us, or so we thought.

After we got the OK from the landlady and from the ball club, we got our luggage over to the house. Everything seemed to be better than we thought. The house sat on a big lot with a lot of space around us. We would have some privacy. There was a big vacant backyard with trees and behind that a cemetery. We thought that was pretty cool. It turned out to be our sanctuary. Our house was just down the street from a Veterans of Foreign Wars Club. I don't know why, but all those VFW clubs seemed to be located downstairs and were very private. Most of the time they stayed open all night.

The bars in Fort Wayne were dry on Sundays and closed, except for private clubs. So, from the very beginning we had a solid connection with the veterans. They were a bunch of great guys. They hauled our luggage and us from the hotel to our new home. With Fort Wayne being dry on Sundays, we could join the vets after the game and hoist a couple of cold ones, without being spotted. It was kind of like a "speakeasy." You would sneak down the stairs, give a secret knock on the door, say the password and you were in. They were delighted to have us and most of the time wouldn't even let us pay. They would stay open as long as we wanted, and they knew how to keep their mouths shut. They even delivered beer camouflaged with food to our house! On top of all that, most of them were good dancers. Ah, what a different world it was then!

At first, I guess, we were all a little scared of getting caught. We soon got over that because we were no longer considered rookies. We were vets now and we felt like we had established our stardom and we could get away with some stuff. We knew we were the heart of the team. We had Tex, the catcher, Kellogg at first base, Faye Dancer in the outfield and me at short. We had Dottie Wiltse, our right-handed, ace pitcher and Annabelle Lee was our left-handed starter. We knew we were all darn good ballplayers. So the stage was set. We lived in the "Caca house" and the "Caca season" was about to open, and we were the "Cacafaces."

We had bought ourselves some farmer-style straw hats and elegantly decorated them with slogans of all kinds. Those hats were not suited for our public image, with stuff like S.D.D., which stood for "Slightly Daffy Dames," and Cacafaces, and of course, our names. Stuff like that. But then again we only wore them in privacy and it did help us to let off some steam. We were to get a "Cacacar" and even a "Cacadog," but that's for later. Now we were focused on opening night and winning for our town.

The local papers had been running stories about us for weeks. We were the headlines, and we knew there would be a crowd at the ballpark to greet us. They knew all about us and we were touted as contenders. They knew all about our charm-school images, our famous managers and our famous uniforms. So, we had a lot to live up to, and a lot to live down, too! Ballplayers in bubble-gum pink dresses? While they knew a lot about us, we didn't even know the name of the mayor of Fort Wayne. He was going to be introducing us at the Opening Day ceremonies, along with all the rest of the town's dignitaries, socialites and church leaders, etc. We were the event of the century in Fort Wayne and it was a big, big deal. Coach Wamby reminded us of our duty to play great baseball for our fans. Our Chappy Ellen cooed to us about the classy ladies we had to be, and there was that double standard again. Talk and walk like a lady at all times, and yet play rough and tough, hard-nosed baseball, just like a guy. But don't look like him! Slide in that skirt, rip your leg up and you don't even get to say, "Oh fudge!" Those uniforms fooled a lot of people. We just didn't look like ballplayers in them. We had to make believers out of the fans, and it was still to be seen if we could do that in Fort Wayne.

All of these things were going through my mind as we ran out of that clubhouse and onto the field that opening day in 1945. We ran right into the pages of history. Sure enough, the stands were packed. The crowd overflowed out of the grandstands, down along the foul lines, all the way to the outfield fence. Talk about butterflies! Well, I had giant "bee moths" flying in my belly. I think at that point all of our cockiness left us and we became scared little girls. "What if we failed? What if they didn't like us? Oh Lord, please help us!" When we ran out on that field that day showing hustle and some of our legs, we heard the crowd buzzing. They were looking us over. Both teams lined up along the first base and third base foul lines with the catchers at home plate.

That was our V for victory formation. The crowd stood and applauded. The gentlemen removed their hats while they played "The Star-Spangled Banner." We removed our hats, too, and placed them over our hearts. That became one of the first rituals I established in those 10 years. That was to place my hat over my heart while they sang "The Star-Spangled Banner." I would ask God to take care of those I loved and to help us win the ballgame and if he had any favors left over, could he please let me get a base hit or two.

About this time, a little girl recited the pledge of allegiance. Then there was a great deal of applause and the announcer asked everybody to be seated. We took our place on our bench on the third base coaching line. There were no dugouts, just a couple of benches right in front of the crowd. The fans were right behind our backs, separated by about two or three feet. I could hear them talking about us. "Oh my, don't they look cute?" I heard a lady say. Then a man's voice interrupted, laughing, "Pink dresses? Look at that. They're wearing dresses. I bet they can't play baseball."

The comments were flying, negative and positive. The guys were laughing at us and the gals were defending us. It was starting to get embarrassing, but we were trying to live up to our billing and be perfect ladies, so we didn't respond in any way. We acted like we didn't hear it. I learned early on in baseball, that you can't have rabbit ears. That will kill you if you start hearing what people say and reacting to it. The announcer's voice cut in, "Quiet, please. Would everybody please stand and greet our new mayor and his wife?" Everyone silently stood and you could hear a pin drop. We all looked expectantly toward home plate as the announcer said, "And now let's have a big round of applause as I introduce you to our wonderful mayor and his wife. Ladies and gentlemen, I give you Mayor Harry Balls." I kid you not. That's what he said, "Mayor Harry Balls." I even have the clippings to back it up.

The crowd was silent for a moment. There was a collective gasp on our bench as we all tried to maintain our composure. But it wasn't meant to be. Tex was at one end of the bench. Faye was in the middle, and I was on the other end. We were holding our breath and choking to keep from laughing. Then Faye broke the spell and let it all hang out. She leaned forward looking down at me and bellowed out, "Pepper, did you hear that? Pepper, Harry Balls! His name is Harry Balls!" She turned her head and fairly shrieked at Texas, "Texas, Harry Balls. Do you believe that? Harry Balls!" And then she burst into loud uncontrollable, uncouth laughter and fell to the ground holding her stomach and repeating, "Harry Balls, his name is Harry Balls!"

That did it. We all looked at each other and cut loose, laughing up a storm. We couldn't help it! Somebody should have warned us, or at least they could have said "Harold." So, there went our ladylike images right down the tube, the first night. Even Coach Wamby and the chaperone were laughing. They tried not to show it, but they were. At this point, the fans were all looking at us in a very disapproving manner (so much for charm school). We were going to have to win them over with our baseball. But, that didn't happen either that first night. We were playing our traveling teammates, the "Chicks," and I guess we were tired and so nervous about Opening Day that we all had the jitters.

Everything went wrong, especially for us. The pitchers were wild. We kicked the ball all over the place and couldn't hit our fannies with both hands. The score was something like 10-7, with us on the losing end of a very lousy ballgame. The crowd went home in disgusted silence. On top of that, our ever-loving coach imparted to us, "OK, girls, I'm not going to call you ballplayers, just girls. On the practice field at 8 a.m. It's obvious we need it." We trudged home in mournful silence. We didn't even want to think about what the papers would write in the morning. But we did have one bright note on which to end the evening.

When we got back to our house, the vets were there to meet us, with smiles and cheers. Surprise! Surprise! Also, there was a small group of fans there, waiting for us. They applauded us and asked us for our autographs. They told us they knew we'd do better next time. We met our first "Locker Room Leonards" and "Clubhouse Clydes," as we called them. They call them groupies today. Things weren't so bad after all. Somebody liked us! We all vowed to do much better in the future and make believers out of all our fans. But deep down, I had this nagging fear. I was worried, and I felt like it was our fault. We had let the fans down. I didn't want what happened in Minneapolis last year to happen here!

I didn't need to worry however, because after our rocky start, we started winning baseball games and playing great ball. We were right up there in first or second place all year long, duking it out with Rockford for first place and having a good time while we were at it. We had made believers out of the fans, indeed we did. We were outdrawing all the major sports in town. We were first on the sports page and first in the hearts of our fans. We were outdrawing even the world-famous Fort Wayne Zollner Pistons. They were the men's national champion softball team. The Pistons even gave their tickets away. We also outdrew the local Triple A, minor league men's baseball team and their tickets were cheaper than ours. A lot of people weren't too happy about that!

There was a newspaper strike that year, and they took an official survey during that strike. It showed that every sporting event lost attendance during the strike, except the All American Girls Professional Baseball League. Our attendance shot up dramatically, actually proving that we were the best show in town. As I mentioned before, I knew the Pistons and the men's minor league baseball team really didn't like us, but I didn't realize just how strong their dislike was. However, I was soon about to find out.

Top Row:
Chaparone- Ellen Townsen - Doris Marsh
Bird Dog Jackson - Vivian Kellogg - Audrey Haines
Faye Dancer - Coach Wamby

Middle Row:
Arlene Johnson - Irene Runkey - Penny O'Brian
Helen Callahan - Yolande Teillet

Front Row:
Annabelle Lee - Pepper Paire - Tex Lessing
Moe Trezza - Marge Callahan

My Grandson & his wife
Scoot & Jill " The Bikers"

Nephew & Wife
Bud & Joannie

Chapter 18
He Was Definitely a Foul Ball!

Between the strain of the war and our own personal war with the Rockford Peaches, 1945 was turning out to be a really tough year — both mentally and physically. Faye and I were beginning to mature as ballplayers. I was having a great year at shortstop — second best fielding average in the league, as well as leading the league in doubles and RBIs, and rarely striking out. Faye was leading the league in stolen bases and home runs. She also was on top defensively. We pretty much had things covered and we were feeling our oats.

The fact that I came into the league as a shortstop, and eventually wound up catching was a little tragic for me. The stats will show that I was a fine shortstop, and I loved that position, but catchers are just hard to come by and you don't win pennants without them. They get hurt a lot! This year, I wasn't worried about that because we had a very good catcher in Tex. She was a good receiver. She had a fine arm, and while she didn't hit for an average, she hit when it counted!

Actually, the whole team was going great guns! Our cute little second baseman, Audrey Kissell, was still with us and we still made a great double-play combination. She was also quick on the bases! The pitching staff was holding up well. Our knuckler, Annabelle Lee, and our curveball artist, Dottie Wiltse, were shutting down the other teams pretty regularly. Kelly was covering the first base bag and slugging away. Runky Dunky and Faye and our right fielder were covering the grass pretty well. They were getting their base hits when it counted! Faye and I nicknamed our right fielder "Bird Dog." Faye told her it was because she could smell out fly balls. Actually, it was because she had a sharp, pointy nose that twitched when she laughed. (I don't know if she knows the truth yet!) (Now she does!)

We had a solid ballclub and figured to be in it all the way. We had an off day coming up and we were all pretty happy about that, but, as usual, they thought better of it and changed plans on us. They scheduled us to play an exhibition game against a local men's team. We were kind of disappointed at first and then we found out that we were going to play the Fort Wayne minor league ballclub. Faye and I had boyfriends on that club so we thought that sounded like fun. My boyfriend was a pitcher, and sure enough, he was pitching that night. I was pretty nervous my first time up to bat, but I took his curve to right field with a clean base hit. He didn't like that very much, but he figured I just got lucky. So, the second time up, he threw his "screwgie" (screwball) inside. I stepped away from it and ripped it down the third base line for a double. Now he was really steaming! All the guys on his club were getting all over him and razzing him.

The score was tied 3-3, bottom of the ninth, two outs, winning run on third base and guess who's up to bat? He stood with his back to me for a little while, roughing up the ball. When he turned around, I saw the gleam in his eyes. I knew I was in for trouble! He took a full wind-up, despite the runner on third base, and fired his fastball right at my head. I dropped the bat and hit the dirt in an unladylike fashion, landing flat on my backside. I could see the guys laughing in their gloves, including him.

The umpire called time. I got up and dusted myself off. I could feel my temper rising. My ears were getting hot. I was thinking, play chin music with me, huh. Max Carey tried that, you turkey! Slowly and deliberately I yanked my hat down over my eyes, taking my time, and dug in, patting the plate with my bat. I guess he thought he had me scared because he pumped his fastball right down the gut. Once again, luck was with me and I lined it right back through the box. Just like I did to Max! My boyfriend's hat flew off and he hit the dirt. The run scored and the game was over. As I rounded first base, I hollered, "And now who's laughing?"

Well, folks, that did it! He dumped me. He could dish it out, but he couldn't take it! But, you know what? I really didn't miss him because I was too busy playing hard, and doing my best for the team and for the fans. Plus, I was having fun dating. I told all the guys before we even started dating that it couldn't get serious because I was waiting for my "Fly Boy" in the South Pacific. I had an excess of boyfriends to fall back on, including Fuzzy. Well, that's what I called him anyway because his hair was black, curly and so short it looked like black fuzz! He was about 6 feet 1 inch and very well built, with dark eyes, and he looked great in a tux! When I found out his real name, I learned that he was the son of the lieutenant governor of Ohio. He was also a councilman or something like that. Well, he took me home to meet his family and they were all pretty sure I'd give up baseball for him. But, of course, I didn't. Politics wasn't the game for me.

Tex, Faye and I had something going on all the time that year, but when we were out there on the ballfield, we were always fighting to win and giving 110 percent! This was a real crunch time in the war. Our Allied Forces had invaded Europe and a lot of American boys were dying. There was a lot of tension built up inside all of us. We had to have an outlet or something was going to blow! Our chaperone thought she was doing her job, but she wasn't really someone you could talk to, or trust. She was strictly management, if you know what I mean. She wasn't one of the ones that could really handle the job properly. There weren't too many of them that could.

Sometimes, when it seemed like the pressure was unbearable, Faye and I would turn to our cemetery sanctuary. Late at night after everybody had gone to bed, Faye and I would take a six-pack of beer and go visit the cemetery. Now, I know that sounds disrespectful, and a little creepy (if not downright crazy) but we meant no disrespect. We were very careful not to damage anything, not to step on the graves or the new grass or the headstones. We just talked together quietly, mostly about my bro Joe and her bro Richard. We were remembering all the silly, funny little times we had growing up together. We asked God to protect them and to protect all of our guys. Faye's boyfriend Johnny was a GI fighting in Europe, and, of course, my Bob was on that B-24 in the Pacific with my beloved bro. As I said, it was a tough war year and we were very worried about our loved ones coming home safely. My poor Mom was so worried. I could read the pain and the heartbreak between the lines in her letters. We didn't know it, but things were going to get worse. Somehow it helped to be in the peace and quiet of that reverent place. We felt like the people there were listening to us and talking to us. I can still remember a name on one of those stones. It was Mrs. McGillicutty. I was to visit her more than once.

We had some great times in that old Fort Wayne house. For the most part, our landlady left us alone. She was just glad to get the rent and grateful that we weren't prostitutes. We actually behaved pretty well at the house. We had to or someone would have snitched on us. It was well known where we lived. We still pulled a lot of funny pranks at that house. One of them was "hide the clothes." We teased Tex and Kelly a lot. They were both bashful and careful about their privacy. We were all pretty bashful about running around in our all-together! Tex and Kelly were <u>really, really</u> bashful. So, while they were taking showers we would grab their clothes and hide them. They would have to come out, wrapped in their towels and chase their buddies around to find them. They would get back at us though, by snapping those wet towels at us!

While we had those good times, we had some hard times too. There are always some people who are just born users. I won't mention any names. They know who they are. We all bought our own food and stored it in the refrigerator. Everybody had a spot for their stuff. You were on the honor system. You weren't supposed to eat someone else's food, but our food would come up missing a lot. Tex, Faye and I bought different stuff than the other gals. Some of them were kind of thrifty. They'd squeeze those Lincoln heads (pennies) pretty hard.

You were supposed to clean up after yourself, too, but again, some of them didn't. Sometimes they would wear our clothes. We didn't have a washing machine available, so we had to either take our dirty clothes to the Laundromat (there was only one of these in town) or to the cleaners. That was pretty expensive, and the timing was never right. Maybe once in a while we could run a batch through with the landlady. However, most of the time we had to hand wash a lot of our clothes and hang them out to dry on the clothesline in the hall or out in the backyard, when weather permitted. Unfortunately, a lot of the times things turned up missing -- panties, bras, socks, etc. Sometimes we'd come home weary from a road trip and find a lot of dirty dishes on the table. That was disturbing.

There was this vacant lot behind our house and right behind that was the cemetery. So, this one time, Faye and I got home from a road trip and we found this tough, hard-crusted, garbage-filled, leftover mess in the kitchen. We had cleaned it just before we left on that road trip. That was one time too many for the Cacapot and she decided "to heck" with this. She just took all the dirty dishes (pots and pans and silverware) and wrapped them up in the tablecloth. Then she tied it all up in a knot and flung the whole thing out the window down to the vacant lot below. They landed with a crash that could be heard for miles! I'm sure Mrs. McGillicutty and her friends in the cemetery heard it.

That was the last time we found dirty dishes in the kitchen. Of course, we didn't have many left! Maybe that was part of the reason. Tex, Faye and I decided we needed some form of transportation, so we figured that we needed to buy a car. Enter the "Cacacar." We went to a used car lot and bought a 1940 two-door Chevy sedan. It was a beautiful steel blue color and had all the extras, including new white sidewall tires. We paid $250 and thought we really got a great deal. We didn't find out until later that the white sidewall tires weren't new. Just the white was new (new paint, that is) and the tread was mostly paint also! The beautiful new paint job? Well, that was the only thing that held the car together. The used car salesman really did a number on us. The Cacacar was all rusted out underneath, but it ran great and it looked good, so why worry? We sure had a lot of adventures in it. One of our favorite stunts was to drive over to the Van Orman Hotel, where the visiting ballplayers stayed. We would drive down the alley because there was a "no fraternizing" rule and we would park the car under the fire escape. Then Faye would get up on top of the car and pull the fire escape down. While I held it down, she would shoulder a case of beer and up the fire escape we'd go to visit our friends. This was after the ballgames, of course, when everybody was supposed to be tucked snuggly into their beds. At least that's what the manager and the chaperone thought as they stood guard in the lobby.

The Van Orman Hotel was located in the downtown section of Fort Wayne, all six blocks of it. I had a date one night and didn't go with Faye and Tex. I had been trying to teach Faye how to drive and what a chore that was. But Tex had a driver's license, so Tex and Faye went to meet some of the girls from the other ball club in town, the Rockford Peaches. We knew there was a no fraternizing rule but we thought that was silly. We had some good friends on the ball club, including some Californians. We had all played softball together. There wasn't any way we weren't going to see them, not if we could help it! The league thought that if the fans saw us fraternizing with the other ball club, people might think we would lose to our friends on purpose. That was a ridiculous idea! Tell me this much, if you had a pal, who wasn't on your team, who would you rather beat? You need to have bragging rights, right? There was never any doubt about trying our hardest and, if anything, we would try harder while opposing our friends.

On this particular occasion, we had a rare night off! The visiting ball club was in town early. I got home from my date at about 11 o'clock and I got a phone call from the police. The police were very friendly to us, because they knew who we were, and they kept us on a long leash. It was pouring down rain and it seems that Faye and Tex got to the hotel and couldn't find a parking place. So they just locked the car and left it in the middle of the street in front of the hotel. The police really couldn't do much with it without breaking into it. Would you believe, they came and got me and drove me down to the hotel. They let me pick up the car and drive it home, and promised not to tell coach!

Of course, I had to turn around and go back and get Tex and Faye, but what the heck, the party was just beginning anyway. Now that wasn't such a bad thing, was it? I guess it wasn't exactly a good thing, either. It occurs to me that I talk a lot about drinking beer and partying, so let me get this straight. We were not alcoholics or party girls. We couldn't have done that and played the grueling schedule that we did! It was just that we were under a lot of pressure at all times! We needed to have an outlet of some kind. Our social life was nonexistent most of the time, except for what sneaking out we did. We just had to blow off some steam one way or another and sometimes drinking beer was a way to do it.

It wasn't for everybody, of course. Some of the gals had other ways of dealing with the pressure. For some it was music, for some it was knitting, for others it was writing letters all the time or playing cards. Some just plain couldn't handle it and went home. For Faye, Tex and me, it was music *and* beer when we had the chance. To this day, I believe that beer goes with a ballgame. There should be popcorn, peanuts, hot dogs with lots of mustard and relish, and beer. Ninety-nine percent of the time, we consumed beer moderately, and only after the game.

I won't say 100 percent of the time because I do remember one time when we had a day off and Tex, Faye and I drove off to Chicago in the Cacacar. We had some wild adventures that day. (I wouldn't do that again if we had the chance to do it over.) For some dumb reason, it was fashionable to throw eggs, so we popped a few Chicagoans with some eggs. We didn't actually throw at people but we missed sometimes and we could have hurt someone. That was one prank I'm not too proud of. However, it seemed funny at the time, especially when we hit a hot dog vendor and the egg bounced off him and landed on his grill. We justified that by telling ourselves that he probably cooked the egg and sold it to somebody. We also nailed a couple of streetcars.

We just threw at objects, not people, but there were rare misses. Thank God no one was hurt! You learn not to do things like that when you grow up! It was a long drive from Chicago back to Fort Wayne. We weren't supposed to have a ballgame that night, but they had rescheduled an exhibition game at the last minute. Coach was in a bad mood because we were in the middle of a losing streak. We got back just in time for the ballgame -- Faye, Tex, Kellogg and me. And you know what? We played a great ballgame that night. I can remember making one of the greatest plays I ever made. This little Texas leaguer was hit right over the third baseman's head. She leaped for the ball but couldn't get a glove on it. I crossed over from short, dived through the air and caught the ball barehanded. I landed on my belly and still hung onto the ball. It was a great game, but we still wound up losing.

After the game, Bill Wamby bawled everybody out and said, "If you had the guts and stayed in shape like Pepper Paire and Faye, making those miraculous catches like they make, we wouldn't be losing ballgames. Why can't you all do that?" Oh boy! Did we get some dirty looks that night? The rest of the girls had not been partying and they knew we had. We were loosey-goosey and diving through the air because we were flying anyway. Our consciences hurt a little bit with that one but, again, no one could ever say we didn't give our all on the ballfield and that was a rare occasion.

We still were feeling kind of high after the ballgame, so we had a couple more beers and decided to go corn and watermelon raiding. There were farms all around us and the corn and watermelon were growing in abundance. We'd done this successfully before, a couple of other times, but we made the mistake of revisiting one farm once too often. There we were, just munching away on fresh corn and loading up the car with watermelons. All of a sudden, we hear this loud booming voice, "Ah ha! I got you varmints now!" BAM! A shotgun fires. We can hear the buckshot hitting the leaves. We hopped into that car and took off, forgetting about Kelly -- that is, until she passed the car running. She'd been playing on an injured knee, but it sure didn't slow her down any! Her bandage was flying in the breeze when we picked her up and hightailed it out of there.

Well, that scared the heck out of us. We had a road trip coming up in the morning so we went home and went to bed. We forgot about our stolen loot in the car and we didn't get back until 10 days later. Now, in May in the Midwest, it gets muggy and very, very hot! It was in the middle of the night when we got back from the road trip. We climbed off the bus in front of our house. As we got out, Faye says, "What's that smell?" Something must have died! We were so tired we just shook it off and went to bed. When we got up the next morning (to go to practice, of course), we discovered where the smell was coming from! I cannot describe to you what that car looked like. I swear that thing was moving! It was breathing in and out. It was full of mold and slime and all kinds of disgusting moving little creatures. The smell alone was enough to knock you out! We hosed it down, cleaned it out, sprayed it with all kinds of stuff. No matter what we tried, we never got that ugly smell completely out. We figured God got us back for swiping those veggies. After that, it truly was "the Cacacar"!

Chappie &
Coach Wamby

"Pepper" Paire Davis
All American
Girls Professional
Baseball League
1943-1954

Pepper's Ginger Rogers look

Ruth Lessing

Alma Ziggler
Annabelle Lee

Dottie Wiltse
Pepper Paire
Helen Callahan

Helen Callahan
Margie Callahan

Chapter 19
Fear Strikes Out, and Love Does, Too!

We were well into the meat of the 1945 season, still battling Rockford for first place. No matter how well we played, we couldn't shake that peach tree! They always seemed to be one jump ahead of us. When I think back, I realize my old enemy Bill Allington and his foxy ways probably kept them ahead of us. That and their first baseman, Dottie Kamenshek, and their fine California shortstop, "Snookie" Harrell. Something was about to happen that made everythin else seem unimportant to me.

On a dark, dark day in 1945 my Mom got the "black letter" from the war department. My bro Joe's plane was down. That B-24 Bomber that carried my bro and my smiling Bob, was missing in action. Mom and I were devastated. We were in a state of shock and denial. This couldn't be! There had to be a mistake somewhere, but there wasn't. They had flown out on their 30th bombing mission in the morning and they didn't come back that night. I got the phone call from Mom in the afternoon, and I had a ballgame that night. We were in a tough pennant fight playing those ever-loving Rockford Peaches! It seemed like every time something went wrong, we were playing the Peaches.

I went out that night and played that game on what was the worst night of my young life. The night of that black letter! I played a good game (they told me). To me it was as if I was in a black cloud, and it wasn't really me. My bro Joe's B-24 Bomber was out there somewhere in the South Pacific. I prayed it was in one piece. I played baseball that night with a heart that was breaking and with tears sneaking down my face. Yet, I did not give in to the misery that the war brought. I continued to play every night for three weeks straight, not knowing if Joe or Bob were dead or alive. After each game, I'd go home and, when all was quiet and the lights were off, I would silently cry myself to sleep, if I could sleep.

Then came wonderful news. Joe was alive and OK! We found out later, however, that all the news was not so wonderful. Mom got a V-Mail letter from Joe. "V-Mail" stood for "V for victory mail" and it was a little envelope-type thing that unfolded and became a letter. Many of the words were censored. They were blacked out or cut out by the war department. Joe wrote, "We had a little bit of a problem; I can't explain it now, but everything is OK." He wrote, "All the crew members send their love," and he emphasized and underlined, "All the crew members." Then he proceeded to name them all off one by one, each with a little message. He did not name my Bob in that letter! I knew that Bob's name would have been first on that list. So, that's how I knew that my handsome Bob had been killed. I went out that night and I played the ballgame. Then I wandered around the tombstones again with Faye. I finally went back to bed and cried myself to sleep again.

I wasn't the only one to lose a loved one. There were many loved ones over there fighting and dying. We saw it all around us. Unfortunately, Faye lost her Johnny, too. We found out later that he was killed in Europe on Invasion Day, also known as D-Day, June 6, 1944, but her bro Richard made it, so we just had to be grateful that our brothers lived through it. It was happening all around us. Mickey McGuire was a catcher for Grand Rapids and one night while we were playing them, just about five minutes before game time, they came down on the field and handed her a telegram that informed her that her husband had been killed in action in Europe. She said, "Please, don't announce it," hung her head down, and handed the telegram back. She pounded her mitt for a while, then turned around, went back behind the plate and caught the ballgame. She caught every game after that. It was our job. It was what we felt we had to do. We felt that we were doing our part helping the war effort, so we had to take it in stride. All around us, fathers, mothers, sisters and brothers were dying. That was the price of the war. That was the price of our freedom. Even with all our victories -- V.E. Day, Victory over Europe, May 7-8, 1945 -- the fighting was still fiercely going on!

I guess in today's world that may sound corny, but to us it was the only thing to do. We found out that when my brother's plane crashed, the revolving middle gun turret had pinned Joe down. It would have crushed him if it had come all the way down. Thankfully, it only came part way down. They said that even on a rough landing it usually comes down all the way and that it was a miracle he wasn't killed. He had some ribs cracked and an injured shoulder, but he was OK. When the plane landed, he and his buddy were the last ones out. They stayed behind and pulled out a crew member with a broken leg. Then my tenderhearted, world friendship brother Joe, remembered the little mascot dog and he went back to get it. At any moment that plane could have burst into flames and exploded, but he went back to get the dog!

Later on, they heard that the co-pilot, who jumped out of the cockpit window up front, claimed he rescued the crew member and the dog. I think he got a medal for it. Joe and his buddies said nothing. I guess that was protocol. You don't correct your superior officer in the military. They can make it tough for you if you do. Anyway, they all deserved medals out of it, but Joe and his buddy really earned theirs. I guess they were so glad to be alive they thought that was the important thing. I know Mom and I were sure glad that they were alive.

1945 was a blockbuster year in many ways. As I said, the war was escalating. We were winning, but soon we would suffer a very tragic loss. In April 1945, after brilliantly leading the U.S. and the whole world out of Hitler's and Japan's darkness, FDR lost his own battle for his life. Our president had been told if he served that third term, it probably would kill him. He chose to give up his life for this country and win the war. Whether you're a Republican or whatever party you might belong to, I don't think anyone can deny that the third term cost FDR his life. Some might not have liked what he did, but no one can deny that. My family thought he was wonderful and we cried like babies for our president. We felt lost without him. How could we go on?

We did go on, and Harry Truman was going to be a better president than anyone ever thought he would be. Thank God! When we left town in August for another long road trip, we left with hearts that were heavy and tired! It was turning out to be a long hot summer! We were traveling to Racine, to battle the Belles. Our preacher/manager just kept reminding us that whatever happened to us was God's will, and God wanted us to keep playing and win the championship. At least that's what he believed. I don't know if we believed it or not at that point, but I do know it was a very weary bunch that crawled on that bus and headed for the Racine Hotel. We were all half asleep and really ready to hit the sack that night, even us Cacapots.

When the bus pulled up in front of the Racine Hotel, we witnessed a strange sight. Across the street in front of the hotel was this big square with a big pond and a fountain. In the middle of the pond there was a huge statue that spouted water. At night when it was dark, they turned all kinds of colored lights on the pond and the statue, and it was quite a beautiful sight. This night, all the rest of the lights in town were on, including the statue lights. There was a mob of people surrounding the pond and overflowing into the streets around the hotel. The people were all wildly cheering, and there were a lot of soldiers and sailors and Marines in the middle of the crowd. Everybody was waving their arms and throwing their hats in the air.

We couldn't make out what they were saying. We woke up in a hurry. "My Lord, what's happening?" We piled out of that bus in our sweaty, dirty uniforms, and then we heard, "The war's over! The war's over! It's VJ Day." To this day, I can remember the overwhelming joy in my heart. The war was over! My bro Joe would come home safely. Thank you, God! It was August 15, 1945! I jumped off that bus and right into the arms of a big, tall, handsome Marine in full dress uniform. We looked into each other's face, and he lifted me up off the ground in a gigantic bear hug and kissed me. Then in unspoken unison we jumped into that pond in full uniform together. Everybody followed. We were all cheering, splashing and crying wildly, soaked to the gllls and up to our knees in mud! It turned out that the pond had a mud bottom. Boy! Was the chaperone unhappy about that! We all had to have our uniforms cleaned before the next game.

What a wild, wonderful night that was for all of America! VJ Day! Victory over Japan! We thought the war was over and our loved ones would be coming home soon. Our hearts were overflowing with joy. There were also bitter tears also for the loved ones we had lost, for the ones who wouldn't be coming home. I don't think anyone slept that night. We all danced in the streets. The people were going around with coffee, beer and sandwiches for everybody. It was like a gigantic picnic. The restaurants and the bars were open and serving everyone. No one was charging any money -- but the people were all leaving money on the tables. It was a giant love celebration! Not love like in sex, but love like "love in your heart" for everyone.

They called the game the next day, and that was a good thing because no one went to work that day. Everybody went to church and thanked God in their own way. That was one of the few nights I can't remember who won the last ballgame. It just didn't matter! It turned out that my bro wasn't to come home for a while. We thought he'd be right home but it was going to take some time. It's a massive undertaking to end a war; so many things have to be dealt with and changed. Some people got to come home on ships and some had to stay in some places for a while. Unfortunately, although the war was over, the fighting wasn't. There were still some isolated pockets of fighting going on. They were still flying missions. We had scary thoughts that something might go wrong at the last minute.

It was going to take more time of sweating and worry and uneasiness, but at least we got to talk to Joe on a regular basis. We got to hear his voice, and he wasn't in the danger he was before. The rest of that year turned out to be very anticlimactic. Even my baseball was sort of on hold, on the back burner. Of course, we were still playing and winning ballgames and fighting our way into the playoffs (and still getting into trouble).

I can remember one incident in particular. We had this special place we liked to go. It was on the main highway on the outskirts of town. We called them roadhouses in those days. Anyway, they had this big private room in the back where we could sneak in after the game and party in private. They had a beautiful painting of a bird dog hanging on the wall. It was about 2 feet by 3 feet. Faye made a $50 bet that we could steal that picture off the wall and not get caught. It was about 4 feet up over our booth. She had to stand on the table to reach it, and the outside door was right behind us. So, I stood guard and directed the operation while she stepped up and grabbed it off the wall and then slipped it to me. Then I slipped it under the table, just in time to beat the waitress coming to our table.

We sweated it out because there was this big faded white spot where it had hung. We kept hoping that nobody would look up and see it. Nobody did, and we finally got it out to the car. We had to get it home to win our bet. We were feeling very smug about our victory as we drove home laughing about it! Well, we thought about returning it that night after our payoff, but it was late by the time everybody was done playing and we were tired. We decided so what! We'll take it back tomorrow!

When we got up the next morning, we got dressed and were ready to go to practice when we hear Dottie and Lefty talking in the kitchen, "Wow, a big robbery! In this town? Wonder where it was?" We looked at each other and thought, "Uh, oh!" Tex brought us the paper and put a quiet finger to her lips and there in the headlines it read, "$40,000 painting stolen off the wall." Oh me! Oh my! It was a valuable painting and who knew? Wow! We hustled and got that thing back in a hurry! The owner took it well; he was so glad to get it back. He took it home and he put a picture of our team in its place. When we looked at that picture of the team we could visualize the striped suits and numbers under our faces. Like I said, he liked us and he took it well, and he didn't tell anybody. But he sure kept an eye on us the rest of the year.

The season passed and, as hard as we tried, we never caught the Peaches that year. We wound up staying in second place, just a couple of games out. That meant we played the fourth-place team in the playoffs. That turned out to be the Racine Belles. At that time we had the O'Shaughnessy playoff system. This meant that the first-place team played the third-place team, and second place played the fourth-place team in a three-out-of-five series. Then the two winners played each other in the finals, the best four out of seven games series for the world championship.

We played the Belles for the first two games at home, we lost one and won one. The next two games were to be played in Racine and, if necessary, the final game back home in Fort Wayne. By this time, several of the girls had cars besides us. So, somehow we convinced the team bosses to let us drive three cars to Racine. We got the travel money instead of the bus company. They went for it because it was a lot cheaper. Well, it sounded great but it didn't work out that way. It should have been just a four-hour drive to Racine, and it was a night game, so we all left at about 7 a.m., figuring to be at the Racine Hotel before noon, the day of the game.

We left from different directions so we traveled independently. We were going along just great in the Cacacar, when the temperature gauge suddenly went wild and the car started boiling over. We were just outside a little town called Valparaiso, Indiana, so we pulled into a gas station. The attendant came walking up to the car. He leaned down and looked at me through the window and said, "Well, you got some trouble, little lady?"

I swear to you it was Babe Ruth. I said, "Good grief, it's Babe Ruth!"

He laughed at me and said, "I've been told that before. Who are you? Ginger Rogers?"

I said, "I've been told that before!"

We both laughed. I could tell by now that he was much too young to be the Babe, but boy, he was a dead ringer for him. I could also tell he liked what he was seeing. I explained who we were and how desperate our situation was. We were still two hours away from Racine. We had stopped for breakfast on the way and it was now noon. He said our car trouble wasn't too serious. We had blown a head gasket, but he would have to hunt around town for the parts, and it was a two to three hour labor job. That guy, whose real name turned out to be Bud, really worked his fanny off for us, but, it was still about 3 o'clock and a $125 job before he was done.

We were all pulling out all of our meal money and trying to make it add up to $125. He saw our problem and came to me. He took the bill from my hands and said, "Write your address here and come back by. If you let me take you to dinner, the bill's paid! If not, I'll send you a bill." Well, from what I could see, he was a lot like the Babe, also a good guy. I gave him my Fort Wayne address and let him hold my hand for a while and then nervously hopped into that car, and we started hauling out of there. It was 3:30 p.m. and we had to be on the ballfield at five for batting practice. We didn't make that, but we did get there in time to take infield practice. Unfortunately, Dottie Wiltse's car didn't get there either. They had car trouble, too. Only the Canadians made it on time in the third car.

Since we got there before game time, we could at least put a makeshift team on the field, but it wasn't our regulars and we were in for trouble. Dottie was supposed to start the game, but we had to start a Canadian pitcher, who normally wouldn't have pitched. Dottie and her gang didn't get there until the third inning and unfortunately, by that time, the Belles had scored a lot of runs and we were out of the ballgame. Everybody was out of position and we had the jitters. Pitching was bad and we threw the game away.

After that, the league never let that happen again, which was for the best, because I think it really did cost us the series, even though we had the better team. Everybody was so upset and angry we just blew the next game in Racine and we were done for the year. I'm ashamed to tell you, I detoured around Valparaiso and "Babe Ruth" on the way back to Fort

Wayne. However, I did intend to pay the bill when he wrote me, but he never did, and I didn't have his address.

Faye, Tex and I were so disgusted with ourselves when we got back to Fort Wayne, that we passed up all the invitations to dinners and parties and dates. We just paid our bills and packed up our luggage. At least some of us paid our bills. Then we packed up the car and headed for Chicago. We were going to drop Tex and Kellogg off and head home. Well, folks, that was 1945 and the Cubbies and Detroit Tigers were in the World Series. Yep, I was at Wrigley Field watching it! It really did happen! The Cubs made the World Series! We picked up another Californian, Tiby Eisen, in Chicago. She was going to ride home to California with us, but we decided to drive to Detroit and watch the final game of the World Series first. So, off we went to watch Andy Pafko, Peanuts Lowery, Hank Greenberg and a bunch of others in Detroit.

On the way to Detroit, I was driving along this two-lane highway, which was bordered on both sides with tall cornfields and I was singing to stay awake. It was barely starting to get light when this black and white blur darted out of the cornfields and across the road in front of me. I slammed on the brakes and blew a tire, skidding and sliding to a stop. We got out and sure enough, the tire was wrecked. The spare we had was bald in spots, but it was all we had. So we were jacking that car up with a crazy bumper jack and it was swaying back and forth. Bumper jacks always made me nervous.

We heard this whining coming from the cornfields. We could tell it was a dog, so we started calling and whistling and out comes this beautiful English setter.
He was limping and shaking because he was so scared. He looked just like the dog in the picture we had swiped! It was instant love. He wasn't really hurt. He just had really red and sore feet because apparently he had been running around for a few days. His tongue was hanging down to the ground and he was thirsty and hungry. We gave him some water and bologna we had in the car. He gobbled that up in a hurry. When we got ready to go, we opened the doors to get in the car and he jumped right in the backseat and refused to get out. He was a big dog! We weren't going to argue with him. So, we put Tiby in the backseat with him, over her protest. Then he showed his love by drooling all over her. Despite her protest, off we went.

We knew he was a valuable dog and that somebody was missing him, so we made the rounds of all the farms we passed. Nobody claimed him or seemed to know anything about him. We didn't know how long or how far he had been traveling, so, he became the Cacadog! We loved him and we wanted to keep him, but we knew that wouldn't be right. He was a hunting dog and he belonged in hunting country, not in Los Angeles. We didn't know what we were going to do about that. Besides, we barely had enough money to get ourselves home. Fortunately, the situation was taken out of our hands.

We stopped for gas at a roadside tavern and had dinner there. It was also a hunting lodge. The owner took one look at the Cacadog and fell in love, and we could tell it was mutual. So, we made a deal. He filled our gas tank, bought us dinner and gave us 50 bucks. We said a tearful goodbye to the Cacadog and headed for Detroit. Tiby was so glad! She was tired of getting drooled on. We got to Detroit and spent a couple of nights with Marge Wenzell and her family. Marge was a fellow All American and a pal. Her dad Ed was a scout in our league and her mom was a champion bowler! So Marge came by her talent naturally. We watched Hank Greenberg hit some homers, and then we decided to head for home.

Faye and I were unhappy about the way the season had ended. Plus, we were all homesick by now. If you went by the stats, we both had a good year. Faye led the league in home runs, and in defense in centerfield, and she got a lot of stolen bases. Even though I only hit .196 (remember, that's like .296 in the majors), I was at bat 396 times and only struck out six times. I also drove in the second most runs in the league with that average. As Pete Rose says, "See the ball, hit the ball!" And I saw the ball good! Even though individually we each had a good year, we really felt like we had failed. Our team had failed to win the title and again we felt like we had let the fans down.

We were ready to call it quits for 1945 and just go home and get strong and rest up. We vowed to come back in 1946 and win it all for the town. So Faye, Tiby and I said our goodbyes to Tex and Margie and started home, praying that nothing important would fall off the car on the way home, like a wheel or an axle.

The trip home was an adventure all in its own. Flat tires, listening to the rattles and hoping a fender wouldn't fall off. Bologna and peanut butter sandwiches in the car. I drove the whole time. Tiby didn't drive and while I was trying to teach Faye, she could not be depended upon. One night I got so tired I let her drive. After I warned her: "Now listen, if you have a flat tire, don't hit the brakes 'til you slow down. Don't hit the brakes." Well, of course, she did have a flat tire, and she let it roll to a complete stop. The tire was strung out for miles along the road and completely ruined. You used to be able to get tires fixed in those days. They could put a boot in them, or they could patch them or plug them, but nothing could fix that tire but a resurrection.

Anyway, through the grace of God, and about 15 used tires and 30 quarts of oil and a lot of nights sleeping in the car, we made it home to the land of fruits and nuts, and we were darn happy to get there! I walked up those steps and into my Mom's arms. It felt so good! I hugged Pop and kissed baby bro Russ, and I let my Mom baby me. I enjoyed every moment of it! I needed that tender, loving care. I had been dreaming about Mom's cooking all the way home. And you can bet it tasted every bit as good as I dreamed -- and better!

Joe's
B24 crew
at March Field, CA
"1944"
"Joe" top row second in from the left and to his right is Bob

Bob and Joes's Plane
Before the crash

Bob and Joes's Plane
After the crash

Girl Diamond Stars In Debut

Curiosity of Fort Wayne's fans concerning the heralded skill of the nation's best girl baseball players will be satisfied tonight, at least partially, when the All-America Girls Professional Ball League makes its debut here, with this city's new entry playing Grand Rapids at North Side High School Athletic Field.

The girls in the All-America League are the best talent available in the diamond game and are recruited from all over the United States and from Canada as well. Baseball is a business with them, for the present at least and like men in the same game, the more skillful and more valuable to their teams they are, the better they fare when it comes to signing contracts.

The game the girls play is not softball, but more on the order of modified baseball. This is the third year of the league's existence. While Grand Rapids and Fort Wayne clash tonight, Kenosha will be at South Bend and Rockford at Racine. They play a series of four games including Saturday night.

Some special opening day ceremonies, starting at 8 o'clock, will precede tonight's meeting between Fort Wayne's Daisies and the Grand Rapids Chicks. Henry Herbst, president of the Fort Wayne Association, will be in charge. He will introduce Ottomar Krueger, president of Concordia College, who will in turn present Max Carey, president of the All-America League and former Pittsburgh Pirates star and Bill Wambsganss, manager of the Fort Wayne club. Both are products of Concordia College.

Mayor Harry W. Baals will be on hand to participate in opening night ceremonies, but he has been asked to turn over the traditional first ball tossing ceremony to Mrs. Baals. Players on both teams will be introduced individually before starting the game.

"V" For Victory

Single Handed Triple Play

Faye & Pepper

PEPPER BOX — Lavonne (Pepper) Paire is the shortstop for the Fort Wayne Daisies and she is one of the players who has attracted attention by her handling of the ball and hitting in the first three games of the All-America Girls League. She hails from Los Angeles.

Racine Newspaper write-up

Dottie McGuire
Got a letter about her husband killed in war
D-Day 1944

180

Chapter 20
Jim Thorpe's Thunderbirds!
Winter '45

I finally got rested up, and then I ran out of money. I was ashamed of myself for just lying around, so I shook off the dust and went out job hunting. I took a job driving a school bus, but that really didn't last long. It was a lot of fun, but it just didn't pay enough for me to get by on. I could never figure out the American wage system. We pay technical and professional people in high-profile jobs lots and lots of money. We pay movie stars and athletes "boo-koo" bucks, but teachers and school bus drivers are low on the pay scale. Yet, these people are at the very heart of our foundation! Taking care of our most precious possessions ... our children. They shouldn't have to fight to make enough money to exist on. The war effort was still in effect and the defense plants are still going full blast, and they paid top dollar. Packard Bell opened up a new plant on Bundy Avenue in Sawtelle right by Faye's house. That was very convenient! They advertised that they were accepting trainees at a decent wage. Mom, Faye and I all went down and applied and we all got jobs, but we weren't able to work together. Mom had to go on the swing shift because of little bro Russ. Somebody had to be there to take care of him. Faye and I had to work days so we could do our softball at night. I wanted to help my Mom because she had never done that kind of work. She was hired on as a trainee and she hung in there and got the job. I was so proud of her!

I had picked up where I had left off on my softball and my boyfriends, still playing on my two regular teams, but I added a new one. It was "Jim Thorpe's Thunderbirds." Yes, that's right, our very great Olympic hero! Please remember, I was only 20 years old in the winter of 1945, and what a dumbo I was. I didn't know I was playing softball for an Olympic legend, and perhaps America's greatest athlete. All I knew was that he was an Olympian, a football player and a nice guy -- happy-go-lucky most of the time. There would be times when he was very quiet and humble and seemed to be brooding. I could see the hurt in his eyes. I really didn't understand why at the time, but now I do!

He won three gold medals in the 1912 Olympic Games and they broke his heart when they took them away from him. He received some expense money for playing in a baseball game. It was a small amount, but he didn't know to hide it the way the rest of them did. That's hypocritical! Just like the other things we found out recently about our Olympic committee! There's no doubt that Jim Thorpe was treated unjustly and it hurt him a great deal. Before our softball games he would don his old-fashioned football uniform, with his funny little brown leather helmet and his skimpy little shoulder pads. Then, he would put on an exhibition of passing, running and drop kicking the football. The poor guy was up there in his 60s, but he would run around out there with just a few hundred people in the grandstands. There never was a big crowd, but he still would put on the best exhibition he knew how! It was sort of pitiful and pathetic.

We simply didn't realize the magnitude of his greatness. In football at that time, you could kick and score a point after a touchdown, by dropping the ball and kicking it after it hit the ground. It's called drop kicking and Jim was great at that. I don't know if anybody today even knows what a drop kick was or is? The kicker didn't need anyone to hold the ball. He could just suddenly drop it, kick it and catch the other team by surprise.

Jim Thorpe was a real nice guy but not too well educated. He also had a little drinking problem. I think some woman had gotten ahold of him and was running him ragged. We called them gold diggers in my day. At that time, they were making a movie of his life story called "The Jim Thorpe Story." It starred Burt Lancaster. Jim was badly overdrawn on his movie funds and struggling financially, as so often happens to great, innocent sports figures, they get drawn into the Hollywood scene and get in with the wrong people.

So, here was the very great Jim Thorpe managing this little rinky-dink softball team! We played quite a few games but there wasn't any real money being made by anybody. Expenses were about all anybody was making. With the boyfriends and the job and the baseball, my time went by quickly. Too fast for me and for Mom and baby bro Russ. I'd take Russ to the movies and out for hamburgers. My Mom came to my Sunday afternoon bowling league and cheered me on. Then we would all get a burger together. The family would make all the weekend softball games.

Once again, it was time to go. I knew that they were going to miss me. Joe was still not home yet, so Mom was going to have that big void in her heart again. But baseball was calling me, and before I knew it, it was time to leave for spring training. Again came the tearful goodbyes. This time we would be driving back with Betty Luna, another Californian teammate. Betty also played in the All American. We figured that it would be a lot cheaper if we drove and shared the car expenses. Then we could drive straight through and save our plane fare.

Well, it turned out that we left the same weekend that Jim Thorpe's Thunderbirds were driving down to Phoenix to play the Phoenix Queens. They were the same championship amateur team that I played before, when we had our car accident. The amateur association here still wouldn't let us Californians play in tournaments, but we often played in exhibition games against the amateur teams. That's why we weren't world champions, they didn't want the competition. As I said before, the only difference between us was that we were paid expense money above the table. They were paid expense money under the table. We decided to take Highway 60, the southern route, so we'd be going right through Phoenix. Then we could go early enough to stop and watch them play a ballgame.

The Phoenix promoter paid Jim Thorpe a $500 fee for the games and Jim accepted it. Some of the gals on the team decided they weren't getting enough money, and they left the team and went home, taking their equipment with them. Coach Thorpe couldn't put a team on the field. He didn't have enough players. Now, if you can believe this, we were told the Arizona promoters were going to put Jim Thorpe in jail for accepting the guarantee and not being able to furnish a team. When we found out that those girls had stiffed Jim, the three of us, Faye, Betty and myself, stayed the weekend and played the games that way Jim Thorpe could put a team on the field. This meant Faye and I would both have to fly out after that or we would be late for spring training and lose two weeks' pay.

So, we didn't save any money and Betty had to drive back alone. After the game, the great "Jim Thorpe" wrote us a little two-line letter, very simple and very beautiful, thanking us very much for playing. That made it worthwhile. It took Jim a great effort to do this. His college training didn't help him learn much of anything. They just let him do what he wanted as long as he played good football for them. From what I see and hear, this is still going on. For the first time in my young life I was starting to understand that even famous people had heartaches. Nothing was easy. It was a sad thing to see a great man fall so far.

We said our goodbyes and Betty drove us to the airport after the last ballgame. We caught a red eye to Pascagoula, Mississippi. We hoped the town wasn't anything like the name sounded! You know, "goula, goula, pass the goula." We were to sing that a lot later. As usual the league was training together and there were going to be six teams again this year.

We were to be picked up at the airport in Pascagoula. We were pretty happy about everything because we were going to get to see all our buddies (on the QT, of course). By now we knew we'd always find a way. So we planted our wide bodies on that wide-body airplane and settled in for the ride. It was late, but neither of us could sleep, even though we were tired. We really weren't that comfortable about flying. When things would start bumping, we'd start jumping! We talked for a while and Faye was wondering if we were still going to have Bill Wamby and the same chaperone. We both hoped not. The thought never entered our minds that we wouldn't be Fort Wayne Daisies. After all, we were the two best ballplayers on their team! Weren't we?

Faye finally dropped off to sleep, but I found myself thinking about home. When I closed my eyes, Mom and Pop and baby Russ came filtering through. I was wondering when the Army would let go of my bro Joe and let him come home. My mind took me back and I started remembering precious things: like how Joe would always let me take him down and beat up on him. He would always let me pound on him, until one time when I was about 11 and he was 12. He got this funny look on his face, grabbed me firmly by the arms, spun me over and pinned me down. I was fuming, hollering and frustrated, but I couldn't move and he wouldn't let me go. Then he looked at me with those big soft brown eyes, full of concern, and said, "I can't let you beat me up anymore, Sis! I'm too big, and people will think I'm a pansy." That was the word for a sissy in our day. I was furious at him. I didn't understand until much later. I wound up crying and not speaking to him (for about 15 minutes)! I could never stay mad at him. I loved him too much and besides, in this case he was right. Reflecting on that, I smiled to myself and thanked God for my wonderful brother, as I often do!

That brought to mind my little bro Russ. What a funny little duck he was, so different from Joe. I wondered how he was doing and how he was handling being alone again. What a little character he was! Again I slipped back to memories, when Russ was about 5 years old and hadn't started school yet. He used to play in our front yard on Armacost Avenue. There was a fence around our house, about 4 feet high, and he was not allowed out of the yard, so he would be safe. When the other kids used to walk by on their way to school every morning, he'd walk along the fence and talk to some of them. There was this one little gal that he especially liked, but she was Japanese and very quiet and modest. She would just look down and not answer him when he would talk to her, but he kept on trying.

This one morning, she looked up and answered him when he said, "Good morning." Well, I'll tell you, he was so excited he didn't know quite what else to say. So he said, "What nationality are you?" And she said, "I'm Japanese." Well, he thought on that one for a while. He wasn't quite sure what Japanese was. So then he said, "Well, I am Japanese Bohunk!" She laughed and he laughed and they eventually became good friends. "Bohunk" was a slang name for a Bohemian or Czechoslovakian. Russ was willing to do anything and be any nationality if it would please that cute little Japanese gal. He always did have the eye for the ladies. Mom had been standing at the screen door watching him and had heard the whole thing and related it back to me.

I said a prayer for him and my thoughts drifted back again. This time I was filled with warm and wonderful thoughts of my little doggies and their unconditional love. I wondered how my silky little black Mickey, our little cockapoo, was doing? And our cute little Boston bull, Jerry? I had pictures in my mind of Mom standing on the front porch holding Mickey in her arms and waving goodbye to me when I left for spring training. Jerry was at her feet barking goodbye, too. My Mom's smiling face came shining through and, as usual, she was trying to hide those tears. I vowed to spend more time with her when I came back home. A promise that I was forever making, and forever breaking, and living to regret!

I felt a jolt and woke to a not-so-perfect landing and Faye's loud tone, "We're here!" And indeed we were. But where in the heck was "here"? They practically dumped us off the plane on a very dimly lit runway. They threw our baggage out after us and immediately whirled around and took off. They couldn't wait to get out of there. That should have told us something. It was about 3:30 a.m. and nobody was around to help us with anything. Fortunately, we didn't have much luggage with us, just what we needed for spring training. Betty was bringing the rest. So, we grabbed our stuff and headed into the lonely terminal.

Cacapot Faye observed with sarcasm, "Guess they took the sidewalks up already."

I replied, "Yeah, well, at least we won't have autographs to sign."

There was a sleepy-eyed attendant sitting at a desk and he told us that the bus would be there at 4 a.m. Then he pointed to a small group of people sitting on benches by the door. This was the bus station too, so we sat and waited. Already we knew this wasn't going to be like Chicago. There wasn't going to be much class around here. After about an hour, making it 5 a.m. instead of 4 a.m., a rickety old school bus showed up. Everybody got on and away we went.

It was a terrible road, an old two-lane blacktop road with a lot of bumps sticking up through the blacktop. Between the bumps and the bench seats, there would be no sleeping on that bus. There were only about eight people on the bus, including us. As we drove along, they got off one at a time at various farm roads. I guess they were farm workers. By the time we got to our stop, we were the only ones left on the bus. The grumpy old guy driving practically threw us off while he grumbled about being late, turned around in a cloud of dust, and away he went. So we grabbed our stuff and started looking around.

We could see what looked like old Army barracks or bungalows. It was getting light by now, and Faye pointed to a big building that still had its lights on. It was about a hundred feet away. "Well, Cacapot, looks like there's some life in there," she said. We grabbed our duffle bags and dragged them over to it. Just as we got there, the screen door flew open and out popped Tex. "Hey, Cacapots, I knew you'd make it," she said in that Texas drawl of hers. She rolled those big blue eyes and laughed, "but you'll be sorry!"

Jim Thorpe 1887-1953

Pictorial Parade Inc.

"Jim Thorpe was probably the greatest natural athlete the world has seen in modern times."
The New York Times Book of Sports Legends(1991)
edited by Joseph Vecchione.

Jim Thorpe of the Thunder Clan of the Sac and Fox Tribe, was born May 22, 1887, on the Sac and Fox Indian Reservation, Prague, Oklahoma.

Chapter 21
No Buttons, No Bows -- Just Bugs and Bats and Belles
The Joint Was Jumping

It appeared that Pascagoula was going to be as gruesome as it sounded. We found that out immediately when Tex took us to our bungalow. We just had time to dump our bags and jump into our practice sweats and then we had to hit the ballfield to report on time. The visit to the room shocked us. Bare and well-worn wood floors, not too clean, used Army cots with sag-bag mattresses. One big room and then there was the bathroom and that was it! There were two light fixtures. The lights were still on, and there were just bulbs stuck in them. The bathroom didn't look too clean. As a matter of fact, nothing looked too clean! Faye gave me a look of disbelief and exclaimed, "Wow! What a dump this is!"

Tex was laughing at the looks on our faces as she spoke, "Yeah, no plush Chicago hotel here! Just you all wait, you haven't seen nothing yet!"

We didn't know what that meant, but we found out later. We grabbed our spikes and gloves and followed Tex out. I noticed that the lights were still on, so I switched them off (conservationist me) as we went out the door. We were way out in farm country somewhere, and that figured, because when we got past the bungalow to the ballfields, we saw four cow-pasture diamonds. Boy! They were really rough. Bumps and holes and clumps of grass. "Wow!" Faye observed again. "They must have really got this place cheap!"

I responded, "Yeah! Real cheap, maybe they're paying us. Boy, oh boy, there's going to be some bad hops out there!" We found our "diamond in the rough" by spotting Bill Wamby!

Faye gave a big groan, "There he is!" He was standing tall and foreboding in the middle of the diamond with a big clipboard. But then she brightened a little, saying, "Hey, at least it looks like we got a new chappy."

We went over to sign in and say hi to everybody we knew and just started gabbing away -- but not for long. Bill immediately called roll from his clipboard. Then he had one of the gals lead us in 15 minutes of calisthenics. After that he pointed to the outfield and said sternly, "OK, gals, let's run sprints this morning!" That meant we'd run 50 feet, then walk 50 feet, and run 50 feet, and so forth, and so on, for about the next hour.

Then the fun stuff began. Coach would be hitting ground balls to the infielders and, I was right, you really had to duck and load. The hops were terrible. Other coaches were hitting fly balls to the outfielders. Pitchers and catchers were throwing (it went on that way for a while). Then we had a quick box lunch and the <u>real</u> fun started. Batting practice! Everybody loves to hit! It was getting late and I noticed that some of the teams had already knocked off, being the first day and all. But not our beloved Wamby. He was still hitting ground balls and rotating the infielders, while the outfielders shagged fly balls. He hadn't changed. We went right down to the wire at 5 o'clock before he called out, "OK, time to eat."

By this time, Faye and I were really beat. It had been a long 24 hours. We were dragging our tails off the field when Tex caught up with us. "Hey, you guys, are you going to shower first, or eat first?"

In unison we answered "Eat!" We looked at one another and then echoed, "And sleep!"

Tex laughed a strange laugh and said, "Oh yeah?" Then she passed us saying, "I'm showering first. I'll see you at the mess hall. Save me a seat."

That described the food perfectly! A mess! Cafeteria-style food, the kind they slop together in trays. I got some runny mashed potatoes and some watery corn and picked out what looked like roast beef, along with gravy and some Jell-O on my tray. Faye followed me with much the same. Then she went back and got us some milk and orange juice. The milk was almost warm, and the orange juice was watery but, actually, we were so tired we didn't care. In fact, I was pretty grateful I had all my teeth to eat with after all those bad hops on that ballfield. I needed those molars too, because the roast beef was really stringy.

We were just about done and kicking back when Tex came in. She grabbed a tray and joined us. I noticed that she had mainly fruits and vegetables on her tray. She saw me looking and said, "Well, you know they can't hurt this stuff much."

Faye said, "Hey, what's good for dessert?"

Tex answered, "The tapioca's not bad, and the coffee's not bad, either."

So Faye grabbed a tray and headed for the line, saying over her shoulder to me, "I'll get it, Pep."

I remembered what Tex had said that morning and asked, "Is it the food you meant when you said we hadn't seen nothing yet?"

"Nah," she grinned.

I went on, "Well, the bad diamonds? The rooms?"

"Nah," she shook her head and went on eating with a grin still on her face.

I said, "Come on, what is it? Nothing could get much worse." Then seeing the look on her face, I said, "Could it?"

She just nodded her head and said, "Just wait!"

We finished up dessert and coffee while Tex finished eating and then we walked wearily out the door and headed for our bungalow with Tex in the lead. It wasn't quite dark yet, but all the lights were on in our room. I said, "Hey I turned those lights off!"

Tex answered, "I know. I turned them back on, and don't turn them off again! Ever!" she added emphatically.

"Why?" I asked. I was starting to get exasperated now. What's the big secret anyway?

Faye joined in, "Hey, what's going on?"

Tex said, "OK, you asked for it. I'll show you." Stopping us she said, "Stay here!" She reached inside the doorway and switched off the lights. "Wait," she said.

After what seemed like about five or 10 minutes, but probably was only a minute or two, we started hearing noises. Clicking and rustling noises. Like dropping rice or beans on the floor. I looked at Tex and she wasn't laughing now. In fact, she looked a little scared. The joint was jumping.

Faye's eyes were wide open and she had a funny look on her face. "What the heck is that?" we both said at the same time.

Tex flipped the light switch back on, and the floor was crawling with big, black bugs! They scrambled and zipped out of sight when the light came on. Tex said, "Well, how do you like your roomies?"

"Oh, my God!" I exclaimed. "Cockroaches."

She nodded, "Yep, and they're big enough to ride on!"

Some of them looked to be 2 inches long, and those suckers could fly, too! Faye hollered, "They're almost as big as the airplane we flew in on!"

From that time on, we knew that we didn't dare turn the lights off or we'd be swatting and ducking all night long. The lights kept them quiet and out of sight. Really, those guys were big enough to go to work. They could have starred in a sci-fi flick today, maybe something like "The Cockroaches That Ate Mississippi."

That started what was to be the worst spring training experience during my 10 years in the league. The place had been an old housing project that had been converted to an Army base. It had really been misrepresented to the league. I can honestly say that that was probably the only time things weren't first class. Mr. Meyerhoff, who had purchased the league from Wrigley, was later asked by a newspaper reporter about the terrible living conditions in Pascagoula. He was quoted as saying, "Well, those weren't really cockroaches! They were pinch bugs."

I'll tell you what. I don't know what a pinch bug is, but I _do_ know what a cockroach is, Mr. Meyerhoff. It wasn't your fault, and I know you're up there on cloud nine now, but those were cockroaches! There was a lot of spraying with DDT and poisonous stuff in an attempt to control things, but no way did that put a dent in the population. It probably did us more harm than the bugs.

Somehow we got through those two weeks without dying from food poisoning, or worse yet, by getting bitten by one of those flying giants. Of course, there wasn't a lot of sleeping going on. We dealt with it by doing things like staying out on the porch late at night, playing cards, writing letters home or just talking baseball. Sometimes in the middle of the night, we'd make trips down to the laundry room and do our wash. There were only a couple of washers and dryers and there were six teams training there. They were constantly busy, and you had a long line during the daytime. We did whatever we could to keep our minds off those bugs.

Town was about five miles away and hard to get to and there was nothing there when you did go. Even the baseball that we loved too much wasn't that much fun. The diamonds were so bad that playing real games was dangerous and you risked injury. Our slave-driving Bill limited his ground ball hitting, so we had a lot of "skull practice" sessions and lots of exercises. Oh yes, exercises! Our coach didn't like talking all that much, so with us it was mostly those boring exercises. I often wondered what, as a preacher, Coach Bill's Sunday sermons were like? Maybe he would just hold up a picture of the devil and say, "OK now, everybody be good or else!" Or maybe he would just have a Bible slide show. But then, I don't know whether or not J.C. plays baseball? Let alone slides? (Little joke there, Lord ... Only kidding!) And thank you for getting us through those two weeks!

We were more than ready to leave that place when the three charter buses finally came around to pick up all six teams. We found out ahead of time that the official Allocation Day wouldn't be happening this year. We were told that the teams were all pretty much set, with just assignment of the rookies still needed. So, we joyfully piled on our buses with our fellow teammates and drew comfort from the fact that at least we would know most everybody on our team. We also knew that we had a good team and we felt like we could make a run for the pennant.

That was good, but what wasn't so good was that we found out we'd be traveling with the "Pride of the Midwest" for the exhibition tour, the snooty Racine Belles. They had beaten us the year before in the playoffs and they didn't let us forget it. They were known in the league as a very cliquish team. Oh well, we didn't care. This year we'd show them! Right? Our preseason tour schedule was the worst ever in my 10-year history. It was a mess of back and forth, and doubling back to towns; up and down more times than the market.

1946 was going to turn out to be a true test of my endurance and my love for baseball. The bus staggered around the country for seven days, while we were playing the cold, unfriendly Racine Belles, and beating them most of the time (I might add). I guess that was part of why they didn't like us. Finally, we made our way up north to God's country (where the bugs were smaller) and ended up in Chicago. That's where we were to separate and go to our own hometowns. We had to get settled in our living quarters and get the season under way.

Again, I think we had a generous two whole days in which to do that. It was the middle of the night when we got to Chicago and we were all sitting on the bus waiting for our charter buses to show up to take us home. The Cacapots, Tex, Faye, Kelly and me, were discussing quietly how glad we were to be able to dump the Racine Belles. Coach Bill stuck his head in the bus and called my name. He had a funny look on his face and I thought, Oh, oh! What did I do now? He stepped up on the bus, pointed a finger at me and said, "Get your stuff." Then he dropped the bomb, "You've been traded to Racine."

I couldn't believe my ears. I was dumbfounded. I cracked a faint smile and asked pleadingly, "Bill, is this a joke?" But I knew by the look on his face it wasn't. I also knew that he didn't make jokes.

He answered me grimly, "Nope, Pepper, I wish it was. I tried to stop it." Then he turned and headed off the bus, and looked back over his shoulder, "Hurry up, no time, their bus is here."

I was in shock! My buddies were in shock! We were all staring at each other with our mouths hanging open. I grabbed my duffle bag and my jacket and headed down the aisle. My other bags were underneath. I got to the bus steps at the front door, turned and choked out, "Bye, everybody." There were faint answers in return. I climbed down those steps, sick to my stomach. I felt like I had swallowed my bowling ball. This couldn't be happening to me, Pepper Paire, shortstop extraordinaire, second best-hitting shortstop in the league, tops in RBIs, second in defense! What more could they want? Marty "Slats" Marion? I could be better than him.

The bus driver transferred my bags to the other bus while I just stood there in the dark, cold wet Chicago night, wanting to cry. But no way would I! My pride was suffering a mortal blow. I had this terrible feeling of betrayal. Tex and Faye were hanging out the windows, waving and choking back the tears. I heard someone holler, "Come on, come on! We want to get home." Then it really struck me, "My God, the cliquey, snooty, Midwestern Racine Belles! Oh Lord, why me?"

I took one last look at that Fort Wayne bus pulling out. There were some mighty angry thoughts racing through my mind. How soon they forget! I got a broken collarbone for them! I know I'm a good player! Eventually I thought, I'll make them sorry they did this! You can bet on that! I mentally shook my fist at them and then I turned and climbed sorrowfully onto the Racine Belles' bus. I found my way to a lonely back seat and sat down. Most of the team was already asleep and curled up, in the best seats, of course. So, I didn't speak much to anyone and vice versa. I just cuddled up to that cold, dark window, thinking it was warmer than the atmosphere on the bus. I was miserable!

For the first time in my baseball life, I felt lonely and rejected. Giving a big, trembling sigh, I pulled my jacket over my head and silently cried myself to sleep. It was a fretful, three-hour trip from Chicago to Racine. I kept waking up every time we hit a bump, and that was often. I stopped crying and was trying to make sense out of the whole thing. I was trying to find something positive to think about. "Oh, well," I thought, remembering 1944, at least I don't have a broken collarbone, and after all those bad hops down there in spring training, I still had my bridgework (so I don't have to eat corn on the cob through a picket fence). That's a plus! But one very ugly thought kept creeping into my mind. I'll make them pay! They'll be sorry!

It was still dark when we arrived in Racine. I guess it was about 6 a.m. when the bus pulled up in front of the Racine Hotel. There was that big fountain across the street, the one I had jumped into with the Marine on VJ Day. It seemed so long ago. By now everybody on the bus was awake. I sat up to face the music. I was surprised to find out that everybody seemed to know that I was joining them. What surprised me more was that they seemed to be glad about it. Hey, maybe this wouldn't be so bad after all. At least I was wanted. The gals I knew were introducing me to the ones I didn't know. Cars were pulling up and the players were piling into them and taking off. They all had a place to go to. I wondered what I was supposed to do?

By now there was just the manager, Leo Murphy, and our first baseman, Margaret (Marnie) Danhauser, and I left. Marnie was the team's only local girl. I had been talking with Coach Murphy for a while, and I learned that he had been a catcher in the "Bigs"! I was beginning to think things might not be too bad. Murphy had let me know how glad he was to have me on his team. I was starting to feel better about everything. A catcher, huh? Well, he must know what he's doing. You see, catchers are the unspoken leaders on the ballfield, sort of like the quarterback in football (usually the brains on the team). But they don't get the credit the quarterbacks do.

So, I'm thinking, this is a smart guy, maybe this won't be so bad after all. About that time, Marnie broke into my thoughts by grabbing my arm and saying, "Come on, pal, you're staying at my house." She flashed me a friendly smile and added, "At least for now. So grab your bags 'cause I live just around the corner."

I hopped off the bus and grabbed my bags from the sidewalk. Turning around, I asked, "OK, which way?" thinking we were walking. Marnie laughed and replied, "This way. Here comes my bro." Then she looked at me and added, "My, oh my, just wait 'til he sees you!"

I looked over to the curb just in time to see this old Plymouth pull up and a tall, blond man jump out and come running around the car. "Hi, Sis!" he flung at Marnie, as he came up to me. He stuck out his hand and I started to give him my name, but he stopped me. "I know who you are. You're Pepper Paire! I'm Jim, Marnie's brother. I've watched you play, Pepper. You're the shortstop who's going to help the Belles win the pennant this year."

I grabbed his extended hand, looked up and answered, "Yeah, that's right. You bet we are!" and my heart skipped a beat! Wow! What a good-looking guy! Friendly brown eyes, wide, wide smile, built like Paul Bunyan, and I was staying at his house! How great was that? Marnie also seemed like a swell gal. In fact, everyone on the team was going out of their way to be nice to me. They told me that all they needed last year was a good shortstop that could hit, and they seemed to believe that I was going to fill that bill, and that we'd win it all. I felt good about that.

After we had loaded the car, Marnie told me to get in the front seat. We took off and slid around the corner, and there was Lake Michigan! What a beautiful sight! Blue, blue water stretching out as far as the eye could see. Gentle waves were sparkling in the morning sunrise. The new morning light revealed a crystal white stretch of beach. The pristine beauty of Lake Michigan took my breath away. "Wow!" I exclaimed, "Look at that!" Then my immediate thoughts spilled out, "Boy, oh boy, there must be some fish out there!"

Jimmy answered me enthusiastically, "You bet there is!" Then he looked at me with surprise and asked, "You like to fish?"

I echoed back his enthusiasm with a positive "You bet I do!"

"Look up here," he pointed. There on the right was a long pier, sticking out into the beautiful blue water. Then he pointed back to a house directly across the street from the pier saying, "That's our house!"

I was speechless. It was too good to be true. But it <u>was</u> true. Then he gave me another look and smiling a shy smile, he echoed my thoughts. "You're all too good to be true!" His eyes complimented me. "My, oh my!" he went on. "Great shortstop, cute as can be, and she likes to fish! I've got a feeling that this is going to be a great summer!"

Looking up into those eyes, I blushed and blurted out loud, "Me, too!"

From the back seat Marnie mimicked us with a "Me, too." Then we all burst into laughter.

Jimmy pulled up to the curb, and Marnie and I piled out. She grabbed my hand, saying, "Jimmy will grab your bags. Come on and meet my mom." We climbed up some gray stone stairs to this beautiful, old, classic-style wooden home. It was a gray and white, two-story, Old World home! I loved it! The door flew open and out came Marnie's mom, who wrapped Marnie up in her arms. "Welcome home, my baby girl!"

With her came a most delicious assortment of smells. I hadn't smelled anything that good since I left home. I was about to find out that there was another great cook around besides my Mom. Marnie's mom extended an arm to me and urged: "Come on, Pepper. I'm Marnie's mom and I know you've got to be hungry. Come on in and have some cinnamon rolls and hot coffee."

All I could think was, Wow! I've died and gone to heaven. It can't get any better. But it would! Even though I didn't know it yet, despite its rocky start, 1946 was going to be the greatest year yet! In my baseball life and also in my love life ... the whole shebang! After consuming three delicious cinnamon rolls and an ample amount of coffee, Marnie's mom insisted on both of us hitting the sack for a while. She knew that we had been up all night long. Like a typical mom, she thought we needed some rest, and she was right!

Marnie's room was a beautiful large room with a window overlooking that gorgeous Lake Michigan. It had beautiful hardwood floors with thick, warm-looking braided rugs, complete with this giant old-fashioned brass bed perched on them. It was piled high with real feather pillows and homemade, colorful-looking, soft and fluffy quilts. It was perfect. Marnie pointed to the right, "That's your side of the bed kid," and we crawled in.

Out loud I said, "Man, this is great!" Mentally I was thinking, boy, I sure hope I can stay here.

As if reading my mind, Marnie mumbled a muffled sentence, "Hey, Pep, it's yours for the season, if you want to stay."

She dozed off as I answered, closing my eyes with a "Yes, ma'am, I sure do!"

And we were both out like a light.

Seated Left to Rt 1946 Belles Bat Girl
Maddy English — Heather Black — Claira Shillace

2nd Row Seated L to R
Irene Hickson — Pepper-Mae Trezza — Sophie Kurys — Edie Perlick
Betty Emery — Ruby Stevens —

L to R
Back Row — Standing — Mildred Wilson (Chaperone)
Dodie Barr — Anna May Hutchison — Marney Danhauser
Joanne Winters — Betty Russell — Elly Dapkus.
Thelma Walmesly — Leo Murphey
Coach —

"1946 Racine Belle"
Champs —

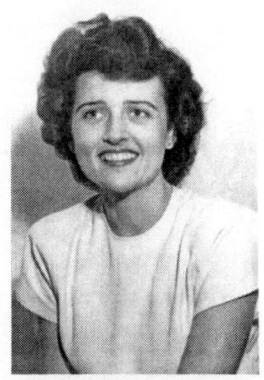

Chaparone 1946
Willie Wilson

Marnie, Pepper and
Bill Watawitz,
President Western Printing.

Pepper 1946 Belle

Me-pop Murphy -Marnie
"Looks Like Murphy Found The Beef"

Horlick Field, Racine
Factories in background

House on Michigan Ave

Chapter 22
It Just Keeps Getting Better

The next thing you know, there was a light tapping at the door. I opened my eyes and was shocked to see that it was dark outside. I could hear Jimmy's voice filtering through the door. "Hey, come on, sleepy heads, wake up! Let's go get a beer."

My eyes popped open wide! Wow! It just keeps getting better. Come to find out, we had slept all afternoon. So, I guess Marnie's mom knew what she was talking about -- we were tired! There was only one bathroom downstairs and Marnie went down the hall first. When she came back, I was surprised to see that she had on jeans and a sweater. "Hey," I asked, "don't we have to get all gussied up to go out and get beer? What about the rules?"

She looked at me and laughed, "Heck no, gal. We're just going around the corner. I'm home grown here. They know me. Besides, the season doesn't start for two days." She added, "Wear something warm and comfortable." Then she laughed again "no California wardrobe, mind you … it's cold here."

"You got some boots?" she asked.

"Yeah. Cowboy boots," I said. "Put them on, gal." she advised.

I said, "Great!" and grabbed my jeans and a sweater and went down the hall to clean up. Jimmy was sitting at the kitchen table, waiting patiently for us. He had on a typical Midwest flannel shirt, jeans and cowboy boots. So I thought, Hey, I'm right at home.

Marnie came in and sat down. After I got out of the bathroom, I joined them in the kitchen and wondered what we were waiting for? But not for long! In came Mom Danhauser dressed in her jeans and sweater. Also, she had on a knit cap over her ears with a whisper of gray hair just peeking out around her weathered face. She smiled and said, "Come on, gang. Let's go."

I thought, well, what do you know? Mom's going too. Just like home! I grabbed my windbreaker and out the door we all went, laughing and joking and all talking at once. Boy! It was brisk out! Lake Michigan in April was still pretty crisp. I learned that in a hurry. Especially when I got into my little short dress and went out on the ballfield. It wasn't going to be as warm and comfy as the jeans were.

The tavern, as they called it, was just around the corner. When we got inside, it was warm and toasty and loaded with local people. Everybody knew everybody, and they all seemed to know me, too! I guess they all came to the ballgames. They kept coming up and introducing themselves and buying me beers and saying, "Here's to the championship!" We weren't having any problems drinking the beers, including Mom Danhauser.

In fact, we were all doing a pretty good job of getting those beers down -- right there in public! I was getting a little nervous. Poking Marnie, I asked, "Don't we have to worry about the coach, or the chappy, or somebody finding out?"

She looked at me like I was crazy, and said, "Don't worry, pal. We're OK." But she looked at Jim and said, "It is getting crowded in here, maybe we'd better move."

He said, "Yeah, if we want some privacy we'd better go."

I thought, Oh well, shoot, the fun's over.

Marnie told me to grab my stuff and follow her and Jim. I was thinking, I guess we were going out the back door. But when we opened the door, we walked into a whole new room, with a bar and a little bowling alley with five little fat pins across it. "What's that?" I asked.

"That's Duck Pins," Marnie answered. She continued, "We bowl for the tavern team and there's a tournament tonight. Jimmy and I and another guy are special members and only special members are allowed in here." I thought it looked like great fun, so I asked Jimmy to show me about this bowling bit. You had a hard round ball that felt like a hard rubber ball, about the size of a large orange -- no holes in it. You just rolled it at the five pins across the alley. If you got all five with one ball, it was a strike. If you got them with two, it was a spare. But if you didn't get them all, you had to get the first pin on the left side to score or nothing counted.

I picked up the game in a hurry and was scoring on every roll. By this time the other team had arrived and they were all getting ready to start. But Marnie and Jim's teammate was late, so I was having a great time practicing with Jimmy. I was hoping the other teammate wasn't a gal and a friend of Jimmy's, when he looked behind me and said, "Here comes our partner now!"

I turned around just in time to see our coach, Leo Murphy! ("Pop" to the girls.) Murphy's silver head was making his way back toward us. My heart sank to my boots! Oh, my God! The coach! I'm in trouble now! Murphy was greeting everybody along the way and I'm thinking, wait a minute, they all know him. What's going on here? I couldn't imagine Bill Wamby coming in a tavern.

Coming up to me, Murphy's round, reddish Irish face cranked into a smile and he laughed, "Don't look so scared Pepper. Here, I brought you a beer." He had four frosted mugs in his big hands. He set them down and greeted everybody with a hug, and then he turned back to me and said in his Irish brogue, "Sure and be gory, you're a sight for sore eyes, and a pennant winner if I ever saw one!"

I was dumbfounded -- and elated -- all in one. Wow! It just can't get any better! I wanted to pinch myself to make sure it was real. They bowled three games and Marnie's team won. The table was covered with beers. We had one beer after another, and finally Murphy got up. I thought, this is it! Curfew!

"Well," he says, "I've got to go ... 6 o'clock mass, you know!"

I said, "OK, coach. What time's practice tomorrow?"

He looked at me like I was nuts and said, "Practice? What practice? That's for our rookies and bad ballplayers. That's not for you two gals. See you Tuesday at the ballpark for a meeting, and a skull session on the rules and the signs. Maybe a little practice, too," he added. Then he gave us a wink and a wave and he was gone.

Marnie laughed at me and said, "You should see your face. You look stunned."

I said, "I am stunned. Excuse me, but don't we open the season Wednesday?"

"Yeah," she said, "but not 'til Wednesday. Pop knows we're in shape." Seeing my worried look, she patted my hand and said, "Don't worry. I'll go over the signs with you tomorrow and we'll run for while -- and we'll throw a little."

I let out a big breath. Boy, this was going to be a great summer!

About that time Jimmy came over and asked if I wanted to dance. I found out we could do that well together, too. There was a big table loaded with some great sandwiches, potato salad, baked beans and all kinds of good stuff to nibble on. After we ate, Jimmy said, "OK, it's midnight. If we're going fishing tomorrow, we'd better hit it!" So we left the bar the back way. We were breathing frost all the way home, but it was only around the corner. We were all back at the house and into our bed in nothing flat. I was pulling up those big warm quilts and crawling under them. Once again, I was thinking, it just can't get any better!

Somehow, I knew that it would. Soon as the sun came up, I was up. There was one thing that could always get me up really early, and that was fishing. Checking out Marnie, I whispered, "Come on, it's light!"

She rolled over. "Come on, let's go. The fish are up!" I urged.

She opened her eyes. Well, actually, just one eye blinked at me and she moaned, "I can't believe you're really going." Then she closed both eyes and said, "Not me. See you later, 'gator!" and pulled the quilt back over her head.

I thought, oh darn, we're not going. Since I didn't hear any other sounds, I figured everybody was still asleep and Jimmy wasn't going either, I might as well get undressed and go back to bed. I was disappointed, but I thought, "Hey, maybe another time." As long as I was up, I decided to go down the hall to the bathroom. I quietly opened the door and was tiptoeing down the hall to the bathroom when I noticed a light in the kitchen and I smelled coffee.

Jimmy's head poked out that kitchen doorway and he said, "Well, what do you know? I don't believe it, you meant it!" He had a great big smile on his face as he said, "Hurry up, Mom's packed us a lunch and I've got hot coffee. We got cold beer and sandwiches for later." I hustled in and out of the bathroom and joined him in the kitchen. We threw on our jackets, and tiptoed out the door. He had a cart out in front waiting, equipped with fishing poles, chairs, blankets and a picnic basket. He had a big jug of coffee under his arm -- hot coffee! It was freezing outside, but I felt great!

We trekked across the street to the pier and walked clear out to the end. The sun was glorious in all its golden beauty and the rays soon warmed us up. We unpacked and set up our chairs. I asked, "OK, what do we do for bait?"

Jimmy pulled out a can and said, "Well, we got some great night crawlers in here. (For those of you who don't fish, those are great big fat worms that come out of the ground at night.) Then he pointed down and said, "We'll probably net some of these."

I looked down and in the crystal clear water were schools of minnows wiggling all over the place. I just about died. All of this and live bait, too! What a paradise! As soon as our lines hit the water I got a hit. Nailed a couple of little bass. Jimmy came up with a nice-sized perch. The fish were practically jumping in our sack. In a fast couple of hours we had a stringer full of about 20 nice, fat fish. We had lake bass, perch and blue gills. Up to that time we had only had coffee. We didn't eat anything because it was too much fun fishing to stop. But now my stomach was starting to growl.

About that time, Jimmy asked, "Are you hungry?" and handed me a hard-boiled egg.

I answered, "You betcha! You must have been reading my mind!"

He looked at me and said, "You know what? Why don't you eat this egg and keep on fishing. I'll clean what we got here and let's go back home and fix breakfast for everybody." He finished with, "We can save the lunch for later and come back out this afternoon."

I said, "You bet. That sounds great to me," thinking in my own mind, if you want an argument you have to change the subject! Nothing tastes better than fresh pan-fried blue gills and bass, cooked in butter with scrambled eggs. Oh boy! We looked at each other, pure enjoyment was shining on my face, I know!

He said, "Pep," and then impulsively bent down and kissed me. "You're the greatest." Then he blushed and apologized, "Oh, I'm sorry. I couldn't help myself." I said "I'm not!"

We both broke into huge smiles again. It was a wonderful world and, just like that, I was in love, and so was Jim! Thank you, Lord. That was just the first day of that magical summer. There were many more to come and everything would seem to get better. I knew it was going to be a great year in every way! I was truly happy for the first time since "Smiling Bob" was killed. I was finally able to put the negative, sad thoughts of the past behind me. My brother was safe and coming home. The war was over. The world was safe again!

Even my negative thoughts about the team and the trade faded away. I'd had a long discussion with Pop Murphy, and he told me the story of the trade. The league had a policy of balancing the teams. They did the trading for attendance' sake. That way the teams could be more competitive (the major leagues could learn from that!). Anyway, Bill Allington, my ever-loving nemesis was now the coach of the Rockford Peaches and he had complained that Fort Wayne was going to be too strong in 1946, so they decided to trade me to Racine for a weaker player. They thought that this would help Racine, who was struggling. That was the official explanation.

The unofficial explanation was due to the fact that the "Cacapots" were known for their antics in Fort Wayne --on and off the ballfield! The board thought this was a way to split us up. I guess it boiled down to the fact that they thought I was the main mischief-maker. Afterward, they found out that Faye got into a lot more trouble by herself, that I actually had held her down a little -- but they found that out too late! In my 10-year career, I was traded three times, and I made the team that traded me sorry every time. Each time I took the pennant with me to the team I was traded to. I <u>know</u> I had a lot to do with that.

Well, the league really goofed there, because by trading me to Racine they gave the Racine ball club the missing piece of the puzzle they needed to win a championship. They turned a good team into a great team. As we played our ballgames that summer, I discovered that it was true, we did indeed have a very good team. Our third sacker was Maddy English, a cute little gal from Boston, well-built, black curly hair, dancing brown eyes and the world's cutest accent. She was an all-star third baseman with a great arm. She was a fine fielder and an all-around good ballplayer. That allowed me, as shortstop, to slip into the hole and roam back over to second base and cut off those base hits. I had an arm to do it. I knew that I was one of the better shortstops in the league and I was out to prove that, and show them, in 1946. My dignity was still hurt from that trade.

Our second sacker was Sophie Kurys from Flint, Michigan. She was known as the "Flint Flash," base thief extraordinaire. Sophie simply couldn't be thrown out! She knew how to read the pitchers. She'd get a great jump-start and then she had an assortment of slides for every occasion, from headfirst to hooking the bag. Whatever it took, to beat the ball! Better still, she had a great eye at the plate and a good stick. Since you can't steal first base that made her an unstoppable offense. She was also a fine fielder. She and I made a great double-play combination. She didn't get the credit for that because she had a funny way of flapping her arms when she threw, but she got the job done!

In my opinion there were two players in our league that stood out head and shoulders above everyone else. One was Dottie Kamanshek, the first basemen for the Rockford Peaches, and the other one was our second sacker, Sophie Kurys. There were many other great players, and I don't mean to slight any of them. Some of the other players might name somebody different. There were players like Jean Faut, who was a great pitcher, a good third baseman and also a good hitter. Jean played for the South Bend Blue Sox. There was Connie Wisniewski, the "Polish Rifle," a great pitcher, a good right fielder and great hitter. There was Doris Sams from the Muskegon Lassies. She also pitched and played centerfield and hit a ton! Then there was Dottie Schroeder from the Kenosha Comets. She probably was the smoothest-fielding shortstop in baseball, man or woman. There were the Weaver sisters from the Fort Wayne Daisies, and many, many more. I don't mean to leave anybody out. Kammie and Sophie did what they did for 10 years straight and many of those players didn't have that kind of playing time. I think the stats will bear me out. You could flip a coin as to who was the best. We were going to find that out in 1946.

Well, my conscience is bothering me and I need to add one more player to the mix, my buddy and my gopher-toothed whistling friend, Alma Ziegler. Alma "Gabby" Ziegler, was the franchise second baseman for the Grand Rapid Chicks. She would dispute what I'm saying, heavily. She'd be the first one to tell you that her bat always had a hole in it. She had trouble hitting her weight, and she didn't weigh much! But, you know what? She could do all the little things at the plate that it took to beat you. Like laying down a bunt or getting a walk when you needed it. She wasn't above sacrificing her body and sticking out a leg or an arm and taking one for the team. Then, after she got on first base, she'd steal second. She had a great arm and was probably the best fielding and smartest second baseman in the league. Then after all that, she'd step up on the mound and win you 20 ballgames. She had a fast, hard-breaking curve ball, a pretty good fastball and great control. Besides that, she had a heart as big as Yankee Stadium. Now, how about those apples?

In 1946 they made some big changes in our ballgame. They lengthened the base paths to 72 feet and they pushed the mound back to 43 feet. They lengthened the season from 107 ballgames to 113. The pitchers were actually starting, unofficially, to throw sidearm because it was difficult to throw effectively from that distance underhanded. They also went to an 11-inch hardball specially made for us.

It didn't matter to Sophie how far apart the bases were or how small the ball was or whatever way the pitchers were throwing. She stole 201 bases for us that season. Imagine 201 bases in one year! She would go on, in her 10-year career, to steal 1,114 bases. (Eat your heart out, Ricky Henderson!) When she got on base, you could just move the monopoly piece to third base. It was automatic and, remember, she wasn't wearing sliding pants, not even long pants, just a short little skirt with satin shorts underneath. When she had plenty of time, she would slide on her socks from the knee down, but if the play was close, she couldn't do that.

Most of the time in baseball, you steal on the pitcher. A catcher can have a shotgun arm and not get the runner, if they've got a great start. I think in my career as a catcher, I only got Sophie once, and that was at third base, when she slid past the bag. Of course, Sophie says, "In your dreams, Pepper, in your dreams."

My pal, Marnie, was at first base, and she made us all look good. Until I joined the Belles, I hadn't realized how really good she was. Not slick and spectacular like some, and maybe a little awkward-looking in fielding the ball. But all you had to do was throw the ball in the direction of first base and Marnie would come up with it. Flapping that pancake glove, she'd snag that ball out of the air, or surround it in the dirt, and somehow she'd always come up with the ball, and with her foot on the bag.

It was really scary how much I was enjoying myself. I was having fun playing shortstop again. To make things even better, we had a great little catcher, so I didn't have to worry about getting back behind the dish, and getting "bit" again! We had Irene "Choo Choo" Hickson, as some of us called her. She was from Chattanooga, Tennessee. I don't think she was more than 4 feet tall. I probably weighed more than her when I was born! She was tiny in stature but she was tough. Some of the other teams called her "Tuffy."

That ought to tell you something.

She had a pretty accurate arm and was definitely a smart catcher. When she ran she pumped her arms and legs straight up and down. Somehow it reminded you of a choo choo train, thus the nickname, "Chattanooga Choo Choo," given to her by her teammates. She kind of reminded you of "Mammie Yokum." Nobody seemed to know how old she was, and she wasn't about to tell. Her face was a little wrinkled and weather-beaten. She said that was from the sun. Nobody cared about her size or her age because she played like she was 16, and 10 feet tall.

As I said, we were very strong down the middle and we were a great all-around defensive team. We had a good, hard-hitting outfield behind us. We had shy Ellie Dapkus in right field, a big, raw-boned country gal. She could hit with power. Then she'd come in and pitch when we needed help on the mound. Ellie and Choo Choo were very close. They were roommates and buddies. It was really kind of cute, sort of a Mutt and Jeff relationship. We'd be having a gabfest after the game, up in their room, or maybe playing a little poker, or maybe crying in our beer if we lost, or bragging if we won. You would hear Choo Choo bawling Ellie out for this or that. Yelling at her for some reason. She didn't mean it, it was just her way. Catchers just sort of like to have the last word. If Choo Choo kept it up, we would hear Ellie finally say, "Shut up, Choo Choo, or I'm going to put you in the drawer."

Now, that would usually shut Choo Choo up. I always laughed at that, thinking that Ellie was kidding. But you know what? One night Choo Choo wouldn't shut up and Ellie really did it! She grabbed Choo Choo, pulled out the middle dresser drawer (those hotels had pretty good-sized dresser drawers), stuffed Choo Choo in it, legs and all, and shut the drawer. She actually did it! She shut the drawer! I was astounded. We heard this pounding and screaming, and scratching. "Let me out! Let me out! I'm going to kill you, Ellie! I'm going to kill you!"

Ellie just stood there calmly and said, "Are you going to be good?"

There was a long silence, then we heard a meek little "Yeah."

Then Ellie said, "Are you going to be quiet?"

Another exasperated, "Yeah."

Ellie said, "OK, but one word and you're right back in the drawer." And she opened the drawer.

Well, Choo Choo just stuck her legs out and let them hang there for a minute, cooling her temper down. Then she crawled out, her face beet red, but she never said another word. (That night anyway!)

The Racine Belles really turned out to be a bunch of great gals. Joannie Winters and Anna Mae Hutchinson were our two ace pitchers. Joannie threw a solid assortment of junk: up, down, in, out, curves, change-ups, drops, plus a mediocre fastball. Her secrets were a lot of heart and good location. In other words, she never threw it where the batter wanted it. Anna Mae's strength was her sidearm, cross-arm delivery and speed. We also had a Canadian, Dodie Barr, on our staff. Dodie was a typical lefthander. Her secret was that she couldn't throw the ball straight and she had a great, spinning rise ball.

Then Ellie would come in on the mound and throw some steam when needed. It was great to have three good pitchers on staff in the All-American. We had Claire Schillace in centerfield (she was a fleet-footed, fly-catching genius) and Edie Perlick in left. Edie was fast in the field and on the bases, and swung a powerful bat. We had just the right combination of chaperone and coach for this savvy veteran team. Our chaperone, Willie Wilson, was beautiful, as well as a great gal; and Pop Murphy knew all the right buttons to push. I found out that I had the Racine team pegged all wrong, after I got to know them. As the old saying goes, "Don't judge a book by its cover!"

Two Infield Newcomers Spark Belles' Assault on First Place

Paire Fills In for Absent Catcher

RACINE, July 25—(Special)—Two reasons the Racine Belles are currently engaged in a red hot battle for the lead in the All-American Girls' Professional Baseball League are LaVonne Paire and Betty Trezza.

Both are new to the Racine roster but neither is a stranger to the fans who follow the activities of the league.

LaVonne Paire, better known as "Pepper," got her start with Minneapolis in 1944, and quickly developed into one of the best shortstops in the league. She hails from Los Angeles, Calif. "Pepper" bats and throws right handed. She is 5 feet, 4 inches tall and weighs 140 pounds. She was born May 29, 1924.

PAIR WERE TEAMMATES

When Ft. Wayne took a franchise in the All-American Girls' League in 1945, replacing Minneapolis, Paire went along. She continued at shortstop and the final statistics showed "Pepper" second in both fielding and batting in the league. Her timely base hits while in the Racine lineup both as a shortstop and catcher have helped the Belles climb to second place.

Paire's catching experience acquired with Minneapolis was put to use during the past few weeks when Irene Hinkson, regular receiver, was called home because of the fatal illness of her mother.

Mrs. America to Join AAGL *1947*

Beauty Contest Winner to Train in Cuba

Max Carey, president of the All-American Girls Baseball League announced today that Mrs. John Acker, the present "Mrs. America" of Anderson, S. C., has signed a contract to play ball in 1947. Mrs. Acker was chosen from hundreds of contestants as the most beautiful married young woman in the United States, and is at the present time touring the states as a model in fashion shows in each city she visits.

Mrs. Acker, who is a sister of Viola Thompson, for three years one of the top hurlers in the All-American circuit, will report for spring training at Havana, Cuba, on April 21st.

Carey stated that "Mrs. America" comes from an athletic family and typifies the All-American sports girl. "I give her a good chance to win herself a position on one of our eight clubs," he said.

Newspaper article about Americans in Cuba!

Jimmy

Marnie Danhauser
"Our local IST Sacker"

American Team in Cuba 1947

210

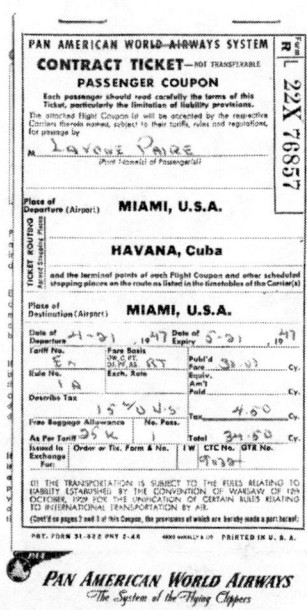

Airline Ticket to Havana

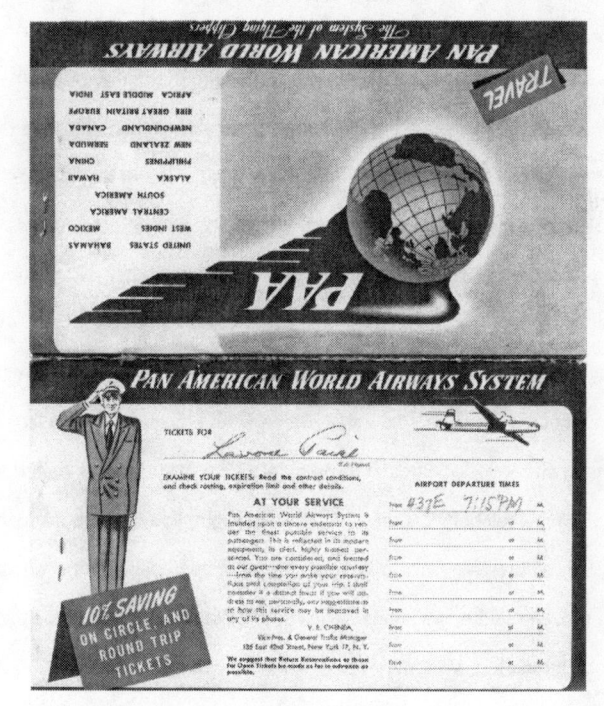

Chapter 23
For Whom the Belles Toiled

The year was flying by. We were winning games, and you always have fun when you're winning. I was still playing a great shortstop and hitting well. By this time, it was clear that the "All American Girls" had taken the Midwest by storm. We were the most popular game in town. Our attendance was growing by leaps and bounds. Our team was stronger than ever because my little rookie friend from Fort Wayne, Betty "Moe" Thezza had been traded to our ball club. Betty was from New York and she would prove to be a more valuable player than we first realized. Right now she came in as a backup shortstop and she doubled in the outfield when Ellie came in to pitch. She was fast on the base paths and could lay down the bunt. She occasionally hit the ball with power. Being small, she was tough to pitch to, so Moe was definitely a help to our ball club.

By now, I had established a tradition of breaking in the rookies. One way to do that was to drive out to the cemetery, which was on the outskirts of town, late at night. It would be after the game to show them this phenomenon called the "Rising Tombstone." It was actually featured in "Ripley's Believe It Or Not" column. So we took Moe out there after the ballgame one night. As we turned into the cemetery our car lights hit the side of this big hill that was covered with hundreds of tombstones. There it was, right in the middle of that big hill. One tombstone that would appear to magnify and rise up into the air, radiating all kinds of flashes of color. It got larger and larger as it rose up, and then, just as you turned toward it, it would suddenly disappear.

It really was a fascinating and scary sight! So we backed up again to get it in our sight again. Then we told our little rookie, "Now wait, Moe." (And Moe really was a little rookie.) She was about 5 feet tall and weighed about 110 pounds. She had curly black hair, dark Italian eyes and a shy smile. So we'd tell her, "Listen, Moe, if you get out, you can see it a lot better!" We'd all get out. Well, her big brown eyes were about as wide as pumpkins, but she took our word and she climbed out. Of course, we jumped back in and slammed the door. I shoved it into low gear and we pulled out on her. We left her alone in the graveyard at midnight! Well, she started screaming at us and we're howling with laughter, and I shoved it into second gear. Then we heard the pounding of feet, and little Moe went by us like a streak of lightning! Those little Italian legs were pumping up a storm. So we knew Moe would make the team because she sure could run!

Moe was from Brooklyn and came by her nickname honestly, because she called everybody "Moe." She taught me a song that she used to sing. It's called, "I Come from Brooklyn" and goes like this:

> I come from Brooklyn,
> And Brooklyn is outta dis woild.
> I come from Brooklyn,
> Everyone dere is hard-berled.
> President Roosevelt thought it was great,
> He was going to make it the 49th state.
> I come from Brooklyn,
> And Brooklyn is outta dis woild.

Well, Moe was a little out of this world, too! She fit in perfectly and was going to prove to be a necessary component in a winning situation.

Life was great in Racine. We had the perfect coach for our team in Leo "Pop" Murphy. He knew his ballplayers and let the vets pretty much do their own thing. He took charge of the rookies and the ballplayers that needed to work and learn. He was a great motivator for everyone. We would all go to practice. But it was mostly just hitting practice for us vets. Sometimes we worked on other things if we were having a problem. Usually, we would have a little bit of a skull session and then we would head for breakfast or lunch at the Ace Grill.

Larry Lowe, our number-one fan and a buddy of the coach, would generally take us there. He hauled us all around town. Actually, he was there whenever we needed a ride. He was a short little heavyset guy, built kind of like Danny DeVito. He was quiet and reserved acting. He had this little round face and just kind of said, "Huh?" once in a while. But there wasn't anything he wouldn't do for us gals. He was a real great fan! If you needed something done, wanted to know anything, wanted to go somewhere, just ask Larry, and he was right there. Larry was one of those wonderful fans that I think the baseball players of today are missing. Most players today don't have that kind of loyalty. Basically, they don't have it because they don't give it. They don't have much personal contact with their fans.

Anyway, as long as we kept a low profile and kept out of sight, we could pretty much do whatever we wanted (those of us you could count on). Our chaperone, Willy Wilson, was great! She was a beautiful black-haired Hedy Lamar type of gal. She had been a model before, and also a ballplayer, so she knew the ropes. She knew just how far to let us go, and when to draw the line. We were all giving our best on the ballfield! Oh yes, one more thing, we were all dedicated to beating the hated Rockford Peaches and winning the whole works!

On the weekends, when Jimmy was off work, we would go fishing. He'd tie a quart of beer to his toe and drop it down in the lake and we would happily fish away. And neck a little bit, too. Of course, sometimes when the fishing was slow, the necking wasn't. That was great, too! But I also knew when to draw the line. My mother had taught me to save the best for my husband and I did! Of course, I didn't know that Mrs. D was watching us with unapproving eyes. Trouble, though out of sight, was ahead in more ways than one. Jimmy's and Marnie's dad had died young and the kids were Mom's pride and joy. Jimmy had been their father figure for a long time and Mom D. wasn't about to give him up to a redheaded Hollywood gal who was an unconventional, worldly ballplayer.

I was blissfully unaware of all this at the time, and life was sweet until out of the blue came the fly in the ointment. Our catcher, "Choo Choo," got her foot stepped on and broken. She was out for the season. Our backup catcher couldn't throw back to the pitcher. If we were going to win, we needed a catcher. Nobody in the league would give us one. So, once again, I proved that I earned the title to wear the tools of ignorance (as catchers' equipment is jokingly called) and I stepped back in behind the plate, quietly leaving my beloved shortstop. If we were going to win I had to do it. I knew it and so did everybody else on the ball club. I defy anyone to ever say that I was not a team player, because I was from start to finish.

Fortunately, little Moe could play a good solid shortstop. She also had the arm to do the job. So she covered my position at short. What could have meant a devastating loss to the team barely caused a ripple. Only I knew and realized what I was letting myself in for. I will say this, however, as time went by, I did grow to love catching. I wouldn't advise anyone to be one, unless you're a glutton for punishment. You get hurt all the time, and you have to play hurt! To me, catching is the most important position on the team. That's not because I wound up being one; that was always my opinion.

They say that pitching is 75 percent of the game, but many people, including me, disagree with that. Pitchers are very important, but they only pitch one to two games a week. In the big leagues the catcher is out there every night. Physically and mentally, it is tough. They've got to handle the young pitchers and steer the game that's laid out in front of them. The catcher is as important to baseball as a goalie is to hockey. Goalies look like armored bugs. They turn themselves inside out and crawl all over that net to keep the puck out. It's fascinating to watch them. They get the wins, of course, but they get the blame too, if they lose!

A good catcher could qualify for a degree in psychology! You really need the couch to keep the pitchers performing. You have to recognize their temperaments, and deal with them. You handle all of them in different ways. Give them what they want. It's really the manager's job but if you have a catcher that can handle it, that takes the pressure off the manager; that allows him to deal with the other problems. A good catcher plays a heads-up game all the time, like the time we played the South Bend Blue Sox in Racine, after I took over for Choo Choo.

It was a Sunday afternoon doubleheader and the games were being broadcast. All our home games were on the radio in Racine. We played the first game and won. Then, the broadcaster, Don Black, did a dugout interview between the games. He interviewed Sophie Kurys, our second baseman, Claire Schillace, our centerfielder and me. He complimented me on my timely hitting and taking over behind the plate. Then he asked me about our pennant chances?

Well, I answered enthusiastically, "Yes, I'm Pepper Paire and we are going to win everything, and we have a doggone good team, and we have a doggone good manager and chaperone, and we're going to win the doggone pennant!" I sounded like a little munchkin. The reason I know this is because, incredibly and miraculously, that tape survived and surfaced all these years later. It reads like a Pepper Paire commercial.

That particular Sunday afternoon, the second game captured what I mean about catchers having to have brains. The South Bend Blue Sox were definitely a running team. They had a bunch of rabbits in their lineup. I had to be able to nail them if we were going to win. This one inning they had "Shoo Shoo," their speedy shortstop, on first base and the gal on third was their outfielder, Lib Mahan. Lib had stolen 114 bases that year. Shoo Shoo had 88. You don't throw through to second base if Shoo Shoo runs because we didn't want the runner on third base to come home. So, I walked out to the mound and said: "Let's set up this play for the cut-off play, but I'll throw to second. Fake a cut off, then let the throw go through. I've got a hunch that the runner on third won't try to score."

Sure enough, old Lib was asleep at third base and didn't move. Shoo Shoo was just sort of nonchalantly drifting down to second base and we nailed her. We got the next hitter out, and lo and behold, we got out of the inning. You usually don't take the chance of throwing with runners on first and third with less than two outs, because the runner on third would usually score if you did. But, in this case, I out-thought them! Later on, in the same game, the situation repeated itself, with the same runners. I knew it wasn't going to work again. So, I walked out to the mound meeting and said, "Let's set this thing up again, but I'm going to try something different."

Well, sure enough, Shoo Shoo takes off. This time, she's ready and she's really hotfooting it to second base. Meanwhile, Lib is all set at third, chomping at the bit. She's determined not to get caught napping again. I fake a hard throw to second base, following through with my arm but hanging on to the ball. Lib breaks for home plate and I turn and snap a throw to third, and we pick her off. You don't see that play pulled off successfully very often, even in the majors. On the tape, you can hear the crowd screaming and you can hear the announcer shouting over the noise, "What a great play that was. Pepper set them up, folks!" He explained it to the crowd.

I played that tape for my son the other day and I told him, "You hear that? You hear what he's saying? Your Mom was a pretty good ballplayer."

He said, "Mom, you were a regular Pete Rose."

I said, "Thanks, but I don't think I have some of his personal habits." Incidentally, I was still catching with a finger mitt, because a catcher's mitt at that time was a huge pillow with a tiny little pocket in the center. No hinges, no webbing. You had to use both hands to catch the ball. But with that finger mitt I could dig the ball out of the dirt or snag it one-handed if it was a wild pitch. However, it was tough on the fingers and hands. My hands would be like raw meat when the game was over. But it did the job. That's one of the reasons I can point in so many different directions now, with one finger at the same time. My fingers are not exactly digits of beauty. But even with those fingers I could still throw to second on the line and on one knee, which wasn't too shabby. My bro, Joe, still says, "Sis, if I had an arm like yours, I'd have been in the majors."

It was undeniable that Sophie was our leader. Every-thing offensively was geared around her and she'd let you know if you crossed her. You could accept it from her because she always put her money where her mouth was. She was a very smart player and she was usually right. "There goes Sophie after her trophy!" they would say. You know what? She got it! I gave them the hustle and heart and the RBIs they needed, by driving Sophie in, 'cause even Sophie couldn't steal home, well, not too often anyway. I turned out to be the hitter that consistently drove those ducks on the pond home.

The pitcher's mound was moved back again that year to 43 feet and sidearm pitching became legal. I only hit .216 that year (good for our league) and there were a lot higher averages than mine. But, I drove in 59 runs, a lot more than the higher averages and big swingers did. I was second in RBIs in the league and one of the main reasons the Racine Belles had a shot at winning the whole enchilada in 1946.

In that magical year, even bus trips were fun, and we had a lot of them. Most of the time, we had to ride all night long. Our superstitions played a part in that too. Like when you would pass a bone yard (cemetery to you guys), you crossed your fingers. (Well, that's worked so far for me. I still do it.) Now I cross everything I can cross! When you passed cows lying down that meant it was going to rain, and it usually did. If you passed horses and saw a white one, you kissed two fingers on your right hand, slapped them in the palm of your left hand hard, and then slammed it with your fist (that meant base hits). The more horses, the more hits. It seemed to work. Of course, you <u>never</u> stepped on the chalked line on the ballfield. There were many more superstitions, I'll tell you about some more of them later on. The strange thing is, they really did seem to work. Like I said, I don't know if we really believed in them so much as we used them as crutches. They took our mind off technicalities and allowed us to relax. That's probably a lot of what they really did. It helped that we were in farm country and there were a lot of cows and horses around. We also sang and played a lot of cards on the bus -- whatever it took to get through the long night and get to the next town. I guess I could include here the song I wrote about road trips, "We're on a Road Trip":

We're on a road trip,

A lovely road trip.

We'll travel all night long,

We lost our ballgame.

Ain't that a darn shame?

We'll talk about what went wrong,

Later on, we'll sing a song.

It's tough to lose when you tried so hard.

Forget those boo's,

Come on and let's play cards.

And yet the memory lingers,

Forget, but cross your fingers.

Here comes another bone yard.

The cows are lying down on the ground.

Look there's a bridge we're going under.

Listen to the thunder, here comes a train.

And you know darn well,

That cow can tell -- It's gonna rain!

The town is dead ahead,

But we won't see the bed!

A doubleheader's on the menu --

Shake off the rust,

Stay on the bus —

Get into uniform

Come out and play two!

Rumble, rumble, rumble!

Well, we had just left on this 10-day road trip in August. We were going down to Muskegon, Michigan, and we had to pass through Chicago to get there. To go through Chicago meant you had to go through Gary, Indiana, and by the slaughterhouses. We always dreaded that! That smell could wake you out of a sound sleep. On top of that, Murph informed us that we had to make a stop in Chicago to pick up a passenger. He was being very mysterious about the whole thing. He told everybody not to go to sleep because we had to stop anyway. He made a special trip back just to tell me, "Don't go to sleep now," and he had a funny look on his face.

Well, I just assumed that it was a ballplayer that we were going to pick up. Someone who wanted to try out, or maybe a league official? Pop kept checking on Marnie and me, making sure we stayed awake. I said grumpily to Marnie, "What's the big deal? You'd think Wrigley was joining us!"

She laughed and said, "Maybe it's the president?"

I hollered up at Pop. "Hey, Coach, is General Eisenhower going to join us?"

He turned around, grinned at me, and said, "Well, it is military personnel, but he is much more important than a general."

We were all pondering that one and getting really curious. By the time we pulled up in front of Union Station in Chicago, everybody was wide awake and sitting up. We were staring out the windows, anxious to see who this mysterious military visitor was. Straining my eyes, I saw this soldier coming toward the bus. He was dressed in an Army Air Force uniform with his hat pulled down over his eyes, and I could see his stripes. "Well," I said, "he's only a staff sergeant. That leaves Ike out."

Then I looked again. He was still 50 feet away, but there was something so familiar about that walk. My heart started pounding, "Oh my God, could it be?" I jumped to my feet, "Oh my Lord," I hollered. "Marnie, Marnie," I exploded. "It's my brother! It's my brother!"

I climbed over her and went running down the aisle with happy tears running down my face. I reached the front of the bus just as the doors flew open and there he stood. His officer's hat off now, that curly black head was looking up at me with those big brown eyes and a huge smile on his face. (I have to stop writing now and wipe the tears from my eyes. It still overwhelms me with joy, all these years later.) I jumped off those steps. He dropped his bag and hat and caught me in his arms and we just hugged and hugged. I was sobbing with joy and tears were running down my brother's cheeks. I couldn't even talk.

He finally untangled me, put me down on the ground, patted the top of my head, and said, "How's my baby sis?"

I answered in between sobs, "Wonderful, just wonderful, now!"

It was one of those moments in a lifetime you never forget. The overwhelming joy in my heart threatened to strangle me. I grabbed him again just hugging his chest, trying to control myself. It was as if a huge weight had been taken off my back. My bro was home. He was safe. God was good. I grabbed his hand and said, "Come on, let me introduce you to everybody." The gals were all hanging out the windows and whistling and laughing, and some were crying, too. Some of their loved ones hadn't come home from the war.

We climbed on that bus, and I was gabbing like a fool. "Everybody, everybody, this is my bro, Joe! The most wonderful, the most handsome, the bravest, smartest guy in the whole world." Everyone was talking at once. I gave Murph a big hug and a "Thanks!" He had taken the phone call from my bro and set the whole thing up. Joe was with us that whole road trip. That was one of the few times in my life that baseball was sort of secondary.

Of course, I had to show off and play great for him. Luckily the road trip included Fort Wayne so I was able to introduce him to Tex. Faye had some big hugs for him. She was happy because her bro, Richard, was coming home, too! Tex had eyes for him. In fact, all the eligible girls were very eager to please Joe. He could have had his pick. But I could tell he was holding back. He was very polite and very nice to everyone, but not really interested. When I asked him about it, it seems like that little gal in St. Louis still had the strings to his heart. He didn't want to mislead anybody. I guess I knew then that the St. Louie woman was going to be my sister. What I didn't know was how lucky that was going to be for me!

Those days flew by, and Joe had to leave and return to St. Louis to be mustered out. Then he was going home to see Mom. We burned up the telephone wires talking to her on the road. It was so wonderful all being together again. We won eight out of 10 games on that road trip and everybody wanted to keep Joe. But he had to report back. I came back to Jimmy in Racine. Our team was in first place, and I was the happiest that I'd ever been in my life. The

Belles were riding high! All of us were of one mind and one thought. First, we were going to win the pennant! Then we were going to win our World Series! We had grown close together as a team now. Even when we were at home, we practiced together, we ate together and we spent our spare time together. We had fun being with each other like a real team does.

We had a lot of fun with Maddy, our little Boston gal. We really gave her a bad time about her accent. We always made sure her fork was missing when we ate at a restaurant. Because when Maddy innocently asked a waiter for a fork, it turned into an X-rated conversation. The waiters' eyebrows would rise way up and they would say, "A what?" Maddy would blush, then spell it: F-O-R-K. She once called an umpire a bastard and got away with it. It came out like "Bastud." He thought he was being complimented.

We wound up that season winning the pennant easily and then we headed into the playoffs. We had Mrs. Momentum on our side and we made short work of the Daisies in the first round of the playoffs. Then we headed into the World Series with, well, who else? The Rockford Peaches, of course, and my old enemy -- the nasty, wily, Silver Fox, Bill Allington.

Winter 1947

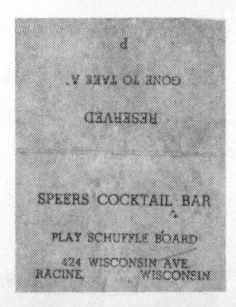

Racine - 1946

Brother Joe & Me- Racine- 1946

Chapter 24
The Catcher Who Didn't Drop The Ball

We had a celebration dinner at a prestigious restaurant in Racine. All the big shots where there, including Bill Wadsworth, president of Racine's "Western Printing." He was the board chairman of the Belles. At that time, Western Printing was the biggest printing company in the United States. Judge Kenshaw and Gib Lance came in from Kenosha to honor us. They were both on the board of directors for the Kenosha Comets (the Comets never did win anything). Kenosha was just 10 miles outside of Racine, so it was <u>almost</u> like winning for them. The Kenosha Comets were headed up by Judge Kenshaw, who was one of the founding fathers of the league, and Gib Lance, who was one of the original guys behind Jockey shorts.

Now that I think back, I guess we were probably the first women to wear Jockey underwear? Unofficially, that is! I don't know when they actually came up with marketing designs for women, but I know it wasn't until years and years later. I do know that in 1944 they made them for men and then they modified them for us, with a few necessary changes to make them acceptable for women's attire. They did that especially and exclusively for us All American gals. (Another first! Wake up, Jockey, what a great advertising campaign that could be: "Jockey shorts have always been in "A League of Their Own.")

Anyway, it was a fabulous dinner. You could order whatever you wanted. I ordered prime rib, which was my favorite (rare, end cut!) Murphy taught me that you get a lot more for your money when you order an end cut. It's charred on the outside and rare on the inside. (Boy, I wish I could chew that now!) It was a great celebration. Before the night was over, the whole town turned out for a parade around that famous fountain in front of the hotel.

Once again, I'll point out that the ballplayers of today are missing a lot. We made a whole town happy, and they all wanted to thank us personally. The admiration in their eyes and the happiness in their voices compensated us far more than money ever could. For a brief moment, they forgot their grief and their hardships and reveled in pure joy and pride at our accomplishment, in their name! What a gift it has always been to be able to make people happy.

Jimmy, Marnie and I wound up in the wee hours of the morning, sitting on the end of the pier, watching the beginning of another glorious sunrise on Lake Michigan. This time Jimmy had a bottle of champagne (instead of our usual beer) tied to his toe and dropped in the icy cold water. We toasted the brilliant, colorful sunrise and raised our glasses to the Racine Belles, 1946 League Champions! How great that sounded!

Then we returned to the house and Marnie and I rested our weary bodies. Poor Jimmy headed off to work. But he had a big smile on his face. It was Wednesday and we had two days to go until the series started with Rockford. Murphy let the vets rest while he went over everything with the rookies and the reserve players. The pitchers threw a little and ran a little just to stay loose. Everybody had to report early Saturday morning to go over the signals and take hitting practice, including the pitchers. They had to practice hitting, too. Especially their bunting, so they could be counted on to help themselves at the plate at the right time. Major leaguers could learn something from that.

Everything was sold out! The radio and papers were full of us. They even added 500 temporary seats to the first base and third base lines. Excitement hung in the air all over town. And then it was time. Saturday night was the kickoff game of a seven-game series. It was our ace, Joanne Winters, against their ace, beautiful Carolyn Morris. Carolyn was a model in her own hometown of Phoenix, Arizona. Carolyn was gorgeous on the mound as well. She had a windmill delivery, very fast, and a rise-ball that fooled you, coupled with a beautiful change-up. When she was on, she was almost untouchable.

We had our ace going, our warhorse, Joannie Winters. Joannie had sort of a sidearm delivery, along with an assortment of pitches that dipped and ducked and backed up. She had a big, wide-breaking curve, a rise-ball, and pinpoint control. Her pitches ranged in speed from medium to slow. But her fastball appeared to be faster because of her ability to change speeds. Her secret was never to throw it where the batter wanted it. Inevitably, they would beat the ball into the ground and we had the defensive team to handle it!

Joannie threw well against Carolyn in that first game and we won it 3-2. It was a good tight ballgame. But, even though we won, one bad thing happened during the game. When I was going for a pop fly by the batting rack, I stepped on a glove and twisted my ankle. I gutted it out and finished the game, but by midnight my ankle ballooned out. I soaked it all night but it was a bad one. So, every night before the game they would spray my foot with a little bottle of silver nitrate and freeze it. Then they'd tape it up. I couldn't get my spike on, so I had to wear Murphy's size 12 spike on my left foot.

Then, every night after the game they would rip off the tape and I would sit up all night, soaking it in the tub. My ankle became raw meat before it was over. I had to bat for myself and run out the hit balls. Bill Allington reluctantly agreed to that, since we didn't have a back-up catcher. If I got on base safely, I could have a pinch runner. In the second game I hit a triple down the third base line. It rolled so far even my grandmother could have circled the bases twice. I fell down at least three times and barely got to third. I couldn't feel my foot hit the ground, and that threw me off balance. (After I got back home that year, it took almost three months before I could walk normally again.) Anyway, we took the second game by one run, 2-1.

We headed for Rockford. The next two games were to be played there. Then we would come back for two more in Racine. If necessary, the final game would be decided in Rockford. It was a best four-out-of-seven series. One thing I knew was, the quicker we could get it over the better for me! I knew I was doing a lot of damage to my foot and ankle. By the seventh inning, the freezing would wear off. I wound up in a lot of pain every night. I didn't know how long I could hold out. Well, we played those two games in Rockford and split them with the Peaches. They were both one-run ballgames.

We headed back to Racine for the next two games. We now had three games in the bank and we only needed to win one of the two at home to win it all. I prayed it would be the first game. My leg was getting really bad. The only way I could sleep was to down two or three beers until they knocked me out. There were no painkillers to take. You just didn't do that. Aspirin didn't touch the damage I had. Unfortunately, we lost the first home game. Again by one run, 3-2. So, as we headed into that sixth game, I prayed harder. "Oh Lord, please, if we have to travel back to Rockford for that last game, I just don't know if I can do it!"

Joannie was pitching again, against Carolyn, of course. It was her third game in four days. She already had 30 wins and 19 losses that year. Overworked was putting it mildly. Before the game started, I came out to the mound and pounded that ball hard into her mitt. We looked wearily into each other's eyes and spoke with our hearts, "We've got to do it tonight." Our whole ball club was tired and beat. We knew if we didn't win this one, we were in trouble. We all joined hands on the mound and I said, "Let's hold them for Joannie, everybody," I was answered with a chorus of "Yes!"

We all knew it had to be tonight. We also knew that it wasn't going to be easy. When Joannie pitched there were always a lot of balls hit. Very few walks and very few strikeouts. But the balls hit were usually catchable, and that's what we had to do. Joannie was in trouble from the first inning on. She was letting them get two or three on base almost every inning. Miraculously, we kept them from scoring and kept getting out of the innings.

Carolyn, well, she was just breezing. Her fastball was dynamite and she was hitting the corners and throwing it right by us. By the ninth inning, we still had not been able to get a hit. Carolyn was pitching a no-hit, no-run game against us. They had 11 hits and no runs. Dottie Kamenshek, the Rockford Peaches' first baseman, got four hits herself in that game. She was on third in the ninth inning with one out and they tried the squeeze play. We got Kammie at the plate! Bill finally pulled Carolyn in the 12th inning for a pinch hitter. We were glad to have her out of the ballgame!

That game went on for 14 innings. Our pitcher Joannie went the distance, giving up 15 hits and zero runs. They had 19 runners left on base. We had five hits with five runners left on base. I got six runners at the plate and four of them were on squeeze plays. We nailed them all. I remember we made some fantastic plays. Our left fielder, Edie Perlick, went way back, leaped up into the air and caught a ball we thought we'd never see again! Marnie was all over the place, snagging desperate last-second throws from diving infielders. Joannie herself got three of the runners at the plate.

Finally, in the bottom of the 14th inning, Sophie got a single. Of course, she immediately stole second. Then, even with two out, that sucker Bill walked me again. Little Moe came up to the plate. She hit one off the end of her bat and shoved it through the infield and Sophie came home to score. We wound up winning the game 1-0, and the World Championship was ours!

Branch Rickey, the general manager of the Dodgers, and Max Carey, who was now the president of our league, were at that game. They both agreed that they had never seen a better-played ballgame in the big leagues, or anywhere else -- by man or woman. We beat the great Rockford Peaches in six games. They were always the most dominating team in the league. There was no doubt about that! They won more championships than anyone else! But they didn't win <u>that one!</u> They had a great team, from their wily, silver-haired, foxy manager to their fine first baseman, Dottie Kamenshek.

Kammie had 109 stolen bases that year and a .319 average. That was like hitting .419 in the majors. She had a lifetime .292 in the All American for 10 years. The last two years she was going to the University of Marquette in Wisconsin and getting her master's degree. She would arrive just in time for the ballgames, go in cold, without any batting practice, and still play a great game. It took a lot of talent to do that. Wally Pipp, Yankee H.O.F. first baseman, said she was the best fielding first baseman he had ever seen -- man or woman. Kammie turned down offers to play AAA baseball because she thought it was just an attempt to capitalize on publicity. Besides, she was making more money in our league. She was a complete ballplayer and for me that is the ultra-best compliment you can give a ballplayer. There are very few complete players in baseball today, despite the millions they make.

Rockford also had the best shortstop in our league, in my opinion. They had fellow prune-picker, Snookie Harrell. After I went to catching, that is (a little joke there!). She had a good arm and was a beautiful, natural infielder. She was so smart and so quick. She could field the ball and get rid of it faster than anybody I ever saw. She had a strong sidearm throw and just flipped the baseball very accurately to first base. Snookie could also hit the ball with power and got her share of base hits, and she hit when it counted. She ran the bases well and she could lay down the bunt and steal a base when you needed it. She could slide well and think well!

We had some other pretty good shortstops in the league, like "Teeny" Petras of the Grand Rapids Chicks, Dottie Schroeder of Kenosha and Fort Wayne, and "Slats" Myers in Peoria. They were all good infielders. But, in my opinion, none of them could do it all -- hit, run, think and throw -- as well as Snookie. So, all in all, we beat a very fine team that year. The Racine Belles earned that championship!

It was like a dream come true, and when it was over there was a happy ending to the baseball story. We were hometown heroes and I stayed some extra time in Racine to bask in the glory and heal up a little before going home. Jimmy and I were getting closer and closer and Jimmy was becoming more open about his feelings for me. As happy as I was about that, I saw problems coming. I would catch Mrs. D looking at me with a funny look at times, and it didn't look friendly. She never said anything but her actions showed me she didn't approve. She didn't want to lose her Jimmy and I really couldn't blame her.

Jimmy and I talked about it and he straight-out informed me that he would never leave Racine and his mother. No Hollywood for him, but he saw no problem with my living in Racine. He was unaware of his mom's feelings! I really couldn't picture this California gal stepping out to get the paper in her shorts in December and sinking down to her buns in snow. So, while the baseball had a happy ending, I knew that the romance was going to strike out. I think deep down inside Jimmy knew it too.

Marnie had a similar problem. The guy she was going with and engaged to gave her a big rock and he wanted her to quit baseball, get married and settle down. Like right now, or yesterday! He had given her an ultimatum. So, she decided to come to California with me and end her romantic relationship. She knew it wasn't going to work out. When we left Racine that day in September, Jimmy and I tried to pretend that everything was OK, but we knew it wasn't. It was a long goodbye and a very hard, hard hug. We smiled our tearful goodbyes. It had been a great roller-coaster ride for me that summer, but I knew that I probably was getting off here, or if I wasn't, Jimmy was!

I took comfort in knowing my wonderful brother was home safe! My wonderful baseball triumph had made me happy, but in the pit of my stomach there was that big cold rock. I knew that my "pie in the sky" romance was over. Mrs. McGillicutty wasn't around, but once again, I cried a lot of silent tears when the lights were out. Marnie was feeling the same way, so despite her mom's objections, I knew that it was good for her to take a California vacation.

We passed on the streamliner because neither one of us felt like socializing and splurged on plane tickets. We both needed to get out of Racine. Marnie had never been to California, so this was a bold adventurous step for a small-town gal. She was very quiet on the

229

plane. I knew she was nervous about meeting my folks and staying in a strange new place. I told her not to worry and I promised that my Mom and Pop would love her and she would love them. When they met us at the airport, my Mom spread her wings and took us both in her arms, and Marnie's doubts flew out the window. Pop was pleased, too. He had someone new to talk to. And little bro Russ, well, he was smitten with my shy, brown-eyed beautiful pal. In fact, everybody was. Marnie was such a sweet gal and a great pal! You couldn't help but love her.

Mom was just full of plans for us. She wanted to introduce Marnie to all our available bachelor friends, of course. But first we just wanted some R & R. Since September in California is still definitely beach weather, we took full advantage of that. We went down to the Santa Monica Beach, lay in the warm sand, basking in the California sun, and carefully picked up a Hollywood tan at the same time. It took awhile but I was finally walking without pain. Marnie's heartache was healing and so was mine, so we finally started having fun!

I didn't worry about going to work that winter, like I usually did. Mom said that the defense plants could get along without me. She loved having me be a ballplayer, but missed me when I was gone. So I just took my time, let my body heal and showed Marnie the town, introducing her to family and friends. Financially, things were better. Pop was now a foreman at the shipyards, and the good times were starting to swing on down the road. We lived that one block off Wilshire. Two blocks down Wilshire from us was a unique restaurant called "The Toad's Inn." It was a historical monument because it had been there a long time. It was actually built in the shape of a large toad.

Mom knew Lil Rosen, the owner, real well. In fact, she and Mom were great pals. Lil was a good lady and a lot of fun. So sometimes, Mom, Marnie and me would go over there, play cards, drink beer, dance and just have a good time. It was small and had a friendly atmosphere and Marnie was comfortable there. It reminded her of her hometown. Lil would cook special things for us, like chicken livers and gizzards for Mom and Marnie (while I was saying, "Ugh, ugh, yuk, yuk"). She'd make a chiliburger and fries for me. She was a great gal.

One night, I was waiting at the pick-up counter for our food and beer and, as usual, I was saying, "Ugh, ugh, yuk, yuk," making fun of the chicken livers, etc., when I heard this deep voice behind me say, "I agree, yuk, yuk." I turned around and stared into the most electric blue eyes I had ever seen. The owner of those eyes was dressed in an Army uniform and definitely tall, dark and handsome. He quickly removed his hat as he laughed at me and said, "Hey, let me carry that for you." He grabbed my tray that now held four beers and a couple of chiliburgers and the "yuk, yuk" chicken gook on it. He knew right where to go and carried the tray to our table in the back room. I followed him, thinking, "Well, this boy's not bashful!" Then Lil introduced him to us and it made sense. "This is Norman, Jackie's brother. You know my waitress, Jackie?"

Well, Jackie was also a close friend of Mom's. I started to tell Norm who I was and he cut me off. "I know, you're Pepper, the ballplayer, and this is your friend Marnie." He took Marnie's hand briefly, but he was staring straight at me when he said, "So glad to meet you ... " Then he looked down at Marnie and said, " ... both." He was really cute. One wavy lock of black hair dipped down to his eyes and there was a smile in those eyes. Then he flashed his white teeth at me saying, "I've heard about you, gal."

My heart skipped a beat! I replied, "And I've heard about you. You're Stormin' Norman."

He laughed and said, "OK, OK, so my sis has been talking!"

Hey! Well, it was happening again. I had the butterflies. I was always so surprised and pleased when a handsome man took an interest in me. I could never figure it out, but I was always very grateful. I didn't think I was that good-looking. Joe and I used to talk about how neither one of us thought that we were attractive. I knew my bro was handsome but he didn't realize it. I guess I wasn't too shabby either. Many people told me I looked like Ginger Rogers. I can see the resemblance now in the old photos, but I didn't believe it at the time. One thing I did know was that I was over Jimmy because of the way I felt when handsome "Stormin' Norman" looked at me!

Carolyn & the Peaches
greet a fan.

Bill & his Rockford "Pitchers"

Carolyn Morris- Beauty Queen
Peaches-1945

Murph-telling us like it is
1947 Bells Opalocka, Florida

Faye DANCER

THE RUNNER IS SAFE

DANCER DUST

PEORIA'S CALIFORNIA SLUGGING OUTFIELDER. SHE'S ONE OF THE LOOP'S TOP HOME RUN HITTERS, PLAYING HER FIFTH YEAR IN THE LEAGUE AND HER SECOND SEASON HERE... HER SPEED AFOOT SWIPES MANY BASES.

PICK ME AND YOU'LL HIT A HOMER

HAS LOTS OF CHATTER AND TEAM SPIRIT, WHICH MAKES HER A COLORFUL PLAYER. HER LONG PEGS FROM DEEP CENTER TO HOME HAVE CUT OFF MANY OPPONENTS' RUNS. EASILY IDENTIFIED BY THE WAY SHE WEARS HER CAP AND DIAMOND SOX...WEST LOS ANGELES IS HER HOME.

1947 Peoria, Illinois
Faye Dancer

Chapter 25
Stormin' Norman

We had a lot of fun that night, Norman asked me for a date for the weekend. He told me that he had a good buddy who was a nice guy for Marnie! So we said OK to the double date. On the way home that night, Mom told us more about Norman. I knew that he had been in Hawaii (in the Army) but I didn't know he had been on the Bataan Death March in April 1942. The Japanese marched our boys 63 miles in five days and then put them on a Japanese prison ship. Then he survived a three-month journey in the hull of a Japanese prison ship to Japan. He spent another year in a Japanese prison camp before he was finally found and freed.

Much has been said and written about how unfair it was to put Japanese-Americans in prison camps in California during the war. It broke up their families, and in some cases they lost their businesses and homes. I definitely agree that it was very unfair to the local Japanese-Americans, the ones that grew up here. The ones I went to school with. I'm sure things could have been handled a lot better. But, in all fairness, there wasn't much time. How could our government do anything else? It was later proven that many of the Japanese pilots who flew those Zero planes, had gone to USC and UCLA. (Surprise?) That's what brought Pearl Harbor down. The government couldn't very well make appointments and interview everyone who was Japanese, check out their birth certificates, and ask, "Are you a spy? OK, I'll take your word for it." They had no time. Invasion was on the way! I do not condone the inhuman treatment, or the seizing of their land, and I'm ashamed of the Americans who did that. But I can tell you this, when Norman finally was able to talk to me about it (and it was a long time before he could), when you compare what was done to him and our American boys, I think the Japanese in America got off easy! The Japanese have never financially reimbursed any American for their loss of life, or sanity, or anything else. I guess we're just supposed to pay because we won the war they started.

Norman and I became an item, and I told him about Jimmy. He knew we had problems and that I wasn't totally committed to Jimmy. He also knew that I was attracted to him. He told me that he would wait until I sorted things out. Day by day, we grew closer. Marnie and I had fun dating but she grew homesick and wanted to go home for Christmas. She was over her guy, too. In fact, I bought her diamond engagement ring for $200 so she could fly home for the holidays. Mom never had a real diamond ring, so I gave it to her for Christmas. Marnie wrote me after she got home and let me know that Jimmy was moving on, too. He was making his mom very happy by seeing a local gal whom he had gone to school with. She was a strict Catholic. That made Mom Danhouser even happier.

So the summer romance was over, and it was clear sailing for Norm and me for a while. Once again, I thought maybe I had found the right guy. But there turned out to be a fly in the ointment, as always. Norm wanted to get serious right away. After what he had been through, he wanted to enjoy life as much as he could. He was already thinking about a home and children. Who could blame him? He felt that life was short and that you needed to live it while you can. But I wasn't ready to commit. I wasn't ready to quit my baseball. 1946 had been such a great year I wanted to bask in the glory a little longer and maybe help Racine win another championship at the same time.

Norman finally agreed to wait and give me another baseball year and we were both happy. One beautiful thing was that Mom loved Norm. She thought he was the greatest. The feeling was mutual. Norm loved Mom and was very good to her. It was great fun to include her in a lot of our dates. Dad was still working nights and Russ was 16 and had interests of his own. So, it was clear sailing for Mom. We had a lot of good times together. Mom couldn't wait for us to get married. She and Norman talked about it all the time. How we were going to have a little girl and name her Tessie after my Mom. I told Mom that she had to teach her to cook and I'd teach her to hit! We told Norm that he could just stand around and change diapers. We had a lot of laughs about that, but he was ready, willing and able to do whatever I wanted him to do.

The next thing I knew, the time had rolled around again and even though I was having a great time, deep down inside, that old baseball itch was starting. I had to admit to myself that I was excited and anxious to start the new baseball season. I had to report early because I found out that we were going to Havana, Cuba, for part of the 1947 spring training. Wow! What a thrill! Larry Lowe was driving Pop Murphy down to Florida, so I flew to Racine, and Marnie and I rode down with them. Larry knew people in New York, so we stopped over for two days and saw some of the sights. It was my first time in New York City. What a thrill it was to see and touch the Statue of Liberty. Marnie and I took the elevator part way up and then climbed those narrow winding steps all the way up to the torch. I'd never make it now, even if they would let me. What a glorious feeling it was to stand in the palm of that lady's hand, look out over New York and Long Island, and thank God for America and our freedom.

The league had made a deal with the Cuban government to tour Havana. It was called a goodwill tour. What a laugh! It did get us a lot of publicity, but things weren't as glamorous as they were cracked up to be. We stayed at the Seville Biltmore Hotel. It was the best hotel in town. The food was good, but eating wasn't much fun. If you sat on the balcony and looked over the rail, there would be a woman nursing her baby with small children huddled around her. There would be hungry eyes staring at you, while the mother held out her hand and said, "Leche! Leche!" (which means "milk"). We gave them whatever food we were eating and whatever change we could spare. It got so bad that most of the time we just ordered food in our rooms, because there were just so many of them and we couldn't help them all. We learned there were only two classes of people there: the very rich and the very poor. The military ruled for the rich. We also found out that the majority of Cubans hated Americans. That was 1947.

May 1947 ... that's when I learned that May Day was Communist Day. We almost didn't make it through that day. All the hotel employees took the day off and they even shut the power off at the hotel. We only had flashlights and the candles the Army had furnished us. The soldiers surrounded the hotel to protect us. We didn't understand that until we saw what happened later. We had to make ropes out of sheets and bedding to lower baskets to the street vendors to bring up fruit and beer. You didn't dare drink the water! What a beautiful excuse! But, hey, I was thirsty, not dirty! We thought it was funny for a while, until we found out what was really going on. We didn't know what the heck it was all about!

May Day in the United States was just another springtime holiday, but we soon found out in Cuba it was about communism and hating American capitalists. That was us -- American capitalists. And we didn't even know it! We didn't know why they hated us. People gathered on the rooftops of the surrounding buildings and we found out what obscene was. The guys dropped their drawers and proceeded to put on a pornographic show aimed at us that would have made Howard Stern blush! We finally realized that we were surrounded by a mob of angry communists. That was a bad day, and scary, too!

It wasn't all bad, we did have some good times in Cuba. When we first got to the hotel we had a lot of laughs. We noticed that they had two toilets in the bathrooms. One was a regular-looking one and the other one was kind of a narrow and streamlined-looking one, with no lid. We just figured that was probably for the men when they didn't want to sit down. There were also no doors on those bathrooms. One of our gals decided to try the new toilet just for fun. We heard a flush, then we heard a scream, and then our gal comes running out, screaming: "It's broke! It's broke! Help, help! It just shot water all over me! It's overflowing!" Well, we unsophisticated, innocent Americans didn't know that it was a European toilet called a "bidet."

There was an Americanized restaurant in Havana called "Sloppy Joe's Bar" that made the greatest sandwiches you've ever tasted. They were about 6 inches tall. Cheeses, ham, roast beef, with all the trimmings, piled high on this great hand-pounded, homemade rye bread. They took a picture of us and put it on the wall right next to the <u>Dodgers</u> and the <u>Yankees</u>. I wonder if it's still there! The <u>Dodgers</u> and the <u>Yankees</u> were there at the same time for their spring training and we actually outdrew them. They were also playing exhibition games and we had thousands more people come to our games! Now, how about that?

In Cuba at that time the power was in the hands of a select few. The poverty was something I had never seen before and never want to see again. We felt so sorry for those poor women who sat on the pavement holding their scarecrow babies with their little potbellies and begging for milk, "Leche! Leche!" Somehow the people showed up by the thousands for our games. I don't know where they got the money for the tickets. They would just go wild when things started happening. Such as hitting the long ball, running the bases, and so on. They got especially excited if there was physical contact. They loved to see blood, and they got it. One of our Canadian gals slid into home plate and caught her spike and broke her foot. The way her foot twisted around was sickening. It was twisted clear back with the toes pointing backward. I can still hear the crack and pop and her screaming until mercifully, she passed out. Well, I'll tell you what, the crowd loved it. They roared and went wild. No wonder they love bullfighting. The sight of blood whipped them into a frenzy!

That, indeed, was a spring training to remember! We bought loads of all those wonderful liqueurs: cream of banana, cream of cocoa, cream of cherry, cream of strawberry and all the wonderful rums. It was very, very cheap. Faye, Tex and I really loaded up on it, thinking about having some wild parties. Nobody told us you could only bring home two bottles, then the duty laws and the taxes kicked in. You had to pay so much duty on them! That made them too expensive to bring back. Boy, I bet those customs workers sure had a party when we left there.

Well, that did it! After witnessing all that hatred and the communism and the poverty, we counted our blessings and just wanted to get off that island. We'd had enough of Cuba, for the time being anyway. When we hit the U.S. shore, we were glad and grateful that we were Americans. We didn't even mind the exhibition games and the bus tour back to Racine. It was great to have Americans rooting for us and to be able to understand them and not to have them screaming for our blood. Incidentally, Cuba's resentment started long before the JFK incident, long before his showdown with them, but no one in our government seemed to know it! Or maybe it was that they didn't want us to know it! The government just turned a blind eye to the situation (kind of like Pearl Harbor). It's no wonder there was trouble coming in later years!

When we got back to Racine, we opened the season on a winning note. Choo Choo was back behind the plate. My ankle was healed, and I was back to short. It looked like the Racine Belles were going to win another pennant, or at least have another shot at it! I was injury free for a change and ready to have a good year. The whole team was healthy, for a while anyway. We cruised along, easily staying in second place and within striking distance of first place. However, living at Marnie's now was a little uncomfortable, for both Jimmy and me. Old memories kept popping up. However, as time moved along, it grew easier to put things behind us. That, I think, is the great thing about being conservative sexually, like we were in my era. You don't wind up with all the emotional baggage that you might have otherwise.

Eventually, Jimmy and I were able to forget about our romance and enjoy each other as friends. We enjoyed being in each other's company. We still had a lot of things in common. We always had a good time going fishing, bowling and having a couple of brews together. I lost a boyfriend but gained a friend and things turned out fine. I even became friends with his new girlfriend, and Mom D? Well, she was happy as a clam. She could now like me wholeheartedly. I could feel her resentment drop away. Personally, life was definitely looking good.

The 1947 baseball season, however, was going to wind up being a disappointment. Sophie hurt her knee and went down for the count, halfway through the season. While Moe Trezza came in from centerfield and played a great second base, she couldn't supply the offense Sophie did. Nobody could! The whole team seemed to lose its pop and go into a mental funk when Sophie went down. We weren't the only team with problems. The Fort Wayne Daisies had encountered problems, too. Secretly, I kind of reveled in that one. "Trade me, would you?" I thought they had it coming.

Halfway through the season, things got so bad in Fort Wayne that they were dumb enough to trade both Tex and Faye in an effort to change things. "How about that? Trade off two All Stars." Well, things changed all right! Tex became the "All Star Catcher of the Year for Grand Rapids." Faye went to a very happy Peoria team and became the "All Star Centerfielder." Meanwhile, Fort Wayne headed straight to the bottom. They received inferior players in the trade and that just made things worse. We all had a big laugh out of that one.

I didn't laugh for long however, because the second half of the season without Sophie became a big struggle for Racine. As often happens when a team is having a bad time, the team became divided and we started losing a lot of games we should have won. Our board of directors was very unhappy with our year and we got the feeling things were going to change. I hoped that they didn't blame Murphy and cause him to lose his job.

Even though we still finished second, we got knocked off early in the playoffs in the first round by South Bend. I went home early. I was so disgusted I didn't even hang around for a little R & R, fishing and partying. Of course, it helped to know that I had an eager Norman waiting for me in California. I didn't have to have a guilty conscience now about falling in love with him. My ever-loving Mom and my family were always so happy to have me home; it made me feel like a million bucks. So, for a change, I was not reluctant to leave when the season was over. I was happy about it. I had done my part. I played a great shortstop, hit .226 and was second best in the league, driving in 50 runs — even without the great Sophie on base. So, no one could blame me, could they?

By the time I got to California, I was ready to put that 1947 season behind me. I stepped off that streamliner and there was Mister Blue Eyes waiting. He took me in his arms and whispered in my ear, "Are you my Pepper now?" My answer was to grab that lock of dark curly hair, pull his face down to mine and whisper, "Yes." Well, he planted a big loving, long, long kiss on my lips that took my breath away. Coming out of it, I saw my Mom's beautiful face over his shoulder and broke away embarrassed and hugged my Mom. The happy look on her face said she didn't mind waiting and that she approved. Oh yes, Mom definitely approved of Norman!

As usual, it was wonderful to be back home. Seeing Mom's happy face always made me feel great. That was one of the wonderful perks about being gone so much of the time. It was always such a treat to get back home again. Everything was new again. Things never got dull or tedious. We didn't have time to get mad at each other and quarrel like some families do. Because of Norman, things were even more special this time. I had never met a man like him before. He was so kind and so gentle, and yet so strong and firm when he had to be. I had to be careful, because if I mentioned anything I wanted, he'd buy it for me, or make it happen. He wanted to give me everything.

Mom shared in everything with us. It was like a dream, too perfect to be real. Norm wasn't working yet. He was in therapy after his war experience, and I knew he still needed it. Sometimes there would be a tone in his voice and a cold look in his eyes that scared me a little. There was a dark side lurking inside him somewhere. It was always a momentary thing and then he would flash those white teeth and the love would reappear in his eyes. Mom said it would go away. The government was giving him some sort of settlement for what he went through. I never did know the details there. Just that he had money and didn't need to work at that time.

That made everything fun because we got to go places and do fun things all the time. We could go to Las Vegas or to the Hollywood racetrack. Naturally, we went to the ballgames. We could go to the beach and down south to Tijuana. Norm gambled quite a lot and he gambled big! He usually won. I worried a little about that. How long would that winning streak last? Then there was his drinking. While I dearly loved my beer, and Mom did, too, we usually just drank in the right places at the right time. With Norm, it was always the right place and always the right time. There were some warning signs lurking, but I would put those thoughts behind me. Because by this time, I felt this was a man I could marry, settle down with and be happy.

Hiding behind all that blue sky, there were clouds. I knew that I was not ready to give up my baseball yet. I also knew that Norman (though he denied it) wasn't really in a position to settle down. He was staying at his sister Mickey's place, waiting for his complete settlement from the government so he could get a house. Also, he still had to finish his therapy. Mickey's apartment was right across from us so we had a perfect setup! Norm had a 1937 two-door Ford convertible and he let me drive it while he drove his sister's car, which worked out great for me. Having transportation I decided to get a job before Christmas and make some extra spending money. I didn't want to keep freeloading off of Norm and Mom and Pop for everything, even though they wanted me to.

Hughes Aircraft in Culver City was advertising for all kinds of electronic help. Faye was back home, too, so we decided to give it a try. They were advertising top salary for experienced electronic technicians. There was a lot of extensive interviewing, much more than we had ever gone through before. We wound up getting a job because we had the experience they wanted. Apparently, they investigated everything about us, right down to how many fillings we had. We went to work as electronic assemblers in what they called the "White Lab." It was an isolated building where they did special research and everything was a secret.

We had to wear white lab coats over our regular clothes, white gloves, and we were carefully checked in and out at work. Actually, we were X-rayed when we went in and out. (I wonder how much cancer we picked up from that?) We found out that the project we were working on was for Howard Hughes himself. He was personally involved in it. It was this huge wooden airplane. Sound familiar? Yep, that was the "Spruce Goose." We had no idea what was going on or what a Spruce Goose was. I thought maybe it was something you stuffed for Christmas. What we did know was that we got paid good money and it was an interesting job. We heard that Hughes himself would be coming to see us. Then we thought, Wow! Hey! This must be some special kind of job.

There were only a few of us gals working there, along with about 20 guys. That was all the personnel in the whole building, besides the security. Then one day, sure enough, here comes Howard Hughes with all these dark suits around him, guys with nervous eyes. He worked his way up to our table, talking to people on the way. We were pretending to work, but secretly I was looking at him and I thought, Hum! What a handsome man he was: tall, well-built, dark hair slicked back in the very popular style of the '40s. He wore a pin-striped suit, also a very popular style in the '40s. He didn't need the shoulder pads. He had big brown eyes and was very soft spoken.

He worked his way around to our table, picking up a P.C. board or a plug here and there, examining the parts and examining the work. When he got to me he stopped. He looked at me, smiled, and said, "Well, well, how are you, Pepper? How's baseball these days?"

I was floored. I had a nametag on, but it said Lavone A. Paire, my given name. How did he know? I was so flustered I stumbled all over my words and mumbled something dumb about the Dodgers.

He raised his heavy, beautifully shaped eyebrows and stopped me cold, saying, "Oh, no, I mean <u>your</u> baseball, Pepper."

My mouth dropped open and I eked out a faint "Fine."

He smiled at me and, seeing my confusion and embarrassment, took pity on me and turned away. Wow! How about that? Howard Hughes knew my name, and he knew that I was a ballplayer? Once again, that strange pattern of association with famous people had established itself. It turned out not to be as big of a mystery as it seemed. One of our bosses told me that Howard Hughes always went over all the personal files of everyone who worked in this special white lab. So, he had all the facts. Every time he would come to our building, he made a point of stopping at our table and talking to me. I took quite a ribbing about that. I don't know if I imagined it, or if he really wanted to ask me out, but I had the feeling that he did. He always seemed to make leading remarks like, "What movies are playing around town? Where's a good place to have dinner?"

I felt like he wanted to ask me out and if I would have shown a little personal interest of any kind, he would have asked. I didn't respond because I was totally in awe of him and I had Norman! So, I just kept my head down and my eyes on my work and answered, "Yes, sir. No, sir." Then he would move on. I didn't let my "Pepper" personality show at all. Seems like that might have been a good thing though, who knows what might have happened? The way Howard Hughes' life turned out, I might have ended up on a couch somewhere in some psychologist's office. It might have been a rich couch, but my life might have been totally different. Anyway, perhaps it was all in my mind. Heck, maybe it was just the red hair that made him keep stopping.

About the Spruce Goose ... Some of you might remember how Congress tried to nail Howard Hughes for fraud. They claimed he was just ripping the government off and that this huge wooden airplane would never get off the ground. Well, its true purpose always was that it was meant to be a flying laboratory that was ground-based. The laboratory part was what was important, not the flying part, but Hughes showed them. He got in that big "rubber ducky" and flew it around in the Los Angeles Harbor, and that was that! He shut those big-mouthed senators up!

We also worked on this huge experimental helicopter. It could pick up a loaded freight train car on one side of a mountain and set it down on the other side. It would prove to be a huge military asset when fighting in rugged, impassable terrain. I don't remember its name. It had a long military-number name. What I do remember is the day they tested it in Culver City at our plant. We were invited to watch the test on the airfield right there. We were standing behind a huge chain-link fence next to Hughes and his accompanying security. You could almost reach out and touch this huge thing. It looked like something out of Flash Gordon. (For you younger ones, that was one of the original space heroes from the 1940s, maybe even the 1930s.)

Anyway, this big thing looked like a huge grasshopper, with a spinning hat. When they started it up, I felt a big vibration and heard a deafening rotating roar. It picked up that loaded freight car and moved it about a hundred feet and then set it down right in front of us. The wind was blowing and the ground was shaking. We had white smocks on and Howard was dressed completely in white, from his Panama hat right down to his shoes. That's a frozen picture in my mind, his face smiling at the success and oil splattering all over him from head to toe. His white suit was polka dotted with oil. Seems it was normal for machinery of that kind to throw off a ton of oil. Howard didn't care. It was a success! Howard Hughes was such a brilliant and wonderful man. It was so sad that he died such a tragic death! They do say that being a genius is just a hair away from being insane! Who knows? Maybe that's true?

Spring training
Havana, Cuba

Spring training
Havana, Cuba

Stormin Norman

Racine Belles At Spring Training
1948 Havana, Cuba
Pepper Second From Right

Chapter 26
The Crash -- And I Don't Mean Wall Street!

My Hughes job was so interesting and, with everything else going on, I stayed pretty busy in the winter of 1947! We worked out every Sunday at Brookside Park in Pasadena. They had a big baseball complex there. The major leaguers moonlighted in the winter and played there for some big companies like the Ford Motor Company and Signal Oil. It was just a little semi-pro baseball league, but players didn't have the million-dollar salaries like they do today. They played year-round and made some extra spending money that way. So, while California didn't have a big league ball club, we did have some big league stars in town in the winter. We got to meet some of them because we were invited to dinners at the Sports Ambassadors Club in South Pasadena.

Ziggy was acquainted with the guy that ran it. I remember when Ziggy, Faye and I were invited to a banquet that was held to raise funds for the 1948 Olympic Games. (What a dream night that was!) We met Joe DiMaggio, my hero, and Ted Williams, the "Splendid Splinter" and "Stan the Man" Musial, and many other great sport stars. The secretary of the Olympic Games gave a speech, asking us to support them. Then they asked me to sing our league song that I had written in 1944. I got a standing ovation.

After dinner, the secretary of the U.S. Olympic team came over to me and asked if I could adapt my song for them. Well, of course, I was thrilled and said yes. But it wasn't going to be. I simply never did get the changes made and get back to the Olympic committee. Actually, I think that turned out to be for the best because that way it remained our All American League song only. Somehow, it seems that's the way it ought to be, because all these years later the movie "A League of Their Own" came out. It was just natural for the song to be in it. It was brand new and all ours! The real reason I didn't get it done was because Lady Fate stepped in again.

When I was driving home that night from the banquet it was raining. I took Faye home first, then came back up to Wilshire Boulevard to get to my house because Santa Monica Boulevard was flooded. It was raining very hard. I was driving Norm's little 1938 Ford convertible. It had a built-in safety feature in the ignition to keep it from being stolen. When you turned the key off, it would lock the steering wheel! Well, they had had some troubles with that, but I had never given it a second thought. I was in the inside lane with the rain pouring down on the windshield and I could barely see. I decided to cut over because oncoming traffic was splashing even more water all over my windshield. I turned the wheel to pull over to the outside lane and when I went to turn it back, it wouldn't turn back. It locked up! I tried again desperately, but it didn't budge. I was going maybe 30 to 35 miles per hour and I tried my brakes. I tried to put them on gently but the car started skidding sideways. I could see the parked car up ahead that I was going to hit. There was nothing I could do. So I ducked my head down, held on hard to the steering wheel and kept trying to put the brakes on. There was a brilliant explosion when I hit and everything went black.

The next thing I remember, I was in the hospital. I could hear people talking at the foot of the bed and I could hear my Mom's trembling voice, "Oh my goodness, my poor little girl! Oh, please God, please make her be all right!"

I could hear her sobbing and I tried to raise my head but a brilliant flash of pain hit me. I spoke out, "Mom, I'm OK, I'm OK." My voice sounded hollow and far away.

Breathing, "Thank you, God! Thank you, God!" Mom put her arms gently around me and it felt so good. That's the last I remembered for a while! I had some broken ribs and 21 stitches in my head. They told me that hanging on to that steering wheel probably saved my life. It kept me from being thrown through the windshield. I was in the hospital for 10 days; then I went home to my own little bed and my Mom's loving care. It took another week before I could get up and move around again. There I was, up and around, with stitches in my head counting down the days mentally, because it was time.

It was time to go to spring training. I knew I had to get moving and I knew I'd have a battle on my hands this time because Mom and Norm were dead-set against me going, especially now that they had an excuse. They were constantly bombarding me with words like, "You're too ill, you shouldn't go, you'll hurt yourself even more," and so on. That's all I heard from them, but my own gut was telling me I needed to go. If I didn't go, I knew my baseball career would probably be over, and I just couldn't accept that. Deep down, I wasn't ready to marry Norm. Maybe that was part of it and I didn't know it. But I did know I had to go. Spring training was only three weeks away.

I really didn't have time to heal, so I faked it! The doctor put a brace on my knee and I tried not to limp when Mom and Norm were looking. The stitches in my head had dissolved, but the doctor had to put some back in because there was too big of a gap in the gash. He said it might require plastic surgery if he didn't. Fortunately, the gash ran across my left eyebrow and in the middle of my forehead. It just looks like a wrinkled brow line. I was very lucky. Mom was really concerned and used every excuse she could think of to keep me home. She told me that I had a great job and I shouldn't give it up, and she had a point there! I really didn't know how to get out of that one, but it was solved for me. My boss at Hughes came to see me and told me there would be a job waiting for me when I got back in the fall. So, that was handled. I got my way. Norm and Mom finally gave in because I reminded them that they had never seen me play in the All American. I wanted them to come back, see me play and be proud of me before I quit. Mom had wanted that for a long time and I knew that. We just couldn't really afford it before. So, they both finally caved in and said, "OK, one more year!" And they both were excited at the thought of visiting me and watching me play!

So in 1948 I found myself on a plane headed for Opalocka, Florida, for spring training. My ribs were still taped and my knee was still stiff and very sore.

I still had 17 stitches in my head. I had to wear a bandage over my stitches to protect them from the elements, but I made it and I was happy about it! My baseball blood was flowing again, as always. I was visualizing another great year in Racine, going fishing at the lake, doing all the fun things, and, of course, winning the pennant again -- not knowing that the road ahead was still rocky and would prove very difficult to travel!

When I got down to Opalocka, Florida, I found out that our spring training site was at a naval training base. (Shades of Pascagoula!) Oh, my Lord, I thought, but the Navy guys were still there, so everything turned out to be class A. There were barracks and a mess hall, but it was not like Pascagoula. Everything was sparkling, military clean, and the food was great! The Navy always has the best food. At least in the '40s and '50s they did! It was kind of nice being surrounded by all those cute little swabbies in their tight, little bell-bottom pants. When I was down there I learned why sailor's pants have 13 buttons. Not for the original states as you might think! It's because you've got 12 chances to say no! And I did!

Right about then, I had all the romance in my life I needed. Fact was, I was missing Norm and wondering if I had made a mistake! I was really hurting from my injuries and the rugged pace of spring training only aggravated my knee and my ribs more. I was gimpy and, although I tried to hide it, I guess it showed. I was missing Mom's tender, loving care. Mentally and physically, I really had to push myself.

Oh yeah, besides being a military base with a lot of cute servicemen around, there was something else that Opalocka had in common with Pascagoula, and that was critters! Everywhere you went they had these little bugs that looked like crabs crawling along sidewise. They called them crawdads. Well, I didn't care what they called them and I didn't like them going to the bathroom with me. No matter how clean everything was, they were still around. I guess they came up out of the water and had to be endured. Everybody laughed and said, "Oh, they won't hurt you. They're good eating." Well, I didn't want to eat them and I didn't like to go to the bathroom with them. But I did endure them.

Then came the capper! I was put on the block again. I couldn't believe it. I was betrayed again! How soon they forget. No matter how much I had done for them, the town fathers in Racine didn't want a shortstop with a gimpy knee. They weren't willing to wait and see if I'd be OK, no matter how many championships I helped them win. I found out about the trade when Pop Murphy came to see me at midnight the night before the camp broke. He told me that I'd been traded to the Grand Rapids Chicks. He had tears in his eyes when he told me. He said: "Pepper, I know this is unfair, and they're making a huge mistake here, but I couldn't stop it. Just know that me and the team will miss you a great deal."

I hung my head down and cried with him. He put his arms around me and whispered in my ear: "Just remember this, Pepper, great players get traded because everybody always wants them. If you weren't any good, they wouldn't want you. I know you're going to make them sorry." That night when I laid my head down on my pillow and turned the lights out once again, I vowed through my tears, "You bet I will, Murph. I'll make them sorry." And I did! That year, the Chicks were going to beat out the Belles for the division championship and I helped them do it.

In fact, the Belles were never again to be a contender -- just like the Fort Wayne ball club never did much winning without me.

The sun still came up the next morning and I found myself wearily climbing up the steps of the Grand Rapids Chicks' bus. All of a sudden Ziggy swooped down on me, "Peppy," she squealed. "Peppy, we're finally on the same team. Give me that duffle bag. I've got a seat saved." Looking up at her beaming smile, things didn't seem so bad. I had forgotten that my buddy Zig was a Grand Rapids Chick. She turned back to me in the aisle, "How's my fat little redheaded friend?" she laughed.

I broke into a smile and replied, "I'm just fine, and how's my gopher-toothed whistling pal?"

Right about that time, another head popped up and I heard that familiar Texas drawl. "Hi ya, Cacapot. It's about time you got here! Now we've got a team!" It was Tex. I forgot she was a Chick now, too! Well, we high-fived all around. (It wasn't called that then. We just "slapped hands.") I knew most of the gang already and Zig introduced me to the ones I didn't know. The blues were dropping away again. I was welcomed and wanted and, by golly, that was something to be happy about. Murphy's words came back to me. Maybe he was right! Wow, Tex and Zig and me on the same team! Back together again. Life wasn't so bad after all and we definitely had a good team. I knew I was going to miss Murph and the Belles, particularly my brown-eyed buddy, Marnie, and Maddy, my cute Bostonian third sacker, and all the rest of the team. But, hey, I'd see them when we traveled and we'd find a way to get together. I was confident of that!

I was a Grand Rapids Chick now, so I settled right into that Grand Rapids nest and was ready to do my share! Our coach, Johnny Rawlings, was another ex-big leaguer. He played in the National League from 1912 to 1925. He was a very smart man and a good teacher. The trouble with Johnny was that there was no letup with him and he had a very poor sense of humor. He was a small, rangy-looking guy, white (gray) hair, with slitty eyes. You could never tell what he was thinking. He narrowed those eyes even more when he was talking to you about baseball. He'd get to talking real softly, like he was telling you a secret! But, I'll say this, if your hearing was good and you were listening to Johnny, you could learn a lot!

The trouble was, his disposition needed help, and he was a tough, tough taskmaster. He didn't forgive or forget mistakes. Usually, he would make you pay for them. Our chaperone was a Canadian, Dottie Hunter, and what a great gal she was. Dottie had been a ballplayer and she quit because she thought she was too old for the game. She was perfect for the chaperone job. She had a fiery disposition and wasn't afraid to tell you off if you were wrong. Dottie could take charge, but she also had a soft side. If you needed help, you knew she would be in your corner. She had black, curly hair, snappy brown eyes and a great smile. Those eyes had a twinkle in them, unless the fire showed up, then stand back!

Dottie was an attractive, well-built gal, and a lot of coaches tried to hit on her. She handled it and put them all in their place: "Hey, I'm a pro, why don't you be one, too? Sex doesn't go with the job. You do your job and I'll do mine." It always worked for her (maybe because she did her job so very well). Dottie was not only a great chaperone but she was a strong authority figure. She knew how to handle us gals. She knew when to bend, but she would never break. In the years to come, she and I became close personal friends, but it took a while. I used to constantly challenge her. Nothing good ever comes easily. That's something you learn with age.

When we got back to Grand Rapids, I settled in with Tex at the home of the Sullivans. They were a big friendly Irish family. They had a huge two-story, wooden-frame house with lots of space, lots of bathrooms and all the luxuries. Tex had been there for the last couple of years. We were rooming with Corky Olinger, our shortstop, and Dorie Ried, our centerfielder. Corky was a friendly gal, but a little naïve. She was from Ohio. She was very cute with curly brown hair and eyes to match. They crinkled when she smiled. I kidded her about being curvaceous, like all us good shortstops. Corky covered the ground at short and she had a strong arm. Not too great with the stick, but she could bunt and run.

Dorie was a mousy-looking, little blond gal who never talked much. She probably weighed a hundred pounds soaking wet. She had a way of looking down and appearing very shy. Dorie had rather expressionless eyes. You never knew what she was thinking. When you got to know her, she was a lot different! That little mouse could really roar when she wanted to. Dorie covered centerfield like a blanket. She was very fast and had an adequate arm. She was also good on the base path and she could bunt. But she had a weak stick! I could see why they needed me.

As for my buddy Tex, well, she was aces all the way! Great receiving catcher, good arm and power at the plate --when she got a hold of the ball.

She told me that the Sullivans had this cottage, as they called it. It slept 12 people and was about 90 miles north of Grand Rapids on Big Star Lake. They had their own private bay with two piers, a Chris Craft speedboat and a couple of rowboats with outboards for fishing. We were invited to go there anytime, and I could hardly wait. Mr. Sullivan told me that the fishing was really great. He was a roofing contractor with a very prosperous business. They weren't hurting for money. They just charged us a token rent payment of two bucks a week and didn't want to take that. Most of the time they made us eat breakfast. They kept food there for us. So we had cereal, oatmeal, or whatever we wanted. They were great fans of ours and came to every ballgame. The kids were grown and both of them worked during the day so we had the run of the house.

I fit in just fine with everybody and Tex and I just took up where we had left off, laughing and joking and loving our baseball together. It was even more fun now because we had Zig. Of course we missed Faye! But we got to see her when Peoria was in town!

Since the Chicks had Tex, they didn't need me behind the plate, and they didn't need me at short because they had Corky. But they did need me at third base. They also needed my firepower at the plate. Once again, I filled the bill and proved to be the added ingredient that helped to make us a winning team. It was really good that they didn't need me at shortstop because the knee and the ribs were still healing. My injuries slowed me up and that would have really showed at shortstop. I could handle third base fairly well. Most of the plays were do or die plays, where you had to dive for the ball --- instant reaction plays. My strong arm made up for my slowed-down movement. I was not myself by a long stretch but, being me, I kept it to myself and didn't make any excuses. I tried to act like I was OK. I thought I had everybody fooled, but I didn't know Johnny very well. He knew something was wrong. But since we had jumped off to a good start and kept winning, he said nothing at the time.

Gimpy or not, I still had the bat that talked and drove in runs. It was just like old times. Tex and I were double-dating and having a ball. Better yet, I was with my longtime pal Ziggy. My little gopher-toothed buddy Zig roomed and palled around with our chaperone Dottie. Actually, we called her "Dorth from the North" because she was from Canada. We all learned the Canadian national anthem. Every chance we got we would all stand up and sing it. Even on the bus, just to bug her! I had some great times with the Chicks all year. Later, I came to realize that I was more of a Chick than I ever was a Belle or a Daisy. We were a complete team, and we enjoyed being together -- even on those long bus-riding, butt-busting road trips.

Boy! What we used to put those rookies through on those bus trips! On Sunday mornings, Zig and I used to deliver what we called our "Sermons on the Mound." Reverend Alma "Maudie" Ziegler and pastor Pepper "Augusta" Paire really gave them their "Hallelujah, Lord, I've seen the light!" I think we missed our calling because I'll tell you, some of them really took up religion after our sermons! Of course, our sermons were all about baseball and rookies taking care of the vets, shining shoes, carrying bags, and so on. If they were good and humble, we'd put in a good word for them! We were not being blasphemous and we were not making fun of the Lord. We were having fun with the Lord. We were instilling a team spirit and awareness at the same time. It kept us close together as a team. If they didn't know how already, they learned how to pray. If only to pray that we would leave them alone. I don't think there was a player in the league who didn't pray for base hits.

Then, of course, there were our card games, mostly canasta and gin rummy. They were for blood. There was Dorth from the North and Ziggy against me and the "Big Hook." That was our nickname for Inez Voyce, our hefty left-handed first baseman. She could reach out and snag balls with her big hook glove. The "Big Hook" also had a big hard stick that helped me out in the RBI department. Sometimes we'd get mad if we lost, and sometimes even call each other names, and Zig would wind up throwing the cards out the bus window! Sometimes we wouldn't even speak for a while, only to start laughing at some silly little thing before it was over.

On those bus trips the superstitions really showed up (and we had an awful lot of them). I've never seen a baseball player or a football player or even any athlete who wasn't superstitious, whether they would admit it or not. We had some dillies, as I mentioned before, like if you passed under a bridge with a train going over it, you made a wish and you were supposed to hold your breath until the next intersection. Well, that got dangerous in the country, you could turn blue and choke to death. We told jokes and we laughed until we cried. Sometimes, if we made an error, or didn't get a hit and lost the ballgame, we cried until we laughed. We didn't have portable boom boxes or tape recorders, like we have now, and television was still relatively unknown, so we had to entertain ourselves.

Music was one way we dealt with the hardships on those road trips. When the loneliness and the frustration, and the hurt and the pain got to be too much for us -- or when we made errors that lost the ballgame, or when we got news that something was wrong at home == then we turned to our music.

Some of us had better voices than the others and sometimes we would sing all night long by request. My buddy Ziggy always performed any request, but the request was usually "Don't sing!" Seriously, the requests were mostly for songs that really meant something to somebody, like, "I'll Be Loving You, Always," "Back Home Again in Indiana," "My Buddy" or "White Cliffs of Dover," or other World War II songs. Songs that really made us feel close to home and our loved ones. The music and the superstitions were the crutches that got us through, along with our love for our families -- and our faith in God.

1948 Grand Rapids Chicks

Our Fire Power
Jaynne Bettner
Alma Gabby Ziegler
and Erlene "Beans" Risinger

Our Polish Rifle
Connie Wisnoski

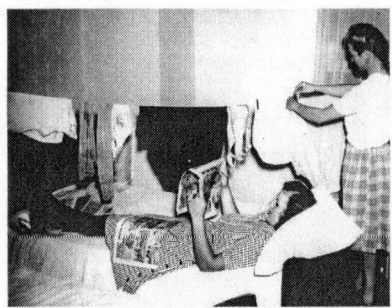

Tiby doing the wash & Whitey loafing

Chow line at Opa Locka

Alma Zieggler- 2nd base
"Grand Rapids Chicks"
The bat with a hole in it!

Alice "Sis" Haylett

Chapter 27
Jaws or A Whale of a Fish Tale

Speaking of the Chicks' road trips, we really had some dillies. Sometimes they would only last two to three days, but sometimes they could last as many as 10 days or more. We were just finishing up this 10-day trip and we wound up having an off day in Racine before finishing the series. It had rained and the field was too muddy to play on. Boy! I'll tell you, that took some doing for them to give us the day off. It had cleared up in the afternoon, but this time, no matter how much gasoline and oil the ground crew poured on and burned off the field, they were still knee-deep in mud. So they decided to call off the game. Incidentally, that's the way the baseball leagues dried their fields in those days (pour on gas and oil and keep burning until it got halfway dry). Lovely for the environment.

Well, I was really delighted because we were in Racine and I managed to sneak out and go fishing with Jimmy and Marnie. I know I've talked about "Chappy Dorth" being a strong lady and being Scottish with a fiery temper, but I don't think I told you about her weakness. She hated and feared fish! Yep, a fish phobia. The only thing she wanted to do with fish was eat them, and with fiendish pleasure, I might add.

As usual, we had caught a lot of fish, so I kept three lively, pretty good-sized perch. I put them in a bucket with some water and sneaked them back to the hotel. We knew Dorth's routine to a tee. We usually had a whole floor at the hotels, so our team would just leave the doors open and wander around the halls. Dorth would make her rounds after the game, check everybody in. She would check on all our bumps and bruises, and see if we had any problems. Then, when she was done, she'd go back to her room and draw this great big bubble bath, jump in and relax for the night. She might even fix a little "toddy" for the body, to help her relax.

This night, she checked on all of us and then went back to her room. When we knew she was there, we had Jaynne, one of our pitchers, call her room and ask, "Gee, Dorth, I know you're about ready for your bubble bath," (which she was) "but my arm is really hurting me." Jaynne was pleading. "I didn't tell you before because I thought it would go away. But it's just getting worse now."

So Dorth put on her robe and went to check on Jaynne's arm. Jaynne faked her injury for a short time, while Dorth rubbed it down and iced it. Finally she said it felt better. While she had Dorth occupied, I had sneaked into her room and deposited those three live perch in Dorth's big old bubble bath. Well, now, "Dorth from the North" came back to her room and, with a sigh of relief, unzipped her robe and stepped into that bubble bath. And here comes these three live perch, "Dum de dum dum," just like "Jaws."

I tell you, there was this loud bloody scream and out the door flew Dorth. She was streaking down the hall yelling, "Oh my God! Help! Help! Fish! Fish! Live fish! Help! Help!" Now, if she'd been yelling, "Help! Help! Fire! Fire!" she might have gotten a response, and that could have been big trouble for her because she was in her altogether, but who answers to, "Help! Help! Fish! Fish!"?

We laughed until we cried. That episode was not to end there, however. She knew I was to blame because I was the only one who had gone fishing. So, I'll tell you how she got even.

In our clubhouse in Grand Rapids, we had three big community showers. About four or five people could shower at the same time in each one. For about three weeks straight, no matter how close I tried to watch, when I wasn't looking, a hand would reach into that shower and give me about three quick hard whacks with a wire coat hanger across the rear end. So, I paid in the end, literally, for those fish.

Those bus trips were exhausting because, remember, we had no days off to travel. So, it was play the game, hop on the bus, ride all night to the next town, hop off the bus, play a game, stop for a short time at a hotel here and there. Then, back on the bus and so on and so forth. We were together so much of the time that if you didn't have a sense of humor and some kind of diversion, life could be tedious and miserable.

As I said before, that's where the music and the superstitions came in. You had to amuse yourself on those 12-hour bus rides and at times everybody did their own thing. There was letter writing, singing, playing cards, knitting and some sleeping, occasionally. But those buses didn't allow much comfort. They had straight-back bench seats and half the time the windows wouldn't open. Then, if you got them open, you probably couldn't get them closed. So we didn't get too much beauty sleep.

Radio was the big thing at the time. But remember, the portable boom boxes weren't around. You had to plug in your radio, and there was no way to plug them in on those buses. So that's why learning the songs, and singing the ones we liked, was what we did! They say music soothes the savage breast (or was it beast?) In our case, I think it was breast, or maybe both!

As for superstitions, we knew they wouldn't change the world, but as I said before, they were definitely our crutches. They helped take our minds off the bad things so we could go out and do the good things. And that helped us to relax. The nicknames and the superstitions were a big part of the whole picture. You could bet that if you didn't have a dirty uniform or a nickname, you weren't much of a ballplayer. I seemed to have it all going for me all the time.

The best thing about the road trips was when they ended! Getting back home after a long one was so great. Kind of like hitting yourself on the head with a hammer, so you could feel good when you stopped.

Tex and I had a great time resuming our double-dating again that year. I remember this one time that she made this date and then changed her mind, which was an old habit of hers. Since I wasn't busy that night, she asked me to sub for her. Remembering Percy Jones Hospital, I said, "Oh no! Oh no, not again." But she pleaded with me, used that Texas charm on me, and I finally said, "Well, maybe. Who is he?"

It turned out that his name was John Dennis. He was a really nice guy, as I remember. Good looking, and everybody said he could sing like Vaughn Monroe. I also remember, he had a beautiful Chrysler station wagon. Vaughn Monroe was a famous bandleader in the '40s and '50s, and I think he's still around. Among his hits you might remember "Racing With The Moon," which I already told you about (we changed it to "Racine With The Moon"). Another of his hits was "Ghost Riders In The Sky."

Anyway, I forgot that I had made the mistake of subbing for Tex before. Well, John comes to pick me up and he's dressed in a beautiful blue suit with a carnation in his lapel. He jumps out and runs around that snazzy blue Chrysler station wagon and opens the door for me. I said, "I hope my subbing for Tex is OK?" and lied about her being sick.

He answered that he would be proud to have me on his arm and held out his hand to assist me into the car. So, I took his hand, which I found cold and clammy. I thought, Oh, what's this? Oh well, cold hands and warm heart. He's probably nervous. So I dismissed it from my thoughts. He closed the door and went around to get in. As I looked up at our bedroom window, I saw Tex and Corky waving at me. I waved back and then noticed that they were both laughing up a storm. That puzzled me and I started to think, uh oh, what do they know that I don't?

I had an uneasy feeling now about the whole thing. But John started talking to me and it seemed like we had a lot in common. I talked him into singing, saying, "Can you really sing like Vaughn Monroe?"

He said, "Well, Pepper, you be the judge." And he launched into "Racing With The Moon" and "Ghost Riders In The Sky." He sounded great, so I joined in and we found out that we sang well together. We were really getting along great when he says to me, "I hope you don't mind, but I have to stop and pick up a box, and then drop it off at my place of work. It will just take a minute." I assured him that it was fine, and that his business came first.

He pulled up in the back of this weird-looking place behind the police station. It had cement walls, with little barred windows high up. I said, "Wow! This place looks like a morgue."

He said, "It is. I'll be right back," and out he hopped.

A guy came to the door, let him in, and now my stomach is starting to churn. Pretty soon, they were back, carrying this big oblong wooden box. I thought, Oh, Lord, please don't make that be what I think it is. But it was.

They loaded it into the back of the station wagon. They shoved it up so close to the seat that I could have touched it, if I wanted to. He climbed back in and said cheerfully, "Poor guy, didn't duck when he should've." Then, he looked at me and saw I was pretty upset. "Oh goodness," he said, "Don't worry. I don't have to take care of him 'til tomorrow. I just have to stop and put him on ice at my place."

Well, "my place" turned out to be the "Rest in Peace" Funeral Parlor. I went strangely silent. He dropped off the box and then took me to a wonderful restaurant in Grand Rapids called Safey's. We dined and danced, but not for long. I ate very little. I was seeing pictures in my mind that I didn't want to see, and when we danced, those cold white clammy hands really turned me off. They conjured up thoughts I didn't want to think about. I told him, "Something I ate didn't agree with me. I need to go home."

I also told him that we were hitting the road in the morning and we had an early bus call. All the time I was thinking, that dirty Tex! She knew! She did it again! I silently cussed her all the way home, and I knew she'd be waiting up. John escorted me to the door, kissed my hand and asked if he could call me. I said, "Sure," but I knew I wouldn't be answering. I know that was totally unfair to the poor guy, but I was young and just didn't want to deal with death and taxes! So, forgive me all you undertakers out there!

The minute I got inside the door, I could hear Tex and Dorie and Corky. They were in the kitchen laughing and giggling and pretending like they were just having a late-night snack (beer and sandwiches and so forth). I walked in, playing it real cool, grabbed a beer and one of the bologna sandwiches off the table, and acted like nothing was wrong. Never said a word. I knew they couldn't stand it for long. Pretty soon, Tex said, "Did you have a nice date? " I just nodded.

She proceeded. "Did he take you to a nice place?" Now the three of them were trying to keep from laughing.

I said nonchalantly, "Oh yes, but first we stopped by and picked up a box and dropped it off at his place." Then I stopped and just kept on eating.

Now, they're thinking, "A box?" Tex said, "What was in the box?"

I was shaking my beer under the table before I opened it, and then I just exploded up with it and aimed it at Tex, spraying her and yelling, "A body. A stiff, you turkey, just like you're going to be!"

Well, she took off running and I took off behind her. By the time I caught her, we were both soaked in beer and limp with laughter. So we made Dorie and Corky help clean up and toddled off to bed.

Over the course of the following days, I found out that a lot of people had known about my date and I endured a lot of teasing and good-natured remarks. Like, if I kicked a groundball or something, someone would be sure to say, "A little stiff today, Pepper?" or "What's wrong, Pep, are your hands cold?" Even worse, when I got up to hit, "Hey, Pep, make sure you get into the right box."

Anyway, baseball was fun again, but harder work than ever for me because I was fighting my auto accident injuries and trying to deny them. It was a tough row to hoe, but I hung in there and never missed a game. Johnny Rawlings wasn't happy with me. He knew that I wasn't performing up to my capabilities. He thought I was just dogging it, pretending I was hurt and using it as an excuse. He didn't like that. I was too proud to tell him how bad it was. Besides, he might have taken me out of the game, and they needed me in there, and I <u>wanted</u> to be in there.

As a result, our relationship was getting really bad, and deteriorating more every day. Dorth knew the truth. I couldn't hide the pain from her when she taped me up. She wanted to tell Rawlings, but I wouldn't let her. I think he was just about ready to lower the boom on me when his attention got focused on another target. I was happy about that, but I wasn't happy that it was my buddy Zig.

John could never understand how come Zig wasn't a better hitter. She was such a great ballplayer in every other aspect. He just couldn't believe she couldn't hit and was always searching for ways to improve her hitting. We were losing ballgames by one or two runs and it always seemed like Zig would come up to bat with a chance to win the game. Unfortunately, a lot of the time she seemed to pop up or strike out or hit into a double play to end the game. Johnny was finding it harder and harder to accept this. He was constantly after Zig about it.

Well, one morning at our workout, he came up with this brilliant idea. "Ziggy," he said, and shoved his hat back on his silver white head. "You're a pretty good bunter, so here's what we're going to do." He always talked out of the side of his mouth like he was telling you a secret, and we all had to strain to hear him. Johnny also always looked like he was tasting something sour. We found out later he was; he had an ulcer.

Anyway, we were all ears. Johnny continued, his eyes narrowed down even more, tapping Ziggy on the emblem with one finger, he repeated: "You're a pretty good bunter and they respect you for that, and they expect it from you! So, here's what we're going to do. You're going to fake a bunt." Johnny was emphasizing every word by poking Zig in the emblem. "That will pull the infield in. Then, you're going to take a half-swing and slap the ball right over their heads or right through them on the ground. They'll be playing in short, so they won't be able to react quick enough to grab it."

Well, Zig practiced for two hours that morning. She did a pretty fair job of learning how to push the ball over and through the infield by choking up on the bat and taking that little half-swing. Sure enough, that night, Ziggy comes up to bat in the bottom of the ninth, with two outs and runners on second and third. We needed a hit to tie the game. Ziggy fakes the bunt and that brought the infield in close. The next pitch, she squares around, chokes up on the bat, and the infield comes charging in, thinking sure as heck she's going to bunt. So Ziggy takes this "half" swing and hits the longest ball she has ever hit in her life. It went clear out to the left-field wall, but unfortunately the outfielder caught it for out number three.

Whenever Johnny was upset or flabbergasted, he would turn his hat sideways and say, "Holy suffering jumped up J_____ C_____" and then he would do a stiff, straight-back pratfall and land flat on his back, hard! How he did it without breaking his back or his neck I'll never know. Well, Johnny did his flop and when Zig saw that, she didn't even come back to the bench. The game was over so she just rounded second and took off straight for the clubhouse. Zig remembers that to this day.

The next day, Johnny got Zig out there at 8 a.m. in the morning on the ballfield, working and working and working. He was really rough on her. Many of our managers, like Johnny, were sometimes too tough. Zig ended up with blisters and tears, but Johnny never knew it because she never complained. Dorth could see Zig was exhausted but, when she tried to stop Johnny, he said sarcastically, "Well, I'm sure Zig wants to help the ball club!" He kept her out there so long that she barely had time to shower, grab a bite to eat and get back into uniform to play the ballgame that night.

The beauty of the whole thing was, that night our starting pitcher got knocked out of the game and Johnny had to ask Zig to come in and save the game for us. So, when he went out to the mound and took the ball from the starting pitcher, he turned around to Zig at second base to wave her in. Well, she just turned her back on him and acted like she didn't see him and just sort of strolled out toward right field. She made Johnny keep following her and pretended that she didn't know he was there. Eventually, he had to holler at her and ask her if she would "please come in and get the third out!"

She finally turned and said graciously, "Why, certainly, Johnny. I would do anything to help the ball club."

Major league ballplayers today wouldn't put up with that kind of treatment from the managers. The discipline, the practice, the hard work, the bad-mouthing, and so on. But they're the ones who are missing things. They're forgetting about the game, the wonderful fun, the comradeship and the great feeling you get from giving it your all. I can't help it. I know I preach this a lot. I still have to say that baseball today is secondary and money is first. It should never be that way. It destroys the teamwork. To me, teamwork is the most important thing in any sport. And maybe not just in sports, but in life itself. When you work together, you can get so much more work done than by trying to go it alone.

Somehow Mom and Norm never got around to visiting me -- seems like something was always popping up to prevent it! And the season seemed to fly by!

We had a good, solid team in the 1948 Grand Rapids Chicks, and we won the pennant. We had nine teams to beat out because that year they added the Springfield, Illinois, "Sallies" and the Chicago "Colleens" to the league. The home games in Chicago were televised and that was a new experience for all of us. You really had to watch out what you adjusted in the dugout. It was uncomfortable, but we got used to it. And we kept our dugout from looking like a pigpen, too.

We were now throwing a specially made 10-inch baseball completely overhand, with the pitching mound at 55 feet. The bases had been pushed back to 85 feet and that was truly the game that was best suited for us gals. You could hardly tell the difference from baseball by looking. But it was just short enough to make it suit our physical capabilities fine. The dimensions were great for us.

The Chicks sailed through the first round of the playoffs and then, well, what else? Next we came up against the fuzzy-skinned Rockford Peaches for the Championship World Series of our league. It ended up being a close, hard-fought series with a break here and a break there deciding every game, but the important breaks going the Peaches' way. They beat us in the seventh game and wound up being the champions again. I felt like I should have done better, but my body just wouldn't obey me.

Even though it was the first time I played third base, I think I did an adequate job. But my knees and my ribs never really got a chance to heal completely. I just kept aggravating them when I played. By playing hurt all year, I had the worst season of my All American career. I hit only .186 and struck out 34 times, more than all the rest of my 10 years put together. This was an indication that my ribs and my knee would not let me turn on an inside pitch or reach out to punch the curveball.

I knew that Paire was not up to par! And my coach, Johnny Rawlings, knew it, too. Only he thought I was lying down on the job and just dogging it. He didn't know the extent of my injuries. So when we lost, I actually felt glad the 1948 season was over. I was worn out and tired. I needed to get home and let my Mom baby me, like she always did. Once again, I needed to lay out on that beautiful beach by the blue Pacific and let that golden California sun heal my body.

I was beginning to wonder if maybe, just maybe, it was time to quit. After all, maybe Mom and Norm were right. I had promised Norm that we would get married and maybe I should live up to that promise. He and Mom were elated. They were already making wedding plans, but I thought they were jumping the gun. Somehow, it didn't feel right to end my career on such a down note.

263

After I rested for about a month, I started to feel like my old self again and I knew I had to go back and prove myself (if only to Johnny Rawlings). I figured I still had time to talk Norm into letting me go. It was only October and I had until April, when spring training would be starting. I was sure I could swing it. I knew where I was going to be Easter!

Then in November came the news that an all-star team had been picked to go on a post-season tour to South America that winter, and I was on the team. Well, my feet started itching and I said, "Who can resist that?"

"You!" said Norm. "It's me or South America. Make your choice." I said, "Well, I guess it's 'adios' 'cause I'm going to South America!" Of course, Mom was very angry and upset, and she told me that I would be sorry. Norm didn't say anything else. He just stared at me with a cold, dark look, turned his back and walked out the door. That was to be the last I saw of him for a long, long time.

Inez Voyce
Tina Petras

"Grand Rapids Chicks"

G.R. Chicks Johnny Rawlings "1"
Pepper 1948

LETS GO! LETS GO!
A LITTLE PEPPER!
A LITTLE PEPPER!

1948
Chicks

265

Chapter 28
Latin Knights and All American Women

I tried to put the image of that straight, stiff back walking away from me out of my mind, but it stuck in the corner. I had made a lot of people unhappy, including my Mom, and that hurt me. I knew that I might have lost a very good man. A man like Norman didn't come along too often. I prayed that I wasn't making the biggest mistake of my life, like my Mom thought I was doing. Well, I would just have to be Scarlett O'Hara again and think about that tomorrow. For now, I would concentrate on what a great time I was going to have in South America.

Checking the list on who was going, I found out that a lot of Chicks were going. That was the good news. But then I got a big jolt when I found out who the chaperone and coach were. That was the bad news. You guessed it -- "Bull Dog" Johnny and Dorth "I'm the Boss" Hunter, the loveable leaders of our Chicks. There were fireworks ahead, I knew. I also knew that I was headed into an adventure of a lifetime, and I was going to enjoy it, no matter what.

We ended up touring Central and South America for about nine weeks -- flying more than 40,000 miles (I was told). The games were billed as the "Americanas against the Cubans." Actually, there were only four or five Cubans on that tour, and only two of them were good ballplayers. It's kind of different in the majors today, isn't it? They showcased the Cubans and put them up in front where they could be seen. The rest of us filled in on either team as needed. Most of us were blondes or redheads, and the "Latin Lovers" went for us big time.

Our first stop was Guatemala. We barely got out of there in one piece. (They were having a revolution.) I hear they still have them and the saying goes, "If there's not a revolution going on now, just wait 20 minutes." Well, we waited 20 minutes, played a couple of games and got out on the last flight before the revolution started. They were shooting at us as the plane took off. Fortunately, I guess they missed because we made it down to Venezuela and wound up in Caracas.

We stayed there for a couple of weeks and played a lot of towns in the area. We'd go walking down the street and it was strange. We'd see this blond-haired, blue-eyed handsome

American (we thought) coming toward us, so we'd give him a smile and speak to him. He would speak back in German. A lot of Nazis were hiding out down there. To escape punishment they had taken their money and gone to South America. We completely ignored them when we found that out. We didn't want anything to do with Hitler's buddies.

There were also a bunch of British and Americans in Caracas who worked for the big oil companies. So there were plenty of men around to choose from, all eager to date an American baseball beauty queen. I met George Ashley at our hotel. He was British and a big shot with Standard Oil. He was a handsome, mature "man of the world" and he had his own Jeep, which he let me drive around.

I was double-dating with my buddies, Inez "The Big Hook" Voyce from the Chicks and Sophie "The Flint Flash" Kurys from the Belles and a gal named Jane Stolle. Jane was the centerfielder for Kalamazoo and a good ballplayer. We nicknamed her "Jeep" because she was built low to the ground and ran well.

Anyway, this one night we all had dates and went out together. There were two cars of us. I was driving George's Jeep up front with Inez, "Jeep" Jane and George in the car. Their dates were following us in the other car. We never went anywhere that we didn't all ride together. We didn't let anyone get isolated, even though I knew we could trust George. There were stories about women, especially blond-haired women, disappearing in South America in those days.

Here we go ... I'm driving along in the Jeep. I come up to this stoplight and it turns to green, so I go through it. Lo and behold, an old guy in a big old truck ran the light going the other way and hit us broadside. Our Jeep kicked over. It was a soft-top Jeep and fortunately no one was hurt. As a matter of fact, our "Jeep" Jane came crawling out from under the back seat of the Jeep, still smoking her cigarette.

We got out of the Jeep and I started to go over to see how the old guy was, but George just grabbed me and started hollering at all of us, "Come on! Come on! You've got to get out of here!" He hustled us into the other car. Everybody was sitting on somebody else's lap. I couldn't understand why he wanted to get us out of there so fast. Clearly, it wasn't our fault. The old man had run the light.

Well, the next day, we read in the paper about the accident and found out that if you get caught driving down there without a Venezuelan driver's license, no matter whose fault it was, that was a life prison sentence. That would have been me! I was the one driving. Oh boy! No wonder George wanted to get us out of there. I thank the Lord that he did. That was a close call.

We had a lot of exciting adventures down there in South America, particularly in Caracas. It seems like something was always happening. You couldn't take your laundry anywhere. You might not get it back in time and you didn't have time to wait. Laundromats were unheard of. The people just washed their clothes by hand. So, most of the time, we wound up doing our own wash, as usual. We had these little portable irons that we used. We didn't have any of the no wrinkle, wash-and-dry stuff yet, either. We used to put a towel down on the mattress or table or desk and do our ironing.

One night, we go out and play our ballgame, and we come back to the hotel and there are fire engines surrounding the hotel. We're thinking, good Lord, what happened? Well, it seems "Jeep" had done her ironing and left the iron on the mattress and forgot to turn it off. That was a little scary because there was a lot of smoke, but it really only burned up the bed. The bill for damages came out of our proceeds.

We played some games in little towns around Caracas, and one of them was a little mountain town. We went down to the airport and looked for a wide-body plane to get on, but all we found were two little planes. Each one held 10 to 12 people, along with the flight attendant, who was a guy, and the pilot. That was it. Hopefully, we figured, the flight attendant could fly, too, just in case. But we really didn't know, and didn't ask. One was a little two-engine plane and the other, a little single-engine plane. They both looked like little wind-up planes.

We were really laughing because we lucked out and got on the two-engine plane. The single-engine plane took off first, and then we took off right behind them. We were laughing like crazy, saying: "Boy, oh boy, at least we've got two engines, if something goes wrong. We just hope the rubber band doesn't break." The flight attendant did everything from backing up the pilot to winding up the rubber band.

We were still laughing about having two engines when I looked out the window and said: "Hey! Wow! Wait a minute! The propeller on the right-hand side isn't going around!" I hollered at the pilot, who you could reach out and touch.

He said: "Oh, si, Senorita, don't worry about that one. She never works."

Well, so much for two engines.

We got up to this little mountain town, which, if I remember correctly, was called Leon (but don't hold me to that). We weathered the landing, which was at a little postage-stamp airport. It was really just another big cow pasture. And there were hundreds of people there. I don't know where they came from because we were on the top of a mountain and you couldn't see any buildings.

I don't know how many pesos they paid to see us, but I bet it was a lot. Again, I wondered where they got the money, because these people were beyond poor. Some of the boys didn't wear pants or shoes, even up to nine or 10 years old. And you could tell that just by looking!

Once again, the ballpark was something else. It was just another cow pasture. The game was something else, too. We just got it over as quick as we could and were thankful nobody got hurt. The people didn't seem to care about the game. They just wanted to see us run the bases and slide in those skirts. Our team benches consisted of all kinds of old-fashioned chairs, some metal, some wood, stools, whatever they had, lined up along the first and third base lines. There was what looked like a chicken-wire backstop behind us, and the grandstand consisted of two weather-beaten wooden benches and big rocks.

Mainly, the people just stood around. It really got kind of funny because when we went out on the field to play and then came back in to bat, somebody would always be sitting in your seat.

We finally got the game over with and they took us to eat at a little sidewalk café. They were so proud to have us. You couldn't actually tell what the food was. It was a lot of rice and stuff all mixed up. We really didn't want to know what was in it, but it tasted pretty good and we knew we had to eat it. If we didn't eat it, that would be an insult. The people crowded around us, just to watch us eat. Once again, that made me feel so guilty, because you could see all the hungry eyes. One man had an epileptic seizure and fell down on the sidewalk right beside me. We tried to help him, but nobody else paid any attention. The soldiers came and dragged him off, apologizing to us for the trouble.

It got a little scary when we left the restaurant. We had to wait outside and about 500 people crowded around us, at least it seemed like that many (it may have been more or it could have been less). They surrounded us and kept closing in on us. They were laughing and not threatening us in any way, but they kept squeezing us in the center and trying to reach out and touch us. Then the soldiers came and moved them out of the way, jabbing them with their guns and even firing off a couple of shots. I can tell you from my experiences, the South American people are hot blooded and explosive. We were really happy to climb on that airplane and fly out of there, even if it did take our flying experience to another level.

Maybe one of the main reasons the people are so hot blooded was because the weather itself was so doggone hot. The heat got up there between 115 and 120 degrees in the shade, and that was the average temperature. Remember, this was our winter. So we played early morning games, at about 8 a.m., and then everyone would take a siesta. Then we played a night game. That way, we beat the heat a little. We had two catchers and we rotated.

Once, I played the morning game and when it came time for the night game the other catcher couldn't be found. She had disappeared. So, I got nailed to catch the night game, too, which started at 9 p.m. What I remember is that I got a double and then didn't remember anything else until I was on second base. I guess I sort of passed out from the heat but kept on running. It was a long day and even a longer night. The big "Hook" and I came dragging into the hotel lobby at about 1 a.m. We were pooped out and hungry and thirsty.

Looking around, to our surprise, we found out everything was locked down. We couldn't even get a cold beer, which we were dearly thirsty for, or a bologna sandwich or a burrito or anything. There was nothing to be had -- to eat or drink. It was some kind of religious holiday and everyone was gone. The lights were down in the lobby and as we walked by a big liquor cabinet, we saw this huge bottle of wine beckoning to us from behind a sliding glass door. We were thinking, "Oh boy! That would taste so good!"

Well, you know what? That cabinet wasn't locked! Just in fun, Hook pulled on the handle in front, and the thing opened. We couldn't resist the temptation so we grabbed up that big bottle of wine and snuck it up to the room. Then, under pressure, of course, we shared it with everybody. It was one of those big jugs, maybe a couple of gallons, or more. I don't think they make them anymore. I think it was Virginia Dare wine.

The next day, a big team meeting was called, bright and early. "OK," says John out of the corner of his mouth, "who stole the wine?" He was looking directly at me.

Dorth said, "John, let me handle this." He gave her a dirty look, but he left mumbling. "OK," she says, "is everybody going to suffer, or are the guilty parties going to step out and fess up?"

Hook and I stepped out and confessed, "We did it." We explained, and amazingly, Dorth understood. She said she would explain it to John, and she did. He didn't get on our backs too bad. He just gave us dirty looks thereafter. Of course, it cost us $25 apiece, which was a lot of money for a bottle of wine, and none of the other "yea-hoos" offered to help us.

From that time on, John was all over me; pressuring me on the ballfield, as he had done Ziggy. I got into a hitting slump, from trying too hard, I think. He just made it worse with his attitude. He left "angel" Hook alone. He thought I was the "big bad influence" on her. And I guess I was, because Hook was from Iowa and was really bashful. But at that particular time, the whole wine business had been Hook's idea and once again "innocent" Pepper got the blame (well, maybe I wasn't that innocent).

My relationship with John went from bad to worse. This one time I was coming up to bat and John was all over me. He practically snarled at me out of the corner of his mouth, "Get your arms out away from your body and you just might actually hit the ball."

Well, I went up to the plate and stuck my elbows way out. I took the exaggerated swing, flapping my arms like a chicken, and hit the biggest, tallest, "can of corn" you ever saw. (A "can of corn" is a pop fly in baseball talk.) Dottie told me later that I made John so mad that he threw up. He actually went down to the end of the bench in the dugout and threw up. That did it! He stopped speaking to me from then on. He just glared at me. And from that time on, I gave up trying to please him and decided to just completely ignore him and have fun.

One of the fun stops was Managua, Nicaragua. The Samosa family was in power there. To us it seemed like they didn't like people very much. They didn't treat them very well, at least not the common people, when we were there. They invited us to the presidential palace for a big dinner and dance party. They picked us up in armored Jeeps. Going down narrow streets in those army Jeeps and trucks, they herded the people out of the way, just like they were cattle. If they didn't get out of the way, they ran over them!

We met General Samosa and his son, Phillip. Believe it or not, Phillip was attending West Point. Rumors had it that General Samosa had been a used-car salesman in Philadelphia. He built up a bankroll and went back home to Nicaragua, bought himself an army and became their military dictator. There was no doubt that the military ruled for the rich. We were in this long welcoming line and General Samosa and his son were graciously kissing our hands as we were being introduced and the line filed by them. It was kind of like meeting the Queen of England.

One of our ballplayers on the trip was the beautiful and talented Dottie Schroeder. Dottie was the only ballplayer in the entire 12 years of the All American League who played every year from 1943 to 1954. She was only 15 years old when she came into the league and she was a great, natural ballplayer. Dottie also happened to be a very beautiful young lady. She looked a lot more like a movie star than a ballplayer. She had golden-blond hair that was braided and hung down to her waist. She had beautiful blue eyes and golden skin, with naturally dark eyebrows and eyelashes. Dottie had a dazzling smile and was truly an all-American beauty.

General Samosa's son Phillip was a great big, tall, really handsome dude and he couldn't take his eyes off Dottie. He took her hand and kissed it and asked if there was anything he could do "to" her. He meant "for her," of course, but we got a big kick out of that. We said, "Oh yeah! Oh yeah!" We know what he'd like to do to you, Dottie.

It was a fun-filled evening of wining and dining. There were all kinds of fabulous hors d'oeuvres and food, flowing champagne and whirling waltzes on the huge marble floor. It was sort of like the Cinderella fairy tale, in more ways than one. When the clock struck time to go home, it was sad because there would be no fairy-tale ending. The coach turned into those armored cars again and the wicked witches started shooting at the people.

The people were just trying to get a look at us. It was almost as if they thought it would be worthwhile to get shot if they could just see us, or touch us. We were glad to get out of Managua because of the military being so violent. It made us realize how lucky we were to be Americans, living in a free country. We felt so bad for the people, but it wasn't really much better anywhere else down there, not at that time, at least.

We made a short stop in Panama and went to see the Panama Canal, of course. They let me operate the levers on one of the locks and I let a Russian ship go through. It was so close I could almost touch it. The canal is very narrow at that point. We were still war buddies with Russia then, and the sailors were smiling and waving. So we waved back and threw them kisses. If I had known what was to come, I might have thrown rocks instead! We went from there to Puerto Rico. We had the most fun there because it was the most Americanized stop on the trip, and the people there were all very nice to us. We got there at the same time the American submarine fleet was there on maneuvers, and you can bet there were some great maneuvers attempted. We were very happy to see those American sailors and they were happy to see us, too. They hadn't seen any American gals for a while and we were yearning to see our American guys. So, that made us all happy.

Hook, Kammie and I were invited to go onboard a sub. They submerged and gave us a ride around the bay. That was some experience, knowing that you're cruising along under all that water and everything was dry as toast. I won't forget walking down those narrow aisles and having all those guys hanging out of their narrow bunks, whistling and grinning from ear to ear as we passed. They had on T-shirts and would flex their muscles for us as we went by. We'd just give them a big smile. You could tell they were homesick and happy to see us. It wasn't disrespectful, just a heck of a lot of fun.

We had dinner onboard with the officers, of course. That's the way it goes in the military. The brass gets all the fun. And the food was something else: filet mignon, corn on the cob, fancy desserts and anything we wanted to drink. They seemed to eat very well on those subs, but then they have to put up with being underwater for months at a time. Psychologically, that would take a lot out of you. I understand they have to take a lot of tests to be stationed on a submarine. They have to make sure that everybody is mentally sound when they start out because they'll sure be tested by the end of a tour.

That made me think about this young man I had been dating a couple years ago, Dale Portuno. He had been stationed on a sub. Dale was Italian and there was no doubt that he had the cutest round dark face, with big brown eyes. He had black curly hair, a broad white smile and this Rollie Fingers handlebar mustache, all curled up at the ends. He was quite a guy. I met him in Hollywood right after the war started, but our romance didn't make it through the war. He wore two little gold earrings.

One time, we were having a drink and this guy came up to him and wanted to know why a "red-blooded American sailor in the American Navy" was wearing two gold earrings. Dale just quietly told the guy, "Well, if you knew what they meant, you would understand." It seemed the tradition was that if you had a sub shot out from under you, you wore a gold earring. Dale had two of them. He had lost two subs and unfortunately, he went down with the third one and didn't make it back home.

Seeing all those lonely faces and dining with those wonderful guys brought all that back to me. So in a way, it became a sad experience. But, I just became Scarlett O'Hara again, put that behind me and devoted my time to entertaining the Navy.

There were a lot of nightclubs in San Juan, and we visited a few of them. A couple of times we were with our Navy boys, and a couple of other times we were with those Latin lovers. I sang in one of them for a couple of nights. The Cuban gals had taught me some Spanish songs and I had taught them some American songs, like "three itty bitty fishes," you know, "down in the middle of the itty bitty pool." I still remember one song they taught me called, "La Ultima Noche." I remember it because I wrote English words to it. It was such a beautiful song that I learned it in Spanish and then wrote my own English version and sang it in the nightclub. They loved it.

I'm not going to try to recreate the Spanish version, but here's my version in English:

"La Ultima Noche" ("My Last Night With You")

"My last night with you

I'll always regret it.

Somehow I knew

I'd never forget it.

I've tried and I've tried

but all in vain.

Thoughts of you

keep bringing my heart pain.

You held me tightly,

caressed me lightly.

And then you whispered

'Yo te amo.'

But when I woke at dawn

it was to find you gone.

Oh, my chiquito,

why did you go?

My last night with you

I'll always regret it.

Somehow I knew

I'd never forget it.

I've tried and I've tried,

but all in vain.

Thoughts of you

keep bringing my heart pain."

(Pepper Paire Davis, 1948)

I do believe if somebody like Andy Russell would have made that record, he probably would have had a huge hit. I might even have made some money, too, if he liked my words! At that time in the '40s and '50s, Andy was very popular on both sides of the border singing both Spanish and American songs.

While we were in San Juan we stayed at the Normandie Hotel, which was built and shaped like a huge ship. I recently inquired and spoke to some people who say that it is still there, that it has been totally rebuilt, but still looks like the "Normandie." It was a huge building shaped like a ship, with a swimming pool in the middle of it.

From Puerto Rico we went to Costa Rica. They were supposed to have the most beautiful girls in the world in Costa Rica. But, I'll tell you what, the guys weren't following those Costa Rican girls around; they were following us around. So, who knows, maybe America has the most beautiful girls.

We had a really wonderful time on that trip and I have to admit that, while I had thoughts that maybe I was doing the wrong thing by walking out on Norman, I was glad I didn't miss that trip. It was a once-in-a-lifetime experience for me. Besides, I kind of felt that when I got back, I could probably talk Norman into coming back to me. At least that's what I told myself. I also knew that I wasn't even going to try until after the next baseball season because I still had things to work out.

By the time that trip was over, I knew I was really in the doghouse with Johnny Rawlings but one good thing came out of it. Dorth and I had established a friendship based on mutual respect. And thank God for that because that was how I was going to survive the coming years with the Chicks.

When I got back home, I knew it was time to straighten up and fly right. Forgotten was my retirement plan. Not forgotten, but buried deep, were my feelings for Norm. I had an urgent need to prove that the bad year I had in 1948 was the result of my injuries and not because I was over the hill, or not trying! I had to prove all these things to John, and myself, maybe, more than anybody else. So, I set out to do just that.

"Venezuela" 1948
The Oil Man from Caracas

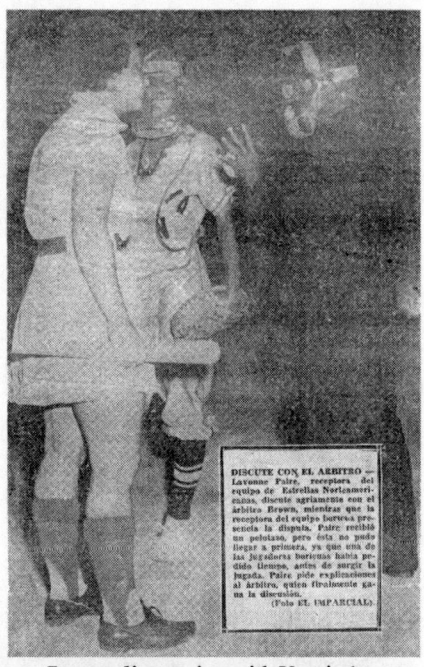

Owner of the Jeep!

Pepper disagreeing with Umpire!

Pepper Paire
Jeep Stoltz

Pepper Paire, Shirley Starvoff, Annabelle "Lefty" Lee

BASE - BALL CLUB
ESCUELAS INTERNACIONALES

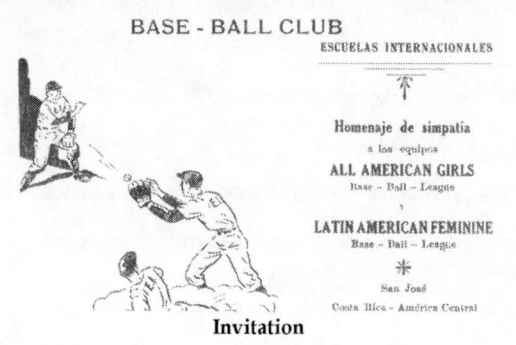

Homenaje de simpatía
a los equipos
ALL AMERICAN GIRLS
Base - Ball - League
y
LATIN AMERICAN FEMININE
Base - Ball - League

San José
Costa Rica - América Central

Invitation

277

Chapter 29
A Reconditioned Chick

After getting back from South America, there wasn't really time for me to go back to work again. The holidays were coming up and people were taking vacations and the 1949 spring training wasn't that far off. Besides, I needed to rest and get into shape to achieve my goals. Mom wasn't giving me a hard time anymore about Norm. She had resigned herself to the fact that it was over and she just wanted to enjoy me while I was still here.

Unfortunately she had another disappointment from Joe. He had been discharged from the Air Force and came home to visit a couple of times. But eventually he decided to stay in St. Louis and go to St. Louis University. He wanted to nail down his St. Louie gal. She wasn't the same girl he had been carrying a torch for. This was long, tall Sally, my wonderful sister-in-law! He met her while working at the post office during income tax time. I guess it was love from the beginning for both of them, and this time he married his St. Louie woman.

At that time, they lived with Sally's mom. Joe sent pictures home (they were glamour shots). Sally was a tall, shapely blonde and had done some modeling. She looked like Carol Landis, a blond movie star. Carol was known as a "blond bombshell." She came before Marilyn Monroe. Sally was a beautiful gal. Mom was really worried that Joe had fallen into the clutches of a siren. Mom was also upset because she had not been able to attend the wedding. Joe and Sally didn't have much money; they were both working hard and Joe couldn't afford to come out to California or send for Mom. They had a nice, but small wedding, because they decided to save their money for when they had kids.

Sally was Catholic and Joe was converting to Catholicism, so you knew there would be kids. Big bucks just weren't around in those days. You had to save to buy anything and you had to pay for everything. You couldn't charge it. And I'm not so sure that wasn't a good idea. I think when you have to save and you have to wait, things mean a lot more when you get them. They're much dearer to you because you worked so hard and waited so long to get them.

Somebody said that anticipation is the better part of realization. As you get older, you do realize that is true!

Mom was also worried about Russell. He was getting ready to graduate and running around in his own circle, and he was becoming draft bait. Even though the war was over, the draft was still in effect. Russell was probably going to get drafted and Russell in the Army would be a disaster -- both for him and for the Army! Russ wasn't home that much of the time. He was out and about in his usual fashion. He could disappear at the oddest times.

With all this going on, Mom was not really herself, so I just stayed close to her. I tried to keep her laughing and happy and we did a lot of things together. She went bowling with me all the time. At least she didn't have to worry about working because Pop was making enough so they could get by. Working the graveyard shift brought in a little extra money. I was thinking it might even be good for her to go out and get a little job! Then she wouldn't be alone to think all these negative thoughts. Since Pop was working the graveyard shift, she didn't see much of him. When he came home he'd stay up a little while, doing things around the house and then he'd go to sleep. That would leave Mom just sitting there at the dining room table.

Well, the time really flew by, like it always did after we got through the holidays. Mom seemed to be sad all the time. She didn't have that cheery smile and that big laugh. Things just weren't the same for her. Everything had changed. Joe settling in St. Louis upset her a great deal. She had thought he'd come back home to live. After my marriage had been called off, Norman was not around. They had really gotten along great together and I knew that Mom missed him, probably even more than I did. I did have feelings in my heart for him and at times I wondered if I had made a mistake. My pulse would quicken a little when I would see his car drive by. He still lived right across the street at his sister's apartment. But his car never stopped. It slowed down a couple of times, but it never did stop. It just kept going by.

I knew I shouldn't make a move because I wasn't ready to stay home. I was going back again to play ball and he had made himself clear about that. So I decided to stop thinking about him and concentrate on my bowling. I was in the middle of final playoffs at Santa Monica Bowl and Mom had come along to root me on as usual. I noticed that when I was standing there talking to her, Mom would be smiling and applauding me like she always did. But when she didn't think I was looking, I would catch her with her head hanging down and looking very sad. My breaking up with Norm had hit her hard. She had thought her baby girl was going to settle down and she would have a lot of fun being a Mom and a Grandma. My Mom always had so much love to give.

I guess my baseball years stole a lot from her. Not that we all don't grow up and go our own ways, but usually you're in the same state and you still have lots of time to be together. I guess Mom was dearly missing that time. I had all these other diversions. Even though I carried her in my heart always, as I think back now, I could have been a better daughter. Well, after bowling was over and we knew we were going to the playoffs, we went into the bar to have a beer or two and our usual hamburger and fries. Mom said no to the food. She was trying to hide it but I could see tears in her eyes. "Hey, Mom, what's wrong?" I asked, "We won! Why are you crying?"

She tried to smile but she just couldn't do it. She just shook her head and then everything came out in a torrent of words. "My baby girl will be leaving me again and my little boy is married and he'll never come home again and my baby boy, Russell, well, the Army is going to get him." She broke down and sobbed, "I'll never get to see my grandbabies that I thought I was going to get to hug and kiss."

I put my arms around her and I hugged her hard. I was crying too. I could feel her pain. My Mom had always been so brave and cheerful, so ready to laugh and ready to tell a joke. It killed me to see her this way. "Hey, Mom," I said, "You know what? I bet Joe will be out here before you know it. He's a California boy, Mom. He won't be able to stay in St. Louis forever. When they start having grandbabies, they'll be here for you to hold them."

She brightened a little and said, "Do you think so? Do you really think so, Lavone?" She blew her nose and said again, "Do you really think so?" I said, "I'm sure of it, Mom" and I was.

I've been a lot of places and there's no place like California. Joe knew it too. My heart was aching for her. After all the sacrifices she had made for us, we had been her whole life. It hurt bad to see her so desperate. She got quiet again and said, "Now it's time and you're going again and you just got home and I won't see you for a long, long time."

She was going to cry again and I couldn't take that, so I said, "How about July?"

She looked at me with her eyes questioning, "What do you mean July? You won't get home 'til October or November, sometimes even December."

I took a deep breath and told a lie. "Well, I wanted to surprise you but I'll tell you now. I've made arrangements for you to fly back and see me for your birthday present." Even as I spoke I was thinking, where am I going to get the money? How am I going to pull this off? But the happiness in her voice and the look on her face made me know that I was doing the right thing.

Mom said, "You mean it?"

I said, "Yes, you're coming to see me!"

"Oh my! Oh my!" she cried. "I'm going to get to see you play?"

And now she's crying with tears of joy. I knew I'd raise that money somehow -- I had to! I loved my Mom far too much to let her down. So I said: "OK, mark your calendar. The last two weeks of July you're coming back to the All American and I'm going to show you what a good ballplayer your daughter is."

She gave me a big hug and a kiss and said, "Oh I've always known that. You're better than anybody else in the world."

Well, that made me want to cry, so I laughed at her and I said: "Mom, I don't know about that, there might be a couple better ballplayers than me! But on the other hand, they did call me Babe Ruth in South America!"

We both laughed up a storm and I felt good because I had my Mom back. She was giving me that hardy belly laugh again. She said, "Hey, I'm hungry."

"Yeah, me too," I said. I don't know why, but at bowling alleys hamburgers and french fries always seem to taste awfully good. So, we ordered some and we ate them and we both went home happy.

Now I really had goals to achieve. But I was ready for them. I had a little secret stash of money stuck away in the bank that I'd been saving for a car. That would take care of Mom's trip. I figured I'd just start being very responsible and save some of that baseball salary. It was time! I was going to be 25 years old and I needed to start thinking about my future. I vowed not to party so much and start concentrating on being the best ballplayer I knew how to be. So, this time when Mom drove Faye and me to the airport it was with a happy heart. It wasn't such a tearful goodbye, although we shed a few tears. It was "I'll see you soon, my baby girl" and our hearts were happy.

I loved my Mom so much and she loved me right back. Our family always had that deep love -- quick to hug and quick to kiss. I've always been so grateful for that. You see so many families that not only don't love, they seem so full of jealousy and hate. And then, some love but can't seem to show it. They can't cry or laugh with their loved ones. I'm so blessed to have a Mom and a Dad and a bro that show that unconditional love. Some people don't know how to do anything but take. They don't know how to give and they're missing all the fun. The whole point in life is loving and giving.

I turned and waved goodbye to Mom and threw her a kiss and said, "See you soon." The joy on her face almost made me not need the airplane. The Cacapot Faye and I slept the first part of the trip and then I noticed that Faye was very, very quiet, not her usual self. She wasn't harassing the stewardess or going up front and demanding to see the pilot. I said, "Hey, what's wrong, Cacapot?"

She just laughed and said, "Nothing. Just wish I could be on a winner for a change."

I said: "Hey pal, it's not your fault. You're always doing your share. Your team, Peoria, just needs to get you some help."

She brightened a little. "Well," she said, "they've got me. I'll keep those fans interested." And she always did.

I felt like something else was bothering her, but she wouldn't say. So I just said, "Listen, pal, you know that I'll be coming to town and if you need help, I'll be there for you."

She gave me a warm look and said, "I know you will, Pep." Then she flung her arm around me and said, "Just you wait! I'll get us some great dates when you're in town; guys that will buy us some steaks and beer."

I said, "Yeah, I bet. Probably be hamburgers and hot dogs." We both laughed and vowed that our friendship would last forever, and it has, and it will.

In 1949 the league was trying something new. Each team was going back to their hometown for spring training. There were not going to be any all-league tours. Apparently, they thought this would save money, even though we had drawn more than a million people in 1948 with the 10 teams. The two new teams, the "Chicago Colleens" and the "Springfield Sallies," weren't bringing their teams back. They dropped out and we had an eight-team league again. The league was billed as a nonprofit organization, and although they made lots of money, they weren't smart with it. They gave a lot away to schools and scholarships and charities. That was commendable and I'm not knocking it, but they should have put some money away for a rainy day and set up some kind of a farm system.

Now we were playing with 85-foot bases and a 55-foot pitching mound and a 10-inch baseball and all baseball rules. No softball player could come in from softball and play the game right away. Even if they were really good ballplayers; it took time and some of them never did make it. It was too big of a jump to make. It was the same way in major league baseball, too. You couldn't bring in a man from softball and have him make it overnight to major league baseball. Very few would ever make it at all, and if they did, it took a while. Sooner or later the talent was bound to grow thin but, hey, not to worry. Be Scarlett O'Hara again.

When I reported to spring training in Grand Rapids, I was in great condition and loaded for bear. I knew I had a lot to prove to John Rawlings. I was really dreading what was coming because I knew that he would make it hard on me. But I was ready for him. So John saw a totally different Pepper Paire than he had seen before, and one he never expected to see. This one was healthy and in shape. Eager to hustle and eager to show him that she was still a darn good ballplayer. I was the first one on the field and the last one to leave. I caught hitting practice. I even shagged fly balls in the outfield. He ran my buns off. Running me from one side of the outfield to the other side. But I hung in there and came up with the ball most of the time, causing John to comment to Dorth from the North, "She looks better than those regular outfielders."

I stuck my nose in the dirt and kept it there for as long as anyone would hit grounds at me. John was amazed. He told Dorth, "I knew she was a good ballplayer but last year she didn't even try." Well, I guess Dorth told him how hurt I was and why. When John found out everything, he gained respect for me. And when I found out what a great teacher he was, I gained respect for him. Then we came together in mutual respect. It was then that I became a Grand Rapids Chick. Up to that point I would have to admit that I was still a Racine Belle in my heart, but not anymore. I was now a Grand Rapids Chick.

Our 1949 team was fit and looking good and we were looking forward to a winning season. Well, we did have one little glitch. Tex hurt her shoulder in spring training diving back into a base. The doctor said it was just a bruise. Tex had had a sore arm before and didn't come out of the lineup. She just said, "I'm OK," and kept playing. As for me, well, I was ready to show the world that Pepper Paire was back and in one piece. I was all set to be an All-Star third baseman, knock in a lot of runs and help the Chicks win the pennant.

Things looked very good. We jumped off to a great start, winning at home and on the road. My bat was singing and so was I. I was doing all the things I was supposed to do: going to bed early, eating the right food and saving money. The only time I went out was when Tex and I would date, or maybe one of our California buddies would be in town. Actually, I was kind of enjoying it. I was devoting everything to baseball and wondering if I shouldn't have been doing that all those years.

It was coming up on July and we were in first place and looking good. I could hardly wait for Mom to get there, thinking how great it would be for her to see our team on top. I was still a little concerned about Tex. She was hanging in there but the soreness in her arm just wouldn't go away. Her shoulder would seem to get better and then it would stiffen up on her again if she had to throw too much. Tex just shrugged it off and would say, "Hey, I'll be OK." But I knew from experience that it wasn't much fun playing in pain.

July 1 finally came. We had moved the date up so Mom could meet us in South Bend. Her plane was landing in Chicago and that wasn't far away. Our coach's wife, Mrs. Rawlings, had volunteered to pick her up at the airport and bring her to the ballpark. I just kept watching that gate, looking down that crowded aisle trying to see that curly black hair coming down it. I so wanted her to make it by game time. It was getting close and we were just about ready to take our infield practice when there she came, walking, almost running. She had that familiar black coat on and I could see her curly black hair. That curly black hair my bro Joe got and I didn't. She was stretching her neck and trying to peer over the top of the crowd, looking for me.

    I ran to the fence behind home plate and we met there. Our fingers entwined through the backstop fence. "Oh, my baby girl," she beamed at me through her tears. "The best ballplayer in the whole wide world." We were both crying now. Then I heard John over my shoulder, "Come on, Pep, time for infield practice." So I said, "I love you, Mom. See you after the game," and ran out to third base.

    They had a seat for her and Mrs. Rawlings right behind our dugout on the third base line. So I knew she had a good view of me. I was so excited and so happy I hollered at John, "OK, coach, I'm ready." Mom had never seen me play third base before and I was eager to show her how good I was. Well, John usually hit bullets at us for ground balls, but I guess he wanted me to look good because he hit this little bouncy, twisting ground ball at me and I booted it. I guess I was over-adjusting, so he hit me another dribbler that bounced off my wrist. Then he hit another easy bouncer and I kicked that one.

    Now the crowd's laughing and I'm turning red with embarrassment. I swear, in my eagerness I must have missed five or six of those easy ground balls right at me. I lost track. Sometimes an easy ball hit right at you can be the toughest to field. You're just so sure of it, that you kick it, especially if you over-adjust like me. I finally hollered at John in exasperation, "For crying out loud, John, hit the ball! Hit the ball!"

    John, who was just trying to be nice, raises an eyebrow and says, "OK hot shot, I'll let you have it." And he belts a line drive down the third base line, low and whistling. Well, it sinks down, cuts in, and I dived through the air and speared that thing with my bare hand. The crowd stopped laughing and gave me a huge ovation and I was finally able to sneak a peek at my Mom. She was standing up and clapping like crazy with the rest of the crowd. She had this huge proud smile on her face. We went on to win the game.

After the game, Mom went out with us and we had our usual hamburgers and french fries and a couple of beers and I proudly introduced Mom to everybody on the team. She gave them all a big hug. She was so warm and wonderful. Some of them were homesick for their moms and they had tears in their eyes. On the bus ride back home to Grand Rapids, we just gabbed instead of sleeping and Mom caught me up with all the happenings at home. I had made arrangements for her to stay with us at the Sullivans'. Their whole family was going to be away on vacation so we had the run of the house. Corky and Dorie and Tex (the whole team actually) got to sample that cooking I was always talking and bragging about.

Mom outdid herself. She cooked everything from a juicy, golden brown turkey stuffed with her scrumptious dressing, to her famous chili. I tried to take her out to dinner, but she just wanted to be near me, watching the ballgames, rooting for us, and then come back home and cook for us. We had a 10-day home stand and I enjoyed every moment of it. I think the whole team put on weight. We were winning our games and Mom was so happy that time just flew by until suddenly it was time for her to go. Actually that was the way it ought to be because she was worrying about how Pop and Russ were doing, bacheloring it. She worried about the poochy pups, little Mickey and Inky, our little loving dogs. So she needed to go.

I knew she had had a great time and we were both happy. Peoria had come into town and she got to see the Cacapot Faye and give her a big hug from her mom, Olive. Faye, as outrageous as she was, was always a favorite of my Mom's. So, Mom went home with a happy heart and a lot of stories to tell, and she never forgot that 1949 trip for as long as she lived!

1949 G.R. Chicks
Front Row: Pepper & Sadie
L to R: Tex-Dorie Reid-
Mid Earp Beans- Connie-Corkey-
Inez Voyce Stand

Ruth "Tex" Lessing
Chicks 1948

"Pepper" Paire Davis

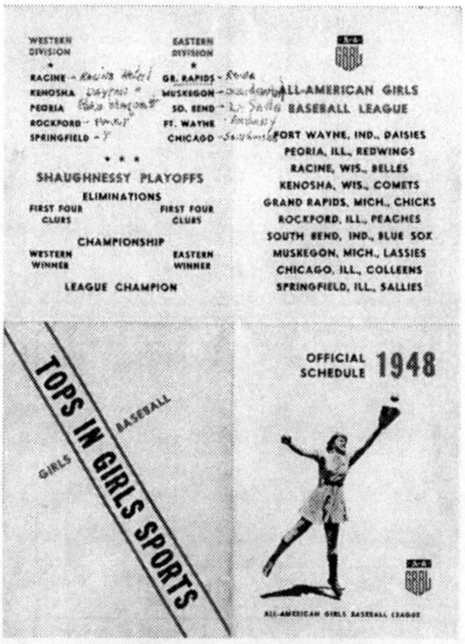

1948 Original Schedule
Showing the 10 teams expansion

287

Chapter 30
Big Daddy Wore Cement Scuffies
Sopranos Relatives

After Mom left, everything just seemed to fall into place. It was so great to have her come back and see me. I thought, "Maybe we'll do that again next year." (I already knew that there would be a next year.) I was healthy and happy, and I was playing the field again, as far as the guys were concerned! While I was at it, I was playing a great third base for the Chicks and driving in runs by the bunch.

I was really beginning to like third base and I felt my game was now more suited for third base than for shortstop. My injuries from catching had taken their toll, but at third base, I could still handle everything. My reactions were still great and I still had the cannon arm that a third baseman needed to dive in and field a bunt or that little dinker and throw the batter out. The whole ball club was doing well, playing great and hitting up a storm. They all credited Mom for being their good-luck charm (including me). We went on this winning streak and I went on a hitting streak at the same time. The strange thing about it was that it all started when I started finding pennies, right after Mom left.

Here we go with the superstitions again. The Grand Rapids clubhouse was up on a little hill. If you were on the field, you really had to take a hike to get to that clubhouse bathroom and back. If you got caught short during a ballgame, there was a good chance you wouldn't make it. One night, I decided to go to the bathroom at the last moment and coming into the clubhouse, I was looking down and found this penny. Well, our superstition says that if the penny's heads up, you put it into your left shoe and it's good luck. Well, I put that penny in my left shoe and we went out that night and won. I think I got two or three hits.

The next night on the way into the clubhouse from the outfield I found another penny and I put that one in my left shoe, too. We won again and I got a hit again. Now, if the penny is heads up, you put it in your left shoe and that means good luck and money. If it is heads down, you put it in your right shoe and that means good luck and good friends or whatever. Well, I have to tell you, it just kept happening. In the meantime, we're winning 15 straight ballgames and I'm getting hits in 15 straight ballgames. But, I'll tell you something. My shoes were getting heavy.

I was carrying enough weight as it was and I never was a phantom on the basepaths. I could always run well enough and my knowledge always allowed me to get an extra base when it was called for. I knew <u>who</u> was going to throw <u>where</u> and <u>if</u> they were throwing. If I got a single and they were throwing to the plate or third base, you could bet I went down to second and got my extra base. If I was on second and there was a runner going home on a fly ball and the throw was to the plate, then I got my extra base down to third. I knew how to run the bases. Later on, I really slowed up, after all those ups and downs behind home plate.

At any rate, the pennies went on. Somewhere along the way from the clubhouse to the diamond I kept finding them. This was now getting to be a cross to bear. But we had won something like 16 or 17 straight games and I hit safely in all of them. Well, any superstitious ballplayer knows I'm not going to pass a penny at this point. I'm carrying about five pounds of pennies in my shoes. This one time I decided I better go back to the bathroom before I went out to the field. So I turned around and went back to the clubhouse. The bathroom was right by the door so I just sneaked in and went to the bathroom and when I came out, who did I spot? Tex! Down on her hands and knees planting pennies! She'd been planting those pennies the whole time and I caught her red-handed.

Well, I chased her all over creation trying to "knock her in the noggin," but all I got was her laughing. I never really caught her. In the meantime, I went back and picked up that penny she planted. We won again. I really don't remember but I think we went on a road trip and our winning streak finally got broken. Then I got to unload all those pennies. That was my buddy Tex, that "little penny planter." She got me again. I'd get so mad at her little stunts. But I couldn't stay mad at her. She'd give me that big old Texas smile and say, "Now, Pepper, you know you love me. Just think how dull it would be without me?" She was right and I was going to find that out the hard way, and a lot sooner than I ever expected to, unfortunately.

We took off on a 10-day road trip, and we were looking forward to this one because we were going to Peoria for a four-game weekend series. We knew that we would have a great time with Cacapot Faye. She told us that she had dates set up for us for the weekend. We were looking forward to seeing her and we were also looking forward to the ballgames. Even though the Peoria Redwings never won anything, they still always gave us a tough game. Faye would always prevent an inside-the-park home run by kicking the ball under the fence and converting it into a ground- rule double.

Even though the Redwings weren't big winners, there was always a crowd on hand. This time there was to be a special ceremony and some kind of raffle. We were told that they expected the biggest crowd of the year and, sure enough, there were about 20,000 people at that game. That was a huge attendance for those days. Well, the first game was close but we won it 2-0. We had gotten permission from Dottie for Faye to join us at the hotel for something to eat. So Tex and I were having a drink and waiting for her. Tex kept looking over her shoulder and saying: "Where the heck is Faye? I want to get to bed early. I've got to catch a doubleheader tomorrow." She was mumbling and sounding really grumpy.

I looked at her and said: "Hey, let's just sneak in an extra beer. You know Dorth from the North isn't counting."

"I don't want one," Tex fired back at me. Then she slammed her glass down on the bar.

Wow! I was shocked. I had never seen Tex react like that. I just kind of looked at her in surprise and was about to ask her what was wrong when Faye's loud voice filled the air, "Hiya, Cacapots." She came up behind us and threw her arms around our necks and hugged us. Tex pulled away from her and snapped, "Damn it, you're hurting me!" But then she added to Faye quickly, "How the heck are you?" and gave her that big smile.

I was staring at her. This wasn't the Tex I knew, but Faye shrugged it off. So we got a table and ordered our sandwiches and brought each other up on the news while we ate. Tex excused herself early and as she walked way, Faye's eyes met mine and she asked, "What's wrong with Tex?"

I answered: "I don't know. I guess her arm's hurting her and she just doesn't feel well." But we both knew that something was drastically wrong. We called it an early night because Faye's date ("Big Daddy" as she called him) was on business in Chicago and he was coming in tomorrow (Saturday night) and we were going out after the game. Faye told us he was bringing two of his business associates as our dates.

When I got back to our room, Tex was asleep so I didn't get to talk to her. The next morning when I got up, she had already gone to breakfast without waking me. Again, that was unusual for Tex. I was really getting worried but when I went downstairs to the hotel dining room, she was sitting with Zig and Dorth and seemed fine when I joined them. I decided not to mention anything until later.

That night we lost the ballgame. We couldn't get any hits off the Peoria pitcher, while they hit our pitcher pretty hard and ran wild on the bases. Texas didn't even bother throwing to second most of the time. We thought it was just because they had a big jump on the ball. But I also noticed that she was wincing on every ball she threw, almost bouncing the ball back to the pitcher. No doubt about it, she was in pain. After the game when we jumped into the shower, I tried to talk to her about it, but she just shrugged me off and said: "Hurry up. Come on and get dressed. We've got dates, remember? We've got to be downstairs and meet them in the lobby."

We had talked it over and decided we didn't want to go out anywhere. The hotel had great food and they could come over and take us to dinner there. So, we were sitting in the lobby of the hotel and we see these two long, long black limos show up with smoke glass windows, chrome wheels, white sidewalls, the whole bit. The door opens and out steps Faye and a short, roly-poly, middle-aged guy in a black suit rolls out behind her. He's got a red carnation on his lapel and he's wearing a white tie and a snap-brim fedora. He has an overcoat flung carelessly over his shoulder and he's smoking a stogy about the size of a small baseball bat.

Tex and I look at each other in amazement. "What is that?" Tex asks. About that time, two other guys pile out of the limo dressed the same way, but they have white carnations in their lapels. There isn't a uniform among them. Neither are they spring chickens. Well, they all head into the lobby followed by two other guys in dark suits who get out of the second limo. The big guy is just laughing and smiling at Faye as she rambles on and on, gesturing and laughing. She must have been telling him a joke. Faye introduces him as her "Big Daddy," or "Geno," and she introduces the other two guys. They all had Italian names.

We figured the white carnations were our dates. The other two guys just hung back and kept looking nervously around. I whisper to Tex as we head toward the dining room, "You didn't set this up, did you? Are these guys undertakers?" They were strangely overdressed for a regular date (strangely dressed indeed).

She whispers back: "You know, I think I saw this in a movie once. I'm really glad that we are not going out somewhere in those cars with them. I'm glad we're just going to dinner in the hotel here."

I answer emphatically, "Me too, kid!" The two guys that we hadn't met had gone ahead and negotiated tables with the waitress. Then they sit down at another table. The six of us all sit at this one big table. I ask, "Aren't your friends going to join us, Geno?"

He gives me kind of a strange smile and, removing that stogy for a minute, he says: "Well, they're really not friends, Pepper. They are, shall we say, employees. They make sure everything goes OK."

Well, things were really getting stranger and stranger as far as Tex and I were concerned. But Faye seemed to be oblivious of everything and was just having a good time. She was calling all the shots. There was no doubt about it; her Big Daddy Geno was the boss. Nobody did or said anything until he asked or approved it. When he laughed, they laughed, and when he pulled out a cigar, they lit it. And we had the best of everything for dinner. Faye made sure of that. When she spoke, he snapped his fingers and everybody jumped. We had all kinds of hors d'oeuvres and we had champagne. Then Geno ordered oysters Rockefeller. Well, we gave Cacapot a look! She roared back at both of us. "Oh don't worry guys. He's not getting any, he's just hoping."

Well, we all burst out laughing at that and Geno laughed louder than anybody. She ragged him all the time and he loved it. After dinner, Tex and I made our excuses and they all kissed our hands as we offered them to be shaken and escorted us to the elevator. We waved at Faye. As soon as the elevator door closed, Tex and I burst out laughing. Wow! "How strange was that?" Tex said. "What was that?"

I don't know," I answered, "but they sure got bucks. I wonder what they do for a living." Well, believe it or not, even though we had our suspicions, we did not really realize until that winter, and after Faye told me about all her suspicions, that we had dated the mafia. I didn't even know how to spell mafia, let alone recognize them. Faye told me that Geno had asked her if there was anyone that she wanted eliminated. She thought he was kidding, of course, and said, "Yeah, the umpire." When she saw he wasn't laughing, she quickly added, "Oh, wait. Only kidding, Geno, only kidding."

She also told me that he wanted to set her up in business and buy her a sporting-goods store and have her settle down there in Peoria. He also sent plane tickets to her folks, brought them out to visit her and wanted to buy them a new car. She finally put it all together and then got really worried. While Geno had always been a gentleman, one day he said to her: "We won't get married 'til you're through playing baseball and we won't be having sex until then, either, because in my family there is a tradition. We always marry virgins." Faye got really worried then and realized that she might be in some kind of trouble. But, fate stepped in on her side.

One night, Geno came to her house very late and told her he had to leave town for business reasons but that he would be back. Faye said that when he left, he had tears in his eyes and he had four guys walking him to his car and they just shoved him in. She thought the big bosses took him for a ride, put some concrete scuffies on him and dumped him in the river.

Anyway, after leaving Peoria, we went down to Rockford and Tex was acting stranger than ever. She and I were sitting in the dugout that night waiting for infield practice to start, when she hung her head down and said to me, "Pep, I can't do it. I can't throw!" When she raised her head she had tears in her eyes and she said, "It hurts too much." She said, "Make excuses for me, Pep. I can't do it." Then she turned and ran out of the dugout and up toward the clubhouse holding her arm to her side.

I started after her, calling, "Tex, Tex, wait." Then I heard John behind me saying, "Come on, girls. It's time to take the infield!" I turned back and saw Dorth talking to somebody at the fence. I said, "Dorth, Dorth, follow Tex." And I pointed, "Please follow Tex. Something's wrong. She's hurt." Dorth took one look at Tex and saw the way she was holding her arm and she took out after her. John was calling again for the infield, so I went up to the plate to John and said: "Coach, I'll take infield as the catcher. Send Dorie or Doris out to third. Something's wrong with Tex."

Well, Tex didn't come back. Dorth took her directly to the hospital. We knew that it had to be something really bad because Tex never quit! She played no matter what. She was like me. She never gave in to the pain unless it was too bad to go on. They took her to the hospital but it was too late. Her injury had been misdiagnosed as a bruised shoulder. It was bruised all right but she also had a torn rotator cuff, and by playing and throwing with it, she injured it beyond repair. When she first hurt it, if she would have been able to rest, it could have healed, but now it was too late. In those days, there were no miracle operations.

My buddy Tex's career was over and she was going to have to live with that pain for the rest of her life. I was going to miss her more than words could say, both on the field and off. The whole team was going to miss her. She was the heart of our ball club, laughing and smiling and always ready to do her best. Now, this meant that I had to forget about being an all-star third baseman, step behind the plate and put those "tools of ignorance" back on and take my beating. That pretty much ruined the whole season for all of us, even though we did finish in second place and went to the playoffs.

Tex stuck around for a little while to see us finish but it wasn't the same. All the fun was missing. She tried to root us into the playoffs. She even tried to throw a couple of times, hoping for a miracle, but the pain was too great and she couldn't do it. For our ball club, without her around, it was kind of like somebody turned the lights out on the ballfield. We missed her sunny smile. We did make the playoffs but we got knocked off in the first round.

Personally, I had a great year, hitting .205, driving in 40 runs, striking out only 11 times out of 370 times at bat -- proof that I was healthy once again. But it wasn't enough to carry the ball club or take us anywhere. The Rockford Peaches won it all again, going away. No one ever gave them any real competition that year. That was something I could never figure out. Nobody ever took any players away from the Rockford Peaches -- no matter how powerful they were or how many titles they won. Whatever happened to evening up the teams? I could never understand that. The old Silver Fox, Bill Allington, really knew how to play his cards.

Once again, I decided to take off immediately and head home. I'd picked up a halfway decent car at a bargain price. It was a 1940 two-door Pontiac sedan. This time it was from a dealer who was a great fan and I really did get a good deal. I knew I could drive it home and sell it and make a profit. By driving, I could then stop over and see my bro Joe and his gal Sal, and meet my new little nephew, "Baby Jody." More and more I found I was looking forward to going home almost as much as coming back to play ball. Maybe that "siren's" hold on me was weakening.

When I got to the Chain of Rocks Bridge in Missouri, I knew by my directions that I was fairly close to Joe and Sal's apartment. They were staying with Sally's mom and Joe had told me that she was a wonderful German lady by the name of Steena. I got kind of turned around; to tell you the truth, I got lost. Not being a man, I knew I had to stop and ask for directions, so I was looking around for a place to stop and I found this café and bar. It was appropriately called "Jody's Rumpus Room." It was around midnight so I thought, "Well, OK, I'm tired and hungry and thirsty, and I'm sure they have a public phone in there, so I'll just go in and have a beer and call Joe from there." So, I parked the car and went in. It was Saturday night and the place was almost empty. I thought, wow, I guess business is not so good.

The bartender was kind of a sleazy-looking character and he gave me a strange look and asked, "Out kind of late, aren't you little lady? What can I do for you?"

I asked for a beer and telephone change, thinking he was kind of nosy. Then, I went into the phone booth and called Joe and Sal. Joe answered on the first ring. "Hi, big bro Joe," I greeted him.

He answered back in a relieved tone. "Hey Sis, it's late. We were getting worried about you."

I said, "I got lost so I stopped to call you and wet my whistle and get directions."

He laughed at me. "What an excuse. Where are you?"

I answered, "Well, I'm at a very appropriate place. It's called 'Jody's Rumpus Room.'" I expected a laugh and a retort from him but all I got was dead silence and then Joe's worried voice came back and said, "Did you say 'Jody's Rumpus Room?'"

I started to say, "Yeah," when he cut me off. "Sis," he said, "Get out of there, go to your car, get in and lock the doors! Then drive to the corner gas station and wait for me."

I started to protest, "But I just paid for a beer ... "

He cut me off again and angrily ordered, "Sis, get out of there! Do as I say. I'll be there in five minutes." And he hung up.

I knew by his urgent tone that something was wrong, so I just grabbed my purse and slipped out of there. I hopped in my car and did what he said. It was only about three or four minutes and here he came barreling up. He didn't get out of the car, he just motioned me urgently to follow him. But, there was a big relieved grin on his face. They had an upstairs apartment, or flat as they called it. We parked and hopped out. He gave me a big hug and then he hustled me up the stairs. He explained on the way up that "Jody's" was a very bad place where bad elements hung out. There had just been a murder there the night before. He said, "Boy, Sis, you sure know how to pick 'em."

I met Steena, Sally's mom, for the first time, and she was just as sweet and wonderful as Joe had said. Even though I had only seen Sally a couple of times, I already was beginning to love her. She was so sweet and so much in love with my bro Joe, and she was such a beautiful lady on top of all that. I've only grown to love her more as the years have gone by and she's only grown more beautiful, inside and outside. The Lord has been so good to me, giving me such a wonderful family. Their apartment was a two-bedroom upstairs flat. The kitchen was the family room, as it so often was in those days. It had lots of counter space and was the center of family life.

The apartment had windows going all the way down one side with old-fashioned blinds. The kitchen table was covered with an old-fashioned oilcloth. We sat there until the wee hours of the morning, laughing and talking and drinking "teakettle beer." When you looked out the window you could see a friendly little tavern on the corner blinking its lights at you. They knew the owner and Joe would run down the stairs with Steena's old-fashioned aluminum teakettle. It had a big black handle and a long spout, and for a quarter, the bartender would fill it up with some good old St. Louis draft beer. I believe it was Schlitz. Steena fixed us snacks of all kinds. We just sat there and gabbed the night away.

I met my new little nephew, Jody, the next day. He looked so much like my bro Joe that I fell in love with him immediately. It was like he was my own son. That was such a wonderful visit. I didn't want to leave. I met some of Sally's family and got along great with her big sister, Oda and her husband, Paul. But, when we called Mom, she was anxiously awaiting my homecoming and worried about me driving home alone. I knew she wouldn't sleep well until I got home, so I didn't stay long. This time when I jumped into my car and hit the road on Route 66, I knew I had real family in St. Louis. Steena and Sally were locked in my heart forever.

If I had sis' arm
I'd be in the majors!

Joe and his St. Louis woman

Proud father Joe and Jody

Steena - Sally's mom

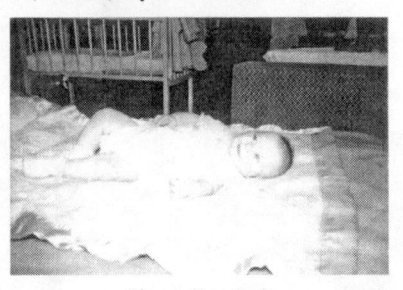

Pin-up Boy Jody

298

Chapter 31
The End of the Caca Era

As usual, arriving home was great and the warm welcome by my family seemed even more touching. They were so proud of me; they showed me off to all of their friends and I made the rounds of my relatives. Grandpa and Grandma Ote were getting up in their 80s, still they remained young at heart. They didn't understand everything, yet they seemed to realize and revel in my limited amount of fame. On the West Coast, the AAGPBL was not well-known. The publicity barely reached us. It wasn't like the hub of Chicago in the Midwest where we were well-known. Only the big things like Life magazine and newsreels reached the West. While the AAGPBL wasn't a household name, it was enough to let everybody know that I was at least doing something newsworthy. Of course, things were different with the media in those days. There wasn't the media blitz that you see now. It took awhile for things to get around the country by newspaper and radio. Something that happened five minutes ago didn't go from the East Coast to the West Coast immediately like it does now. Television was coming into its own, but it was very limited coverage. Grandpa Ote and Grandma Rhea had a TV and they were hooked on wrestling. Can you believe that? Grandma Rhea was in love with Baron Leone and Grandpa Ote liked Gorgeous George. They had some great battles with each other, as well as the wrestlers. It was a riot! I still can't get into it as a sport. Granted, they put on a great show. It's a little too violent for me, even though I know some of the guys personally and they are nice guys. What the heck, I guess everybody's got to make a buck. Then, of course, in those days there was the Art Linkletter Show and "This is Your Life," which was Mom's favorite show. Mom also loved a young comedian who did a standup routine about a travel agency. I think his name just might have been "Johnny Come Lately Carson." Then there was her secret romance, Arthur Godfrey. I had bought her a new 1948 Zenith 12-inch round-screen TV the year before. She was one of the privileged few to have a TV at that time. (It still sits in my garage.) On the surface, everything seemed pretty much the same. Russ was in and out, as usual, and he still knew how to work on me. I had the radio on one day in my room and Jo Stafford was singing, "See the pyramids along the Nile. Watch the sunset on a desert isle. Just remember, darling, all the while, you belong to me." Russ walked into the house and said, "Sis, where are you?" I hollered, "In my room." He comes in saying, "What are you singing? You sounded great!" Well, to be compared with the pure, beautiful voice of Jo Stafford, this was a compliment I couldn't ignore. So when he mentioned there was a movie playing that he'd like to see, of course, I took him. Things were changing. The shipyards were cutting back because the war was definitely out of the picture and Pop changed his profession. He got weary of that long, long drive to San Pedro, so he went to work in "Security" for a friend of his in Santa Monica. Russ was also working part time with him in security. It didn't pay as much, but the hours were much better. Pop helped his income by a little part-time bartending and he was still doing weekend caddying for golf tournaments, a job he loved doing. He'd been friends with the great Walter Hagen in the past. I think I mentioned about Dad caddying in those golf tournaments before. I also think I mentioned that I still had a set of Walter Hagen clubs that he gave to my Dad. They're old wooden shaft "jobbies." Those are the only ones I ever used in golf. Pop could have easily been a "pro" if he could have held his temper while putting. You know that old saying goes, "Drive for show and putt for dough." I was into golf in the winter now, along with bowling. Bowling was becoming my favorite form of competition. I still played softball on teams here and there, now and then. It just wasn't the same after having played baseball for so many years. Actually, I found that I did need a little vacation from it, which was very unusual for me. So I turned to golf and bowling. All ballplayers love to play golf whether they're good or not and you can tell that by one swing. I can tell you the reason why we all love it. It is such a great pleasure to hit a ball that's sitting there, just sitting there! Standing still, so to speak. Waiting for you to hit it. So I now had three passions besides baseball and guys. Bowling number one, golf number two and I guess I didn't mention horseback riding, number three. I had met a young man named Kenny Morgan who was a "drug store cowboy." He took me riding at the Griffith Park stables. We went with a group on moonlight rides up into the Griffith Park hills. Then we would polish the night off at an open fire with a pan-fried bacon and eggs breakfast with pancakes. There would be an old-fashioned, huge granite coffee pot sitting on the coals and just boiling away -- it was wonderful, grounds and all. Of course, every once in a while we'd add a little "liquid" firepower to the coffee!

I had gone back to work at Hughes, as usual. They were still going strong. Actually that's where I had met Kenny. Though I was having a good time, the thoughts that kept creeping into my mind were: "Wow, I'm getting older. Twenty-seven and I'm not even married yet. How long can I keep playing baseball? What's my future? How long will this body of mine hold out as a catcher?" I started taking some writing courses again and I was saving to buy a new car. I figured I'd drive back to the 1950 spring training, that way I could stop and see Sal and Joe. But I was no longer counting the days until I <u>could</u> leave. I kind of put it out of my mind and I now counted the days until I <u>had</u> to leave. I became more and more worried about my future because I knew my body wouldn't let me be a catcher forever. The Cacapot Faye was working with me at Hughes. They kept taking us back every year, anytime we wanted to come in and out. That was great because we really had no financial worries. We were paid good money because they knew we knew the work and that we did a good job. Another worry popped up there because Faye confided in me that her back was really bothering her and she didn't know if she could make it through the year. But when I got too worried, I could fall back on my old friend Scarlett O'Hara and think, "Oh, well, I'll worry about that tomorrow."

Another thing that had changed was my Dad. "Charles E. Paire the Plumber" was starting to show up again. In fact, he lived in the neighborhood. He was showing signs of shaking his own personal bottle demons. He was going great periods of time without drinking. He and Pop were actually able to be in the same room. Granted, just for a few minutes, but without blows. Dad was living only a couple of blocks away. Just a couple of blocks up from Uni High School. He had moved in with a sweet old widow gal named Mary Taylor. She had a little house on Barry Avenue. Mary had a big crush on Dad. Her house was one block off Wilshire Boulevard. Dad was taking care of her and the house. He still had the eye for the ladies and the silver spoon in his mouth and the charm to captivate them. This time he had a wonderful gal in Mary. Thanks to Mary, Dad had a few bucks now and he would slip me a "twenty" every now and then. I didn't want to take it, but Mom was OK with it. She said, "It was about time he paid his dues." So finally there was peace in the family and I could begin to form a relationship with my Dad and his little Grandma Mary. She was only about 4 feet 5 inches tall, or something like that. She was slumped over a little bit because she had a broken hip as a child and no doctors to fix it. So it healed without being set and it was uneven. It sort of gave her a little bit of an uneven gait. You'll hear a lot more about her later. She was truly a remarkable lady who lived a lot of great history. I would come to know her and love her as time went on. For the time being, I decided to set myself some goals I would have to work hard to obtain. I grabbed all the overtime I could get at Hughes, and eventually with my baseball savings I had enough to buy myself a car. I had a significant amount to pay down, $500. Big bucks! Mom got to have the old Dodge at her disposal. Russ was always gone. Dad was gone pretty much of the time working his three jobs. Mom was getting stuck home alone a lot and she didn't like it. She even talked about going back to work now that she would have transportation. She had catered a couple of parties at UCLA for the sororities and word had gotten around that she was a great cook. So a couple of sororities had asked her if she would come and cook full time for them. She asked me what I thought and I told her that I thought it would be great. UCLA was just around the corner from us. Mom loved cooking and she loved young people and she got along just great with them. I knew she needed to have something in her life to look forward to. She was still brooding about not having Joe and Baby Jody and his wife close by. I just kept telling her, "Well, you just wait. Just wait. They'll come. They'll come." But Mom was impatient and unhappy just sitting around, so this sounded like a good idea. I shopped around for cars and finally settled on a brand-new 1950 two-door Nash sedan. If I remember correctly, it cost me a total of $1,750 and they brought it down to $1,500, so my $500 down did the trick. It was a black beauty with lots of extra chrome and all the rest of the extras including white sidewalls. I thought it was beautiful. Of course everybody else called it a black bathtub. But that car always did all right for me. In fact, I like Nash's. You'll hear more about them later. I picked it up the day before I was supposed to leave for spring training. In those days you couldn't drive a new car more than 40 mph. They had a "governor" on them. You had to break them in slowly. They didn't think it would be good for your engine to drive fast, until you had at least a thousand miles on it. So I needed to leave early for spring training and drive slowly, giving myself extra time to get there. I was driving alone because the Cacapot was staying home until the last minute and then flying back. The season was a large question mark for her. I would get a dismal feeling in my stomach when I thought about that. Mom and I said our tearful goodbyes but it didn't seem so bad this time because

Mom had stuff to look forward to. She also knew that more and more I was starting to come home early and thinking about ending my baseball career. My plan was to drive straight through to St. Louis, stopping only at truck stops now and then to grab a cup of coffee and an hour or two of shut-eye. As I said before, you could trust the truck drivers in those days. They were the knights of the road and they watched out for me all the way, even when I was sleeping in my car. I arrived in St. Louis and this time I knew where I was going so I found Joe and Sal's house without visiting any gangsters' hangout. I knew I could only stay a couple of days even though they wanted me to stay longer. I had to report on time to get those 200 bucks. I stayed just long enough to hug Baby Jody and hug my bro Joe and tell him how much I loved him, have a few laughs and a few teakettles of beer with Steena, Oda and Sally (along with some of Steena's great German cooking). Then I was off to Grand Rapids to spring training. The teams were now all conducting their own spring training in their own towns because it was a lot cheaper. The league's coffers were getting a little empty, despite the fact that in 1948 they had the 10 teams and drew more than a million people to the games. In 1949, the attendance had dropped and the two new teams, Chicago and Springfield, dropped out of the league after only one year. Again, lacking media support contributed greatly to that. But the league, being a nonprofit organization, gave away too much money. They needed to survive the loss of Wrigley, his money and his press power, and they weren't doing too well at that. Anyway, we completed our spring training and still had a preseason tour to look forward to. That was necessary to pick up a few extra bucks and perhaps maybe line up some new towns to sponsor teams in our league. I wasn't rooming at the Sullivan's anymore. I just couldn't go back there. Things just weren't right. Corky and Dorie remained there but I couldn't do it. There were too many ghosts there without Tex. So I got permission from "Dorth from the North" to rent an apartment. There was a rookie pitcher I became friends with whose name was Mildred Earp. We called her "Middie." Actually, John and "Dorth from the North" asked me to take her under my Chick wing, so we decided to share the apartment together. This was going to be a new experience for everybody. Imagine me, Pepper Paire, "The Cacapot," being a good influence? Wow, I guess I really was settling down. I realized now that I was going to be behind that dish for the rest of my career. There would be no more roaming around free at shortstop. I decided to strap on that gear and really work at being the best catcher I could be. That's where the team needed me, so that's where I'd be. We had a very good pitching staff and a good solid ball club. We had some veterans on the mound. There was Ziggy, my buddy and Connie Wisnewski. We also had a couple of young gunslingers. We had Erlene "Beans" Risinger, who was about 6 feet tall and skinny as a rail, thus the name Beansie. Beansie was from Oklahoma and she threw a speedball. My new roommate "Middie" Earp was from Arkansas. In Middie's case, she came by the name "gunslinger" naturally. She was a distant relative of the famous Wyatt Earp. Both Middie and Beansie blew the ball by you and they had decent curveballs. But both needed help in the confidence department and that's where my experience would come into play. My "on the couch advice" would be needed. With me behind the dish and good pitching, it looked like we had a championship year going for us. We went down south on our preseason tour and it was pretty uneventful. We played local men's teams, as well as women's teams. I do remember a couple of things that were a lot of fun. Since we were going to be roommates at home, Middie and I became roommates on the road. We were exact opposites. Middie was a quiet gal with brown curly hair and big blue eyes. She was tall, with a solid build and a good figure. She had a shy little smile and she had this cute little dimple that would show on one side when she was really tickled. Middie must have had a bad romantic experience early in her life. She didn't talk about it — but you could tell she didn't trust men. I think she grew up with a brother like me and she pitched for their local boy's team in Arkansas. Middie had the talent and the desire. You could catch Middie in a rocking chair. Just put your glove there and wait for her to hit it. She threw an assortment of pitches that ranged from drops and curves and sinkers, to a great changeup that you could count the stitches on. Combine that with a high, overhand hard fastball in the high 80s, maybe 90s, and it made her one of the toughest pitchers to ever pitch in our league. Most of our pitchers threw in the range of low 70s to 80s. But there were, in my opinion, about three or four that threw in the high 80s and 90s, and Middie would be one. Jean Faut from South Bend and Lois Florich from Rockford were very fast also. Maybe our Chick "Beansie" got the speed up there sometimes. Middie turned out to be one of the best pitchers in our league, until she ruined her arm pitching every night. Like her counterpart relative, Wyatt Earp, she could shoot from the hip with accuracy! Middie could spot the ball on a dime and give you 9 cents change. She was pitching this one night down south in Tennessee on our little tour. It was a twilight game and it was cloudy and dark and there was a storm coming. They were telling us that the storm was an hour away and that we'd be able to get the game in. The storm was forming directly behind us and there was a huge light show going on behind home plate. It was still far away and mostly covered by clouds. Middie was looking right at it when she was pitching. Now we knew that Middie was scared of thunder and terrified of lightening. So we were a little nervous and anxious to get the game in. Everything was going fine. We were leading in the bottom of the ninth 1-0 and they had a runner on first base with two outs. Middie was throwing a two-hitter and it looked like we had the game won. Just as Middie started her wind-up, shooting her leg way up in the air and leaning way back to fire that fastball, she looked up into the sky for a last-minute prayer and guidance! Right then the lightening strikes right behind home plate! It was a jagged bolt of lightening that went all the way to the ground! Well, I see those eyes get terrified and then they started rolling like Groucho Marx's eyes. I'll tell you what! I don't know how she did it, but you talk about Elgin Baylor or Kobe or Doc J. You talk about "Hang Time!" There she was with her leg thrust way up in the air, her arm reaching way back almost touching the ground, her head way back; I don't know why she didn't fall on her head. Then, she froze when that lightening bolt struck. I'm telling you, it was more than "hang time" -- it was suspended motion! It seemed like about an hour later, the foot came down by itself. Then another hour later her arm came through and the ball came back to the plate. Well, immediately, up went the umpire's thumb. "Balk," he hollered and the runner goes to first base. Now they have runners on first and second. John comes out and we have a meeting on the mound. "Middie," he says, "Are you OK? Can you get it done?" Well, Middie says yeah, she's fine and we start the game again. And, oops, the lightening strikes again. Same thing! Middie goes into that wind-up, thrusts that leg way up to the sky, rolls the eyes as the lightening strikes again and suspended motion again! Half an hour later, the arm, the leg and the pitch followed through and instantly the umpire hollers, "Balk!" Well, this went on until we lost the game. John didn't think it was funny, but it was! After all, it was only a practice game. The whole team was trying not to laugh, but you couldn't help it. It was one of the funniest things I have ever seen! I tell you what, John got so mad he frothed at the mouth. He fell over backwards in his dead flop, turned that hat around and said, "Holy

305

jumping up suffering J__ C__." Middie, I wonder if you remember that? Another thing I remember about that particular spring training trip was meeting baseball's great "Joe Tinker." We actually played at Tinker Field in Orlando, Florida. Joe Tinker goes way back, even before my time. It was long-mentioned and often said that the greatest double-play combination in baseball was "Tinker" to "Evers" to "Chance." (Chance was the first baseman.) I don't know if anybody reading this is old enough to remember that but me. It was a thrill to meet the great "Joe Tinker." He seemed like a nice guy. He had his own little rinky-dink dirt diamond ballpark. He took care of it himself and kept it in good condition. No small feat, as he only had one arm. He had lost the other one in a hunting accident. I am proud to say that I have met some of the greatest ballplayers in history.

When our tour ended we headed back up to Grand Rapids the day before the season opened. Naturally, they weren't leaving us any spare time, as usual. John decided to have a short practice the morning before the season opened, just a little infield practice and maybe a little batting practice. I got behind the plate to catch a few balls and loosen my legs up and disaster strikes! I got a foul tip off my index finger on my throwing hand. You could tell it was bad right off the bat (so to speak). My finger was pointing in a lot of different directions all at once and pretty sick looking. Well, off we went to the "butchers," I mean to the doctors. Sure enough, the finger was broken in three places and the doctor says, "You'll be lucky to be able to play in three months." So he put one of those huge wire bird-cage splints (that's what they called it in those days); the kind that resembled one of those wire trellis things that you grew tomatoes on. Well, you've got to understand, I was the only catcher we had. At least the only one we could win with. So Johnny says, "Pep, are you willing to try catching with that finger?" I said, "John, how can I with this thing on?" I was waving the tomato cage at him. He said with that out-of-the-corner-of-his-mouth speech, "Well, I'll tell you what we're going to do. Wait 'til we get back to the hotel." Then Johnny took that wire contraption off, got a Popsicle stick, broke it in half and taped it to my finger; one piece on the side and one piece on the bottom. Then he said out of the corner of his mouth again, "Now, Pepper, we'll tape the second finger to the first finger and you'll be able to throw just as good as new." Seeing the look on my face he said: "Well, Pepper, I know it will hurt, but I also know you, and your team needs you. We're not going anywhere without you." He repeated, "Of course, it will hurt a little, but you'll be able to throw." I thought, "Oh, yeah, sure Johnny, easy for you to say." But, of course, I said, "Sure, John, I'll give it a try." I had to grip that ball with three fingers and that would cause the ball to float or drop. I knew that I was going to be in a lot of trouble trying to throw somebody out and I was going to be in for a long, hot, pain-filled summer. And I had been so ready to go. I don't know, sometimes I wondered what did I do wrong? We opened in South Bend the next night and they still had those rabbits on the basepaths. I took a little hitting practice and it felt really great when you got the ball on the handle. But I couldn't show any pain, so I retreated to the dugout. I stayed down in the dugout and tried to keep out of sight and avoid questions. I kept my hand closed so all they could see was the little pieces of tape. I tried to keep the hand hidden. The Blue Sox had heard rumors and as they went by the dugout they were saying things like, "Hey, I heard you hurt your hand. I hear you hurt your finger?" I nonchalantly denied it, of course. They had Shoo-Shoo at short and Bonnie Baker catching and Ole Libbey was hanging out in left field, and Shorty in center. They were small, fast and very good baserunners and they could slide. Our pitcher, fortunately, had a very good move to first base -- one of the few pitchers who did. She also got the ball to the plate quickly, so they couldn't get a big jump and that would help. Bonnie Baker was the first one up. She laid down a bunt for a base hit. Then she immediately took off on the first pitch for second base. Luck was with me and I fired one to Zig and we got her. I guess they thought that was an accident. So "Shoo-Shoo" came up next, got on and she immediately took right off for second. Wham! By the grace of God and the wind blowing the right way, I nailed her! The very next inning Shorty got up. Same thing, and I cut Shorty down at second. Well, they had wasted quite a few runs, so they didn't try to run anymore for the rest of the game. The gang was all asking me how I could do it with a bruised hand and finger that looked like a big red sausage and felt like, well, I can't put it into words. I don't know how I did it. I guess God was with me and I guess it was all instinct. Well, maybe not all instinct; maybe a lot of guts. I just shut the pain down. So I guess it was God and the wind and good luck. Our pitcher, Alice "Sis" Haylett, held them close to first base and that's what really stopped them. If your pitcher doesn't hold them close, your grandma can steal a base. The rest of that year, whenever I had to dig a ball out of the dirt, that Popsicle stick would hit the ground and send a shooting pain up my hand

and wrist. At first, the girls would all come running to see if I was OK. But I wasn't about to holler or complain. My answer was to do something fierce. I'd grab the ball and throw it as hard as I could at whoever was coming at me. That eased my pain and frustration a little. I hung in there because I knew I was important to the team. They needed me to win. Later, after they found out what was happening, the minute I got hurt, they would all go backing away. They didn't want to be on the other side of that fireball that I threw. As I said before, my fingers are not digits of beauty and my hands are not a pretty Palmolive sight. But you know what? I'm proud of them. I earned them.

We had a great pitching staff and they all did well, some of them performing in two positions; like Zig who excelled at second base and then came in on the mound and won for us. Then we had our "Polish rifle," Connie Wisnewski, who played right field and hit consistently, including the long ball. Connie, in 1946, set a league record by winning 33 games on the mound. She was a constant threat to win 30 games. Then there were Beansie and Middie, our fireballers! Our "ace in the hole" turned out to be Alice ("Sis") Haylett -- "Sis" surprised everybody that year. She came out of the pack as a rookie and pitched up a storm. She was a quiet, shy gal from Michigan. She had soft brown eyes and a lovely shy smile. She was every inch a classy lady, but, boy, could that lady "Hum Baby!" I remember one night I caught Al in a 20-inning ballgame. It was once again against those South Bend rabbits! We won it 1-0. Al and I both went the distance. That's the kind of baseball we All American gals played. All the way with all our hearts. "Sis" won 25 games that year and lost only seven. But she really shouldn't have lost a game. Her ERA that year was an unbelievable, fantastic .077. To put it in perspective, that means less than one run per game. In today's baseball world, a 3.7 is considered a great ERA. What kind of money bracket do you think that would put Al in in today's world? That's why when I look out there at the major league scene today, I just have to shake my head and wonder.

I had a pretty good year in 1950, despite my injured hand. In fact, I finally had to admit I liked being a catcher and I knew I was good at it. I enjoyed running the show. I had the knowledge and the experience and the pitchers knew and respected me for that. Of course, it would have helped to have a degree in psychology as I have said before. You had to know your pitchers inside and out to get the best out of them. They were all individuals and required different methods of handling. When I could have a year like I did, with a bad hand and still enjoy it, then I knew I was finally a catcher. A good example of what a catcher can do for a pitcher was me and Beansie! When she first came on the club, she had a hard time! She was more than 6 feet tall and definitely on the skinny side. She was all arms and legs and she could really fire that apple. She was from Oklahoma and not used to the big-city ways. When the game would heat up and the crowd got on her sometimes, she would get flustered. Then she would hang on to the ball too long and throw it low and into the dirt. This was happening in a late inning in this one game. Johnny came out and bawled her out. I tried bawling her out and nothing seemed to work. So I decided to try something different. I went out to the mound, took my mask off and peered up at her from my 5-foot-5-inch frame. I stared into her scared eyes and said in a very stern voice, "Beansie, if you can't get this next pitch over I'm coming back out here and I'm going to pee all over your left leg." Well, she looked down at me, eyes wide with amazement and her mouth dropped open. She turned beet red and pulled her hat down over her eyes. She turned her back on me and I could see her shoulders hunching up as she laughed. Then I went back behind the dish. Low and behold, Beansie started firing strikes. Her problems were forgotten. She had relaxed and started throwing that "Oklahoma Heat" and we were out of the inning. We had some great fans in Grand Rapids and despite missing Tex a heck of a lot, I still had a pretty good time. One of our fans was going to be the President of the United States of America down the line. Who knew? Yeah, President Gerald Ford was either a councilman or a senator? I think he was a senator for Michigan at the time. He used to climb up the stairs and sit behind home plate — and then fall down them (little joke there)! With John and Dorth at the helm, we won a lot of ballgames. We were good.

Middie and I had a great time in our apartment. It was a one-bedroom apartment on the second floor. It had a kitchenette and a front room with a couch that made into a bed. We had a lot of nice windows overlooking Division Avenue (that was the main street in Grand Rapids at the time). As a matter of fact, all the Chicks enjoyed our apartment (along with our out-of-town buddies). We were all from five- to eight-year veterans in the league and acting in a responsible way now. All maturing. I like to say maturing instead of saying getting old! I'm still maturing. This one time we really had a full house. It was on a day our game got rained out and the visiting team was our friendly enemies, the Rockford Peaches. We invited some of them over because, by this time, we knew everybody very well. We had a little rookie named Anita Foss on our team and she discovered a giant bottle of Virginia Dare wine that night. She kept saying, "It tastes just like grape juice. It tastes just like grape juice!" I bet you the next day when that grape juice was coming up it didn't taste as good. Anyway, Charlene Barnett was our second basemen and she was tanked. It didn't take too much to get Barney feeling good! She only had two beers, and when we turned around, Barney was missing. Now, the front door was the only way in or out of the apartment and it was blocked by people and chairs. Yet, we couldn't find Barney? Then there was this knock on the door, so we moved things to get the door open and there stands Barney clutching two very handsome policemen by their arms. Barney was a beautiful, blond-haired, blue-eyed, sexy-looking gal. She was a flight attendant in the off season and had a full boat of charm. She had that goofy look on her face that told you she had too much to drink and she pops out with a cheery, "Hi, everybody, look what I found!" The guys were in love with Barney. They were looking at her with adoring eyes. They escorted her in and said, "We found this little lady wondering around and we thought she was lost so we brought her here." They had a beer with us and left saying, "Have fun, gals." They knew who we were, but they were good guys and understood our need to relax once in a while. Funny thing though, we never could figure out how Barney got out of the apartment with only one door. We finally figured that she must've fallen out the window, and as loaded as she was, she didn't get hurt when she landed on the grass below. After that, I locked the windows every time we had a party. That year flew by faster than usual. We did all our usual things, such as our early-morning breakfasts at the "Toddle House" restaurant. If on a date, we ate at "Safey's," a great restaurant in town that made the greatest au gratin potatoes in the world. Also, the bartender taught me how to make the most wonderful brandy Alexanders you ever laid a lip on. Brandy Alexanders are usually made with cream, brandy and crème de cacao, with a little cinnamon and nutmeg on top and some crushed ice. But the secret is to use ice cream, not regular cream. Wow! It makes them taste like a thick malted milk with a depth charge in it.

We won our division title that year and I had a great deal to do with it. Despite my bad hand, I drove in 70 runs and hit .250, while striking out only six times out of 379 at bats and 110 ballgames. Playoff time was coming up!

**Alma K. Ziegler "Ziggy"
Grand Rapids Chicks!
1944-1954**

**Alma "Ziggy"
Ziegler**

Pepper with Jaws

**Bigalow Field
Grand Rapids, Michigan**

Chapter 32
Go Bear Hunting with a Stick

Disappointment was straight ahead. We won our division and were hoping to move forward, but we had to climb that Peach tree again. And, sure enough, we got eliminated in the first round. Again it was to be another Peachy year. I didn't want to stick around and see it, so I got in my big 1950 black bathtub Nash and took off for home via St. Louis. Once again, I would sip on the teakettle beer and visit my beloved brother Joe and my St. Louis relatives. Little Baby Jody was now walking all over the place and he was such a cute little guy. My bro Joe was happy as a clam because his gal Sal was pregnant again. While I was happy for them, inside I was thinking, "Uh oh, no California this year!" Mom would be disappointed again. Joe had been talking about coming back home, but I knew Sally would want to be near her mom and her family when having a baby. Joe was on vacation, so I got a great idea and said, "Hey, why not ride with me to California? We'll surprise Mom." Their money was tight and Joe said he didn't think he could go. Sally wasn't able to work now, so that's what made the money tight. I told them that I would pay for everything. Well, it wound up that Sally let Joe and Jody ride along with me. She said she just wasn't feeling well enough. She needed to stay close to home and her mom. It was pretty close to her time. So, off we went in my rub-a-dub-tub down that old Route 66. We planned to drive straight through. Since there were two of us to drive, that would eliminate having to get a motel. We could save some money and it would only take us a couple of days to get there. We were buzzing along Route 66 through that great Colorado River country and up through Kingman, Arizona. It was late afternoon. We were passing through those beautiful, purple mountains with those majestic, huge pine trees with patches of snow tipping them off. It was a breath-taking sight! It was starting to get dark and we were having trouble finding a place open for little Jody to go to the bathroom. He had to go really bad. So I gave him 50 cents and told him to hold it. Boy, he was concentrating on holding that 50 cents and it took the bathroom off his mind. I finally pulled over on a really wide spot in the road and Joe took him out to go potty with the bears. Of course, Jody insisted on going into the trees where I couldn't see him. Soon they came back, both looking relieved and smiling, and off we go again. We got about 15 to 20 minutes down the road and the smile disappears from Jody's face and he starts yelling, "Daddy, Daddy, my 50 cents. We've got to go back! I lost my 50 cents!" Well, we turned around and went back and I found the spot in the road where we pulled off. After all, 50 cents was a pretty good chunk of money in those days. That could buy two teakettles of beer. Joe and Jody got out and they went looking for Jody's money, but it's almost dark now and all the trees look alike. I don't know how many piles they found, bear or human, but they didn't find the right pile with the 50 cents. So they finally had to give up. That 50 cents is probably still up there. But maybe under a huge bear pile. Yuk! We'd have to wash it -- then wouldn't it be called laundered money? We all still get a good laugh out of Jody losing his 50 cents in the mountains while taking a dump!

    What a glorious surprise for Mom when I arrived bringing Joe and Jody with me! It worked out really well. Mom was now working, cooking for UCLA's sororities. They hadn't started their fall semester yet, so we could all spend time together. Pop could more or less name his own hours, so that was no problem. It was just real good, old-fashioned family time. To make things even better, Joe told Mom he thought he had Sally talked into giving California a try after the new baby was born. He had a job promised to him by Northrop Aircraft in Inglewood, California, and he could finish his schooling and get his engineering degree at UCLA. Mom was in seventh heaven. It wasn't so hard to wave goodbye to Joe and little Jody when they got on the Greyhound bus to go back, knowing that they would be coming back in the near future. Mom was also happy at her cooking job at the sorority. So I felt kind of good about things. I went back to Hughes for my winter job. Faye did too. But I definitely saw a big change in Faye. She was missing a lot of work and running around with a fast crowd. She told me that she had been released early from the Peoria ballclub because of injuries. Well, I heard differently. I had heard that she was being reprimanded, but she didn't care. Her back wouldn't let her be the carefree all-out ballplayer she always had been and she couldn't settle for less. She decided to hang up her spikes and move on. She was bravely trying to act like she didn't care, but she was hiding from the truth. Alcohol was starting to get a strong hold on her. She found out, as so many lost souls do, that while it relieves pain from the mind and body for a while, it's a temporary cure at best. It leads them deeper and deeper into the quicksand until it gets such a hold on them, they may never get out. It got so I barely saw her anymore and I guess it hurt her too much to see me and be reminded of what she was going to miss and what she had lost. It hurt me a lot, too, to see her like that! So when I headed back to spring training in 1951, it was a quiet and somber Pepper, knowing that I would be a lonely Cacaface without Tex or Faye. My baseball life would never be the same again and I knew it. That siren's call was still there, but it was weakening. Now it was just going to be me and there was no one else but Zig and Grand Rapids Chicks to share it with. While I loved her dearly, Zig did not do the wild and crazy things that Tex and Faye and I did. She was always a totally dedicated ballplayer. Not that we didn't have a lot of fun with our card games, our sermons on the mound on the bus, but it was a different kind of fun. Baseball was the focus of it. We had a few beers on those hot midwestern nights together and shared a lot of laughs. But we dedicated ourselves totally to baseball and winning for the team. So, Pepper Paire decided to devote her final years to serious baseball and make sure she ended her career on top. The wild streak was over. I was maturing again and I set out to prove it. Middie and I decided that the 1951 apartment was too expensive and it had gotten us into trouble. So she decided to room with Corky and Dorie at the Sullivan's. I ended up rooming with Jaynne Bittner. JB, as we called her, was from Lebanon, Pennsylvania, and had been traded to Grand Rapids from the South Bend Blue Sox. She was a pitcher with great possibilities. She threw a heavy ball with a lot of natural movement on it. That made her hard to hit. Trouble was control and lack of it. I figured I could help her with that. After we got to know each other, we got along great. We had a lot of fun together. I found out one of her problems was her eyesight. She needed glasses, but she kept it a secret. She thought they might release her if they knew that she needed glasses. Well, between her poor eyesight and my before-mentioned little fingers, JB really had a hard time seeing the signals. It is very important for pitchers and catchers to communicate. So I devised a special set of signs for JB. A pitchout was, I would pat myself on the head several times. Fastball, I'd shake my fist at her. The signs were so simple and so obvious no one caught on. It was a riot with me going through all those contortions. We'd all be laughing a lot when Jaynne was pitching. But the opponents didn't laugh too often. When Jaynne was on, she was very tough to beat. The year once again seemed to fly by. I was growing closer with Zig and Jaynne and Dottie; we did everything together, including the ever-popular canasta on the bus and our sermons on the mound. Our team was doing well but trailing the Rockford Peaches (as usual). Grand Rapids was fond of its Chicks and the fans gave us picnics, parties and barbecues all the time. That helped to pace ourselves. I missed the Cacapots a lot. But I heard from both of them regularly and they said they were doing OK. Matter of fact, to my astonishment, I found out that Faye was working for my Mom as an assistant cook at the sorority. Now what a riot that had to be! The last time I heard, Faye couldn't even boil water without burning it. For that matter, I wasn't so great at cooking either because my Mom did all the cooking. I think I inherited a little bit of her talent later in life. Faye's job was just to chop and grind and toss up the salad, take out the garbage, serve food, do dishes and whatever chores Mom had for her. She still didn't know how to boil eggs. She had lost her job at Hughes and, reading between the lines, I knew that she was still having trouble with alcohol. I was hoping Mom could help her with that. They had always been close. Since Faye and I had grown up together, she was almost like a daughter to my Mom. Except, they could relate a little better by just being pals. Faye's folks came off as "parents" and, of course, Faye was obstinate and stubborn with them. But sometimes she would listen to Mom. It sounded like they were having fun together on the job and I was happy that Mom had company. Meanwhile, I was living up to my "dedication to baseball promise" and having a really good year. Everything was going great for me on the ballfield, even against the Rockford Peaches. I remember in particular this one night when we were playing the Peaches in Grand Rapids. The game was locked in a 3-3 tie. The Silver Fox was still at the helm of the Peaches and, of course, every time I got up to bat, that "Silver Fox" would have the pitcher walk me. No matter what the situation was, they would walk me, even if they had to force runners over on the bases. They kept getting out of the innings without us scoring. So, I came up to bat in the bottom of the 12th inning with the score still tied. Lefty Lee was on the mound for the Peaches, getting the sign from Bill to "pitchout" and walk me again. The catcher moves outside the plate and Lefty throws the ball. Ball one, outside. It was a pitchout. Then, ball two, outside. Another pitchout. I noticed that the ball was almost reachable. So I act really nonchalant and ball three comes. Well, that one I was pretty sure I could have hit. So I just kind of let my bat hang loosely and acted upset and really aggravated, but I knew I could have reached that pitch. I just played like I was disgusted and hung my head down and waited. I was watching for the next pitch and gripping my bat tightly. Here comes the toss and, sure enough, the ball was barely outside the plate and at the last moment, I just reached out, took a swing and snapped my wrist and boom! The ball goes over the right field fence for a home run to win the game. The next day the sports writer James Martin wrote, "Pepper Paire went for a bad ball, she swung at a bad pitch and was lucky enough to hit it out of the ballpark." I guess he didn't know enough to realize that I had hit a pitchout for a home run. Of course, I had refused to go out with him several times. Maybe, just maybe, that had something to do with that, and the fact that I never got any credit from him. But what really amazed me was I did get the credit from the "Silver Fox." After the ballgame, he had come up to me and looked me right square in the eyes with those cold, blue eyes and he was smiling. He shook my hand and said: "Pepper, I'm proud of you. That was a heads up, great piece of hitting. I'd like to have you on my ballclub, girl." I was to remember that later. By now we were playing almost complete baseball, though the dimensions were a little shorter. We had a special 10-inch hard ball instead of the regulation nine inches and our base paths were 85 feet instead of 90 feet like in baseball. Our pitching mound was at 55 versus 60 in baseball. But everything else was completely baseball. It was really a great game for gals. You still had to look twice to tell that it wasn't actually the same dimensions as baseball. While the game was good, the attendance wasn't. It was dropping with the quality of the play. Having no farm systems was finally catching up with us. When a regular player would quit or get an injury, there was no one qualified to take her place. Though we had some junior teams in some of the towns and a traveling team in the winter, they really couldn't match the veterans' quality of play. They had already implemented a rookie rule in the league, demanding that each team had to play at least one rookie in the lineup. That got them some playing time and evened up the competition a little. Now they had to change it to a two-rookie rule. The fans were not seeing the excellent quality of play that they had come to expect. New management had taken charge in Grand Rapids. A promoter named Jim Williams, who operated several sports businesses and promotions in Grand Rapids, including midget car racing, had taken over our team. He was cutting every corner he could. We didn't actually realize that when he stepped in, he saved the Grand Rapids franchise. We didn't know that until later on. We thought he was just a cheap businessman.

None of us really knew how bad it was getting. We were blissfully unaware of the storm cloud brewing. It was happening in the big leagues also. The attendance was hurting. People had discovered television and they were released from their wartime jobs. The economy was still OK, so they had money to travel. Staying home and going to ballgames were not priorities at the time, especially when you were offering less and less quality teams. Once again, we went down to the wire in first place in our division, and we made the playoffs. But this time we got beaten by South Bend. Surprise, surprise. The South Bend Blue Sox went all the way. They even beat out those ever- winning Peaches. Once again, I had done my part by having a good year. For the first time ever in my career, I didn't play the full 110 ballgames (aside from when I was injured). I played in just 84 ballgames. John had tried to take it easy on me in doubleheaders because we had a pretty good backup rookie catcher. However, I drove in 56 runs in those 84 ballgames. I got six doubles, two triples and even a home run (which was a rarity for me). I hit a career high batting average of .264, absolutely great for our league. It showed that the rest helped. So I lived up to my dedication and had one of the best years of my career. Once again I hit the road for home just as soon as we were knocked out of the 1951 playoffs. I was anxious to see Joe and his family and anxious to get home. Again, I started realizing that I had to end my baseball career one of these days and get on with my life. But then there would come that sinking feeling in the pit of my stomach. What would I do without it? Once again, I would become my friend Scarlett, and I'd forget about it. On the way home, as usual, I stopped and visited Joe, Jody and Sally and their new little addition "Linda." She was trying to talk and walk and conquer the world all at once. She was a little blond-hair, blue-eyed beauty like her mom. What a rough time she gave her bro Jody. Boy! That struck a familiar note. It really reminded me of Joe and me growing up. Jody had this little wooden tool set with a cute little metal box. Well, he was just playing away, making believe sawing and hammering with his little wooden mallet. Little Linda was playing with her toys beside him on the floor. He kept reaching in and out of his toolbox, so pretty soon little eagle-eye Linda reaches over and slams the lid down on his hand. Well, Jody lets out a holler and shook his head and looked at Sally. Little Linda thought that was pretty funny. Sally says, "Now, Linda, don't you do that again." Time goes by and it happens again. Jody hollers, Linda laughs and Sally says, "No, no, sweetie pie, don't do that again." But she doesn't take any action. So, of course, Linda does. She thinks it's a real riot now watching Jody holler. Well, this happened about five more times and Jody keeps looking at his mom for help. All Sally does is say, "No, no, little girl, don't do that again." So, the next time it happens, Jody reached over with his little wooden mallet and calmly bops Linda a good one right on the noggin! Well, of course, she wailed up a storm, but she never did that again. Jody didn't say a word, just went right on playing. Linda was a real little pistol! Something told me that there was a lot of "Auntie Pepper" in her. Well, I had my visit with the family and my bro Joe told me that they were coming to California soon. I left happy! I hit that old Route 66, driving straight through, as usual. It was so funny how I couldn't wait to get back there and then couldn't wait to get back home again. One of these years something had to give, because now the urge seemed to be equal. One would tug me one way and then one would tug me another way. But for now, I was just happy to be bringing Mom good news. I wanted to get home and slide into my winter routine. After my usual warm welcome and a little rest time, I went back to work with Hughes and settled in with my old gang. I knew I could have a permanent job there anytime I wanted it and that was great. It took care of worrying about finances for the future when I wouldn't be making the good time baseball money in the summer. I knew my job and I was good at it and I had made a lot of friends there. They all asked me about Faye and, unfortunately, I couldn't tell them much because now she had quit her job with Mom and we didn't really know what she was up to. She would call me once in a while, maybe late at night, and we'd laugh and talk and get into all our memories. But I could tell she wasn't in good shape. My heart hurt for her, but there was nothing I could do. She had to win her own battle. So, I just kept her in my prayers. I had quit playing softball in the winter altogether now. I needed to save my body and my legs. By now I was really getting into bowling. I was on teams in a couple of leagues and I was getting pretty good at it. We had a team at Hughes. Dottie, June, Harriet, Gladys and me; we had a good time with that. I got so good I was asked to join a Ladies Major League travel team. I was carrying a respectable 170 average. Pretty good for a beginner (rookie, that is). I met some good buddies that way. I met Betty and John Rothmund, Lulu and Kay at Van Nuys Bowl. There was a gang of us that bowled on Friday nights, including Carol who worked there! We usually bowled pot games for high scores and a few bucks after the league was over. Then we would all go to dinner afterwards, so that kept my competitive spirit going. Also, my social life was still active. I was meeting a lot of guys, but not meeting anyone special. That gets harder as you get older.

I stayed in touch with my Grand Rapids Chicks. Ziggy and I were Californians and "The Big Hook," our first baseman and Anita Foss, our little rookie infielder, had moved to California. So we had all become close friends, especially after this one road trip. Our little grape-juice rookie had really crawled into an embarrassed shell after the wine incident. She had not spoken three words to anybody after the party. She wouldn't have said you know what if she'd had a mouthful. She was so quiet and so bashful until one night when we were coming back to Grand Rapids after a long road trip. It was one of those hot, muggy, midwestern nights and we were all peeled down to our traveling outfits; you know, the ones you wouldn't want to be caught dead in. We talked the bus driver into a quick, quiet, bus stop into the wee small hours of the morn, and I do mean "wee-wee" hours. We got off, did our thing, and back on the bus and off we drove. Good thing I was sitting by the window because I was half asleep when I hear this high-pitched squeaking sound. I rise up, look around, saw nothing, so I was about to lie my head back down when I heard it again. Leaning over, I looked out the window and saw our silent little rookie. She was running full speed, really pumping those little "gamms" up and down. She was in shorts and a T-shirt, hair in pin curlers, the whole bit! She was screaming at the top of her voice: "Wait for me! Wait for me! Help! Help! Wait for me!" -- you could barely hear her over the bus motor. Well I stopped the bus and "Nita" came puffing on. Her mouth flapping like a duck's rear end. "There I was in the middle of nowhere, in shorts and a T-shirt, no money -- yackety yackety." We shushed her up real quick so she wouldn't wake John. But after that, we could never shut her up. She made sure we all knew where she was at all times. And that led to a great friendship.

As usual, we were still working out on Saturday afternoons keeping in shape during the winter. After our workouts, we would have a couple of beers at the "Goats Nest." Then on Sundays sometimes we'd play golf at a municipal course. The Goats Nest was a little bar way up on top of a hill in Pasadena. We had to walk up the hill from Brookside Park where we practiced our baseball, so we nicknamed it the Goats Nest. I'll tell you what, when you're tired and hot and thirsty, cold beer tastes like chicken! They used to serve it in pitchers with big chunks of ice in it! Their hamburgers were fat and juicy with crisp, hot, homemade fries! Mmm, mmm! I can still taste them! Zig and I would pair up in the golf games against Nita and the Hook. The Hook and I being sluggers were the best golfers, and Zig and Nita, well, they were the best competitors. They would bet on anything. Best drive, longest drive, best putt, longest putt, so forth and so on. They even bet on which way the flag was blowing when we got on the green and they were very, very verbal about it. They would be hollering across the fairway, "My drive was longer than your drive." "No, it wasn't." "Yes, it is." "Here's mine. This is my ball." "No, it isn't. You moved mine!" "No." "Yes," etc. Hook and I would walk ahead and act like we weren't with them. We would tell the guys behind us when we got up to the tee, "Don't worry, guys, we're not good but we're fast." Most of the time we golfed at Griffith Park. At one time they had four golf courses there: two regulation 18-hole courses, one nine-hole course and a little pitch-and-putt course. I believe they were called the Wilson, the Harding and the Roosevelt. I can't remember the other one. They were beautiful courses laid out in the middle of the hills, with beautiful trees all around us and lots of green grass and shrubbery and wild flowers. There were always lots and lots of wildlife moving around! There were all kinds of birds and lots of squirrels and rabbits, too. When we would tee off real early or if we would finish late, the deer would come down and munch on the greens. We would have to holler at them to get them off. I bet they're not there anymore, sad to say. Hook and I got so we could break 90 on the big courses. Not bad for rookies. Of course Zig and Nit, well, I guess they broke everything else. One time Zig was teeing off and instead of hitting off the closest women's tee, she decided to go back to the men's tee. So she slugs the ball and it's a grass cutter. That thing whipped along and hits the women's marker and whistles right back and hits her in the hip. Well, before it even hit her, she's yelling, "I get a Mulligan." I don't know if you non-golfers know what a "Mulligan" is. But we used to give each other one "Mulligan" on the front nine and one "Mulligan" on the back nine. That just meant that if you hit a bad shot, you had the choice of taking one over. She could have been killed, but she's yelling, "I get a Mulligan." Well, as you can see, I really kept myself busy, not thinking about the inevitable. Trying to convince myself, "Maybe I won't go back to baseball this year." Everybody wanted me to stay home. My friends, my boss and, of course, my family. But that voice started in on me again and began wailing at me. "One more year, just one more year!" And I gave in!

Pop, Jody and Linda

Joe, Sal, Jody and Linda
California

Pepper Paire

Jimmie Foxx

Jimmie Foxx

Jody-Sally-Linda
Bathing Beauties

Boots, Jody, Linda, Mickey and me
California

Jody, Me, Linda and Joe

Pop & my black bathtub and little Jody

323

Chapter 33
One More Time

Despite all the signs and all the persuasions, I just couldn't do it. I couldn't say no to that siren's call. So I made up excuses to go: like, Mom wouldn't be lonely anymore because Joe and family were in California; I wanted to buy another new Nash, because I liked them and I needed my baseball money to pay for it; and, as far as my Hughes job was concerned, it was mine anytime I wanted it. So, of course, I made the decision to go back in 1952. My baseball siren won again! I was sure I was going to help the Chicks win that elusive championship that we had never won. We kept winning our division and we had the team to win it all, but for some reason we just hadn't gone all the way. Zig and I vowed that this would be the year!

American Motors had a new little 1952 model called the "Nash American Rambler." It was expensive -- $2,500. A lot of money for a car in those days. But it was so cute. It looked like a foreign sports car. I could get a real good down payment from my 1950 bathtub because I almost had it paid for. I decided to make the car deal here. So I traded my 1950 in and flew back to the plant in Kenosha to pick up my new car. I no longer had to make a stop in St. Louis, because St. Louis was now in California, meaning my bro Joe and family. They had stayed with Mom and Pop for a while and then they rented a little house on the next street over from Mom and Pop. Mom was finally getting to be a full-time Grandma and she loved it. She even quit working so she could spend more time with Joe and Sally and the kids. Pop loved it, too. He taught Sally the art of garage-sale shopping and they had a great time running around finding all these bargains while Mom watched the kids. So, this time I could take off without any guilty feelings. I flew back to Kenosha and my roomie Jaynne Bittner met me there and we picked up my little Nash beauty and drove it back home to Grand Rapids. It was a first year model. It was not the little "teenie weenie" Rambler, but it was a midsize car. It was a two-door convertible and looked a little like a T-Bird (to come later) or a foreign sports car. Classy black with a black top, it had gray and black upholstery with the cutest little continental tire kit on the back, along with white sidewalls. It had all the extras, including lots of chrome. Later on they wrote a song about my car -- "and the little Nash Rambler went beep, beep and the little Nash Rambler went beep, beep" -- or something like that.

We hit one of those midwestern thunderstorms on the way to Grand Rapids and my convertible top leaked like a sieve. That maybe should have told me something. But it really wasn't a big thing and they fixed it later. That little Rambler got about 35 miles to the gallon. Boy, I've got to tell you it was a beautiful little thing and it made me very happy. I found out later on that they only made a few hundred of those models. They made them only the one year because people didn't want to pay that kind of money for a Nash. It would be worth a mint if I still had it now.

After we got to Grand Rapids, we found out that since the Chicks had been taken over by private ownership, they were no longer a part of a nonprofit organization. Making money was going to be the new priority! We soon found out that the new ownership was going to squeeze expenses down to a minimum. We had heard financial rumblings going on all over the league and we were now back down to just six teams. Some teams were even taking up special collections from the fans to help pay the salaries. Giving away all that "good time" money was catching up to the league in a big way. So, while the writing was not on the wall yet, the wall was definitely being built. Corners were being cut all over and we all knew that we needed a really good attendance year to keep the Chicks finances solid. What better way to do that? Of course, win ballgames. Win a lot of ballgames! Win the championship! Zig and I and Jaynne and Connie and all the rest of the Chicks set out to do just that. Statistically the 1951 season could be called the greatest year of my career and I was determined to top that in this 1952 season. I felt there was no reason I couldn't. I had the desire and I was dedicated solely to baseball. I was healthy and happy being with Zig and my friends. Matter of fact, our whole team was happy and we were winning a lot. I had really settled in the nest and figured my career would end as a Grand Rapids Chick. How wrong can you be? All the teams were cutting corners all over the place and our new owner objected to the big cleaning bills that our uniforms cost. We usually had to wear our uniforms for a couple of days, maybe three days if you weren't a catcher. Catchers had to really stretch it to make that. Sometimes our uniform would really get racked up in one night, if it was a doubleheader. Now, the new rules said we had to wear our uniforms at least a week or we would be fined. A whole week! Then maybe longer if it wasn't too dirty. We got this message after a doubleheader in South Bend from Dorth from the North. They had a real dirty, dusty infield. "Are you kidding me?" I asked Dottie, "Look at me." I was grimy and dirty and soaked with sweat. "Smell me," I added. I had started out with a clean uniform that night. She said, "No thanks, Pepper. Thanks for the offer, but no thanks." Then she added, "I'm sorry Pep, but those are the rules." I couldn't believe it. It was the middle of June and those midwestern nights were hot and muggy. On top of that we had all those dirt diamonds. Well, you might say, wash the uniforms yourselves but they weren't made of the material that you could wash. Actually, they put a rule in that you would be fined if you tried to wash a uniform, they had to be cleaned. Well, I wore this one uniform for five days and I just couldn't stand it anymore without saying something. It was so stiff and sweaty, I could hardly move in it. I felt like the "Tin Man" from "The Wizard of Oz." Besides, it smelled like something out of a dump. Well, that night the owner, Jim Williams, was seated right behind our dugout and I stood up and offered to let him smell my armpits. He got very upset and I knew that I was probably in for trouble. Probably I would be fined. That night I got five hits and drove in seven runs. South Bend had really collapsed and I single-handedly won the game for us. We won it like 12-6. Connie Wisnewski, our Polish rifle, had gotten hit five times by a pitcher that night and my old newspaper buddy, Jamie Martin, wrote in the headlines, "Connie Wisnewski gets hit by pitcher five times." My name wasn't even mentioned, except in the box score. Well, after that game, the next night we were all laughing and talking in the clubhouse. We were laughing about how ridiculous that write-up was. Even Connie was laughing. In the middle of our laughing, John knocks on the door and then peeks in the clubhouse and points at me and says he wants to see me outside. He had that look on his face. I thought, "Oh no, not again." Yep, that was it, traded again! Dumped from the Chicks' nest. John told me that I had been traded to Fort Wayne and I had 24 hours to report. The owner had labeled me a troublemaker. My little speech had done it and they made a package deal trading Jaynne and me, my roommate, to Fort Wayne, of all places. Back in the Daisy chain. Really, all Jim Williams wanted was an excuse and I had given it to him by popping off. The real reason was because I was making top salary and we had a halfway decent rookie catcher who could at least stop the ball and she got paid half my salary. He didn't care whether or not we won. So, once again, I became expendable. I couldn't believe it, even after having a great year and the year before leading the league in runs batted in and the least strikeouts. I started the year way on top and I was playing great ball. They were still dumping me. This time I didn't even cry, outwardly. I was too angry, but my heart was broken and full of bitterness. I actually thought about packing up and going home, but I wasn't a quitter. The Chicks had needed some help in the pitching department and Jaynne only seemed able to win when I was catching her. Since they wanted to get rid of me, it didn't make sense to keep Jaynne. They also needed some help at third base. These were all their excuses. So, they wound up getting four players for Jaynne and me and still only paid out about half of the salary. I guess that made sense to the owner. Dollars and cents, that is; never mind that it gutted the team! Jaynne and I knew that they would miss us a lot and we also knew that we would miss Zig, Dottie and all the Chicks. But we were pros, so we held our heads high and took off in the middle of the night at about 3 a.m. After we packed, ate and cried in our beers a little bit. We said our goodbyes. We took off in my classy little Nash Rambler ... beep, beep! We only packed what we needed because we didn't have much time and we were told we would be back and play them in a week and we could get the rest of our stuff then. It was a rough way to treat us, but that's the way it was in those days. I guess it was the same way in the majors. You were a piece of meat and if they wanted to chew you up, or grind you up and spit you out, they could do that. The owners had complete power. They were on the honor system and we were under contract and a lot of them didn't have any honor. Ballplayers had no rights. Maybe that's what led to the way things are today. If they had shared that big pie, even little pieces of it, and had they been more honorable, perhaps today the owners would still be bosses instead of the players. Anyway, we took turns driving because we really had to push it. We had to report in time to be on the ballfield by 5 p.m. that next day and ready to play or we would be fined! We tried to think positive things all the way there. At least we didn't have to wear those bubblegum-pink uniforms anymore. Fort Wayne had classy-looking one-piece uniforms that zipped across the whole body and you just stepped in and out of them. The home uniforms were white, trimmed in red and blue. They even had road uniforms. Home uniforms and road uniforms! Wow! That was a biggy! The road uniforms were blue, trimmed in white and red. They were really great looking. Fort Wayne was still doing well. They had good attendance and good financial backing. So at least I wouldn't have to endure those stinking, plastic-feeling uniforms anymore. Jaynne and I vowed to make them sorry! After talking things over we decided it might not be so bad. We were bringing them talent. We just might be what they needed to win. We had heard that the Great "Jimmie Foxx" (known as "XX") was their manager now and it would be great playing for him. At that time he had hit more home runs than anyone else in baseball except Babe Ruth. In 1932 he had hit 58 to almost break Babe Ruth's record. After only stopping for coffee two or three times, we finally got to Fort Wayne about 8 a.m. in the morning and checked into the Van Norman Hotel as per our instructions. My old stomping grounds. It was a Saturday twilight game starting at 5 o'clock and that meant we had to be on the field at 3 p.m. at the latest. When we got there we were very surprised to find out that there was no one to meet us. We had expected a chaperone or maybe Jimmie to greet us because we had been told that they were living at the hotel also. Our stay there was only going to be temporary until we found living quarters. But there was nobody in the lobby. I guess they couldn't get up that early, but boy! we knew John or Dottie would have been there. So right away we knew things were going to be different. We were very glad because that meant that we could grab maybe three or four hours sleep. Actually it sounds bad, but it wasn't much worse than on our bus trips. Except my car was much more comfortable riding, and of course, there was much more depression involved, too. We laid our weary bodies down thinking it would be hard to go to sleep but it wasn't and suddenly it was time to get up again. Looking at the clock I saw that we had overslept and we weren't going to have time to eat. I hollered at J.B. on my way to the bathroom, "Come on gal. We're late." She mumbled something unintelligible about food and I just hollered back, "No time." So we rushed through our bathroom duties, grabbed our ever-loving duffle bags that were always packed with our necessities for the game like gloves, spikes, extra underwear, extra socks, sweatshirts, sweatpants and whatever. I don't know what a ballplayer would ever do without a duffle bag. As a matter of fact, I think they made the world "duffle-bag conscious" because everybody has realized how handy they are. Now they come in many different sizes and many deluxe models. Anyway, we grabbed ours and jumped into the car and headed for the ballpark. We played at North Side Field in Fort Wayne. We knew we were going to be late and I was sweating it out and J.B. was too because this would have called for a fine and a good old lecture from John. We didn't know what would happen here. We parked by the clubhouse and walked through the gate. There was no one to ask directions from. So we go inside the clubhouse and there was nobody there either, not even the chaperone. It seemed like there was nobody around, so we just jumped into our sweats, grabbed our spikes and our gloves and headed back out the doorway and across the parking lot to the ballfield. We thought that's where everyone was because there was a crowd of people just standing along the backstop and lined up around the third base line, including some of the ballplayers. That looked kind of strange. I said to Jaynne, "Look at that, must be some kind of show going on." She said, "Yeah, whatever it is, everybody's watching." As we looked out to the diamond, we saw what looked even stranger. There were only players in the outfield and nobody in the infield, except for the pitcher. She was standing on the mound and she had a ballplayer standing about 2 feet in front of her on each side of her. They were crunched down and ready for action. The catcher was in full gear kneeling behind the plate and waiting for the hitter. Jaynne said, "Wow, what a strange way to take batting practice." "Yeah," I answered. "Maybe they're working on a special play or something." I was puzzled too. About that time up comes the hitter, strolling to the plate. So then we saw what it was all about. It was Jimmie Foxx. The Great Double X as he's known in baseball's history. They call him "Double X" because his last name is spelled F-O-X-X. He was swinging about four bats like they were toothpicks. He was built like a "Mac truck," with arms that looked like tree trunks. He had on a sleeveless shirt. His chest looked to be about 3 feet wide and about 4 feet deep. "Wow!" J.B. exclaimed, "No wonder they call him 'The Beast.'" We both were standing there with our mouths hanging open. We weren't the only ones either. He dropped the extra bats and he steps up to the plate, swinging his bat over his head and warming up his arms. Looking at those muscles, Popeye came to mind. "OK," he smiled at the pitcher and spoke softly, "OK sweetheart, let's see what you got." She winds up and throws a decent fastball right down the middle and whap! The ball was a blur going through the infield. It stayed about 3 feet high and blazed its way to the left field fence making a loud whacking bang when it hit the wall and careened off it wildly. Jimmie says: "Whoops, sorry I didn't get a good look at that one. Let me have another one." Then he points to the two girls in front of the pitcher and says, "Watch out girls, just in case." He nailed the next pitch up into orbit and it went out of the ballpark and bouncing down the street. That's one we would never see again. He hit about two or three more and each one he hit seemed to get harder and harder and go further and further. Then he says, "Well, I guess that's all, I better not use up anymore balls," and he drops the bat and goes back down into the dugout. Everybody applauded and he tipped his hat with a big smile. We gulped and went over to introduce ourselves in the dugout. Jimmie saw us coming and he stood up, took his hat off and extended his hand, saying, "Hi." He had one of the baseballs in his other hand; that thing was totally flat on one side. He said "Well, they don't make them like they used to," and smiled again at us. His smile was complete with big dimples and a big round face and beautiful blue eyes. Wow, he was much better looking in person than in his pictures. "Sure glad to have you, Pep," he told me. "We need a catcher with some punch," and he added, looking at Jaynne, "We can always use some pitching on the mound." Well, we talked for a while, and I asked "where the chappy was" because we needed to get our uniforms and equipment. He laughed and said, "Well, she's probably shopping, she'll be here by game time." J.B. and I exchanged surprised looks. He continued: "Don't worry about it, just go back to the clubhouse, grab your stuff off the uniform racks. Take whatever number you want. I got to get out of this sun. It's too hot. Too many cold ones last night you know." Then he gave us another big smile, "Let me know if you need anything." Then as he turned around he said: "Hey, Pep, if you guys are too tired, you don't need to play tonight. You don't need to suit up, and hey, by the way, I know you didn't have time to eat. So if you want to go over and grab a hot dog, go ahead. But I'll tell you what, we could use you, Pep; we lost last night. Needed some more bat power." I protested, "Hey no, I'm ready coach, I'm ready." He said, "Well OK," and he flopped down in the corner of the dugout where it was shady. "That's better," he says and he flipped his hat down over his eyes muttering, "Somebody wake me at game time." Well, we went back to the clubhouse. Both of us were dumbfounded. Boy, was this going to be different than John and Dottie. We found the uniforms and got what we wanted. I picked out my favorite number seven. What a change this was. About that time some of the gals came in from hitting practice and we got formalities out of the way saying, "Hi" to everybody. Tiby Eisen, my California buddy, was now playing centerfield for the Daisies and she introduced us to the gals we didn't know. We already knew most of them. Tiby had played for John, and I said to Tiby with a big smile, "Wow, what a different atmosphere here, eh, Tiby?" "Oh yeah," Tiby says. She's laughing, "Yeah, we got a pretty cool deal going here. So just relax and enjoy it." After hitting practice was over for both ballclubs, we found out that we were playing the Kenosha Comets that night. Jimmie woke up long enough to take infield practice with us. I took turns with their starting catcher Shirley Bolder and I could tell that Jimmie was really impressed with my arm. After we were done he told me: "You don't need to start Pep, let Shirley start. She can take the first couple of innings and if we get out in front, well, then you can take a little rest. We should be able to beat this ballclub because they sure aren't going anywhere. Unless we need that bat of yours, you can have the night off." I said, "OK, coach, but remember that I didn't get any batting practice. I might strike out every time." He looked at me and laughed: "Are you kidding me? You don't need any batting practice and I know you're not going to strike out. I know your record. That's the reason we gave up four ballplayers for you. We need the RBIs. You already struck out twice this year. You probably won't strike out again the rest of the year!"

Well, the starting catcher did OK that night. As a matter of fact, she whacked a home run. The rest of the team did OK also. We won going away. So I got to rest and observe. The grandstand was still in touching distance behind us, although we did have a recessed dugout now. Not just some benches out in the open. The top of the dugout served as tables that the people used to lean on. The back portion of the dugout was paper thin so we could still hear the comments of fans. When the catcher whacked her home run, I found out that it was unusual, because the comment I heard was, "Oh my goodness, that's different. Better give her a saliva test." It was an unkind remark but it got a big laugh. Horse racing was going through a rocky period at the time involving drugs and putting the "fix in"; that remark was a reference to that. It was not a very nice comment, but it told me that I was more than welcome on the team. Shirley was a decent receiver, but she could only hit the size of her hat at the plate; that was about 6-1/8. I knew I was going to get the call a lot! So I was beginning to feel comfortable real early!

Once again I could prove to be the missing piece of the puzzle. J.B. and I both knew we could help that ballclub win a pennant! So, eat your heart out, Grand Rapids!

Gabby's flair enlivened Chicks

Former captain of Grand Rapids baseball team

BY GREG JOHNSON
THE GRAND RAPIDS PRESS

Alma "Gabby" Ziegler is remembered for more than the gift of gab that earned her a nickname from the local newspaper reporters.

She was a flamboyant captain of the Grand Rapids Chicks of the All-American Girls Professional Baseball League, a leader on championship teams in 1947 and '53, one of the best players in the league and even had a brush with movie stardom.

"She was our leader, and a lot of fun to be around, quite a character," Dolly Konwinski of Caledonia, a former Chick involved with the league's alumni association, said.

"She was also one of the best players in the league. The fans and the press loved her."

Ziegler played second base and pitched for the Chicks.

The World's Greatest Ballplayer - Friend

Ft Wayne Daisies 1952
Pepper Paire-Pat Scott-Rita Briggs

Chapter 34
Let the Good Times Roll

There was no doubt about it now. Jimmie appreciated me and I was beginning to feel a whole lot better about everything. It didn't take long to get settled. There were no rules to worry about so Jaynne ("J.B.") Bittner and I got a great apartment, just off one of the main drags in Fort Wayne, on Miller Avenue. It was on the second floor with two bedrooms and a big kitchen, and a large front room with a fireplace. It had windows that overlooked the roof. We could catch the sun in the daytime and sit out there and cool off on those hot muggy midwestern nights. The kicker: $25 a month! The owners were so happy to have us "famous ballplayers." They would have paid us. So, with my car, great apartment and no rules, we were "styling"! Oh yeah!

It was pretty obvious that Fort Wayne had a strong team. To start with, we had the remarkable Weaver sisters, Jean, Joanne and Betty. Jeannie was an OK utility player and played both infield and outfield, but she didn't have much of a stick. Then there was Joanne, who was the younger sister. She played left and centerfield, and hit up a storm. The last year of our league she hit more than .400, something that no one else had come close to in the past. I have to qualify that by telling you that by 1952 many of the good pitchers had long retired or quit for various reasons. The talent was thin and the quality of play was definitely headed in a downhill direction. Joanne was also a very good outfielder. She was tall and rangy with long loping strides and she covered a lot of ground. She had a strong arm, too, and plenty of speed on the bases. She was the complete package! Except maybe being so young she needed a little help in the knowledge department, because of her lack of experience. But that would come later.

Joanne was a top-notch player, but her older sister, Betty, was, in my opinion, the best by far. We called her "Fossie" because that was her married name -- Betty Foss. She could qualify as perhaps one of the best players in our league. Fossie was built powerfully, like a man; she was close to 6 feet tall and weighed about 180. I don't mean in any way that she acted or looked like a man. She was an attractive gal with a handsome husband who towered over her.

That was a good thing for him because Fossie was very strong. She was one of the few gals in our league who could have competed physically in a men's league.

Fossie was a natural for first base, being left-handed and having a great reach. She could hit from both sides of the plate. We didn't have too many successful switch hitters in our league, so this was quite a plus. Fossie was amazing at the plate. It didn't matter where you threw the ball, she could get the good wood on it. If it was a high pitch, she'd just reach up and club it; if it was a low pitch, she would golf it. She had great power, and, as big as she was, she could still run like the wind. The ground shook under her and you better get out of her way. There was no blocking the plate on Fossie, unless you wanted to end up with your head in the clouds. I was really glad that I was her catcher and not playing against her. Joanne and Fossie were both remarkable players and very good hitters.

By now, the dimensions of the field had changed again and we were almost playing complete baseball! Believe it or not, as the ball got smaller and the dimensions got bigger, we got better. The smaller ball went a lot farther when you hit it and it was easier to throw. Of course, it took some getting used to, but all our averages went up when our game changed completely to baseball. The problem was that the rookies were coming in from softball and their skills were suited to the small diamond and the underhand pitching. It was very hard for them to break into the starting lineups. The teams with the most veterans would win, most of the time. That was why the league established those rookie rules. As I said before, everybody had to play at least one rookie in their lineup and that was now changed to two.

We didn't have to worry about that, because we had some great rookies on the Daisies. We had our third baseman, Katie Horseman, from Pennsylvania, and she could hit with power. As an added benefit, she had a strong arm and could come in on the mound and throw, as well. "Horsey," as we called her, was a cute, little, curly-haired, blond gal with a broad smile and a laugh you couldn't ignore -- and all the hustle in the world! I think she was only 16 when she came into the league and she still had a lot to learn, but she was willing and able to learn it.

Our second baseman, Jeannie Carter, was also a rookie and a good all-around ballplayer. She could hit with power and she could also run. Jeannie was a very pretty gal with big brown eyes and a shy little smile, and a very soft voice most of the time. But she could fool you and she could be tough when she needed to be. When she got excited, her voice would go up about 10 notches and it sounded like she was squeaking. So we nicknamed her "Squeaky." I remember this one time we were passing through Gary, Indiana, on the outskirts of Chicago, where those ever-lovin' slaughterhouses were. (I've told you about that before -- the smell could wake up the dead.) We had all been asleep but now our eyes were watering and we were gagging and trying to act like we were sleeping. From the back of the bus comes this squeaky little voice: "Who sh-t? Who sh-t? I don't mind the smell, but when it gets in my eyes!" Well, that broke us all up and we were laughing like crazy. Squeaky denies it now. I was talking to her at a recent reunion and she says it never happened -- but it did happen and it was funny!

We also had the experience on the ballclub to carry those rookies through their mistakes. At shortstop we had the before-mentioned, beautiful Dottie Shroeder, probably the classiest shortstop in the league. Then we had old friend Tiby Eisen in centerfield. She was a fellow Californian like me. Tiby had learned to do it all. She had the experience to be a leader. She was a champion ballplayer in her ninth year. She covered the ground and knew how to play the hitters. She also had a good bat; I think she hit .265 that year. We also had veteran outfielder Wilma "Willie" Briggs, a good, solid right fielder and left-handed power hitter. She could run and she could slide. "Briggsie" also had the whole package.

We had a powerful ballclub right down to the pitching staff, although we did have to depend on some rookies -- but that's where a good catcher comes in. We had the veteran Maxine Kline who was always a 20-game winner. She was anchoring our staff. The rest of the pitchers were talented but maybe a little shaky, and that was going to be my job. I knew how to handle them and give them confidence. We had a round little rookie named Pat Scott, a cute, black-haired, chubby gal who could really fire that ball. She had a good fastball, a good curve and a little bit of a change-up. Pat Scott would become a 20-game winner with my help. We had Jaynne "J.B." Bittner and I knew Jaynne would be good for 10 to 12 games. When we needed more help on the mound, Horsey or Jeannie Weaver would come in and throw some fire. They would win on speed alone.

We knew we had a great shot at the pennant, but the trouble was, did Jimmie Foxx know or care? A lot of the time he would retreat to the end of the dugout and pull his hat down over his eyes and then the veterans would run the ballclub. Tiby handled the outfield and sometimes hit infield practice when Jimmie didn't feel like it. I handled the pitchers and helped with the young ballplayers. We gave them the insight that we had gained from 10 years of experience, and it was going to pay off.

Jimmie was a great guy but he was very unhappy about being out of organized baseball. He found it very hard to deal with "women" ballplayers. He just couldn't understand it. There were similarities between Jimmie Foxx and Jimmie Dugan (the character that Tom Hanks played) in the movie "A League of Their Own," but the movie went way over the top on that portrayal. There's no way I'd put Jimmie Foxx down. He was a great guy and the movie portrayal of him was greatly exaggerated. Sure, he had a drinking problem, but a lot of ballplayers did at the time. Jimmie was not alone. Jimmie was also neither vulgar nor rude. He was a quiet, classy, polite man. He had a heart that was hurting from being out of baseball sooner than he should have been. Maybe he was hurting because he couldn't defeat his problem.

At that time there was honor in journalism and journalists didn't blow things out of proportion -- they didn't try to make the news -- they just reported it. There's no comparison, then to now. The problems today are a lot worse than just alcohol. There's just no comparison between ballplayers of my day and those of today. I feel Cooperstown standards have been compromised. Ballplayers who get in the "Hall" now sometimes don't qualify for the right reasons.

Jimmie Foxx's stats were awesome. He played from 1925 until 1945 and amassed some impressive numbers. His career batting average for 20 years was an awesome .325. He had almost 2,000 RBIs with 538 home runs. He was voted the American League's Most Valuable Player in 1932, 1933 and 1938, and won baseball's coveted "Triple Crown" in 1933. He hit 458 triples, got 2,646 base hits and had 1,751 runs scored. He had a total of 8,134 times at bat in 2,317 games. He did it the hard way! Jimmie was nicknamed the "beast" because he once hit a home run ball so hard that he was credited with splintering the back of a seat in the left field upper deck of Yankee Stadium. Jimmie was actually close to 6 feet tall and weighed more than 200 pounds. He didn't look that tall because he was so powerfully built across his chest and shoulders and his arms. He had been inducted into the Hall of Fame in 1951. We didn't realize that when we were playing for him in Fort Wayne.

It took years before I realized how fortunate I was to play for such great men as Jimmie Foxx, Jim Thorpe, Max Carey and also Bill Wambsganss. (Bill is still the only man to have made an unassisted triple play in the World Series.) James Henry Foxx was born in Suttersville, Maryland, on October 22, 1907, and they're very proud of him in that city. He was married twice and had three sons and later adopted two more children. Sometimes his kids would come to the games and take turns being batboys and batgirls. I could go on and on about his greatness, but check the records -- he was amazing!

Later, Jimmie and I got to be good friends and sometimes I would sit with him on the bus in the front seat behind the driver. Jimmie would tell me baseball stories over and over. About how many home runs he could have hit if it wasn't for those screens and nets they put up on that short porch in Boston. They made a ground-rule double out of a lot of balls that he hit that could have gone for home runs. About the only time Jimmie talked was on those bus trips! When we were at the ballpark, most of the time he would just hide at the end of the dugout and sleep. But he didn't curse anyone, or spit tobacco, nor was he rude or crude. Jimmie would sometimes have a case of champagne on the bus and a case or two of beer. He would share those with some of us as he told us stories. Besides that, he had his little "pocket-pal" that he shared with no one. We loved hearing his stories.

The 1952 Daisies proved to be a powerful machine, capable of winning it all. Once again, I had arrived in the right place at the right time. With my experience behind the plate and my punch at the bat, I had a good second half with Fort Wayne, doing all the right things they needed. Helping the young pitchers and coaxing good games out of them. When the veterans were on the mound I helped them outsmart the hitters. My nine years of experience was paying off for our pitching staff. After the trade I wound up playing in 67 games for Fort Wayne and I hit a respectable .238. Jimmie was right: I went the last 200 times at bat without striking out. It was a cakewalk as I remember it. J.B. won 11 games and was definitely an asset on the mound. Again, I had made them regret trading me!

Jimmie grew to like and respect all of us ballplayers and he appreciated us as a team. At the end of that 1952 year, one of my fondest memories was our championship banquet. Jimmie shook all of our hands and told us "that we were all major leaguers in his book." I have a program that has the complete lineup of the team with me at one end and Jimmie at the other. It is autographed by the entire team. I went back home for that 1952 winter with a vindicated feeling in my heart and a good feeling about the whole year. I was looking forward to another year playing for Jimmie. I felt that he was on the mend with his problem and he would probably be taking a much more active part in running our team. He was a very likable man, and he really knew baseball. It was great playing for him and I knew I would be very proud to have him as our manager again.

When I got back home, I fell back into my winter routine, being babied by Mom and Pop. It was great having Joe and Sal nearby and we were definitely a happy, loving family. I was back working at Hughes during the week, golfing on Saturdays and practicing my baseball on Sundays. Our same group was there, except for Faye -- she wasn't around much. There was Nita, Inie (the "Big Hook"), Ziggy, Annabelle Lee, Snookie and myself. Some of the local softball gals were coming out to work out with us also. Bill Allington joined us and helped us work out. He seemed to have changed and was much more friendly and kidded around a lot with all of us. I was beginning to think that maybe I had been misjudging him all these years. Maybe after I got to know him, he might be a pretty decent guy.

Once he invited all of us to dinner at his sister's house. After dinner there was going to be a séance. It seems that Bill's sister had just lost her little 6-year-old daughter to some kind of illness, and Bill's sister believed in life after death. Her best friend was a medium and we were going to visit the spirit world after the dinner. Well, Zig and I thought that would be pretty cool, a real kick in the pants. We couldn't believe that Bill was going to be there and that he had asked us to come. The Silver Fox believing in spooks? We knew there would be no hanky-panky going on because Bill's sister, Emily, "believed" 100 percent, and it would be at her house. There would be no props, no tricks involved.

Well, the medium comes in and she looks like any ordinary middle-aged woman, carrying her purse and that was all -- no bags or packages or anything else. She was laughing and talking with Emily like a regular person for a while. Then we formed a half-circle with chairs. Bill, Zig, me, Emily and her husband. The medium sat in a chair in a doorway with the closed bathroom door right behind her. They had replaced the regular light with an ultraviolet ray light. That was the only prop. You could just see the outlines of faces and bodies and forms and movements -- you couldn't see any details. The medium tells us that she's going to contact her Indian guide and the Indian guide is going to the spirit world and bring out some spirits to talk to us.

She then asks us to join hands with her, making a complete circle. Well, Zig and I are cracking up, but we do it. The medium starts this strange chanting and suddenly a loud male voice fills the room. It seemed to just come out of the air. We look at her and her lips aren't moving. The voice is telling us he's chief so and so, and he's taking us to the spirit world. We're still laughing under our breath and I'm thinking, "Gee, she's a good ventriloquist" -- and that explains that! This went on for a while and then the man's voice goes away and the medium's voice returns and asks, "Is there anyone here that speaks Danish?"

Well, the hair on the back of my neck stood up a little, but I didn't answer. This was just a trick; she could have said any language. Then she says, "There's a little old lady here that can't speak much English, she speaks Danish. She wants to talk to her granddaughter."

I'm thinking, are they going to tell us that's my Grandma Paire? But I still don't answer.

The medium goes on, "She's telling me that her name is Chris, Chris," and she's fumbling for words. Then she says, "I think it's Christina."

OK, it's getting interesting. No one there knew that I had a Danish grandma who didn't speak English, let alone her name. So, I thought I'd better speak up. I said softly, "Well, my Grandma Paire's name was Christina Bodina and she was Danish."

It turns out that was supposed to be my grandma and she wanted to speak to me. So, I agreed to let her come out of the spirit world and talk to me. The medium said I had to wish for it and believe in it strongly. I'm feeling a little nervous, but I'm saying, "OK, God, if it's really her, let her come out."

There's a hissing sound and this white, milky mist comes out from under the medium's chair and forms a ghostly little figure in misty white flowery robes. Now I can't say it looked like my Grandma Paire but it was tiny and chubby and sort of built like her. The head was shrouded and you couldn't see any of the features, only the eyes. They were like radiant ruby red spots glowing out of her head. Well, my supposed grandma speaks to me for a while and I couldn't understand this spirit any better than I could the real grandma. She could barely speak English and had this heavy Danish accent. She talks to me for a while and the only thing I could understand was when she said, "Can I give you a kiss?"

I said OK and felt this cool little touch on my face and then she was gone, back to her spirit world, I guess. Different forms and shapes come out, supposedly representing people. Ziggy talked to a couple and then they would disappear. This was getting spookier by the moment. Our hands were cold and clammy. Eventually, the medium brings Emily's little girl out and she talks to her momma for a while and then she goes and plays with her little doll. You could hear the doll crying. Finally, the little girl disappears and then the whole thing is over and the lights come back on. Zig and I were definitely relieved and we were brave again, whispering and laughing, both of us were wondering how the tricks were done? There were probably pills for the mist, and she is definitely a good ventriloquist. Then I had a weird thought! I guess I had a funny look on my face because Zig says, "What's wrong, Pep? What's wrong?"

I didn't answer, I just pointed, and said, "Ziggy, the doll!"

"Yeah," she said. "So what?"

I said, "Ziggy, the doll! It was in the other corner, clear across the room."

"So what?" Then it dawned on her. "Oh yeah. How about that! How did they do that?"

Well, we never did figure that one out. While I still find it hard to believe that we were actually talking to spirits, I couldn't figure out how that doll got clear across the room before anyone left their seats. I could explain a lot of it -- trick pills under the chair, the mist, but the doll physically moving 20 feet across the room without any help? Even the Silver Fox couldn't explain that one. So, maybe we actually did speak with spooks!

Once again, what with working, baseball, going to the beach, doing all my fun things, the 1952 winter was flying by. I was becoming good friends with Sally and by now we all knew that Joe had picked the right gal. I was getting more serious about my bowling and was bowling in a league in Santa Monica, along with some of the other ballplayers, and I was making new friends there also. We always had a good time at the Santa Monica Bowl. It wasn't far from the house and Mom would come down and watch me bowl in the ladies' major bowling league. Nobody wanted me to leave and play ball again. Of course, I was telling myself and everyone else the same story. That voice was nagging at me, "One more year, one more year." I wanted to win the whole thing in 1953 for Jimmie Foxx.

    I didn't have any reason not to go and I knew we had the team to do it. So off I went. Everybody knew we had a strong team -- and I do mean everybody, and that included the Silver Fox. His Rockford Peaches had been struggling these last couple of years. Now I don't know how he did it, but when I got back to Fort Wayne for spring training, expecting to find Jimmie Foxx, he's gone. Who's the boss? The Silver Fox, Bill Allington. Somehow, during the whole life of the league, Bill Allington always seemed to get what he wanted.

    So, there it was. Bill Allington knew that the Fort Wayne ballclub was going to be a powerful team and he wanted to manage it. I would now be playing for my old enemy. I hoped that my new image of him was true. I wasn't alone in my apprehension. From Jimmie Foxx to the Silver Fox was quite a transition and everybody on the Daisy ballclub was waiting to see and check out how Bill would be as manager.

Rockford catcher Ruth Richards
making the tag.
The way we played the game!

Silver Foxs
L-End standing - Bill Allington
R-End standing - Doris Tetzlaff (Chaperone)
Back row standing fourth from left - Jaynne
Front row kneeling 4th from right - Pepper

Chapter 35
On the Rocks with the "Silver Fox!"
(For the Last Hurrah!)

I felt that Bill Allington might object to J.B. and me having an apartment, but when I asked him, he just smiled and said, "No problem. Just don't let it interfere with your baseball." Bill was a charming man when he wanted to be and still very handsome, with chiseled features. He kind of resembled Charlton Heston. He always had a great tan and cold, steel blue eyes that complemented his wavy silver crown. His hair had been prematurely white from the age of 18. Given our past history, I had to wonder how we were going to get along. I had been looking forward to 1953 and winning a pennant with Jimmie Foxx -- but with the Silver Fox? I had my doubts!

Things started off good, however. I still had my fine catcher's arm and the brains to go with it. I had proven I had the ability to hit with all the ducks on the pond and Bill seemed to appreciate the job I was doing behind the plate. We still had the same strong ballclub, but a couple of our pitchers had developed sore arms out of spring training and that made us a little short in our pitching staff. Bill asked me how I would feel about pitching a game or two. He knew I could throw hard and I showed a little promise when I pitched batting practice. He also knew that I knew where to throw to those hitters.

I said, "Sure, I'll give it a try." I knew my arm could take it because I had never had a sore arm in my 10 years as a pro. It was about the only thing that wasn't sore or broken or hurt. I always warmed up my legs first. Then I just tossed the ball before throwing it hard. I also had a pure straight overhand throw. I fired it right by my ear most of the time, unless I had to throw from the side to beat a runner on a bunt. I wound up pitching three ballgames that year -- and I won them all, with a 1.00 ERA. Not bad for a rookie!

One Sunday in Fort Wayne, I pitched the first game of a doubleheader and caught the second game. We won both games so I was the winning pitcher in more ways than one. By the second half of the season, I was getting tired and had lost a little bit of my gung-ho, so I tried to take it a little easy at practice and save it for the games. Bill didn't like that, even though he knew I was doing double duty and was always hustling and ready to answer the bell at game time. He also didn't like my social life. Bill had a reputation with the ladies and I think he might have wanted to add me to that list, but that wasn't for me. I think Bill knew that and resented it.

We had a good young catcher named Rita Briggs. Rita was a left-handed hitter, a fast runner and a good receiver. Her legs were still strong because she was a rookie. Bill was partial to left-handers, being one himself. I think I was a better receiver and better with the pitchers, as well as a better RBI hitter. At first, I got most of the duty, but as the year went on Rita started getting more and more of the starts. This seemed to start after we had a little party at our apartment on one of our nights off.

The Chicks were in town and I invited some of my old buddies, along with some of the local guys, to a party at our apartment. We were dancing and drinking a little bit, not doing anything really wrong. It was a typical Fort Wayne night, hot and humid. Some of the guests were sitting out on the roof to cool off. There was a knock at the door and there stood Bill. I guess a couple of beer cans sort of rolled off the roof (accidentally, of course) and rolled on down the street (again, accidentally) and hit or got run over by a taxi cab. The cab driver called the cops and said there's a wild party going on, and the cops called Bill. That broke up the party and we sent everyone home. Bill told me that if I didn't have anything else to do on the next hot and humid off night, I could visit him in his nice cool, air-conditioned hotel room. Well, I told him, "Bill, it will never get that hot!"

From that time on, I noticed that my playing time was really diminished. When I asked why, Bill said it was because we were way out front and Briggsie needed the experience. So 1953 turned out to be a long and grueling season and even though we won a hard-fought championship, I was physically and mentally drained. Time and injuries were taking their toll on me. I knew I couldn't last forever. I was tired of everything, and I was disillusioned at not getting the number-one call from Bill. What the heck, maybe they were getting ready to deal me again. It just wasn't the same. The spirit wasn't there anymore. My body was hurting and the quality of the game wasn't the same. I had been at it for 10 years and I knew I sure wasn't the same.

My temper was getting short, even with the umpires. As an example, I can remember one night when we were playing against the Chicks, my buddy Zig was one of the best there was at the "phantom tag." This one night when I slid into second base, the throw had beat me by quite a bit and Zig tried to lay a tag on me but I slid away from the bag and she missed me by a foot. Lou Remkus, a pro football player from the Chicago Bears, was moonlighting as an umpire in our league. Pro football wasn't making it big yet in those days. There was no money in it, so they had second jobs.

Well, "Big Lou" was on the wrong side of the play and he called me out. He bent down with his thumb in the air. I jumped up, whirled around and my right hand hit him right under the chin, and I decked him. It was an accident; I guess Big Lou had a glass chin. Actually, Lou was about 6 feet 4 inches and weighed about 280 pounds. Boy! Down he went! He was as startled as I was. There he was, lying on the ground, looking up at me and saying, "Pepper, I guess you know you're out of the game for this." He knew I wasn't the kind that would do that on purpose, but the contact was made. He had to do it. Walking off, I had a parting shot. "Well Lou, you might have thrown me out, but that catcher didn't!"

That cost me 10 bucks -- no small figure in those days. Max Carey sent me a telegram saying, "You better watch it, Pepper. This could get expensive." I've still got that telegram from him. It's in my scrapbook. It wasn't so much the 10 bucks but when you get thrown out of a ballgame, it really hurts the ballclub. That was one thing I was always careful of as a catcher. You could hurt your pitcher if you got too smart with an umpire. I don't care how bad he was, you had to deal with him. It's no different in the majors. If the umps have it in for you, close calls will never go your way. That's just the way it is.

You can get away with a lot if you don't turn around on the umpire and make him look bad in front of the fans. With my gift of gab, my approach always was to say something like, "Hey, I know you can miss one, but that was a good pitch." I would not look back and I tried not to sound angry. You have to do what is best for the team. Suck it up and bite the bullet. That's the way you win ballgames. In my 10 years as a ballplayer in the All American, in more than 1,000 games, I only got tossed out twice. So you see, I did practice what I preached.

Once again, we won the pennant, being the best team for 112 ballgames, but we lost out in the championship series in the first round, ironically, to the Grand Rapids Chicks. I was almost secretly glad about that because Bill really hated getting beat by Ziggy and the Chicks. When it was over, I got out of there as quickly as I could. I breathed a sigh of relief and headed home.

This time it was my Mom's voice I was hearing, "Stay home, baby, stay home. Quit while you're still in one piece. I'm afraid later in life your body is going to pay for this terrible beating you're giving it." (And she was right.) Her voice was drowning out that siren's wail. Maybe, just maybe, I could do it this time. It was on my mind the whole trip home. I drove the 2,000 miles straight through from Chicago to L.A. in my ever-loving Rambler, once again just stopping at truck stops along the way.

When I stopped for gas, everyone would ask, "Hey, what a great car! It's a foreign sports car, right?" Well, I got tired of explaining so I would just agree with them, whatever they said. But it was fun having everyone admire it. It was such a great little car. I think it would be a great retro car for today. It was just too far ahead of its time.

I was home again in a couple of days and once again under my umbrella of love and so happy to be there. I needed to rest my body for a while and get reacquainted with my family and friends. In the last couple of years, I had lost Grandma Rhea and Grandpa Ote, and Grandma B and Grandpa B were gone. They had died while I was back playing ball and it seemed like I was just realizing it. I looked around and my family had become smaller. It seemed like I felt their loss more now than I did when it happened.

When I looked in the mirror, I saw this 29-year-old woman with short, curly red hair and tired-looking eyes, ready to turn 30. Where had she come from? Where did the redheaded, high-spirited, pig-tailed Pepper Paire go? It was as though the last 10 years had happened so suddenly. When I took a good look at Mom, I realized that she was aging and looking older, too. Oh my God! What had I missed? There was this panicky feeling in my heart and I didn't know why. I just hugged my Mom really hard and vowed to tell her I loved her every day. Something was telling me I needed to do that.

I tried to put all these thoughts behind me and went back to work at Hughes Aircraft for my loyal bosses, Chuck and Carl. The gang was still all there and glad to see me. June, Gladys, Dottie and Harriet, and our cute little boss, Don Belle -- who was now making eyes at Dottie. I was still having all those disturbing thoughts of what I had lost and what my baseball had cost me, and was it worth it? Then a tight knot would form in my belly. Where was I going from here? It seemed I couldn't be Scarlett anymore. I didn't have time to wait until tomorrow. I guess I was going through a withdrawal from baseball, a midlife crisis. I don't know what you would call it, but there were sure a lot of disturbing thoughts in my heart and on my mind.

I needed competition, so I started bowling again at my Santa Monica Lanes in the Ladies Major League. Every Friday night Mom would come with me, and that did my heart good to see her laugh and have fun. As usual, I would stay after and bowl in the "pot" games. That meant that we would put money in a "pot" and the high game would win it. I won more than my share of those and I began to notice that quite often I would be duking it out with this handsome, blond-haired guy by the name of Bob Davis. It was a friendly war and Bob and Mom and I would often wind up buying each other a beer afterward. We didn't bowl on the same team but it got so that I'd find myself looking around for him while the league was going on. When I spotted him, I'd feel this little flutter in my throat because he'd be looking right at me with a smile on his handsome face.

Pretty soon, it became a steady thing. After the "pot" games, Bob and I, and Mom, too, if she was there, would go into the bar and have a couple of drinks and something to eat. I was learning a lot about Bob and I liked what I learned. He had been in the Naval Air Force, enlisted like most of our guys did. He was a tail gunner on a two-man dive bomber called The Douglas Dauntless! They flew off of a carrier in the South Pacific, stationed in Hawaii. After Pearl Harbor, he had been discharged in San Francisco. Bob was originally from Kalispell, Montana. He had decided to stick around Southern California for a while and see what big-city life was all about. He had met and married a young gal and they had a couple of kids right away, but it didn't work out -- both too young, I guess. Bob didn't talk much about it.

He was a great athlete and built like one. He was about 5 feet 11 inches and weighed about 180 pounds, all muscle. He had wavy blond hair with sky blue eyes, that kind of poked fun at you when he looked at you. There was something in those eyes and that whimsical smile that took my breath away. I was in love again, and this time I knew it was for real. Bob had won the Montana State College Golf Championship and was an all-star shortstop for Whitefish University. On top of that, he was also an all-star point guard for their basketball team. He probably would have had a shot at the pros but the war ended his career before it got started.

We had a lot of fun talking sports. Bob couldn't get over the fact that I was a pro baseball player and he admired my bowling, too. I was doing pretty good, carrying a 180 average. Now that's not all that great and I've seen times when I'd settle for that as a batting average. But it's a pretty good average for someone who only bowled one night a week and was kind of new at the game. When Bob found out I also golfed, he really got excited. Not too many women were good at golf in those days. I could tell he admired me a lot.

Mom was usually along through all the bowling but she started going home after we'd get done eating. She knew something was happening between Bob and me, and she didn't want to be in the way of anything. After the "pot" games were over, some of us would go into the bar and we'd dance to the jukebox. I found out that Bob was a great dancer and that he loved to dance, like me. He had a very unorthodox style and couldn't get over how I could follow him so easily. He was not used to that because he was one of those dancers with whom you never knew what step was coming next. There was never anything that was really routine, and it was inventive and good. Actually, I could always tell the way he was going by his touch -- actually, I could tell a lot by his touch! I'd kick off my shoes and we'd jitterbug to Jimmy and Tommy Dorsey, Bill Doggett, Glenn Miller, Artie Shaw and all the rest of those great big bands. They ruled the swing era. I'd usually come home with holes in my socks. I wore them out regularly.

After a little while of being with Bob, I realized he was getting to me. There was a competition that I had never felt before. We had a mutual love of sports and our natural competitive natures seemed to make everything a lot of fun. He didn't get mad at me when I beat him -- and I did beat him sometimes! Most of the other guys I went with couldn't handle that. But, instead of getting mad, Bob was always very proud of me and my athletic skills. I thought: "Hey, wow! Wait a minute here. This is different. Maybe I'd better stay home and see if I can hook this guy."

That's the real reason I didn't go back to the league in 1954. I wanted to make sure I could get my handsome Bob for myself, and I had plenty of competition. There were a lot of girls after him, in particular, the glamorous barmaid Millie at Santa Monica Bowl. He had been going with her before he met me. Well, I decided that this was the time to test myself and see what life would be like without baseball. I found out, to be honest, that it wasn't going to be easy. I didn't know what to do with myself at night when I wasn't with Bob. When I went home and went to bed, I couldn't sleep! I was so used to going out for that steak at midnight and those two cold beers. I missed the laughing and talking about the win or the crying over the loss. I even missed riding on that bus until the wee hours of the morning. I missed singing our songs or listening to the birds while watching the farm fields go by and counting the white horses, all the while praying for the rain.

I kept having to put all that in the back of my mind. For the first time, I wasn't going to be playing baseball at Easter. I got a telegram in April 1954 from the Silver Fox asking, "Where are you going for Easter, Pepper?" He told me that Briggsie, who was now the number-one catcher, was hurt. She was out with a broken wrist and I could name my own price to report. I was tempted but I was out of shape, and I also was deeply in love with my man. On top of that, I was still trying very hard to see what life was like without baseball. I could always go back next year, couldn't I?

The telegrams came all the way into July, saying, "Name your price." I was very tempted but I said no to the 1954 season. I put those telegrams into my scrapbook and closed it. It was the first time in my life that a man became more important to me than baseball. I figured that I'd sit out this year, make sure I hooked Bob and then talk him into letting me play one more year in the All American. I figured I could go back as a pitcher. I knew I could do a decent job on the mound.

Bob and I got engaged and it was easy to talk him into letting me finish one more year and play in the 1955 season. He was even talking about coming with me because he wanted to see me play. I had failed my test! I had missed baseball too much, and I knew I wasn't ready to give it up, even though I had found the man I wanted to spend the rest of my life with. So, we were making plans. Bob and Mom were going to come back in the middle of the season and visit me in Fort Wayne. They still wanted me on the team. Then I figured that would be the end.

Spring training was just around the corner and I was all set and ready to go when, out of the clear blue sky -- literally, out of nowhere, came the abrupt collapse of the league. One of the teams had dropped out at the last minute, leaving only five teams and two of those were shaky! You can't have a five-team league; it just wouldn't work. After 12 glorious, successful years, the All American Girls Professional Baseball League folded. It went down in the books as "play" being temporarily suspended. But it turned out to be a long way to "temporary."

I have never regretted not playing that 1954 season because of meeting my Bob. But I have to honestly say that, had I known it was going to be the last year, I probably would have stuck it out and played until the end. My destiny might have changed. I might not have married my Bob. How strange and complicated life can be. Things don't just happen by accident. There is a master coach calling those plays from that diamond in the sky.

I now had some pretty tough roads to travel. I was caught totally by surprise and left feeling lost and vulnerable. I had always thought that I would be the one leaving baseball. I never dreamed that baseball would leave me. To me it was like breathing -- you had to do it! How could I get along without it? Once again came the need to prove myself. I put away my suitcases, put my scrapbooks into the closet, closed the door and went out to work in the electronic work field. I thought my Cooperstown dream was over and gone forever. There were many more tests to come before my feet would again travel the path back to my dream. But I didn't know it at the time. For a while I was completely lost.

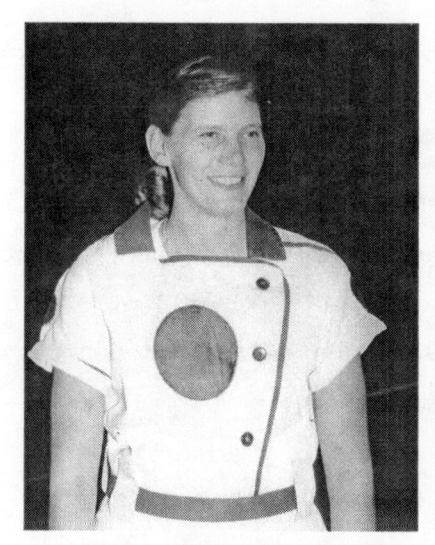

Jaynne
Bittner

"MY HANDSOME BOB"

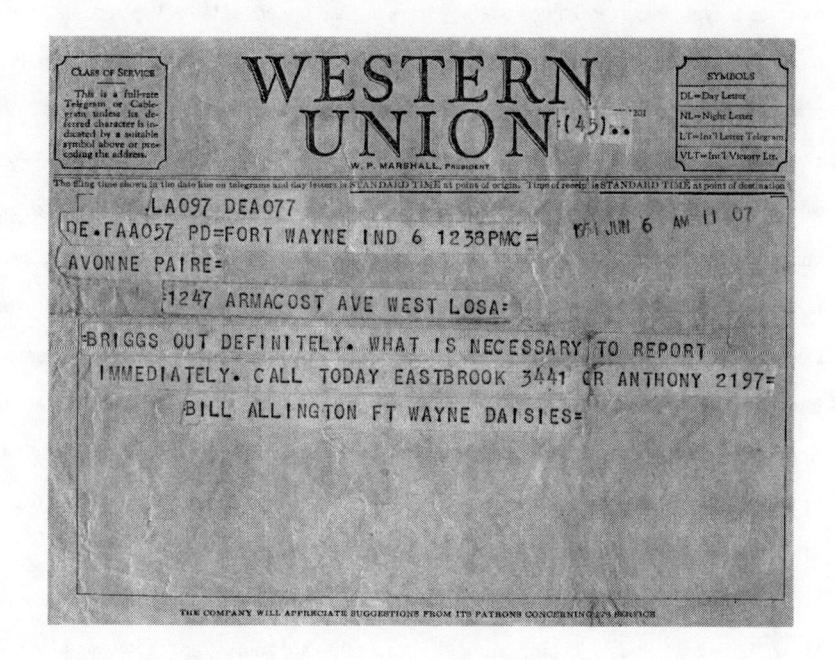

LA097 DEA077
DE·FAA057 PD=FORT WAYNE IND 6 1238PMC= 1951 JUN 6 AM 11 07

AVONNE PAIRE=

1247 ARMACOST AVE WEST LOSA=

BRIGGS OUT DEFINITELY. WHAT IS NECESSARY TO REPORT
IMMEDIATELY. CALL TODAY EASTBROOK 3441 OR ANTHONY 2197=

BILL ALLINGTON FT WAYNE DAISIES=

Chapter 36
There is Life and Death After Baseball

I put the suitcases in the closet and the "siren call" was gone! I packed Scarlett away, because tomorrow had become today! I decided that I'd better get serious about my electronic technician job at Hughes. I needed a year-round job now to support myself. That quick, good baseball money wasn't there for those four or five months. The war was over, but fortunately for me, the 1954 post-war boom was still going strong with all the defense plants. There still was a place for me at Hughes and they still paid me very good money for my know-how!

I still needed to include sports in my life to satisfy that competitive desire that burned within me. I tried softball again for a short period of time but that didn't do it. Softball was still going strong all over the U.S. The city leagues had sponsors. They called it "amateur ball," but that was a hypocritical term, because they were all paid under the table. We accepted our gas money over the table in California and by doing that we were not eligible for the national tournaments. The competition and the game itself was just not the same after baseball, like chess versus checkers.

I was bowling a lot more now but you don't have the personal contact and fierce competition in bowling, like you have in baseball. I was missing that. I had my bowling average up close to 190 and I was doing well in the tournaments. I was also playing golf about every weekend now instead of baseball practice. Ziggy and Nita, and Inie and I, formed a "fearsome foursome." We would tell the guys behind us, "Don't worry, guys. We're not good but we're fast." Sometimes I would play in Bob's foursome. Of course, he was far better than me, but I could hit the ball 200 yards or better off the tee. Everybody would marvel at how I could take a two wood on the fairway and get 180 to 200 yards with it, without teeing up.

I didn't play in Bob's foursome too often, just when he wanted to show me off! You know, "Boys will be boys!" I could break 90 on a 7,000-yard course, and that wasn't too shabby. I could give the guys some competition once in a while. I definitely astonished them at my ability to get that ball up on the green. My strong eye and hand coordination was still there, and I could putt up a storm! You know how that golf saying goes, "Drive for show and putt for dough." That's where I got them all the time.

I was having fun doing all that and working at the same time. I was dating only Bob and we were making plans for the future. Still nothing seemed to fill that huge void that All American baseball had left in my heart. As time went on I finally realized that nothing ever would! The future was here. It was time to settle down and do what I was supposed to do by all the standards in the world of the '50s -- get married and raise a family. Mom had babied me my whole life. I didn't know a heck of a lot about being a wife and a mother, but I knew it was time to learn.

The years now seem to fly by quickly -- it was 1958 before I knew it! Although I sensed that Mom wished it had been Norman I chose, she never said anything. It had been my choice and she went with it. She liked Bob all right but I think she thought Norm was a better man, maybe more trustworthy. My Bob had a little wild streak in him. Maybe that's one of the things I loved about him. I always figured that after we had children that would change. He never really got carried away, he just liked to have fun and for that matter, I did too! After putting it off for a while we decided to go to Las Vegas and got married in February 1958.

We drove up there in my little old black Rambler and had a great time. Something should have told me that something wasn't quite right because when we got married, Bob wore the same blue suit that he wore when he got married the first time around. He had two small children from that marriage. After the divorce Bob really missed those two little kids. I told him we could get involved in their lives if that's what he wanted. I'd been through that. Little children need fathers they can depend on.

We went to the courthouse in Vegas to get the permits and on the way back out going down the stairs, Bob fell down. That was another bad sign, but I was in love with my man and happy, so I put any negative thoughts behind me and February 28, 1958, I became Mrs. Robert Davis. Being a superstitious ballplayer, it didn't surprise me that we ran into bad luck as far as gambling was concerned. We had a good time but definitely bad luck. We soon went broke and came back home.

Bob was doing building contract work on his own. He was a carpenter and a cabinet maker and he was always quick to tell me that a cabinet maker was actually a furniture maker, not just a carpenter. It was the top of the ladder as far as being a carpenter was concerned. He never wanted to settle for anything but the best in materials and perfection in building it. Bob had lost everything through his divorce -- his car, his house, etc. Everything went to his ex-wife, Rosemary, including custody of his two kids -- 6-year-old Bobby and 8-year-old Suzy -- actually that's the way it should have been.

He was also supposed to be paying a hefty sum of alimony and he wasn't doing a very good job at it, so I supplemented that and helped out with my salary. I knew that moms need alimony to support the kids when the marriage is broken. Mom and Pop said that we could live with them. This saved us some money, although we did pay some room and board. They said we could live with them until we could afford our own place. I figured with both of us working we could cut down on expenses, save up a little money and rent a place of our own in two to three months.

We were seeing Bob's children, Bobby and Suzy, every weekend now. We would pick them up and take them with us somewhere. Sometimes it would just be a ride up the beach and cooking some hot dogs over an open fire. Most of the time on weekends, we'd go see Sally and Joe. They had a home in La Mirada. It was out by Disneyland and Anaheim. Mom wasn't happy about that because it was quite a jaunt -- we didn't have all the freeway links yet, although they were being built. It was more than 40 miles to get there, through traffic-congested L.A. and surface streets.

We would all pile into the Rambler, singing "One-eyed, one-horned, flying purple people eater," and away we'd go. We would get to Joe and Sal's and they would welcome us with open arms. They had a nice home with a huge backyard and a park right behind it. Our kids had a great time together. Jody and Linda were very close to the ages of Bob's kids, Bobby and Suzy, so they all got along great. That was our recreation. Most of the time, Joe and Sal footed the bill, although I would cook and bring stuff and we would bring drinks.

Our family get-togethers have always been the greatest times in my life. I've always been so close to Joe and Sally. Their kids are like my kids and mine are like theirs. We have always felt that close connection. I know that I have always been very lucky that way.

By now I had formed a close relationship with my Dad and little "Grandma Mary," as we called her. They were talking about selling her little house because, actually, she was being forced out. The people with money wanted that Wilshire Boulevard property. Any property that was anywhere near Wilshire Boulevard was going to prove to be very valuable, and Mary's little house was in the first block south of Wilshire. As usual, the guys with the big bucks knew how to make more. They were buying everybody out and those who didn't want to sell were just being forced out. They had a huge apartment complex planned for that area. They were paying good money so those who didn't want to sell were at least getting good money for their homes.

We were trying to save money for a down payment on a house, but that was a long way off. We knew we were wearing out our welcome at Mom and Pop's, although Mom didn't want me to go and Pop would never say anything. The house was crowded. It was really just a one-family house. So, when Dad started talking about how he and Grandma Mary and we, should buy a place together, we listened. The idea was that they would make the down payment, and we would make the monthly payments.

Well, it sounded good. It sounded like it could work. Dad was sober now for months at a time and he and Bob seemed to get along fine. I asked Mom how she felt about it. I knew she still had some bitter feelings about Dad, which was understandable. She surprised me. She shook her finger at me and said, "Good, it's about time he did something for his kids." So in 1959 we started looking for a house.

We couldn't afford to buy in West L.A. or Santa Monica. Property there was untouchable, simply because they were running out of it. Culver City wasn't the greatest area to live in, so the San Fernando Valley became our solution. It took a while to get over there by Old Sepulveda Road. You had to go through the pass and the old tunnel in those days. They were building the San Diego (405) Freeway and they said it would only be a 15- to 20-minute drive when it was done. But they overlooked a little thing called traffic, which was to come in the future. So, we started looking in the Van Nuys area, that was close to West L.A.

After searching for a while we found this little house on a street called "Marlin Place" (like the fish). Later it became "Marlin Manor" because it was home to a lot of people and its doors were always open. We had a large lot -- 75 feet by 140 feet deep -- I think they called it a quarter of a commercial acre. We had lots of trees, lots of front yard, a little side yard patio and a big backyard. We had a black walnut tree, a regular walnut tree and an orange tree. We also had plum, apricot and peach trees. The Valley in those days had been strictly farming country with lots of trees and walnut and citrus orchards. The house was a little two-bedroom, one-bath house. It had a dining room, living room and kitchen. It also had an addition built across the entire back of the house that was just like an apartment. It had its own separate bathroom and a big sliding glass door in the back. That gave it its own separate entrance.

It looked like it would be very suitable for Dad and Grandma Mary, so in 1959, I was about to become a "Valley Girl." Grandma Mary sold her house and gave us the $5,000 for the down payment. The total price was $14,500. We had all hit-and-miss furniture donated by the whole family. Sal and Joe gave us some. Mom and Pop gave us some. We also got some from Bob's sister Billie and her husband Clyde. Bob and Clyde were buddies. They had both been in the Naval Air Force and stationed in the South Pacific, not together, but they were both Swabbies. The house also had its own stove from the '40s (which, incidentally, I still cook on).

Bob was now working at The Sawtelle Lumber Yard in West Los Angeles. It was located on the corner of Pontius Avenue and Santa Monica Boulevard. The same Pontius Avenue where Grandma Rhea's home had been, the house where I was born. It was now the parking lot for Pacific Bell -- small world. It was another six to seven miles from the lumberyard to Hughes Aircraft, so I could drop Bob off on my way to work.

We had our happy little home filled with Dad and Mary, Bob and me, and my little French poodle called "Baby." She had been the runt of the litter from Mickey, my Mom's dog. Mom had saved her for me and we called her "Baby" because she was so small when she was born. She turned out to be a standard-size French poodle. Most of the time she looked like a big black hairy sheepdog. We just clipped the hair out of her eyes and cut off her tangles and let it go at that. She was definitely my dog and didn't want anything to do with Bob for a long time. She got up on our bed the first night we brought her home with us and took a dump right in the middle and Bob didn't like that. But when they got to know each other, they finally bonded. Baby was a very shy, gentle dog. On the other hand, Grandma Mary had this little old cocker spaniel and she was mean and only Mary's dog. She used to bully Baby.

Everything seemed to be working out fine except for one thing. My Mom was lonely again. Joe and Sal had bought a home in far off La Mirada and now her baby girl had moved and bought a home in the Valley. There was Mom stuck at home and alone again. I would stop by and see her on my way back and forth to work whenever I could and we had numerous family get-togethers for all the occasions. Sometimes we would have what we called cork-offs. If it was a special occasion, Joe and Sal would buy some Andre's champagne and we would line up and take turns to see who could pop the champagne corks the farthest. I think I wound up being the champion -- at least I'll claim it. As we got older, our kids have settled in areas far apart. It's hard to get together as much. We don't miss the important events though!

I didn't see much of my baseball buddies anymore. I was too busy working and traveling back and forth to work and taking care of a family. I was a piece of work in transition. Pepper Paire was trying to become Mrs. Lavone Davis, wife and homemaker and mother-to-be (I hoped). It wasn't easy! The Cacapot Faye would drop by or call up once in a while -- she was still living with her folks and she was still drinking and running around with a fast crowd. We were moving in totally different worlds now.

The next thing you know, nature takes over and I become pregnant. It was kind of a surprise because we had been married for two years and nothing had happened, and we weren't doing anything to avoid it. I was beginning to think that perhaps it was me. We knew it wasn't Bob because he already had two children. I was starting to think that maybe I couldn't have children, that maybe, by playing baseball, I had done something to my body. My body had been bumped and banged around so many times. But lo and behold, I became pregnant after two years of not expecting it. I kept on working and bowling -- the doctor said it was OK, my body was used to it.

More and more I would stop by and see my Mom after work. She was so excited and so sure I was going to have a baby girl. Her baby girl was going to have a baby girl! I would lie down and take a nap on the couch and she would sit beside me and feel my stomach. It got hard for me to keep on working because I was unlucky enough to be one of those people who was half-sick all the time, all through my pregnancy. I felt like throwing up all the time but never could. It was a miserable feeling. I had to make myself eat, and I had to keep working because we needed the money. I also kept on bowling because the doctor said physically it was OK. But it was a struggle. When I was seven months along, I actually weighed less than I had weighed before I got pregnant. It was hard because I had to cook for Bob, Dad and Mary, and sometimes the smell would get to me.

      To my surprise, I found out that I had actually absorbed some of my Mom's cooking talents without knowing it. When I would get stuck and didn't know how to make something, I would just get on the phone and call for help and Mom would be there for me, just like she had been for my whole life. Now Christmas 1959 was approaching and I was thinking, I need to get a good briefing from Mom on how to stuff that bird. I had been home from work three or four days straight, not feeling well. I figured I'd stop by on the Friday before Christmas, get my bird briefing and give her a hug. To my dismay, when I got to her house, I found that Mom was in bed. She was sick. She had been sick for about a week, since I'd been there last. Pop and Russ hadn't called and told me, and I was mad at them for not doing so. They knew and I knew that it took a lot to get my Mom down -- something had to be really wrong to keep her down. When I got there she didn't look good at all. She looked and acted listless. Her eyes looked glazed over and she just didn't seem to care. She knew me; she had all her faculties, but she was definitely struggling. I called the doctor and we got her right down to Santa Monica Hospital for an examination and tests. They said that maybe it could be her heart. After I checked her in, I sat holding her hand and I was terrified. "Oh, dear God, please don't let anything happen to my Mom. How could I exist if anything happened to her? God just couldn't be that mean."

      I sat there holding her hand until they made me go home. We didn't talk much because they had an oxygen mask on her and she was struggling a little to breathe. They were afraid that pneumonia was settling in. I had brought her a little stuffed poodle for company. It looked like her dog, Inky (Baby's daddy). I perched him on the rail of her bed and reminded her that I had a turkey to cook for the family and, since it was usually her job, she had to at least walk me through it. She tried to laugh, but she was gasping for air. Then she whispered, "Oh, baby girl, I just hope you don't have to cook it alone." Those words I will never forget.

I hugged her and kissed her and told her how much I loved her and Bob dragged me out of there backward. The nurse was saying we had to go. Mom was breathing hard and trying to pull her oxygen mask off. Her face looked so white and so scared. I stopped at the desk to tell the nurse to be sure to check that she had on her mask. I wanted them to tell the doctor that maybe she should be in an oxygen tent. They said they would tell him. They said the doctor would be in shortly, but that I had to go, because they wanted Mom to rest.

I walked the floor that whole night and my Dad walked the floor with me. He had always loved my Mom, even though he had been a lousy husband. He was trying to comfort me the best he knew how. He told me, "Your Mom is too good and God would never take her away from you." But deep down in my gut, I knew my mother was in big trouble. I berated myself over and over for all the times I had not stopped to see her and for all the things I hadn't done for her. Then I prayed and prayed all through the night.

The phone call came the next day, Christmas Day 1959! "Come quick to the hospital." Mom was in big trouble. By the time we got there, she was gone. I think she was probably gone before the call and they just said that. I collapsed by her bedside. My heart couldn't hold my body up. My Mom, the greatest Mom in the whole wide world, my number one fan, my friend, was gone. God had taken her from me. How could he do that? She was only 55 years old. My grief was inconsolable. I was almost out of my mind. No one could comfort me, not Bob, not Dad, not Joe -- no one. Joe and Bob made the funeral arrangements. I wasn't capable. I was a vegetable living in a nightmare. A lot of the funeral is blacked out in my memory. I was in a daze. I remember when I bent down to kiss her in the casket, her cheek felt cold and when I held her hand it was cold. I finally realized she was gone. I wanted to die with her. But when I touched her hand, my baby kicked. I could feel it in my stomach. I could hear Mom whisper, "You've got to be strong for your baby, my baby girl." I put my other hand on my stomach and looking into Mom's face, I realized that there was a part of her inside of me. I would have a little "Tessie" to heal my heart. Mom would always be with me in my baby! I knew I had to straighten up and fly right for her, and that's what kept me going. The next days and weeks were a great struggle, but from that time on, I made myself eat and sleep, and with the help of Bob, Joe and Sally, and little Grandma Mary, I kept my baby. On March 12, 1960, my little "Tessie Marie" was born "William Joseph Davis." I had been so sure that I would have a girl, but I was wrong. Bob named him William Joseph. William after his father and Joseph after my bro Joe. We had made a deal. I would name the girl, he would name the boy. Afterwards, I told Willie I wanted to name him "Monty" Cal Davis (after Montana and California). Willie said, "Thank God, Dad named me. If you had, I would have had to be a used-car salesman."

  Our little guy only weighed 4 pounds, 3 ounces and had to be taken by Caesarean section because they thought his head was too big for my pelvic opening, plus he would have been a difficult breach birth. They gave me a spinal, because it was safer for the baby. They had a big tent-like sheet in front of me so I couldn't see what was going on. There were people holding me down on both sides. But when I looked up into the operating lights I saw the reflection. I could watch the whole thing. The doctor drew a line of X's across my stomach with a marker. I had a big smile from hip to hip. When he started cutting across the X's and black blood started oozing out, I quit watching. I just shut my eyes and hung onto the people who were holding me down.

  My heart felt like it was beating in my throat. The whole table was surrounded with doctors and nurses. There must have been four or five of each. They had to reach in and actually drag that little guy out. I could feel my body being tugged and then, suddenly everybody gasped and stepped back. It scared me and I choked out, "What's wrong? What's wrong? Is my baby all right?" The doctor answered, "Don't worry. _He's_ fine. He just baptized us all."

  My little William sprayed everybody with his little dinky hose as he came into the world. So, my little William Joseph Davis, or "Wee Willie" as the nurses christened him, became my heart and soul. He was my last link to my Mom and the love of my life. They brought him to me while I was on the table and showed him to me. I was startled because his head was covered with blood. "He's bleeding. He's bleeding," I panicked.

  The doctor said, "Oh no, don't worry about that. That's your blood." Well, I breathed a sigh of relief and said, "Oh, well that's OK." About that time I started to slip into unconsciousness because they had given me a shot to relax me so I could rest and recuperate. When I came out of it, I was in my room. It was the next day and there was no Willie around. The nurse told me that he had to stay in an incubator for three days because he was so small. So everybody else, Joe and Sal, Bob, Pop and Dad and Grandma Mary, all got to see him, but not me. But I knew he was doing fine from all the daily reports I got.

I was a pretty sick lady for a while. I did need to recoup and to rest. I discovered that it was pretty tough work to have a baby. I thanked the Lord I didn't have a doubleheader. It was a week before Willie and I got to go home. It turned out that he couldn't breast-feed because he was so small, so he became a little bottle formula baby from the start. I had to put up with a lot of pain while my milk dried up. But he was worth it. He was so beautiful and my heart was so full. I was wishing my Mom could hold him and he could feel her love. He would never get to know the most wonderful grandma in the world.

After a little while, I threw aside my bitterness because I knew Mom was with God and she was at peace. So I was finally also at peace with God again. He had done what needed to be done, taking Mom out of her pain. I thanked him for that, and I thanked him for Bob. I had planned on staying with Mom for a while and letting her show me the ropes. I knew nothing -- zip, zero -- about handling babies. I could handle a ground ball OK and I could handle a curve, but babies and diapers and formulas? He was such a tiny little guy. I could hold his head in my hand and his feet didn't reach my elbow. I had to buy doll pj's for him. He had such short little legs. I was afraid he'd break, but Bob took over and showed me how to be a mom.

Bob was so proud and so happy, and so were Dad and Grandma Mary. They all loved Willie dearly, from day one, and so did my poor Pop. He and Russell were devastated at the loss of Mom. Russell had just disappeared for a while, his usual style, and Pop, well, he just lived and breathed "Willie Joe" as he called him. We would take him to see Pop so there would be no conflict between him and Dad. Although Dad was doing OK, I could now only count on one or two sober months, and then he'd be on a binge for maybe two or three days and nights straight.

Dad pretty much stayed in their back apartment with Mary and didn't get mean. He was just a pest and a worry. At times, he would go out driving while he was drinking, and he was never a good driver, even when sober. He now had my little "purple people eater Nash

Rambler," and we had a brand-new Vista Cruise Oldsmobile; Bob's first new car, and he loved it. It was a beauty. We called it "Baby Blue." It could carry eight people with a turn-around backseat and all power windows. The windows all along the sides and the top, and it was all automatic. The windows and the transmission!

Bob was now a yard boss and making good money and he needed a good car to make the daily drive. As a mechanic, he was a great carpenter. He never heard a noise in a car. The wheels could probably fall off before he would notice. The new car made me feel like he was much safer in his 30-miles-a-day drive, which was considered a big drive in those days. So Dad rambled around in the little Rambler, which was going strong with more than 100,000 miles on it. It never had the head off -- of course it smoked a little, but that was to be expected. It stood up to the beating Dad gave it and kept on ticking. (Must have been that bunny again!)

I took a year and a half off work to be with Willie, and then in 1962, I went back to work, this time at ITT Gilfillan Electronics here in the Valley. They made big electronic cables and sonar equipment for the Navy. That way I could be closer to home in case there were any problems. I took the swing shift and little Grandma Mary would watch Willie for about an hour until Bob got home. Dad couldn't be trusted alone with Willie but he would help. When I left for work, Grandma Mary would walk Willie in the stroller down to the end of the block. They could watch the big diesel trucks work on the freeway. Willie called the trucks "choo choo's" because of the smoke coming out of their top exhaust. That way he wouldn't see me leave and cry. Bob would be home in about an hour and then take over.

Everything on the surface was going OK. But I was uneasy, not knowing why. Both Bob and Dad were drinking more now and it was starting to be a worry. I decided I would try to concentrate on the good things and have Scarlett O'Hara out of the closet and worry about bad stuff tomorrow. I was taking Mom's place as the chief cook and bottle washer. All our dinners and family get-togethers were now being held at Marlin Manor. While I couldn't compare with Mom's cooking skills, I was becoming a good cook! A transformation was taking place and I was doing my best to be like my Mom, though I knew I wasn't really in her league. The family now seemed to look at me with new respect as "Pepper Paire Davis," wife and mother.

Mom & Pop's
25th Anniversary

Jody, Pop, Linda & Mom

Mom & Me at the
Santa Monica pier foolin around

G-Ma Mary & Dad

Wee Willie Arrived
3/12/60

Shower for Wee Willie & Me

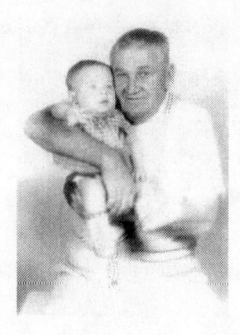

Pop & Willie

I hooked him

Bob & Me

Mom wins cake contest

363

**Chapter 37
A Whole New Game
(God and the Grunion)**

By the time he was a year old, my little "Wee Willie" was showing signs of becoming a good ballplayer. He was knocking the heck out of the ball from both sides of the plate with a little plastic bat. He also threw the ball with either hand, equally well. He definitely had natural talent. That was the good news. The bad news was, he was showing signs of allergic reactions to some medications and he also developed a touch of asthma. Allergies ran in Bob's family but they didn't in mine. So, the doctor felt he had a chance to outgrow them. He was the apple of everyone's eyes. Such a cute little guy, so smart, too smart! You had to watch him closely.

I was elated over his baseball talents, because I was afraid something was wrong with him. He never crawled a lick. Just couldn't seem to get his fanny up off the ground. So, most of the time he just kind of laid around on his tummy, pushing himself up like he was doing push-ups and then down would come the fanny. He would play lying down and play sitting up. He really didn't need a playpen. So, we just folded a quilt in the corner of our sectional in the front room. He was perfectly happy there. It didn't seem to bother him any that he couldn't crawl. He would just sit there or lay there, with my little "black Baby girl" lying right beside him. For amusement he would pull "Baby's" hair out. He could have pulled her head bald and she never would have hurt him. She just kept on kissing him. But he learned to love her and learned not to do it after he realized he was hurting her. She loved every single inch of that little guy. The fact that he couldn't crawl had turned out to be a blessing. I had worried about what might happen when he started to crawl, because Dad and Mary were getting up there in years. They didn't have the greatest eyesight or perhaps the greatest balance. They both used canes to walk and I guess I could just visualize Willie crawling up behind one of them and kaboom! -- them getting broken bones and Willie getting squashed. When Willie was about eight months old, Bob went off to the kitchen one night to get a beer. Willie just got up and walked right behind him. I guess he was tired of fooling around with trying to crawl. He had barely even tried to walk. He just bypassed everything else and took off walking. From that time on, I knew he was normal. Then we definitely needed the playpen and the walker. I had this little side yard patio, with lots of shade trees and roses. It was fenced in with a locked gate. So, Bob built a sandbox with a roof on it. Willie loved to play out there. I could see him through all the windows on that side of the house and could hear him with the windows open, even from the kitchen. Baby would lay right beside him. She wouldn't let anyone near him that she didn't know. This allowed me the freedom to do the housework. I could hear everything that went on. Actually, when you don't hear anything, that's when you worry. Willie was a blabbermouth so all was well. I remember this one time Dad got all dressed up. He still liked to dress in white from head to toe. He goes out the front door, elegant in his white Panama hat and white patent-leather shoes, white shirt, white pants and then his silver cane with the silver handle (for effect only). He went down the steps and stops under our big English Elm tree by the house and he waves at us. I was holding Willie up on our sectional couch so he could see his Grandpa through the big front window. Willie was hanging on to the back of the couch and we were waving at Dad. It was a beautiful sunshiny day with the beautiful blue sky capping it off. Willie's just giggling and laughing as Dad is performing for him. He's waving, he's tipping his hat, he's making faces and he's pointing his cane. We're all having a great time. Then I see Dad; he gets a puzzled look on his face and he looks up and he holds his hand out like it's raining, but apparently he sees nothing and of course, the sky is still solid blue. So, again he's clowning for Willie. Well, this happened a couple of times and Dad is looking up and getting that puzzled look. I'm wondering what the heck, what's going on? Dad looks back at us and all of a sudden, a torrent of brown stuff comes tumbling down on Dad. It covered him like syrup on a pancake. It was a squirrel and he really cut loose. He nailed Dad, dead center. Stuff was dripping from his hat to his shirt to his pants to his shoes, the whole works. The squirrel must have eaten up a ton. Even Dad's face was dripping. The look on his face was one of astonishment; he was flabbergasted. Willie thought Dad had done it for him and really cut loose laughing and I couldn't help it, though I tried not to, I had to cut loose laughing, too. It was a sight that no one could have resisted. Well, Dad of course, was not amused. In fact, he was furious at Willie and me. He would have killed the squirrel if he could have caught him. He came back storming into the house shaking his cane and his fist at us. "Fine thing laughing at your Grandpa in this catastrophe." He also said a few unprintable things to the squirrel. Well, that only made it funnier. He didn't speak to Willie or me for about a week after that. He just stayed in his room and buried his nose in his library books. Dad really didn't have a great sense of humor. Although he was very intelligent, there were times he just didn't get it. He would check out 15 to 20 library books every week. He read them all and would go back and get another 15. He knew a lot about a lot of things, but sometimes I think he didn't interpret them the way they were meant. If there was something he didn't like or didn't think could be done, he just refused to believe it. He had a closed mind at times. I think maybe the drinking all his life might have accounted for that or at least contributed to it. Now, on the other hand, Grandma Mary had a very open mind. She hadn't been educated like Dad. Dad went to Montana University for a while and was considering a legal career. But little Mary had more common sense than Dad. She was up there in her 80s and life had taught her a lot. She was proud to say her birthday was the same day as the telephone's birthday. She had lived a rough life, a hard life on a farm in Illinois. Her mom died at a very early age and she took charge and took care of her father and the family. Her little body was twisted because of an unset, broken hip, but she didn't let that bother her. She laughed a lot and she loved a lot. Every night she thanked me for everything and told me that she loved me, just in case she didn't wake up the next morning. She was a courageous, wonderful, classy little lady. She had some great stories to tell. She told me she campaigned for Teddy Roosevelt and that she was sitting on a platform with him when he was giving a speech. She said he put his straw hat down on the seat and then he got so excited and so carried away by the enthusiastic attitude of the crowd that he forgot that his hat was on the chair and he came back and sat down on it and crushed it. She was also in Chicago when McKinley was shot. I think she was a distant cousin to President McKinley. Grandma loved TV. I watched that little lady, who was born when the telephone was born, sit on a chair as close as she could to the TV and watch Neil Armstrong step on the moon and she comprehended it! Dad wouldn't watch TV. He didn't believe it was possible; it was just a hoax in his mind. Mary loved it. She loved to watch "Bonanza." Only in her vocabulary she called it "Bonsai," and she loved Mickey Rooney. He was "macaroni." She told me the one thing she would like to do was to go out to the "Vesper" and see that play called "Ammonia." Well, of course, she meant she wanted to go to Hemet and watch that classic Indian story of "Ramona." But I tell you what, she laughed with us when we laughingly told her how to say those things.

When Dad was sober, he was a great help to me. He would spend a lot of time outside working in the yard and helping fix up the house. Dad, Bob and I actually roofed our house together. At night, he would return to his room and read all his books. Sometimes he would write poetry and, if he wasn't too loaded, sometimes it was pretty good. If he was, then it would become gibberish. Unfortunately those bad times were coming now frequently and I could see signs of Dad becoming jealous of Bob. There was trouble ahead. Bob was also drinking more now but he kept on working hard and he was good to the kids and good to me. When he'd get home, I'd barely keep him awake long enough to feed him and he would go to sleep on the couch. That got to be a regular routine. Our love life was practically nil but I was so tired that I really didn't mind. I was putting in a pretty full day myself taking care of Dad and Mary and the house and then going to work on that swing shift. Sometimes on the weekends we had Bob's children, Bobby and Suzy. That made for a pretty tough schedule for me. But I did get Friday night off. That was my night out. After work, a group of us would either go bowling or go to somebody's house and play cards, just to do a little something different. Sometimes we would just go out to eat and then go home. Bob always came home early and sober on Fridays, so I could have that night off. He made up for it on Saturdays. He only worked a half day on Saturday and then he played pool with his golfing buddies and came home around seven or eight. He would bring us some great steak sandwiches as a treat. He just seemed to be completely involved with his work. So, all of the family duties fell on me. I had to be Mom and Pop to Willie and Dad and Mary and Bob's kids. I would take the kids to the dentist, to the doctors, go to the store, etc. Sometimes Bob would golf on Sunday morning and while he was a good husband and father in many ways, he wasn't around a lot for the kids. I came to learn there was a private part of Bob that he never shared with anyone, at least not with me. He told me that he would always love me and would never leave me and I believed him. I loved him too much not to. But sometimes I would wonder because he was so withdrawn. To me, marriage meant for the good, the bad, forever. My belief has never changed on that, although I know I may be in the minority on that one. But life goes on.

This one Friday night at work, we were all taking our usual break and we were laughing and talking in the lunchroom and drinking a cup of coffee. I was reading the sports page, as usual. "Hey, look," I said. "The grunion are running!" Rod, one of our inspectors, answered me with a question. "What would a grunion be, Pepper?" I told him, "It's a little fish that runs." He interrupted me with a laugh and went on in his lazy Texas drawl. "A fish that runs? Yeah, sure," he said in disbelief. Just like snipe hunting I bet," he added. That's how it all started. A cup of coffee at work and a casual statement that the grunion were running. When I explained that running meant they came in with the tide and laid their eggs by dancing in the sand, he snickered in his coffee. When Ellen told him the only legal way to catch them was to turn your back to the waves and trap them with your bare hands, Rod broke out in hardy laughter! Then he said, "You mean instead of ending up with an empty snipe bag you end up with a wet backside?" Well, we decided that it would be fun to prove to Rod that there was really such a fish as a grunion. There were about 10 of us in the act, including me. I should have had enough sense to forget it and go home to Bob and Willie. But, I still couldn't resist a challenge so I found myself on my way to the beach with the rest of the gang. There were a couple of carloads of us. The object was to prove the existence of this little silver fish with peculiar mating habits. Thus, the stage was set for the drama to come. We decided not to go to a popular beach because when the grunion are running, hundreds of people have been known to flock to the ocean. They risk life, limb and pneumonia to catch those little elusive silver fish. So, we headed up north of Malibu on the Coast Highway looking for an isolated spot. After about a 10-minute drive, we pulled off on a dirt shoulder overlooking the ocean. We parked the car to check it out. The place was perfect. There wasn't another grunion hunter in sight. As we pulled up, the car lights had shown a winding path going down to the beach. Jumping out first, I ran ahead of the group, and just as I reached the path it became dark. They had cut the car lights. It had seemed so wide and safe before, but now it was ominously different. I started cautiously down, feeling for the side of the cliff with my groping right hand, like a blind man. After about two or three hesitating steps, I sensed something was wrong. I started to turn back and wait for the others when it happened. My feet dropped out from under me. It was like coming off a step you didn't know was there. Then as the ground gave away completely, I found myself scratching and scrambling and clawing wildly at nothing. Time seemed suspended during that long silent drop. There was nothing but the velvet blackness and the sound of the air in my ears. They say your life passes in front of you at times like that. Mine didn't. I found myself praying. I prayed that I might hit something ... anything. I knew I needed to hit something soon or it would be too late. Then in a violent explosion of colors, I did hit. I felt a shattering, jolting motion followed by complete nothingness. I was floating in silence. Slowly the brilliant balls of fire stopped flashing. Everything seemed to steady a little and I opened my eyes. At first, I saw nothing but blackness. Then to my relief, lights began to appear in the spinning night. They seemed familiar. Stars I thought ... stars. I tried to sort things out. What had happened? Where was I? A sharp stabbing pain interrupted my thoughts. I stared at my whole body. It was like I was somebody else, standing off in the distance looking. I was stretched out flat on my back, on a narrow sandy ledge. The pain eased off and numbness set in. Again, I tried to think, "What had happened?" Coffee and grunion, that was it. Gradually, I was becoming aware of some very ugly feelings growing under my back and my legs. My senses seemed to be returning one at a time. I was also beginning to hear things. Soft, sighing sounds. The soft sighing became a rushing sound. It turned into a roar and exploded with a crash. The smell of salt air came alive in my lungs and I recognized the sounds. Somewhere in the darkness below me, waves were breaking. Sharply, coldly, reality returned. I remembered, I had fallen. "My God, I had fallen." The pain came on again violently, this time bringing foaming waves of white hot blackness. They rolled over my body and threatened to blot out my thoughts. I tried to hang on. It was like trying to hang on to a slippery piece of ice with my fingertips. Just when I was about ready to lose the fight, new sounds penetrated my semiconscious. I could hear voices in the darkness above me. Of course, my friends, they were up there? I tried to catch some words but all I could hear was laughter. Laughter? Why would they be laughing at a time like this? A chill swept over me. Something was wrong. I managed to raise my head and Rod's voice came floating down. "This all looks pretty steep." Helen's voice answered him, "Hey, too steep." Then another voice inquired, "Hey, where's Pepper?" The truth hit me like a blunt axe. "Oh my God, they didn't know that I had fallen." I opened my mouth to shout, nothing came out. Frantically, I tried to raise myself to my elbows to holler again. This time came blinding pain and only a hoarse whisper. I fell back seeing those flashing fire bolts again. Then as I lay there shaking with pain and frustration, I heard my "sentence" pronounced. Helen's voice came clearly down from the blackness above me. "I think Pepper is back in the other car, it's too cold," she complained. "Let's get out of here." The waves were momentarily quiet. In shock and disbelieving silence, I heard the voices trailing off and ending with a car door slamming faintly and then they were gone. I was left alone hanging half off an unknown ledge with nothing but the darkness and the rocks and the cold wet sea underneath me. My thoughts rambled on by themselves without direction or purpose. I found myself wondering if Bob had paid the phone bill. I could feel grains of sand oozing slowly but surely out from under my right shoulder. Just like my timer, I thought. When they all ran out, that will be it. My goose will be cooked. I wondered how long it would take for the sand to crumble away and let me plunge to my fate below. I had never faced death before, but I felt its presence now. My mouth went dry with fright as I realized my right arm was hanging loose in space. The cold, gray fear in my throat spread to my stomach and I felt sick. Silently, desperately, I cried. I don't know how long I stayed like that with my eyes closed and my mind a dark blank. Perhaps I wasn't fully conscious. But gradually I became aware of an urgent need to open my eyes. It was without thought that they must open and open they did. At first, all I could see through my blurred tears was a hazy blackness. Then out of the haze, as clear and bright as the morning sun, I saw my little boy's face. Corn yellow hair, soft like gold dust; little snubbed nose, with a hint of freckles to be on his soft skin; and happy little blue eyes staring at me. "Oh my God," I moaned. The thrust of pain was almost unbearable, as though the words were ripped out of my heart! I knew now that death was not the fear, the real fear was that I couldn't get back to my husband and my little 18-month-old boy. Willie needed Bob and me to guide him as he walked on those stubby little legs. I could see Bob's crooked smile as he pointed his finger at me and said, "Hon, I'll teach him to spell, you teach him to hit." Tears ran down my face and into the already wet sand. I prayed silently now; my eyes seeking the stars as if they were God's eyes. Funny, when no one can hear you, you don't make unnecessary noises. The waves were getting quieter now and I knew it must be getting close to daylight. I wondered if I would see the sun. Again, I felt the dreaded movement under my shoulder. My despair was complete. Yet despite my hopelessness, something inside wouldn't let me quit. Maybe, just maybe, if I tried again, I could move. I dragged my right arm up and with a supreme effort, I tried to throw my right leg over and turn on my side, away from the edge. It brought an involuntary scream of pain from my lips; my leg didn't even move and my arm flopped back down again. The sound of my scream echoed in my ears; then it died away. Then I heard something. It sounded like a voice. I heard it again. This time I was sure it was a woman's voice. They had come back for me! The overwhelming joy in my heart rose up and threatened to choke me. More sounds came down from above. I tried to make out the words. There was a moment of almost complete silence and then I heard a voice loud and clear say, "Steve, over here, over here. This is the spot, Steve." There was no Steve in our group. Who was up there? The unfamiliar voice came again, even louder. "I tell you, this is the place. There was a path right here! I'm sure this is where we caught the most last time." My heart sank momentarily. They weren't my friends looking for me. They were grunion hunters. I prayed fiercely. "God, don't let them give up the hunt too soon." Again the woman spoke. She sounded as if she was directly above me now. "Steve, I tell you this is where the path should be." There was impatience in her voice now. "Oh boy, this is it," I thought, calling on every bit of strength I had left. I raised my head and screamed. My raw soul reaching up to God and whoever else was up there in the night. Pain bit into every fiber of my broken body. I gasped for air. My ears roared, my eyes felt like pure fire was coming out of them. Fighting unconsciousness, I searched the blackness above me listening for that unknown voice one more time. For an eternity, I heard nothing and then blessedly, I heard my prayers answered. "Steve, come quick, somebody's down there." Somehow I screamed again and this time a man's voice came excitedly drifting down to me! "You're right, you're right, there is someone down there. Someone has fallen!" "Hang on down there," he hollered. "I'll go get some help." I let my body go limp and gratefully slipped into oblivion, those last beautiful words ringing in my ears. It wasn't safe to climb down to me. They were afraid my sandy ledge would collapse. So they had to bring in a helicopter, lower a basket and pluck me off of that ledge. They said I made little jokes as I was being brought to safety in the basket. I told the firemen not to drop me on the way up, as that first step was a big one. Later, I told the X-ray technicians at Malibu emergency station to be sure and get my good side. I don't remember, I guess I was just so glad to be alive that everything was beautiful. I had a broken back; three vertebras were crushed in my lower back and I had some cracked ribs. I was bruised so badly that my feet and legs were black. But when I realized that I had fallen 50 feet (equal to a five-story building), somehow things didn't seem too bad. At first the doctors feared that I may not live. Then they feared I might not walk again. Next came the fear of many operations. But through the long pain-filled weeks, I never feared. I knew I would beat it. Whenever my courage would falter, Bob and little Willie were there for me. Dad and Mary, too. But Bob was wonderful. He stopped his drinking and came right home from work every single night. He and Mary did the cooking and took care of Willie and he helped me in every way he could. Financially we made out great because both Bob and I had good medical coverage from our jobs and both of them paid off. We came out of it with enough money to fix the house up. Bob told me that he was so scared that he would lose me and that he would always love me and take care of me and I guess he meant it. Right in the middle of all this, little 8-year-old Bobby and 10-year-old Suzy asked to come and live with us. Their mom was having trouble getting her feet on the ground and life was tough for them. They wanted a family life with Bob and me and our family. So, of course, I said yes. It made things rough, because Bob was worn out from burning the candle at both ends. He needed help and I knew I had to "play hurt" again. So, we were now a family of seven, eight counting my dog Baby! We had a full but happy home, and we all made the best of it. I had been in the hospital for 31 days. So Joe and Sal, and Pop and Bob's sister, Aunt Billy, or Aunt BB as the kids called her, had taken turns in taking care of Willie while Bob worked during the day. Pop used to take him for part of the day. Then Aunt BB would take Willie when Pop had to go to work. Then Bob would pick him up after work. Pop used to have a bathtub full of diapers all the time. We used the real diapers in those days. If you had money, you could have a diaper service or buy throw-aways! But we didn't, so it wasn't that easy. Joe and Sal took Willie for a couple of weeks to give Bob a break. I guess it gave them ideas because after a 10-year hiatus, Sally came up pregnant and their youngest daughter, Jeannine, was born. They always blamed me for that. When I look back now and think about my fall, I become very sure of a couple of things. One is, if anyone ever asks me again if there really is such a thing as a fish called a grunion, I'll tell them "yes, definitely," but if they don't believe me, I'll make a bet and then I'll get them a dictionary and let them read all about the grunion. The second most important point I'm sure of is that there is a

God. If you don't believe in him, there's a famous book I could refer you to. But I won't make you a bet, because if you doubt him, you'll have to find out for yourself, like I did. Funny thing though, I never did meet those two people who saved me. I guess they're still out there, roaming up and down the dark foggy coast in the wee hours of the morning looking for those little silver fish. Well, anyway, they're two very dear people, whose identities remain unknown to me, but they have been blessed in many prayers by me. As for those grunion, well, I don't know if I want to bless them or not. They almost got me killed, but then I guess you could say they also got me saved. God and the grunion, that is. While this story had a happy ending in many ways, in one way, it didn't. Those injuries put an end to my baseball career. Period. In fact, my body was never ever going to be the same. The doctors wanted to do fusion surgery on my back but at that time there was only a 60-percent chance of success. You could wind up with a completely stiff back. I didn't want to risk it. They said that I wouldn't be able to stand the pain if I didn't have the surgery and they put me on Percodan. At that time they didn't realize how addicting and dangerous a drug it was. But they didn't know me and my pain tolerance. When I saw what that drug was doing to me, I took myself off it. I wanted to live in the real world, not a fantasy world. I had too many responsibilities to live in "la-la land." So, I settled for aspirin and a couple of beers now and then. I learned to sleep with my back propped up and my legs propped up; that way the pain was less. "Pepper Paire" the ballplayer disappeared and Mom Pepper Davis and caretaker took over. I was determined to be a good mom to all the kids. But it wasn't going to be easy. Bobby and Suzy both had a will of their own. They listened to me and respected me and I'm sure they loved me, but a stepmom is never completely the boss. You need the dad to back you up and for a while it worked and we were a happy family. But it just wasn't in the cards for things to stay that way.

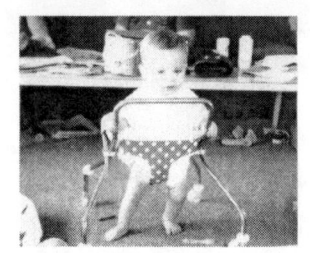

Wee-Willie

Marlin Manor Gma Mary, Jeannine & Willie

Bob & Willie

Me & Willie

Bob, Clyde & Me

Willie & Uncle Clyde

Gma Mary

Bob - cabinet maker

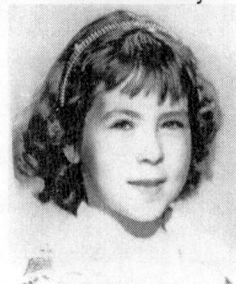

Suzy

Willie & Baby

Pepper, Willie,
Gma Mary & Bob

Bobby

My Ballplayers

Bobby

Willie

My Two Catchers

Willie the Tramp

Elvis

Chapter 38
Hair Today, Gone Tomorrow

From that time on there was no longer the option of Mrs. Davis working. I had all I could handle at home with Dad, 78 and Mary, 83. Then I had Bobby, Suzy, Willie and Bob, all to take care of. It was a full-time job and then some! Financially, we were OK. I was able to draw disability for a while and Bob had been promoted to foreman, so we were trying to make it on his salary. As long as I cut corners and stretched things to cover the necessities, we were sliding by. By the time Bobby and Suzy were in high school there were a lot more expenses: clothes, shoes, school supplies, etc. Doctors and dentists, well, we made payments on those. Bob didn't spend much money. He was only doing his golf on Sundays and I was back to bowling one night a week, actually, more for recreation than anything. I was trying to get myself back in physical shape. I didn't have the physical capabilities I was used to. I couldn't get down low and fire the ball. I was only carrying around 150 or 160 average, which, everybody but me thought was respectable. We were not fashion conscious or socially active. We just had our family get-togethers on holidays and birthdays. Both of us really looked forward to those. Joe and Sal were still my rocks. It was still fun to be with them and Bob got along great with them, too. We kind of lost track of little bro Russell for a while. He had gone through a really rough time after Mom's death. I tried to keep in touch with him, but he had moved out and Pop didn't see or hear much from him anymore either. Pop said Russell was drinking a lot and running around in bad company, but then so was Pop. He was now a bartender full time and had met a woman who had reminded him of Mom. He thought she looked like Mom! We didn't! Boy, was he wrong! She was not a saint like my Mom. This woman was the devil. She was actually supposed to be a dietician and she worked at a hospital formulating diets for sick people. Every time we would visit Pop, who had sugar diabetes, "Ethel" would have a table full of pies, cakes and cookies that she had baked for him. This from a dietician for a man with sugar diabetes. Then the inevitable happened. He had a stroke and she took over. She came up with a marriage certificate and sold the home. We believed that she forged Pop's name along the way. She bought another home and sold that. More and more of Pop's money kept disappearing. All the while, she kept stuffing Pop with sugar. We tried to talk to him, but she had him convinced that <u>we</u> were after his money. To end the tragic story, she sold the second house in 1965 and took Pop to Torrance to live with her family. This made it a long drive for us to see Pop. When we would drive down and try to see him, she wouldn't answer the door. After she got all the money completely, she stood him on a corner with a suitcase and a little change in his pocket and gangrene in his leg. She called Joe from a phone booth and told him that we had better come get him, because she was through. That was the beginning of a long, pain-filled death for Pop. He had to have his leg amputated. It was too late to save it. He spent a lot of time in the County Hospital. Then the nurses or attendants, got him out of bed and let him step on a piece of broken glass someone had carelessly missed. That took care of his other leg. It got infected and they had to take it off. He became a double amputee and pretty helpless. I tried to take care of him for a while at home, but I couldn't do it. Physically, I just couldn't do it. He had to be lifted and carried. Medically, I couldn't do it either. He needed professional care. So, we had to put him in a home near us in the Valley. Joe came over faithfully to see him about every other week and Willie and I went to see him a couple of times a week. He just had us to live for and he really didn't care that much about life anymore. I hope that woman met the fate she deserved, because basically she was a murderer. For poor Pop it was the beginning of a long, hard struggle that would eventually end with his death. Sometimes life is not fair.

    In the meantime, back at Marlin Manor, things were plugging along. "Wee Willie" had developed asthma and the allergies started to come out. We ran the gauntlet of tests, and he was allergic to many things. The doctors said the only thing we could do was to move to another state and give up everything. That meant all the animals and everything else and we couldn't do that. Besides, they said he'd probably come up with new allergies in a new state. So, we just tried to figure out a way that he could live through it with medication. It led to him being a very spoiled little guy. You don't make a kid clean up his room or clean off his plate when he's struggling to breathe. We knew all about it because Suzy had gone through an asthma period and outgrew it. So, we just hoped that Willie would too. I didn't know it, but my life was starting to run away like a loaded freight car going downhill with no brakes. I was finding it harder and harder to stay on those tracks. Dad was drinking more and more and he was getting meaner. It was mostly verbal, but somehow little Grandma Mary came up with a broken arm. She claimed she just slipped and fell, but I suspected that Dad had something to do with that. He was at the point now where he couldn't stay sober for even a week. Dad and Bob were now openly hostile to each other and barely speaking. Our next-door neighbor, who was a retired nurse, had a drinking problem too. Her name was Irene. Dad was still a lady's man, so he used to go next door and visit with her for a while and then come home. This one time he went to see her she was drinking also. She called the cops on Dad. Bob had to go over and bring him home in order to keep him from being arrested. The cops realized that Irene was as much to blame as Dad and that he really didn't do anything wrong, so they allowed Bob to bring him home. Bob had to force Dad home and that sent Dad off the deep end as far as Bob was concerned. Dad was only looking for a reason anyway. He was always jealous of Bob being my husband. I was his little girl. I wonder how many fathers feel that jealousy? Anyway, the next-door neighbor's name was "Irene" and Dad would always say, "Irene, Irene, The Village Queen." At that time the song, "Good Night, Irene" was popular. I went to bed many nights hearing and thinking, "Good Night, Irene." Dad never forgave Bob for forcing him home, even though it had kept him out of jail. From that time on, he did nothing but make constant threats. He stayed in his room most of the time when Bob was home, but there was always that underlying threat.

  Willie, in the meantime, was growing up and his asthma took him away from the sports that he loved. He just couldn't perform like he wanted to because you can't do it when you can't breathe. His physical activities were limited. He took a liking to karate and I squeezed out the money for him to take lessons. By the time he was about 9 years old, he was a brown belt. He was very good at it. Then his artistic talents took over in school. He excelled in drama and starred in all the plays. In one of them, he even taught himself to tap dance. He told me, "Mom, get me a pair of tap shoes." He told me that in January and his birthday was March 12. He said, "Mom, get me the shoes and I'll be ready to do this tap dance number by my birthday." He then starred in the musical "Gypsy" in high school and the whole family attended, including Joe and Sal. Willie was great! He brought the house down. He did a dance number all dressed up in top hat, white tie and tails singing, "I've got my top hat, I've got my tie. All I need now is the girl." Then he did this terrific dance number up and over a table and ended up on a drum. The woman behind me was saying, "Well, yes, he's good, but he probably took lessons all his life." I just had to turn around and say, "No, madam, he taught himself to do that." He learned it from last January to March. I think Willie really had a career in front of him in drama. But, I couldn't afford to send him to a dance school or to New York where he could have studied, so it wasn't going to happen. At that point in time, his girlfriend was Dee Dee Bellson, Pearl Bailey's daughter. Willie had a complete set of drums and was teaching himself to play them. He was getting pretty good! Dee Dee's father was Louie Bellson, the great drummer and band leader. He was very fond of Willie. Willie might have had a career there also, but it did not work out.

The home environment wasn't helping. Dad would make threats to me about what he was going to do to Bob. Bob would just laugh and treat him with contempt, which, of course, just made things worse. I begged and I pleaded with both of them and I lived in constant torment trying to keep them apart. Nothing was working and Dad was starting to take it out on the kids. They, of course, would stick up for their dad. He was actually starting to worry me because he was now verbally abusing them, too. Bob would come home from work and I would feed him his dinner. After eating, as usual, he would go to sleep on the couch. I now would have to sit up all night, many nights, guarding him. Dad would sober up and apologize all over the place and tell me how sorry he was and that it would never happen again. For a while there would be a little peace and quiet and a little rest. Then it would happen all over again. The bad times were getting closer and closer together. The peace time had been cut down to nothing. I was in a constant state of worry. I was worried about little Mary. I was worried about the kids. I was worried about Willie's asthma. I was worried about Bob's drinking. I was worried about Dad's drinking. I was worried about Bob becoming less and less of a father and less and less of a husband. My loaded freight train car was picking up speed with a lot of trouble on the track ahead. I really didn't realize it. I was just too busy trying to make things work for everybody. Bob was becoming more and more distant and withdrawn, even from the kids. But I tried to support him because he had been there for me when I needed him. The only time he acted like a father always seemed to be at the wrong time. Of course, alcohol was the reason for most of it.

It was the era of long hair, the late '60s, and Bobby sported a ponytail like all the rest of his buddies at school. Parents were known as the "establishment" and the enemy at that time.

Of course, we didn't like the long hair. Bob would grumble about it all the time. But I reasoned with him and I'd been able to keep things level pointing out to him that Bobby got passing grades, didn't do drugs and was respectful to us. But this one night, after one too many six packs, Bob got violent about the hair and ordered Bobby to get a haircut or else. I tried to talk to him and pointed out that peer pressure would make it tough on Bobby if he got a haircut and that Bobby was basically such a good kid. But once he said it, Bob wouldn't take it back. Bobby had always been laid back and a happy-go-lucky, relaxed little guy. But this time, he rebelled and went to live with his mom in Santa Monica. I really missed him and so did Bob, but he wouldn't admit it.

We thought Bobby was going to school in Santa Monica, but we started getting phone calls from Birmingham High in Van Nuys, where Bobby had been going to school. He was still attending there, but he was missing a lot of days and he was late a lot. They didn't know that he wasn't still at home with us. Then we got a letter from the police department. Bobby had gotten a number of hitchhiking tickets in the same area. The poor kid was getting on that 405 Freeway and trying to hitchhike from Santa Monica to Birmingham High to go to school. He was only 15 years old and that was dangerous. So, Bob finally saw the light. Bobby could have gotten into so much more trouble hitchhiking than he could have for having long hair. Bob let Bobby come back home with his long hair, and, of course, one of the first things Bobby did was get a haircut. I was very happy that he was home because Bobby and I always had a very special relationship. He was always such a good natured little guy. He loved coming to live with us because before that, he had to exist in a woman's world: shopping, nail doing, beauty shops, all the girly things with his mom and Suzy. At "Marlin Manor," the guys ruled with Dad and Charlie and Willie. At least, we let them think they did! I still had my curly hair, so I didn't make Bobby go to the beauty parlor. I'm the one who played catch with him and showed him how to take two strikes and hit the curveball to right field. We were always close. He wasn't a very graceful little guy. I knew he wasn't going to be a ballet dancer. He was all boy and he went through a very awkward period. He liked to run around barefooted. We had a hard time keeping shoes on him. The entire time when Bobby was growing up, I cannot remember a time that he did not have a nasty-looking, bloody, stubbed toe. He would come in the door, and no matter where Willie's toys were (I'd try to get them out of the way), Bobby would find them and fall over them. I was extremely worried about open manholes. We could have lost him! He was a good athlete and, for a while, he wanted to be a catcher like me. But the unfair prejudice and tactics of "little league" put an end to that. His team was run by a father whose son was a catcher! The boy wasn't near the ballplayer Bobby was, but he was playing and Bobby wasn't. When I went down and tried to talk to them, the coach wouldn't respond to me at all. He didn't want a woman anywhere near the baseball field. When I tried explaining to those gentlemen that I played professional baseball with some great Hall of Fame baseball players as my coaches, they just looked at me disdainfully, as if I was crazy, and said, "You mean softball," and walked away. So, for Bobby, baseball faded away. Since he was always very good in the water, he joined the swim team at school. He was like a cork in the water, so Bobby became a surfer. He didn't get the best of grades, but he got passing grades. Suzy was our scholar. She got A's and B's all the time. Suzy really loved ice skating and roller skating. But like most teenaged girls, she was really majoring in boys.

    We knew that her mom allowed her to wear full makeup at an early age. This was before she came to live with us. We allowed only lipstick, but we couldn't follow her to school and follow her around for 24 hours. I suspected she was putting on more makeup at school. We took her to the skating rink and picked her up. But you can't be a watchdog, you have to trust your kids at some point. I worried, because I knew she was very young to be so interested in boys. In the long run, we lost the vote and Suzy did what she wanted. She got married at a very young age and was pregnant by the time she was 16. She paid the price for it. We all did. In 1967, a wonderful thing came out of it -- my little grandson Kent! The little guy was going to wind up living with me for a lot of his life. For Suzy, it was the beginning of a long, hard search of trying to find the right guy. She was very beautiful, very young and very trusting. "Wrong" guys are so easy to find and so hard to identify (until it's too late). I knew my Suzy might be in for some hard times before she found happiness. I had failed again.

    Things were going from bad to worse. Bob and Dad rarely spoke now, other than to curse at each other, even when they were sober. The hate in Dad's eyes frightened me. My heart was torn. Had it only been myself I had to worry about, I would have stuck it out with him and tried to take care of him because I knew that inside, Dad really loved us all. But alcohol was robbing him of his reason, like it does so many times. The situation was becoming embarrassing and fearsome for Mary and the kids. I had to protect them. I knew that something had to give, so I made a decision. "Marlin Manor" was almost paid for, so I borrowed $5,000 on it. Then I found this beautiful house in Northridge on Burton Street, which was only about three miles from Marlin. It was the bargain of the century. It had four bedrooms, a huge family room, a large floor-to-ceiling slump stone fireplace, paneling, a high-beam ceiling overlooking a beautiful landscaped pool. It was a nice, large pool. It had a formal dining room and a large see-through kitchen to the family room. It had a washer and dryer built in off the kitchen, a two-car garage and a nicely landscaped front yard with palm trees and a lawn. The owners were in a bind. They had to move into their new home and they needed their money to close escrow. It was the rainy season and no one was interested in their pool. They were asking $39,000, a large sum then, and the house was worth every penny of it. I offered $24,000 and they took it because they were out of time. With our $5,000 down, the bank picked up the balance and they got the full amount of cash. I was in heaven in one way; I had my dream home. But I was also devastated in another way. The plan called for us to make the payments on Marlin Manor, only $50 a month. So we decided to let Dad live out his life there. Our whole payment on Burton Street was only $147, so that was less than $200 a month for both houses and Bob said he could handle it. So, I had to walk out on Dad, taking everybody with me. Little Mary still loved Dad, but she feared him now. Dad could be a wonderful guy when he wanted to be. But, the drinking was making him impossible to live with. He would apologize every time and say he wouldn't do it again. But sooner or later he did, and the "sooner" now always came quickly. It looked like this was the only solution. I had warned Dad over and over that this would happen, that we would have to leave him, but he didn't believe me. He really didn't think that it would ever happen. I had to sneak out on him. I felt bad about that. I had to blindside him. He didn't even guess that it was coming. In February 1969, we moved out gradually and slowly. We moved all the little things first and then … Boom! We moved the big things overnight and we were gone. The house was empty except for his little room in the back. Of course, I came back that night and told him what and why and how, but I couldn't give him a phone number and I couldn't give him an address. When he sobered up, he was devastated and so was I. He was in a state of shock. I told him that I still loved him and I cried when I saw him. I can still see his face. He had the saddest, most brokenhearted look in his eyes that I have ever seen. But he patted me on the back and he told me softly, "Don't cry, poulette. I know it's my fault." Of course, I cooked for him and went and saw him daily. I put food in the refrigerator, but I could see that he wasn't eating much and he was drinking more. His heart was broken. Dad had always stayed quietly in his room for most of the time when he wasn't drinking and he never ate at the table with us. He always had these little pots and pans of things sitting by his bedside and he would nibble on things and read his 15 to 25 library books. He would come out occasionally and heat his food up. I cooked and filled those little pans for him and now I could see those pots were just sitting there and the food was going bad. I kept trying to talk to him. Over and over I would say: "Please, Dad, sober up. Go to the VA and spend some time there and then you can come and live with us again. We've got a big house, there's room." But I could tell each time he was slipping deeper and deeper into the world of alcohol. He just didn't care anymore. I kept praying for a miracle, but I knew in my heart, there would be none. Dad had given up and I felt totally and completely to blame. My heart was sick for him, but I didn't know what else to do. I knew something would have to give and it did. It was May 29, 1969. It was my birthday and I was taking Dad his dinner. I had cooked for him and Mary and the kids. Bob was coming home early to take me out for dinner. I was apprehensive as I pulled up to the house thinking, "Gee, I hope he's sober." I hadn't been over for two days and our last encounter hadn't been too pleasant. He had been on a three-week binge and was openly sarcastic to me. He had promised me once again that he would quit that night and I was hoping that he had kept his promise. When I entered the house, I felt strange. I always did ever since we moved out. It was so empty and so hollow. Dad had never moved out of the back room and into the house that had been so full of life before. It was now strangely silent and empty. I had made lots of noise as I always did when I came in. I unlocked the door and slammed it. I did this because Dad was now pretty hard of hearing and I didn't want to startle him. So, I would go around slamming doors and purposely setting things down with a bang and I would holler, "Dad, Dad, it's me." When I set the food down in the kitchen, I could see through the window that his bathroom light was on. I tapped on the kitchen window and hollered again, "Dad, Dad, it's me."

Then I went back through the dining room and down the hall to his little bathroom still hollering, "Dad, Dad, it's me." He had not answered, but that was not unusual because sometimes he would be napping. I came to the door of his room and I could see that it was slightly ajar. It also opened into his bathroom if he didn't have that little door closed. I knocked hard on the door and repeated my greeting, "Dad, Dad, it's me." Somehow my words seemed to hang hollow in the air and a shiver ran down my back. Something was wrong. I pulled the door open slightly and peeked in and I could see my Dad's knee. The bathroom door was slightly open and you could see through the crack! Dad was sitting on the "pot" and somehow I knew immediately that he was dead. I could not see his face, but I <u>knew</u> he was dead. I choked out, "Dad? Dad?" I reached out and I touched his knee and it was ice cold. I opened the door and looked into his cold, gray face. His eyes were closed and he looked peaceful, like he was asleep. I fell to my knees in anguish moaning: "Oh, no, God, please! Oh, no, God, please! Dad? Dad, it's my fault. It's my fault." I don't know how I got out of there. I don't know how I drove home. I knew that I had called Bob and I knew that I had called Joe and that's all I did know. They said they didn't recognize my voice. They couldn't tell who I was. My voice was wrenched out from my gut. My Dad was gone and I felt this terrible, terrible burden of guilt. This was the same guilt I felt for my Mom, for my Pop and now I felt it for my Dad. I still carry that guilt today. I don't know what I could have done to change things. I honestly don't know if I could have made things any different but somehow it seems like I should have been able to take care of him and make things better. Dad was yet another link in the chain of tragic events that seems to happen on holidays. My Mom died on Christmas Day 1959 and now my Dad dies on my birthday. So, the chain continued. I felt haunted. I began to dread the approach of holidays.

"Sheriff Russell"

Bob, Me & my Rambler

Bobby

Will & Scoot

Suzy & Scoot

Willie & Scoot

Jody

Mom Suzy & son Scoot

Chapter 39
Shake and Bake

By now, my new, beautiful dream home seemed to be more like nightmare alley for me. We now had Marlin Place to worry about. Should we fix it up and rent it? Home sales were down, so it didn't make sense to sell it. It needed a lot of help and real estate wasn't doing well. If we fixed it up and rented it, maybe that would be a way to pay it off and make a profit at the same time. We were thinking that situation over. In the meantime, Suzy's marriage had broken up and she had a little 1-year-old boy to take care of. She was only 17. She was struggling. She needed help to raise that little guy. I talked Bob into letting her come back home with little "Scooter," as we nicknamed him. He was just learning to walk. He was such a cute little guy. Suzy got a job and went to work. I started taking care of him along with Willie and Mary. Once again we had a full but happy home. At first it seemed that Bob was happy again without Dad's interference and with Suzy back home. But it didn't last long and he started withdrawing again. It was February 1971 and along came the big quake -- the "Sylmar Quake." Actually, while it was a really bad night, we were very lucky. It scared the heck out of us, but it really didn't do all that much damage on Burton Street. It broke all the dishes in the kitchen, threw water out of the swimming pool and up over the garage, but it didn't crack it. "Marlin Manor" faired even better. We had been fixing it up a little bit and we had some shelves leaning up against the wall while we were painting. Those shelves didn't even fall over! We got some money from the quake on both houses. It was just a little cosmetic money, not a lot, but enough to buy some materials. We started to get serious about fixing up Marlin. Bob seemed to lighten up and get excited about the whole project. He and I were painting and fixing and cleaning on weekends. Sometimes we brought Willie and our dog, "Baby," with us and they played in the yard. Sometimes they stayed home. Suzy would take Scooter and Willie to the movies or they would swim and she would watch them, so that situation was handled. I'd make us a nice lunch with some cold beer, of course.

After the quake, when people asked where I was from I would say the San Fernando Valley, you know, "Shake and Bake Country." Bob seemed like his old self again as we worked side by side. That old Marlin manor was built in 1922 and while we had upgraded and fixed a lot of things, you can never get done with an old house. We were always finding a crack, or something missing, or something wrong that needed fixing. Instead of tearing it out and adding all new stuff, I'd say, "No, no, Bob. Let's just get a bigger piece of molding." He always wanted everything perfect, but sometimes he would give in to me. Then he would laugh and say, "OK, but you know what you are? You are the 'Molding Queen.'" That's what he nicknamed me, "The Molding Queen." I'd say, "OK, just as long as you're not saying 'Moldy Queen.'" It almost seemed like old times when we were newly married. When Bob and I were alone together, he seemed to be much happier, but I didn't pick up on that soon enough. I just thought, "Hey, he was coming out of it."

My Bob was back again. After we got Marlin fixed up and cleaned up pretty well, we rented it to a lovely woman (we thought). She had two teenage boys. Her husband had dumped her for another woman. We thought she needed a break and we rented her the house at a very cheap price. Well, she paid the rent for about the first two months and then she started getting later and later and later. Before we knew it, we had a heck of a time collecting any rent at all. I think it was about here that the silent song I nicknamed "And Bob Blamed Me" started. I guess by this time Bob was tired of having Suzy living with us and so, of course, Bob blamed me! Suzy decided to try again and she married a nice young man named Tim. He was a good dad to Kent. He was going to school and trying to work two jobs. Neither job paid very much, so they moved in with us. Of course they paid rent, but they couldn't pay much. "And Bob Blamed Me."

My poor little Grandma Mary was heartbroken, like me, about Dad's death. She also blamed herself for Dad's death and she wasn't doing well at all. She was sick with the flu and I really believe that at 92, she decided just not to live anymore. I took the best care of her that I could. I served her food in her room and tried to get her well, but the only time she was happy was when "little Scooter" would sit and eat strawberries with her. She kept failing and the writing was on the wall. There wasn't much I could do about it. I was helpless. She had lost the will to live and no one can give you that back. You've got to do it yourself.

Eventually she developed pneumonia and she didn't fight it and boom! -- she was gone. That was on Valentine's Day 1971 and there went another holiday. We all loved her very much and it hurt a lot to lose her. Even Bob cried at her funeral. But, as he was crying, he looked at me and though it was unspoken, I heard the song again, "Bob Blamed Me!" Somehow whenever a bad thing happened, he would focus on it being my fault. I didn't know why. Actually, pretty soon I started to believe him, and mentally and physically I was breaking down. That warning my mother had given me a long time ago, about what I was doing to my body and what would happen when I got older, was coming true. I was keeping everything inside of me and not telling anyone. Meanwhile, the kids were growing up and Bobby was now taking driver's education at 15. We got this chance to buy a Pontiac at a good price. It was silver and wine colored. We called it the "Burgundy Bomb." I talked Bob into buying it. He did some work for the woman we bought it from, so we didn't have to pay very much for it. We made a sizable down payment and Bobby, who had a part-time job, was going to pay it off. I gave him driving lessons. It was a little harder for Bobby to learn things than Suzy. But I finally felt that he was ready and he and I headed for the DMV. Well, he turned into the driveway at the DMV and an old guy comes out of nowhere and rams right into us. It wasn't Bobby's fault; it was the old guy's fault, and that was proven because Bobby passed his test and the old guy didn't. The old guy didn't have very much insurance, so we had to fix the car up on our own. There wasn't much damage. It had a dented bumper and some minor dents. Then, of course, came the melody, "And Bob Blamed Me!" It turned out to be too much of a car for Bobby. Sixteen-year-old boys and high-powered automobiles just don't work out. We had to take it back from him and sell it. What 16-year-old boy doesn't get tickets and have car problems? You're lucky if you get through it without them getting hurt or hurting somebody. And we were lucky! But, of course, through the whole thing, the song kept playing, "And Bob Blamed Me!" Again, Bob was showing signs of discontent and drinking more. I was worried about him. I was also very worried about my beloved bro Joe. He was having health problems. My world friendship, softhearted brother was suffering from bleeding ulcers and I knew where they came from. They came from those 33 bombing missions that he flew during the war. He worried about all those bombs that he perceived were dropped on innocent people in the South Pacific. He worried that maybe he had hurt a lot of innocent people.

It went from bad to worse, and on the Fourth of July 1969, my bro Joe was hospitalized with a bleeding ulcer. He had an oral hemorrhage while he was there and he lost two-thirds of the blood in his body and we almost lost him. If he had not been at the hospital, he wouldn't have made it! I was out of my mind with worry. But, through the grace of God, and all of our prayers, he made it through. I was so grateful for that. I was starting to think life was worth living again and I was pulling out of my depression. Then Suzy's husband, Tim, and Bob got into an altercation over some little thing about the kids. Suzy and Tim moved out in a huff. The song, "And Bob Blamed Me," had now taken on a life of its own and was becoming a concert. By this time, our Bobby had finally graduated and that was a good accomplishment. He made it through. He didn't have the greatest grades, but, he made it. Then he decided he wanted to see the world. So, he joined a one-elephant traveling circus as "Ringmaster." But don't let the title fool you. They headed for Alaska and he found out that he had to sleep with the elephant. (That must have been great fun.) Of course, I heard the song again, "Bob Blamed Me" because I had encouraged Bobby to see the world. I knew that traveling was a lot of fun and I told him if that's what he wanted to do, that's what he should do while he was young enough to enjoy it. Through all of this, my health finally broke down completely and I had to go to the hospital. The doctor said I needed complete rest and I also had an abscess that had to be removed from my bowel area. That's when I knew that my marriage was really in trouble. Bob only came to see me once at the hospital and when he did, it was like he was a stranger. I even wrote a song about it. I was writing a song about everything in those days. It helped to express my emotions. Don't know if I ever finished it, but it went something like this:

> "Like a bolt from the blue,
> You said we were through
> How come I never knew?
> Now, as I look to your chair
> There's a stranger sits there
> With a cold, unloving stare
> Like a bolt from the blue
> How come I never knew?"

© Pepper Paire Davis, 1970

Man, I was deep into the blues on that one.

Bob just didn't seem to care as he sat like a "stranger in his chair." I was in the hospital for five days and when I came back home, that very night, as I laid resting on the couch, Bob came in the door late from work. It was about 8 o'clock. He didn't even pick me up from the hospital. Suzy had done that. He walked in the door and he had a tall can of Coors beer in his hand. He left the door open, didn't even close it behind him. Looking straight at me he said, "Pep, I'm leaving you. I want out!" Then he walked across the room, stood in front of me and I could see the hate in his eyes. He said: "You don't love me. You just loved your Dad, you just love the kids, you just love the dogs. That's all you ever cared about. You don't love me." Then he turned and he threw that full can of beer across the room and it bounced up against the wall and foamed all over. He turned and said, "You don't love me, you never did. It's all your fault." And he walked out the door slamming it behind him. He sang the song for the last time! I was in a state of shock. I was gasping for air with his words ringing in my ears. "You don't love me. It's your fault!" My God, was this real? Was that my Bob? It couldn't be! I was having a nightmare but I was awake. It did happen! The truth finally dawned on me. All that time that I thought I was doing everything for Bob by taking care of his children, by taking care of everybody, he was resenting it. He thought that I loved them and not him. I had never neglected him. I had always fixed him his dinner and kept his clothes clean. I would always be ready for him whenever he wanted to make love, which wasn't a hell of a lot in those final years. But Bob didn't see it that way. I guess he didn't feel the same way I felt about the kids coming first. Apparently, Bob resented not being first. Had I been able to wake up to that fact earlier, I could have possibly done something about it. But now it was too late. After he left, he didn't come back home for quite a few days. But he did come home for the Easter weekend.

My nephew, Jody, was getting married on July 8, 1972, and Bob had promised to go to the wedding with me. He still loved and respected my family and, for that matter, they loved and respected Bob. As far as they knew, he was being a good husband and father, and they knew I loved him very much. They did not know what had happened. Bob did still love my family, just not me! I asked him not to tell them. I didn't want to spoil the wedding. So, we went to the wedding together, arm in arm. I sat in that church listening to Jody and his wife take those wedding vows with such pain in my heart and tears running down my face. The reception was held in the backyard of Joe and Sal's. I wasn't fully recuperated physically from the hospital. Mentally, I could barely keep it together. I kept busy helping in every way I could just to keep myself going. The tears just kept rolling down my face. Everyone thought that I was really sentimental over my little Jody getting married. I was, but they didn't know that my heart was breaking all the way through it. I didn't want to dampen the spirit of the wedding and I didn't want my brother to know. I didn't want his ulcer to act up. After we got home, Bob grabbed some clothes and walked out again.

So, there we were, Willie and Baby and me, in my big old four-bedroom, two-bath, dream house with a swimming pool. Just my 11-year-old son and my little black Baby girl doggy and me. It seemed like Dad's death, Mary's death, my mother's death and all my sacrifices had gone for nothing. They were all gone. My 15-year marriage was over. I was in my 40s, the most vulnerable time in a woman's life. I was sick mentally and physically. I don't know why, but like a lot of other women, I felt it was totally my fault. I guess I had been listening to that song for so long, I believed it. I felt like a complete and utter failure, and the freight train crashed and for a little while, I drank too much. But I did it late at night and in my own home mostly! I had my Willie and I needed to take care of him, so I snapped out of it. After that, Bob came out a couple of times and gave me a few dollars. But that didn't last too long. I was getting deeper into financial trouble. Bob had told me that he didn't want anything but his personal belongings. He signed everything over to me. That was right because it was Dad's and Mary's money that had originally bought Marlin. But, while Bob didn't claim anything, he didn't claim any of the bills either and there was a lot owed. I had to leave things in his name because nobody would give me any credit. I was a woman in her 40s who hadn't worked in 10 years and you can forget it, baby. There was no credit for me! I was in a place called "No Woman's Land!" What I tried to do was pay a few dollars on everything that I could and write letters. Once in a while, Bob would get bills and then he would call me up and say, "Hey, how come you haven't paid this?" And once in a while he would help me out. But that didn't happen too often and things were getting worse. The nice woman -- quote, unquote -- that we had rented to, turned out to be not so nice at all. She wasn't paying any rent. She was on welfare and because of her two kids, as a landlord, I couldn't get her out unless I needed to move into my own residence or unless the property was sold. Once again, I found out that sometimes landlords don't even have control of their own property. There are some laws that are not very fair. I tried many times to sell Marlin, but when I would bring people over there, she wouldn't even let them into the house. She had two dogs that she let crap all over the house and she left it there. The people never got past the front door because she kept the house so filthy. I didn't want to worry Sal and Joe because I didn't want them to know how bad my troubles really were. Finally it got to the point that I was in danger of losing both homes. So, I had to put my dream house up for sale. It sold in five days for $35,000. I got enough out of it to pay the bills and get caught up on Marlin Place. But, what a bad deal that was for me. It was the beginning of the real estate boom and property was just starting to escalate. That started in the 1970s. A year later, that house was worth $90,000. Had I been able to hang on, all my financial worries would have been over. But, at least I was finally able to get the parasite woman out because we needed to move back in. We went full circle. So, Willie and me and the "little black 'Baby' girl makes three," went back to "Marlin Manor" where we were all alone with all the ghosts.

Clark of my heart & Boo-Boo

"My black baby girl"

Willie, Me & "Tina"

Happy & "Lonesome Pete"

Clarky - Barky

My little black baby girls, Licorice & Tina

Chapter 40
A New Low Point -- Single With Shingles

I knew I had to buckle down and do something. So, I went out and bought some drugstore eyeglasses and got myself a job at ITT Gilfillian Electronics. My confidence was shot and I was pitiful, but I managed to get the job anyway. So, I was able to start making payments on everything. I bought an old Rambler station wagon for transportation and Willie and I started going fishing off the Malibu Pier. That little pier used to stay open all night on those hot valley nights in the summertime. On the weekends, I'd pack a lunch, maybe peanut butter sandwiches and hard-boiled eggs. We would dig up some worms (night crawlers).

Sometimes we had enough money to buy a little live bait at the pier. We would go down in the afternoon and fish. Sometimes we would stay until midnight or 1 a.m., when the sharks would come in. I hooked a six-foot blue shark off that pier. After I pulled it up, the guys had to net it and shoot it. It was too dangerous to land otherwise. Willie still has a couple of the razor-sharp teeth, I believe. As time went on, I was slowly but surely getting it back together again; at least for outward appearances. But, I had lost all my confidence and all my self-esteem. Being "Willie's Mom" was all that kept me going, for a lot of years. It was still touch and go with his asthma and there were many nights we spent in the hospital for emergency treatment. But his asthma got better as time passed. Funny thing, when we went to the pier, even though it was foggy and damp, he never got an asthma attack. That was another reason we loved fishing. Seems that the ocean wouldn't let it happen. I wrote a little poem about us fishing that I really like. It's about the ones that got away.

My Son and Me and the Malibu Sea

One fine day my little son and me,

We drove down to the Malibu sea,

We walked out to the end of the pier,

Sat on the bench and rigged our gear,

Willie was first in the water with a proud look,

I smiled with my eyes as I tied my hook,

We changed this and we changed that,

But caught not a fish,

Spit on the hook and turned 'round our hats,

Still didn't get our wish,

But the sun was bright and the sky was blue,

So we stayed on to see it through,

We caught not a thing that wonderful day,

But, oh what fun we had, with the ones that got away.

Like I said, fishing was our salvation. My bowling pal, Betty, and her husband, John, lived nearby and they had a little fishing boat. Sometimes we went fishing with them. Once in a while, when I could scrape up a little money, we would go on one of the sport-fishing boats. It didn't cost very much then at the Malibu Pier. Betty and John didn't have any children, so John kind of filled in as a father figure for Willie. He taught Willie how to clean and filet the fish. Willie was so proud when he learned how to do it.

Betty and John were very good to Willie and me through those bad times. We had gone from a family of seven to a family of three. Me, Willie and our little black dog, Baby. Bob's sister Billie was a great help, morally as well as financially. She never had children and she loved Bobby, Suzy and little Willie dearly. Actually, right here, I have to give her credit for helping me spoil Willie. Many a night, when the despair was getting me down, Willie and I would climb into the old clunker and we would sing, "Over the hill goes Mom and Will as they go by-de-bye. Riding along, singing a song under the blue, blue sky." Off we would go to see Aunt BB. Sometimes it would be 11 o'clock or midnight, if there was no school the next day. I would have a beer or two with Billie. She would have a Coke or two, maybe with a little something in it, or maybe not. She would cook hamburgers for us, or maybe we would go out to dinner. Billie might make cookies or popcorn and we would play cards. She would always insist on paying the bill. We always had fun with Aunt BB. That's what the kids called her. She was a lifesaver. She loved her brother, Bob, but she knew that he had let us down and she helped in every way she could. Joe and Sally did too, but they both worked and they lived too far away for me to make the trip in my old clunker too often. I always put on a good show for them. I didn't want my beloved bro to worry. They were always right there for me if I asked. I don't know what I would have done without the help of Joe and Sal, and my loyal friends. At one point in time, Bob asked me to get a divorce and I told him, "Go ahead, that is your job. You are the one who wanted out." He never did get one. It turned out that there was more to that story than met the eye. There was a gal at work that he thought he loved. She was married also, and supposedly loved Bob. So, he walked out on me and became available; then, I guess she didn't want him. The old grass is greener in somebody else's backyard. She never left her husband. I was finally beginning to feel better about everything and getting over my bitterness. But Willie wasn't. He was angry at his dad for leaving. Bob had literally forgotten about him, so I couldn't really blame him. I used to try and fake it and buy cards and presents for him on special occasions and put Bob's name on them. One day he just flat-out turned and said: "Mom, I know they're not from him. He doesn't care, so cut it out. I know they're from you." It was true. It was just him and me, and our little black girl, "Baby" most of the time.

If it got too lonely, off we'd go fishing! I don't know what I would have done if God had not made that ocean and put fish in it. Anyway, I had saved up a couple hundred dollars and we bought a little 16-foot boat. It was a "Wolverine," Lake Michigan fishing boat. Boy, the guy really sold me a bill of goods! We didn't get to try it in the water. He convinced me that I could tell if the motor was OK by running it in a big 50-gallon metal drum, filled with water. Well, in the drum it worked fine, until we got it in the water. Then we discovered that it would only go backwards. The forward gear was shot. But, we had fun anyway. We went up to Lake Castaic and putted around there, backwards! The patrol boat guy saw us. It didn't take him long to realize that we could only go backwards. He could have kicked us out because it really wasn't safe, but, he was a good guy about it. This one time he went by and he looked over at me and laughed. He said, "Hey, that makes it kind of tough to pull a skier, doesn't it?" We had a lot of fun in that old boat. We named her the "Beer Barge." We still had our old clunker station wagon, too. What guts I had launching that boat down a steep hill with no reverse gear in the car! Being on the freeway, in high-powered traffic, with no reverse gear. I'll tell you, you learned not to pull up close behind a car because if it stalled on you, you were stuck! You also went around a lot of blocks looking for front-end parking spaces, so you wouldn't get pinned in.

    Bob's nephew, Buddy, came down from Montana and lived with me for a while. He and his wife slept on the couch until they had money to find a place to stay. That started a great friendship. His early marriage didn't last, but later on, he married a great little gal named Joanie. We became good friends. Buddy could fix anything with wheels on it. If it didn't have wheels, he could put them on for you. He fixed up the boat and the car for me. As a matter of fact, through the years, Buddy has fixed a lot of cars for me. Even though he was Bob's nephew, he and I remained close. Bud and Joanie were always around when I needed them. Bobby would drop into town now and then, and Suzy was generally around. She would come back home when a relationship would go sour on her and her marriage would fall apart. Suzy was trying desperately to get back those young years that she had lost. Scooter was now starting to grow up and be a little boy. Actually, his real name was Kent, but we had nicknamed him "Scooter" from early on. When he was just a little baby, when we would lay him on the bed, that little guy would scoot all over the bed. Suzy and Scoot would move in and out as Suzy kept trying to find the right guy. She met and married a man from Denver in 1975. She took my little Scooter and they were gone for three or four years. I missed them both greatly. But time flew by and the next thing I knew, they came back. By now, Scooter had become Kent, because he decided that Scooter was a baby name. They moved back in with Willie and me at Marlin Manor. Willie was growing up and was starting to discover girls. He was having a good time at school keeping busy with his drama and karate.

There was a little rivalry between Kent and Willie for my affection. A little jealousy perhaps. Willie wasn't home that much and my little Scooter filled the void he left. The rivalry faded out with time and eventually they became good buddies. They are now more like brothers than uncle and nephew. The years were flowing like water and through those years, a lot of people came and went at Marlin Manor and came and went in my life. It was kind of like what is written on the Statue of Liberty, "Bring me your poor, your humble and I'll give them a home at Marlin Manor."

Bobby was still coming back every now and then to see us. He was seeing the world. He was now a very handsome young man. He always had a female companion with him. At least one! The doors at "Marlin Manor" were always swinging open and closed. Various people came to live at Marlin -- sometimes guys with wives and kids that I felt sorry for! So, I would try to help them. The deal was, they were supposed to pay a few bucks for expenses. They were supposed to earn their keep by fixing the place up, doing yard work, repairs and so forth. I don't know how many times I fell for that one!

By now, my little black dog, "Baby" was getting up there in years. She was 18 years old in doggie years. That's 126 years old in human years. The inevitable was straight ahead of me. I just couldn't stand to think about it. She was the last link to my Mom and Willie's pride and joy. She was starting to have heart trouble and she would fall down and shake, and bang her head on the floor. Then she would be all right for a while. I took her to the vet, but he told me he couldn't do anything. He said to bring her back when the pain got too bad and the inevitable would have to be done. So, the time came; I didn't tell Willie (he was at school). Bobby was in town. He had bought an old truck and had built a wood camper for it. It was shaped like a house with a slanted roof. He took us on the death ride. I sat on the floor of the camper and held my little black baby girl in my arms, as close to my heart as I could get her. Bobby carried her in and the deed was done. I held her when the vet gave her the injection. She passed away with those dear, loving eyes staring into mine. If you have never loved and lost an animal, you may not know how bad it hurts. It was the last of the ties to my Mom. It was the loss of 20 years of undying and unconditional love. Then I had to go home and tell my son, Willie. He was already lonely with his dad, sister and brother out of the picture, most of the time. Now, he had lost his best friend. He had never known life without Baby and her love for him and his love for her. It was indeed a sad and lonely time for both of us. I wanted to get him another dog, but he wouldn't have it. He didn't want to go anywhere or do anything. He just sat quietly and the tears would roll down his face. He said he never wanted another dog because it just hurt too much! Actually, I agreed with him. We were both in a world of pain.

Bobby finally got his camper finished and he was quite proud of his accomplishment. He had built his little house on wheels. He was bragging about the fact that he had inherited some of his dad's carpenter genes. And looking at that cute little thing, I was inclined to agree with him. He decided that he was going to take it on the road and I think that was probably the first time I was maybe glad to see Bobby leave. That little camper was a constant reminder of the last trip with Baby to the vet and it was a heart-hurter. By now, Bobby had turned into a full-fledged flower child and was bent on seeing the world and sowing his oats all along the way. Unfortunately, the first time he pulled out, he wasn't gone long. He got about a mile down the freeway and the roof of his little shanty blew off, all in one piece; off it blew! He was very fortunate that it didn't hit anything. He was actually able to go back, pick it up and bring it back home. He nailed it back on and then he took off again. I guess he wasn't quite as good a carpenter as he thought he was. He definitely was not a cabinet maker.

I was working swing shift as an electronic assembler at ITT Gilfillian's in Van Nuys now, so I could take care of the house and all the things that needed to be done during the day. I didn't get home until about 11:30 p.m. After Willie got home from school, he had to stay by himself in the evenings. I was only two or three miles from the house and we were in constant touch on the phone. It was still a worry, him being alone. I let him stay up on Friday nights until I got home and we would make popcorn or he would make us cookies or something. Then, we would watch scary movies together. This one night, I was coming home and it was pouring down rain. It was an electrical storm, which is unusual for California. I was worried because I knew he would be scared of the thunder and the lightning rolling around in the sky. When I rounded our corner, a black-and-white shadow darted across in front of me. I had to brake hard to miss it. It looked like a large dog, but I could not really tell what kind, because it was raining too hard. I couldn't see that well. By the time I got to the end of our block and pulled into our driveway, there it was, on our driveway waiting for me. Black and white and spotted; I rolled my window down and the paws went up and this big head came through the window. It was a beautiful dalmatian, with big frightened eyes. I said, "What's the matter, baby, are you lost?" Well, I got kisses all over my face. I guess she knew my tone of voice was friendly. She spun around in a circle and lit out for the porch. Willie had every light on in the house and he was waving at me through the window. So, I opened the door and that dog dashed in, water flying everywhere! She ran into the kitchen, then into the hall and finally into the bedroom. She was checking out everything and then she came running back out. She jumped through the air from about 20 feet away and landed on Willie's lap. She started kissing the daylights out of him. God had sent her to take the place of our "Baby." Willie named her "Happiness," or "Happy" for short. We tried for a little while to find the owner, with fear in our hearts that we might actually find them, but we never did. So, we would not be alone anymore. Willie was so proud of her. He would put her leash on and take her for a walk. Everybody admired her and wanted to pet her. She was such a beautiful, loving little girl.

Time does have a way of flying and healing and the hurt grew less in my heart. I found I could think of Bob again with love and not hate. The years seemed to pass without knowing. One day, I looked around and my Willie was a senior in high school. He was having his first live romantic fling. Well, that was traumatic, but I dealt with it. He was still playing his drums but he had given up the idea of a future in music. He was now into photography and making a feast or famine living by taking pictures of school graduation classes. One day he'd have a lot of money, then he'd be broke if the pictures didn't sell. However, he was having fun and really enjoying himself.

I continued working and doing all the same things such as bowling a little, fishing a little and of course, going to see my bro Joe and his gal Sal and "Aunt BB" whenever I could. But I did make a new friend named Sylvia Evans. I worked with her at ITT Gilfillian. Sylvia was a great little gal and she was married to a good guy named Jerry. She was about 30, going on 21, anyway, looking like 21. Sylvia was a great friend and we had a lot of fun together. Of course, she was a little nuts but then so was I (we had to be to make it). Sylvia was beautiful enough to be a model but way too sweet and way too shy and not confident enough to even try. She had a heart about the size of the Pacific Ocean. She was naïve and sometimes her child-like actions got her into trouble. She had beautiful brown eyes that were almost hypnotizing. They were surrounded by a large mass of flowing auburn-colored curly hair. When you looked deep into those eyes, you could see tragedy. She had been forced into an early marriage when she was very young to an older man who turned out to be a bad guy -- a brute who left her with many emotional scars before she got out. She was tiny and petite and built to perfection. All the guys were fascinated by her, and as Jimmy Carter said, "They lusted in their hearts for her!" But she just ignored them. In spite of differences in our looks, our demeanors and our age, we became soul pals. We hid our sad secrets by laughing and clowning and enjoying beer and fishing together. We had some great times. The only problem was Jerry -- although he was a really great guy, he was very jealous of Sylvia. He loved her so much he couldn't stand her caring for someone else. He resented anybody she liked, man or woman. But we managed to have fun anyway. Sylvia would come over late at night and we would talk until the wee hours. Sometimes we would eat junk food and drink beer. Then we would go out fishing early in the morning, maybe to Malibu or Oxnard or Marina del Rey. Sylvia had a friend named Frank, an older guy who was an ex-skipper on a fishing boat. He had his own 24-foot fishing boat, so he'd take us out with him a lot. What great times we had. Sometimes Willie would come along with us. Frank was teaching him to be a skipper and showed him all the good fishing spots. Like I say, time does fly.

  The next time I turned around Willie was majoring in girls (and the girls did find him). He wasn't home much, but Kent or "Scoot the pot" as I called him, took Willie's place, so I wasn't so lonesome. Suzy had moved in and out several times in the meantime. But the last time she left, Scooter chose to stay with me. Marlin Manor was home to him and I was his grandma, who had always been there for him. He had brought his little dog "Tina" with him, and we had picked up another little girl doggie named "Licorice" who needed a home. Both dogs were black fuzzy cockapoos. So, we were getting lots of love there. Unfortunately, our poor "Happy" had developed problems in her hips. Like so many pedigree dogs do, she had passed on and that was another heartache for both Willie and me.

Suzy was always there for all the occasions for Kent. Birthdays, holidays and family get-togethers but she was still trying to find her lost youth and the right man. So, it was better for everybody that Kent stayed with Willie and me. Kent was now growing up and getting near that driving age. So, I taught him how to drive, like I taught all the kids down through the years. I also taught him how to cook, like I taught all the other kids. But once again I was assisted by "Aunt BB." She helped me teach them everything. Including the best way to spoil them. She's to blame (along with me). I was still working at Gilfillian when my mind and my body started acting up on me again (just like Mom said it would). Both of my knees were very bad and my right one needed replacing, and my back was really beginning to give me a lot of pain. But I had no money to do anything about it. So, I just kept on taking my aspirin and biting the bullet and putting the bad thoughts behind me. In the past, I had dated a few times but I never really found anyone that I liked being with. I just didn't want anything more to do with a man after Bob left me. There was no desire and no attraction. I meant it when I said, "I do until death do us part!" I never loved another man since Bob, and I still love him. I would see him every once in a while at Aunt BB's, but not that often. He had a little apartment close to her house. He was still working at the lumberyard and drinking was still his main hobby. He spent his weekends drinking in his apartment and at the bowling alleys. My Willie, although he came with me often to see Aunt BB, did not want to see or speak to his father. The Cacapot Faye was still in and out of my life. She had finally quit drinking and she moved out of her folks' home and into a little hole-in-the-wall apartment close by them. She was working in a little electronic factory down in Santa Monica. She only made slave driver wages, but her wants and needs were not much, so she got by. Her dad had long since passed away. Funny thing, she quit drinking and I was still drinking beer and she was lecturing me, like former addicts do. Once in a while, when I was at home alone, I still drank too much. She was worried about that, but I have come to learn that certain people become addicts and other people do not. I knew that I was one that did not. When I got to the point where drinking was interfering in my life, I would quit completely.

It was the '80s and Faye and I used to go to dinner now and then at a little restaurant over in West L.A. by her house, called "The Turkey Bowl." That is, when we got two-for-one dinner coupons. So, here it was my birthday again and Faye was going to buy my dinner. I knew

I always had to be careful of holidays. They were killers for me. I worked half the day because it was Saturday and I headed her way. All day long I felt funny. My neck itched and burned. When I got to Faye's she said, "What are all those little blisters on your neck?" I hadn't looked in the mirror at work. I answered, "I don't know. What do they look like?" She said, "They look like shingles to me." Her mom had come down with shingles awhile back. Well, that was the beginning of a complete breakdown that was going to push me over the edge. By the time I got back home, I was in misery. It was a four-day holiday weekend, and there were no doctors available until the following week (by then it was too late). I understand that if you catch those shingles early enough, they can do something about them. They have a lot more sophisticated treatments now. By the time I got to the doctor, the shingles were in full bloom. The doctor said he had never seen a worse case. I had big runny green and black sores on my head on the right side. They went all the way inside my ear and down the side of my face. I think the doctor called it the triangular nerve. They say it's the largest nerve in your body. Shingles are infected nerve ends. They come to the surface and become runny, ugly sores (at least they did in my case). Sometimes people get away with just a little red itchy rash. You can't get shingles if you've ever had the chicken pox. That virus lodges at the base of your skull and activates sometimes, later in life. They don't know why, but they believe that stress can bring it on. It acted like palsy on me. I couldn't close my right eye. I had to hold it shut with my fingers. The corner of my mouth drew down on my right side. Thank God, it went away in about 10 days, but those runny black and green sores didn't. They ran down on the right side of my face, neck and shoulders. I had terrible, sharp, shooting pains. I looked like the "Creature From the Black Lagoon." I just curled up on my couch and wanted to die, but I was too sick to die. It was a horrible nightmare. Medicine and pain pills couldn't touch it. The only thing that helped me was my big old aloe vera plant in the backyard. I would strip a leaf, put it in the refrigerator and then lay it on the sores. Everything was really kind of hazy through that period. I don't remember eating or drinking very much. Scooter stayed with his mom for a while and Suzy brought me food and things. Willie came over once in a while and tried to help me. But, no one really could help! I just laid in the dark. The light hurt. Everything hurt. I prayed for it to stop hurting. After about two months, it finally started letting up. I had to go on disability and that's what I was living on, but it was running out and I was still in too much pain to work. They warned me that if I didn't come back to work I would lose my job. Well, they couldn't fire me because when you're on disability they can't fire you. But they know how to get around that. They just eliminate your job! They name it something else, so they don't need that job anymore. Call it what you will, but I was out of a job! Meantime, because of the economy, they passed a bill to allow more disability and unemployment. So, I used up my sick leave and then I went on unemployment and got an extension on that. I lasted for about a year before everything finally ran out. At this time, I had mainly only myself to support so I was able to get by. Scooter was working a part-time job himself and was still going to school. He helped me when he could. I never really got over that dumb disease. It did chronic damage to the nerves in my neck, face and shoulders. The doctors were amazed that I wasn't scarred a lot more than I was. I really think that my aloe plant accounted for that. The unemployment rate had reached an all-time high level and it looked like a depression was finally setting in. So, I had to apply for my Social Security early. Mentally and physically, I couldn't work full time, even if there was a job open. I got my Social Security but it wasn't enough to live on. So, I took a part-time job at a pizza parlor and learned how to make great pizzas. I did some volunteer work for the Chamber of Commerce and that led to another part-time job. I was stuffing envelopes for them for their monthly mailings, their newsletter and some other mass mailings. It was a job that suited me perfectly. My boss, Nancy, being the great person she was, let me bring the work home, so I could work at my own pace. That was important because I was still suffering from those shingles pains and from mental depression. Even though I really didn't know it at the time. It was as if I was in this dark tunnel, traveling along and trying to find the light at the other end. I didn't know if I was ever going to find that light. Nancy paid me $5 an hour, which, of course, wasn't very much, but along with my $300 a month Social Security check, at least that gave me enough money to get by on.

  My pizza parlor job helped with the food! While working there I met a young man, who shall remain John Doe, also working there and he rented my back living quarters. But he only paid by dibs and dabs and was always behind. He didn't help with the work like he was supposed to either. He wound up being a very bad influence on Willie. Years later I found out he was growing pot in his closet. That accounted for all the cars that used to park at the curb with their motors running, while young boys and girls ran in and out. I was incredibly naïve and lucky. It's lucky that I found out before Willie or Kent got hooked on it. John Doe went to Europe on a vacation and I caught Willie watering his plants in the closet. That's how I found out. I used to wonder what those funny little palm tree-like plants were. They were growing here and there in the backyard.

Anyway, John Doe and I parted ways and he left me his little 1972 Datsun truck for all the back rent he owed me. It had been stolen and stripped and needed a lot of fixing. But with Buddy's help, I fixed her up and called her "Patches." She had a white hood, one black fender, one blue fender, a yellow body, one red door and one white door. Cosmetically she needed a lot of help, but the motor ran so quiet, she sounded like a mouse in tennis shoes. Mechanically she was perfect. All she needed was a paint job. She was really a, "going Jessie" of a little truck!

My little bro Russ & me

My little bro Russ & big bro Joe

Willie

My nephew Jody
& his gal "Dolly"

Mr & Mrs William Davis

Mr & Mrs Kent Canaday
"Scoot Pot"

Me & Suzy

Russell & JoAnn Blazek
Alias Mr & Mrs Santa

Betty & John (Cat-Caper)

Me & Sylvia

Me & Willie

Our Boat

Chapter 41
On a Roll, Downhill!

Well, by now my little Suzy was back home again at Marlin Manor. She was still searching, trying to find a life of her own; still trying to figure things out. Of course, my "Scoot pot" Kent, was still with me. Suzy and I got to talking and we figured out that "Patches" would be a great little truck for Kent. He had taken his driving course at school and got his permit. I had given him some driving lessons, like I did with all the kids. So, we went to the DMV and he got his license. I was letting him drive every now and then, but he really needed more experience. What I had in mind was to give him that slowly, but Suzy decided she could trust him and let him drive it to school right away. I agreed and we let it happen. Well, the same old story, 16-year-old boys and unsupervised cars just don't mix. Unfortunately, he flipped that truck the first weekend after we let him drive. He totaled out "Patches" and sideswiped two cars at the curb. He had kids with him and nobody got hurt. It also turned out that nobody sued. We wound up just having to pay for the damages. Of course, we were out one truck, but it was by the grace of God that everybody was OK, and Kent really learned his lesson the hard way. But poor little "Patches" was terminal. Buddy couldn't fix her up without spending a lot of money, and we just didn't have it. So, she was towed back to the house to rest in peace in the backyard. That was kind of good in a way, because she was a constant reminder to all of us, especially to Kent, and probably the reason that he became such a good driver. He never really got into any big trouble on the road after that. I have had cars all through my life, some good and some bad. When you think about it, that's how men are, some good and some bad. I didn't make Suzy pay for the truck. I took the loss and life went on. I was now existing in a world where there was really no "me" left. I was a composite (the character that stood up when somebody needed something), like Willie, Suzy, Kent or some of the people I befriended and gave a home to. They moved in and out, owing me money. Worse yet, some stole from me. I guess that is how they repaid me for my kindness. Actually, that really didn't hurt. I was more or less in a numb state. I knew I was doing the right thing and they were doing it wrong. In the end, right would win out, I thought. I lived for the times when I was with Joe and Sal or when Willie would show up. He was out of school now and would bring me love and flowers and update me on his life. Suzy came around now and then, and helped me out when she could, but her visits were getting farther and farther apart!

Scooter had now become an avid surfer. He was like his Uncle Bobby. He was a cork in the water. He bobbed up and down and you just couldn't sink him. He was going to high school now and I didn't want to think about when he would graduate and be gone, and I would be alone, except for my little black doggies, Tina and Licorice. I now knew how my Mom had felt!

By this time, Bobby had found the right girl and moved to Colorado! He turned his surfboard in for skis. He was living in a little town called Minturn, which was just outside of Vail. He will probably be mayor of that town one of these days. With his looks, personality and willingness to work, and with Debbie beside him to help shoulder the load, he can't miss.

Now, I was *not* only *not* Pepper, I wasn't even Mrs. Robert Davis anymore, or Lavone Davis. I was "Lavone nobody" and not really caring much about anything except the kids and that non-dimensional front that I put up for my loved ones, Sal and Joe. Sometimes I came alive on the phone with the Cacapot, or when I talked with my old baseball friends like Marge and Kammie and my buddy Ziggy. Sally and Joe never knew the depths of my despair until long after it was over. I couldn't do that to Joe, I held it together in front of all of them (including Willie and Scooter). I was still very worried about Joe's ulcers. He had another bad bout with them, but he made it through. I was still bowling a little with Kay and Betz, my brown-eyed buddy, and Lulu. Sometimes we would bowl on Friday mornings and then go to lunch, taking turns at each other's houses. Sometimes, we would play word games like Password or cards. Kay had a great rec room complete with a pool table and a dart board, which leads me to the "Over-The-Hill" kidnap gang story, also titled "Who Purloined the Feline?"

We had gone over to Kay's to play poker but we ended up playing pool instead. I had just called the eight ball into the side pocket and made it. Since I'm no "Minnesota Fats," this was a remarkable feat for me. I turned to my partner, Betz, expecting applause and flowers and found her staring out the window instead. She had completely missed my shot. "Hey," I hollered, "Did you see that? We won!" "Yeah, yeah," was her slightly less than hilarious answer. I looked closely at her and I thought that I detected a tear leaking out the corner of her eye. "What's wrong, Betz?" I asked. She didn't answer. She just swallowed hard and continued staring out the window. "Bartender Kay" joined the conversation in her own sweet lovable way, "Yeah for Christ sakes, Betty. What the hell's the matter with you?" The words trickled out of the corner of her mouth, sarcastically. The game being over anyway, we all tabled our pool cues (pool expression), and we joined Kay at the bar. Kay's den was a warm paneled room, loaded with lots of bowling trophies. It had a lot of windows that gave you the view of a lot of nice trees, blue skies and sunshine. You could see it all without actually having to endure it. It was our favorite gathering place. You could see the neighbors' atrocities without being seen yourself. Kay was mumbling to herself and we knew she was about to boil over. Now Kay was our "pro bowler" in the group and really quite good at it. She carried about a 185 average. She was also probably the one who most needed the couch, although there were times when we could all flip a coin for that honor. Kay almost always knew everything about everybody, and if she didn't know it, she knew somebody that did. She had a beautiful, sarcastic, brutal way of putting you down. At times she seemed to have a very hardened look on life, for no outwardly apparent reason. She stopped her mumbling and impatiently barked, "Well come on Betty, let us in on the secret." Betty just shot her a withering look and continued her nature study out the window. At this point, Lulu walked over to Betty and picked up the conversation in her deceitfully charming way, "Come on Betz, you've got us all worried. Tell us what's wrong. Maybe we can help," she pleaded. Betty just kind of shook her head and still gave no answer. Well, Lulu shrugged her shoulders and pointing at me with an "I give up" look, went to join Kay at the bar. We considered Lulu our pro pool player and artist! She was a pretty smart cookie, when she wanted to be. She was proficient at almost anything. Lulu, as I called her, was a petite blonde who wore jeweled glasses and tight hip-huggers and she looked good in them. She was pure female, although it took awhile to figure that out, because her claws were pretty well hidden. Lulu didn't care who she got her therapy from. The rest of us were a little bit more selective. By now, I realized it was up to me to get my brown-eyed buddy Betz to open up. Betz batted third in our lineup and she was our pro, intellectual and animal lover (like in pets). She could very often be happily unhappy about a lot of things. She had a couple of years on the rest of us. Unfortunately, she never had any children. I guess this accounted for her fondness of animals and for her sometimes caustic outlook and impatience with anything she considered imperfect or unnecessary. Betz knew almost as much as Kay thought she knew. Only Betz didn't quite know what to do with this knowledge. Since her husband John knew even less what to do with Betty, that sometimes resulted in frustration for both of them. Looking at her, I was wondering just how serious this thing was. She really looked upset. I decided that I better fortify myself with another screwdriver before making my move to solve this thing. Of course, I bat fourth in our lineup, but only because I'm the ex-pro ballplayer in the game. I couldn't do much of anything right these days and I think it showed. It also took a pretty wide couch to tell you about it. By this time, I had put on a lot of weight. Lack of activity and my physical condition would not let me work it off. I was pretty hefty. I wore bad bras and bad baggy pants in the misguided hope that they would cover up my big boobs and my rear-end problem. I took a deep breath and a big slug of my screwdriver and I grabbed Betz by the arm and made her look at me. I said: "OK Betz, this has gone far enough. I want some answers. You arrived late, that's not like you. You're on the verge of tears, again, that's not like you. What is it? Can we help?" "Yeah," Kay piped in. "It's your turn to get smashed today anyway, so, come on and open up." Betz just kept playing "Misty" looking out the window and not answering any of us. Kay's rough style never wavered, as she spit out: "Come on Betz, don't drag it out anymore. Is someone sick? Has John screwed around? For Christ's sake, what is it?" In spite of her crude words, in reality, Kay was concerned, as we all were. Betz didn't cry too often. Finally, as we sat there in exasperated silence, she drew in a jagged breath and answered Kay's barrage. "No, no, no, it's not anything like that!" Then she added, "I don't want to say, you guys will just laugh at me." Her voice trailed off with a sigh. She was close to tears again. Then she looked hard at Kay and said, "At least I know you will, you jackass!" Well, Kay was the picture of injured dignity as she denied the accusation. We all protested making noises all at once and continued questioning, until Betty finally agreed to level with us. "OK, OK, I'll tell you! It's nothing really serious, I guess, but no laughing," she warned shaking her finger at Kay. She fumbled for words, "Well, you see, it's this, well it's this, it's this cat!" We all sat trying to focus on her words listening as she continued: "No, it's not a cat really, it's just a kitten. I had to go to the pound for a permit and I saw this little kitten!" She choked up again and couldn't continue. Then she blurted out, "Well, damn it, they're going to kill it!" There was a moment of stunned silence. Kay's mouth dropped open and then she exploded, "Jesus key-rist," and she slammed her glass down! "And I thought something was really wrong." She didn't laugh; I'll give her that. But she shot Betz a dirty look that said it all. Betz just looked at her with tears welling up in her soft brown eyes and said, "See, see, see I knew I shouldn't have told you, I knew you wouldn't understand." Lulu jumped into the breach with a sharp, "Shut up, Kay," then she said to Betty, "Wait, wait, I don't understand. Tell us the rest." With more urging, Betty explained. Seems she had seen this little orphan kitten at the pound. It was lonely and sick, in a huge cage. She tried to buy the animal, tried to pay for shots, have it spayed, the whole works, and can you believe it? They wouldn't let her do it. There was some kind of cockamamie law on the books that says if a cat is less than six months old, which Betty was sure this little one wasn't, then only the owners can claim the animal. Since the cat obviously wouldn't have been there if the owner wanted her, it would be curtains for this skinny little waif in the morning. Betty had even gone to her vet to protest and ask for help, but he just said, "Forget it, you can't fight city hall!" We all got to feeling pretty indignant about it, even Kay, who decided her rights were being violated and felt, "If it had been a G-d damn tomcat, it probably wouldn't have happened!"

    We chewed it around for a while and it got bigger and bigger, just like a tough piece of meat. We spit it out and chewed it some more. All the while we were polishing off a little more of the old sauce. Maybe that's why we did what we did. All of a sudden Lulu says, "How far is the pound from here?" Betty said, "About two miles, why?" and then we all looked at Lulu wide-eyed. We saw the gleam in her eyes. Then we looked at each other and unanimously agreed. A great vendetta was born! The agreement was silent but the planning was loud and wet. The mouths began flapping and didn't stop until the mission was set. Finally, we blasted off with one last toast to each other and the mission was on its way. We peeled out in two cars, one for getaway and one for diversion tactics. As we tore down Victory Boulevard, I swear I heard strains of the "William Tell Overture" and "Hi-ho Silver" was ringing in the air. We parked Betty's car close to the door of the pound and left her there with the motor running. She was frustrated at being left behind but we couldn't risk taking her in. She might be recognized. Kay took the lead as always, with Lulu following along behind her with an innocent look and swinging a duffle bag in her hand. I brought up the rear, because that's what I do best. We nonchalantly staggered down the aisle stopping here and there to talk to the poor poochy pups in the cages. The young doggies were leaning against the wire bouncing and licking, trying to get our attention. The cat room was all the way back in the building. It was like walking the last mile. A few feet from the entrance of the cat room, we noticed an attendant. It was a long way from the front to the back of the building. He looked tired and bored as he was unloading something or other. He didn't really look like he wanted to talk. We looked at each other and broke formation. Lulu and I headed for the cat room with Kay staying behind to talk to the attendant. He wasn't very friendly, but when Kay wants to talk, you talk. We staggered on. We entered the cat room and saw it! An ugly, little, skinny ball of dirty orange. It looked like an old sock trying to unravel after too many washings. It was crouched alone in the corner of the cage looking terrified and yet bravely defiant. We could see why Betz had been so taken with her. She was the only cat in the room. Damn good thing too, because Lulu just had a small duffle bag. I glanced around the room and noticed a young girl standing over by the window. I thought, "Uh oh," a witness. Lulu hadn't seen her and before I could say anything, she crossed over to the cage and was unlatching the door. "Here kitty, kitty," she called. Sounded pretty loud to me, but the attendant didn't hear her "little kitty voice." The girl in the corner just stood and watched with her mouth wide open. I was still in the doorway blocking the view from the outside, which I also do very well. I pointed a finger at her and commanded: "Quiet now, don't you fink on us. This cat is going to get the chair in the morning and we're going to save it." That gal never moved and she never made a sound. She just stared. I often wondered about her to this day. There was a teenager somewhere in Van Nuys that had an interesting and different view of the establishment. The little ragamuffin in the cage hesitated only an instant and then came right to Lulu. She jumped right into that bag, without hesitation or sound. It was as though some sixth sense was telling her this was her chance. Lulu zipped her in, and out the door we went. I mumbled to her, "You go ahead and I'll get Kay and we'll be right behind you." I was rehearsing blocking and delaying tactics just in case. Lulu started on ahead, walking just nonchalantly enough to cover up her hurry. When Kay saw us coming by, she left the attendant somewhere in the middle of his, by now enthusiastic, oratory on the overworked, underpaid position he had. Kay hurried to catch up to Lulu, who was a few feet ahead, swinging the duffle bag. Do you know that that cat never made a sound? Of course, she hasn't been quiet a minute since then. Kay caught up with Lulu, and I followed behind, stopping at various cages and looking at the poor doggies. I paid more attention this time, seeing little old gray-mouthed poochies. They just laid there quietly, with their sad eyes looking at me, as though they knew what was coming. I was particularly fond of old dogs and was remembering my big old French poodle, Baby, who had lived to be 20 years old. It bothered me to think about these guys ending up this way and not having any kind of good family life. Well, after about three cage stops and with the juice and the adrenalin flowing, I began to snivel and talk to the doggies, losing all track of time and purpose.

Meanwhile, the getaway had come off clean. Betty had taken off with the loot and the other two were out front racing the motor and wondering what the hell had happened to me. Well, there must have been 40 to 50 cages in there, each one with four or five dogs in them. Time was passing. Kay and Lulu decided I must have been nailed. I'll hand it to them, they weren't going to leave me hostage. Kay edged back into the door looking for me. I was only halfway down the aisle by now. The tears were streaming down my face and I was in a full-fledged crying jag. I had lost control completely. I was talking to myself and the doggies. I must have been a sight. Kay took one look at me and hustled over to me, grabbed my arm and started kneeing and pulling me out the door. All the while, I'm blubbering and bellowing in loud, uncouth tones: "It's not right, it's just not right, let's get a truck. We can clean out the whole joint. Let's at least give them a fighting chance. Let's turn them all loose." Kay just kept pushing and pulling and dragging and shushing me toward the door until we were finally in the parking lot. She poured me into the car and off we went with a whoop and a squeal. I finally stopped crying and listened to "William Tell" again. I often wondered what that attendant thought when he found that cage empty and bolted shut from the outside. I would have loved to have seen the look on his face. Anyway, to bring a short story to a long conclusion, Betz returned home triumphantly with her bedraggled trophy. Through the grace of God, and good luck, we all made it home safely. Unfortunately, the happy ending didn't come right away. "Tina," as Betz named the cat, was very sick with cat fever. She had to be hospitalized and wasn't expected to live. But, I guess someone up there decided she'd earned another chance and gave it to her. When Betz went to pick her up, she had her checkbook in one hand and her tranquilizers in the other to take after seeing the bill. The vet, who has to be nameless, hadn't been fooled when Betz brought Tina in. He hadn't figured out how we had done it, but there was no doubt in his mind that we had done it. So, when Betz asked how much the bill was, he said: "What bill? What cat? Do you think I want to get involved in a mess like this?" He turned his back on Betz to hide his smile and said, "Get out of here you criminal and take your stolen goods with you." Tina turned out to be the most beautiful white and gold lady you ever saw. And ornery? Wow, it was like she knew how close she came, twice. She was determined to make the most of her seven other lives! As I look back now and think about it all, I wonder what would have happened if we'd been caught. It might have made the news and it might have been worth it, if only to point out a cruel and heartless law concerning animals; one that is still on the books, I'm told.

Of course, we're not doing too well for people these days. Maybe no one cares about cats or dogs, for that matter. I think if I had a lot of money, I would buy a huge ranch, a big piece of property with lots of acres and I would build a big complex on it. I'd hire old people, sick people and handicapped people. They would all have living quarters. We would grow our own food, and have our own doctors and dentists, including good medical facilities. Then we would take care of every kind of animal that needed a home and every kind of a person that needed a home. Some dogs could be trained to be guard dogs or watchdogs and seeing-eye companions. We would give them to people with needs and free of cost. The animals that wanted to run around free would be allowed to run free in contained areas. The ones that wanted to stay inside and be companions could do that; whatever made them happy, meaning both people and animals. It could be a community of people dedicated to the poor and the lonely and sick, animals as well as people. We could grow our own food, make craft things and sell them, and teach school. We could take care of all our own needs. I'm not talking about a cult here. I'm just talking about people and animals in need of sharing their love and helping one another with God in their hearts! Of course, it would take a person with a lot of money to fund it, and that definitely wasn't me!

Bratty teenager Will

Tina "The Feline"

"Bruce Lee" Will

Suzy & Scoot

The drummer

Sue High School

Bobby High School

Scoot riding the Bull

High School Scoot Becomes Kent

Pat White, Scoot's Dad

Beautiful Suzy, Scoot's Mom

415

Chapter 42
Happy Days Are Here Again

Financially, things were looking tough, but I was still bowling and fishing when I could. I was still working part time at the chamber job, and with my Social Security, I managed to get along. I was just eking out a living but didn't need much to live on. I mainly just wore the same clothes, old stuff. Clean but worn, it didn't matter. You don't need outfits to go bowling or go fishing in. The bowling was getting harder all the time, because of the pain in my knees, my right knee especially. Between that and a stiff back, it was hard to get down and give the ball the lift required. I went from a 16-pound ball to a 14-pound ball to a 12-pound ball, in an effort to do better. I was thinking about going to a tennis ball or maybe a ping-pong ball, but you don't carry the pins with a light ball, so I realized it was about time to give it up. I couldn't hold to the standards that I had always set for myself. Besides, I still had fishing. It cost nothing and didn't hurt!

Sylvia and I got out with Frank on his boat as often as we could. Willie, too, if he was around. Incidentally, Frank's boat was named "Fish." We would pack a little lunch, take some cold water and some cold beer, and help with the gas money. That was my form of fun and recreation. Bob had moved back in with his sister (Aunt BB). His health was breaking down. He was still working, but he was struggling to keep going. He always seemed happy to see me, and he would keep asking me about Willie. Sometimes we would play cards and sometimes we would talk sports. Since the Lakers had come to California, Bob had turned into a big basketball fan. He had been a great player and, of course, enjoyed the game. He wanted to take Willie to some Lakers games but Willie was still being stubborn. He didn't want to see his father, even though he had picked up some Lakers tickets himself and had turned into a fan.

By now, Willie had met the right gal. A pretty little gal named Phyllis Erdman. Willie was still working at his feast or famine camera job. Phyllis was a very good influence on Willie. I thought as soon as he settled down and got a steady job, there would probably be a wedding in the future.

I was still doing my darndest to get Willie and Bob back together again. I had been working on Willie, and I felt like he was softening. I didn't want Willie to have regrets or bad feelings about his dad when it was too late and Bob wasn't in the greatest of health. Our Lakers were the catalyst to get them together in the long run. The doctors had diagnosed Bob with heart problems, and he was going to need a very serious operation. So he was resting up for that. One night Bob called me and told me that he had tickets to a Lakers game. He asked me again to bring Willie over to go with him. That's when they played at the Sports Arena, before the Fabulous Forum. To my surprise, this time Willie agreed to go.

There was an awkward moment when they first met. When Willie stuck his hand out, his dad just ignored his hand and hugged him with tears in his eyes. I could see that Willie had tears in his eyes, too. After that first awkward moment, Willie hugged him back and then they went off to the game, arm in arm, just joking away. Aunt BB and I were happily watching.

After that, the Lakers games turned out to be a regular thing. Magic Johnson was here and "Showtime" was born. We were all turning into Lakers fans. In fact, we all were turning into die-hard Lakers fans. Bob later bought season tickets for himself and Willie. Willie was able to love his father again. He brought his girl Phyllis over and introduced her to his dad and to his Aunt BB. Bob and I were getting closer. We seemed to fit like an old pair of shoes. Very comfortable! My life wasn't so lonely anymore, and he told me he was sorry. I didn't feel like such a failure anymore. There was no romance involved but there was love.

Bob wasn't working now, and Aunt BB was faithfully taking care of him. She was always more like a mom to Bob than a sister. Every now and then Bob would go with me to Joe and Sal's, just like old times. We even went to Las Vegas with them, and we all had a great time. Kent was always there for me at Marlin Manor, holding the fort and watching out for our two black baby girl doggies, Tina and Licorice. They kept each other company.

I was still driving the old clunker Rambler wagon with still no reverse gear and we still had the old beer barge boat that only went backwards. Bob said if only I could have gotten the boat on the freeway or the Rambler in the lake, I could have gone both ways. We both got a great laugh out of that.

In 1979, after almost a 25-year hiatus, June Pappas, one of our All-American Girls, had put out an All American Newsletter. Some of us had always kept in touch at Christmas and holidays, but this started everybody writing back and forth, checking to see who was still around and who wasn't. That led to the All American Girls' first reunion in Chicago in 1982. Faye and I managed to scrounge up enough money to make it. I wrote a script and Faye and I put on a little play and we were a big hit.

It was great seeing everybody again. Granted, sometimes you had to look at name tags, but it didn't take long to figure out who it was. Most of the time the eyes told you who it was. Our spirit was still alive and doing well. It was there in Chicago that I first asked, "Where does it say 'Men's Baseball Hall of Fame?'" My impossible dream was alive again! We all went to a Cubs ballgame and listened to Harry Caray sing, "Take Me Out to the Ballgame." June Pappas threw out the first pitch. We had not been forgotten. A group of about 30 fans paraded around the grandstands with a huge 50-foot banner that read, "All Americans, we still love you! Rockford Peaches, we still love you." After 40 years of no publicity, they still remembered us. So, the media rediscovered us, and all kinds of publicity followed -- magazine articles, television. The story of the All American Girls Professional Baseball League hit all the newsstands. Once again, I asked, "Where does it say, 'Men's Baseball Hall of Fame?'"

Things began to snowball, and all hell broke loose with the media who had neglected us all those years. We got coverage on lots of news broadcasts. We appeared on TV shows and talk shows; shows like "The Third Degree," hosted by Bert Convy. It was a new version of "What's My Line?" The Smithsonian magazine did a huge article on us. People magazine also did an article, as well as Parade magazine. There were newspaper articles all over the country and people were starting to write books about us.

After I got home from Chicago in 1982, I got a phone call from David Hartman of "Good Morning America." He asked me to come to New York and be on his show. My fellow All American buddies Marge Wenzell and Dottie Kamenshek were now living in California and I talked Dottie into going with me. It wasn't easy because she didn't like flying. She was the best ballplayer in our league, and I thought she should be there. We stayed at the famous St. Moritz Hotel. It overlooked Central Park. You could see the horse-drawn carriages down below and the beautiful grass and trees and lakes from our big plate-glass window. That New York skyline, with all those stars shining above us outlining the Trade Center twin towers was a beautiful sight. I swear I looked for Liza Minnelli to come waltzing down out of the sky and start singing, "New York, New York."

David Hartman turned out to be a really great guy. We found out that he was an avid baseball fan. He had a tryout with the Dodgers in his youth. We sang our league song for him and followed a script that was prepared. But I threw David for a loss with my ad-lib. I told him that we didn't really come to New York just to be on his show, that actually we had been traded to the Yankees from the Angels for Reggie Jackson (Reggie had been traded the day before). Well, David got a big laugh out of that. Right after us, Dolly Parton came on, and David was kind enough to say we should be in the Hall of Fame, while he was talking to her!

After returning home from New York, I received numerous media phone calls, and one of them was from Scott Ostler. Scott had been California's Sportswriter of the Year. He came out to the house and wrote an article about me. Also, the great Hall of Fame sportswriter, Bob Hunter, did a three-part series on me. I was getting headlines the same time Reggie was hitting his 500th home run. That was pretty great; my family was having a ball. They had always known that I played baseball, but they didn't realize what a big deal it was. For that matter, neither did I. I was totally surprised when Scott Ostler's article came out and I started getting movie offers.

After more phone calls from producers, through Scott, I met Leigh Steinberg, the great sports agent. He was truly an extremely nice guy and about as handsome as you could get. He drove down from Berkeley just to see me and take me to lunch. He really tried to help me, but I don't think he knew the entertainment game as well as he did the sports game. He turned me over to one of his assistant attorneys, and they decided I should accept a contract from HBO. They had passed on several other offers from well-known producers. The contract read in figures of hundreds of thousands of dollars, but it boiled down to an option of $1 until it was sold. They assigned two young women to sell my story. They were very nice gals, but they were not "sports knowledgeable." I gave them my scrapbooks and told them to be sure to call me when they had interviews, but they didn't involve me, as they should have. So, after a year went by, they said no one wanted the story and they passed on the option. I didn't even get the dollar! Boy, oh boy, I wonder what they think now about passing on a movie like "A League of Their Own"?

In the meantime, I had resumed writing my book, in sort of a half-hearted way. I had started it in 1940 and called it "From Hot Dogs to Tamales." Even though I had struck out, I knew ours was still a great story and that it should be told. I was going to write it, if only for my family and friends, to set the record straight. In the meantime, the All-American Newsletter had started to fail. June had turned it over to one of our All-Americans, and she was having a hard time getting it out. It was funded by donations and was not a paying job. There had not been a letter out for about a year. So with the help of Marge and Kammie and Faye and my daughter Suzy, I decided to utilize my writing skills and make an effort to write the newsletter. In 1984 I took it over and kept it from failing. I made it truly an All-American Newsletter. I named it "Extra Innings." I picked up our baseball threads and wove them back together. I called on my memories and wrote about the great times we all had together, using my numerous photos and my memorabilia. The newsletter picked up steam, and we all became close again.

Meanwhile, pockets of publicity were still going on here and there all over the country. Articles were still being written about us. Sports Illustrated did some articles on us. This led to another reunion being planned in 1986 in Fort Wayne. I didn't know if I was going to be able to go because Bob had had his operation and was recuperating. Aunt BB, who was taking good care of him now, had another problem. She had two sisters up in Montana who were alone. They had lost their husbands and were both sick. She felt that she needed to go help them, but she didn't want to leave Bob alone. So, I volunteered to help Bob and check on him so that Aunt BB could go. Bob was doing fine and was well enough to take care of himself. In fact, he was due to go back to work. So, he told me he wanted me to go to the reunion because it would only be three or four days. He actually gave me some money to help pay my way.

There was a documentary being planned for that reunion. A lot of it originated here in California. We had several meetings at my house. I invited the California ballplayers over and served soft drinks and snacks. I really couldn't afford it, but I wanted this to happen.

Unfortunately, in the long run, I didn't get much credit for my input. That wasn't going to be the first time that my help and talents weren't appreciated. It wouldn't be the last time either.

"Kent the Scoot-Pot" promised me that he would watch Marlin Manor and the poochy pups. Willie said he would be checking on his dad. Willie and Bob had renewed their Lakers season tickets and they were enjoying the games together, especially since the Lakers were winning championships. Faye decided to go to the reunion also. She didn't have much money, but she had credit cards.

So, off to Fort Wayne we went. "All the Way Faye" and myself, the catcher. Once again, it was wonderful to see everyone, to laugh and sing and talk about old times. There were tears, too, for the ones we had lost. It was happening more and more now. We were all getting up there in that endangered age. I laughingly suggested that we have reunions every weekend to keep up. Seriously, we did decide that we needed to have them more frequently. Perhaps every year!

The documentary took place and it was made by Kim Wilson and Kelly Candaele (Helen Callahan Candaele's son). They were afraid that Faye and I would not participate because we were both unhappy about some things that had happened. I convinced Faye that it was a good thing and that we wanted to be a part of it. They called it "A League of Their Own." Due largely to the efforts of the director, Mary Wallace, and the great input of Faye and myself and all the rest of the All Americans, it turned out to be a very good documentary. Kim and Kelly did a great job, I have to admit, but I didn't agree with some of their methods. They used my song in the documentary and that turned out to be a break for me later on.

We found out at the reunion that the "Hall of Fame" was going to make a place for us! They were remodeling and they promised us that as soon as they were finished, they would put us in! They were getting requests about us from all over. I triumphantly returned home with the great news! The publicity was still escalating and it was not uncommon to see All Americans in the news and on the tube and in various articles and shows all over the country. We were back, but how long would it last?

In the meantime, my younger brother Russ and his wife JoAnn had come back into my life and everybody was having a good time. Along with my kids, Bob and Aunt BB, they were all riding the fame train with me. Granted, it was a little train, but it was big enough for all of us. Everything was going so well, it was hard to believe. I should have known that it couldn't last. Experience should have taught me that! Aunt BB had brought her two sisters to California with her. Her older sister Aggie was Bud's mother and she went to live with him. Grace stayed with Bob and Aunt BB. They all got along fine together. Bob was their baby. I would go over there often, and we would play this addictive card game. It was a Montana game and they taught it to me. They called it "Spite and Malice," and that game was just as deadly as its name. It was a little bit like canasta. You could get so mad when you lost out. Bob and I would drink a little beer and Aunt BB would make popcorn. If Bob and Willie weren't off to a game, Willie would bring Phyllis and we would all play cards.

In the meantime, big things were happening at Marlin Manor. My little Scoot Pot Kent was all grown up. He had done well at school getting good grades and winning awards. He was taking auto mechanics in school and working part time for an auto repair shop. He had inherited a natural knack as a mechanic from his Uncle Bud, I guess. He won the Art Piner all-city award for mechanical skills and good citizenship. I was so proud of him when he graduated from Birmingham High School in 1986. He then went to work immediately at a pizza parlor. He was now holding down two jobs and helping me out financially. He was paying his grandma back. He has always been very deep in my heart. More great news came. Willie and Phyllis were making plans to get married.

I was so happy that Willie was starting to settle down. On the surface things were fine, but I had noticed that there were times when Bob didn't seem to feel well. He never complained and when you asked, he would just say that his teeth were hurting and that he would have to go to the dentist one of these days. I knew what he meant about that. I don't think anybody wants to go to the dentist, at least I know I don't. So, it didn't seem like it was anything to worry about at that time.

KCET had bought the "A League of Their Own" documentary. It came out in February 1987 in a "California Gold" series and became an immediate hit. It won several awards and captured the attention of a lot of people, including Cooperstown. As I said before, Faye and I were prominent in the documentary and so was my song. I was getting a lot of phone calls. One night I received one from Penny Marshall. I still have the tape. Penny said that she was thinking about making a movie about us, and that if she did, she wanted to use my song (the one I had written for the All Americans all those years ago). I was ecstatic that it was happening. The world was finally going to know our story.

I resumed writing my book in a frenzy. I had originally titled it "When Diamonds Were a Girl's Best Friend," but Scott Ostler had stolen that title from me, but he had written such a nice piece on me, it was OK. So, now I'm thinking, well, what do I call it? "Pepper Games," "No Crying in Baseball," or "Dirt in the Skirt"? I think you might be familiar with some of those phrases. In the meantime, another All American Girls Baseball reunion had been set for October 1988 in Scottsdale, Arizona. My old pal "Sophie the Trophy," my old pitching buddy Joanne Winters and our "Iron Woman" Connie Wisnewski, and the rest of the Arizona gang had decided to host it. They got the OK from our league president. We now had a board of directors and a league president. She had taken over the newsletter and she was also our treasurer, so things had become complicated. Somehow when money is involved, they always do.

The All American Girls Professional Baseball League Board changed their minds after they had already given their OK. They wanted to cancel the reunion. The Arizona gals had already gone to a lot of work and expense. The board felt that it would interfere in the "Hall of Fame" ceremonies that might be coming up in November 1988. There was no way that Sophie and Connie and Joanne were going to cancel their reunion after planning it. So, that became an issue in our league and caused some conflicts. People were choosing up sides as to who was going to go and who wasn't going to go, and for a time that wasn't a good thing. Then, something happened in my world that took the reunion completely out of my mind.

Bob was sick again. He had gone to the dentist, but it wasn't his teeth. It was the dreaded Big C. There was a tumor in his throat and in the back of his mouth. They didn't know yet how advanced it was. That really put the damper on everything. I realized that I still loved Bob, and that in my heart, I felt that we would get back together again. I was sick with worry. I started driving over the hill on a daily basis. My old clunker was now barely making it up and down those hills. I was taking Bob for all kinds of tests. They weren't sure of anything at this point. The entire family was worried and saying prayers for Bob. Willie was devastated. He had just gotten his father back and now this! Secretly, I was worried about my car's transmission going out completely. Aunt BB had never learned to drive, and Bob, not being able to drive, had given his old Ford to Willie a year ago. It turned out that I wasn't the only one worried about my driving home late at night and my car breaking down. My good friends, my 50-year buddies Marge Wenzell and Dottie Kamenshek came out to my house one day and took me out and bought me a little used Toyota truck. They had offered to buy me one before, but I had refused to accept it. I didn't feel like I should do that. This time they wouldn't take "no" for an answer, and in desperation, I had to gratefully accept. Thank you, dear friends.

Well, that took a great deal of worry off all our minds. Bob was under the care of the UCLA Veterans Medical Center. After many kinds of X-rays and testing, we found out that the tumor had spread to one lung, but they said the other lung was clear. So, they led us to believe there was hope. The radiation treatments began. They were set up for three times a week for three months. I don't know how many of you are familiar with that process, but just let me tell you, it's like cooking in hell. When I would bring him back home to Aunt BB, his face and neck would be beet red and he would be too exhausted to speak. We were told from time to time, that the tumor was shrinking and that things looked good. Bob was rapidly losing weight and strength. He was down from 180 to 130 pounds and from a 34-inch waist to a 24-inch waist. But the news was good and they finally said that he didn't need any more radiation treatments. The timing was right, and they sent Bob home to rest for a while and told him just to take his pills and that he would be OK. They said he was in remission and that after he rested he was to come back and get his dental work done. Things looked great and we were all very happy.

Our prayers had been answered, and it was a wonderful world. That was in April 1987. We were all so happy and Bob was feeling much better. His appetite seemed to be coming back, and he was making himself eat. He was starting to get his strength back, gaining a little weight and acting like his old self. He was really looking forward to life again, and so was I.

Kent with trophey

Graduation with honors

Willie

Beautiful Sall
& my handsome Bro.

Will & Jeannine
Graduation

Joe-Sally-Linda-Me-Jeannie & Jody

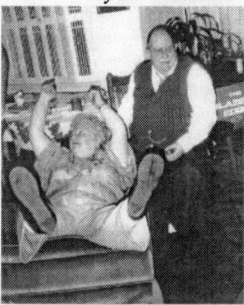

Me & my little bro Russ
Bottoms up

Faye & me the two
Cacapots putting the
moves on Santa

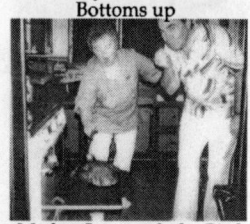

Willie and his Javalyn

My bro Joe, me & the Bird

My gal Sal & me

Me and my truck

Bob

Bob & me

The American beauty!
She paid for the Marlin Manor roof

425

Chapter 43
You Win One, You Lose One!

Bob's recovery wasn't the only good news we got in 1987. Soon came the news that Willie and Phyllis had set the wedding date for August 22, 1987. That made everything perfect. Bob and I and the whole family were really looking forward to seeing "Wee Willie" tying the knot. Plans were going ahead for an old-fashioned formal wedding. It was going to be held in Westlake at Rancho Calamigos. It was a <u>beautiful</u> outdoor setting with a lovely lake. It was famous for its natural beauty of tall oaks, weeping willow trees and wild flowers, all nestled in among the rolling green hills. Once again, it just seemed like life couldn't get any better. We were a family again, even though Bob was still living at Aunt BB's and I was still living in the Valley. In heart and spirit we had come together. We were the proud "Mom and Pop" of our son who was going to be married. Phyllis' mother, Alice, had been divorced for some time and had basically raised Phyllis and her sister, Cheryl, on her own. Phyllis' father had remarried and raised another family. But he was always in the picture and financially he had helped Phyllis in college. While he had been an absentee father at times, he was stepping up to the front and paying the main share of the wedding cost. That really helped, because neither Alice nor I had that kind of money.

Bob was really kidding me about his new trim waistline and how good he was going to look in a tux. I was still roly-poly. I decided (out of self-defense) to start dieting. I started looking for a draped-style wedding gown and shoes, purse, the whole bit. I had nothing in my closet that was suitable. Funds were limited and I was at a loss as to what I was going to wear, never being any kind of great shopper. Joe's gal, Sal, really helped me out there. Sally always had impeccable taste and always looked beautiful. She always wore coordinated outfits. So, she took me shopping to her favorite spots. She knew where to get all the deals. I never was a fashion plate. I was always choosey, very hard to fit and to buy for. But Sally found me the perfect dress at an unbelievable price. It was a beautiful chiffon draped-style gown in lovely delicate shades of lavender, trimmed in white. We bought gray sandals with matching accessories. Everything was perfect and the outfit really flattered me. I was worried about not looking good. Remember, I had lost a lot of confidence in myself. Now, I was starting to feel like a woman again and thought, "Hey, I do look good in this outfit!" I wanted Willie to be proud of me.

I was thinking maybe I could talk Bob into getting some matching gray slacks and a matching gray shirt with a white dinner jacket. We would look so great together! We were having so much fun laughing, talking and planning. It was like a fairy tale, like all my long lost dreams were coming true. But once again, it wouldn't be that fairy tale ending. Bob decided that he wanted to get his teeth fixed before the wedding, so he could really look sharp. The timing was right. His rest period was up and it was time to go for his checkup anyway. So, I took him to UCLA for his tests and to see his doctor to get the OK to go ahead with the dental work. They did all the blood things, all the X-rays and all the tests. As usual, the doctor told Bob to come back in a week and he would set up the dental appointment.

Bob had a new doctor. He was Asian and spoke very broken English and was hard to understand. At first, I was a little apprehensive, but Bob liked him. So, we made the appointment, came back the following week and waited for our turn. Instead of taking us into the examining room, the nurse ushered us into the doctor's office. I got a bad feeling in the pit of my stomach. Usually the nurses would set up appointments, not the doctors. The doctor had Bob's chart lying on his desk and he said "hello" to us. He was sitting in his swivel chair and had his back to us. He said in his broken, hard-to-understand English, "You don't need appointment. I just send you there." Immediately I said, "You mean just go to the dentist right now, and we don't need an appointment?" He wheeled back around in his chair and laid the folder down. Without even looking up, he started writing on a pad. Then again, in broken English, he mumbled something that we couldn't understand, but it ended with the word "hospice!" I said, "What? What did you say?" Then he looked up at Bob with his expressionless face and eyes and said, "Hospice, you need to go to hospice." I looked at Bob and the blood had drained out of his face and he was silent. He looked white and shocked. We both knew that word hospice! I jumped up and leaned on the desk and shouted at him, "What do you mean, hospice? We're just here for a dental appointment." Without changing his expression, he coldly said, "No dentist, no use, go to hospice" and held out a slip of paper to me. I looked at it dumbfounded. Fumbling for words,

"You, you mean, you mean?" Then Bob spoke for the first time. He quietly asked, "How long?" He had to repeat it louder, as it was obvious the guy didn't understand the first time. "How long do I have to live?" He repeated himself, speaking slowly and deliberately. Again came a cold, unfeeling and expressionless look and a broken-English answer: "Two, maybe three months. If lucky, maybe six months to year. Do you want to go to hospice now?" My body went limp and I had to hold onto the desk to keep from falling. My legs had turned to jelly. I looked at Bob. He had closed his eyes and his face was a mask. But I could see the muscles bunching in his jaws as he gritted his teeth. Then, he answered again, calmly and quietly, "No thanks, no thanks, no hospice. I'll go home." Then he got up and walked slowly out the door. I gave that cold-hearted doctor a withering look and I'm sure he understood, because he turned his back to me again. I followed Bob out the door. I was shaking and still jelly-legged but trying hard to pull it together for Bob.

Now, I don't mean to put down any race or creed. It didn't matter whether that doctor was black or blue or whatever race he was. He was wrong, so very wrong. It was an inhumane thing to do. It would have been kinder to take a gun and shoot both of us. But, I suppose the doctor was just the fall guy. He shouldn't have been put into that position, probably. Maybe no one else had the guts to tell us, after all the fairy tales they had told us before. Well, fairy tales or misinformation or whatever you want to call it, we found out later that the tumor had activated and came back to spread to his other lung, and then throughout his body, and left no hope. I still don't know how that could have happened. Someone, somehow, should have prepared us. It just wasn't right to have a bomb dropped on us like that.

When we got back to the house, Bob just went straight to his room and closed the door. Aunt BB saw him come in, and when she saw his face, she knew. Of course, we all vowed that it wasn't over and that we would fight. We refused to believe it. We would do something about it. We would get the best doctors in the world. But nobody could help. The reality was that it <u>was</u> over.

From that time on, all Bob wanted to do was lie quietly in his room and try to live long enough to make the wedding. He didn't want Willie to postpone the wedding no matter what, and he asked me to promise not to let that happen. Aunt BB and I watched him die before our eyes, and it didn't take long. He wasn't going to make that wedding. He suffered terribly, going down to an 18-inch waist and maybe to 80 or 90 pounds. They were giving him the maximum painkillers that they could give him, but when it gets to that point, nothing helps. He never complained. What a brave man he was!

At the last moment in June, a few days before his 65th birthday, we rushed him to the hospital. They went through last-minute efforts and emergency efforts that were doomed to fail, and they did. Our son Bobby had flown in from Colorado and we were all at the hospital. Waiting for the final curtain, we knew that it was coming. They called us in for one last visit and we stood bunched around Bob's bed. He seemed to know all of us. Suzy stood at his shoulder and Bobby and Willie held his hands. He was saturated with tubes and all kinds of strange-looking attachments. He was hooked up to a respirator, and his thin chest was sucked in and out with that terrible raspy sound. But his eyes were still alive and a big tear ran down the side of his face while he silently said goodbye. I had to turn away and leave the room. I couldn't stand it. The rest of that night we all huddled in the waiting room. He was unconscious but still alive. We were all praying for that last-minute miracle that never came. About 5 o'clock in the morning they came in and said he was gone. God had taken him. I almost slipped into unconsciousness, but my Willie grabbed my hand and squeezed it hard and said, "Mom, Mom" and that brought me back. It was over, the rasping of the respirator had stopped, and Bob's life stopped with it. In my heart I said goodbye to the only real love of my life. I told him, "Thank you for Willie, and I will always love you." That was June 30, 1987, two days before his 65th birthday.

Bob was buried with full honors at the VA cemetery in Riverside, California. Aunt BB's husband, Clyde, was buried there also. So, they were side by side and buddies again. Aunt BB and I took it very hard and so did Willie. It was a tragic ending to what had started out to be such a happy time.

We had the wedding ahead of us, and we knew that Bob wanted it to go on. We just had to believe that he would be there with us, looking down and enjoying every happy moment. So, the big day came, and it was truly a lovely, wonderful wedding, despite the sadness of losing Bob. As I sat under that brilliant blue sky, gazing at that beautiful lake and the fragrant flowers, surrounded by tall, stately trees nestled in the rolling green hills, I knew Bob was with us. I could feel him in my heart. I talked to him in my heart. "Bob, look. Look how handsome your son is and how beautiful his bride is. You can be proud. We did a good job. Thank you for Willie, Bob." I told him that, and I still tell him that every night in my prayers.

Everything calmed down after the wedding, and life went on. It was missing pieces, but it went on. By now the AAGPBL reunion disagreement had been hashed out, and the Scottsdale, Arizona, reunion was going to happen as scheduled in October 1987. Faye and I were really looking forward to going. We knew Joannie and Sophie and Connie (our Polish rifle) and all those Arizona girls would put on a good reunion and they did. In my opinion, it was the best one we ever had. The topper was, while we were there, Cooperstown named a date, and they made it official. They were going to accept us November 5, 1988. That was the magical day. My impossible dream was coming true. So, I say to all those little boys out there, all those years ago who told me, "Girls could never be in the Hall of Fame." Wherever you are now, guys -- Nanna! Nanna! Nanna!

Scottsdale was a scene of a great triumph. Finally women were going to pass through those hallowed, men-only doors. I wrote a song the year before, about us All Americans getting in the Hall of Fame. I sang it in Scottsdale for the gals on the night we found out that it was going to happen. They all stood and cheered. It's called "Move Over Boys." I wanted to go to Cooperstown and sing it on that wonderful day, but I didn't think I would make it, even though I had dreamed about that trip for so long. I just didn't have the money or the clothes. But my All American buddies took care of that. They took up a collection and gave me enough money to buy me a wardrobe and a ticket and even spending money. Some of the gals who pitched in couldn't even afford to go themselves. That made me feel very special and very proud and made up for some of the hurt in my heart that some of the All Americans had caused me. I promised them that I would be there and that I would sing that song for them.

Just before I was ready to leave for Cooperstown, Penny Marshall called me and reminded me about using my song. She said that she was going to Cooperstown, also to talk to our league's board about making the movie. She asked me if she could take me to dinner and anybody else I wanted to invite. She said she wanted to discuss the movie. Well, I told her that if she wanted to get into an argument she would have to change the subject, and the answer was yes, with a big emphasis on "Yes."

The time came for us to leave. The Cacapot took out another credit card to make the trip. She didn't have any money, but she had a steady, long-term, bad-paying job. Finance companies let you get in all kinds of trouble that way. Alice "Lefty" Hohlmayer, an All American buddy who lived in San Diego, also maxed out her cards to go, and we all wound up headed for Cooperstown together. We hooked up with Tiby and the other gals. That six-pack was formed and we all piled into that limo and headed for Upstate New York to (up until now), my mythical Hall of Fame. Faye had reserved her room earlier, so she was staying at an inn with a lot of other gals. Lefty and I had made our reservations at the last moment, so we wound up at this little dinky upstairs hotel. It had been built maybe in the 1800s. For that matter, everything in Cooperstown was built in the 1800s. Time just seemed to stop there. That's part of the charm of this famous little town -- all original, old-fashioned buildings and houses and streets. It was right out of a Mark Twain novel. It is a quaint little town that is truly America's history, where baseball rules. Cobblestone streets -- some had sidewalks, some didn't. The shops were tiny and they overflowed onto the streets. They were all full of baseball memorabilia, both old and new. In certain areas you couldn't drive a car at all. There were no parking lot areas, only behind houses or buildings down by the lake. Some people make a living just by letting you park cars in their yards and garages. The tiny stores had a lot of counters and tables on sidewalks that were overflowing with people, all hours of the night and day, all fascinated by the legend.

We had to crawl up little stairs and walk down this little narrow hallway to our little kiddie room. Our potty was little, even the bathtub was little. It looked like a child's bathtub. The closet consisted of coat hangers on the wall behind the door. It had to have been built in the late 1800s or early 1900s. For that we paid $95 each per night, and we felt very lucky that we got a room. But at least our location was great. There was a souvenir store right under us. We were on the main drag, and the store was like a 5-and-10-cent store, and right next door there was a quaint little café called "The Short Stop Inn." They served great breakfasts and sandwiches. Just down the street was the Hall of Fame museum. Because neither of us could walk too long or go far, it was a great spot for us.

Unfortunately, I found out after I got there, that things were not as they should be. Like I said before, when organizations and union-like tactics set in, you sometimes lose important things along the way, like personal contact and control. It happens a lot in the world of business. When something really big happens, people sometimes lose their perspective. They mean well and do a lot of good things, but sometimes they try to control too many things. The people who organized our league had worked very hard to promote us, and I think they have done a great job in many ways. But, I personally disagree with some of their policies. Again I'll say, I know that doesn't make me right either.

When we became a nonprofit organization, it meant that none of the money could go personally to any All American. These were the gals who made the league what it was. Many of them needed financial help in their old age and many still do. They didn't get it. To my knowledge, a lot of money has been made on the movie and afterwards, selling memorabilia and a lot of things, but precious little has gone to help All Americans who really needed it. Many secrets were kept and I don't think very many All Americans even know financially what we made? I know I don't. Some have died who could have used help financially. To my knowledge, no All American other than the board has received a penny out of the whole thing. Well, I'll take that back. I think plane tickets and reunion expenses have been bought for some people. Most of our girls are too proud to accept anything like that because they had to go through a procedure to get it. They were too proud for that. Of course, we funded schools and museums and charities and so forth, just like our league counterparts did so many years ago. But they didn't take care of their own backyard. That just doesn't seem right to me. Of course, my views didn't make me very popular with a lot of people, and as I said before, it doesn't make me right either. But in my heart, I feel that I'm right. To my amazement, after we got there and had our first meeting, I found out from Penny that the All American board had refused to talk to her. They even went so far as to tell other All Americans not to talk or to associate with her and called her a bad influence. They refused her admission to our main banquet and meetings. The reason they gave was that they had signed options with another company and for some reason, God only knows why, they labeled Penny an outsider. I couldn't see the logic of that and went to dinner with Penny and co-producer Elliot Abbott and Helen Callahan Candaele and Marge

Callahan, the Canadian sisters whose son had made the documentary. Another of Helen's sons, Casey Candaele, was also there. I invited a lot of All Americans but only a few came with me: Tiby and Peggy and Faye and Lefty. The rest were warned off by the league. They had refused Penny's admission to the main banquet. I guess they thought they had the better deal with this small company. I really don't know why. It made no sense.

But, I can tell you that it was a good thing that I went to dinner with Penny and the other girls. Penny could have said the hell with it and gone home. It would not have been the movie that it was without Penny doing it. We had a great time at dinner with Penny and Elliot, talking and laughing together. Faye told some of her outrageous stories! We sang songs for Penny, and the gals all shared some of their memories. Elliot had asked if they could tape things before we started, and we all said "Yes." As a woman doing what was strictly considered a man's job, Penny really could relate to us. She knew how hard it was to break that barrier. She felt that our story was a story that was long overdue in the telling.

So, it was there in Cooperstown that she decided to make the movie. She made a deal with the other company, "Long-Bow Productions," and they probably got more out of it than our league did, if the truth was known. In my opinion, some bad decisions were made in Cooperstown. Of course, once again, I have to say that it's my opinion and that doesn't necessarily make it true!

Beautiful Bride & Groom

Willie & me

The Bride & Groom

Ronnie, Phyllis & Willie

Willie & Phyllis Davis

Me, Willie, Phyllis & Alice

The Groom & me

The Beautiful Ruth "Tex" & Me 1993

Ft. Wayne "86" Faye laying down

Phoenix "07"
Annie Meyers Drysdale & me

Joanne Winter

1993 50th Reunion Ziggy & Pepper

Pepper & Joanne Winter

Chirpie - Tex & Me San Antonio, Texas

Lefty, Ziggy, V. Kellogg, & Pepper

Lefty, Ziggy, V. Kellogg, Pepper, Chirpie, Kammie

Chapter 44
That's the Tooth, the Whole Tooth and
Nothing But the Tooth

My association and cooperation with Penny in Cooperstown once again made me very unpopular with the powers that be in our league. I began to think that there might be an underlying campaign of some sort against me. At least, that's the way it seemed. At our big banquet and meeting they bypassed me. Without my knowledge, and at the last moment, they had someone else lead the girls in our league song. I had always led them before. They knew I was supposed to sing my Cooperstown's song for the gals that couldn't make it, but they left it out of the program and they tried to dismiss the meeting without me singing. I didn't let that happen. I walked to the center of the room and without the aid of a mic I got the attention of my fellow All Americans. "Wait gals," I asked, "Please wait, I have a song to sing for you." Many of them knew about the song and had been waiting for me to be introduced to sing it! I told them that I had promised some of the gals who couldn't make it, that I would sing my song for them in Cooperstown, and by golly, I was going to do it! I had no microphone, so I had to really belt it out. At the same time I had to be careful because just before I left home my two front teeth caps had broken off and I had to have a temporary two-tooth bridge put in my mouth. So, I had to sing carefully, but I belted out my Cooperstown song anyway. I was doing beautifully, until I got almost to the end. Then I got carried away with frustration and emotion and when I belted out that ending, out flew my front two-tooth bridge. You know what? With the help of Frisco, one of my pals, we caught it in midair and I went right on singing.

"MOVE OVER BOYS"

"Cooperstown Song"

"After 40 years or more, we've finally got the floor

We had to wait for this important date and now we're gonna score!

Move over boys, in Baseball Hall of Fame

Make room for the gals, who played the All American game.

While you boys were out winning World War II

We were the women, picking up the slack for you.

We swung the bat, and we ran the paths,

And yes, we could hit the dirt!

We did it all, we played baseball,

What's more, we even did it in a skirt!

So, thank you, Cooperstown, for making a space,

and putting us in our rightful place!

Come on, let's hear, a mighty big cheer (right about here my two front teeth took flight)

For the All American Girls Professional Baseball League is finally here!"

© Pepper Paire Davis, 1987

There were rumors circulating and a big deal was made out of the whole thing. The rumors were untrue. I knew that my real friends knew that, so I took the high road and ignored it and made my own decisions. It was kind of hard on me after finally realizing my greatest dream and then have negative reactions around me, but as I said, I took the high road and just enjoyed the standing ovation that I got for my song. By the time I got back home I was "Scarlett" again and I put it behind me, and what do you know? Pepper Paire was emerging again. I found that important people were interested in what I had to say. The more I became my old self, the more they liked it and the more they listened. By now, we had baseball fans all over the country coming to life. When they found out that we had surfaced, they became hungry for our stories and our history. The movie plans were also moving forward. Penny was in the middle of making "Awakenings" for 20th Century Fox. So, she convinced 20th Century Fox to hire David Anspaugh to direct the movie. He directed the basketball hit "Hoosiers" and was well known as a talented sports- minded director. We had heard that he was very, very good. Then we heard that Jim Belushi was to be the coach. The female leads were unclear and they were still up for grabs. Nancy McKeon from "Facts of Life" was the only name we had heard. Penny had assured me that they would use my song and that I would be given a contract for that. She was going to co-produce the movie along with Elliot Abbott. Our All American League board had named one of our players as technical advisor and the rest of the board had options on their life stories. I was told this inside information. Well, I guess that was fine but it seemed to me that some of the league's finest should have been involved to some extent. Not that everybody wasn't perfectly legitimate, but maybe some of them didn't have the longevity or the stats. The main technical advisor had only been in the league one year and that was the last year of our league. As technical advisor, I wondered how much she could know about what really happened? However, that's the way it came down. It looked like I was going to be bypassed, as well as Faye and Dottie Kamenshek and a lot of other deserving All Americans. A lot of Californians were being bypassed, but we just wanted the truth to come out of it and we just wanted it to be a very good movie.

      The studio called me many times asking me technical questions and I gave them all the help I could. In the meantime, I had met a great little gal by the name of Joie Collins. My pal Joie was an assistant to producer Elliot Abbott. We had only talked on the phone, we hadn't met in person, but it was one of those things where you instantly feel comfortable and at home with someone. We were friends from the moment we said hello. Joie was in my corner from the very beginning and if it were not for her, you might not be reading this book right now. From the beginning, she was pitching for me to have more involvement in the movie. She said it needed me. She listened to all my stories and she was captivated by our league story. We talked many late nights on the phone for hours. I would tell her my troubles and she would tell me hers. She's a poochie pup lover like me and we both swapped our doggie stories. A few months earlier the "Scoot-pot Kent" and I had lost our little black doggies. We had lost both Tina and Licorice. Tina was 21 years old and had grown up with Kent. That was probably something to be expected. We had to accept that. But little Licorice was only 11. After Tina died, almost overnight, Licorice developed cancer of the lymph glands and she was gone within a month. So, after 21 years of a wonderful, loving companionship, both of my little black baby girls were gone. Scoot-pot and I were very lonely and heartbroken. I sure chewed Joie's ear off with that one. I didn't want another doggie, because I didn't want to be heartbroken again. But, then my Willie brought me this great big 6-month-old mutt. He had been mistreated badly and was left to die next door to Willie, when the renters moved out. You couldn't tell what kind of dog he was, except that he had big feet and big ears. His hair was coming out all over. I didn't want a big male dog, but he was so scared and so sick, I said I'd take care of him. He had a broken hip and the big guy just needed help. So, I took him to the vet and babied him and got him well. In the meantime, I named him "Clark" after Clark Gable, because he had such big ears. I swear that if you cranked on his tail, that guy could fly. After he felt safe with me, he started eating and came out of his shell. He turned into the most beautiful German shepherd that you have ever seen. It was a reincarnation of Buster all over again. So, he became "Clark of my heart." I guess God sent him to me to fill an empty, aching heart. Well, I told Joie all about that. Joie had lost some loyal and lovely dogs too. She had a German shepherd named "Elvis." So you might say we shared some "doggone" good stories.

   We also used to talk endlessly about our children. She would talk about her daughter Melissa, whom she was very proud of. Melissa was in the movie industry and had a small part in our movie. I would talk about all my kids, Kent and Willie especially! Joie also kept me up to speed on the movie. She was as devastated as I was when they went on location to Indiana and didn't take me with them. Again, I received calls from them requesting technical information. (Can't imagine why!) The technical advisor was with them. Anyway, I was still holding out hope of getting there, sooner or later. Then one day Joie called me and told me the bad news. She wanted me to hear it from her. Out of the clear blue sky, in June 1989, 20th Century Fox had called off the picture and put it on the shelf (at least for the time being). They said they couldn't find any good female leads. I think that they didn't believe in the movie and just didn't want to risk the money. I was devastated, along with all the other All Americans. So close, and now our story probably wouldn't be told. Joie tried to comfort me and told me that it didn't mean that it wouldn't be made, just not right now. She assured me that both Penny and Elliot believed in the story and felt it was worth telling. I thought she was just trying to make me feel better and that once again, there wasn't going to be a fairy-tale ending. I figured we would have to settle for the documentary. It was indeed a huge disappointment for our league. But, we did make Cooperstown! No one could take that away from us. So, I thought I'd better go back to work on my book again because that might be the only place our whole story would ever be told.

While that 1989 news was very disappointing, I also got some other news that was wonderful. Right around Thanksgiving I had a real reason to give thanks! While the movie "A League Of Their Own" had been called off, Willie and Phyllis had decided to start working on "A Family of Their Own." I was so happy about it! It was about time! We needed a new little baby in the family. Everybody was excited! My Willie was going to be a daddy! I had told him so many times: "Just wait son, just wait until you hold your own little child in your arms. Then you'll know why I worried. You'll know why I scolded you, why I did so many things that you didn't like or thought wasn't fair! It was because you are a part of me. I had to protect you! Now you will find out what it's all about. When you hold that precious little body in your arms." I felt very blessed! Because of this great news, I had some very happy holidays for a change. I was looking forward to the future.

So, 1990 came and then I got more terrific news. My little Suzy decided to try one more time. This time she found a real live cowboy! She had always loved horses and the whole western scene. At times she had dated one or two cowboys, but they were more like "drugstore" or "Hollywood" cowboys. She found the real thing in Ralph Gardener. He even owned a throwback "bunk house" on his mini ranch in the Palmdale-Lake Elizabeth area in the San Gabriel Valley. I hadn't met Ralph because for a while Suzy and I had grown apart and I hadn't seen her for a while. But I hoped and prayed that this time she found the right man! The wedding date was set for June 30, 1990. It was held at Three Points Roadhouse in the Lake Elizabeth area. The whole family attended and it was quite a shindig! Western theme all the way -- including line dancing, 10-gallon hats and the whole works! Suzy looked so cute out there in her boots and her little denim skirt, just kicking up those boots to guitar music! Ralph really seemed like a very nice guy and it was obvious he was very much in love with Suzy! I felt like she had finally found a good man and I asked God to please let her have the happiness she deserved! It really was a great wedding and we had a wonderful time! I got to wear my cowboy hat and vest and I didn't look too shabby! I only wished Bob could have been there to see his little girl finally find her happiness she worked so hard to get. But then, you know I think he was there, looking down on us and smiling!

Then came some disturbing news. My "Scoot pot" Kent had moved out for a short period of time for his first live-in romance. It was brief and he came back home. He had an unhappy experience with an older woman. I was relieved that it didn't last, unfortunately, he had not been told the truth. He wound up being a father at a very young age. He wanted to be a part of his son's life but he didn't have any rights as a father because there was no marriage. He wound up paying child support for his son, Scott. Even though it was an unhappy situation, I was proud of him for taking care of his responsibilities.

After his graduation, and with the help of his father, Pat White, Kent went to school and studied as an apprentice elevator mechanic. He passed all the tests and became a full-fledged elevator mechanic. He was set for life in a good-paying job. He worked hard to get it, but he made it. He was now paying rent money and helping with the groceries. That made things a little easier financially. So, we weathered the storm.

Then more good news came. I found out that when Penny finished making "Awakenings," she took our story off the shelf and took it to Columbia. She told them, "If you let me make this movie, I will come and direct for you." They wanted Penny, so they said "yes"! "Awakenings" was being heralded as Academy Award material! So in 1991 the real story began in earnest. They sent me out a contract to sign for my song. They offered me $5,000 for use of my song and Elliot Abbott told me it was a fair price, so I signed. My pal Joie kept me advised on everything and I started to really get excited again. It turned out that 20th Century Fox calling it off wasn't such a disaster. Actually, it was a huge break for us because now, with Penny directing and Columbia behind it, it was going to be a much bigger, more spectacular film. Through Joie, they had me come out to the studio to a huge cast and crew conference.

Everybody important was supposed to be there. I finally got to meet Joie face to face. I recognized her immediately when she came walking toward me. She was tiny but well built. She had long black hair and big brown eyes that smiled at you out of such a sweet face. They made you want to hug her and I did! I said, "Well, I finally get to meet my pal Joie." She laughed at me and said, "And I finally get to meet my friend Pepper." When I tried to thank her, she just waved me off and said, "It was a privilege to help you!" About that time, Elliot Abbott (Penny's co-producer) came up and pulled her away saying she had work to do. She smiled back over her shoulder and said, "I'll call you tonight." Then she winked at me and said, "Tell them how it was, Pepper!"

Indeed, everybody was there: the scriptwriters, Lowell Ganz and Babaloo Mandel; all the young actresses were there that were playing the Peaches; the directors and some of the technical people were there, too. Penny was there. We had a big round-table discussion. I had brought my scrapbooks and some actual film footage from 1946 that belonged to Sophie Kurys, my Racine Belle buddy. They fired questions at me from all angles and I answered all of them. They asked me about sliding in a skirt and I told them, "Hitting the dirt in the skirt wasn't easy, it hurt!" I told them how we played with sprained ankles and broken fingers. I told them how one of our gals had received a telegram during a ballgame that told her that her husband had been killed in the war in Europe. She continued to play and never missed a game. I told them how I played for two weeks without knowing whether my brother and my boyfriend were still alive. We had received notice from the war department that their plane had crash-landed on Okinawa. We didn't know whether they made it or not. They asked me, "How could you girls do that, wouldn't you be crying?" I told them: "There was no crying in our baseball. When you went to bed at night and turned out the light, that's when you cried." Some of this may sound very familiar to you!

When I got back home, Joie called me and told me I was great. She also told me that she would send me the script when it was done, for me to look it over and see what I thought should be changed. She was pushing hard to get me more involved. But, they already had a technical advisor that the league had assigned them and they didn't want to pay another one. (Even if she was a more experienced ballplayer.) Once again, I said, "Oh well, as long as it's a good movie that's what's important."

Meanwhile, they had taken over the University of Southern California baseball field to hold tryouts and baseball clinics. At this time the word was out and every actress in Hollywood wanted to be in this inspirational, historical, groundbreaking movie! With Penny Marshall directing and a big Columbia budget, it could only be a winner. By now, big names were being tossed around. Tom Hanks as the coach, Debra Winger as the catcher. Even Madonna's name was being mentioned. I was beside myself, wondering what was going on? I wanted so much to be a part of it. I knew that I could help them tell the real story.

Joie kept pushing and one day she called me and said, "Hey Pep, are you doing anything tomorrow afternoon?" I said, "No," and she said, "Well, Debra Winger wants to stop by and see you around 1 or 2 o'clock, after practice." I echoed in surprise, "Debra Winger wants to see me? Why?" Joie told me that Debra was going to play the catcher and she had heard about me being at the studio, and was sorry that she missed me. She wanted to get my input. Well, I called everybody in town and told them. I called my kids and they conveniently set their schedules so they could accidentally drop by. I told my son: "Debra Winger is coming to my house, what can I get to serve her? What should I buy for her to drink or to eat?" Well, my son advised me to get some appetizers of some kind and get some chips of some kind and get some Perrier water. I said: "I'm not getting any Perrier water. We can drink water out of the faucet; besides, I'm thirsty, I'm not dirty. I've got some pretzels and beer and I've got some 7UP and some chips and some cheese and that's what I'm going to serve." Willie mumbled something about me being old fashioned but I ignored him. I got out all my scrapbooks and all my memorabilia. I also cleaned my house and nervously awaited her arrival. About 1:30 p.m. a limo pulled up in my driveway and what looked to be a little girl, hops out of the car and steps up to my door. Sure enough, Debra Winger was actually knocking on my screen door. She had on faded blue jeans, a baseball cap on backwards, a sweatshirt and a Windbreaker. She looked every inch a ballplayer. Well, big old "Clarky Barky" beat me to the door and he was booming and barking up a storm and looking vicious. By now he was real brave, he had scared the dickens out of many a pizza delivery guy. I ran after him, grabbing him by the collar and I said, "Wait, wait, wait a minute Debra," figuring he would scare her. "Wait, I'll put him outside." Well, she whacks open that screen door and says, "Don't you dare!" Clarky jumped up and plants his feet on her shoulders and it was instant love. They were hugging and kissing. He was as tall as she was. It turned out that she had just lost her doggy "Buck." He was a big old German shepherd that she had had for 15 years. My Clarky Barky seemed to just fill a big hole in her heart. After the love fest, I showed her all my pictures and memorabilia. She couldn't get enough of us. She kept asking all kinds of questions and kept telling me how great we were and how happy she was to be playing the catcher. I played a cassette that I have, of a radio transcript of a doubleheader in Racine in 1946. I had just been traded there and the announcer interviewed me and Sophie Kurys and another one of our Racine Belles, Claire Schillace, in the dugout in between games. We sounded like munchkins. I was saying, "We have a doggone good team and we have a doggone good coach and a doggone good chaperone and we're going to win that doggone pennant." You know what? We did! We won that "doggone pennant." Whenever I tried to explain something to Debra, she would shush me. She was fascinated. She kept on telling me that she had goose bumps. That doubleheader read like a Pepper Paire commercial. I got some hits and pulled off a super play and the crowd cheered and the announcer explained the play, saying that, "They didn't even make that play very often in the big leagues." Well, Debra stayed at my house for four hours and all the while the limo driver sat in the driveway with the motor and the air conditioning running. I wondered what my neighbors were thinking. Of course, my kids happened by. I confessed that it was a setup, but she was very kind and friendly and she took pictures with all of them and gave them autographs. When Willie was there, I asked her if I could get her something to eat or drink and I told her that I had some 7UP and some pretzels or some chips. What could I get her? She hesitated for a moment and said, "Well, you know what? I would rather have a cold beer and some pretzels, if you have it?" I said, "Is Colorado cool aid OK?" And she said, "Coors just happens to be my favorite." When I started to get up to go get it, she said, "Hey! Let me wait on you!" and headed for the fridge. I shot Willie a look of triumph! Wow! Debra Winger was waiting on me. She couldn't have been nicer. I had always liked and admired and been a fan before, and now I always will be! It was getting dark when she left and she gave both Clark and me a big hug and a kiss and she thanked me for a wonderful time. As she went out the door she turned and pointed at me and said, "You'll see me again. We need you on that set."

The next day I got a beautiful basket of goodies from Mrs. Beesley's Elite Bakery: cookies, brownies, candy, a lot of good stuff and a beautiful thank-you note. That wasn't all, she was as good as her word. Joie called me two days later and excitedly told me that Debra went back and told Penny and Elliot that they needed me and my input and my inspiration on the set. Well, Joie had been telling them that all along and they finally caved in and told her to call me. They arranged to have me picked up by a limo. I was now named as a consultant on the movie "A League of Their Own" and I can honestly tell you that there is a lot of Pepper Paire spread out in that movie. After the first day I rode with Wendy in her Jeep. Wendy is Penny's niece and a great gal. She worked on the movie also. Sometimes I would have my bro take me or somebody in my family, like my daughter or Willie. I was just trying to get all my family there so they could see what was happening and meet some of the movie stars. This one day my bro Joe brought my niece Jeannine along and it was great. Joe spent the whole time talking to Janet Jones' mother in the dugout. It turned out they were from St. Louis, so they were talking about St. Louis things. Janet Jones was Wayne Gretzky's wife; she was a fine ballplayer and had a great arm. She could really fire that apple. She played a pitcher on the Racine ballclub. She only had a small part and she had been promised a larger one, but she stuck it out.

That first day when I walked onto USC's "Dedeaux Field," the magic started! This roly-poly gal comes running up to me and starts singing and talking to me. "For we're the members of the All American League ... I know your song, I know your All American song." I said, "Hey, that's great, that's great. I wrote it in 1944!" Then she really got excited! That was Megan Cavanagh who played the ugly duckling, "Marla Hooch." Then Debra Winger comes up to me and grabs ahold of me and my bro and says, "Come on, I want you and your brother to meet someone." She pointed to this tiny little girl. She had a baseball cap on pulled down over her eyes and a long brown ponytail. She wore a blue baseball jersey over shorts. Debra hollered at her, "Come over here, Mo, there's somebody here I want you to meet." Well, the little girl skips over with a big boombox on her shoulder, sticks out her hand and says, "Hi, Pepper" and Debra says, "Pepper, Joe, meet Madonna." Well, Joe and I just about swallowed our gum. She looked so different. So cute and so demure, so tiny and so reserved, and so nice, I might add. Well, that whole day was full of surprises. I found myself the center of attention, with all the big stars around me. It was unbelievable. I walked over to the hitting cage and watched some of the gals swinging. They were hitting off an "Iron Mike" pitching machine. I recognized Rosie O'Donnell, and she was having trouble fouling off those inside pitches. I told her, "Rosie, open your stance a little and lay off the inside pitches." I could see she was not getting her arms out. "Go for the outside pitches and take them to the right until you get your timing," I said. Well, she started belting the tar out of the ball.

      While I was standing there, this beautiful little gal with a striped shirt and a green baseball hat on backwards came up and said, "Hi, I'm Tracy." Then she softly asked me if I would watch her hit and see if I could help her. I said, "Sure," but before she got her turn, Debra came over and introduced me to Tom Hanks. I could see the disappointment in the little gal's face as I walked away and met handsome Tom Hanks. Such a nice guy, and so cute and so talented. Yeah gals, he's just as good-looking as you think. While I was talking to Tom, I looked back over at the cage and I saw Tracy was taking her turn at hitting and she was having problems. I asked Tom to excuse me and went back over to the batting cage. Tracy's face lit up like a Christmas tree when she saw me. "Oh," she exclaimed, her big brown eyes glowing with joy. "I thought you would stay with all the big shots." I said, "Hey, I said I would help and I always keep my word." Well, I gave her a tip here and a tip there and by the time she was finished, she was doing much better. She thanked me profusely and then she had to go take fielding practice. About this time, Joie came up and said, "Well, I see you have met everybody." I said: "I guess so. I sure hope that little gal Tracy makes it. She's trying so hard." Joie looked at me and said, "Oh, don't worry, she'll make it. Don't you know who that is?" I answered with an innocent, "No. Who?" She said, "That's Tracy Reiner, Penny Marshall's daughter." Well, you could have knocked me down with a feather. I had just made a loyal, faithful friend, one who would turn out to be in my corner, one with a lot of influence. How could I miss with people like Joie, Georgie, Debra, Tracy and Megan in my corner? How lucky could I get? The tide was changing and Pepper Paire was indeed back!

Suzy, Ralph & Me
(Bride, Groom and Mom in Law)

The Bride dancing
with her son
Suzy & Scoot(Kent)

Willie, Phyllis, Debbie, Bobby & Little Kelly

Sally, Suzy & Pepper

My boys Willie & Kent
(Scoot-The-Pot)

Me leading them in song

Zig, Me & JoWinters

Two of me at Cooperstown

Leading them in song once again

Dottie Hunter & Me

Faye & Me (HOF)

Rick, Me & Paula
My two best friends

Reunion Group - Faye & Pepper

Faye & Me
Sacramento, CA"

Ro & Mo

Faye, Lori & Me
Chicago

Debra & Me at my Memorabilia Bar

Jo Winters

Chapter 45
Showtime

So, showtime began in earnest. It was such great fun to get up early and head for the USC ball field. Sometimes I would take friends and relatives with me to watch everything that was going on. I would flash my pass and get them in. Actually, now I was getting so well-known that all I had to do to get in was flash my teeth. Of course, there was a little, tiny downside. My brother Joe and I are true-blue UCLA Bruins fans, so for the time being, we had to forget our rivalry with the USC Trojans. Rod Dedeaux and Bill Hughes were the coaches at USC. They turned out to be very nice guys. There was no doubt about USC being a baseball power. They won many championships while Rod Dedeaux was head coach. My official title at this time was "technical advisor." One of my jobs was to help rate the baseball skills of all the actresses that were trying out. They gave me a big clipboard, a bunch of rating charts and a long list of young actresses. Some of these actresses were known and some were unknown. When I look back at that list now, I see so many famous names, it boggles my mind. Many gals on that list went on to be famous and they all took a swing at our movie. Some of the names I recall are Teri Hatcher, Tea Leoni, Helen Hunt, Mariel Hemmingway, Rosie O'Donnell and Tracy Nelson.

It wasn't easy to eliminate anybody. They were trying so hard and they all wanted to be in the movie. Unfortunately, some of them just couldn't catch or hit, or even stop the ball. If the movie was going to be good, the baseball playing had to at least look decent. I worried a great deal about that. Fortunately, the gals really worked very hard on their skills and I did my best to help them. I gave them my approach to the game. All the baseball coaches were very qualified. One was even an ex big-league catcher. They had been teaching men's and boys' baseball for a long time. These boys and men had grown up playing ball. They cut their teeth on a baseball, not on a doll -- well, at least I don't think they did? They learned the technical way: catch the ball the same way, hit the same way and thrown the same way. A girl sometimes grows up without being taught the technically right way. They all had different styles. The coaches were telling them that the correct way was to kick their legs way up in the air and throw

450

like the pitchers in the majors. Some of the girls were finding that difficult to do. I advised them, "If it feels good your way and you can get the job done, just follow through and you'll get a good result." I showed them little tricks on how to get it done their way. Tracy was still having a little trouble at the plate. She was good, but she wanted to be better. In fact, she wanted to be the best. She worked very hard at it. She hadn't played very much baseball growing up; she was one of the gals that was handed a doll. She was determined to make it on her own skills. I know you might think, "Oh yeah, tough stuff. Penny Marshall's daughter will have it easy." That was not the case! Sometimes I think Penny was tougher on Tracy than anyone else. So, I told her Pete Rose had the best definition of hitting that I have ever heard. I know that I have said it before, but it bears repeating: "See the ball, hit the ball." Of course, you need to have some talent to go along with that, but that's a very important thing. Then, you let your hands and arms do the natural thing. I told Tracy to relax and follow through and it worked for her. She really turned into a good ballplayer. Her hard work paid off! In my opinion, sometimes they overcoach in schools and even in the big leagues. If a player gets in a slump, he's not going to be able to hit a cow in the rump with a shovel until he relaxes and gets his timing back. They need to get back to basics: "Keep your eye on the ball. See the ball, hit the ball." A lot of the gals did better after I talked to them. I got to know all of them pretty well and became sort of a "baseball mom" to some of them. I kept an endless parade of my friends and family going to the practices with me and some of the things that happened were really a riot. One of those times was when my bro Joe brought my niece Jeannine with him. Jeannine was a great fan of Madonna and she was thrilled to meet her. Madonna accepted a small role in our movie and she was great in that role. "Mo" wasn't the world's best ballplayer, but she worked hard and got to the point where she could fake it pretty well. No one can deny that Madonna definitely has all the moves. The "Material Girl" is "big- league material." Sure, sometimes she is outrageous, but that's her job and she does it very well, as she laughs all the way to the bank. Deep down inside, I think she is a good friend, a good sport and a good gal. Even though we were never close friends, I gained a lot of respect for her after I got to know a little bit about her. At first glance, I saw a street-wise, hard-nosed, outrageous but courageous person and an incredibly sexy and intelligent woman with a "yen for men." After I knew her for a while, I saw a lost little girl who grew up too soon without a mom to guide her, and desperately seeking genuine affection and love. In my opinion, she was looking for it in all the wrong places. Once again I'll say that doesn't make me right, that's just my opinion. So, as I was saying, this one day my niece Jeannine, who is 28, Lori Petty and I were all sitting on the bench in the dugout at USC. About six or eight feet in front of us some of the girls, including Madonna and Rosie, were playing catch. They met on the movie set and had become good buddies. We called them "Mo" and "Ro." So, anyway, Mo and Ro were playing catch and Madonna looked over at me. There was a lot of chatter going on, so she hollers to get my attention. "Hey, Pepper? Hey, Pepper? Did you girls say the 'f-word'?" Well, the chattering stopped and there was an awkward silence. Everyone was listening. I could feel my face warming up and I knew I was blushing, so I pretended I didn't hear her and I asked faintly, "What?" I could hear Jeannine and Lori start to snicker. Well, Mo gave me a disgusted look and said loudly: "You know what I mean! Did you girls say the 'f-word'?" I think my mouth dropped open and my bridge was in danger. Lori cut loose now and my sanctimonious niece was busting a gut, too. Normally she wouldn't say "s_ _t" if she had a mouth full. I guess I turned beet red, at least I felt like it. I didn't even think that word, let alone say it out loud. If there was a reason I really had to, I would spell it. Everyone was now laughing at me. I had to do something to save face. I answered loudly and clearly: "Hey, Mo, hell no. We didn't even do it." Well, Mo put her hands on her hips, looked blankly at me for a minute and then exploded with "b_ll s_ _t." That did it. Everyone exploded laughing. Lori fell on the floor of the dugout and Jeannine was down on her hands and knees and they were laughing up a storm. That was a typical, honest Mo answer. No frills. Just tell me like it is. What a circus. (Please forgive the language, but that's what really happened.)

    Well, the girls got picked and the show went on for three months. The girls were getting pretty good at their baseball skills. Once again, I have to criticize a little bit. Most of the gals had never worn baseball shoes with real metal spikes on them and they all had a little trouble walking in them. If you have ever walked in them you will know what I mean. It's kind of like a beach walk in the sand, you have to get used to it. You pick up your feet or your cleats will "hang up" and trip you. This one day I noticed that they had all the girls in left field and they were trying to teach them how to slide. They were in the outfield on the grass and dirt, and, of course, their spikes were "hanging up." I suggested that they dig a sawdust or sandpit to slide in. With their spikes hanging up, they were heading for sprained ankles or worse. I knew that they were also headed for some humongous strawberries from sliding on that surface. Strawberries are bruises and burns, like a cement burn but worse, because they are usually a deep bruise. They decided to forget it for the time being and decided they would take care of that when they got to Chicago. The casting seemed to be pretty well set by now. Tom Hanks was the coach and Debra Winger was "Dottie Hinson," the catcher. Lori Petty would play Dottie's sister, the pitcher "Kit Keller." My gal Tracy was "Betty Spaghetti." The ugly duckling, "Marla Hooch," was my buddy Megan Cavanagh. The "All The Way Mae" character was based on my friend, "All The Way Faye." She was played by the one and only Madonna. Rosie played her friend "Doris." That was all the biggies. The cast included some newcomers like Anne Ramsay, who played the first baseman; Renee Coleman as "Alice," the catcher; Bitty Schram as the "no crying in baseball" gal; and Ann Cusack as "Shirley Baker," the little gal who couldn't read. "Ellen Sue," the beauty queen, was Freddie Simpson. Robin Knight was "'Beans' Babbitt." The rest of the class included some big names such as the very accomplished actor David Strathairn. Jon Lovitz, a very funny guy from "Saturday Night Live," played the scout. The prestigious and funny Garry Marshall played "Mr. Harvey," of the Harvey Bar, which, of course, was a takeoff of P.K. Wrigley of Wrigley's Chewing Gum. No wonder the movie was going to cost $40 million, it had a very high-salaried cast. Finally we got to the winding-down point in practice and they were getting ready to break and head for Chicago and start the filming.

Tracy decided to have a kickoff party for the cast, and me. She told me that I could invite anybody I wanted. I asked her if I could include the All Americans, and she said, yes, she wanted to meet them and honor them. So I made dozens of phone calls and I did my best to include everyone, like I have always done. We only had one more day left, so that night Tracy threw this big party at Penny's house. For some reason only my grandson Kent went with me. I think the kids had something else they had to do. I don't remember why, but anyway, Kent took me. Penny's house is way up in the Hollywood Hills, pretty close to that famous "Hollywood" sign you always see on TV. When we got there, it was so beautiful. It was just a great big one-story rambling home, California style. It had beautiful gardens and trees surrounding it. Penny has great taste. The furniture, the drapes, everything was class. Of course, it had a big, shiny, beautiful, blue swimming pool. It had all the luxuries, including a huge recreational room in the basement filled with a whole bunch of exercise stuff. It had a Jacuzzi and many of her movie souvenirs, including the fortuneteller from "Big." I loved her kitchen. Penny had a thing for cows. All kinds of cows covered the walls. Cows in all shapes and sizes. It was so great. Now, remember that. Remember cows! There turned out to be very few guys there. Maybe half a dozen. It was just mostly all us gals so we had even a better time because we could let our hair down.

My "Scoot-pot" Kent was only 23 and had a steady girlfriend but he was in for a big night. Annie Cusack's brother was there, too -- the popular actor and handsome guy John Cusack. He showed up on a motorcycle. It was a different image of him, kerchief tied around his head and a leather jacket. He was very handsome and very nice. There was wonderful food, all kinds and lots of it. There were cold drinks of all kinds, from soft drinks to beer and champagne. And, yes, there was Perrier water. It was a great night and we all had a ball. All of the All Americans were telling stories and giving tips to all the eager young actresses who were just eating it up. At one point, my conservative grandson, "Scoot the pot," who usually went to bed early, was considering taking a dip in the Jacuzzi with Renee Coleman. Renee played the assistant catcher "Alice." Renee was not only a good actress, but she was beautiful enough to be a model. In fact, I think that she was one. The champagne was working on everybody, including Scoot, so he was going to take his dip in the Jacuzzi with Renee. But, when he found out that there was no swimsuit and the girls wanted him to skinny dip, he backed off. We finally went home long after midnight. The next day at practice, a lot of hind ends were dragging and a lot of baseball hats were too small for heads, and the water coolers, well, they were very busy places. There was a lot of moaning and groaning going on and a lot of sweating. Not glowing, sweating! Everyone agreed that we had a great time, but it sure was a long, hot day. I hadn't seen Debra all day and she hadn't been at the party. I spotted her and waved and I hollered, "Goodbye for now. I'll see you in Chicago." She motioned for me to come over and she quietly said to me, "So, Pepper, I'm afraid you won't see me in Chicago." I looked at her thinking she was kidding, but I could see by her face that she wasn't. She continued: "I want to be in this picture in the worst way and I think I belong in it, but a lot of other people don't. Sometimes you can't fight city hall." There were tears in her eyes and she hugged me and thanked me for my help and she said goodbye. Well, I'm not putting Geena down, but Debra would have made a great catcher. She wore her hat on backwards, her fingers taped up, she had a pretty good throwing arm and she could hit the ball. She had all the tools. She looked every inch a catcher. I was devastated and flabbergasted. I found out later that there had been an argument with the cast and the studio. I never did know the real story, but they bought Debra's contract out. I felt so sorry for her because I knew she wanted to be in the movie. I know that there have been a lot of controversial things written and said about Debra Winger by the studios and by the media, but all I saw was a classy individual, a great actress and a gal of her word! I found out that they had to pay her $3 million to buy her contract out. So, she got $3 million NOT to make the movie. I didn't feel quite so sorry for her then. She did all right. Good for you, Debra! But now who was going to play the lead? The next day the newspaper headlines read, "Geena Davis to play ball." Seems she had gone over in the middle of the night and tried out by Penny's swimming pool. They sealed the deal. Of course, Geena was fresh from "Thelma and Louise" and the Academy Awards attention, so how can you argue about that!

The night before leaving, I found out that Debra wasn't the only one that wasn't going to Chicago. I wasn't either. At the last moment, I was told that they didn't need me. They were just going to get set-up in the hotels and get people and equipment in place. Then they were going to shoot the charm school scenes. I was very disappointed again, because I figured, "Uh-oh, they really don't want me." But Joie promised that I would be there sooner or later. She told me that Tracy would see to it. Once again, I was left waiting at the church. I waited for a phone call. I got it because, as usual, Joie kept me briefed on all the happenings. There were some funny things going on. They thought that they had solved the sliding problem, but not with a sawdust pit or sandpit like they should have. Somebody got the brilliant idea of using a Slip 'n Slide. Well, on the surface it might have sounded like a good idea, that is if you didn't know anything about Slip 'n Slides! They are dangerous! I had to take ours away from the kids because they were getting hurt. The first day they were using the Slip 'n Slide on the set, they came up with two concussions. Fortunately, they weren't too serious. They finally did what they should have done all along and used the sandpit. Another thing that happened that was funny, but could have been tragic, was the glove incidents. The girls had all been practicing with today's modern equipment in California. That means that big glove with big, long fingers and with the big, long hammock-like webbings. Those gloves were huge. They were twice the size of the gloves we used to play with. We used to call our gloves "drug store" gloves. They had little short fingers and practically no webbing at all and very little padding. They had been looking for period gloves and had found some of the old gloves and they distributed them to the girls. Well, the first day, again, two broken noses! The gals put up their gloves to catch the ball and forgot that they didn't have a six-inch hammock webbing, and "boom!" right in the schnozola! Once again, they were fortunate, no serious injuries.

      Joie's phone calls weren't the only ones I received. I also got a couple of calls from Elliot Abbott. He wanted me to talk with Geena Davis. Seems she was really getting down in the dumps and discouraged. She was getting hurt. She was getting a lot of balls in the shins and a lot of fingers banged up and she was having a hard time in general being a catcher. This was not surprising, because a lot of real players don't want to be catchers for those same reasons. They don't like getting hurt. Geena had legs like a model and they were not made for catching. Elliot wanted me to inspire her and make her feel better. Well, I tried. I talked to her for a while and I think it helped because I had her laughing about the whole thing and she went back out with renewed efforts. I told her that after she got her legs strengthened, that it would be a lot easier. The catcher's crouch isn't an easy position to sustain if you don't have strong legs. Seems the ball would get about half way to the plate and Geena would fall over sideways like that old guy on a tricycle on "Laugh-In." I told her: "Geena, go down on one knee and rest your legs part of the time when nobody is on base. Then get back up when there are runners on." Well, her legs got stronger and exercising helped. Geena hadn't had the time for conditioning like everybody else had. She had to get in shape overnight. But after she got those legs back under her and straightened out, she started looking really great and she did a very good job of looking like a catcher.

The call finally came. Joie and Tracy had convinced Elliot and Penny that they needed me and I convinced them that they needed my friend, the Cacapot Faye, too. I knew that Madonna wanted to meet her. So, off to Chicago we go. They were having tryouts in Skokie, Illinois, for all the real All Americans that could still play ball. There were scenes to be filmed in Cooperstown that included a reunion at the Hall of Fame Museum and a reunion ballgame to be played at Doubleday Field. So, where else could they get women in their seventies with all the moves? Even Hollywood would have a hard time faking that. It was wonderful when we got there because we got to see all our old buddies: the Cacapot Kellogg and Beansie and Moe Trezza and JB and Lou Arnold (sweet throat). There were over a hundred of our gals at the tryouts, including Slats Myers and Briggsie. It was great seeing all of them. Unfortunately, some of them weren't going to be around much longer, although, I didn't know it at the time. I noticed Beansie didn't have a red tryout shirt on and I asked her why. She looked very disappointed and said, well, she had a gimpy knee and our league officials told her she couldn't do it. They had set physical requirement rules for the girls. Well, Beansie wasn't crippled or anything, just a little gimpy. Penny was standing right by me and I said, "Wait. Wait a minute, Beansie." I got Penny's attention and I said, "Penny, I want you to meet Beansie, one of the great pitchers in our league." Penny said: "Well, hi, Beansie. What a great name. Why aren't you wearing your red shirt and why aren't you out there trying out?" Beansie just kind of shrugged her shoulders and Penny looked at me and I said: "Gee, I don't know why not. She's perfectly capable." So, Penny turned around and hollered to one of the assistants and said: "Hey, get this young lady a red shirt. I want her in this movie." Beansie gave me a big grin and I winked at her. Once again, Pepper disagreed with the head honchos. I knew I couldn't make the tryouts because my knees were so bad. Faye had to go back to work and couldn't afford to stay in Chicago on an "extra's" pay and do the whole thing. So, we weren't in those scenes, but at least, by gum, I got Beansie in there. We stayed at the very prestigious Omni Hotel, but not for long. We only stayed for about four days. And to my dismay, an airplane ticket for home was stuck in our box. They still weren't convinced that they needed me. So, it was back home for Faye and me. All the girls had welcomed me with open arms. None of them wanted me to leave. Tracy told me again: "Don't worry, Pep, I'll get you back here. We need you." I was very disappointed when I had to climb on that plane and fly back with the Cacapot. At least I got her there and we had seen our old buddies and had a great time! It just seemed like fate was against me and they just didn't want two consultants on this movie! Even if they did need me!

Zig & Me

Beansie

Bitty Schram & Me

(Chaperone on the set)

Me and
Annie (15 Year old)
Meyers

Sweet Throat Lou Arnold

Faye & Pepper at Tracy's party

Tex, Renee and Lefty Lee

Kent, Me, John Cusack & Lefty Hohlmayer

Debra & son, Me

Chapter 46
To the Set by the Jet

So, in August 1991 I found myself headed back home again and while I was disappointed in one way, in another way, I wasn't, because it was coming up on Phyllis' "time." The sonogram showed that it might be a boy, but it wasn't positive. Phyllis was really struggling and going through a lot to have this baby. Poor little gal was in a lot of pain and had to spend a lot of time in bed. Things had been tough all the way. Finally, August 22, 1991, along came our precious little "Riley." We were all at the hospital. Willie was right by Phyllis' side. After it was over and everything was all right, Willie hugged me and whispered: "Now I know, Mom. I held him in my arms. He's wonderful! You were so right, Mom!" I smiled at him through my tears, saying, "I'm so happy for you, son! The best part of your life has just begun!" It hadn't been easy, but everything was going to be all right! So, in the end, there wasn't any place I'd rather be!

This time I kept my suitcases packed while I listened for the phone calls. I knew that I belonged on that set for it to be a really good film. They needed to know a lot of little personal things that would make it real. They needed to get inside my head and hear the sad stories, as well as the funny ones. All those things that made us different. As a 10-year veteran and a good ballplayer with a good memory, I could tell them those things. The calls came; first, from Chicago. They were filming the charm school scenes and the recruiting scenes where the scout goes to the farm. They had picked my brain at the studio about the charm school. They had seen my scrapbook with the streamliner menu in it. So, they thought they really didn't need me for all of that. Remember, Jon Lovitz and the cows? Remember I told you to remember the cows? Well, in the middle of those very funny charm school scenes in Chicago, a cow started to give birth in Penny's honor! They had to stop shooting, name the baby "Penny" and then go on! That was in all the papers. In fact, everyday now we were reading about the movie. I was also getting a lot of calls for interviews and doing my best to promote the movie. There were more technical questions, first from Chicago and then from Huntingburg, Indiana. Then from Evansville, Indiana, when they went there for shooting. That's where all the baseball scenes were going to be shot. I was a technical advisor all right, but just on the phone! I just didn't have the title and I wasn't being paid for it. Money wasn't what I was worried about. That was the last thing on my mind. I just wanted to be a part of it. The writers had asked me at that studio meeting, about my greatest baseball accomplishment. I told them about the series where the Racine Belles beat the Peaches for the championship, in the 1946 playoffs. That's the big series you see in the movie at Bosy Field in Evansville, Indiana. That was supposed to be the Racine Ballpark. Then in Huntingburg, Indiana, "League Park," was the Rockford Home Ballpark. At one point in time, they asked me, who I considered the greatest player in our league. I said that the stats would show that it was a toss-up between Sophie Kurys, my Racine Belle second baseman and Rockford's All Star first baseman, Dottie "Kammie" Kamenshek. If it were my pick, I would probably have to pick Kammie, because the Rockford Peaches won so many championships. Kammie was an All Star and led the league in hitting for many years. Well, you will note that the catcher's name, as the best ballplayer, was "Dottie." At that particular time, there was five or six "Dottie's" on the Peaches, so they were safe there. They couldn't get sued. If they had called her "Pepper," that would have been a different story. I now had a copy of the script and I had rewritten it and sent it back. They did make some of the changes that I suggested but I'll tell you about scripts. They don't tell the whole story. A lot goes on that can't be written. A lot of improvising and the way the actors and actresses interpret and say those words, mean so much. A good director knows what's good and what isn't good. I found out a lot of things and gained a lot of respect about how hard it is to make a movie. As Geena said to Tom, "It just got too hard," and Tom said: "It's supposed to be hard. The hard is what makes it good. If it was easy, anybody could do it." There is a reason why actors and actresses get paid a lot of money. It takes a lot of hard work and a lot of real talent to be a competent actor.

    Well, finally the call came from Tracy from Evansville. "Pepper, you are in; you will get your airplane ticket tomorrow." Seems like they finally caved in and decided they needed me. All the girls were having tough times. The morale was real low on the set. They were tired and they were spent and they didn't know the little things they were supposed to know. It just wasn't coming out right. They needed someone to tell them like it was. Someone to revive them. Someone to remind them that this was a real story. Someone to give them a fresh look at things. Joie and Tracy finally convinced them that they needed me. I flew out at the end of August 1991 to the set! The limo picked me up at the airport and took me straight to Huntingburg to League Stadium. It was in the middle of the day and they were shooting baseball scenes. Wendy greeted me with a big smile and told me to "be quiet" and took me to the left field gate. We walked down the line a little toward third base, then stopped and waited for them to finish shooting. Lori was on the mound being "Kit." She looked over to hold a runner on and she saw me. She jumped into the air and screamed, "Pepper, Pepper, it's Pepper." Well, I kid you not, they all saw me and started squealing, "Pepper, Pepper! She's here!" They all took off in a dead run for me. The camera was still going. I heard Penny's voice hollering in an aggravated tone, "Cut!" Then they mobbed me. Tracy was first, throwing her arms around me and whispering in my ear, "See, I told you, I told you I'd get you here." I hugged her back. Lori was jumping all over me in joy, and so was Megan, Annie Cusack, Robin, Patti and all the girls had come running up. Rosie and Madonna waved to me from the outfield. Even Geena, who I didn't know that well, came over to see me. She walked slowly and she was carrying a big umbrella. She gave me a big smile and a warm "Hello." It was great! I had tears in my eyes. They had a director's chair all set up, with my name on it right next to Penny's, with one of those big umbrellas over it. It was a typical hot, muggy July day in the Midwest, but I loved it! At last I was where I should be! After I got settled down, the questions came from the gang endlessly. From Penny I got technical questions and I got trivial questions from the girls. I told Tom all about Jimmie Foxx; about what a great guy he was, and I told him the funny stories, as well as the sad stories. Everyday I grew closer to most of the gals. They seemed to relax and started enjoying things again. Some of them did better after I told them things about their baseball. I know at least they had a little more fun with me being there. Relating to a woman helped them to relax, especially a woman who had been there and done that. I told them all my old stories and jokes, they were so old they were new again. I sang them all my old songs. All those songs that we sang on those buses. That helped them to feel like this is a real story. These women were real! They really did all these things. It's not just Hollywood make-believe. They respected us, for what we had done and what we had accomplished in women's sports history. They became proud to be All Americans. That's when Joie told me that the movie came alive. I knew those feelings would come through in the movie. I just knew they would and they did. That's one of the things that made it a great film. I think you laughed with us, you loved with us and you cried with us, and you played a lot of baseball with us and that's what it was all about!

      Tracy had rented a house in Evansville. It was a big house with a lot of bedrooms and she assured me that I was staying with her. Well, we filmed until after dark that first day and then headed back to Evansville from Huntingburg. It was about a 20-minute drive on the freeway back to Tracy's house. Megan and her husband, Lori, Robin, Patti and Annie were all staying in the area. So, they all came over to see me and we had a celebration party for my arrival. I met Megan's husband, Todd, and I met Tracy's boyfriend, Dan. Dan was a very nice, handsome guy with brilliant blue eyes and long brown curly hair. He was very well built and in top shape. He was, and I think he still might be, Robert DeNiro's personal trainer. Tracy and Dan were very much in love and it looked like marriage was in the future. Well, we played poker and word games and we ate popcorn and peanuts and snacks. We drank some beer and had an all-around good time. I made lasting friendships on that movie. Little Robin Knight was a kind of reincarnated Pepper Paire. She was a good ballplayer, too. Lori Petty, Megan, Annie and all of the gals were great to me. We all seemed to be soul mates. It was wonderful. Tracy became like my daughter and she's still my baby. Only, we had a lot more fun together because I wasn't her "Mom." She has always been very considerate and very protective of me. I have a very special place in my heart for Annie Cusack. She is warm and outgoing and laughs at all my jokes. My affection for these gals has lasted, even though I may not see some of them for a long time. They still stay fresh in my heart.

      The next few weeks were fun-filled, but crazy and hard. Sometimes they filmed for 14 to 16 hours on the set. There were so many things involved to get it right. Matching the lighting caused lots of delays and scenes had to be shot over. Many technical things went wrong and caused more delays; equipment breaking down, etc. Those actors and actresses (mostly the gals) were out there in that heat for long hours! Their dressing rooms were little trailers and big trailers. Of course, the big trailers were for the big stars and little trailers were for the little stars. The little ones are called honey wagons.

They served food at all times, from craft food service trucks. They had breakfast trucks, lunch trucks and snack trucks. There were trays going around all the time of very good food, like homemade root beer and lemonade, chicken sandwiches and snacks of all kinds. Almost anything you wanted to eat or drink was available. There was a big main tent that was the dining room where they served the big meals. That menu included everything from Maine lobster, to steak, to ham, to caviar. Anything and everything with all the trimmings. I think I put on a few pounds when I was there. I think everybody did. I know Tom did, but then he was supposed to.

The baseball field was surrounded by a large park area with waterfalls, rock gardens, grass, flowers, tall oak trees and maple trees for shade. It was a beautiful setting. They had tent-like structures set up all over for all the services they needed. They had a makeup tent, wardrobe tents and equipment tents. They needed enough tents to handle the 2,000 extras that were on hand at all times. It was like an army camp. People and things coming and going at all times.

The ball diamond itself had not been used for a long time. It had housed an "AAA" baseball team that the town had given up on. The field and the grandstand were run-down and in lousy condition. The studio rebuilt the whole thing from the "grass up!" They built it to match the "Rockford Peaches Home Field Park." So, since it was brand new, they had to "age it!" They spent more than a quarter million dollars on everything. Then, after the movie, they donated it back to the town. Now, Huntingburg has a men's minor league baseball team again!

Both Evansville and Huntingburg were picked because the surroundings matched up well with our AAGPBL towns. They had little old double- and single-lane highways, surrounded by green, green cornfields. The funny thing was, when it came to shoot those cornfields scenes, they had to spray paint them all green because they had a drought and the corn had all died and turned yellow. Talk about "painting the town" (er, corn)! But it wound up looking very authentic. So, it worked. Ya gotta do, what ya gotta do!

What I had to do was answer a constant stream of questions. Penny believed in letting the girls improvise and she knew when it was good and left it in. If it was bad, she knew when to leave it out. The gals all came to me with their questions. They asked me what the boyfriends' names were, the names of the songs we sang and the names of the bands and the singers. I made lists of all of them. I told Megan that my favorite song that I liked to sing was "Embrace Me, My Sweet Embraceable You." Boy, oh boy! What Megan did to that song in the movie! It was great! If you check the musical score you'll see that they did a wonderful job at picking great bands and artists and great songs for the film. Hans Zimmer wrote such a beautiful score. It should have won an Academy Award. Carole King's "Now And Forever" is a classic. It says what's in my heart, and Madonna's "This Used To Be My Playground" was very, very touching, and hey, that "All American League Baseball Song, that wasn't too bad either! I wonder who wrote that? Rosie and Lori wanted to know what swear words they could use. I told them, darn few. After all, we had charm school. But they had a scene coming up, where they get into a fight. "Well," I said, "You might get away with 'damn' once in a while. You might say 'tush' (rear end), that goes by many other names like 'jackass.'" Maybe you could get away with that if you didn't say it too often. You could call somebody "T.P." or "bung-hole-fodder," which meant toilet paper. Again, I made more lists. I said, "Remember, we were ladies, remember charm school? We couldn't use swear words, we couldn't even sweat, we had to glow!" I told them about Maddy English and how in her Bostonian English she called the umpire a "boss stud" (bas-tard). He couldn't understand her so he thought he was being flattered. I told them, "If you really wanted to insult a ballplayer, you would call them a 'bush-leaguer' and that would make them want to fight. But, we couldn't do that because we were all ladies at all times and we would have been fined." Penny asked me "If we chewed"? Well, I thought she meant gum and I said, "Yes, but Wrigley wouldn't pay for it. We had to pay for it ourselves." Well, she looked at me kind of blankly, then I realized she meant tobacco. I said, "Oh, oh no, I meant gum. Some of the gals who came out of the South did have to rid themselves of a habit or two." Again, I made more lists -- lists of baseball expressions and baseball memorabilia -- literally, a baseball dictionary. I was asked how we dealt with our periods. Well, you weren't supposed to talk about it. If you did, you said things like, "I fell off the roof last night" or "I fell on an ax" or "I'm back in the saddle again." We really weren't supposed to say those things out loud in those days. They asked me what kind of a band played at the ballpark. I could only describe it as an "oom-pah-pah" band, with a big tuba, a slide trombone, a trumpet and a big bass drum, and they went "oom-pah-pah, oom-pah-pah." Penny wanted to know what went on in the dugout. I told her that we could be having a delightful time with the chappy, putting methiolate or iodine on your "strawberry," while you had two people holding you down. Boy, that was an eye-opener! Rene Coleman, who played "Alice," the second string catcher in the movie, found out about all that. She got a "strawberry" and you saw it in the film. It was a beaut of a sliding burn! It wasn't planned, but when it did happen Penny said, "Keep shooting, keep shooting." They asked about what else went on in that dugout. I told them about a lot of practical jokes and equipment maintenance. Our dugouts didn't wind up being a pig sty, like they are now in the majors. They were old and crummy, but we kept them clean. One of the things we did in the dugouts was work on our bats. The bats came in untaped. Some of the gals liked the handles taped, so they would do it! I liked mine clean and smooth so I sanded them down a little bit and then cleaned them up. We definitely weren't loading them with cork. You might be trying to repair your shoes or your glove or your bra, with shoestrings and tape. You might be taking care of a blister with the chaperone's help. Guess what we fixed those blisters with? Nail polish! That sure felt good. The chaperone might also be helping you fix or adjust something personal. Then again, you could be playing a practical joke on somebody. That could be anything from a hot foot, to sticking something uncomfortable in a glove, to tying their shoe laces together (when they weren't looking). Or maybe hiding their hat somewhere when they were ready to take the field. They would be frantically looking for it. Just all kinds of crud. Those were some of the tamer ones. Actually, we really didn't do anything that would injure anybody. We were very careful when we gave someone the hot foot. We'd wake them up before they got burned if they didn't wake up soon enough. We couldn't afford to lose a ballplayer to a joke. We wore rally caps, but we called them good luck caps. We would put them on backwards or sideways with the brim up, twisted them around every which way, whatever way they worked best. As I said before, superstitions were a great part of our life. I told them a lot of the little funny ones and they used some of them in the movie, like crossing their fingers when they passed a bone yard. They used many things that I told them.

Tracy and I would drive back and forth to Huntingburg for the shootings every day and we had a lot of time to talk. Tracy wore my number seven on the back of her uniform and she called her husband "George" in the movie, after one of my boyfriends, whose picture she saw in my scrapbook. She wanted to use "Bob" but that was taken. Tracy did a fine job of acting in the scene where her "Betty Spaghetti" character was handed a telegram that her GI husband had been killed in Europe. I cried with her, just like I did when it really happened almost 50 years ago.

Every day on the set was a new adventure and I'll tell you, if you never have seen a movie filmed (and I hadn't), you don't realize that most of the time nothing is filmed in sequence. A lot of the scenes that are in the same setting are filmed all at once, whether they occur early in the movie or later in the movie. You can't really tell what exactly is going on, or how good it is, even if you read the script, because the script leaves a lot open. But, you sure can tell what's funny and what's sad, if the acting is right, and the acting was so right in our movie, most of the time. The day they filmed the "No crying in baseball" scene it took a lot of time to shoot it. They had to do it over many times, not because Tom or Bitty Schram ("Evelyn" in the film) weren't doing good, in fact they were doing too good. Everybody was laughing so hard that they would have to stop; even the cameramen were cracking up and losing control. That same day, they shot that scene where Freddie Simpson, who plays "Ellen Sue," the beauty queen, does the "catch a fly, get a kiss" scene. The sailor who was supposed to catch the pop fly was just about to catch it on top of the dugout, when a little boy about 12 sneaked through his legs and caught the ball. He wanted his kiss! I thought they should have left that scene in. It was a riot. He was insisting. They finally bought him off with some M&M's. Things like that were happening all the time. Sometimes Geena, Tom and Madonna would put on an exercise show and the rest of the girls would join in. They would entertain the crowd of 2,000 extras at the ballgame.

When there were delays, there was always a long hot sun out there, and the crowd would get restless. So, the cast would dance and lead them in songs. It kept the extras entertained and enthusiastic and laughing. Geena Davis is a multitalented and beautiful actress, but she surprised me with her other creative talents. She built the cutest little pipe organ made out of plastic and cardboard and I don't know what else. It looked great and it looked real. It was about 6 inches long, but the surprising thing was that it actually worked. It played our league song. She also directed when she and Tom starred in a musical that they put on for the cast and the crew. So, those guys and gals were working all the time, even when they weren't acting. Geena was quiet and reserved and pretty much stayed in the background in her big air-conditioned trailer while I was there. She only came out when something was going on. She and I were not close, but she was always very nice and polite to me. As far as Tom was concerned, well, Tom is an ace! He was so friendly to me. He is always nice and friendly to everybody from what I was told. He has constantly said that he had a great time making the movie and said: "What's not to like? I got to play baseball, I got to eat all the time, I didn't have to shave and I was around beautiful women! It's great! What's not to like?" Tom was a fine ballplayer, I could tell that, because when they shot that scene where he was taking hitting practice late at night with the "Iron Mike," I checked out his swing and he had a beautiful one. That was the scene they modified. I had told them about Jimmie Foxx taking his hitting practice. Tom had his whole family with him, including their new baby girl and his son, Colin, who was only 15 at the time. Wow, I guess he's in his 20s by now and starting his own acting career. There goes "Father Time" again, this time he just shot by in a jet. By now, all the actresses had the baseball game down pretty well, and some of them, the ones that had played softball, were so good they might have had a shot at the All American. Gals like Rosie and Robin -- they could hit, run and field. They had the whole package. Freddie Simpson and Tea Leoni were both good and they had previous softball careers. The other gals had to learn it all from scratch. Like my Tracy, Megan, Patti and Annie, but they had worked hard and by now they were looking good. Lori Petty really had that pitching act down good. She would kick that leg back, haul off and fire chin music! As Tom said, "They were hauling it around the field just like real players." They had been playing ball together now, counting the time in California, for nine months or more and they were becoming a real team. Later they would prove it.

While I was there, a lot of All Americans that lived in the Midwest area would visit the set and some of them did cameos in the movie. I did my best to introduce them all to the big stars like Tom, Mo, Geena, Lori and all the rest. I remember when my friend Lou Arnold from the South Bend Blue Sox came to visit. I called her "Sweet-throat." I got her down on the field, and into the dugout, to meet them all and to get pictures and autographs. She did a cameo appearance in the movie. They wanted me to do one also. My kids were upset with me for not doing it and wanted to know why. For the life of me, I can't tell you why I didn't. I think that I felt so privileged to be so involved and to have such a big part of the whole thing, that I didn't want anyone to think I was taking advantage of the situation. I just tried to include everybody else.

Stuart Fink was the publicity director. He took a liking to me from the beginning. He shot two extensive interviews with me in Huntingburg. One was a 45-minute interview with me alone, basically telling everybody my life story. The other one was a 30-minute interview, with Megan, Tracy, Robin, Patti and Annie -- all my favorite gals. We sat on the dugout steps and looked at my scrapbook, while I told them stories and showed them pictures. You can see and hear the sounds of the movie going on around us and behind us. It's a wonderful piece of memorabilia to have. So, just like everybody else, Stuart was great to me. He called me "His Darling of the Media." He turned over the job of dealing with the media on all the All American interviews to me. When they wanted to know about our league, it was my job to talk to the reporters and do TV. Even after I got back home, I still had people calling me for a long time for information and interviews (I still do). It was such great fun! By now I had all the answers and I could deal with any of them, one-on-one or whatever. I've often felt that I'd like to do the "David Letterman Show" and deal with him, one-on-one. All that time I was on the set, and that was around two months, I only saw Karen Kunkel, our league-appointed technical advisor, a couple of times, and at a distance, except this one time in Evansville on the set. She came up to me and asked me a technical question, which I guess they had asked her. I answered it for her. Karen's main job, I was told, was to take charge of the real ballplayers that made up the other teams in the league. They were extras and she was in charge of that. I guess she also did some scouting for them, looking for some suitable sites to match the real All American ballparks. I know she worked hard and I know she did a good job and helped them in every way she could.

But, how could she tell them about those years, like I did? She just wasn't there. It wasn't her fault, she just wasn't there. If you check back, you will find many pieces fit together in the movie like they did in my life, with maybe a different twist here or there -- like Tom and Geena sitting on the bus behind the driver talking and drinking; like the charm school scenes; like the streamliner; like Marla Hooch; like the series between the Belles and the Peaches; like Stillwell; or like Betty Spaghetti getting the deadly telegram. I could go on and on. Those stories were all real stories and they came from me and they came through that way. They came through real. I was just so glad that they listened to me and told it like it was! I will always be grateful to Penny, for telling our story in such a delightful and entertaining way!

My Sacramento Family
Carl & Sue Miller

Alice, Chirpie, Faye & Me

My Mountain Kids Bobby,
Debbie, Eric & Kelly

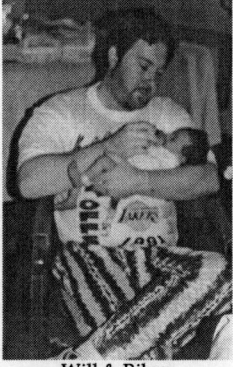

Will & Riley
"Now he knows"

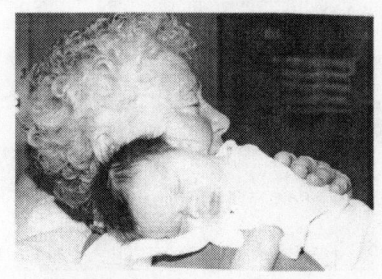

Riley Robert Davis Arrived

My little big man
Riley

Right where I should
have been

My little Bro. Russ as Santa
with Phyllis & Riley

Phyllis, Will & Riley

Chapter 47
Truth or Dare -- Foul or Fair

While everything was wonderful on the set, I couldn't help being worried. Everything that was said or written about our movie described it as a comedy. I couldn't help but think, "Would they be laughing with us or at us?" As I told you, there really is no way of knowing how good a movie is just by being on the set and watching it. Until the movie is actually put together and tied up in one piece, you simply can't tell how good it is going to be. At least I couldn't and that made me nervous. There were about 200 old gals out there that just might blame me if it was a dud and they could still throw pretty hard! I just kept doing all I could to make it good and I tried to put those bad thoughts behind me. I was having so much fun that it was easy to do. This one night a bunch of us went out to dinner at a place called "Bonanza." It was kind of like a midwest version of Sizzler. I was with Tracy, Lori and Megan, as always, and Annie, Patti and a couple of the other gals were along also. So the gals decided they wanted to play "Truth or Dare," Madonna's game. I didn't really want to participate, but when I tried to back out, they called me "chicken." Since they considered me one of them, I sort of, kind of had to play. Well, it was a riot! They would ask a question when it was your turn and if you didn't want to answer and tell the truth, you had to take the dare. The questions were dillies! Tracy was asked a very personal question about her man, Dan, and she took the dare. She had to run around the big restaurant three times singing the alphabet, A-B-C-D, etc. That was something. Then Annie was asked something personal about her boyfriend and she took the dare. Well, there was this huge salad, fruit and dessert bar right by us. There was a bunch of goodies in there, especially one messy dish of whipped cream, coconut and fruit. Annie's dare was to go over and stick her face into it. Sounds easy, but there was this very big waitress guarding it. I guess she was there to keep anybody from taking salad that wasn't entitled to it. So, Annie just kind of circled it with a plate, looking around, acting like she was trying to make a choice. Every time she thought she could make it "Big Momma" would show up. She was keeping an eagle eye on Annie and she didn't look happy. Of course, we were all enjoying Annie's plight immensely. Finally, she thought she had her chance and she did a desperate dive for the dessert tray and, Wham! In her hurry, she misjudged the almost invisible plastic covering around the table. Her head bounced off that thing and went "boing!" It just about scrambled Annie's eggs. She came staggering back to the table to a chorus of cheers and they let her off the hook. Next came Lori. She took the dare, too. She wound up having to take her shirt off behind some signs right by the restrooms. She thought she couldn't be seen because her head was covered up, but there was about 3 inches of visibility right in between the two signs. Lori didn't have a bra on and that's right where her boobs were located. Suddenly, a lot of guys had to go to the bathroom. Tracy ran over and told her that she was flashing everybody. Well, everybody had their turn and then they finally got to me. I was dreading it, and I knew they would ask me a personal question. They asked me a very personal question about my husband and I took the "truth." They actually took it easy on me. Boy, I never told my kids about that and I never told them about the question either. I can't tell you details because it's just not nice to kiss and tell. I made a promise to myself when I started writing this book that I wouldn't write anything that would hurt anybody or insult anybody if I could possibly help it. Every day and every night held adventure. Tracy and Lori made sure that I was included in everything. As I said before, I formed loving and lifelong friendships with Tracy, Lori, Megan, Annie and Robin. I also made lasting friendships with many of the others. I'm sure they all remember me, including Rosie, Mo and Geena, too. I felt like I had a special relationship with all of them, even Penny and Tom.

    Moviemaking is really like magic. They find a way to handle almost anything. For instance, the fences at the Huntingburg Ballpark were about 375 feet down the line and more than 400 feet in the center and in the alleys. All the gals were getting pretty good with the bat, but that was a long way for a gal to hit the ball. Actually, it's a long way for a guy to hit it, too. So, it was tough to hit a home run like Dottie was supposed to be doing. So, they came up with this catapult idea. They made up this big thing, it was like a big slingshot. They could shoot the ball high up in the air and sail it out of there. So, when Geena was supposedly popping her own home runs, they would cut the scene. She would hit it all right, but then they would pick up the catapult ball in midflight and away it would go. It would go out just at the right spot so they could film it correctly.

Sometimes it was worth coming to the set just to watch little "Stillwell." He was a real cute, chubby little guy. He was talented, too. They said he was raised by his grandmother and he was very sheltered and maybe a little spoiled. So, when we finally got to the scene where he was supposed to get hit by Tom with the glove, they had to keep shooting it over because Stillwell started ducking before the glove got to him. That would spoil the scene. He was ducking because he knew it was coming. So, Penny told him: "Give your little speech, Stillwell, and then we will just fake it this time. We will just pretend and not really throw it. Then we will fix it afterwards." So, Stillwell does his "Nanny, nanny, nanny, you're going to lose" speech. Penny winks at Tom and Tom lets it fly. And, whamo! They nailed Stillwell. That look on his face was priceless. He <u>was</u> surprised! "A good director improvises," Penny says as she walks off satisfied.

Just listening to Penny was a riot with her New York accent and her natural comedy flair. If you could understand her, she was very funny. Penny knows comedy when she sees it and she knows drama when she sees it. She knows how to pull the strings to get it out of the actors. What a talented lady she is. Another scene they shot with Stillwell never made the movie and I wish that it would have. It was a great little scene. It was where he was tied to a dugout post during the game to keep him from getting in trouble. When the game was over, everybody went home and forgot about Stillwell (supposedly). It was getting dark and there was Stillwell tied to the post. Well, he had this little wooden rifle toy and he was standing there in the dark, in the moonlight going "Bang! Bang!" He was shooting at those phantom ghosts. "Bang! Bang! Bang!" That chubby little face was wide-eyed and scared. Yep, that was a cute scene. Penny had to cut a lot of scenes before it was over, because this movie was already more than two hours and the studio wanted it shorter. Sometimes good things have to go.

The time was winding down, and according to what I heard, we were way behind on the shooting schedule. They were shooting around the clock. They had a date to make in Cooperstown to film the final scenes. They had to meet that schedule. The weather could wind up being a factor. Cooperstown is a busy place. There is a full schedule of events going on all the time: events at Doubleday Field, events at the Hall and things at the theater. They have to get everything in before the weather really turned cold. They get a lot of snow there.

I wound up having to choose between going home to see my new little grandson, Riley, or going to Cooperstown with the movie. I was anxious to see him and Phyllis. I wanted to see with my own eyes if they were getting along OK. I got all the news from Willie, but Riley had just been born when I left. I wanted to hold him in my arms and make sure he was all right. Phyllis had a very rough time bringing him into the world. I was worried about both of them. I decided that since we had another All American reunion coming up in November in Clearwater, Florida, I would go home and see my little Riley and my family. I would see my bro Joe and my gal Sal, too. Then, instead of going back to Cooperstown, I would go down to the 1990 reunion in Clearwater, Florida. As much as I would have liked to have been at the Hall, I knew that they really didn't need me. There would be a lot of All Americans there and the ending was all written and the scenes were pretty much finalized. So I went back home to get acquainted with my precious little Riley and to see all my loved ones. One reason I decided to go back to the reunion instead of Cooperstown was we were all getting up there to that endangered age. We were losing somebody at every reunion, somebody close. All my old buddies would be looking for me to come down there and tell them all about what went on in that movie. At this age, life is really precious, you just never know. At the next reunion there would be more people missing and, hey, I might be one of them! So, my mind was made up and when I told Tracy, she told me not to worry. She said there would be plenty going on in California after Cooperstown and after the movie filming was over. There had to be scenes rewritten, scenes cut out, scenes added and voice-overs. Many, many technical things have to be dealt with. Things that you don't ever know about when you go sit down and watch a movie. There has to be a lot of promotional things done, also, including documentaries, TV appearances and commercials. There is a lot of publicity that needs to go out to promote the movie before the premiere. Tracy assured me that Penny wanted me to be involved in all of that.

Before I left, there was a ballgame scheduled. This was the last night of shooting. I had told them how we had shot fireworks off on holidays and the 4th of July. So, this was a 4th of July doubleheader that was scheduled to be filmed. Penny asked me if I would go up to the announcer's booth and talk to the crowd of extras to keep them entertained because there had been delays. This was a night shooting and the extras had been on the set all day and they were getting tired and anxious. They had paste-up audiences in the background. They are cardboard people who are placed in a darkened area so you can't tell that they're not real people. This gives you the appearance of a really big crowd. It was supposed to be one of the championship games between the Belles and the Peaches in 1946. When I got up there in that booth and looked down on that field and I saw those yellow and those peach uniforms, I swear I did not see actresses, I did not see baseball players, I saw All Americans. I saw the Peaches and the Belles duking it out. It was 1946 all over again. The skyrockets were going off and shooting up through the sky. It truly was my field of dreams. I saw Marnie, my brown-eyed Racine buddy at first base. I saw my Boston buddy Maddy English at third. I saw "Sophie the Trophy" at second and I saw Joannie on the mound. I was behind the dish wearing those tools of ignorance. My heart was racing right along with those skyrockets. I didn't plan on it or realize it, but I was telling all this to the crowd. They told me afterwards that the rowdy crowd became silent. They said you could hear a pin drop and that they were listening to every word. When the Peaches got out there on that field, I saw Dottie Kamenshek on first base. I saw Snookie at short and I saw Carolyn on the mound. Yes, it was that championship game in 1946 all over again! Well, that game got started and there was no score that first inning. Remember now, the Peaches were all actresses. The Belles were mostly really good, solid ballplayers from softball leagues and universities all over the country. Well, you know what? The Peaches were holding their own. They were making the plays and looking good. Tracy was on the mound and she was firing it by them and shutting them down. Nobody was faking it. The actresses were really playing ball. There was no doubt about it. They had really turned into a team and they wanted to win. It was only supposed to be a two-inning ballgame. Then they would cut and piece the film to get it where they wanted it. It is very costly to film a ballgame. You have to shoot from many angles with lots of cameras. But the score was tied and Penny said, "Keep shooting." Everybody was excited and they were watching the game, including Penny. They were all really amazed at how good the Peaches were playing! That game went four innings. They said that it was the most expensive ballgame ever filmed. And, actually, the Peaches won it. Not like in real life when my Belles won. The crowd roared its unanimous approval and they didn't have to rev them up anymore to get them to cheer. What a night it was. When Tracy and I drove back after the game, I hugged her and told her how proud I was of her. I told her, "You took me back, baby, and it was wonderful. I'm very proud of you all." We were both emotionally and physically spent. Tracy looked into my eyes and she said: "Thanks. That's what we wanted to do because we are so very proud of you and what all of you accomplished. We wanted to do our best for the All Americans."

The next day was Labor Day and Penny gave everybody a day off because everybody needed to rest. They had a tough 24-hour, around-the-clock shoot schedule coming up in Cooperstown. So, Penny decided to give a big Labor Day party for the cast and the crew and the VIPs. She had rented this big villa for her stay. It was on top of some beautiful, grassy hills. It had a man-made lake down below and, of course, a swimming pool. It had park-like surroundings. It was a fitting place for a gala party and it would be my "going away" party. Everybody turned out. There were more than 200 people, including all the VIP guests from Evansville and Huntingburg. Madonna and her whole "Truth or Dare" group was there, musicians and all. As usual, the food was fantastic. It doesn't get any better. There were barbecue grills set up all around and they were grilling everything. There was fish, steak, chicken, lobster and corn, whatever you wanted. You could even have hamburgers and hot dogs, if you wanted. There were huge tables set up all around with all the trimmings on them: salads, desserts, breads, veggies, etc. Boy, I can tell you that on those movies, they work hard and they eat hard and they party hard! It was great. They had a disc jockey, but Madonna and her band performed, too. She got me up there dancing with her. She was teaching me to do the Macarena. So then I was showing her my baseball boogie dance using my cane instead of a bat. It was a fun time. The party itself went on until the wee hours of the morning, I guess. Tracy and I only stayed until a little after dark. She had to take me to the airport early the next morning and we were both emotionally drained and tired.

The next day, on the way to the airport she said, "Wow, I sure don't know how you gals did this for four months and 130 ballgames. It would be awfully hard." I looked at her and smiled and I started to say my favorite line in the movie and she said: "Wait! Wait! I know. I know. It's supposed to be hard. That's what makes it good." I nodded my head and we both laughed. I had talked to Tracy a lot about my little Riley and about my kids. Now I longed to be back and hug them. When we made the video with the girls, I kept mentioning Riley's name trying to get it in. Tracy had told me that she couldn't wait to have her own little baby. I had the feeling that she and Dan were thinking seriously about that now.

When I arrived home, Willie picked me up and after stopping and loving up my big old "Clarky Barky," we went straight to Willie's and I got to hold my little Riley guy. His eyes were open now and he looked at me like, "Where have you been, grandma?" Then he gave me a sweet little laugh. Well, maybe it was a burp or a hiccup, I don't know. I choose to call it a laugh. Then he snuggled right up in my arms like he knew he belonged there and he's been my little "Plum" ever since. There is a lot of his grandma in him, I tell you. He's got a husky little voice and a great sense of humor. He's happy-go-lucky and laughing all the time. And he's a good little athlete. He has turned out to be a loving little guy with a very generous and soft heart. He even lets all his little girl cousins play with all of his toys. I know that he's going to get his heart hurt a lot when he gets it stepped on, but he's going to be loved a lot, too, and he's going to give a lot of love.

After I made sure that he was OK and Joe was OK and Sal was OK and my whole family, then I just relaxed for a while. I was pooped! I just laid around for a couple of days, but I was missing all that excitement and I was kind of down in the dumps a little bit. I thought, well, I guess it's over now. "Clarky Barky" just lay at my feet or crawled on my lap and he tried to drown me with kisses. He didn't want to let me out of his sight. But I knew he had been well taken care of because I have two really great next-door neighbors, Jim and Irene. Irene took care of him during the day and, of course, "Scoot the Pot" was home with him at night, so he wasn't all alone. Irene loved my Clarky just about as much as I did. Irene and Jim are originally from Greece, but they are proud American citizens now. They take good care of me. They have been my neighbors for about 30 years. Jim fixes broken things for me and takes care of plumbing problems. Irene is a great cook and she is always cooking up something special for me. I love them both dearly!

My rest really didn't last too long. The phone started ringing again and the calls started coming in from the media. I had told Stuart it was OK to give out my number and he did. I started doing TV interviews and newscasts all over the place. I did newspaper interviews almost on a daily basis. Everyone was getting really excited now about our movie and the media was really hyping it. Tom Murray was head sportscaster for Channel 7 (ABC) and he brought a crew to my house and did a great interview with me. Then he went to Faye's house and interviewed her and he put it all together. It was a great piece. He was such a nice guy and handsome, too. He left the station to go up north to San Francisco and I miss him a lot. I heard rumors that he wasn't happy with his job. He just wanted to be a straightforward, well-informed sportscaster. He just wanted to report the news in an interesting and informative way. That whole hype thing about newscasting and sports broadcasting was just beginning. You know, the hollering, the bad jokes, the trying to make the news and not break the news. I guess that's what they wanted him to do and he didn't buy it! I miss you, Tom.

      The list of interviews and reporters included some very famous guys: Jim Lampley, Keith Erickson, Jack Snow Sr., Ron Barr of "Sports By-line," old-time radio commentator Robert W. Morgan. I did some TV shows also, like Bert Convy's show called "The Third Degree" and "The Tim and Daphne Reed Show." I did all the "Good Morning" shows, except maybe "Good Morning Vietnam"! It was a blast. I threw out the first pitch for the Dodgers and the Angels. I met Tommy Lasorda. He gave me a jar of his pasta sauce. I tried to get a word in edgewise, but it's not easy with Tommy. Seriously, he is a nice guy. It was great, but it was time to leave again because our reunion was coming up in Clearwater. So, I took off for Florida to see all my old buddies instead of visiting Cooperstown, even though Tracy and the girls wanted me to come back to Cooperstown. It was a great reunion and everybody was full of the news about the movie. The media was there in full force. I got to see all of my old friends, but once again, we were minus a few good ones.

      There was this great little café right across the street from the hotel where we were staying. It had much better food and it was much cheaper than the hotel. I was eating breakfast there one morning and I noticed they had some fishing pictures on the wall and a number to call for sports fishing. We were right down by the ocean and the pier. I asked the restaurant guy, "Hey, if I bring back a bunch of fish all cleaned, will you cook them for us and how much will it be?" He said, "Well, nothing, as long as you buy beer and side orders and give me some of the fish." So I said, "You got a deal!" The next day, bright and early in the morning, a group of us went fishing on a sports boat. There was Rene, Lefty, Julie, Alice and me. We caught about 30 really nice-sized ocean perch. I caught the most and I think Julie caught the biggest. We had them filleted and we took them back to the restaurant. That guy fried those things up in some kind of beer batter that he specialized in. He cooked some french fries and onion rings in the batter, also. Boy, was that good. We had big platters of delicious fish and deep-fried onions and french fries and big pitchers of cold beer. The word got around somehow and All Americans started coming into that restaurant by the dozens. Those big old full platters became empty in nothing flat.

There was more media at this reunion than there ever had been before. By now, we were famous again, only this time it wasn't just in the Midwest. It was all over the U.S. and Canada. The pressure was building and everybody was talking about our movie. It was being mentioned as a possible surprise hit of the summer of 1992. But, articles were hinting that Columbia was getting worried because they had a $40 million budget. That was a big budget for 1992.

When I got back home, they had finished shooting in Cooperstown and Penny and Tracy and all the rest of the gang was back home in California. Tracy and Megan came over to the house and gave me wonderful news. They were both pregnant. Tracy and Dan were going to be married after the movie premiere. It was almost like having two daughters tell you they're pregnant. It was great! They blamed it on me and my little Riley and said that I gave them the idea. Tracy told me to rest up because after the holidays, things would start popping on the movie. The publicity had begun. Joie told me that when the scene cutting and voice-overs and all those technical things were done, they were planning to keep me busy. She said that they had an HBO special and some commercials planned and that Penny wanted me involved in them. Joie and Tracy would make sure it was going to happen. By now I had pretty much established myself as an asset to the movie. So, just when I thought all the fun and excitement was over, it was just beginning again.

Tracy-Lori-Me & Megan at Dodgers Stadium

Tracy - Lori & Maddy

Alice - Margie - Me - Lefty - Kammie - Chirpy
"The Legendary Ladies of Baseball"

Pepper & Dottie Kamenshe

"All the way" Faye & Mae
and me Chicago-92

My brother Joe, Me & Russell

Will & Phyllis
My son and his beloved wife

My #1 & #2 Grandsons

481

Chapter 48
Something Old is Something New

Things started popping again before Christmas 1991; a producer for ABC called me and Faye Dancer. He asked us to be in a TV pilot for a series. It was a story starring Hal Linden of the "Barney Miller" series. It was about a restaurant and a bar called "Jack's Place," kind of a "Love Boat" style show, on land. Hal Linden was the restaurant owner and our episode was called "Something Old is Something New." It was a story about a bunch of, guess what?, over-the-hill ballplayers. The storyline had them getting together at "Jack's Place" every five years for a reunion. But, what made it different was that these over-the-hill ballplayers were girls! How about that? I talked them into including more players and managed to get five of our gals in the episode. I was still being a team player. Funny thing about it was that while I was kind of the star of the show, they all got more airtime than me. Because, in the story, they all think that I am dead and I don't show up until the last minute of the show. Then I come in the back of the restaurant and I throw a baseball about 40 feet across the room -- over the tables, around and up, over the waiters and through a glass archway to Faye. I did it perfectly the first time, and I decked the director. That got me a standing ovation from the cast. Well, I threw it right where he told me to, right at his head. The director said if the series went over, he would like to use us again for a repeat performance. But I guess that they only made a couple of episodes. Then they went to Canada to shoot. I thought it was a cute show but it didn't last. They scheduled it to air on July 7, 1992.

Geena, Tom, Penny and Madonna, all the main characters including Lori and Rosie, were showing up everywhere now. It was the big push that the studios require to get everyone's attention. I was hoping to get on a few of those talk shows with them, but I didn't make it. By now, I felt that I could get the job done but they just wanted star power, and they had plenty of that in our movie. However, my name did show up here and there. Tom did an interview on the "Tonight Show With Jay Leno" and Jay asked him about the movie and about the music. Tom told him about our league and about my song. Jay asked him " ... if he knew it and could he sing a few bars?" Well, Tom launched right into it. "Well, we're the members of the All American League ... " and so forth and so on. At one point, it appeared that Jay was trying to stop him but Tom just kept right on singing and sailed through the whole song. I was saying, "Sing Tom, sing." I think Tom knew that by B.M.I. music rules a song time has to last past 45 seconds or it is just rated background music. It's major if it goes past the 45 seconds; then you get paid more money. So, God bless him, Tom made sure that it went past that time. That was about the first time that I realized the ins and outs of show business. I had all these contracts to read and to sign with the studios. I had the music and a lot of technical things to deal with. My pal Joie helped me all she could, but she told me that I really needed legal advice. She knew that I couldn't afford to hire anyone, so she nosed around and found this really great gal, who was one of the top "legal beagles" for Sony Music. Her name was Georgette Studnika. She knew all the angles. Joie had talked to Georgette's secretary and explained my situation to her. She told Joie that she would be glad to help me out and that she would call me the next day. Well, I kept thinking about that name, Studnicka, and then it came to me -- Mary Lou Douglas, one of my oldest friends, who was a pitcher for the Grand Rapids Chicks, had married a man named Studnicka and that was her married name now. Well, I convinced myself that that was just a coincidence. Mary Lou was from the Midwest and that was 50 years ago. So, how could it really have anything to do with her? So, I forgot about it. Well, Georgette Studnicka called me the next day and we talked for a while. She told me: "Gal, you need help. We'll meet for lunch and I'll fill you in. But we kind of have to make it on the 'QT' because after all, I am supposed to be working for Sony and not against them," she laughed. I said, "Gee, thanks a lot, and can I call you Georgette?" She answered, "No way, call me Georgie." Well, I said, "That's great! Now I have a pal Joie and I have a friend Georgie Girl." Then I told her that I had a friend from a long time ago, who's married name is now Studnicka. She answered, "Really, where's she from?" When I told her the Chicago area, she got a little excited and she told me that her husband's people were from there. Well, if you can believe it, Mary Lou turns out to be a distant relative of Georgie's husband. They had lost touch with her and never knew that she had been an All American. Small world, but they reconnected. From that time on, my friend "Georgie Girl" took care of me legally. I could have been taken for a ride, more than once if it wasn't for her. Joie and Georgie are perfect examples of women who have made it and then gave back. Standing up for the rights of other women in need. You know what? We need more of us to stand up and lean on these guys. Thank you Joie, thank you Georgie from the bottom of my heart.

      The spotlight was now on my family as well as on me. That was another one of the wonderful things that came from the movie, the fun and the pleasure that it has brought to my family and friends. My bro was telling everybody in the state of California about me. His quote, "If I had my sister's arm, I would have been in the majors." My Willie and Phyllis were so proud of me. Willie's line, "Yes folks, that's my mom." Riley, of course, was too little. He just understood that I was his loving grandma and that was good enough for him and me. But the day was to come that he would probably say, "Yes, that's my grandma." Next came a call from Tracy. She told me, "Mom wants you to come over because HBO is going to film a documentary to promote the movie," she said. "They're going to call it 'The Girls Of Summer' and they're going to shoot mom's part at the house. She wants you to be a part of it." So, I called my friend Gina "Chirpie" and asked if she and her sister Alice would like to take a little ride with me and meet Penny Marshall. They were thrilled to death and said that they would love to. Actually, Chirpie's name is Gina but I call her "Chirple," you know like the bird, chirp, chirp, chirp. We had been friends from many years ago. She and her sister Alice were championship softball players from Rhode Island and some of their teammates had played in the All American. Alice had a tryout as a catcher, but didn't make it. Chirpie was a little bit too young. We had just recently gotten reacquainted at one of our baseball get-togethers and had become good friends again. They are both small gals, so I kid them a lot and tell them that everybody from Rhode Island has to be small, because if they weren't, when they fell down, they would be out of state. Well, she got me back and she has a lot of great stories to tell, if you can understand her "Rhode Islander" talk. Seriously, she is another gal who steps up and helps out, without being asked. Anyway, I grabbed some of my scrapbooks and put on my "A League of Their Own" hat and my Peaches "A League of Their Own" jersey that Penny had given me on the set (she had given them to all the cast and crew) and away we went. It was exciting for all of us. When we got there, Penny was very nice to Chirp and Al. She gave them T-shirts, hats and signed autographs. She let them take pictures while the film crew was setting up. They filmed Penny and me. Then they made stills of my scrapbooks and memorabilia. Actually, the whole thing took all day. My interview was about 40 minutes and it was really hot under those lights, especially with all that makeup on. I was nervous, but they all said I did great. Everybody involved with HBO was very nice to me. I got thank-you notes from them and then later they sent me copies of the videos. I was overwhelmed again at the amount of equipment, the technical stuff and the people it took to get it done. It's no wonder that movies cost a lot of money. All we ever see is the tip of the iceberg! When it was over, Penny served us some food and some drinks and just sat and chatted with us, like the down to earth gal that she is! We all had a wonderful time.

So right about now I was living in a dream world. After all this time, the movie was really happening. I couldn't believe it, but it was real! The movie was so much bigger and so much better and more magnificent than I had ever dreamed of or hoped for. Penny Marshall will always have my undying thanks! The cast and crew and writers and studios, everybody that had a part in it, has been blessed by me many times. Right in the middle of my daydream, came the news. The cast and crew premiere was coming up at the "Cary Grant" Theater at Sony Pictures in Culver City. The date was set for June 21, 1992, at 6 p.m. Immediately following the premiere, there would be a baseball theme party, co-hosted by Columbia Pictures and QVC shopping network. It would be held in the ballroom of the prestigious Four Seasons Hotel in L.A. The studio asked me to make a list of who I wanted to invite. They said that I could bring all my friends and family and anyone else I would like to invite. They said I could bring a couple of All Americans. I asked them, "How about inviting all the All Americans in the California area?" I told them that it wouldn't be fair to invite just a few. So they said OK. But then, since there would be a longer list than they expected, each All American could only invite two guests. They said not to ask any of them from out of state because they would be having their own premiere sooner or later in different areas. So, once again, I was a team player. I called everyone I could reach from Southern California to Northern California and I told them what was going on and I asked them for phone numbers of any All Americans who were in town. I spent a lot of time and a lot of money on phone calls. I made up this list of names and addresses and phone numbers and then sent them to Columbia, so they could be sent invitations. You would think I might have gotten some goodwill out of that, but my efforts went unappreciated in some areas. I even had telegrams and invitations sent to players that I knew were out of town or on vacation. I figured that they could at least have them as souvenirs. I called the gals that lived in Arizona. Sophie, my second sacker, and Joan Winters, my pitcher, and I called them and said, tell everybody to come on out and visit us. Then you'll be in California and you can attend. I even got one of my Chick players and her hubby from Grand Rapids, Michigan, to be there by saying they just happened to be in town on vacation, and it worked. Well, I not only didn't get thanked by some, but I got bad-mouthed by a couple. I got one gal special permission to bring seven members of her family. Well, she had something like 28 to 30 members in her family and she wanted to bring them all. She wasn't satisfied and she was mad when she saw I got to bring my whole family. Well, I said nothing then and turned the other cheek as usual, but I'll tell you right now, listen gals, I earned it. I worked many hours and did many things for the movie without money. I spent my own money on phone calls. That was one way that the studio paid me back.

The big day came and I was sitting in that little theater that held about 500 people, holding my breath with my son sitting next to me who was now holding his breath, too. My whole family was there but they had Willie and me sitting in a special place. I wanted Willie by my side. I knew that he was almost afraid to come to the premiere. He didn't know that I knew it, but I knew that Willie thought it might not be a good movie, and that he and the rest of the world would not like it. He did not want me to be hurt. The lights went off and the screen lit up and the music came on. Carole King started out singing that beautiful song she wrote, "Now And Forever." Those are the words that I feel in my heart. I grabbed Willie's hand, squeezed hard and tears welled up in my throat and I had to choke them back. From the very moment the scene lit up, it was magic, from the very start to the very end. The audience was enthralled from the beginning. You could hear a pin drop, when there was no sound coming from the picture. You could hear spontaneous laughter coming from all over, at all times, including my son. You could hear Tracy and Lori and my Peaches laughing like crazy when they saw themselves doing those things. I knew that my All Americans were laughing and crying at the same time, like I was. When they got to the scene where Madonna and the girls did the jitterbug at the roadhouse out of town, I squeezed my son's hand harder and whispered, "I told them that, and your Dad and I could do that, your Dad and I could do that!" He shushed me. I was back there, I was with them on that screen. Tom and Geena were great, and Rosie and Madonna were so funny and all my girls and all the cast were wonderful. It was so real. When they got to the part at the end where they sang our "All American Song," you could hear little soft sounds of people crying, and then came Madonna's song, "This Used To Be My Playground," and it was over. But it wasn't, because then they ran the credits and you saw all those old gals, way up there in their late 60s and 70s. They had all those great moves. You could tell they were ballplayers. They were really hauling it around the field, as Tom said. As the credits ran, my name passed by twice, technical advisor and music credits for my song, and then it was over. There was a tremendous amount of applause and a standing ovation. Everybody was whistling and stomping. No doubt about it, it was a hit! When the lights came on, my son and I were hugging and the tears were streaming down my face. I felt a tap on my shoulder and I turned around to see Penny standing there. She said in her New York style, "Well, Pepper, you hated it, right?" I turned and hugged her and said, "Yeah, sure, right, Penny. That's why I'm crying." I introduced her to my son and with tears in his eyes he said: "I want to thank you, Penny. I always knew what my mom had done all those years ago, thank you so much for <u>showing</u> it to me." I was so proud of him! About that time somebody came up and grabbed Penny and yanked her out of there. There was a mob of people just running around and it seemed like everybody was talking at once, and it was all good. Willie and I caught up with Joe and Sal and Phyllis and the rest of the family. They were all thrilled and letting me know how good it was. I was basking in my glory! So were all the rest of our All Americans. We were hugging and kissing and laughing and crying. I felt a huge rush of relief. The suspense was over and the movie was great! Thank you, Lord. So, pretty soon, somebody announced that the hotel was waiting for us along with the media. There were cars outside waiting to take anybody who needed a ride. We all filed out and headed for the Four Seasons Hotel for the party. Reporters and cameras were roaming around outside the hotel. They were stopping people to interview them before they got inside. They got me a couple of times before I got to the party. It was a big room and already filling up with people. Red, white and blue flags and banners hung from the walls and the ceiling. Simulated bleachers with people in them were painted on the walls. Red, white and blue balloons were bunched and grouped and just floating around the room. There were blown-up pictures of scenes from the film all over the place. There were popcorn and peanut machines scattered around the room. Hot dog and hamburger vendors were positioned in various places, with all the condiments on the side and serving all kinds of stuff to go with it, like chili and chips and ice cream and snow cones. Big tubs of iced cold beer, wine and champagne and soft drinks were scattered around the room. Wow! What a scene, what a scene. It was exactly like what you would think you would see at a ballgame. Baseball indeed. It was like the World Series atmosphere with the blending of excited crowd voices filling the air. As I came into the door, my "Peaches" mobbed me, much like they had done on the set in Huntingburg. They were excitedly yelling at me, "Pepper, Pepper, we did it. We did it Pepper." Tracy and Lori both were hugging me and telling me that they couldn't have done it without me. I was hugging them back and telling them they were what made it so good. You could not have asked for more of a fairy tale-like ending. I sat with my Racine buddies, Sophie and Joanne Winters, and I visited with Zig and Dorth, my Chick buddies. I made the rounds of the tables with all my friends and all my baseball companions. Then I finally settled down at a table with my family, next to Sophie and Zig. Everybody was eating and talking all at once. No one could believe that the movie was so good. We were all talking about the fact that before it had premiered, no one had thought it would be a hit. We couldn't wait to read the reviews now. I was so excited that I really couldn't eat, I just had some peanuts and popcorn. Eventually I knew I would get around to those big old fat hot dogs with a lot of relish and mustard, just slopping all over them and leaking out on me. I just sat beaming with pride and nodding my head "yes" to everything. Penny came over to my table and introduced herself to my family and then she asked me to join her for a couple of minutes. She wanted to introduce me to the gal that was representing QVC shopping network. We talked for a little while and she was very interested in what I had to say. She asked me if they could call me from Pennsylvania when Penny and Tom were on her show. I said, "Sure, of course." They were going to be on for a week selling memorabilia from the movie: hats, shorts, sweatshirts, T-shirts, "Peaches" jerseys and even autographed "A League of Their Own" baseballs. Penny and Elliot Abbott had a company called "Parkway Production" that was involved in the movie. I had noticed that Tom, Geena and Madonna were not at the premiere or the party and I asked Penny why not. She told me they were still out on the circuit telling everybody about our movie. That was part of their job, to make sure everybody knew about it. She assured me that they would probably be at the Academy Awards Theater the next day for our Sneak West World Premiere, June 22, 1992. Then she asked me if I would join her and all the big stars at the big round robin press conference, the next day following the premiere. I gulped and said "yes."

Well, we all partied until well after midnight. After all, a night like that doesn't come around too often. They had all kinds of souvenirs for us -- goodie bags just filled with all kinds of stuff like videos, drink holders, buttons, ribbons, T-shirts, hats, peanuts, pens and lots of goodies. Sony and QVC really put on a great shindig for us. Thanks again, both of you. After all these years, the memory still stands out vividly in my mind. When I got back home that night, again, I had that feeling in the pit of my stomach. The one that I used to get a long time ago, about baseball. I had gotten used to all the fun and excitement of reliving my baseball life again. This was the second time around. Now, what was I going to do when it was over? How could I get along without it again? Scarlett had returned from the dead! Oh well, I'll think about that tomorrow. I'll just go to sleep and dream about the worldwide big, big premiere that was coming up tomorrow night. I would wake up real early and send Willie out to buy all the papers in town. Then we would have breakfast together. Then Willie, Phyllis, Riley and I will all sit there and read the reviews on our sweet premiere, with all that floating around in my mind. I finally drifted off to sleep, trying not to worry about that round robin press junket, as Penny had called it. I could handle it! Sure I could. Right now I would just dream about all the wonderful reviews we would be reading!

Cooperstown

Exhibit

"Dorth from the north" & Peaches

All Americans, Movie Peaches & Me

Me & my Boston buddy Maddy

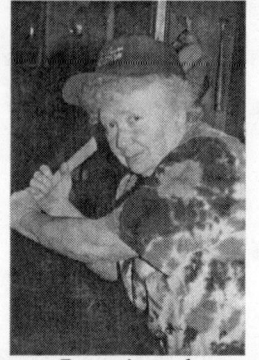

Put me in coach

On my way to Cooperstown in Penny's private plane

"Shooting the" commercial

490

Chapter 49
It Ain't Over 'Til It's Over

The reviews of our "Sneak Peek" turned out to be very good, but you could still tell there was some optimism out there. The critics were writing about what a wonderful story it was, but they were still being cautious. They were waiting for it to open around the country to see what kind of reception it would get from the general public. So, we weren't home free yet. Our premiere was limited mainly to the cast, crew, family and local audiences. So, of course, we would think it was wonderful. I still got the feeling that there were a lot of "doubting Thomases" left out there. "Beauty and the Beast" was premiering the same week and they were definitely touting it to be the blockbuster hit of the summer. "Our little movie," as they called it, along with a couple of others, was being labeled as likely "runners up." So, in other words, the honors were still up for grabs. They wrote things about our movie like, "Well, sports movies are tough to make, and they never go over big." Or you heard, "Well, there's a lot of young actresses in the show and you never know how they'll do." So, I was still worried and I already had one major disappointment that week. I found out that I could only take one person with me to the Hollywood premiere. I wanted to take my bro Joe and Sal and everybody, but the space was limited at the Academy Awards Theater and the guest list of prominent people was long. Everything was filled up. Penny had put Willie and me on her guest list, or I wouldn't have gotten there at all. The big day was here, June 22, 1992. It was time for our West Coast world premiere! Tracy had told me to be at the house by 5 p.m. The plan was to go in limos to the Academy Awards Theater from there. I was really very nervous about what I was going to wear. Not being a fashion plate and having a limited wardrobe presented me with a problem. The cast and crew premiere thing was easy because it was a baseball theme and the party was informal. Dress sweater and slacks were OK. But this was a major Hollywood world premiere. It would be seen all over the world on the tube. Guys have it so easy. All they have to do is throw

491

on a tux or a nice dark suit, shine their shoes, match accessories, slick back their hair and they're ready to go. They don't even have to shave, if they're like my Willie and they wear a beard. My fashion plate, Willie, would be wearing a nice dark suit. I knew that the focus wouldn't be on me. It would be on all the major stars. Still, it was possible that I would accidentally be seen. So, I finally decided on the drape-shaped dress that I had worn to Willie's wedding (that wonderful but sad day). I had only worn it once and I had gotten great reviews on it. The focus would be on the glamorous stars. They would be engaged in their usual, incredible fashion show rivalry that is always going on at all the big premieres. Each glamorous star would be trying to outdo the other one and dress in some incredible world-famous designer's creation. Willie arrived at my house two hours early. He knew me and he has this annoying habit of being on time or early (like his father). On the other hand, I'm notorious for being late. If I happen to be ready, it seems like I can always find last-minute things to do that wind up making me late. Willie knew this, so he came early to light a fire under me. Being late has always been something that I have to apologize for. It's one of my minor faults. I don't know why or how I do it, I don't mean to. This time I fooled him and I was ready because I had been getting ready since I got home the night before. I finally ran out of things to do. So we got to Penny's house early. Tracy had said come on over whenever I was ready, "Just don't be late." Tracy and Penny were in the kitchen getting their makeup on. Tracy asked me if I wanted her gal to fix me up, but I told her, "No, thank you." I knew nothing could make me look like a movie star. Incidentally that's why it's called makeup. In some cases it makes up for being ugly. So, Willie and I had a beer and just watched the whole thing. People were running all around like chickens with their heads cut off. It seemed like everybody had last-minute things to do or ask, and Penny was the one that had the answers. Tracy was ready a little after five, but Penny, who had been answering the phone and being interrupted with all kinds of questions, wasn't ready. A lot of people were telling her "break a leg" and all that last-minute jazz. It was coming up to six o'clock by now, and the limos had arrived. One was a big long white one and looked kind of new. The other was a big black one, but just not quite as new-looking. Tracy grabbed me and motioned for Willie to come on. She says to Penny, "We'll go ahead Mom, see ya down there." On the way out the door she giggles and says to me, "We'll take the big new one." So, away we go, drinking champagne and laughing and talking, leaving the driving to the big tall dude in his chauffeur's outfit. Tracy called her Mom a couple of times and the last time Penny said they were coming right out and they'd only be about 10 minutes behind us. The traffic was horrific as usual. Lines of cars were just inching along because it was the crunch hour. When we finally got to the theater, it was almost seven. People were lined along the sidewalks and roped-off red-carpet areas. We got out at the curb in front of the theater. They were announcing the arrivals over the PA system. I guess they announced who we were, but I didn't hear them. Geena Davis was standing in front of us being interviewed. She waved at me and I waved back. She looked stunning, absolutely gorgeous. Her beautiful long red hair gently framed that angel-like face and she wore a radiant smile that accented those cute dimples. She had on a dress that was molded to her body and it showed her beautiful shape and her sexy-looking legs (that were not made for catching). The dress was a cream-colored tangerine sherbet color. The color beautifully complemented her beautiful long flowing auburn hair that curled gently around her face. A large white baseball with red seams was embroidered on her dress and it wrapped around her body. I really can't do her justice. She was majestically beautiful. She's a tall gal. She's more than 6 feet tall in her stockings and she wears it well. She motioned to me to come over to her and the commentator and they introduced me on the mic. I said a quick "Hi" and got out of there. Tracy said her Mom had the tickets so we would wait for her before going in. In the meantime, the whole gang was arriving and getting their moment of fame and applause. They were all coming up and hugging me. They all looked beautiful, especially Tracy. She was wearing this very plain, but beautiful, clinging dress. It just flowed kind of gently around her. It was a soft black and green color and cool-looking material. Tracy's long, black, shiny hair almost hung to her waist. Her big brown eyes sparkled out of that beautiful olive complexion. Her heart-shaped face glowed with this radiant smile. I was so proud of her. Tracy is beautiful. Tom arrived with his family and with his beautiful wife Rita at his side and a whole gang of family. Colin, his son, was dressed in a tux like his dad. He was mugging for the cameras and cutting up as usual. Tom came over, hugged me and thanked me for my help. Gals, I'll tell you, he was so handsome in that tux. You could call Tom beautiful, too. Inside and out. He has always got that "little boy look" that makes you want to cuddle and kiss him. Once again, only the word "magic" could describe the night. The crowd was "oooing and ahhhing" when the major stars arrived and there were a lot of them. Willie was checking out all the beautiful women when I said, "Hey, I'm going to tell Phyllis." He said, "Go ahead Mom, and while you're at it, tell her she's more beautiful than all the stars here." I smiled at him and patted his hand. The time was flying and everybody was getting ready to go in. By now, Tracy was beginning to get worried. She had been trying to call her Mom but couldn't get through. We had been there more than 45 minutes and Penny was supposed to be right behind us. At this point everything was kind of being held up, waiting for Penny. It was getting serious and Tracy was really starting to wonder. Maybe there was an accident or something? She kept calling, but no answer. Everybody was stalling now and wondering. It was getting scary. I think Tracy was about ready to call the police. All eyes were anxiously straining, looking down that blocked off, barricaded street for a big black limo. Then, here comes this little "Chitty Chitty Bang Bang" Volkswagen. Tracy says, "I wonder who that is and how they got through?" Well, it pulls up to the curb and it was loaded with people -- so many you couldn't tell who or what or even see faces. The door opens and this rear-end comes awkwardly backing out. That's the only way you could get out. Tracy gasped and said, "Oh my God, it's my Mom." Penny turned around and said like only Penny can, "Well, I'm here now. Let's party." It seemed like about 30 or 40 more people piled out of that Volkswagen. Penny comes up and Tracy hugs her and said, "Mom, I was worried. What happened?" Penny said, "What happened was you took the right limo." When they were backing out of Penny's driveway, the other limo's engine had caught on fire and everybody had to pile out of it. When they looked around, everybody else had already gone. The only car left was this little Volkswagen. It was too late to call for a cab or a limo, so that was it. Of course, Penny being the great sport she is, made a joke out of the whole thing saying, "This is one red-hot premiere," and it was! They took us to the second floor and seated us in this special box. It was on a balcony that overlooked the screen. It only had about three or four rows of seats and you could see that they had added temporary seats at the end. Tom, Geena, Penny and all the actresses and families were sitting with us. It was crammed full and the theater was packed. There was standing room only. There was a huge fancy curtain over the screen. It was all very impressive. Then the lights dimmed and the music started and the curtain went up. The beautiful musical score of Hans Zimmer filled the air and I was lost in yesterday again. I was totally involved in what was going on in the movie. This time, my eyes were riveted to the screen, catching all the things that I had missed the first time. Our movie is so packed with action and I was so emotional, I had missed a lot. I found many more wonderful things to like, that I hadn't seen the first time. It was another ride on the time machine. I was aware of the laughter and the crowd's reaction at all times. Then it was over, all too soon and the wonderful credits were running, with all those great baseball scenes from Cooperstown. I was coming out of my time zone and became aware of the fact that the audience was standing, cheering and applauding all the way through the credits. There was no longer any doubt -- with the people anyway! "A League Of Their Own" was the blockbuster hit of the summer. Of course, the critics would still have the last say, but the people had voted loud and clear and they unanimously approved. Afterwards, I talked to Penny and thanked her for the ending and the way that she included all the All Americans in it. She told me that they tried to make her cut those scenes while the credits were running, but she wouldn't do it. She told them that she owed it to the All Americans to leave them in. The studio had wanted the movie to come in under two hours but Penny refused to budge. God bless her! It took a while to get out of there. The people were trying to get at us. They all wanted to compliment Penny and Tom and all the gang. A lot of them wanted my autograph, too. It was a joyous scene of jubilation. What an emotional high actors and actresses and all the people involved in the motion picture industry, go through. We finally made it outside and were making our way to the premiere party next door. Actually, it was an outdoor building site, all cordoned off with fences that were covered in canvas. Inside, there were tables set up with umbrellas over them because we were under the sky. Only in California, huh? Again, it was an informal setup. Food serving tables were lined all around serving all kinds of food and beverages. Waiters were running around with trays of everything imaginable and there were buffet items in heated steel bins all along the fences. There was everything available from Maine lobster to steak to chicken, etc. All kinds of gourmet dishes including hot dogs and all the courses to go with them. Walking on the sidewalk, I looked up and saw Tom and his party in front of me and he was dressed in a regular suit. I patted him on the shoulder and as he turned around, I said to him, "I see you got out of that monkey suit." He said, "Oh no, I'm a different monkey. Hi Pepper, I'm Tom's brother." I don't know if he's a twin or not, but he sure could be. I guess he keeps a low profile. Hey girls, there's two of them! When we went through the gate, we got another shopping bag full of great souvenirs and goodies. It was indeed another magical, wonderful, unbelievable night. There were a lot of people coming to the table asking me for my autograph, interviewing me, asking about the movie and about our league. The interest was totally everywhere. It was very obvious that people were fascinated with our story. But, now "Hey" it was over! Wasn't it? I felt so grateful, so wonderful, so thankful and yet "so empty"! And why? It was like when the league ended all those years ago. I was so strangely empty and spent. I couldn't find the "Scarlett" in me. What tomorrow? Tomorrow was over! Nothing was going to happen tomorrow, I thought! When I laid my head down that night on the pillow, I thanked God as I always do, for keeping my loved ones safe, my list was as long as it always is, and when I reached the end of my thank you's, after a long hesitation I added, Oh! God! What now? What do I do now? Will I be able to handle that heavy-duty press? Would they even want to talk to me, with all the big stars there? Oh my, there went my stomach again. As confident as I was, the thought of being in the spotlight with Madonna, Geena, Tom and Penny kind of floored me. All the rest of the cast would be there also, including Jon Lovitz, Rosie, David Strathairn, wow, and all my "movie Peaches." Wow, again! I prayed God would not let me get stage fright and have my tongue freeze up. That next morning, bright and early, they sent a car for me. Willie went with me. I needed him for moral support and I wanted him to get in on the act, too. They took us up to the hospitality suite of the hotel. Trays of everything good to eat and drink were stacked all around the room including champagne and giant tomato-sized strawberries. Willie loaded up his tray but once again I was too excited to eat. But I did have a glass of champagne with one of those giant strawberries in it and tried to relax a little bit. We were early and pretty soon the actors started to arrive. Tom, Rosie and Geena came in. They said "Hi" and I introduced them to my son. Jon Lovitz came in. He was on "Saturday Night Live" at the time, playing that very funny character who did a lot of lying. Willie was telling him that he was his favorite guy on the show and Jon really seemed to appreciate it. Finally, it was time, and we went downstairs and met up with one of our chaperones. I had told them about Helen Hannah Campbell who was one of the favorite chaperones in our league. She lived down in the San Diego area. Her father was "Truck Hannah," a very famous baseball catcher, especially well known in California because he played in the old West Coast League for the Angels. Later on, I believe he played for the Yankees in the majors. I told them that they should include one of our wonderful chaperones if they had the chance. They saw this opportunity and it was good publicity, so Helen was invited also. We walked down those narrow halls together to the press room. It was kind of like making that last walk to the electric chair. They opened the doors to the press room and it was a scary sight. There were at least 30 tables there; little round tables with five to six chairs around them. They were loaded with press. There were four or five of them sitting at each table. They all had notebooks and tape recorders. Cameras were spread all over the room. They led Helen and me to table number one. They poured us a cup of coffee from these fancy silver coffee pots and everybody introduced themselves. The first table was all from California and it was good to start that way. They took turns taping and writing and asking questions of all kinds, asking both of us personal and baseball questions. You name it! But it always seemed to wind up with me getting bombarded, so Helen kind of moved on ahead of me. I answered the questions straight from my heart as honestly as I could. As we moved around the room, it was amazing. There were representatives from all over the U.S. There were people from Scotland, Australia, China, Japan and France. It seemed like there were representatives from all over the world. Some of them were hard to understand, but as I said, I answered with as much honesty as I could and I found that I really didn't have any worries. It was just like the old days. When the pressure is on, just hand me that bat, er, I mean mic. The only time I reneged was when they tried to get me to say something off-color or bad about somebody or something personal like some dirt on the stars. Then I just laughed and changed the subject and tried to make them laugh by telling them that I did not kiss and tell. I was at those tables for three hours. Everybody else was long gone and I still had people around me asking questions. All the big stars had split and Helen was gone, too. It seemed like they were more fascinated with the real story instead of Hollywood and the big stars and the movie stories. They finally had to announce that the press conference was over, to get me out of there, but they still followed me out. Columbia and Penny complimented me and told me I was great and once again, Stuart told them, "Of course, of course she is. She's my darling of the media." Well, Willie, who had been lounging in the hospitality room just soaking up all the good stuff and living the life of Riley, came down to meet me and they drove us home in the limo. I was tired and emotionally spent. My voice was gone, I could hardly talk and my strength was gone, too. But my spirits were sky high! Higher than they had ever been. I had done it! Once again, I had proven that I was a champion who could perform under pressure!

Me, gussied - up (The other Babe!)

Me and The Babe

Jeannine, Linda & Sally

Jeannine & Jo

Will　　　　　　　Kent
My Boys

Phyllis, Riley and Will

Chapter 50
I Sang! It's Over! Isn't It?

By the weekend, the reviews were out on the world premieres all over the country. As planned, Willie, Phyllis and little Riley arrived Sunday morning loaded down with every newspaper in town. We were going to read the reviews and then they were taking me to breakfast. Phyllis was excitedly telling me that she had caught a glimpse of Willie and me on the news on the tube. But, I was looking at Willie and he had kind of a funny look on his face. I knew he would have read at least some of the reviews, so I asked, "Hey, were they that bad?" He kind of turned away from me and my heart sank as he said, "Well, Mom, to be honest the reviews weren't as good as we expected." I interrupted with, "They weren't? I can't believe it!" Then he turned back around with the broadest, biggest grin in the whole world on his face. He said, "No, Mom, they were not as good as I expected, just a thousand times better." Then he hugged me. We read all the reviews together while we ate breakfast. The suspense was over. We were definitely labeled the blockbuster surprise hit of the 1992 summer. Sony and Columbia could breathe a sigh of relief. It turned out to be their biggest all-time moneymaker up to that time. All of the reviews were acknowledging Penny as one of the great directors of our time. She had done what everybody had said a woman couldn't do. She made a movie that would gross more than $100 million. In fact, Penny did it twice with "A League of Their Own" and "Awakenings." "Awakenings" had been nominated for three Academy Awards: Best Actor, Best Writing and Best Picture. Now, how does it happen that there could be a Best Picture without having the Best Director? But Penny didn't get it and, in fact, they still haven't given her that honor, or any other woman. But, Penny will nail it down one of these days. You just watch and see.

All the reviews were wonderful and, actually, I can honestly tell you I've never read a bad one on our movie. Of course, it was still opening in different towns and different places all over, including Europe. They would be reviewing it also, but there were no worries. The verdict was already in, the people loved it. We were a smash hit! So, we All Americans just sat back and basked again in the glory of it. We were calling each other all over the country. Ma Bell must have made a fortune on us. I got calls from all my close friends thanking me for my part in it. That was very gratifying. I just tried to soak everything up and I kept putting off thoughts of tomorrow, just putting them out of my head. My bro Joe and his girl Sal and all the kids were enjoying everything right along with me. I wouldn't have been surprised if Joe had rented a sound truck and went around town saying: "That's my sister. She's technical advisor. She wrote the song and if I had her arm, I could have played in the majors." Seriously, it was very touching. They were all so very proud of me. It seemed like I was the only one who felt a little lost now that it was over. So, of course, I didn't tell anyone how I felt and I was even mad at myself for feeling that way. What the heck was the matter with me? I had been given this wonderful gift, to live my baseball over, and I'd been a part of giving it to the world. Why was I sad? I couldn't even understand it myself. Something deep down inside of me just wouldn't let it go! I was waking up every night with this feeling of dismay.

Well, things kind of died down a little on the movie until a week later. Then our episode of "Jack's Place" aired July 9, 1992. The timing was perfect and it got very good reviews, so things were moving again. A little while after that, Joie called me and told me that the studio wanted me to make a commercial to promote video sales of the movie. They called it an "in house" commercial, meaning it wouldn't be released for TV or radio. It would just be shown to all the video dealers along with a gift package to promote sales and get them to buy a lot. So, it wasn't over yet! I signed what Georgie told me was a good contract. If I remember correctly, I got $3,000 to make that -- that was like a year's Social Security for me. It was going to be filmed at Sony studio's North Hollywood building. That's where Georgie's office was, so I'd get to see her and thank her again. I went to Georgie's office and she took us up a couple of floors to this little theater they had there. They had a makeup room there and they told me I needed to wear makeup for the commercial. I told them I never wore anything but a little powder and a little lipstick. My eyebrows are naturally dark, so I didn't need that. I really didn't want any makeup, but the gal told me, "You need to wear it. You'll look like a corpse if you don't." So, I agreed to it. Wow, they really spiffed me up. I actually looked pretty good. They had told me ahead of time the best colors to wear to show me off good. So I wore my long- sleeve red "A League of Their Own" jersey with my "A League of Their Own" hat. They had sent me some gray sweatpants and a script to read, which I read and rewrote and sent back. I think they used a couple of my lines. Anyway, after makeup they wired me up like a robot. I had wires and microphones taped all over me and the wires were coming out everywhere. There were electrical wires running all around at my feet. I was positioned between two rows of theater seats and I could barely take a step. They said, "Don't move unless you have to." "Don't move?" I asked. "I'm supposed to throw a ball at the camera, how can I do that and not move?" Well, I got through my lines and I threw the ball at the camera and it worked. Everyone was happy with it. There was an ovation from the crew and then there were a few lines dubbed in pitching Contadina products and the movie. At the end of my spiel, I am sitting in a theater telling them how qualified I am to talk about the movie and that I know it will be a big hit. A really big hit! Then I say, "Did I say a big hit?" and I stand up and I pick up a bat lying there by me and I say, "Throw me that pitch." In the background they're saying, "No! No! No, Pepper!" Well, the theater was dark on my side and I'm looking into these big, bright camera lights and the ball comes out of the darkness right at me. I'm supposed to hit it right over the camera. Well, I did, almost, except I hit the cameraman right in a private place. But he was game and he kept on shooting. You could hear him moan. The camera turns upside down, spins around and then you see my feet only and you hear me say, "Oh, you could have caught that." Actually, they were Robin's feet because I was too wired in and tied down to move up to the camera. I thought it was pretty funny and I guess they did too, because right after that the Contadina Pasta people called me up and asked me if I wanted to make another commercial promoting pasta. They had teamed up with the studio to promote the movie. They told me to come down for tryouts and, again, I asked if I could include some other All Americans. Well, they thought that was a good idea, so they told me I could bring two or three down with me. So, I called up Lefty, Kammie and Marge and I asked them to come with me. Chirpie and Alice came along for the ride. They were going everywhere with me those days, driving and helping me out. It was fun for them and extremely helpful for me. When we got there, we found out that we had to compete with a bunch of pro actresses. There were about 20 old gals trying out for the parts. I won't mention names, but some of them were pretty well known. There were some comedians and character actresses that have been around for a while. They were very nice to us and they all admired us and thought that our movie was really great. Incidentally, some of them were on the Academy Award board and they said they were going to vote for our movie. Somebody must have talked them out of it, because we never heard anything more about that. Anyway, Kammie, Lefty and I got the parts. Marge really didn't want one, she was coaching us. But, we did get them to include a little girl. She was a rookie at the acting jobs and she had never done any commercials. We had coached her and we gave her some tips while we were waiting. She won out over some of the little gals who were experienced. We made a Contadina Pasta commercial about baseball grandmas. We were dressed in Peaches jerseys and hats, cooking and throwing pasta around the kitchen. The little girl was supposed to be Lefty's granddaughter and she was giving us the signs. I was stirring a big pot of real boiling water to drop the pasta in while Lefty and Kammie threw pasta and sauce under my nose. Well, I was a little nervous about that, but we made it, thanks to the fact that they both were good shots. The background music was really cute. It was swing music of our era. It took all day to shoot it and it looked like it might go into overtime. Boy, they didn't want that because it would have cost a lot of money. There were a lot of technical reasons why they had to shoot some of the scenes over before we got it right. The last couple of times I had all my lines right except this one little technical thing that I wasn't saying right for the director. I had come down with a flu bug early that morning and I had a very sore throat. I had loaded up with Contact and aspirin and I was praying I would make it through the whole thing before I started blowing my nose and sneezing. I had trouble with the last line and we only had about 10 minutes to go before it would go into overtime. So, I told the director: "Hey, listen, you get three strikes in a ballgame, so I got one more left. I can do it. I can do it in 10 minutes." So, we shot it for the last time and I nailed it. I knew I nailed it, so right at the end, I gave this great big wink. That wasn't in the script, but the crew loved it. They erupted into a roar and there was a standing ovation for all of us. It was great! By now it was after 8 p.m. and I was so glad to take my sore throat, my headache and my limp body home and put them to bed. I felt great thinking, "Hey, I can still do it. I played hurt and came through for the home team." They gave us a few hundred dollars and they did what you call "bought us out" because they decided to use the commercial with the release of the movie. Too bad, it was really good. At least everybody who saw it thought so. They did send enough ravioli, spaghetti, pizza and sauces home with all of us to last us for years. And you know what? That Contadina stuff is pretty good. The director called me again later on and asked me if I wanted to come down and tryout for another commercial. The timing wasn't right and I would have to go through all those tryouts again and buck up against those professional actresses. I thanked them, but I decided I wasn't going to do it. I figured that it was a little late to start an acting career, even an over-the-hill acting career.

So, while all this was going on, I had lost that feeling. But now it was coming back again. I finally figured out what was bugging me. I had a taste of yesterday's fame and I was having trouble dealing with facing losing it again. I had put so much of me into that movie; I didn't know what was left. Thank God I had my family: my bro Joe, my gal Sal and Willie, Phyllis, Suzy, Scooter and my little sweet Riley. My love for them would see me through. So, I concentrated again on trying to be the best mom and the best grandma that there ever was. I was thankful for the movie and I was also very thankful for the financial help I got from everything involved. I was far from rich, but at least I was able to catch up and pay my bills on time. So, Mom Pepper and Grandma Pepper were back again. They never really left. They never could. I was getting phone calls every day now, a TV show would call or a radio reporter. When it looked like things were cooling off, something would bring it back again. Our movie was refusing to go away. It was going to be well over a year before it was released on video. That was a long time to hold off for a video. In other words, it was still very popular and people were not forgetting it. It was on TV a lot. Finally, things got actually kind of quiet for a while, and then came a phone call from San Diego from Lefty, my Kenosha buddy and my Hall of Fame roommate. The 1992 baseball All Star game was going to be in San Diego. Lefty had been talking to them about us appearing at the big Fan Fest that was to be held in San Diego along with the game. She told me that they were going to have a trailer mock-up of the Hall of Fame with a display of All Americans in it. They wanted us to sign autographs and talk to the people. Well, I asked her, "Lefty, won't it be embarrassing? After all, the movie is over now." She told me that she had some baseball cards made up and she had gone to a couple of the local premieres at the local theaters. She sat in the lobby and signed autographs and sold her cards and she said the people were very excited about it. I thought, "Wow! I guess they still do appreciate us. How about that!" They said they would pay for all of our expenses including hotel, food and gas.

Alice and Chirpie said they would drive, so I thought, OK, what do we have to lose? At least we will have a good time seeing Lefty again. I really didn't quite know what to expect out of a Fan Fest! I had never been to one.

After we got down there, we checked in at the hotel and then we went over to the San Diego Convention Center where the Fan Fest was being held. It was going to go on for four to five days. The convention center was quite a wonderful-looking building. It had this gigantic structure of glass and steel beams and plastic all put together in a fascinating way. You could see the blue sky from almost everywhere. It was beautifully lit. The Fan Fest turned out to be absolutely spectacular. They had all kinds of entertainment on stages, inside and outside food courts, and games; shops of all kinds selling souvenirs of all kinds. Everything hyping baseball, of course. There were hot dogs, peanuts, popcorn and beer. There were so many people meshing around, we couldn't find anyone who knew us or where we were supposed to go. Of course, at the door they had our names and they gave us a goodie bag filled with badges to wear, passes, tickets to drawings and souvenirs and stuff like that. We were early, so we just walked around for a little while and tried to take everything in. Then we decided it was about time we were supposed to be signing, so we looked up where the Hall of Fame was on the video directory and we headed down that way. We were supposed to sign autographs for two hours for two days at the Hall of Fame exhibit. We figured they would have a place set up for us there. We rounded a corner and there it was, a mock up of the Hall of Fame looking just as real as it could be. Of course, it was smaller. It really only had one room that wasn't too deep, but the front was built to look just like the Hall. I saw that brick front with those archways and my heart skipped a beat, like it always did when I thought about my life's journey getting there. I looked at Lefty and she looked at me and she had tears in her eyes, too. We weren't watching where we were going and the next thing you know, we were knee deep in people. Chirpie and Al got up in front of us running interference. There were long lines of people waiting their turn to get in. "Wow," I said, "There must be a really big Hall of Famer in there signing. Let's go see who it is." We had to elbow our way through to get in and we got more than one dirty look for what they thought was cutting in. The crowd just kind of mumbled and grumbled at us. After we got inside, we just stood by the door and looked around. We couldn't see any tables or any place that looked like it was set up for us. We couldn't see too much of anything, the place was so jammed. Then we saw the top of what looked like one of our uniforms in a glass case over by the wall. We kind of edged our way over there and Chirpie said: "Hey, there's a gal in a white Fan Fest T-shirt with a badge on and she has a pager in her hand. Maybe she works here. Let's ask her." The girl looked very annoyed, like she was waiting on someone and Chirpie went up and asked her if this is where the "A League of Their Own" gals were supposed to be? Well, about this time, Lefty and I were starting to feel pretty foolish. We just seemed to be in the way. The gal looked blankly at Chirpie and when I came walking up, I think she was about to tell us to take a hike. I kind of tilted my badge a little bit and said, "We're from the movie. Is this where we're supposed to be?" She looked impatiently at me for a brief moment, then down at my badge and she was about to turn away. Then a light came on and she did a double take. Her jaw dropped and she exclaimed, "Oh, my God! Are you? You're not?" Answering her own questions and finishing with a loud, "You are!" The words came tumbling out of her mouth and she hollered: "Hey! Hey, everybody, quiet. Quiet everybody. They're here. It's them. They're here. The real players are here! The real players of the 'League of Their Own' are here!" The words rang out loudly above the mumbling, grumbling crowd. There was about five seconds of silence while it sank in. Time seemed to stop and her words seemed to hang in the air. Then, you could actually hear the crowd gasp and then they charged at us. Thank goodness Chirp and Al kind of held them back. We were the Hall of Famers they were waiting for! Me and Lefty, what a hoot! It was us! There were people of all kinds and all ages: from little bitty girls and boys to pension- age guys and gals. No longer did we have to worry about whether or not they would like us or appreciate us. No longer did I feel useless.

  I smiled with every autograph I signed. They had T-shirts, hats and books. We signed everything imaginable from baseballs up. One 30-year-old guy even wanted me to sign his belly button. Well, as handsome as he was, I told him no, I couldn't because he had an innie, not an outie. I signed his T-shirt instead. They did not even have a table for us to sign on or chairs for us to sit on. They didn't even have pens for us. We had to use our own or what the people brought. We stood for two hours or more taking only a 15-minute much-needed potty break, after promising that we would come right back. When we did, there was a little card table and a couple of folding chairs. The lines weren't even dented, so we signed for four more hours until they closed down. The line was still running around the building and we told them all that we would be back tomorrow to sign for everybody. A huge cheer went up as we waved goodbye. We came back the next day and instead of signing for two days, we signed for all four days. Instead of signing for two hours, we signed from start to finish. We signed from when they opened, until when they closed. Every day that week we signed for capacity crowds and there were still lines when we had to leave to go home.

Each day everyone greeted us with smiles, including the staff. What a difference from when we first got there. There were long lines formed around the building, and now they had some nice, spacious tables with comfortable chairs, some water and snacks and a lot of pens of all kinds laying around. They had official guards at the doorway directing traffic and keeping the lines organized. We had our own private runner that would go for food or drinks or whatever we wanted. Everyone was treating us with respect and smiles. We didn't take too many breaks because there were just too many people having to wait so long and we felt sorry for them. They just wanted to see us and to touch us. They would get their picture taken and get an autograph. We didn't want to disappoint anybody. We didn't want to leave anyone out. Really, the only time we left was for short, necessary potty breaks, and that was only about two times a day. They asked us to give theater presentations to sold-out crowds. Each time we got standing ovations. We told them how it was and we sang for them. I told them all about the movie and being on the set. They just couldn't get enough of us. So, the stage was set and the curtain went back up. Yes, we sang, but it wasn't over!

Our new careers had just begun. Pepper Paire Davis was back again -- ballplayer extraordinaire -- mom and grandma extraordinaire were still there, too. She was alive, breathing hard, but still alive, and shining brighter than ever. The second time around the Hall was not the end, it was only the beginning. The movie had brought our league back and I felt like it was up to me to make it live for the people again. Oh, yes, my dream was alive, now and forever in a lot of hearts.

I was walking off that last day with my good friends and buddies when I felt a tug on my jersey. I looked down but I didn't see anything, so I started on again. Then I heard a worried little voice say, "Wait. Please wait." and I felt another tug. I turned back around and looked down and saw this tiny little girl. She looked to be maybe 6 years old. She had big brown eyes, surrounded by a mass of curly auburn hair and a sweet little face. She looked very worried. I asked, "Are you lost, little girl?" She said, "No, that's my Mommy back there," and she pointed back. Then she extended her other hand with a baseball in it and said, "Would you please sign this for me?" Her mom was apologizing saying, "No, no, don't bother her. She's tired." I smiled at her mom and said, "It's no bother." I took the ball out of her tiny little hand to sign it for her. She still had a hold of my jersey, tugging on it. I could tell that she wanted to ask me something else, so I bent down and said, "What is it, darling?" She asked me, "Were you really a ballplayer?" She had a very worried look on her beautiful little face. I answered her, "Yes, I was, darling." Then she said, "Is it really all right for a little girl to play baseball?" Her voice dropped down to a whisper as if she was telling a secret. I answered her firmly, "You bet it is, darling. What's your name?" and she answered, "Theresa." Then she pulled me down again and whispered, "I need to ask you another question." I had to bend close to hear her as she said, "Would you please tell my Mommy it's OK." Then she added, "My Mom calls me Tessie." Well, the tears rose up in my eyes and my throat tightened as I thought of my Mom, Tessie, and I laid my cane down and I picked up that little girl and I hugged her tight. I swallowed hard and I said, "You bet I will tell her, Tessie. I will tell the whole world that it is all right for girls to play baseball."

And I've been doing just that ever since. I've been telling the whole world that it's OK for girls to play baseball! In doing so, I've had a wonderful time meeting people from all over. I've been signing autographs for everybody who wants one -- most of the time for nothing. I feel if I can make someone happy by signing my name, that's a gift.

I've been able to help many charities and organizations raise much-needed funds. The list is long: charity organizations like Harmon Killabrew's Children's Foundation, Joe DiMaggio's Children's Hospital in Florida, The Make A Wish Foundation, The Paralysis Project of America and MudCat Grant and the Security Mutual Life Insurance Co. of Binghamton, N.Y., as well as many children's charities.

I've gone to hundreds of little league and girls softball tournaments and signed free autographs. The list is endless -- and it's made me happy to help!

I'm very proud to have received many awards like the very prestigious "Victor Award" from the City of Hope! I've met so many famous people and legendary sports heroes that when I try to name them all, I know I will have left some out. To name a few, I've met three presidents and Buzz Aldrin, the astronaut. Then there is Michael Bolton, Donald Trump, Kobe Bryant, Wayne Gretzky, Howie Long, Emmitt Smith, Joe Montana, Johnny Bench, Tommy Lasorda and Sparky Anderson, Mike Scioscia, Mickey Mantle and my hero Joe DiMaggio, Muhammad Ali and his lovely daughter. We went to Victorville, Calif., and visited the Desert Storm troops, rode around in tanks with them and signed autographs for their fund-raiser! I've visited with Vin Scully and Chick Hearn, and I went to school with Marilyn Monroe. I've met Jean Harlow, Burgess Meredith and Robert Preston. The list goes on and on -- please forgive me for not naming you all.

And, my oh my, the many stories I have yet to tell. The wonderful, happy, inspiring and funny stories I have yet to tell! But, hey, that's another book. This time I know I don't have 50 years to tell it, because I'm in extra innings now! Maybe that's what I'll call it --- "Extra Innings"! What do you think?

Extra Innings

Kent & Jil Canaday

Randy Kern & Linda Kern

Will & Phyllis Davis

Joe & Sally Paire

Suzy & Ralph Gardener

Jody & Lois Paire

Little Fans

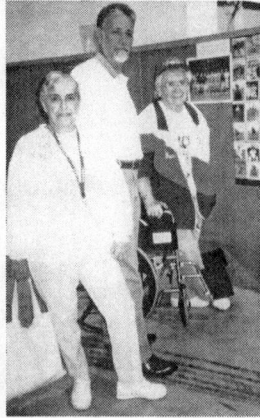

Little Fans

My good buddy Chirpie & Buddy Rick

Me & Rick's beautiful wife Paula, My Mississippi Mudqueen B.B. baseball fans cruise

Little Fans

My Bro. Joe & My Girl Sal

Little Fans

Me & Dirty-Bird

Suzy & Kent

Lisa Leslie & Pepper

Muhammad Ali, Chirpie & Pepper

Chipper Jones &
The Legendary Ladies of Baseball

Pepper & Dottie Kamenshek

Leslie Nielsen

Cal Ripkin

Rookie Kobe Bryant

Don Sutton

Michael Bolton & Pepper 1994

"The one & only Rapid Robert"
Bob Feller - My Friend

Donald Trump

My wonderful Friend Harmon Killibrew

Tommy Lasorda

First time I was ever Benched
Johnny Bench & Pepper

Johnny Longden & Willie Shoemaker

Gene Locklear
& Legendary Ladies of Baseball

Women's Display at baseball's Hall of Fame
Cooperstown, New York

Craig Stadler

William Devane

Steve Garvey &
The Legendary Ladies of Baseball

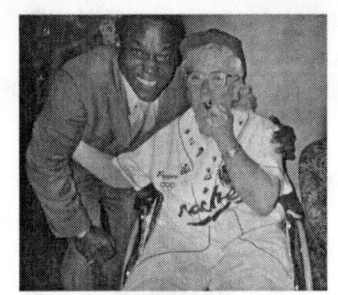

Cliff Branch

Bob Uecker

Bob Costas

Ron Harper

Red Schoendienst
&
Larry Jensen

Mario Andretti

Faye Dancer, Madonna and Pepper

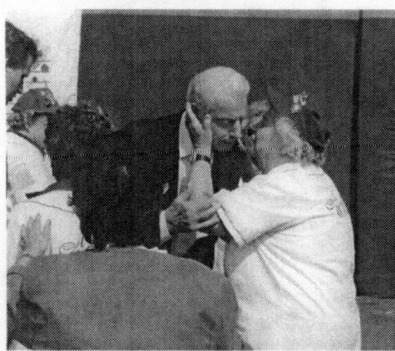

Joe DiMaggio

Dave Taylor

On the set, Pepper and stars from the movie "A League of Thier Own" Geena Davis, Madonna, Lori Petty and Megan Cavanagh

On the set instructions